T0139269

Principles of Verilog Digital Design

Principles of Verilog Digital Design

Wen-Long Chin

CRC Press
Taylor & Francis Group
Boca Raton London New York

CRC Press is an imprint of the
Taylor & Francis Group, an **informa** business

First edition published 2022
by CRC Press
6000 Broken Sound Parkway NW, Suite 300, Boca Raton, FL 33487-2742

and by CRC Press
4 Park Square, Milton Park, Abingdon, Oxon, OX14 4RN

© 2022 Taylor & Francis Group, LLC

CRC Press is an imprint of Taylor & Francis Group, LLC

Reasonable efforts have been made to publish reliable data and information, but the author and publisher cannot assume responsibility for the validity of all materials or the consequences of their use. The authors and publishers have attempted to trace the copyright holders of all material reproduced in this publication and apologize to copyright holders if permission to publish in this form has not been obtained. If any copyright material has not been acknowledged please write and let us know so we may rectify in any future reprint.

Except as permitted under U.S. Copyright Law, no part of this book may be reprinted, reproduced, transmitted, or utilized in any form by any electronic, mechanical, or other means, now known or hereafter invented, including photocopying, microfilming, and recording, or in any information storage or retrieval system, without written permission from the publishers.

For permission to photocopy or use material electronically from this work, access www.copyright. com or contact the Copyright Clearance Center, Inc. (CCC), 222 Rosewood Drive, Danvers, MA 01923, 978-750-8400. For works that are not available on CCC please contact mpkbookspermissions@tandf.co.uk

Trademark notice: Product or corporate names may be trademarks or registered trademarks and are used only for identification and explanation without intent to infringe.

ISBN: 9781032034126 (hbk)
ISBN: 9781032034133 (pbk)
ISBN: 9781003187196 (ebk)

DOI: 10.1201/9781003187196

Typeset in Nimbus font
by KnowledgeWorks Global Ltd.

Contents

Preface

Modern digital circuits are described using a hardware description language based on the semi-custom design methodology. A logic gate schematic is then synthesized by the use of a standard cell library, and the physical layout can subsequently be implemented. Therefore, several electronic design automation tools, especially the synthesizer, should be learned early as a design counterpart.

Key components of computer organization, such as interconnect, memory system, arbiter, I/O controller, embedded processor, first-in-first-out, and accelerator, together with their register-transfer level (RTL) codes, are presented in this book. An embedded co-processor for the Advanced Encryption Standard algorithm is illustrated. Moreover, assembly codes to drive the co-processor are introduced so that readers can fully understand the way every instruction is performed in a processor.

Several application-specific integrated circuit (ASIC) designs are completely provided in this book. Major digital signal processing (DSP) techniques, such as digital filters, fast Fourier transform transformation, source coding, and image processing, will be implemented in RTL designs as well. We also demonstrate step-by-step instructions for a fixed-point DSP design in this book.

In addition to the theoretical background, such as the probability of a synchronizer entering an illegal state, the system-level design for the synchronization of signals across different clock domains is comprehensively presented via three sections: single-bit synchronizer, deterministic multi-bit synchronizer, and nondeterministic multi-bit synchronizer (with and without flow control).

There are ten chapters and five appendices in this book. For your easy reference, they are listed below:

Wen-Long Chin

Acknowledgments

I would like to express my gratitude to my students who contributed to this book, particularly to David Chen and Vivian Pan, who drew illustrations and verified RTL codes used in this book; to Gabriella Williams, my Editor at Taylor & Francis Group; and to the Taylor & Francis publishing staff for their support during this publication project.

1 Introduction

The design methodologies for digital and analog circuits, with an emphasis on the application-specific integrated circuit (ASIC) design flow, are introduced. You will be able to gain a clear picture of what the modern register-transfer level (RTL) design is and the requirements of a workable chip. Timing constraints of setup time and hold time are briefly presented. Further, you can understand the terminology in ASIC design, such as functional verification, logic synthesis, timing verification, and physical implementation in this chapter.

1.1 INTEGRATED CIRCUIT INDUSTRY

Modern integrated-circuit (IC) technology enables the ability to put millions of semiconductor devices on the surface of a small piece of silicon, i.e., chip. Digital and analog ICs are manufactured using semiconductor material. The semiconductor industry is the collection of companies engaged in the design and manufacturing of semiconductor devices, including IC design, mask, fabrication, package, wafer and final IC test, and lead frame and many chemistries, as shown in Figure 1.1. Through the IC layout, the IC mask represents the planar geometric shapes of the patterns of metal, oxide, or semiconductor layers that make up the transistors in the IC. The IC fabrication contains multiple steps of photolithographic and chemical processing guided by the IC mask to gradually create the devices on a wafer. The IC packaging is the final stage of semiconductor fabrication used to encapsulate the die in a supporting case to prevent physical damage or corrosion. The IC testing guarantees that the device works as specified in its design specifications.

The demand of advanced electronic products, such as the high-performance microprocessors and mobile phones, leads to the rapid development in semiconductor industry. Transistors are manufactured by placing layers of semiconductor and insulating materials in rectangular and polygonal shapes on the chip surface. Metals, separated by insulating layers, are formed by putting metal on top of transistors. Consequently, semiconductor device shrinking has plenty of advantages, including the increase in the number of transistors per unit area, decrease in the channel length and threshold voltage of transistors, decrease in the supply voltage, and the increase in wiring layers.

DOI: 10.1201/9781003187196-1

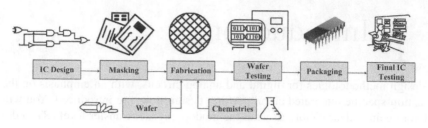

Figure 1.1: Semiconductor industry.

1.2 DIGITAL ERA

1.2.1 A/D AND D/A CONVERSION

The purposes of digital and analog circuits are used to process digital and analog signals, respectively. Typical digital circuits are designed based on logic gates, including AND, OR, NOT gates, etc., while analog circuits inherently compose of passive components, including resistors, capacitors, inductors, and active components, such as transistors and diodes. Though logic gates are made up of transistors as well, they are essentially digital circuits that operate on digital signals. Digital logic circuits respond to two separate voltage levels that represent a binary variable equal to logic one (1) or logic zero (0).

A digital system represents the discrete-time digital signal as a stream of quantized discrete values sampled from the continuous-time analog signal at discrete points in time, as shown in Figure 1.2. Each sample represents an approximation to the analog signal at a given time instant. According to the sampling theorem, a band-limited continuous-time analog signal can be completely reconstructed by the discrete-time samples if the minimum-sampling rate has been satisfied. However, the quantization process will introduce a quantization error or noise. Despite this, the quantization error can be reduced by increasing the number of bits used to represent the discrete-time samples.

Digital circuits process in the digital realm and are generally easier to design. Therefore, current trend is toward the digital signal processing (DSP), which manipulates digitized analog signals via an analog-to-digital converter (ADC) if necessary, or vice versa through an digital-to-analog converter (DAC). Digital circuits operate quantized and discrete-time signals, which are easy to manipulate and store. Each bit of digital signals is assigned two different voltages as two different logic levels: a high voltage (usually the supply voltage V_{DD}) represents logic one and a low voltage (usually 0 V) represents logic zero.

By contrast, analog circuits are much more difficult to design and sensitive to disturbances, such as noise and variation in the signal or supply voltage V_{DD}. Small changes in the voltage level of a continuous-time analog signal may produce significant functional errors. In a modern system, analog circuits are limited to the interface of a system to our nature or a few circuits with special functionality, such

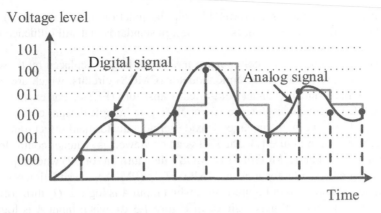

Figure 1.2: Analog and digital signals.

as conversion from analog to digital and vice versa, voltage regulator, phase-locked loop (PLL), and processing of ultra high-speed signals.

1.2.2 DIGITAL SYSTEMS AND DIGITAL LOGIC

Digital systems have such a prominent role in everyday life that we refer to the modernization of information and communication processes as the digital era. Digital systems are designed to store, process, and communicate information in digital form. Examples of digital systems are mobile phones, computers, online gaming, multimedia equipment, and many more.

After the A/D conversion, one promising characteristic of digital systems is their ability to represent and manipulate discrete elements of information. A digital system is an interconnection of digital modules. There may be various components that make up a digital system. For example, a computer has a central processing unit, a hard drive, keyboard, mouse, display, etc. The digital systems have following advantages.

- **Performance**: they have higher accuracy, cost efficiency, and lower power consumption.
- **Reliability**: they are less affected by ageing, noise, and variations in temperature and environment.
- **Flexibility**: they have memory and easier to design. Information and data can be easily stored, processed, and communicate. These systems are more versatile and can achieve highly complicated functions. Moreover, system operation can be changed by interacting with the software.

Digital electronics are the main foundation for the digitized world. To understand the function of each digital module, it is necessary to have fundamental knowledge of digital circuits and their logical operation. Almost every electronics where transistors are used as a switch applies the basic concepts of digital technique. The first family of digital logic gaining widespread use was the transistor–transistor logic (TTL) family within which the logic gates are formed by bipolar junction transistors (BJTs). The electrical properties of these devices led to design standards that still influence logic design practice nowaday.

In more recent times, TTL components have been largely replaced by those using complementary metal-oxide semiconductor (CMOS) circuits, which are based on both n-channel and p-channel field-effect transistors (FETs). For example, the simplest CMOS logic gate is the inverter (or NOT gate in logic design) consisting of one n-channel and one p-channel metal-oxide semiconductor field-effect transistors (MOSFETs) shown in Figure 1.3. The FETs can be viewed as switches controlled by the input A. For n-channel MOSFETs (NMOS), they turn on (or off) when input A is logic 1 (or logic 0), while, for p-channel MOSFETs (PMOS), the situation reverses. For example, as displayed in Figure 1.3(c), when input A is logic 1, Q_2 turns off and Q_1 turns on, and hence, Y gets logic 0. In Figure 1.3(d), when input A is logic 0, Q_2 turns on and Q_1 turns off, which leads to logic 1 of Y. So that, ideally, no static power is consumed from V_{DD} to ground in CMOS logic gates except the leakage power. However, dynamic power is unavoidable and it is consumed during the signal transition.

The most commonly used logic is the positive or active-high logic. In which, a low logic level represents the false condition while a high logic level represents the true condition. In contrast, the negative or active-low logic is used in the reverse condition, particularly for situations that some digital circuits are able to sink more current than drive. Many control signals in electronics are active-low signals, such as reset signal of flip-flops, chip-select signal and so on. Logic families such as TTL can sink more current than they can source, so fanout and noise immunity increase. Active-high and active-low logic are typically mixed: for example, a memory IC may have a chip-select and output-enable signals that are active-low, while the data and address signals are typically active-high.

One of the salient feature of digital logic is the noise margin for possible fluctuation or disturbance induced on the input signals, as shown in Figure 1.4. The output low/high voltage is lower/higher than the input low/high voltage so that disturbance induced on the input signals of a logic gate does not affect its logic function. The symbols for the voltage thresholds are listed below.

- V_{OL}: output low voltage – a component must drive a signal with a voltage below this threshold to establish a low level at the output.
- V_{OH}: output high voltage – a component must drive a signal with a voltage above this threshold to establish a high level at the output.
- V_{IL}: input low voltage – a component receiving a signal with a voltage below this threshold will be represented as a logic low at the input.
- V_{IH}: input high voltage – a component receiving a signal with a voltage above this threshold will be represented as a logic high at the input.

With these thresholds, noise margin exists and signals could not be misinterpreted. For example, in Figure 1.4, the signal with noise is assumed to be the output signal of a logic gate. When the output is logic 0, its voltage level under the effects of noise

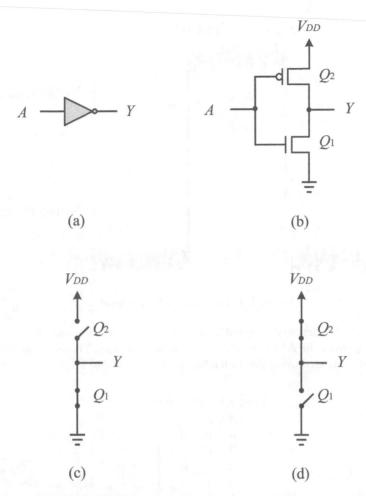

Figure 1.3: CMOS inverter: (a) symbol, (b) transistor-level schematic, (c) operation when the input A is logic 1, and (d) operation when the input A is logic 0.

is lower than V_{OL}, and certainly lower than V_{IL} of the input of another logic gate it drives as well. Therefore, the disturbance will not cause misinterpretation on the input of another logic gate it drives.

1.3   BOOLEAN ALGEBRA AND LOGIC DESIGN

Sometimes, digital circuit design also refers to the logic design. A digital function can be generally expressed by the Boolean equation. Boolean algebra is an algebra that deals with binary variables and logic operations. For example, the Boolean equation of the output Y is written as

$$Y = A \cdot B \cdot \bar{C} + \bar{A} \cdot B \cdot \bar{C} + C \tag{1.1}$$

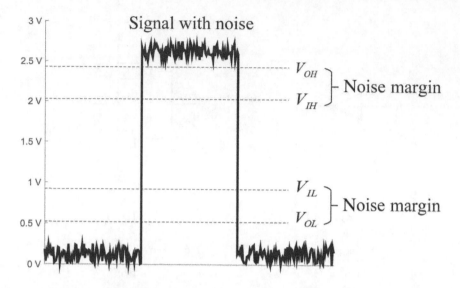

Figure 1.4: Thresholds of logic level.

where $\overline{(\cdot)}$, $\cdot$, and $+$ denote the logical bitwise NOT, AND, and OR operations, respectively. Sometimes, the AND operation is omitted for clarity. The Boolean equation of Y can be visualized using the truth table, as shown in Table 1.1.

Table 1.1: Truth table of Y.

A	B	C	Y
0	0	0	0
0	0	1	1
0	1	0	1
0	1	1	1
1	0	0	0
1	0	1	1
1	1	0	1
1	1	1	1

To optimize the logic function, the Karnaugh map (K-map) is a method of simplifying Boolean algebra expressions, as displayed below.

	AB 00	01	11	10
C				
0	0	1	1	0
1	1	1	1	1

Based on the K-map, the Boolean equation can be reduced to

$$Y = B + C. \tag{1.2}$$

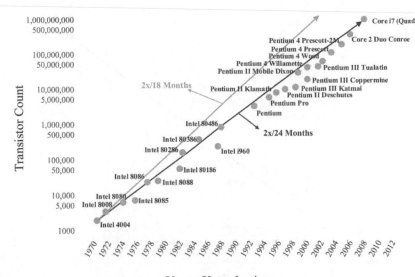

Figure 1.5: Moore's law and the trend in transistor count of Intel processors.

This is not surprising because, according to Boolean algebra,

$$
\begin{aligned}
Y &= A \cdot B \cdot \bar{C} + \bar{A} \cdot B \cdot \bar{C} + C \\
&= B \cdot \bar{C} + C \\
&= B \cdot \bar{C} + (B+1) \cdot C \\
&= B + C.
\end{aligned}
\tag{1.3}
$$

However, the optimization of traditional design method is done by hand, which is not suitable for modern IC design. Instead, current designs rely much on the computer tools, introduced below.

1.4 COMPUTER-AIDED DESIGN

The advances of IC technology obey the Moore's law, named after Gordon Moore, the co-founder of Fairchild Semiconductor and Intel, for several decades since 1965. Moore's law, which has been used in the semiconductor industry to guide long-term planning, is the observation that the number of transistors in an IC doubles about every two years, as shown in Figure 1.5. Moore's law has been quoted by Intel executive David House as "chip performance would double every 18 months (being a combination of the effects of denser and faster transistors)". Notice that, the 1965 paper of Gordon Moore described a doubling every year in the number of components per IC. He revised the forecast to doubling every two years in 1975.

The same trend exists in the dynamic random-access memory (DRAM) capacity, as shown in Figure 1.6.

In the beginning, the designers manually built their circuits on the breadboard, and the IC layout, arrangement of location and connection of circuit components,

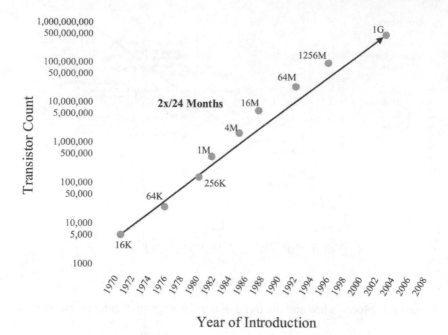

Year of Introduction

Figure 1.6: Moore's law and the trend in DRAM capacity.

was done on paper or by hand on a graphic computer terminal. However, the physical properties of the IC are determined by many important operating characteristics, including switching speed between low and high voltages, which is affected by the current driven and sinked, and the minimum size of each transistor, i.e., the minimum feature size. In addition, according to the Moore's law, rapid and continuous development of IC technology called for effective electronic design automation (EDA) techniques.

Computer-aided design (CAD) is a paradigm shift for design automation to increase the productivity of the designer, improve the quality of design, ease communications through documentation, and to create a database for manufacturing. CAD tools are computer programs that help manage one or more aspects of the design process. Modern systems with high complexity are usually impossible to develop and verify without the aids of CAD. The CAD software is the use of computers (or workstations) to aid in the creation, modification, analysis, or optimization of a design. Its output is often in the form of electronic files for print, machining, or other manufacturing operations. Nowadays, chip designers are using CAD tools, such as simulation, verification, and physical implementation tools, to handle the complexity of their circuits and speed up the design process.

1.5 ASIC DESIGN FLOW

It's not uncommon to see a mixture of analog and digital components in a mixed-mode circuit to save the system cost and printed circuit board (PCB) area. However,

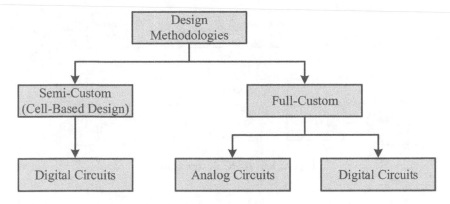

Figure 1.7: Design methodologies.

analog and digital circuits are designed using totally different methodologies and tools. Cares should be given to integrate them into a single chip.

There are two different IC design methodologies, that is, full-custom and semi-custom designs, as shown in Figure 1.7. Full-custom design fully specifies the transistor size, placement of each transistor, and their interconnections manually. Full-custom designs offer the highest performance and smallest die size with the disadvantages of increased design time, complexity, and risk. Small or high-speed analog and digital circuits requiring custom optimization adopt the full-custom design. Traditional microprocessors were exclusively full-custom designs, but engineers are turning to semi-custom designs in this field too.

Semi-custom or cell-based design describes the behavior of digital circuits using a high-level language, i.e., the hardware description language (HDL), which is widely adopted for modern digital ASIC designs. Depending on suitable software tools, logic gate schematic is then synthesized by the use of a standard cell library, and physical layout can subsequently be implemented. A standard cell library is a collection of characterized logic gates that can be used by the logic synthesis tool to realize the design described by a hardware description language. The library needs to update when technology advances.

Digital design based on cells or logic gates thus becomes an easier task without needing to consider physical and detailed information of semiconductor devices. Though cells themselves are developed using the full-custom design. All mask layers are still customized and optimized for placements of logic gates and their interconnects without needing to care about the physical details within cells themselves. Owing to advantages in the cell-based design, it has become the de facto design method for digital circuits.

We introduce the ASIC design flow here. In general, as the design flow progresses toward a physically realizable form, the design database becomes progressively more laden with technology-specific information. After the stage of system specification, where the leader confirms the design feasibility, decides which components take the

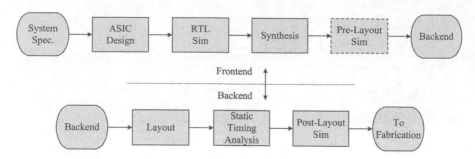

Figure 1.8: ASIC design flow.

in-house or outsourcing solutions, and then partitions the (digital and analog) designs into several blocks including interface definition, the design stage is kicked off.

As presented in Figure 1.8, the ASIC design flow mainly has three stages: ASIC design, synthesis, and layout. Frontend phase of ASIC design (or cell-based design) using standard cell generally ends at the synthesis stage. Once the synthesis tool has mapped the HDL description into a gate netlist, the netlist is passed off to the backend phase, where HDLs do not play a significant role.

In the design stage, the RTL simulation uses the behavioral models of analog circuits and silicon intellectual properties (IPs) to verify the functions of digital designs. In the synthesis stage, the timing models of analog circuits and silicon IPs are read in by the synthesizer ignoring any timing constructs in RTL codes, and then, together with the synthesis constraints, they apply to optimize the digital circuits. The physical layouts of sub-blocks, including digital, analog, and outsourcing IPs, are merged and verified for design rules of semiconductor process in the layout stage. Digital and analog circuits are separately developed by digital and analog teams. Owing to the sensitivity to disturbances in analog circuits, new analog circuits are verified through measurements by test chip in addition to SPICE simulation.

To cut down the design time, traditional pre-layout simulation (pre-sim) with delay annotation, which is used to validate the constraints used for synthesis, can be skipped if designers have enough confidence in their synthesis constraints. For instance, the clock schemes of design are simple, or the design is not or has just been slightly modified for maintenance and its constraints had been verified in its previous version. Annotated with exact standard delay format (SDF) file, the post-layout simulation (post-sim) is very time consuming for a large design. Therefore, designers only select and simulate a few normal patterns. Simulation with SDF annotation is a sort of timing analysis. To differentiate it from the timing analysis based on the design constraints, the post-sim is also named dynamic timing analysis. By contrast, the timing analysis based on the design constraints is very fast, and directly performs on the characterized delays of logic gates. The analysis is also called static timing analysis (STA) to emphasize that the analysis relying on the design constraints does not need time-consuming simulations and dynamic simulation patterns. Finally, the design database is taped-out for masking and fabrication.

ASIC can be manufactured using standard cell or gate array. Gate array is a pre-fabricated silicon chip with most transistors having no predetermined function. Components in a gate array are later interconnected to fulfill the desired functionality. Shared masks can save the cost for advanced semiconductor process.

To give an idea what will fit on a typical ASIC, Table 1.2 lists the number of gate counts for typical digital building blocks. The gate count of a specific component is assessed base on its area relative to that of a 2-input NAND gate. The area size is subject to the processing technology while gate count is not. To evaluate the size of a circuit, we often convert the area to equivalent gate count. Consequently, a gate count equivalent is the 2-input NAND gate composed of four transistors.

Table 1.2: Gate counts of IC components.

Component	Equivalent Gate Count
1-bit of DRAM	0.05
1-bit of ROM	0.25
2-input NAND gate	1
1-bit of SRAM	1.5
Latch	2.5
2-to-1 multiplexer	4
2-input XOR	4
3-input XOR	6
D flip-flop	6
D flip-flop with reset (or set)	8
4-input XOR	9
2-bit carry-save adder	9
D flip-flop with reset and clock enable	12
1-bit full adder	12.5
64-bit carry-lookahead adder	750
32-bit multiplier	7500

Example 1.1. Estimate the total amount of gate counts occupied by the eight-tap finite impulse response (FIR) filter. The output $y(n)$, where n denotes the sampling index, is calculated as follows:

$$y(n) = \sum_{m=0}^{7} h_m x(n-m).$$

We assume that all 8 inputs $x(n-m)$ and 8 weights h_m, $m = 0, 1, ..., 7$, are 32-bit wide. The operands of multipliers and adders are all 32 bits as well.

Solution: There are 8 multipliers and 7 adders in the circuit. Therefore, based on the gate counts of multipliers and adders listed in the previous table,

$$\text{The total gate count of multipliers } (A_m) = 8 \times 7500 = 6 \times 10^4 \text{ gate counts,}$$
$$\text{The total gate count of adders } (A_a) = 7 \times 750 = 5.25 \times 10^3 \text{ gate counts.}$$

To get the total gate count, A_{FIR}, we sum the gate counts of each components. The gate count of a FIR filter is dominated by the multipliers as

$$A_{\text{FIR}} \;=\; A_m + A_a = 6.525 \times 10^4 \text{ gate counts} = 65.25 \text{ K gates}$$

where $\text{K} = 10^3$.

□

Example 1.2. Estimate how many FIR filters of the previous example will, in 2019, fit into the area of a single FIR filter implemented in 2015.

Solution: Based on the Moore's Law, the number of transistors in an IC doubles about every two years, which leads to the following increase N in FIR filter density:

$$N = 2^{(2019-2015)/2} = 4.0.$$

□

1.6 HARDWARE DESCRIPTION LANGUAGE

Besides CAD tools, the HDL forms an integral part of EDA systems. HDL can conveniently represent the function of digital logic independent of physical devices. Specifically, in computer engineering, HDL is a specialized computer language used to describe the behavioral and structure of electronic circuits, and most commonly, digital logic circuits, before they are created physically, as shown in Figure 1.9, where functional blocks, including control unit, buffer, and arithmetic and logic unit (ALU), will be described using the HDL. Finally, the foundry produces the IC according to the layout.

Due to the exploding complexity of electronic circuits in the late 1960s, circuit designers needed standard digital logic descriptions to be performed at a high level while reducing the risk of producing a flawed design. There are two major hardware description languages: Verilog and VHDL. As design shifted to very-large-scale integration (VLSI), the first modern HDL, Verilog, was originated and introduced by Gateway Design Automation in 1983 and 1985, respectively. Later, the VHDL was respectively initiated and standardized by IEEE in 1983 and 1987 under contract from DARPA. Cadence Design Systems acquired the rights to Verilog in 1990 and then released it to public domain in 1991.

During 1995, Verilog HDL was ratified by IEEE as the IEEE 1364–1995 standard, later revised as 1364–2001 (also called Verilog-2001) and 1364–2005 standards. Over the years, much effort has been invested in improving the Verilog HDL, particularly in its verification capability. The latest version of Verilog, formally known as IEEE 1800–2005 SystemVerilog, introduces many new features (classes, random variables, and properties/assertions) to address the growing need for better testbench randomization, design hierarchy, and reuse. Today, Verilog language is commonly

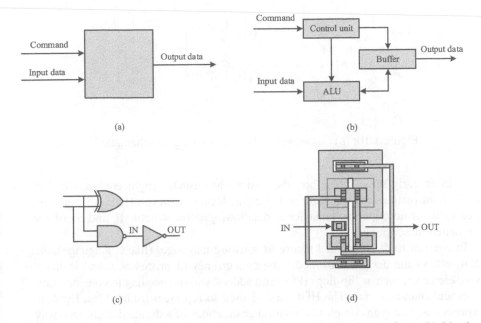

Figure 1.9: From design concept to physical layout: (a) circuit interface, (b) block diagram and its implementation described by HDL, (c) a portion of synthesized logic gates in the circuit, and (d) layout of the inverter.

used by system architects, ASIC and field programmable gate array (FPGA) designers, verification engineers, and model developers.

Prototype ICs are too expensive and time consuming to build, so all modern designs rely on HDL to describe, design, and test a circuit in software before it finally goes into the manufacturing stage. The HDL enables a precise, formal description of an electronic circuit that allows for the automated analysis and simulation of an electronic circuit.

The Verilog HDL had become the popular standard of HDLs and the choice of many design teams. The Verilog HDL simulator, Verilog-XL, developed by Cadence Design Systems quickly gained acceptance from design engineers. The advent of logic synthesis in the late 1980s also radically changed the methodology of digital designs to cell-based design. The Verilog HDL description is synthesized into a netlist (a specification of physical electronic components and how they are connected together), as shown in Figure 1.10, which can then be placed and routed to produce the set of masks used to create an IC. The gate-level netlist describes the logic gate schematic.

As a documentation language, an HDL is used to represent digital systems in a self-documenting form that can be read by both humans and computers. The language content can be stored, retrieved, edited, exchanged, and transmitted easily. The HDL needs not to be tied to a specific semiconductor technology, such as CMOS or

or u1(A[0], IN[0], IN[1]);
or u2(A[1], IN[2], IN[3]);
and u3(OUT, A[0], A[1]);

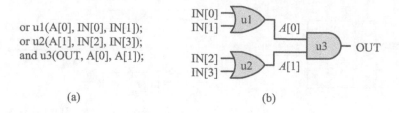

(a)   (b)

Figure 1.10: (a) Gate-level netlist. (b) Logic gate schematic.

BJT, in an early stage. Therefore, the designs are usually engineered at a higher level of abstraction than transistor or logic gate levels. However, HDL still supports four kinds of descriptions: behavioral, dataflow, gate (or structural), and transistor (or switch) descriptions.

In contrast to the sequential nature in software languages (like C language), the HDL allows the designers to model the concurrency of processes found in hardware elements, such as flip-flops (FFs) and adders, without needing to consider their electrical characteristics. The HDL can be used to represent truth tables, Boolean expressions, and even complex behavioral abstractions of a digital design. One way to view an HDL is to understand the relationship between input and output signals of a circuit that it describes.

HDLs can be processed by different computer softwares efficiently and can also be used in major steps of the traditional design flow, such as design entry, functional simulation, logic synthesis, timing verification, and fault simulation. Timing verification is assessed by both timing analysis and timing simulation. Fault simulation is used to confirm the testability for the mass production of an IC. They will be introduced in the following sections.

An HDL looks much like a high-level programming language, such as C, including a textual description consisting of expressions, statements, and control structures. Another vital difference between most programming languages and HDLs is that HDLs explicitly include the notion of time, which is a distinctive attribute of hardware. An HDL supports the co-simulation of digital and analog circuits. In a cell-based design, digital circuits can be designed in different abstract levels, while analog circuits are designed and simulated in the transistor level because detailed electrical characteristics of the circuit is essential for an analog circuit. Behavior models of analog circuits are mainly used to verify the digital circuits. Owing to the complexity in analog circuits, digital and analog circuits are designed and verified separately. Physical analog circuits will be merged into the whole chip in a later design stage.

1.7 DESIGN ENTRY BASED ON REGISTER-TRANSFER LEVEL

The modern semi-custom digital design of choice is the RTL. By contrast, the design entry is the transistor level for full-custom analog circuit and it is also the entry for

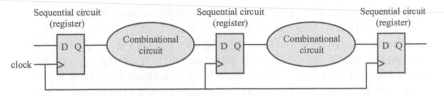

Figure 1.11: Register-transfer level: the transfer of information among registers.

a few digital designs. Operations of modern digital circuits are designed based on clocks and synchronous to the edges of them. The term RTL refers to the fact that it focuses on describing the flow of signals between registers, as presented in Figure 1.11. RTL describes the model in terms of cycles, based on a defined clock. The flow of data in RTL modeling is based on a clock. The result of an operation transfers contents from one register to another through combinational circuits, and then replaces the contents of registers. An RTL model must be accurate at the boundary of every clocked element. Therefore, the timing of the registers (or sequential D flip-flops), such as setup time and hold time, should be guaranteed.

The binary information in a digital circuit must have a physical component for storing individual bits. A binary sequential cell is such a device that is capable of storing one bit of information, i.e., one of two stable states, 0 or 1. A register is a group of binary sequential cells. The Verilog HDL simulation enables engineers to work at a higher level of abstraction than simulation at the schematic level, and thus tremendously increases design capacity. It is mainly used to implement RTL abstraction for the functional model of synchronous digital circuits in terms of the data (signals) flows between hardware registers and the logical operations performed on those data (signals), and timing modeling of a circuit as well.

There are several salient features of RTL designs compared to traditional schematic designs.

- **Easy-to-design**: a concise representation of the RTL design is comprehensive and easy to design and modify. Designers can focus on the architectural exploration until a cost-effective implementation meeting the desired functionality is determined. By contrast, the functionality of gate-level schematics is hard to understand and design. Moreover, a complex system can be partitioned into smaller pieces of RTL designs and, for simulation purpose, a portion of the system can be written in behavioral models using all abstraction levels. Those designs described by their behavioral models can be simultaneously developed by in-house or outsourcing design teams. Designers for ultimate high-speed microprocessors preferred gate-level description because the netlists derived by the logic synthesis may not be optimal. However, owing to the maturity in EDA techniques, RTL designs are also becoming more and more popular for contemporary timing-critical designs, such as ARM processor.

- **Easy-to-debug**: the functional verification of designs described and simulated at the RTL can be done early in the design cycle, which can greatly cut down the design time and risk. A bug found at a later stage, such as the gate-level netlist or physical layout, may necessitate returning to an earlier stage to fix it. However, no matter how long simulation runs, only a portion of possible design behavior will be exercised that might hide serious bugs. Consequently, formal verification and assertion checking techniques have emerged. The advantage of formal verification is quite clear: it can exhaustively analyze a design via mathematical analysis rather than simulation tests. The formal verification relies on assertions about intended design functionality and constraints to keep the analysis restricted to legal behavior. Bugs can be found by violating the input rules or protocols for which the chip was designed. Equivalence checking is formal verification and it is used to check the equivalence between RTL, gate-level, and transistor-level netlists. Assertion checking can also be used to confirm the code coverage by simulation patterns. Furthermore, the programmable language interface (PLI) allows the users to customize their Verilog simulators through interacting with the internal data structures of Verilog.
- **Portability**: designs can be implemented using Verilog constructs without pertaining to a specific fabrication technology. A gate-level netlist can be optimized and mapped to the target technology without changing the Verilog HDL design. Moreover, the same HDL design can be used for different physical implementations, including ASIC or FPGA. Notably, opposite to standard electronic components bought from off-the-shelf ICs, which are designed for a broad range of use, an ASIC is an IC made for specific applications or purposes, i.e., a custom made chip. Most ICs belong to ASICs. The ASIC and standard ICs are designed in exactly the same way by using the same technologies, libraries, and design tools. However, a FPGA is an IC designed to be configured or programmed by a designer after manufacturing. The same HDL files can be used for both ASIC and FPGA deign flows.
- **Integrability**: circuits can be designed at various abstract levels, including RTL, gate level, a mixture of RTL and gate levels. The system-level design can be quickly integrated via designs implemented by themselves or silicon IP (macro cell or megacell) in all abstract levels sold by vendors. For simulation purposes, behavioral codes and even switch level can be co-simulated using the same HDL.
- **Tool-chain support**: various CAD tools, including the verification tools, simulator, design-for-testability (DFT), and formal verification, logic synthesis and layout tools, support Verilog. Also, all vendors of standard cell libraries provide Verilog HDL libraries for various wafer foundries. The productivity advantage inherited from the RTL design and the complete tool chain soon displaced manually-crafted digital schematic.

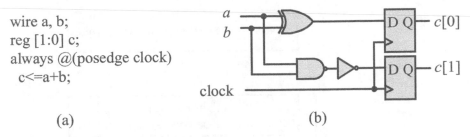

```
wire a, b;
reg [1:0] c;
always @(posedge clock)
  c<=a+b;
```

(a)   (b)

Figure 1.12: Half adder with registered output: (a) a glance at the RTL design (b) schematic.

As displayed in Figure 1.12, a synchronous circuit designed in RTL consists of two kinds of elements: registers (sequential logic, usually implemented by D flip-flops) and combinational logic. The circuit operation is synchronized to the edges of the clock signal by registers having memory attributes. The synchronous design can reduce the design complexity; meanwhile, it can also improve the design performance via skills like pipelining. Combinational logic only consists of logic gates and performs all the logical functions in the circuit. The designer simply declares the outputs of registers and combinational logic similar to variables in traditional programming languages. Then, describe the registers and combinational logic by using constructs similar to assignment, and if-then-else and arithmetic operations in programming languages as well, as shown in Figure 1.12. In the model, it simply describes the function that "at every positive edge of clock, latch (or register or capture or sample or copy) the result of $a+b$ into sequential cells, with a 2-bit output named c including sum and carry". Since a and b are 1-bit, the code fragment clearly specifies a half adder. The output $c[1:0]$ is the output of sequential cells with their inputs connected to the outputs of the half adder.

Modern RTL code definition is "any code that is synthesizable". Consequently, there are three kinds of RTL descriptions: (synthesizable) behavioral, dataflow, and structural descriptions. For clarity, in this book, we will call RTL designs using behavioral and dataflow descriptions as high-level RTL designs, while designs illustrated in structural description are referred to as low-level RTL designs, as presented in Figure 1.13. It must be emphasized that only a portion of behavioral constructs in Verilog HDL are synthesizable. In addition to dataflow description, synthesizable behavioral description is classified as the high-level RTL in this book.

The performances of digital circuits, in terms of speed, area, and power consumption, have increased rapidly. As well as the demand to integrate all sorts of circuits into a single chip. Designers have responded to involved complexity by designing at higher level of abstraction. Consequently, designers pay much attention to the functionality, while EDA tools take care of implementation details. With designer's aids, the timing closure is guaranteed by the sophisticated algorithms of EDA tools.

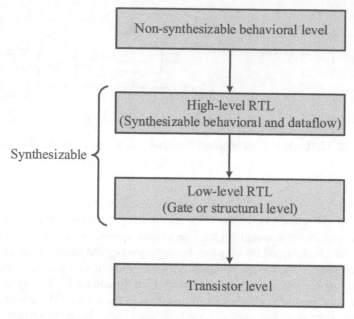

Figure 1.13: The role of RTL in four levels of abstraction.

1.8   FUNCTIONAL VERIFICATION

In addition to timing, the function validation is another crucial factor for a digital system. A successful verification plan can shorten the design cycle and tells whether verification is complete with enough confidence. Threefold functional verification plan, i.e., the verification methodology, must consider what sub-blocks of the design will be verified, what functionality needs to be verified, and how verification will proceed.

First, the blocks under verification depend on the hierarchical partition of the system. Each designer must guarantee sub-blocks they design meet their functional requirements. Therefore, this gives a bottom-up verification strategy.

Second, at the system level, a well-written verification plan is of paramount importance to ensure what the system is supposed to do. However, the functionality of the whole system and the interactions between sub-blocks become much more complex. Thus, it is relatively harder to verify the whole system that meets functional requirements under all circumstances.

Third, there are a number of simulation-based techniques to fulfill the verification methodology.

- **Code coverage**: coverage refers to the proportion of functionality that has been verified. Traditionally, the code coverage is a metric that can help you understand the portion of your HDL source codes that has been tested at least once. The code coverage is easy to measure. It can also evaluate the quality of codes written. It can check the flow of different paths in the HDL source and ensure that whether those path are tested or not as well. However, it does not give a reliable indication that all of the required functionality has been implemented correctly.

- **Functional coverage**: besides code coverage, we can use the functional coverage, even though it is more difficult to quantify. The functional coverage should identify the operations and the sequences of operations that have been verified, the range of data values that has been applied, and the proportion of states of registers and state machines that have been visited.
- **Direct testing**: it uses particular test cases to apply to the design under test (DUT) and then validates the outputs of each case. This approach is very effective for small sub-blocks which implement fairly simple functions.
- **Constrained random testing**: for a complex system, achieving significant function coverage is not feasible by direct testing because it is becoming impossible to simulate all the possible scenarios using traditional testbenches. Hence, the constrained random testing starts gaining attraction. This involves a test pattern generator that can randomly generate input data, subject to constraints specified for the inputs. Specialized verification languages, such as Vera and SystemVerilog, include features for specifying constraints and random generation of data values to be used as stimulus. The constrained random testing allows the user to generate random test patterns in a way of exercising the DUT with more combinations of inputs in less simulation time.

The verification plan also requires a testbench to generate the test patterns or vectors for each applied test case. Then, the outputs of DUT are compared to the golden results, which could be produced offline by other behavioral models written in different programming languages, or produced online by a behavioral model written in Verilog HDL, as shown in Figure 1.14. The checker might make any adjustments for timing differences if necessary.

Example 1.3. Timing diagram is crucial for the functional verification. In Figure 1.15, a pipelined design with 3 pipeline stages implements $y = f(a)$, where the combinational function $f(\cdot)$ can be decomposed into 2 functions $f_1(\cdot)$ and $f_2(\cdot)$, i.e., $f(\cdot) = f_2(f_1(\cdot))$. As can be seen, the pipelined design best suits the RTL design. Without considering gate delays of combinational circuits and timing constraints of flip-flops, plot the timing diagram of the pipelined design.

Solution: In a synchronous digital circuit, processing data are supposed to advance one stage triggered by the synchronous clock edge. This is achieved by synchronizing sequential elements such as flip-flops by simply copying their input to output guided by a clock. For RTL behavioral modeling, the gate delays of combinational circuits are all assumed to be 0. Consequently, the timing diagram can be displayed as that shown in Figure 1.16. As displayed, when stage 3 is processing a_1 in clock cycle 3 leading to the data value of $f_2 f_1(a_1)$ in signal c, stage 2 can concurrently process a_2 leading to the data value of $f_1(a_2)$ in signal b. A pipelined design

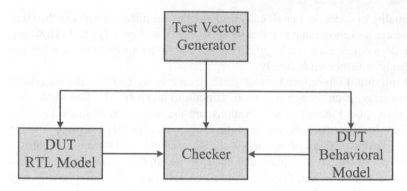

Figure 1.14: A testbench that can automatically compare outputs of behavioral model and its RTL implementation.

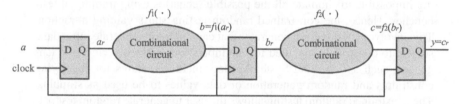

Figure 1.15: A pipelined design with 3 pipeline stages.

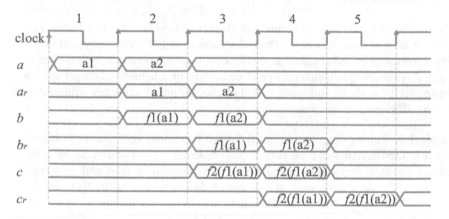

Figure 1.16: Timing diagram of the 3-stage pipelined design without considering the logic gate delay.

can give an output every clock cycle. Consequently, the throughput can be enhanced by the pipelining technique even though the design has a latency of 3 cycles.

□

The problem with simulation-based verification is that it is not feasible to achieve 100% coverage, because the combination of possible input cases and sequences is too large for exhaustive simulation. On the other hand, formal verification does not require simulations and allows complete verification whether a design meets its specification. System-level verification is more difficult for embedded systems. Efficient co-simulation of software and hardware is a challenge we are facing. Before fulfilling the hardware design, the software team can use an instruction set simulator (ISS) and the hardware behavioral model to start software development. System performance can therefore be evaluated at an early stage.

Simulating a circuit in the presence of faults is known as the fault simulation. Fault simulation is used to verify the fault coverage and effectiveness of the test patterns, and guide the test pattern generator program. The test patterns are automatically generated using the tool, automatic test pattern generator (ATPG). To reduce the use of expensive test equipments, testing time should be saved. For a digital circuit, the scan chain is a popular test technique that can make the input signals "controllable" and output signals "observable", including internal input and output signals of combinational and sequential circuits.

1.9 LOGIC SYNTHESIS

Synthesis tools compile HDL source files into a netlist description in terms of gates and interconnections. Writing synthesizable RTL codes is a practice and discipline in modern digital designs. Borrowed from traditional high-level languages, like C, "compiling" often refers to logical synthesis for HDLs in CAD terminology. The tool then infers hardware components for the model by analyzing wire and variable declarations, analyzing expressions and assignments to identify combinational circuits, and analyzing always blocks to identify sequential or combinational circuits.

After RTL design and its verification, the next stage in the design flow is synthesis. That is, the RTL design is going to be transformed into a gate-level netlist. Using the proper subset of HDL, a program called the synthesizer, or logic synthesis tool, can infer hardware logic operations from the HDL statements and produce an equivalent netlist of target library or device to implement the specified functional behavioral. Synthesizer generally ignores the expression of any timing information in the HDL sources. Digital logic synthesizers generally use clock edges as the way to constrain the circuit.

As shown in Figure 1.17, the synthesis tool performs three major steps: translation (to Boolean equation), logic optimization (in terms of area, speed, and power), and mapping (to target library or device). Synthesizer is constraint driven. You set the goals, and synthesizer optimizes design toward goals. For example, two alternative circuit structures might implement the required functionality inferred from the same RTL codes: one with fewer gates connected in a deeper logic depth, which leads to a longer propagation delay; and the other with more gates connected less deeply, which leads to a shorter propagation delay. If our synthesis constraints target at the minimal area, the tool would choose the former implementation. By contrast, if our synthesis constraints target at the minimal overall delay, the tool would choose the later implementation.

Typically, the constraints are set by a given timing specification with the minimal area requirement. Since, in addition to the functionality, the timing specification is

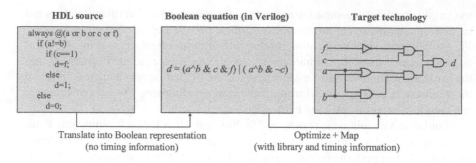

Figure 1.17: Three major steps of logic synthesis.

another essential factor for a workable design. That is, it must be guaranteed. Therefore, the synthesis tool will give priority to optimize the delay of our design. Then the area recovery is performed to reduce the area while attaining the timing specification.

A synthesis tool would start by analyzing and checking the conformability of the model to its style requirements, such as checking design rules, like discovering unconnected outputs, undriven inputs, and multiple drives leading to unresolved signals. Undriven inputs and multiple drives are errors that must be resolved, while unconnected outputs are warning and can be waived by designers. At this stage, the tool uses a simple wire load model to determine the average wire length and its loading, since at this stage the actual layout and wiring has not been done.

Using an EDA tool for synthesis, HDL description can usually be directly translated to an equivalent hardware netlist file for an ASIC or FPGA. Compared to FPGA, ASIC requires long design cycle, and is less flexible and suitable for larger-scale production to reduce its price. From the high-level representation of a circuit, actual wiring and components can be eventually derived.

1.10   TIMING VERIFICATION

1.10.1   DYNAMIC TIMING ANALYSIS

Dynamic timing analysis is carried out by the gate-level simulation with delays and timing checks of logic gates back-annotated using the standard delay format file. There are two kinds of gate-level simulations, i.e., pre-layout gate-level simulation and post-layout gate-level simulation whose standard delay format files are generated by the synthesis tool and layout tool (or RC extraction tool), respectively. Pre-layout gate-level simulation is used to verify the implementation of a RTL design produced by the synthesis tool, while post-layout gate-level simulation is used to verify the implementation of a gate-level netlist produced by the layout tool.

The gate-level simulation allows us to verify functional requirements of a design, together by taking into account physical delays and timing constraints of logic gates produced by synthesis or layout tools. Since gate-level simulations are time-consuming, it is necessary to perform a few normal test cases. Remember that the functionality of a design has been totally assured by the functional verification in the abstract behavioral level. Gate-level simulation can also validate the timing constraints and mismatches between RTL and gate-level netlists or layout. For example, when a signal is wrongly omitted in an always block for a combinational circuit, the simulation results of RTL designs would differ those of gate-level or layout designs. However, such a typo can be easily found by looking into the synthesis report. Therefore, in modern design flow, a design with high confidence can skip the pre-layout gate-level simulation to reduce the design cycle.

On the contrary, the post-layout gate-level simulation must be performed as a final verification for the functional and timing requirements of a physical design, including the confirmation of the high-fanout network, such as the clock and reset nets. Modern design flow also adopts the formal equivalence check between RTL and gate-level designs, and timing verification is done mainly by the STA introduced below to save the design cycle.

1.10.2 STATIC TIMING ANALYSIS

Static timing analysis is a method for analyzing the expected timing of a digital circuit in an input-independent manner, i.e., without requiring dynamic simulations of the full circuit by various test patterns. Synchronous digital ICs are characterized by the clock frequency they operate. The higher the clock frequency, the faster an IC can achieve. Therefore, to meet the design specification, it is essential to measure and optimize the propagation delay of a signal through each path during the design process, such as the timing optimization of logic synthesis, timing-driven layout and in-place optimizations, etc.

In a synchronous digital circuit, sequential elements such as flip-flops simply copy their input to output at every synchronous clock edges. Beyond that, the operation of flip-flops must meet their setup time and hold time requirements. Consequently, there are two kinds of typical timing errors:

- **Max time violation**: when a signal arrives too late before a clock's edge, setup time violation occurs.
- **Min time violation**: when an input signal changes too soon after a clock's edge, hold time violation occurs.

The computational efficiency of the STA has resulted in its widespread use, and it is linear in the number of paths in a circuit. Therefore, the worst-case or best-case delay of the combinational circuit over all possible input combinations can be quickly identified using the STA. Owing to process, voltage, and temperature (PVT) variations, the propagation delay of a signal can vary. Three corners including worst, typical, and best corners are commonly investigated. The STA can consider the clock skew in the synthesis and identify the clock skew after the layout. The clock jitter can be considered as well.

Example 1.4. Considering gate delays of combinational circuits, and setup time and hold time constraints of flip-flops, plot the timing diagram of the pipelined design

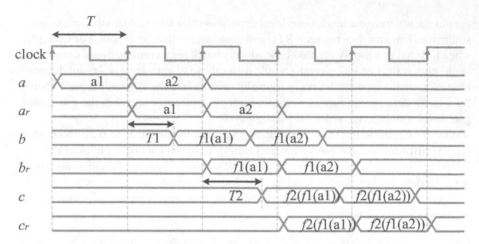

Figure 1.18: Timing diagram of the 3-stage pipelined design considering the logic gate delay.

in Figure 1.15 and explain the relations between gate delay, timing constraints, and clock period.

Solution: The timing diagram is displayed in Figure 1.18, where T, T_1, and T_2 are assumed to denote the clock period, delay of combinational circuit $f_1(\cdot)$, and delay of combinational circuit $f_2(\cdot)$, respectively, and we assume that $T_2 > T_1$. Compared to Figure 1.16, where gate delays of combinational circuits and timing constraints of flip-flops are ignored, the outputs in Figure 1.18 synchronized by flip-flops are the same. Therefore, delays are commonly neglected for functional verification. A pipelined design considering timing information can still give an output every clock cycle. Besides, the throughput can be enhanced by the pipelining technique even though the design has a latency of 3 cycles.

Assuming that the setup time and hold time constraints are T_S and T_H, respectively. To guarantee that the setup time constraints of all flip-flops are satisfied, since $T_2 > T_1$, the requirement of the setup time constraint is

$$T_S < T - T_2.$$

Or, equivalently,

$$T > T_2 + T_S.$$

That is, the clock period must be larger than the max delay (or critical path delay) of combinational circuits plus the setup time.

To guarantee that the hold time constraint of the 2nd flip-flop is satisfied, the requirement of its hold time constraint is

$$T_1 > T_H.$$

That is, the delay of combinational circuit must be larger than the hold time.

The STA calculates the delays and verifies whether the setup time constraint is satisfied under user-specified clock period requirement. The hold time constraint can also be verified by the STA. If, unfortunately, the setup time violation happens in a real chip, the clock period can be extended to solve this issue. However, the system performance lowers accordingly. If the hold time violation unfortunately occurs, since the delay of logics and timing constraint are fixed in a certain operating condition, it is generally a fatal error and cannot be solved.

□

1.11   PHYSICAL DESIGN

The final stage in the design flow is physical design, in which the gate-level design is arranged as physical components in an ASIC, or configured as physical components in an FPGA through a programming file. Design stages are similar for the two kinds of implementations but differences exist in the techniques used for their physical designs.

We enter physical design until functional design and synthesis are done. Physical design information can be brought into the synthesis stage to achieve the timing closure so that the design cycle can be fairly reduced. Based on physical information, such as the placement and routing, that significantly affect area and timing of the circuits, much more accurate timing and area of circuits can be calculated. As such, the synthesis tool can choose among alternative structures that best suit the layout tool. It's better to understand how physical design issues affect the quality of it. Therefore, we are able to make good design trade-offs early in the design flow. The synthesis adds details to the current state of the design. The verification tool, such as the formal equivalence check, checks whether a synthesis step has left the specification intact. The analysis tool provides data on the quality of the design (speed, area, power, etc.).

1.11.1   DESIGN IMPLEMENTATION

The physical synthesis (or layout) has two major steps: 1) The floorplanning & placement fix the relative positions of the sub-blocks, and 2) the routing generates the interconnection wires between blocks. A large portion of delay and power of modern designs is incurred from the wires connecting logic gates, instead of the gates themselves. Managing the floorplanning & placement step is important to ensure that critical paths only travel short distances so that high performance (and low power) can be achieved. A good floorplanning & placement can also reduce the possibility of routing congestion.

Physical design for ASICs mainly consists of floorplanning, placement, and routing. Obtaining a good floorplan is very challenging and important for placement and routing. The EDA tool provides a graphical interface to help us arrange the floorplan and figure out its pros and cons, including the feasibility analysis suggested by the global routing. Aspect ratio of a chip is determined by the designer. Square chips are easier for floorplanning and packaging than rectangular ones. The first step, floor-planning, decides the locations on the chip for each blocks in the partitioned design, particularly for the hard macro cells. Intuitively, to reduce wiring congestion and wire length, connected blocks should be placed closely, and blocks that sink/drive external signals should be placed near the I/O pins of the chip. Pin assignment, in-cluding the arrangement of power supply and ground pins, is therefore also affected by the block location, and vice versa.

The second step, placement and detailed routing, decides the location of each component, i.e., placement, and the routing channel for each interconnection wire, i.e., detailed routing. Due to a large amount of details involved, this step is automated by EDA tools by considering critical paths and area minimization, and other signal integrity issues. If not feasible, the floorplan might be adjusted or we might even go back to the frontend, such as synthesis or even design exploration. Based on phys-ical layout, detailed timing information can be produced for post-layout gate-level simulation. Finally, the chip can be taped-out to the foundry for fabrication.

Physical design for FPGAs consists of synthesis, floorplanning, placement, and routing as well. It implements the design using the resources of a programmable chip which was prefabricated. For FPGAs, the synthesis tool maps the design into logic blocks, look-up tables, or input/output (I/O) blocks in an FPGA. By contrast, the synthesis tool maps the design into cells in a technology library for ASICs. Given a large amount of details involved, the physical design of FPGA is automatically generated by the vendor's EDA tools. Many design issues for FPGA implementation are similar to those of ASICs. However, the problem is much more constrained for the FPGA because its implementation is not customized like an ASIC. The same RTL design implemented by an FPGA typically runs slower than ASIC implementation. If the timing constraints of FPGA implementations are not satisfied, we might guide the floorplanning, specify constraints on placement and routing, or use a larger FPGA to reduce the resource utilization. Finally, a bit stream file is generated to program the FPGA. Based on the netlist and timing information derived from the physical design of an FPGA, we can also verify the timing constraints through post-layout gate-level simulation.

1.12 MORE ON DESIGN FLOW

The largest portion of design modifications are due to functional errors unaware at the RTL design stage. Thus, in addition to rapid prototyping, the FPGAs are often used to emulate the design in a real environment to efficiently find out bugs in a design. The hardware emulation is therefore complementary to functional simulation, which is easy, cycle accurate, flexible, and low cost without any customized hardware for the system being developed. However, functional simulation is often so slow for a large design to complete all test cases. In addition, the application software cannot be developed concurrently. Moreover, manmade test patterns are often too simplistic to reflect complex stimuli that might happen in the physical world. The emulator can be inserted into the system-level design to replace the ASIC being developed. Thus, the whole system, including the RTL codes and embedded software, can be debugged and designed with real data through the use of emulators.

As the more number of wafers integrated in the same package, the more complex its structure is. The difficulty in finding individual bad wafers as well as the compatibility and interconnection between devices can impact the reliability of IC products. In addition, the cost issue and a shortened time-to-market cycle have urged the evolution of conventional test methods. As such, the importance of the final test has been reduced by the wafer level test.

Improving the controllability and observability of signals from the design point of view, i.e., design for test, will also be enhanced by the concept of test for design. Test for design emphasizes the collection of data generated by the test process, and analysis and feedback of them to the design side to adjust design specifications. In the future, design, fabrication, packaging, and testing will no longer be a step-by-step procedure, but a process with continuously optimized loop.

1.13 FURTHER READING

- John F. Wakerly, *Digital design: principles and practices*, 5th Ed., Prentice Hall, 2018.
- M. J. S. Smith, *Application-specific integrated circuits*, Addison-Wesley, 1997.
- Michael D. Ciletti, *Advanced digital design with the Verilog HDL*, 2nd Ed., Prentice Hall, 2010.
- Stephen Brown and Zvonko Vranesic, *Fundamentals of digital logic with Verilog design*, McGraw-Hill, 2002.
- Vaibbhav Taraate, *Digital logic design using Verilog: coding and RTL synthesis*, Springer, 2016.
- William J. Dally and R. Curtis Harting, *Digital design: a systems approach*, Cambridge University Press, 2012.
- Zainalabedin Navabi, *Verilog digital system design: RT level synthesis, testbench, and verification*, McGraw-Hill, 2005.

PROBLEMS

1. Assume that four accidents (A, B, C, D) might occur, where logic 1 and logic 0 denote that an accident occurs and not occurs, respectively. Alarm is activated when (1) more than three accidents occur or (2) the fourth accident D comes together with other accidents. Please design and optimize the Boolean equation of output alarm.

2. A seven-segment decoder that can display the binary-coded decimal (BCD) is a combinational circuit with a binary-coded decimal digit as its input and seven outputs a, b, c, d, e, f, and g for displaying the decimal digit. The seven outputs of the decoder select and light up the corresponding segments in the display as shown in Figure 1.19. Design the BCD-to-seven-segment decoder circuit and derive the Boolean equations for the outputs a, b, c, d, e, f, and g.

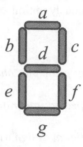

Figure 1.19: BCD-to-seven-segment decoder.

3. Digital circuits are easier to fabricate using NAND and NOR gates than AND and OR gates, which require NAND and NOR gates together with NOT gates. Convert the function

$$Y = A \cdot B + C \cdot D \qquad (1.4)$$

into an equivalent NAND implementation.

4. The eight-tap FIR filter in Example 1.1 is implemented using the architecture in Figure 1.20, where D, $\oplus$, and $\otimes$ denote the D-type flip-flop, adder, and multiplier, respectively. We assume that inputs $x(n-m)$ and weights h_m, $m = 0, 1, ..., 7$, are 32-bit wide. The operands of multipliers and adders are all 32 bits as well. Please estimate its equivalent gate count.

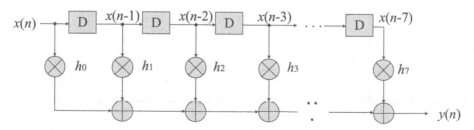

Figure 1.20: The architecture of eight-tap FIR filter.

2 Fundamentals of Verilog

The basic hierarchical modeling concepts in digital designs can be fulfilled using Verilog hardware description language. This chapter introduces Verilog basics, including module, port, data type, four value logic, number representation, primitive, expression, operator, and operand. In addition to the syntaxes of continuous assignment and procedural (initial and always) statement, the way of inferring combinational circuits using continuous assignment, always block, and function, and the approach of deriving sequential circuits using an always block are emphasized. Moreover, you will be able to learn how to write a simple testbench to verify the design.

2.1 INTRODUCTION TO VERILOG HDL

Verilog is used to describe the hardware, and therefore, it is different from software languages. Verilog hardware description language has the capability to describe the propagation delay time of signals and sensitivity of circuits. Consequently, it has the following features.

- Continuous assignment is the most basic assignment in the dataflow modeling. The continuous assignment is suitable for a combinational circuit that can be written as a equation, including the Boolean equation.
- Procedural constructs are the most basic statements in the behavioral modeling. The procedural construct can contain conditional, if-else, case, and looping statements.
- Concurrent (parallel) and sequential execution of statements are supported.
- Arithmetic, logical, bit-wise, and reduction operations can be used in an expression.
- Timing control (introduced in the next chapter) for simulating the delay of a signal produced by a physical circuit.
- Delayed assignment and delayed evaluation (introduced in the next chapter) for modeling the behavior of circuits.
- Blocking and non-blocking assignments (introduced in the next chapter) used to model the combinational and sequential logics, respectively.

Though Verilog HDL is a high-level language, remember that its purpose is to describe the behavior or function of a circuit. Do not learn or write Verilog codes like traditional software programming mindset. Particularly, Verilog HDL is a concurrent language while traditional programming language is basically a sequential language.

Identifier represents an identifiable object you define, such as module name, port name, instance name, and signal name. The first character of an identifier must use a letter, and other characters can use letter, number, underscore, or dollar sign. Verilog is case sensitive, so upper case and lower case letters are different in Verilog.

DOI: 10.1201/9781003187196-2

Keywords, which are marked in boldface in this chapter, are reserved identifiers by Verilog that a user cannot use, such as **module**, **endmodule**, **input**, **output**, **inout**, etc. Keywords define the language constructs and all are in lower case. Verilog keywords are listed in Table 2.1.

Table 2.1: Verilog keywords.

always	**and**	**assign**	**begin**	**buf**	**bufif0**
bufif1	**case**	**casex**	**casez**	**cmos**	**deassign**
default	**defparam**	**disable**	**edge**	**else**	**end**
endcase	**endmodule**	**endfunction**	**endprimitive**	**endspecify**	**endtable**
endtask	**event**	**for**	**force**	**forever**	**function**
highz0	**highz1**	**if**	**ifnone**	**initial**	**inout**
input	**integer**	**join**	**large**	**macromodule**	**medium**
module	**nand**	**negedge**	**nmos**	**nor**	**not**
notif0	**notif1**	**or**	**output**	**parameter**	**pmos**
posedge	**primitive**	**pull0**	**pull1**	**pullup**	**pulldown**
rcmos	**real**	**realtime**	**reg**	**release**	**repeat**
mmos	**rpmos**	**rtran**	**rtranif0**	**rtranif1**	**scalared**
small	**specify**	**specparam**	**strong0**	**strong1**	**supply0**
supply1	**table**	**task**	**time**	**tran**	**tranif0**
tranif1	**tri**	**tri0**	**tri1**	**triand**	**trior**
trireg	**vectored**	**wait**	**wand**	**weak0**	**weak1**
while	**wire**	**wor**	**xnor**	**xor**	

There are two kinds of comments in Verilog to describe or document a source file.

```
1 // A single line with comments
2
3 /* Multiple lines
4    containing comments */
```

You can use white space to enhance the readability and the organization of codes. The Verilog language ignores these characters.

2.2   MODULE AND PORT

As displayed in Figure 2.1, designers usually carry out a complete system from concept to physical design (or transistor-level schematic). The algorithm development and architecture exploration usually adopt the behavioral description. Behavioral modeling enables you to describe the system at a high level of abstraction. At this level, implementation is not as important as the overall functionality of the system. The high-level RTL design uses the synthesizable behavioral and dataflow descriptions, and the low-level RTL design uses the structural description. Going down to the RTL and transistor level increases detailed circuit characteristics and complexity, and going up to system-level concept tends to be more abstract behavioral model.

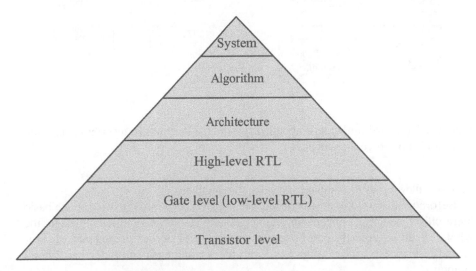

Figure 2.1: A complete system is carried out from concept to transistor-level schematic.

An important aspect of architecture exploration is partitioning of operations into components of a system. Partitioning is essentially a divide-and-conquer method for the system design. We can decompose each component into sub-blocks that satisfy design constraints, until we have reached a level of complexity that is manageable. We then design and verify low-level sub-blocks. Finally, we integrate all of them through a bottom-up approach and verify the design at the system level.

The logical partitioning should take the physical components into account. For example, as presented in Figure 2.2(a), a small embedded system is presented. The system design should consider which components, such as processor core, accelerator, memory or I/O controller, should be included and which tasks should be implemented by which components. As presented in Figure 2.2(b), if our system involves a number of sequential processing steps, we can divide our system into a number of components, each of which performs one of the processing step. Different steps can be simply pipelined to improve the system performance.

Architecture exploration is usually guided by several objective functions that we seek to optimize, such as cost, operating speed, power consumption, or reliability. Therefore, there exists a large space of potential designs that can meet the requirements and design specifications. It is clear that we cannot go through the complete design process for every candidate to derive the optimum design. Instead, we only need to use the spreadsheet for an abstract-level candidate to identify enough information, such as the number of registers, arithmetic and logic units, required memory space, etc. As such, we are able to roughly estimate relevant properties of potential

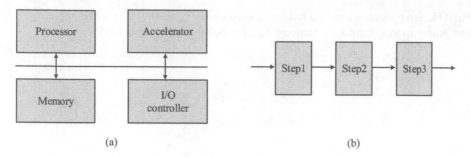

(a)   (b)

Figure 2.2: (a) Partition A: an embedded system. (b) Partition B: a system consisting of a number of processing steps.

designs, allowing us to compare and select among them.

Before we discuss the details of the Verilog HDL, we must first introduce basic hierarchical modeling concepts in digital designs. To obtain an efficient design, the whole circuit is typically partitioned into several blocks (or components), as presented in Figure 2.3. The design has 3 sub-blocks, and each sub-block has 2 basic elements.

Each block may also consist of multiple sub-blocks. Therefore, we can adopt either top-down design or bottom-up design strategies, as presented in Figure 2.4. The top-down design strategy is typically applied, while, for few designs, the bottom-up design strategy is adopted when some blocks have been readily available.

Digital systems described by Verilog HDL adopt the modular design approach. Modules that encapsulate the functionality are basic building blocks in the design hierarchy of Verilog HDL. Hierarchy can be established to manage the whole design. A module can be nested to any depth. You place the descriptions of the logic being modeled inside modules. The modules define (or design) the functionality of those blocks or sub-blocks whether they are written in RTL designs (for digital circuits) or behavioral models (for simulation purpose).

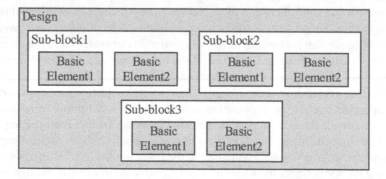

Figure 2.3: Hierarchical Verilog design.

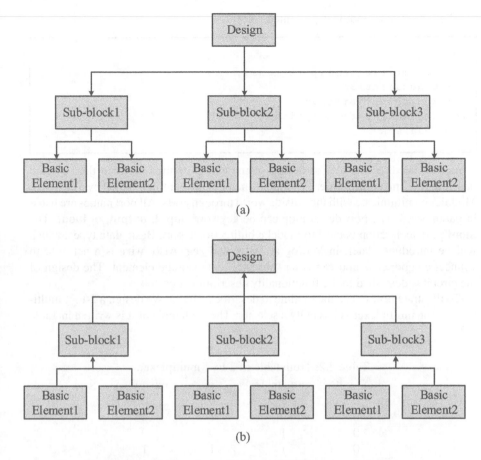

Figure 2.4: (a) Top-down design and (b) bottom-up design.

Ports are I/O signals or interconnections of a module. Module ports are equivalent to pins in hardware. To connect to other modules, all modules have ports except the testbench. The testbench, which will be introduced later, is the top module used to test the device under test and it will not be instantiated in another module. A module hides details in it and enables reusability by instantiation. You can create a larger system or component by listing instances of other modules and connecting those instances by their ports. This allows designers to modify internal functionality of a module without affecting the rest of the design provided that the I/O ports are not changed. Instantiating a module is not the same as calling a subroutine. Each instance is a complete, independent, and concurrently physical realization of the module.

The format of a module is presented below.

```
1// Module definition
2module module_name(port_name);
3port declaration
4data type declaration
5functionality description
6endmodule
```

A module needs a module (or design) name and is defined between the keyword pair: **module** and **endmodule**. The module name is an identifier named by a designer. Modules communicate with the outside world through ports. All port names are listed in parentheses. The port declaration can be keyword: **input**, **output**, or **inout**. The **inout** port declaration is used to model a bidirectional port. Basic data types, which will be introduced later, in Verilog are **wire** and **reg**. Also, **wire** is a net used to connect components, and **reg** is an "abstract" data storage element. The design of the circuit is described in the functionality description area.

To illustrate how to use the module to describe a circuit, we design a 2-to-1 multiplexer. The multiplexer is basically a selector. The truth table of it is written in Table 2.2.

Table 2.2: Truth table of 2-to-1 multiplexer.

mux_in[0]	mux_in[1]	sel	mux_out
0	0	0	0
0	0	1	0
0	1	0	0
0	1	1	1
1	0	0	1
1	0	1	0
1	1	0	1
1	1	1	1

The multiplexer is very commonly used so that it is provided as a logic cell (or gate) by the library provider. The circuit symbol and schematic of a 2-to-1 multiplexer are displayed in Figure 2.5.

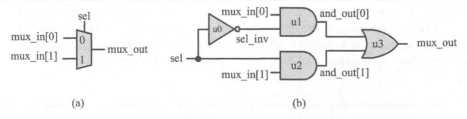

(a)   (b)

Figure 2.5: (a) Circuit symbol. (b) Schematic of a 2-to-1 multiplexer.

A sample Verilog code describing the schematic of a 2-to-1 multiplexer is displayed below, where mux2to1 is the **module** name, mux_out is the **output** port, sel is an **input** port, mux_in is a 2-bit **input** port, sel_inv is a **wire** declaration, and_out is a 2-bit **wire** declaration, keywords **not, and, or** are Verilog primitives, and there are four instances with instance names u0, u1, u2, and u3. The structural description clearly shows what components (primitives) are involved and how they are connected. Notice that ports are default **wire** data type, so they need not be declared as **wire**. The semicolon ";" is used to separate each statement.

```
1// Structural description of the 2-to-1 multiplexer
2module mux2to1(mux_out , sel, mux_in);
3output mux_out;        // Output port declaration
4input sel;             // Input port declaration
5input [1:0] mux_in;    // 2-bit input port declaration
6wire sel_inv;          // Wire data type declaration
7wire [1:0] and_out;    // 2-bit wire data type declaration
8// Verilog primitives describing the functionality
9// They are connected as the schematic.
10not u0(sel_inv , sel);
11and u1(and_out[0] , mux_in[0] , sel_inv);
12and u2(and_out[1] , mux_in[1] , sel);
13or  u3(mux_out , and_out[0] , and_out[1]);
14endmodule
```

Verilog allows a multi-bit wide (or 1-D array) declaration, which is called a vector or bus, for both port and data type declarations. While the 2-D array declaration is permitted in data type declaration, it is not allowed for the port declaration.

Verilog primitives are basic logic elements (or gates), which are synthesizable, and are structural description used for the low-level RTL (or gate-level) design. A structural model in Verilog represents a schematic that is created using existing components. Since Verilog primitives are synthesizable, actual realization of the mutiplexer is determined and optimized by the synthesis tool. You can create a larger system by listing instances (instantiation) of other modules or primitives, and connecting those instances by their ports. There are one **not**, two **and**'s, and one **or** instances in this module. The first port on the port list of Verilog primitives is an output port. In this example, the ports of Verilog primitives are connected in order (or by position association). For example, the wires sel_inv and sel connect to the **output** and **input** ports of **not** gate, respectively.

To build up a 4-to-1 multiplexer based on the 2-to-1 multiplexer through the bottom-up design, we introduce its function table first. When sel[1 : 0] is "00" (i.e., sel[0] is 0 and sel[1] is 0), mux_in[0] is selected as the output mux_out; when sel[1 : 0] is "01" (i.e., sel[0] is 1 and sel[1] is 0), mux_in[1] is selected as the output mux_out, and so on.

Table 2.3: Function table of 4-to-1 multiplexer.

sel[1]	sel[0]	mux_out
0	0	mux_in[0]
0	1	mux_in[1]
1	0	mux_in[2]
1	1	mux_in[3]

The circuit symbol of 4-to-1 multiplexer is presented in Figure 2.6(a). Its hierarchical modeling is realized by the bottom-up design strategy using 3 2-to-1 multiplexers named u0, u1, and u2, as shown in Figure 2.6(b). The same instance name (and signal name) can be used in different hierarchies of a design.

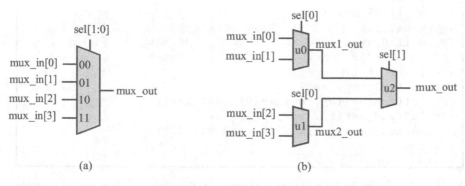

(a)   (b)

Figure 2.6: Hierarchical modeling of a 4-to-1 multiplexer based on 3 2-to-1 multiplexers: (a) circuit symbol and (b) schematic.

The Verilog codes are written below. The 4-to-1 multiplexer has 3 submodules of 2-to-1 multiplexer that demonstrates the hierarchical design. The **module** mux2to1 is instantiated 3 times as u0, u1, and u2. Notice that instance names (u0, u1, and u2) in different hierarchies can be the same. When $sel[1:0]$ is 2'b00, which denotes that 2 bits in the binary format are 00, i.e., sel[0] is 0 and sel[1] is 0, mux_in[0] is selected; when $sel[1:0]$ is 2'b01, i.e., sel[0] is 1 and sel[1] is 0, mux_in[1] is selected, and so on. Notice that the wires, mux1_out and mux2_out, are concatenated using the { } operator to form a 2-bit **wire** connecting to the **input** port, mux_in, of u2.

```
1// Bottom-up design of the 4-to-1 multiplexer
2module mux4to1(mux_out, sel, mux_in);
3output mux_out;        // Output port declaration
4input [1:0] sel;       // 2-bit input port declaration
5input [3:0] mux_in;    // 4-bit input port declaration
6wire mux1_out, mux2_out;  // Wire data type declaration
7// Three instances of mux2to1
```

```
 8 // They are connected as the schematic.
 9 mux2to1 u0 (.mux_out (mux1_out), .sel (sel [0]),
10          .mux_in (mux_in [1:0]));
11 mux2to1 u1 (.mux_out (mux2_out), .sel (sel [0]),
12          .mux_in (mux_in [3:2]));
13 mux2to1 u2 (.mux_out (mux_out), .sel (sel [1]),
14          .mux_in ({mux2_out , mux1_out}));
15 endmodule
```

There are two kinds of port mapping: by name or by position (or in order). In the above example, the ports of the design, mux2to1, are connected by name association. It's a good practice to adopt the port mapping by name, which needs not worry about the actual port positions (that may change in different design versions) in the instantiated modules. Otherwise, functional errors may occur when ports are wrongly connected. Unfortunately, these errors might not be pointed out by a simulator unless a test pattern fails.

A module written in RTL is usually saved in a Verilog file with filename extension ".v". Though a file can consist of more than one module designs (or definitions), it is strongly recommended that a file should contain a module definition and the filename is the same as the module name in it. Doing so makes the management of your designs easier.

2.3   NUMBER REPRESENTATION OF VERILOG

The logic in Verilog has four kinds of values: 0 (logic 0), 1 (logic 1), x or X (unknown logic value), and z or Z (high-impedance), as shown in Figure 2.7.

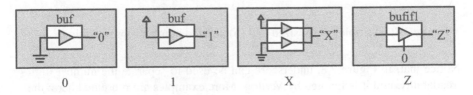

buf	buf		bufifl
"0"	"1"	"X"	"Z"
0	1	X	Z

Figure 2.7: Four value logic.

In a physical circuit, a logic actually has three kinds of states: 0, 1, and Z. In Verilog, a wire that is not being driven to logic 0 or 1 is denoted with a Z symbol. A net is in high-impedance state when the outputs of other circuits connected to the net are physically isolated from the net.

The unknown logic, X, is used for verification (simulation) purpose. When a net has multiple drivers or a timing violation happens, the logic becomes unknown to highlight that something wrong in circuits (either functionality or timing). Another case is that, when timing violation of a sequential cell occurs, its output becomes unknown, X, because it is neither logic 0 nor logic 1. Consequently, actual state for an unknown X may be neither logic 0 nor logic 1 depending on the driving strength in physical circuits or the convergence time owing to timing violation. Either way, an uncertain logic will most likely cause the circuit to fail and requires to draw the engineer's attention to solve it in an early design stage. Unknown logic is displayed in red color on a waveform.

In Verilog, numbers are integer or real constants. Integer constants are expressed as

$$<size>'<base><value>$$

A number may be sized or unsized, as presented in Figure 2.8. An unsized number is 32 bits. The base format indicates the type of number: decimal (d or D), hexadecimal (h or H), octal (o or O), or binary (b or B). The default base is decimal. The base and value fields are case insensitive.

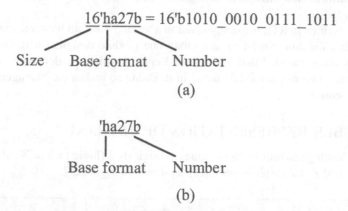

(a)

(b)

Figure 2.8: Examples of (a) sized and (b) unsized number representations.

Notice that, in Figure 2.8, underscore can be used to separate the number digit for readability, and it is ignored by Verilog. More examples are presented here: the most significant bits (MSBs) of the number 6'hCA are truncated to a binary string of 001010 instead of the original number represented by the binary string of 11001010; 6'hA becomes 001010, which is filled (or padded) with two 0's on the MSBs; 16'bz becomes zzzzzzzzzzzzzzzz filled with 15 z's on the MSBs. To represent a negative number, the negative sign should be put before the <size>. For example, to express −3 in decimal, we should use −8'd3 instead of 8'd−3. Finally, real number can be represented in decimal or scientific format.

Example 2.1. We need to design an electronic instrument to measure the time interval between two random events in one week, with a resolution of nanosecond (1 ns = 10^{-9} second). How many bits are needed to represent the time interval as a number in the resolution of nanosecond?

Solution: There are $7 \times 24 \times 60 \times 60 = 604800$ seconds per week. So, the largest number we need to represent is $\frac{604800 \text{ sec}}{10^{-9} \text{ sec}} = 6.048 \times 10^{14}$. Therefore, the required number of bits is

$$\lceil \log_2(6.048 \times 10^{14}) \rceil = 50 \qquad (2.1)$$

where $\lceil \cdot \rceil$ denotes the ceiling function.

$\square$

2.4   DATA TYPE

There are three data types: nets (physical connections between components), registers (abstract storage devices), and parameters (run-time constants). By default, net and register are one-bit wide, i.e., a scalar.

2.4.1   NETS

Nets are connections between structural components, as shown in Figure 2.9.

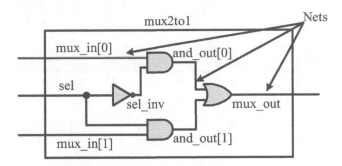

Figure 2.9: Nets are connections.

They must be continuously driven by continuous assignment, module, gate instantiation, function (introduced later), etc. Default initial value for a net is "Z". Verilog automatically propagates a new value onto a net when the drivers on the net change values. This means that whatever value is on the output of a gate will be automatically driven onto the net it connects.

There are various net types including **wire, tri, wand, wor, supply0, supply1**, etc., as shown in Table 2.4. Among them, **wire** and **tri** data types are used most frequently. Other seldom used net types are discussed in Appendix. Multiple driving is not allowed, except for those wires declared as **tri, wand**, and **wor**. The nets **supply0** and **supply1** are wires tied to logic 0 (ground) and logic 1 (V_{DD}), respectively. Nets **wire, tri, wand, wor, supply0**, and **supply1** are synthesizable, while others are non-synthesizable. Undeclared signals are default wires.

Table 2.4: Net types of Verilog.

Net Types	Description
wire	Standard interconnection wires (default)
tri	Tristate wires
wor, trior	Multiple-driven (tristate) wires that are wire-ORed
wand, triand	Multiple-driven (tristate) wires that are wire-ANDed
tri1	Tristate wires with pull up
tri0	Tristate wires with pull down
supply0	Wires for ground rails
supply1	Wires for power supply rails

Truth tables of y, declared as **wire/tri**, **wand/triand**, or **wor/trior** nets and driven by a and b with various logic values, are shown in Figure 2.10.

b \ a	0	1	X	Z
0	0	X	X	0
1	X	1	X	1
X	X	X	X	X
Z	0	1	X	Z

b \ a	0	1	X	Z
0	0	0	0	0
1	0	1	X	1
X	0	X	X	X
Z	0	1	X	Z

b \ a	0	1	X	Z
0	0	1	X	0
1	1	1	1	1
X	X	1	X	X
Z	0	1	X	Z

(a) wire/tri   (b) wand/triand   (c) wor/trior

Figure 2.10: Truth tables of y driven by a and b, when y is declared as: (a) wire/tri, (b) wand/triand, and (c) wor/trior.

2.4.2 REGISTERS

There are four register types: **reg**, **integer**, **real**, and **time**, as displayed in Table 2.5. Notice that **integer** is most commonly used for the index of a **for** loop (introduced later), while **real** and **time** are non-synthesizable.

Table 2.5: Register types of Verilog.

Register Types	Description
reg	Unsigned integer variable with varying bit width
integer	32-bit signed integer variable
real	Signed floating-point variable with double precision
time	64-bit unsigned integer variable

Registers represent *abstract* data storage elements. Hold its value until a new value is assigned to it. Registers are used extensively in behavioral modeling and in applying stimuli. We assign values to registers from procedural blocks. Default initial value for a register is "X". Verilog allows you to assign the value of a **reg** data type only within an **initial** block, an **always** block or **function**. In Verilog, a **time** variable is a 64-bit variable used to represent the simulation time typically used with the $time system **task**, which will be introduced later.

Since **reg** is mostly used in Verilog, below are some declarations for it. Though the 2-D array declaration is permitted in data type declaration, it is not allowed for the port declaration.

```
1// Examples of reg declaration
2reg a;                  // A scalar register
3reg [3:0] b,c;          // Two 4-bit vector registers
4reg [7:0] byte_reg;     // An 8-bit vector register
5reg signed [31:0] byte_reg; // A 32-bit signed register
6// An array of 256 8-bit registers
7// Address index is 0~255.
8reg [7:0] memory_block[0:255];
```

Originally, you can access individual register of a 2-D memory, but you cannot access individual bits of register directly. To do that, you must read a word in the 2-D memory. Then, you can access desired bits in that word. For example,

```
1// Read an element at an address 120.
2byte_reg=memory_block[120];
3bit=byte_reg[7]; // Access desired bit
```

After Verilog-2001, we can access individual bits of 2-D memory. Besides, high-dimensional array with variable addresses is synthesizable as shown below.

```
1reg [7:0] address1, address2;
2// 256x256x8 bits memory
3reg [7:0] memory_block[0:255][0:255];
4// Read an element at an address
5// indexed by address1 and address2.
6out_data=memory_block[address1][address2];
```

In digital designs, hardware (or physical) registers represent memory elements and require a clock to operate and update their states on edges of a clock. They are clocked concurrently. However, a register (**reg** declared) in Verilog, which just means a variable that can hold a value, should not be confused with the hardware register. Verilog registers don't necessarily need a clock and don't need to be driven like a net in Verilog. Values of Verilog registers can change anytime in a simulation by assigning a new value to the register.

2.4.3 PARAMETERS

You can use a parameter anywhere that you have to use a literal (constant). For example, the following module demonstrates a parameterized design.

```verilog
1// Parameterized design
2module param_test(port_name);
3parameter m1=8; // Parameter declaration
4wire [m1:0] w1; // Wire with m1+1 bits
5...
6endmodule
```

Parameterized design is a good coding style. Parameterization increases re-usability. For example, $w1$ can be set as a $(n+1)$-bit wire if we change $m1$ to n (i.e., if $m1 = 10$, $w1$ becomes a 11-bit wire; if $m1 = 4$, $w1$ becomes a 5-bit wire). Parameters can be overwritten when the parameterized module is instantiated. As shown below, the parameter m1 is changed to 10 by instantiation.

```verilog
1// Parameter m1 is changed to 10 by instantiation.
2param_test #(10) param_test(...);
```

Parameters are local, known only to the module in which they are defined, and they can be signed and sized. In you need a global parameter, you can use the 'define compiler directive'.

You can define a parameter, m3, by other parameters, m1 and m2, as follows.

```verilog
1// Parameter defined by other parameters
2parameter m1=8; parameter m2=10; parameter m3=m1+m2;
```

2.4.4 CHOOSING DATA TYPES FOR PORTS

An **input** and **output** port can both be driven by a net or a register, while an **inout** port can only be driven by a net. All of **input**, **output**, and **inout** ports can only drive nets in a module, as shown in Figure 2.11.

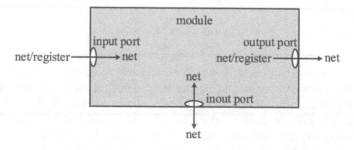

Figure 2.11: Choosing the correct data types for ports.

Finally, before leaving this section, we exemplify some common mistakes of declaration below.

```
1// Ports driven by various data types
2module top(out, in);
3output out;
4input in;
5reg in;   // Wrong! Declare input ports as wire.
6reg sum;  // Wrong! Declare nets connected to output ports
7          // as wire.
8reg op1;  // Correct! Declare variables in procedural
9          // blocks as reg.
10wire op2; // Wrong! Declare variables in procedural
11          // blocks as reg.
12wire out; // Correct! Declare variables in continuous
13          // assignments as wire.
14adder add0(.s(sum), .c(cout), .a(.op1), .b(op2));
15initial op1=1;
16always @(*) op2=in;
17assign out=sum;
18...
19endmodule
20module adder(s, c, a, b); // Full adder definition
21output s, c;
22input a, b;
23...
24endmodule
```

2.5   CONTINUOUS ASSIGNMENT

The continuous assignment is the basic assignment in dataflow modeling with the keyword **assign**. For traditional programming languages, an assignment only performs once, while, for Verilog HDL, an assignment for hard-wired circuits is evaluated whenever its inputs change. An example is described below where the operator "|" is the binary OR operation.

```
1// y changes whenever a or b change
2wire [7:0] y, a, b;
3assign y=a|b;
```

In addition to using gates and interconnect nets, you can model combinational circuit with continuous assignments. The continuous assignment is used to represent a combinational logic circuit that can be conveniently represented by an equation or Boolean equation. During simulations, continuous assignments execute whenever their expressions on the right-hand side change. As its name implies, the execution is immediate and its effect is that the output, *y*, on the left-hand side of the expression is updated promptly once inputs, *a* and/or *b*, change. The *y* on the left-hand side of the continuous assignment is the output of the combinational circuit, and hence, it must be declared as **wire**. The variables, *a* and *b*, are inputs of the combinational circuit. Because the assignment is continuous, the output updates simultaneously with any input change; therefore, combinational logic is implied.

Alternatively, the continuous assignment can be implicitly put into the declaration for shorthand as follows.

```
1// A shorthand for both declaration and
2// continuous assignment
3wire [7:0] y=a|b;
```

2.6   PROCEDURAL CONSTRUCT

Block statement is a way of syntactically grouping several statements into a single statement. Procedural blocks are delimited by the keywords **begin** and **end**. If a circuit has multiple outputs or assignments, we can include multiple assignments using a begin-end block. These begin-end pairs are commonly used in conjunction with if, case, and for statements to group several statements. The procedural blocks, **initial** and **always** blocks, that contain more than one statement require a begin-end pair to group the statements. Instead, the procedural block containing only one statement shall get rid of the begin-end pair.

Procedural blocks have the following components:

* Procedural assignment statements to describe the data flow within the block.
* High-level constructs, such as loops and conditional statements, to describe the functional operation of the block.
* Timing controls to control the execution of the block and the statements in it.

Assignments made inside procedural blocks are called procedural assignments. If a signal is assigned a value from a procedural block, it MUST be declared as a **reg**. The right-hand-side of a procedural assignment can be any valid expression with operands of unrestricted data types.

Procedural blocks are enabled at the beginning of a simulation. Any number of **initial** and **always** statements can appear within a module, and they all execute in parallel.

2.6.1   INITIAL BLOCK

The **initial** procedural block statement is activated only once, starting at the beginning of the simulation. The statements inside an initial block are executed sequentially. For example,

```
1 // Statements in initial blocks execute sequentially.
2 reg b, c;
3 initial begin
4   b=a;
5   c=b;
6 end
```

where "=" is the blocking assignment. The assignments are performed sequentially. Eventually, *c* will have the same value of *a*. Notably, those variables on the left side of an assignment in procedural blocks should be declared as **reg** representing abstract data storage elements. Initial block is non-synthesizable. It is only used in testbench.

If you write codes like this.

```
1 // Initial blocks start at time 0.
2 // Two initial blocks assign different values to a.
3 // The result is unpredictable.
4 initial
5   a=0;
6 initial
7   a=1;
```

The value of *a* is nondeterministic depending on how the assignments are scheduled. If you change the codes to be

```
1 initial
2   a=0;
3 initial
4 // Statements with delay control will be scheduled
5 // at the end of event queue.
6   #0 a=1;
```

The pound sign character, #, is used for the delay control, and denotes the delay specification for procedural statements and gate instances, but not for module instances. Adding zero delay control will ensure the statement to be executed and placed last in the event queue of Verilog. If you write a code like this, *a* will eventually be 1. However, "#0" is a bad coding style and shall be discouraged.

The functional verification is used to ensure that the design performs required operations correctly. To this, we can develop a testbench model that generates input signals to the DUT and checks its outputs, as shown below. You can put all Verilog constructs into a testbench whether they are synthesizable or not. The simplest way to produce the input signal, input_a, is using the initial block, which specifies input signals sequentially after the reset activation (rst_n from 0 to 1) and the edges of a clock signal, clk. The **wait** statement halts the execution until its argument becomes true.

```
1// After reset completes, the input is assigned a
2// new value at every rising edge of clock.
3initial begin
4   wait(!rst_n); // Wait for assertion of reset signal
5   wait(rst_n);  // Wait for de-assertion of reset signal
6   @(posedge clk) input_a=0; // First input signal
7   @(posedge clk) input_a=1; // Second input signal
8end
```

A testbench used to test the module mux2to1, which is a combinational circuit, is described here.

```
1// A simple testbench
2module testbench;
3reg sel;
4reg [1:0] mux_in;
5// Module instantiation by name association
6mux2to1 u0 (.mux_out(mux1_out), .sel(sel),
7                .mux_in(mux_in[1:0]));
8// Input patterns exhaustively generated
9initial begin
10   #10 sel=0; mux_in[1:0]=2'b00; // First input signal
11   #10 sel=0; mux_in[1:0]=2'b01; // Second input signal
12   #10 sel=0; mux_in[1:0]=2'b10; // Third input signal
13   #10 sel=0; mux_in[1:0]=2'b11; // Fourth input signal
14   #10 sel=1; mux_in[1:0]=2'b00; // Fifth input signal
15   #10 sel=1; mux_in[1:0]=2'b01; // Sixth input signal
16   #10 sel=1; mux_in[1:0]=2'b10; // Seventh input signal
17   #10 sel=1; mux_in[1:0]=2'b11; // Eighth input signal
18end
19// Display results whenever monitored signals change
20initial
21   $monitor($stime, "out=%b,sel=%b,in=%b",
22                mux1_out, sel, mux_in);
23endmodule
```

The DUT, u0, is an instance of the Verilog module, mux2to1, that describes the whole design. The testbench is also a Verilog model that, owing to its purpose, without any input and output signals. The testbench is not intended to describe the circuit that we are developing. Rather, its purpose is to apply a sequence of signal values, called test cases or test patterns, to the inputs of DUT, and to monitor its outputs (by $monitor system **task**) to ensure that correct output signals are produced. In the testbench, the $monitor system **task** displays the values of monitored signals whenever they change in a binary format as indicated by %b. The $stime system **task** returns current time as a 32-bit unsigned integer value to notify the event time of occurrence. A simulator executes the DUT and testbench models that assign values to nets and variables indicated by the testbench and DUT with a notion of the progress of time, as presented in Figure 2.12.

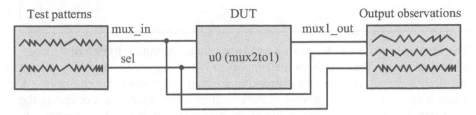

Figure 2.12: Overview of a testbench.

We often investigate the behavior of a circuit depending on the evolution of signals over time using a timing diagram, as shown in Figure 2.13. The signal transition is assumed to be ideal so that it changes suddenly. It can be seen that the timing diagram clearly demonstrates the relation between inputs and outputs.

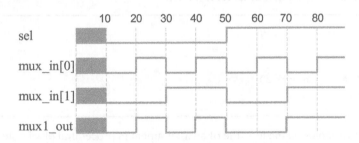

Figure 2.13: Timing diagram of mux2to1 in the testbench.

2.6.2   ALWAYS BLOCK

Always blocks and **initial** blocks are both procedural blocks that contain sequential statements. However, **initial** blocks you have already met in the testbench execute just once. Instead, **always** blocks are always available for execution like what hardware does. The statements inside an **always** block are executed up until the closing **end** keyword. But then they can be executed again.

An **always** block can imply latches (introduced in the next chapter) or flip-flops, or it can specify purely combinational logic. In describing synthesizable designs, an **always** block can contain logic triggered in response to a change in a level (asynchronous triggers) or the rising or falling edge of a signal (synchronous triggers). The syntax of an **always** block for combinational circuits is

```
1 // Syntax for combinational logics
2 always @(sensitivity list) begin
3   statements
4 end
```

The sensitivity list controls the way an **always** block executes. To describe a combinational circuit, the sensitivity list consists of one or more signals. When at least one of these signals changes, the **always** block executes through to the **end** keyword. Then, it can be triggered again when the condition meets what you specified in the sensitivity list. For example, a combinational circuit output, x, has three inputs, a, b, and c. When at least one of a, b, or c changes, the output x must respond to it. That's our sensitivity list. The statements inside the **always** block describe the functionality of the design.

Completely specify the sensitivity list to avoid mismatches between RTL and gate-level netlists, as shown below. If the sensitivity list is incomplete without signal c, the synthesized netlist will still be a 3-input OR gate but the result of gate-level simulation will differ from that of its RTL model.

```
1 // A simple combinational logic of a 3-input OR gate
2 // The sensitivity list must be completely specified.
3 reg x;
4 always @(a or b or c)
5   x=a|b|c;
```

Notably, those variables on the left side of an assignment in procedural blocks should be declared as **reg** representing abstract data storage elements. An **always** block is evaluated whenever the sensitivity list is triggered. In this example, x is recalculated as soon as any input (a or b or c) has a level transition (0 to 1 or 1 to 0). This behavior equals the functionality of a combinational circuit. So, x will be synthesized to be the output of a combinational circuit.

Verilog-2001 introduced additional syntax for describing sensitivity lists.

```
1 // Different ways to describe the sensitivity list of
2 // a combinational logic.
3 always @(a, b, c, d) // Syntax 1
4 always @(*)          // Syntax 2
5 always @*            // Syntax 3
```

Some synthesis tools consider incomplete sensitivity list illegal. You can use (*) to represent all inputs in Verilog-2001. That is, all variables on the right-hand side of all expressions in an **always** block are treated as signals in the sensitivity list. For example, the above example can be rewritten as

```
1 // A combinational logic uses (*) in the
2 // sensitivity list to represent all inputs.
3 reg x;
4 always @(*) begin
5    x=a|b|c;
6 end
```

The **always** block can be used to describe a complex expression that needs multiple assignments. For example,

```
1 // A complex expression described by multiple assignments,
2 // which are executed sequentially
3 always @(a or b or c or d or e) begin
4    y1=a+b;
5    y2=c*d+e;
6    y=y1*y2;
7 end
```

In this example, the equation $y = (a+b) \times (c \times d+e)$ is obtained because the blocking assignments in a procedural block execute sequentially. Notably, the "+" and "*" respectively represent the addition and multiplication. The multiplication has a higher operator precedence than an addition.

The syntax of an **always** block for synchronous (sequential) circuits is

```
1 // Syntax for synchronous (sequential) logics
2 always @([posedge or negedge] events) begin
3    statements
4 end
```

Sequential circuits are storage units. Rising edge (or positive edge) and falling edge (or negative edge) are represented by **posedge** and **negedge**, respectively, as shown in Figure 2.14. It must be emphasized that the sensitivity list of **posedge** and **negedge** for sequential circuits cannot be replaced with (*).

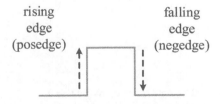

rising   falling
edge   edge
(posedge)   (negedge)

Figure 2.14: Rising and falling edges.

For example,

```
1 // A simple circuit describing both sequential
2 // (register x) and combinational (+) logics concurrently
3 reg x;
4 always @(posedge clk)
5   x<=a+b;
```

Notably, the non-blocking assignment "<=" will be introduced in the next chapter. For the time being, you can treat it as the blocking assignment "=". In this example, x is recalculated as soon as clk changes from 0 to 1 (or at every positive edge of signal clk). This behavior equals the functionality of a hardware storage element. So, x will be synthesized to a true hardware storage element. Using both **posedge** and **negedge** in the same sensitivity list, as shown below, is not permitted for synthesizable codes.

```
1 // Error digital circuit using both posedge and negedge
2 // of clk
3 reg x;
4 always @(posedge clk or negedge clk)
5   x<=a+b;
```

If you opt to do this, the same functionality can be achieved by using a clock clk2x with double frequency of clk and rewrite the codes as follows.

```
1 // Correct digital circuit using a clock clk2x
2 // with double frequency
3 reg x;
4 always @(posedge clk2x)
5   x<=a+b;
```

Furthermore, to write synthesizable RTL codes, never separate the description of an output. For example, the following RTL codes, which separate the reset and normal functions for both a and b, should be avoided.

```
1 // Wrong codes that separate reset and normal functions
2 always @(negedge rst_n)
3   if(!rst_n)
4   begin
5     a<=5'd0;
6     b<=3'd0;
7   end
8 always @(posedge clk or negedge rst_n)
9   if(b==3'd4) a<=a+b;
```

```
10 always @(posedge clk or negedge rst_n)
11    b<=b+1;
```

Codes should be rewritten below. The functionality of a variable described using **always** block should be completely contained in one always block.

```
1 // Describe complete functionality in one always block
2 always @(posedge clk or negedge rst_n)
3    if(!rst_n) a<=5'd0;
4    else if(b==3'd4) a<=a+b;
5 always @(posedge clk or negedge rst_n)
6    if(!rst_n) b<=3'd0;
7    else b<=b+1;
```

To summarize, logic is combinational if its outputs, at any time, are determined directly from the present combination of inputs without clock control. By contrast, if the output needs to keep its value, it will be synthesized into a sequential cell. Logic is sequential if it implies storage. If outputs cannot be determined at any given moment by the state of inputs, storage is implied. When outputs are determined under the **posedge** or **negedge** clock control, sequential flip-flops are inferred. Otherwise, latches are implied.

2.6.3   NAMED BLOCK OF PROCEDURAL CONSTRUCT

We can declare variables (reg, integer, and parameter) locally within a named block but not in an unnamed block. A named block is enclosed by the begin-end pair as shown below. The named block is not commonly used except for the situation that the dummy variables of indices used in **for** loops (introduced in the next chapter) may coincide.

```
1 // Syntax of a named block
2 begin: block_name // Identifier of the named block
3    reg local_variable_1;
4    integer local_variable_2;
5    parameter local_variable_3;
6    statements
7 end
```

For example, each of the following two always blocks contains a **for** loop in it. The index *i* can be used for both **for** loops by the named blocks.

```
1// Example of named blocks
2always @(...)
3begin: loop1 // Identifier of the named block
4  integer i; // Local variable
5  for(i=0;i<8;i=i+1)
6    ...
7end
8always @(...)
9begin: loop2 // Identifier of the named block
10  integer i; // Local variable
11  for(i=0;i<32;i=i+1)
12    ...
13end
```

2.7 VERILOG PRIMITIVES

Verilog primitives provide a means of gate and switch modeling, as shown in Table 2.6. All primitives are simulatable, but not all are synthesizable. Only those combinational logic and tristate gates are synthesizable. The number of pins for a primitive is defined by the number of nets connected to it. All gates (except **not** and **buf**) can have a variable number of inputs, but only one output. The **not** and **buf** gates can have a variable number of outputs, but only one input. Also, the output and bidirectional ports always come first in the port list, followed by the input ports. You can define your own user defined primitive (UDP) to augment the set of predefined primitive elements.

Table 2.6: Verilog primitives.

Combinational Logic	Tristate	MOS Transistor	CMOS	Bi-directional Gate	Pull Gate
and	bufif0	nmos	cmos	tran	pullup
nand	bufif1	pmos	rcmos	tranif0	pulldown
or	notif0	rnmos		tranif1	
nor	notif1	rpmos		rtran	
xor				rtranif0	
xnor				rtranif1	
buf					
not					

We can design an array of NOR gates, as shown in Figure 2.15.

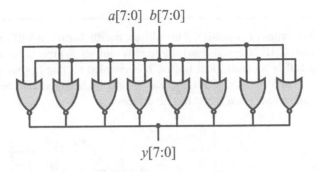

Figure 2.15: Array of NOR gates.

We can intuitively instantiate them in an one-by-one manner using the structural level description, as shown below. You must specify outputs before inputs. The instance name of a primitive is optional.

```
1// A module with 8 NOR gates
2module array_of_nor(y, a, b);
3output [7:0] y;
4input [7:0] a, b;
5// Array of instantiations
6nor nor_g0(y[0], a[0], b[0]);
7nor nor_g1(y[1], a[1], b[1]);
8nor nor_g2(y[2], a[2], b[2]);
9nor nor_g3(y[3], a[3], b[3]);
10nor nor_g4(y[4], a[4], b[4]);
11nor nor_g5(y[5], a[5], b[5]);
12nor nor_g6(y[6], a[6], b[6]);
13nor nor_g7(y[7], a[7], b[7]);
14endmodule
```

To quickly instantiate them, Verilog supports that similar to the use of a vector as follows.

```
1// A module with 8 NOR gates
2module array_of_nor(y, a, b);
3output [7:0] y;
4input    [7:0] a, b;
5// Instantiation using vectorized instance name
```

```
6 nor nor_g[7:0](y, a, b);
7 endmodule
```

Verilog has four types of conditional primitives: **bufif0**, **bufif1**, **notif0**, and **notif1**, as shown in Figure 2.16. They all have three pins: output y, input x, and enable e. For example, **bufif0** is a conditional buffer. It is enabled so that output y is driven by input x when enable pin, e, is 0. Otherwise, y has high impedance because it is isolated (or disconnected) from x and has no drivers.

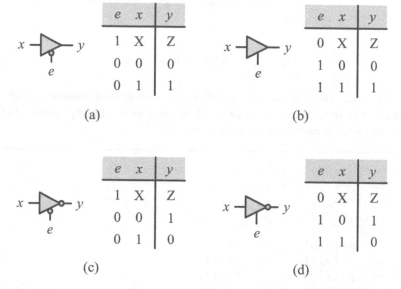

Figure 2.16: Conditional buffers: (a) **bufif0**, (b) **bufif1**, (c) **notif0**, and (d) **notif1**.

2.8   EXPRESSION

An expression comprises of operators and operands. For example. the expression

$$w = x + y - z \tag{2.2}$$

where x, y, and z are operands, and $+$ and $-$ are operators.

2.8.1   2'S COMPLEMENT NUMBER

Before introducing arithmetic operations, we present the 2's complement number here. For an n-bit binary number, $x = \{x_{n-1}, x_{n-2}, ..., x_0\}$, its 2's complement number $y = \{y_{n-1}, y_{n-2}, ..., y_0\}$ satisfies

$$x + y = 2^n. \tag{2.3}$$

For example, the 2's complement number y of 3-bit binary number $x = 001_2$ is $y = 111_2$ because $001_2 (1_{10}) + 111_2 (7_{10}) = 2^3 (1000_2 = 8_{10})$. Alternatively, you can obtain the 2's complement number of x by "inverting every bits of x and then adding 1 to the result". For example, after inverting every bits of x, you got 110_2. Then, add 1 to the result, you got 111_2 as well.

The two's-complement number system encodes 2's complement of x as its negative number in a binary number representation. Therefore, in a two's-complement number system, the 2's complement number $y = 111_2$ of $x = 001_2$ is treated as -1_{10} instead of $+7_{10}$.

Yet another viewpoint, an n-bit unsigned binary number, $x = \{x_{n-1}, x_{n-2}, ..., x_0\}$, is represented in a weighted sum of powers of two by

$$x = x_{n-1} \times 2^{n-1} + x_{n-2} \times 2^{n-2} + ... + x_0 \times 2^0. \tag{2.4}$$

When $x_{n-1} = x_{n-2} = ... = x_0 = 0$, the smallest positive number that can be represented is 0. Likewise, when $x_{n-1} = x_{n-2} = ... = x_0 = 1$, the largest positive number is $2^n - 1$. Hence, the dynamic range of an n-bit unsigned binary number is

$$0 \leq x \leq 2^n - 1. \tag{2.5}$$

A signed number is represented in 2's complement form in a similar way to unsigned binary representation. The difference is that, for an n-bit signed number, $x = \{x_{n-1}, x_{n-2}, ..., x_0\}$, the weight of the left-most bit, x_{n-1}, is -2^{n-1} and negative, so that

$$x = -x_{n-1} \times 2^{n-1} + x_{n-2} \times 2^{n-2} + ... + x_0 \times 2^0. \tag{2.6}$$

When $x_{n-1} = 1$ and $x_m = 0$, $\forall m \neq n - 1$, the most negative number that can be represented is -2^{n-1}. Likewise, when $x_{n-1} = 0$ and $x_m = 1$, $\forall m \neq n - 1$, the most positive number is $2^{n-1} - 1$. Hence, the dynamic range of an n-bit signed binary number is

$$-2^{n-1} \leq x \leq 2^{n-1} - 1. \tag{2.7}$$

If x_{n-1} is 1, the number represented is negative, since the sum of all the powers of 2 with positive weights is less than 2^{n-1}. Likewise, if x_{n-1} is 0, the represented number is positive. Thus, x_{n-1} is well known to serve as a sign bit.

Example 2.2. What values are represented by the 8-bit 2's complement unsigned numbers 00100101 and 10110001?

Solution: The first number is

$$1 \times 2^5 + 1 \times 2^2 + 1 \times 2^0 = 37.$$

The second number is

$$1 \times 2^7 + 1 \times 2^5 + 1 \times 2^4 + 1 \times 2^0 = 177.$$

□

Example 2.3. What values are represented by the 8-bit 2's complement signed numbers 00100101 and 10110001 in the previous example?

Solution: The first number is

$$1 \times 2^5 + 1 \times 2^2 + 1 \times 2^0 = 37.$$

The second number is

$$-1 \times 2^7 + 1 \times 2^5 + 1 \times 2^4 + 1 \times 2^0 = -79.$$

□

From above examples, the same binary number may be interpreted differently by different number representations. Therefore, it is important that one should know the number representations of all variables when they are described using Verilog RTL models.

2.8.2   OPERAND

There are four data objects that can form the operands of an expression, as shown in Table 2.7.

Table 2.7: Verilog operands.

Operands	Description
Identifiers	User specified signal names.
Literals	Integer and real numbers, and bit and character strings.
Index & slice names	A portion of user specified signal names.
Function call	Output of a function.

The following example demonstrates identifier, string literal, and numeric literal operands.

```
1// An example presenting identifier, string literal,
2// and numeric literal operands
3module test_literals(y1, y2, sel1, sel2);
4output [4:0] y1, y2;
5input [1:0] sel1;
6input sel2;
7reg [4:0] y1, y2;
8parameter CONST1=5'b11010, CONST2=10;
9/* sel1, sel2, y1, y2, CONST1, and CONST2 are
10    identifiers */
11always @(sel1)
12   // 5'b0000 is a bit string literal //
13   if(sel1==2'b00) y1=5'b0000;
14   else if (sel1==2'b01) y1=CONST1;
```

```
15  // 5'hOA is a character string literal //
16   else y1=5'hOA;
17 always @(sel2)
18  // 10 and 20 are numerical integer literals
19   if(!sel2) y2=10;
20   else y2=CONST2+20;
21 endmodule
```

The following example illustrates index and slice operands. Index operand specifies a single element of a vector and slice operand specifies a segment of elements within a vector.

```
1 // An example presenting index and slice operands
2 module test_index_slice(y, a);
3 output [3:0] y;
4 input [2:0] a;
5 reg [3:0] y;
6 always @(a) begin
7   y[0]=a[1]&a[0]; // Index operand
8   y[3:1]=a[2:0]; // Slice operand
9 end
10 endmodule
```

The function is delimited by the keywords **function** and **endfunction**. The following example illustrates **function** call operands. Function calls, which must reside in an expression, are operands. The single value returned from a **function** is the operand value used in the expression.

```
1 // An example presenting function call operand
2 module test_function(y, a, b, c);
3 output [3:0] y;
4 input [2:0] a, b, c;
5 reg [3:0] y;
6 always @(a or b or c)
7   y=add_func(a, b)-c; // Function call operand
8 function [3:0] add_func; // Function call definition
9 input [2:0] i1, i2;
10   add_func=i1+i2;
11 endfunction
12 endmodule
```

In the above module, $a - b$ is realized by $a+$"2's complement of b" in 2's complement arithmetic. Overflow happens when the result can not be represented because the value is too large or too small. Provided that there exists no overflow, there are two conditions on the results: 1) a carry out is generated. In this condition, the result is positive. Dropping the carry out, remaining part is the final result; 2) a carry out is not generated. In this condition, the result is negative. Remaining part is the final result. For example, $2_{10} - 1_{10} = 1_{10}$. In binary representation, $010_2 + 111_2 = 1001_2$. A carry out is generated. So, the final result is $001_2 = 1_{10}$. Another case, $1_{10} - 3_{10} = -2_{10}$. In binary representation, $001_2 + 101_2 = 110_2$. A carry out is not generated. So, the final result is $110_2 = -2_{10}$.

2.8.3   OPERATORS

Operators, shown in Table 2.8, perform an operation on one or more operands within an expression. An expression combines operands with appropriate operators to produce the desired function expression.

Table 2.8: List of Verilog operators.

Name	Operator
bit- or part-select	[ ]
parenthesis	( )
Arithmetic Operators	
multiplication	*
division	/
addition	+
subtraction	−
modulus	%
Sign Operators	
unary (sign) plus	+
unary (sign) minus	−
Relational Operators	
less than	<
less than or equal to	<=
greater than	>
greater than or equal to	>=
Equality Operators	
logic equality	==
logic inequality	!=
case equality	===
case inequality	!==
Logical Comparison Operators	
NOT	!
AND	&&
OR	||
Logical Bit-wise Operators	

unitary negation NOT	~
binary AND	&
binary OR	|
binary XOR	^
binary XNOR	~^ or ^~
Shift Operators	
logical shift left	≪
logical shift right	≫
arithmetic shift left	≪≪
arithmetic shift right	≫≫
Concatenation & Replication Operators	
concatenation	{}
replication	{{}}
Reduction Operators	
AND	&
OR	|
NAND	~&
NOR	~|
XOR	^
XNOR	~^ or ^~
Conditional Operators	
conditional	? :

2.8.3.1 Arithmetic Operators

The following example illustrates arithmetic operators, "+", "−", "*", "/", and "%". The arithmetic operators are all synthesizable. The evaluation of the Verilog codes is left as an exercise.

```verilog
1// A module presenting arithmetic operators,
2// +, -, *, /, and %
3module test_arithmetic(y1, y2, y3, y4, y5, a, b);
4output [3:0] y1, y2;
5output [4:0] y3;
6output [2:0] y4, y5;
7input [2:0] a, b;
8reg [3:0] y1, y2;
9reg [5:0] y3;
10reg [2:0] y4, y5;
11always @(a or b) begin
12   y1=a+b; // Synthesizable
13   y2=a-b; // Synthesizable
```

```
14   y3=a*b;  // Synthesizable
15   y4=a/b;  // Synthesizable
16   y5=a%b;  // Synthesizable
17 end
18 endmodule
```

To prevent overflow, one more bit of the result than the operand is required for the addition and subtraction. This can be proved using the dynamic ranges of n-bit operands and $(n+1)$-bit result. The dynamic range of $(n+1)$-bit result is larger than the value of the sum of two n-bit operands.

Similarly, the product of two n-bit operands should have $2n$ bits to prevent overflow. The complexity of a multiplier is much larger than that of an adder because the multiplication needs several adders. As shown in Figure 2.17, the multiplication of two 4-bit operands, M and Q, requires 3 4-bit adders and the product P has 8 bits. One vacant bit exists in the MSB of the first adder. It is padded with 0 because of the unsigned multiplication.

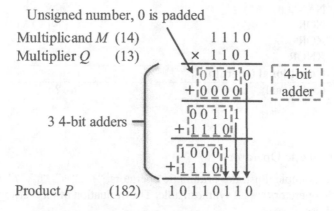

Figure 2.17: Multiplication of two 4-bit operands.

In the above module, if $y1$ is declared as $[5:0]$, two more bits than necessary, the operands a and b will pad 2'b00 on the left-most two MSBs to produce the result. On the contrary, if $y1$ is declared as $[1:0]$, two fewer bits than necessary, the 4-bit result of $a+b$ will be truncated (or discarded) on the left-most two MSBs.

The Verilog introduced power operator, $**$. The $x**y$, for example, means x to the power of y. The most common use of power operator would be 2 to the power of N, i.e., 2^N. The power operator is non-synthesizable except for $x=2$ or $y=2$. When $x=2$, it represents the shift operator introduced later. When $y=2$, it equals the multiplication.

2.8.3.2 Sign Operators

The following example illustrates sign operators, "+" and "−". The evaluation of the Verilog codes is left as an exercise.

```verilog
1 // A module presenting sign operators
2 module test_sign(y1, y2, a, b);
3 output [3:0] y1;
4 output [2:0] y2;
5 input [2:0] a, b;
6 reg [3:0] y1;
7 reg [2:0] y2;
8 always @(a or b)
9   y1=a+-b; // The same as a-b
10 always @(a)
11   y2=-a; // Negate a
12 endmodule
```

2.8.3.3 Relational Operators

The following example illustrates relational operators, ">", ">=", "<", and "<=". The evaluation of the Verilog codes is left as an exercise.

```verilog
1 // A module presenting relational operators
2 module test_relation(y, a, b);
3 output [3:0] y;
4 input [2:0] a;
5 input [2:0] b;
6 reg [3:0] y;
7 always @(a or b) begin
8 // y[0] is the result of comparison: a is greater than b
9   y[0]=a>b;
10   y[1]=a>=b;
11   y[2]=a<b;
12   y[3]=a<=b;
13 end
14 endmodule
```

2.8.3.4 Equality and Inequality Operators

The following example illustrates equality and inequality operators, "==", "!=", "===", and "!==". The evaluation of the Verilog codes is left as an exercise.

```
1 // A module presenting equality and inequality operators
2 module test_equality(y, a, b);
3 output [3:0] y;
4 input [2:0] a;
5 input [2:0] b;
6 reg [3:0] y;
7 always @(a or b) begin
8 // y[0] is the result of comparison: a is not equal to b
9    y[0]=a!=b;
10   y[1]=a==b;
11   y[2]=a!==3'b1X0; // Non-synthesizable
12   y[3]=b===3'bZZZ; // Non-synthesizable
13 end
14 endmodule
```

Notably, "===" and "!==" can compare high impedance Z and unknown X, but only applicable for simulation. You cannot build digital hardware to operate on unknown or high impedance. Thus, the comparisons, "$a!==3$'b1X0" and "$b===3$'bZZZ", are non-synthesizable.

2.8.3.5   Logical Comparison Operators

The following example illustrates logical comparison operators, "!" (logical NOT), "&&" (logical AND), and "||" (logical OR). They are commonly used in the if-else statement. Notably, the operations in a parenthesis are performed first. The logical value of a multi-bit bus a is false only when all bits of a are zero; otherwise, it is true. Therefore, $!a$ equals the comparison $a == 0$. The evaluation of the Verilog codes is left as an exercise.

```
1 // A module presenting logical comparison operators
2 module test_comparison(y, sel, a);
3 output [1:0] y;
4 input sel;
5 input [2:0] a;
6 reg [1:0] y;
7 always @(sel or a)
8    if((sel==1)&&(a>4))
9       y=2'b00;
10   else if(sel==1)
11      y=2'b01;
12   else if(!a)
13      y=2'b10;
14   else
15      y=2'b11;
16 endmodule
```

2.8.3.6 Logical Bit-Wise Operators

The following example illustrates logical bit-wise operators, "~" (unary NOT), "&" (binary AND), "|" (binary OR), "^" (binary XOR), and "~^" (or "^~", binary XNOR). The evaluation of the Verilog codes is left as an exercise.

```verilog
1 // A module presenting logical bit-wise operators
2 module test_bitwise(y1, y2, y3, y4, y5, a, b);
3 output [2:0] y1, y2, y3, y4, y5;
4 input [2:0] a;
5 input [2:0] b;
6 reg [2:0] y1, y2, y3, y4, y5;
7 always @(a or b) begin
8   y1=~a;
9   y2=a&b;
10  y3=a|b;
11  y4=a^b;
12  y5=a^~b;
13 end
14 endmodule
```

About the bit-wise operator, "~", the above statement $y1 = \sim a$ is a shorthand of the following codes.

```verilog
1 // Expanding the bit-wise operator
2 y1[0]=~a[0];
3 y1[1]=~a[1];
4 y1[2]=~a[2];
```

Similarly, $y2 = a \& b$ is a shorthand of the following codes.

```verilog
1 // Expanding the bit-wise operator
2 y2[0]=a[0]&b[0];
3 y2[1]=a[1]&b[1];
4 y2[2]=a[2]&b[2];
```

2.8.3.7 Shift Operators

The following example illustrates logical shift operators, "≪" (left shift) and "≫" (right shift). The evaluation of the Verilog codes is left as an exercise.

```
1// A module presenting logical shift operators
2module test_shift(y, sel, a);
3output [2:0] y;
4input sel;
5input [2:0] a;
6reg [2:0] y;
7parameter B=1;
8always @(sel or a)
9   if (sel) y=a<<B;
10   else y=a>>2;
11endmodule
```

In the above module, when SEL is true, y is the result of left shift a by one bit. Vacant bits will be padded with 0. Therefore, it is a shorthand of the following codes.

```
1// Expanding the left shift by one bit
2y[0]=1'b0;
3y[1]=a[0];
4y[2]=a[1];
```

When SEL is false, y is the result of right shift a by two bits. Vacant bits will be padded with 0. Therefore, it is a shorthand of the following codes.

```
1// Expanding the right shift by two bits
2y[0]=a[2];
3y[1]=1'b0;
4y[2]=1'b0;
```

Multiplication and division by powers of 2 can be implemented using left shift and right shift, respectively. For example, $a \times 8 = a \ll 3$ and $a/4 = a \gg 2$. Also, $a \times 5 = a \times 4 + a = (a \ll 2) + a$.

The arithmetic right shift operator, "$\ggg$", shift the sign bit in instead of 0. For example, if you write 8'b1100_0110$\ggg$2, you got 8'b1111_0001. Notice that signed binary numbers 8'b1100_0110 and 8'b1111_0001 have decimal values of -58 and -15, respectively. Therefore, the arithmetic right shift maintains the sign of the original value, and shifting right by 2 positions got the rounding of original value divided by 4. By contrast, the arithmetic left shift operator, "$\lll$", is similar to the logical left shift operator. If you want to keep the sign bit, you must extend it to enough length.

2.8.3.8 Concatenation and Replication Operators

The following example illustrates concatenation and replication operators, "{}" (concatenation) and "{{}}" (replication). In the example, a is replicated twice by

$\{2\{a\}\}$, which is the same as $\{a,a\}$, and b, $\{2\{a\}\}$, and c are concatenated to form a vector and then assigned to y. The evaluation of the Verilog codes is left as an exercise.

```
1// A module presenting concatenation and
2// replication operators
3module test_concat_replic(y, a, b);
4output [10:0] y;
5input [2:0] a, b;
6reg [10:0] y;
7parameter C=2'b01;
8always @(a or b)
9   y={b, {2{a}}, C};
10endmodule
```

2.8.3.9 Reduction Operators

The following example illustrates reduction operators, "&" (AND reduction), "|" (OR reduction), "~ &" (NAND reduction), "~ |" (NOR reduction), "^" (XOR reduction), and "~^" (XNOR reduction). In contrast to bit-wise operators with two operands, the reduction operation only has one operand and performs the same operation on every bits of the operand. For example, &a is a shorthand of a[0]&a[1]&a[2]. The evaluation of the Verilog codes is left as an exercise.

```
1// A module presenting reduction operators
2module test_reduction(y, a);
3output [5:0] y;
4input [2:0] a;
5reg [5:0] y;
6always @(a) begin
7   y[0]=&a;
8   y[1]=|a;
9   y[2]=~&a;
10   y[3]=~|a;
11   y[4]=^a; // XOR, odd parity
12   y[5]=~^a; //XNOR, even parity
13end
14endmodule
```

2.8.3.10 Conditional Operator

The following example illustrates conditional operator, "?:". When the logic before "?" is true, the result before ":" will be selected; otherwise, the result after ":" will be selected. Therefore, when sel is true, $a + b$ is selected and assigned to y; otherwise, $a - b$ is selected. The evaluation of the Verilog codes is left as an exercise.

```
1// A module presenting conditional operator
2module test_condition(y, sel, a, b);
3output [3:0] y;
4input sel;
5input [2:0] a, b;
6reg [3:0] y;
7always @(sel or a or b)
8   y=(sel==1)?a+b:a-b;
9endmodule
```

2.9   SIMULATION ENVIRONMENT

A top-level simulation environment, also called a testbench (shown in Figure 2.18), for a synchronous design contains an instantiation of the top module of designs, pin/signal declarations for the connections of the I/O of top design model, and clock and reset waveforms. Instantiation of behavioral models for the generation of stimulus, which is also called the input pattern, is optional. The main purposes of a testbench are pattern generation (used to model interface transactions) and output monitoring of the DUT. To verify the logic function of DUT, the testbench allows the user to stop and finish the simulation at any time, log and monitor simulation data of interest, and output (or dump) waveforms for debugging. After a simulation, users can use a graphical user interface (GUI) debugging tool to see the waveform where signals progress with time.

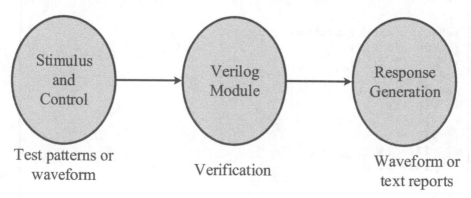

Figure 2.18: Testbench.

We need to design a 3-to-8 decoder with enable control and its testbench. The truth table of 3-to-8 decoder with enable control is displayed in Table 2.10.

Table 2.10: Truth table of 3-to-8 decoder with enable control.

en	x[2]	x[1]	x[0]	y[7]	y[6]	y[5]	y[4]	y[3]	y[2]	y[1]	y[0]
0	X	X	X	0	0	0	0	0	0	0	0
1	0	0	0	0	0	0	0	0	0	0	1
1	0	0	1	0	0	0	0	0	0	1	0
1	0	1	0	0	0	0	0	0	1	0	0
1	0	1	1	0	0	0	0	1	0	0	0
1	1	0	0	0	0	0	1	0	0	0	0
1	1	0	1	0	0	1	0	0	0	0	0
1	1	1	0	0	1	0	0	0	0	0	0
1	1	1	1	1	0	0	0	0	0	0	0

Its gate-level netlist is presented in Figure 2.19.

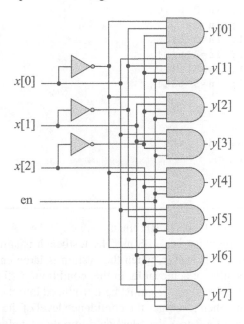

Figure 2.19: Gate-level schematic of the 3-to-8 decoder with enable control.

A testbench for the decoder can be written below. The 'timescale declares the time unit and its precision, which are significant for the delay modeling. The syntax of 'timescale is

'timescale <time_unit> / <time_precision>

For example, 'timescale 10 ns/1 ns declares that the time unit is 10 ns and time precision is 1 ns. Only use timescale in the top (testbench) module, and it is inherited to all sub-modules. If upper module has no timescale but its submodule has, an error occurs. The submodule with timescale will overwrite the timescale of its upper module.

```verilog
1 // Testbench for the 3-to-8 decoder with enable control
2 'timescale 10 ns/1 ns
3 module testbench;
4 reg enable;
5 reg [2:0] in;
6 wire [7:0] out;
7 // Module instantiation
8 decoder dec(.en(enable), .x(in), .y(out));
9 // Stimulus
10 initial begin
11   #0   enable=0; in=3'b000;
12   #10  enable=1; in=3'b000;
13   #10  enable=1; in=3'b001;
14   #10  enable=1; in=3'b010;
15   #10  enable=1; in=3'b011;
16   #10  enable=1; in=3'b100;
17   #10  enable=1; in=3'b101;
18   #10  enable=1; in=3'b110;
19   #10  enable=1; in=3'b111;
20 end
21 // Dump waveform for debugging
22 initial begin
23   $dumpfile("decoder.vcd");
24   $dumpvars();
25 end
26 endmodule
```

The time unit is 10 ns, so #10 delays 10 time units, i.e., 100 ns. As another example, #10.75 delays 10.75 time units, i.e., 108 ns. The testbench is simple that it generates stimulus exhaustively. However, when the system is large enough, exhaustive testing strategy is typically not achievable. In this condition, partial testing strategy is adopted. Some kinds of randomness must be introduced into the verification process. Assertion checking then leverages the confidence level of the test patterns.

Functional simulation for 3-to-8 decoder can dump the waveform for functional verification using the $dumpfile and $dumpvars system tasks, as shown in Figure 2.20. Verilog provides a set of system tasks to record signal value changes in the standard value change dump (VCD) format. Most wave display tools read this format, among others. The $dumpfile system task specifies which file is to be dumped, and $dumpvars system task specifies which variables are to be dumped.

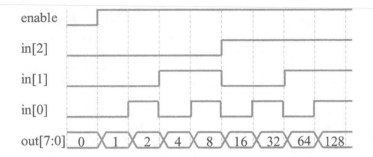

Figure 2.20: Functional simulation.

You can specify the levels and scope arguments to $dumpvars using the following syntax.

```
1 // Syntax of system task $dumpvars
2 $dumpvars (<levels>,<scope>);
```

The scope arguments are indicated by the hierarical names of the modules. We assume that the instance, top, has three instances u1, u2, and u3 within it. When level is 0, such as $dumpvars(0, top), it specifies all signals in top and below are dumped. This is the most commonly used case. When level is 1, $dumpvars(1, top) specifies the signals in the hierarchy of top are dumped, not including those signals in u1, u2, u3, and below. When n is not 0 and 1, the level n specifies the signals within the $n-1$ levels below the scope arguments to be dumped. For example, $dumpvars(3, top.u1, top.u2) specifies the signals within the 2 levels below the scopes, top.u1 and top.u2, are to be dumped.

Timing simulation (pre-sim or post-sim) of gate-level netlist with SDF back annotation for the 3-to-8 decoder can dump the waveform for both function and timing verification, as shown in Figure 2.21. Owing to different gate delays, the path delays from different inputs to output are generally different.

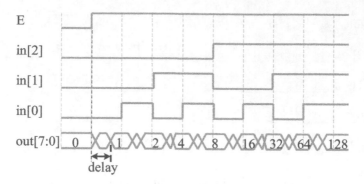

Figure 2.21: Timing simulation with delay annotation.

2.10   FURTHER READING

- Samir Palnitkar, *Verilog HDL: a guide to digital design and synthesis, 2nd Ed.*, Pearson, 2011.
- Zainalabedin Navabi, *Verilog digital system design: RT level synthesis, testbench, and verification*, McGraw-Hill, 2005.
- Joseph Cavanagh, *Verilog HDL: digital design and modeling*, CRC Press, 2007.
- David Money Harris and Sarah L. Harris, *Digital design and computer architecture*, 2nd Ed., Morgan Kaufmann, 2013.
- Donald E. Thomas and Philip R. Moorby, *The Verilog hardware description language*, 5th Ed., Kluwer Academic Publishers, 2002.
- Joseph Cavanagh, *Computer arithmetic and Verilog HDL fundamentals*, CRC Press, 2010.
- Michael D. Ciletti, *Advanced digital design with the Verilog HDL*, 2nd Ed., Prentice Hall, 2010.
- John F. Wakerly, *Digital design: principles and practices*, 5th Ed., Prentice Hall, 2018.
- M. J. S. Smith, *Application-specific integrated circuits*, Addison-Wesley, 1997.
- Vaibbhav Taraate, *Digital logic design using Verilog: coding and RTL synthesis*, Springer, 2016.
- John Michael Williams, *Digital VLSI design with Verilog: a textbook from Silicon Valley Polytechnic Institute*, 2nd Ed., Springer, 2014.
- Ronald W. Mehler, *Digital integrated circuit design using Verilog and Systemverilog*, Elsevier, 2014.

PROBLEMS

1. Let $a = 4\text{'b}1011$, $b = 4\text{'b}0010$, $c = 8\text{'b}00000100$, $d = 8\text{'b}00001111$, and $e = 4\text{'b}0000$, find the results of following expressions.

Table 2.11: Outputs of Verilog expressions.

Expressions	Outputs
$a\|\|b$	
$a \&\& b$	
$a\|b$	
$a \& b$	
$\|a$	
$\&a$	
a	
e	
$!a$	
$!e$	
$\{c[3:0],d[3:0]\}$	
$\{2\{a\}\}$	
$\{2\{4\text{'d}0\}\}$	

2. For the following time scales, find the actual delays of Verilog Model:

Table 2.12: Delays of Verilog Model.

Timescale	Delays
'timescale 10 ns/1 ns, #5	
'timescale 10 ns/1 ns, #5.738	
'timescale 10 ns/100 ps, #5.738	

3. A design called dispatcher has three instantiated sub-blocks in it: rxFIFO, tx-FIFO0, and txFIFO1. The design names of rxFIFO, and txFIFO0 (and txFIFO1) are rx_FIFO and tx_FIFO, respectively. The sub-block, rxFIFO, also contains an instantiated sub-block rxCRC (design name is rx_CRC). Please describe the above design by module and endmodule without considering their I/O port connections.

4. Please declare:

   a. an 8-bit wire, a_in.
   b. a 32-bit register, address, and assign 3 to it.
   c. an integer, count.
   d. an 8-bit memory with 1024 elements, membyte.
   e. a parameter, cache_size, with a value of 512.

5. Find the following simulation results.

   a. latch=4'd12;

   $display("The current value of latch = %b",latch);
   b. #0 in_reg = 3'd2;
      #5 in_reg = 3'd4;
      $monitor($time,"In register value = %b", in_reg[2:0]);
   c. 'define MEM_SIZE 1024
      $display("The maximum memory size is %h", 'MEM_SIZE);
6. Find the declaration bugs in the Verilog codes. After fixing those bugs, evaluate
   the simulation result.

```verilog
1 module SRAM(dout, clk, ce, we, oe, addr, din);
2 output [7:0] dout;
3 input clk, ce, we, oe;
4 input [15:0] addr;
5 input [7:0]  din;
6 reg [7:0] mem[0:65535];
7 wire [7:0] tempQ, dout;
8 always @(posedge clk)
9   if(ce & we)
10    mem[addr]<=din;
11 always @(oe or ce)
12   if(ce & oe)
13    tempQ=mem[addr];
14   else
15    tempQ=8'hzz;
16 always @(posedge clk)
17   dout<=tempQ;
18 endmodule
```

7. Redesign and optimize the alarm function obtained in Problem 1 of Chapter 1.

   a. Using Verilog primitives;
   b. Using an always block. Optimization is done by tools.
8. Verilog number.

   a. Convert unsigned hexadecimal B2EF to decimal.
   b. Convert unsigned decimal 4256 to binary.
   c. Convert signed binary 8'b0110_1001 to decimal.
   d. Convert signed binary 8'b1110_1001 to decimal.
9. Using the continuous assignment to describe the following Boolean functions.

   a.

$$\text{Out1} = (C+B) \cdot (\bar{A}+D),$$

(2.8)

   where $+$, $\overline{(\cdot)}$, and $\cdot$ denote the bitwise OR, NOT, and AND operations, respectively.

b.

$$\text{Out2} \quad = \quad C \cdot (A \cdot D + B) + B \cdot \bar{A},$$

$$(2.9)$$

10. A majority logic function is defined below.

$$\text{Out} = \begin{cases} 1, & \text{if the majority of the input IN}[3:0] \text{ are 1's} \\ 0, & \text{Otherwise} \end{cases}. \quad (2.10)$$

Design a Verilog module that implements a four-bit majority function.

11. Design a combinational circuit whose output Out[3 : 0] is two greater than the input In[2 : 0] when In[2 : 0] is 0, 1, 2, or 3. When In[2 : 0] is 4, 5, 6, or 7, Out[3 : 0] is twice of the input.

12. Develop a testbench for the above design.

13. Express the following decimal numbers in 8-bit unsigned binary format: 9, 88, and 213.

14. Express the following decimal numbers in 8-bit signed binary format: -9, -88, and -213.

15. What decimal numbers are represented by the following 8-bit unsigned binary numbers: 11100101 and 11001100?

16. How many bits would be required to represent an angle in a precision of 0.1 degree between $0°$ and $360°$?

17. Express the following unsigned binary numbers in octal: 101010101, 00000000, and 1111111111.

18. Express the following unsigned binary numbers in hexadecimal: 11100101, 11111101, and 010010111.

19. Perform the following unsigned binary additions and verify them using Verilog. Find the required number of bits for each case.

   a. 01010001 + 01010110.
   b. 11010001 + 01110101.
   c. 10101010 + 00000001.

20. Write a Verilog code that adds three 8-bit unsigned binary numbers to produce a 9-bit result with no overflow detection.

21. Perform the following unsigned binary multiplication to form a 16-bit result: 11101001 × 01010100.

22. Write a testbench to evaluate the Verilog module, test_literals.

23. Write a testbench to evaluate the Verilog module, test_index_slice.

24. Write a testbench to evaluate the Verilog module, test_function.

25. Write a testbench to evaluate the Verilog module, test_arithmetic.

26. Write a testbench to evaluate the Verilog module, test_sign.

27. Write a testbench to evaluate the Verilog module, test_relation.

28. Write a testbench to evaluate the Verilog module, test_equality.

29. Write a testbench to evaluate the Verilog module, test_comparison.

30. Write a testbench to evaluate the Verilog module, test_bitwise.

31. Write a testbench to evaluate the Verilog module, test_shift.
32. Write a testbench to evaluate the Verilog module, test_concat_replic.
33. Write a testbench to evaluate the Verilog module, test_reduction.
34. Write a testbench to evaluate the Verilog module, test_condition.
35. a. Write a behavioral model for the packet generator, as displayed in Figure
    2.22, with format: destination identification (DI) (1 Byte), source identifi-
    cation (SI) (1 Byte), priority (P) (high and low, 1 Byte), random data (DA)
    (16~32 Bytes), and 32-bit cyclic redundancy check (CRC) (4 Bytes). Differ-
    ent packets are separated by 2 clock cycles. Randomly generate packets with
    and without CRC error.

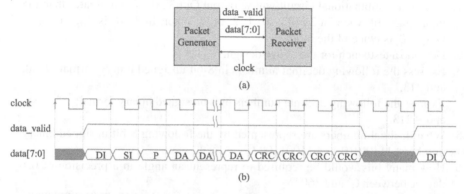

Figure 2.22: (a) Block diagram of packet generator and receiver. (b) Timing diagram
of the interface.

   b. Write a behavior model of the packet receiver. Check CRC of received pack-
    ets and obtain the data statistics for the numbers of high and low packets, and
    CRC error packets.

3 Advanced Verilog Topics

In this chapter, advanced Verilog statements, such as **if-else**, **case**, **for** loop, **function** and **task**, are introduced. We emphasize design guidelines for inferring combinational and sequential logics. The timing of a circuit is as important as its functionality. Therefore, accurate delay modeling is the key to the success of an ASIC. The differences between inter-assignment and intra-assignment delays, and blocking and non-blocking assignments are identified. Finally, the system tasks, approach of timing simulation, and several advanced Verilog features are presented as well. Notably, keywords will be marked in boldface in this chapter.

3.1 ABSTRACT LEVELS

The Verilog hardware description language allows four kinds of descriptions: behavioral description (always block, initial block, while, wait, for, if-else, etc.), dataflow description (continuous assignment), structural (or gate-level) description, and switch-level (or transistor-level) description. Which kind of description is used depends on the level of abstraction, as shown in Figure 3.1. High-level register-transfer level design includes synthesizable behavioral and dataflow descriptions. Among these abstract levels, the transistor level and the initial block of the behavioral description are non-synthesizable.

3.2 IF-ELSE STATEMENT

One of the most important and commonly used statement in RTL design is the **if** statement, which is followed by a statement or block of statements enclosed by **begin** and **end**.

```
1 // Syntax of if-else statement
2 if (expression) begin
3    statements
4 end
5 [else begin
6    statements
7 end]
```

If the value of the expression is nonzero, then the expression is true and the statement block that follows **if** will be executed. If the value of the expression is zero, the expression is false and the statement block following **else** is executed. **If-else** statements can cause synthesis of latches, which are not suitable for synchronous design and static timing analysis. In the following example, if the signal en is logic one,

DOI: 10.1201/9781003187196-3

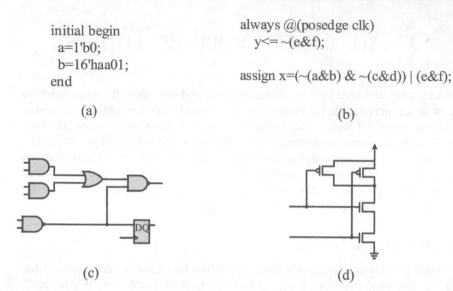

```
initial begin              always @(posedge clk)
  a=1'b0;                    y<= ~(e&f);
  b=16'haa01;
end                        assign x=(~(a&b) & ~(c&d)) | (e&f);

     (a)                         (b)


     (c)                         (d)
```

Figure 3.1: Levels of abstraction: (a) non-synthesizable behavioral level (initial block), (b) high-level RTL (synthesizable always block of behavioral description and dataflow description), (c) low-level RTL (gate or structural level description), and (d) transistor level (non-synthesizable switch-level description).

the output signal, out, will be assigned the result of in1 + in2. Otherwise, out will be assigned in1.

```
1// A module illustrating if-else statement
2module if_else(out, in1, in2, en);
3output [1:0] out;
4input in1, in2, en;
5reg [1:0] out;
6always @(in1 or in2 or en) begin
7   // Completely specified if-else
8   if(en==1) out=in1+in2;
9   else out=in1;
10end
11endmodule
```

The (**output**) port declaration and data type (**reg**) declaration can be combined as follows. Since the **output** port has a default **wire** data type. It's not necessary to combine an **output** port with **wire** data type. Moreover, **input** ports all have default **wire** data types. It's not necessary to combine an **input** port with **wire** data type as well.

```
1// Combining port and data type declarations
2module if_else(out, in1, in2, en);
3output reg [1:0] out;
4input in1, in2, en;
5always @(in1 or in2 or en) begin
6  // Completely specified if-else
7  if(en==1) out=in1+in2;
8  else out=in1;
9end
10endmodule
```

To prevent latches, the outputs MUST be fully specified. This is a basic rule of combinational circuits. If the outputs are not fully specified, latches in Figure 3.2 will be induced because outputs will keep their original states for all unspecified conditions, which coincide with the functionality of latches. Latches are sequential circuits and can be used as memory elements.

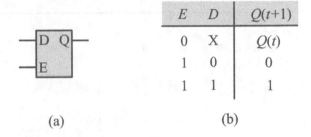

E	D	$Q(t+1)$
0	X	$Q(t)$
1	0	0
1	1	1

(a)   (b)

Figure 3.2: Latch: (a) symbol and (b) function table.

In the following example, the **else** condition is not specified, so latches are inferred.

```
1// A module inferring latches due to unspecified
2// else condition
3module latch(out, in, enable);
4output [3:0] out;
5input enable;
6input [3:0] in;
7always @(in or enable)
8begin
9  // Else condition is not specified,
10  // so latches are inferred.
11  if(enable) out=in;
12end
13endmodule
```

In the following example, signal out is implicitly assigned a default value. If the signal enable is false, the default value will be assigned to out. Therefore, out is fully specified, and no latches are inferred.

```
1 // An example without inferring latches by assigning
2 // default value
3 always @(in or enable) begin
4   out=0; // Default value
5   if(enable)
6     out=in;
7 end
```

If a vector is directly used as an expression, for example, in the if(out) statement, where signal out is a 4-bit vector, any logic 1 bit in out makes the expression true. Be especially careful when using such an expression.

Finally, the following code segment infers a priority-encoded multiplexer, as shown in Figure 3.3.

```
1 // An example of priority-encoded multiplexer
2 always @(sel or a or b or c or d)
3   if(sel[3]==1'b1) // sel is 1XXX
4     out=a;
5   else if(sel[2]==1'b1) // sel is 01XX
6     out=b;
7   else if(sel[1]==1'b1) // sel is 001X
8     out=c;
9   else if(sel[0]==1'b1) // sel is 0001
10     out=d;
11   else // sel is 0000
12     out=e;
```

Though the function of an if-else statement is similar to that of a conditional operator, they may differ in their resource sharing abilities. Resource sharing can assign similar operations to a common netlist cell, and may reduce hardware and degrade performance (due to additional multiplexers). Resource sharing must be kept within the same always block and may not be permissible for a conditional operator, as shown in the following example.

```
1 // Resource sharing may not be done for
2 // conditional operator
3 assign z=sel?a+t:b+t;
```

It may infer the circuit in Figure 3.4, where $\oplus$ represents an adder.

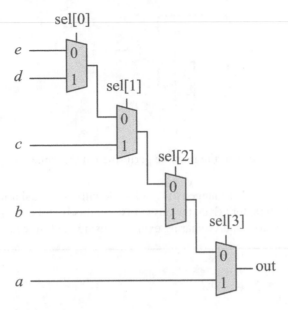

Figure 3.3: The **if-else-if** statement implies priority-encoded multiplexers.

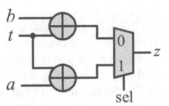

Figure 3.4: Resource sharing may not be performed by a conditional operator.

Rather, the following always block infers the circuit in Figure 3.5. The adder is shared for either case of the select signal, sel, by multiplexing the operand of the adder. The multiplexer may degrade performance.

```
1// Resource sharing in the same always block can be done
2always @(sel or a or b or t)
3   if(sel) z=a+t;
4   else z=b+t;
```

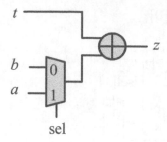

Figure 3.5: Resource sharing must be performed in the same always block.

However, if "$z = b + t$" is changed to "$z = b - t$", will resource sharing be enabled for the adder and subtractor? Even the answer is yes, this is still not a good method. It is always better to do resource sharing explicitly using the following method.

```
1 // Explicit resource sharing on our own
2 assign op1=sel? a : b;
3 assign op2=t; // Or ''op2=sel?t:~t+1'b1'' for subtraction
4 assign z=op1+op2;
```

3.3 CASE, CASEZ, AND CASEX STATEMENTS

The **case** statement is a special multiway conditional statement that tests whether an expression matches one of a number of items and then branches accordingly. A case statement consists of the keyword **case**, followed by an expression in parentheses. It must be enclosed by the keyword **endcase**, and there can be one or more case items (and associated statements) to be executed. A case item consists of an expression (usually a simple constant) or a list of expressions separated by commas, followed by a colon (:). The **default** statement is optional and is executed when none of the items match the expression. If **default** is not specified and there are no matching items, Verilog takes no action.

```
1 // Syntax of case statement
2 case (expression)
3    case_item 1:
4       begin
5          statements
6       end
7    case_item 2:
8       begin
9          statements
10      end
11   . . .
```

```
12  default:
13     begin
14        statements
15     end
16 endcase
```

The following example is a decoder with full case.

```
1 // A decoder module with full case
2 module full_case(out, in);
3 output [3:0] out;
4 input [1:0] in;
5 reg [3:0] out;
6 always @(in)
7   case(in)
8      2'b00: out=4'b0001;
9      2'b01: out=4'b0010;
10     2'b10: out=4'b0100;
11     2'b11: out=4'b1000;
12  endcase
13 endmodule
```

The following example is a decoder without full case.

```
1 // A decoder module without full case
2 module not_full_case(out, in);
3 output [3:0] out;
4 input [1:0] in;
5 reg [3:0] out;
6 always @(in)
7   // Not full-case, latches are inferred
8   case(in)
9      2'b00: out=4'b0001;
10     2'b01: out=4'b0010;
11     2'b10: out=4'b0100;
12  endcase
13 endmodule
```

When signal in=2'b11, the condition is not specified, and just as we saw in **if-else** statements, a latch will be inferred. To avoid such a mistake, it is always a good idea to use a default-case-item fore all conditions to ensure that no latch is implied, as shown below.

```
1 // A decoder module with full case by default-case-item
2 case(in)
3    2'b00:out=4'b0001;
4    2'b01:out=4'b0010;
5    2'b10:out=4'b0100;
6    default:out=4'b1000;
7 endcase
```

If you are using Synopsys Design Compiler (DC) as your synthesis tool, you can prevent lathes by "synopsys full_case" directive to specify all possible branches for if and case statements provided that you know the other branches will never occur. Additionally, if DC cannot determine that case branches are parallel, a priority decoder will be synthesized. By contrast, you can declare a case statement as parallel case with the "synopsys parallel_case" directive, as shown below.

```
1 // Using Synopsys directives to prevent latches
2 always @(in)
3    case(in) // synopsys parallel_case full_case
4       2'b00:out=4'b0001;
5       2'b01:out=4'b0010;
6       2'b10:out=4'b0100;
7    endcase
```

In a short summary, we MUST completely specify all clauses and all outputs for every clause in case and if statements. Failure to do so will cause latches to be synthesized.

If the conditional expression used is parallel and the functional outputs are the same, as shown in the following two RTL codes, then the hardware synthesized will be identical, as shown in Figure 3.6. However, it is always preferable to use a **case** statement instead of an **if-else-if** statement to save simulation time and explicitly infer the parallel multiplexer.

```
1 // Example of parallel case using case statement
2 always @(sel or a or b or c or d)
3    case(sel)
4       2'b00:out=a;
5       2'b01:out=b;
6       2'b10:out=c;
7       default:out=d;
8    endcase
```

```
1// Example of parallel case using if-else-if statement
2always @(sel or a or b or c or d)
3  if(sel==2'b00)
4    out=a;
5  else if(sel==2'b01)
6    out=b;
7  else if(sel==2'b10)
8    out=c;
9  else
10    out=d;
```

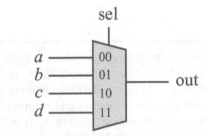

Figure 3.6: Mutually exclusive conditional expressions are synthesized to the same parallel multiplexer.

The case statements consist of the keywords, **casez** and **casex**, which can use (Z or ?) and (Z, X, or ?) in their case items, respectively. Hence, **casex** statements are more commonly used than **casez** statements. The character ? represents logic 0 or 1. For example, the case item 4'b001? contains 4'b0010 and 4'b0011, and the case item 4'b01?? contains 4'b0100, 4'b0101, 4'b0110, and 4'b0111. For synthesis, the characters, Z and X, should be treated as don't case, i.e., logic 0 or 1, as shown below.

```
1// Example of casex statement
2always @(in) begin
3  casex(in)
4    4'b0001:out=2'b00;
5    4'b001?:out=2'b01; // 4'b0010 and 4'b0011
6    4'b01??:out=2'b10; // 4'b0100, 4'b0101, 4'b0110,
7                       // and 4'b0111
8    default:out=2'b11;
9  endcase
10end
```

The priority-encoded multiplexers in Figure 3.3 can be described using **casex** as follows.

```
1// Another example of casex statement for the
2// priority-encoded multiplexers
3always @(sel or a or b or c or d or e) begin
4  casex(sel)
5    4'b1XXX:out=a; // sel is 1XXX
6    4'b01XX:out=b; // sel is 01XX
7    4'b001X:out=c; // sel is 001X
8    4'b0001:out=d; // sel is 0001
9    4'b0000:out=e; // sel is 0000
10   default:out=a;
11  endcase
12end
```

Although in the above Verilog codes **casex** statement is used, it is still intuitively not parallel because, for example, 1XXX contains 8 items, including 1000, 1001, 1010, 1011, 1100, 1101, 1110, and 1111, while 0000 contains only 1 item. If your goal is to minimize the circuit area, the priority-encoded multiplexers in Figure 3.3 suffices. By contrast, if you want to minimize the path delay and maintain a modest circuit area, the circuit in Figure 3.7 might be synthesized. In Figure 3.7, the path delays from all inputs, including sel, a, b, c, d, and e, to the output, out, are balanced as much as possible. However, the circuit area of Figure 3.7 is obviously larger than that of Figure 3.3.

3.4 FOR LOOP STATEMENT

The **for** loop repeatedly executes a single statement or block of statements. The repetitions are performed over a range determined by the range expressions assigned to an index. Two range expressions appear in each for loop: low_range and high_range. In the syntax lines that follow, the high_range expressions will be greater than or equal to the low_range ones. The HDL Compiler recognizes both incrementing and decrementing loops, and the statements which are to be repeated will be bracketed by **begin-end** pair. In the following **for** loops, indices, high_range, low_range, and step are usually represented by integers.

```
1// Syntax of for loop statement
2for(index=low_range; index<high_range; index=index+step)
3for(index=high_range; index>low_range; index=index-step)
4for(index=low_range; index<=high_range; index=index+step)
5for(index=high_range; index>=low_range; index=index-step)
```

An example is given below.

```
1 // Example of for loop
2 integer i;
3 always @(a or b)
4   for(i=0; i<=4; i=i+1)
5     out[i]=a[i]&b[4-i];
```

A for loop is "unrolled" as follows. Therefore, even the variable *i* is declared as an **integer**, it is dummy and does not represent any hardware components.

```
1 // A for loop is unrolled.
2 out[0]=a[0]&b[4];
3 out[1]=a[1]&b[3];
4 out[2]=a[2]&b[2];
5 out[3]=a[3]&b[1];
6 out[4]=a[4]&b[0];
```

All of the elements are then synthesized in the manner shown in Figure 3.8.

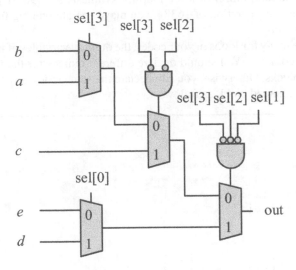

Figure 3.7: Another implementation of the multiplexers described using **casex** statement.

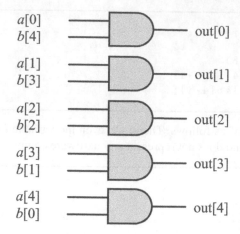

Figure 3.8: The for loop is unrolled and synthesized to five AND gates.

To make the **for** loop synthesizable (and unrollable), the low_range, high_range and step must be constants rather than variables. Therefore, the index becomes predictable so that a fixed number of repeated circuits can be inferred.

The maximum iteration limit of a **for** loop for synthesis is 4096. If your design contains a **for** loop with iteration of 16384, you may separate one big **for** loop into several smaller **for** loops.

When there are many **for** loops in your codes, the dummy variables of indices used in **for** loops may coincide. You should declare different indices for the **for** loops in different always blocks. Otherwise, you can declare the same index, say i, used in all for loops using the named block as follows.

```
1 // Use named blocks to declare local variables.
2 always @(*) begin: y1
3   integer i;      // Local variable
4   parameter I1=8  // Local variable
5   for(i=0;i<I1;i=i+1)
6     y1[i]=a[i]&b[i];
7 end
8 always @(*) begin: y2
9   integer i;      // Local variable
10  parameter I1=16 // Local variable
11  for(i=0;i<I1;i=i+1)
12    y2[i]=a[i]|b[i];
13 end
```

3.5   FUNCTION AND TASK

A Verilog function begins with the keyword **function** and ends with the keyword **endfunction**. The function allows designers to write more reusable and maintainable codes. Its syntax is given below. The 2-D array declaration is not allowed for the input port (and output port) declaration.

```
1 // Syntax of function
2 function [range] name_of_function;
3    input declaration
4    statements
5 endfunction
```

Range defines the width of the return value of the function (default is 1 bit). The input declaration specifies the input signals for a function, and the output of a function is assigned to the function name. For example, the following module demonstrates three different ways to implement the combinational circuit of an adder, including continuous assignment, always block, and function. You can call function in an always block.

```
1 // Three ways to describe the combinational circuit of
2 // an adder
3 wire [3:0] a, b;
4 reg [4:0] c1, c2;
5 wire [4:0] c3;
6 function [4:0] fn1;
7    input [3:0] a;
8    input [3:0] b;
9    fn1=a+b; // Like C language
10 endfunction
11 always @(a or b)
12     c1=fn1(a, b); // Call function in an always block
13 always @(a or b)
14     c2=a+b;
15 assign c3=a+b;
```

Functions are defined in the module in which they are used, and they cannot contain delays.

The concatenation operation is used to bundle several values for multi-outputs of a function. These outputs are then separated, also using the concatenation operation. Function can contain one or more procedural assignment statements (enclosed inside a **begin-end** pair). Function is also a procedural block. Therefore, the left side of an assignment in a function can contain only reg and integer variables. You can also call function in a continuous assignment. In the following example, it should be noted that $y1$ and $y2$ may overflow.

```
1// Example for multi-outputs of a function
2function [9:0] fn1;
3input [3:0] f1, f2;
4reg [4:0] y1_1, y2_1;
5begin
6   y1_1=f1+f2+5;
7   y2_1=f1+f2+2;
8   // Concatenate multi-outputs to a single output
9   fn1={y1_1, y2_1};
10end
11endfunction
12// Separate a single output to multi-outputs using
13// the concatenation again
14assign {y1, y2}=fn1(a, b);
```

A function can also be nested, that is, a function can contain another function, as shown in the following example. Consequently, you can call a function in another function. Notably, Fn1 may overflow.

```
1// Example for nested function
2function [4:0] fn2;
3input [3:0] f1, f2;
4   fn2=f1+f2;
5endfunction
6function [4:0] fn1;
7input [3:0] f1, f2;
8   fn1=fn2(f1, f2)+2;
9endfunction
```

A Verilog Task begins with keyword **task** and ends with keyword **endtask**. It is the section of a Verilog code that allows the designer to write more reusable, easier to read codes. When tasks are placed within a testbench, they can be very handy because tasks can include time delays. This is one of the main differences between tasks and functions: functions do not allow time delays. Tasks without timing controls are like functions. However, tasks with timing controls are non-synthesizable, and therefore, they are typically used in a testbench. The syntax of a task is displayed below. The 2-D array declaration is not allowed for the input and output ports declaration.

```
1 // Syntax of task
2 task name_of_task;
3 input declaration
4 output and inout declaration
5 statements
6 endtask
```

The input declaration specifies the input signals for a task. A task can have no inputs. The output and inout declaration will be similar to that in a module. A task can also have no outputs, although a task can include multiple output, input, and inout ports and/or delays. You can call tasks in an always block or other tasks.

A task used to generate the out signal at clock edges using a sequence of 10101010 or 10100110 selected by the sel signal is shown below. The Verilog code "@posedge clk" in the task is used for the timing control.

```
1 // Example: use task with timing control in testbench
2 reg out, sel, clk;
3 initial begin
4    clk=0; out=0; sel=0;
5    #200; sel=0; seq_gen(sel,out);
6    #200; sel=1; seq_gen(sel,out);
7 end
8 always #5 clk=~clk;
9 task seq_gen;
10 input sel;
11 output out;
12 begin
13   @(posedge clk) out=sel?1:1;
14   @(posedge clk) out=sel?0:0;
15   @(posedge clk) out=sel?1:1;
16   @(posedge clk) out=sel?0:0;
17   @(posedge clk) out=sel?0:1;
18   @(posedge clk) out=sel?1:0;
19   @(posedge clk) out=sel?1:1;
20   @(posedge clk) out=sel?0:0;
21 end
22 endtask
```

The differences between function and task are listed in Table 3.1. Notably, both functions and tasks can only contain procedural assignment statements. Always blocks are not allowed in either function or task.

Table 3.1: Comparison of function and task.

Function	Task
A function can contain another function but not task.	A task can contain other tasks and functions.
A function always executes in 0 simulation time.	A task can execute in non-zero simulation time.
A function cannot contain delay, event, or timing control.	A task can contain delay, event, or timing control.
A function must have at least one or more input arguments.	A task can have zero or more arguments of type input, output, or inout.
A function returns a single value, i.e., the function name itself.	A task can return multiple values through output and inout arguments.

3.6   PARAMETERIZED DESIGN

Parameterized design increases the re-usability of your design. The following module has 3 parameters: WIDTH, HEIGHT, and LENGTH. You can change the values of these parameters by modifying their parameter definitions.

```
1// A module with parameters
2module test(d, a, b, c);
3output [WIDTH:0] d;
4input [WIDTH-1:0] a;
5input [HEIGHT-1:0] b;
6input [LENGTH-1:0] c;
7parameter WIDTH=8;
8parameter HEIGHT=8;
9parameter LENGTH=8;
10assign d=a+b+c;
11endmodule
```

Otherwise, you can change the values of these parameters when instantiating the module. For example, the following module overrides those values of parameters when the above test module is instantiated as WIDTH=5, HEIGHT=4, and LENGTH=4. Therefore, the parameterized test module does not need to be modified and is easy to maintain. In this way, you need to specify all parameters and no parameters can be omitted.

```
1 // Instantiate parameterized module by overwriting
2 // its parameters.
3 module param_1(d, a, b, c);
4 output [5:0] d;
5 input [4:0] a;
6 input [3:0] b;
7 input [3:0] c;
8 test #(5,4,4) u0(.a(a), .b(b), .c(c), .d(d));
9 endmodule
```

Another way to configure the parameters of a design is through the keyword, **defparam**, in testbench. In such a case, the parameter values are overridden during compilation. To specify an object of a submodule in a higher-hierarchical module, such as test_bench, its hierarchical instance name is used and a period (".") is used to specify the parameters in a different design hierarchy. You can use **locaparam** if you wish to define parameters that cannot be overridden by **defparam**.

```
1 // Overriding parameters by defparam in testbench
2 module testbench;
3 defparam u0.WIDTH=5;
4 defparam u0.HEIGHT=4;
5 defparam u0.LENGTH=4;
6 test u0(.a(a), .b(b), .c(c), .d(d));
7 endmodule
```

3.7 DELAY IN CIRCUITS

Regarding the use of a circuit delay, a question may arise, "Where does gate delay come from?" This can be created using a buffer containing two inverters, as shown in Figure 3.9. An inverter is implemented using a p-channel MOSFET and an n-channel MOSFET.

The capacitor shown in Figure 3.10 is charged via the PMOS and discharged via the NMOS of the first inverter. That is, PMOS and NMOS operate in a complementary manner. When the input is low, in the first inverter, its PMOS turns on and NMOS turns off, and vice versa.

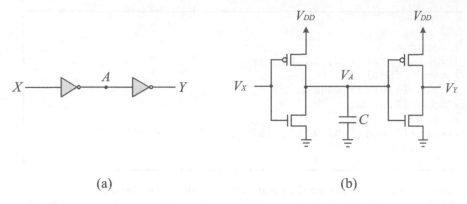

(a)   (b)

Figure 3.9: (a) A buffer with two inverters. (b) Capacitive effect inside a buffer, where V_X, V_A, and V_Y are voltages at nodes X, A, and Y, respectively. The capacitive effect, C, at node A is due to the high-frequency parasitic capacitor in the second inverter.

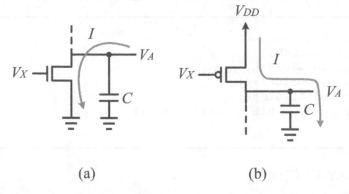

(a)   (b)

Figure 3.10: (a) The current flow when input voltage, V_X, changes from 0 to V_{DD} V. The charge on the capacitor, C, is sinked through the NMOS. (b) The current flow when input voltage, V_X, changes from V_{DD} to 0 V. The charge on the capacitor, C, is driven through the PMOS.

When V_X changes from V_{DD} to 0 V, the voltage at node A, V_A, transitions from 0 to V_{DD} volts as a result of charging through the PMOS. The capacitive effect, shown in Figure 3.11, causes a propagation delay in the first inverter; this is the time it takes for V_A to transition from 0 to $V_{DD}/2$ V. There is also a propagation delay in the second inverter as it discharges through the output capacitor (not shown in the figure) during the transition of V_Y from V_{DD} to 0 V. Similarly, when V_X changes from 0 to V_{DD} V, V_A discharges through the NMOS leading to a transition from V_{DD} to 0 volts. Due to the different charging and discharging paths, rising time and falling time are different, as are the rising and falling propagation delays.

Continuing with this model, we can now introduce dynamic (or switching) power consumption. Through the use of PMOS, as shown in Figure 3.11, when the signal

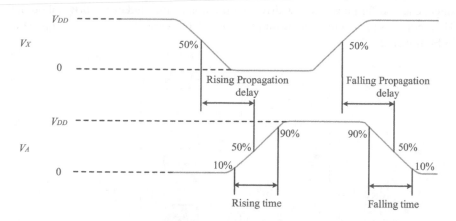

Figure 3.11: Rising time, falling time, and propagation delay of an inverter.

switches once from 0 to V_{DD} volts, energy is consumed by

$$E = \int_0^{V_{DD}} q(t)dV_A(t) = \int_0^{V_{DD}} CV_A(t)dV_A(t) = \frac{1}{2}CV_{DD}^2. \tag{3.1}$$

The same energy, $\frac{1}{2}CV_{DD}^2$, is consumed by NMOS through the discharging path. If the signal switches at a frequency of $f = 1/T$ Hz, the consumed dynamic power is

$$P = \frac{E}{T} = \frac{1}{2}fCV_{DD}^2. \tag{3.2}$$

There are two main sources of power consumption, i.e., dynamic and static. Static power, which is needed for analog ICs, may be generated when the direct current is drawn from the power supply to ground. Ideally, during a steady state, as shown in Figure 3.10, the static power of digital circuits should be 0 because there is no direct path between V_{DD} and GND (0 V) when either PMOS or NMOS switches off. However, advanced semiconductor devices may have a non-negligible leakage of current when they are in a steady state and not completely turned off because of their low threshold voltage.

3.7.1 LOAD REDUCTION BY BUFFER

It might seem unnecessary to waste circuit area and power on a component, such as the buffer, which has no impact on the logic function. However, when taking the capacitive loads of outputs into consideration, it becomes clear that buffers are useful for a given output to drive the many inputs of the next stage to the necessary logic levels, as shown in Figure 3.12. In cases such as this, the output is referred to as a high fanout net. Overloaded outputs use extrapolation of cell library information to characterize the gate delay, which, of course, can be inaccurate and lead to an unreliable circuit. By inserting buffers between the output and the inputs of the next stage, each buffer output is now driving a fraction of the load of the original output. This separates the loading on the output and each buffer now drives four components in Figure 3.12.

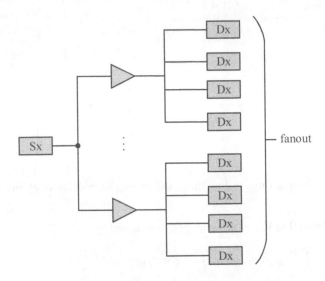

Figure 3.12: Using buffers to reduce loading on the output of a component. Notice that the component marked Sx is the source component, and the component marked Dx is the driven component.

Similarly, when the number of inputs which must be driven for the next stage is very large, such as the clock and reset networks, we can repeatedly insert buffers to the output of another buffer, like a buffer tree. As shown in Figure 3.13, such as fanout is limited to 4. A two-level buffer tree stemming from the original output drives the original inputs of the next stage using four inserted buffers. Increasing the level of a buffer tree exponentially improves the possible number of inputs that can be driven. To achieve a synchronous design, the delays of each branch must be balanced so that the clock skew can be reduced as much as possible. Hence, buffers are inserted, spaced evenly over the chip area.

3.7.2 DELAY MODELING

In addition to preserving functionality, designers must make sure that the timing of circuits conform to the desired specifications. Accurate delay modeling is the key to timing verification. Delays can be modeled in three ways, as shown in Figure 3.14:

- Delay can be lumped onto the last gate driving the output. Lumped delay is easy but does not allow for different delays if there is more than one path to a single output.

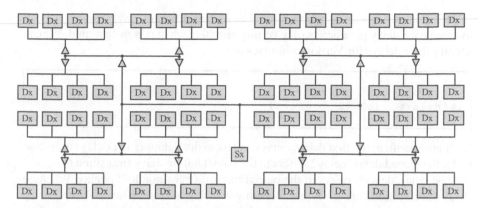

Figure 3.13: Using a balanced buffer tree to reduce loading on a high fanout output, such as a clock network, while keeping the clock skew to a minimum.

- Distributed delays are positioned across the gates. Distributed delays are more accurate than a lumped delay scheme, but may not allow for different delays if there is more than one path to a single output. For example, pins A and B to E have the same path delay, while C to E has a different path delay.
- Specify module path delays in a specify block. Module path delays are easy to model, and allow different delays for different paths.

A gate delay is also called an inertial or intrinsic delay. The physical behavioral of a signal transition is said to have an inertial, because every conducting path has capacitance, as well as resistance, which means that its charge cannot be quickly changed. If the input signal width is less than the inertial delay, the pulse will not propagate through the gate.

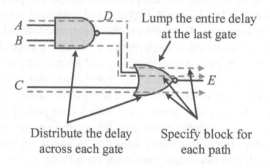

Figure 3.14: Three different delay models.

Delay modeling can be accomplished in several different ways. Firstly, we can overwrite the delay parameters of a Verilog primitive when it is instantiated. We can specify three delays for Verilog primitives as

```
1// Syntax of delay
2#(delay1, delay2, delay3).
```

If all are specified, the first delay, delay1, refers to the output rising delay (transition to 1), the second delay, delay2, refers to the output falling delay (transition to 0), and the last delay, delay3, refers to the output turn-off (transition to Z) delay. When no delay specifications are given, the default gate delay is zero. When only one delay specification is given, the output rising, falling, and turn-off delays are specified by the same delay. When two delays are given, delay1 and delay2 represent the output rising and falling delays, respectively. The turn-off delay is the minimum of delay1 and delay2.

In the following Verilog codes, if the timescale is defined by 'timescale 10 ns/1 ns, the above delays of NOT, OR, and AND gates will be 20, 25, and 36 ns, respectively. If a new in[2] is activated at the 10th ns, the simulated output out will be generated at the 91th ns. If a new in[3] is activated at the 2nd ns, the simulated output out will be generated at the 63rd ns. Delays are ignored by synthesis.

```
1// NOT gate has a delay of 2 time units
2not #(2) u1(temp[2], in[2]);
3// OR gate has a delay of 2.54 time units
4or #(2.54) u2(temp[1], temp[2], in[3]);
5// AND gate has a delay of 3.55 time units
6and #(3.55) u3(out, temp[0], temp[1]);
```

The delay of a circuit depends on the operating condition of process (P), voltage (V), and temperature (T). The higher the voltage and the lower the temperature, the lower the delay, and vice versa. A situation with the extremely worst process, lowest voltage, and highest temperature is the worst-case operating condition. A situation with the extremely best process, highest voltage, and lowest temperature is the best-case operating condition. Therefore, the clock period constraint is the most stringent in the worst case, while the hold time constraint is the most stringent in the best case. A situation between the best and worst cases with a common operating condition is called the typical-case operating condition. Taking the various PVT factors that can influence the delays (including input rising and falling time) into consideration, the minimum, typical, and maximum values for each delay can be more precisely modeled and separated by colons, as shown below.

```
1// NOT gate has a (min:typ:max) delay of
2// (1:2:4) time units
3not #(1:2:4) u1(temp[2], in[2]);
4// OR gate has a (min:typ:max) rising delay of
5// (1.52:2.54:4.30) time units and falling
6// delay of (1.22:2.1:4.17) time units
7or #(1.52:2.54:4.30, 1.22:2.1:4.17)
8    u2(temp[1], temp[2], in[3]);
```

Secondly, delays can be modeled and timing constraints can be checked by using the specify block indicated by the keywords **specify** and **endspecify**. A specify block adds timing specifications to the paths in a module. Parameters can be declared in a specify block using the **specparam** keywords. Tasks which are typically performed within a specify block are giving descriptions of the (state-dependent) path delays and (conditional) timing checks. An example is shown below, with further explanation given in the comments. If timing constraints have been violated, for example, $setup(in1, posedge clk, tS) of the setup time check, the output q of the flip-flop will become X (unknown) and display in red color on the waveform. Besides, some texts used to notify the timing violation will be shown in the simulation window as well.

```
1// A module with specify block
2module buffer_cntl(out, q, q1, in1, in2, in3, in4, a, b,
3                   rst_n, clk);
4output [2:0] out;
5output q, q1;
6input in1, in2, in3, in4, rst_n, clk;
7input [2:0] a;
8input [5:0] b;
9reg [2:0] out;
10reg q, q1;
11always @(*)
12   case({in2,in1})
13   2'b00: out=a;
14   2'b01: out={&b,|b,^b};
15   default: out={in3&in4,in3|in4,in3^in4};
16   endcase
17always @(posedge clk)
18   q <= in1;
19always @(posedge clk or negedge rst_n)
20   if(!rst_n) q1 <= 0;
21   else q1 <= in2;
22specify
23   // Parameters of clock-to-Q rising and falling delays
24   specparam tCQ_Rise=4, tCQ_Fall=6;
```

```
25  // Parameter of setup time requirement
26  specparam tS=2;
27  // Clock-to-Q path delay
28  (clk => q)=(tCQ_Rise, tCQ_Fall);
29  // Setup time check
30  $setup(in1, posedge clk, tS);
31  // Conditional setup time check
32  $setup(in2, posedge clk &&& rst_n, tS);
33 endspecify
34 specify
35  // Pin-by-pin specify
36  // 9 and 10 are rising and falling delays, respectively
37  (in1 => out[0])=(9, 10);
38  (in2 => out[0])=(9, 10);
39  // 11 is used for both rising and falling delays
40  (in3 => out[0])=11;
41  // State-dependent path delay
42  if(in1) (in4 => out[0])=8;
43  if(!in1) (in4 => out[0])=6;
44 endspecify
45 specify
46  // Vector, parallel connection
47  (a => out)=5; // a and out are 3 bits
48  // The same as pin-by-pin specify
49  /*(a[0] => out[0])=5;
50  (a[1] => out[1])=5;
51  (a[2] => out[2])=5;*/
52 endspecify
53 specify
54  /*b is 6 bits, out is 3 bits,
55    their connection is fully mesh*/
56  (b *> out)=9;
57 endspecify
58 endmodule
```

3.7.2.1 Delay Characterization

A more accurate physical delay than delay modeling can be decided following the execution of the synthesis process. A precise physical delay is only possible after the layout has been completed. A physical delay is dependent on the VLSI technology and cell library (e.g., 0.25 um, 0.18 um, and 0.13 um,...). There are only three kinds of delays, i.e., min/typ/max delays, among which to choose, depending on the specific type of PVT. After synthesis, a statement such as #3.55, which is used for simulation, becomes useless. Timescales are also used for simulation purposes, not for the actual physical circuit.

Circuits generated by a synthesis tool have propagation delays determined by their internal gates. The length of delay depends on the particular technology library used and the final placement and routing. The gate delays are specified using SDF characterized by the synthesis or layout tool used for timing simulations. The SDF provides a tool-independent and uniform way to represent timing information, including (conditional and unconditional) module path delays, device delays, interconnect delays, port delays, timing checks, and path and net timing constraints.

Cell delays are calculated using the tables in the technology library. The tables are commonly indexed by input transition versus output load, as shown in Table 3.2. When the input transition is 0.5 and output capacitance is 0.2, the delay is 0.678.

Table 3.2: Delay table.

		Input transition		
		0	0.5	1
Output	0.1	0.345	0.567	0.89
capacitance	0.2	0.456	0.678	0.987

Cell output transition can also be calculated using a table indexed by input transition and output load (however, it is omitted here).

In advanced technology, wire delays resulting from parasitic capacitance and inductance can be significant, and may take up a relatively large portion of the overall path delay in modern systems. Minimizing the impacts of wire delays by various means, such as shortening wire lengths, is an important task of layout tools. Interconnect delays or input port delays cannot be specified in a specify block. To simulate using an interconnect delay, you must annotate the timing using SDF.

None of the delays that we specify in the Verilog code has any effect on the synthesized circuit. A synthesis tool will ignore the delay in the assignment, or perhaps issue a warning. We usually only write assignments with delays in testbench models for stimulus generation. Or, for some designs that interact with macros to impose specific timing constraints and checks. For example, in Figure 3.15, the interface timing diagram of the read-only memory (ROM) is presented, where ren, addr, and data denote the read enable, read address, and read data, respectively.

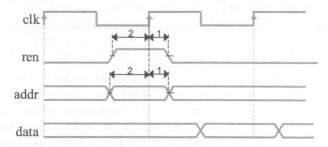

Figure 3.15: Interface timing diagram of ROM.

The timing constraints of both ren and addr require a setup time of 2 time unit and a hold time of 1 time unit. They are checked using the specify block in the behavior model of ROM as follows.

```
1 // A specify block in the ROM model
2 specify
3   $setup(ren, posedge clock, 2);
4   $hold(posedge clock, ren, 1);
5   $setup(addr, posedge clock, 2);
6   $hold(posedge clock, addr, 1);
7 endspecify
```

The setup and hold times can be checked together using the system task $setuphold, as shown below.

```
1 // A specify block in the ROM model
2 specify
3   $setuphold(posedge clock, ren, 2, 1, notifier);
4   $setuphold(posedge clock, addr, 2, 1, notifier);
5 endspecify
```

Since the design is synchronous with the rising edge of clk, if there is no delay for ren and addr signals, they will violate the hold time constraints. Therefore, at the RTL simulation stage, we need to add delays using the delay control (introduced in the next section) to ren and addr signals as follows, where ren_i and addr_i are internal read enable and read address that are synchronous to clk. At the synthesis stage, the delays will be ignored and the hold times will be fixed and ensured by inserting buffers to those paths with hold time violations.

```
1 // Add delays to fix the hold time violations
2 // at the RTL simulation stage
3 assign #1 ren=ren_i;
4 assign #1 addr=addr_i;
```

3.7.3 DELAY CONTROL

The symbol "#" is used to indicate delay control. You can specify minimum, typical, and maximum values for the rising and falling delays in continuous assignments, as can be seen in the following. In this example, the (minimum : typical : maximum) delays for the rising delay are $(1 : 2 : 3)$, the (minimum : typical : maximum) delays for the falling delay are $(2 : 3 : 5)$, and the (minimum : typical : maximum) delays for the turn-off delay are $(3 : 4 : 5)$.

```
1 // (minimum:typical:maximum) delays can be specified
2 // for rising, falling, and turn-off delays
3 assign #(1:2:3, 2:3:4, 3:4:5) a=~b;
```

Only the (minimum : typical : maximum) delays of a single delay can be specified in procedural assignments as follows. In the sequel, the rising, falling, and turn-off delays must be the same.

```
1// (minimum:typical:maximum) delays must be the same
2// for rising, falling, and turn-off delays
3always @(posedge clk)
4  #(1:2:3) a=~b;
```

There are two kinds of assignment delays: an inter-assignment (or regular) delay and an intra-assignment delay. The inter-assignment delay is typically used in the testbench. In the following initial block, Verilog codes are executed sequentially. When executing the delay control #2, two time units must be delayed. After the delay, $a+b$ can be performed, after which, the result will be known as c. Therefore, it looks like that, at time unit 2, c will become (be assigned) 3. In this manner, the inter-assignment delay can be simply interpreted: "the delayed execution of $c = a + b$ by 2 units". This is also called a delayed evaluation.

```
1// An example of inter-assignment delay
2initial begin
3  a=1;
4  b=2;
5  #2 c=a+b;
6end
```

Alternatively, the intra-assignment delay for the code "$c = $#2 $a + b$" in the following initial block takes several steps in Verilog. Firstly, the temp$= a + b$ is executed "at time 0". That is, there is an implicit temporary storage, temp, for each right-hand-side expression. Secondly, the result of temp, i.e., 3, will be assigned to c ($c =$temp) until 2 units of time have elapsed. Put another way, the result of c is not affected by the change of a and b until 2 time units have passed. Therefore, at time unit 2, c will become (be assigned) 3. This is also called the delayed assignment.

```
1// An example of intra-assignment delay
2initial begin
3  a=1;
4  b=2;
5  c=#2 a+b;
6end
```

In the above two code segments, essentially, the same results are produced. That is, at time unit 2, c will become 3. However, if there is another initial block shown below, the additional initial block will cause the value of b to change to 4 at time unit 1, which means that the results of inter assignment and intra assignment will be different. Based on their different operations, the inter-assignment and intra-assignment delays will be 5 and 3, respectively.

```
1 // Additional  initial block that may affect
2 // the result of inter-assignment delay
3 initial
4    #1 b=4;
```

3.7.4   PATH DELAY

Figure 3.16 displays the gate delays and transistor counts of typical logic gates. The area of a gate is proportional to its transistor count.

Path delays, by definition, are the delays from all inputs to outputs through all connecting paths. Among all paths, the one that has the longest (worst) delay is called the critical path; it is this delay which limits the clock rate for synchronous designs. The full adder in Figure 3.17 is an example.

The longest path delays from each input to output are summarized in Table 3.3.

From the table, the delay of the critical path is 6.6 ns. In Figure 3.16, we can also see an AND gate which has 6 transistors and an XOR gate with 14 transistors. The full adder has a total of 46 transistors.

Figure 3.18 is another equivalent implementation of a full adder using simple NAND and OR gates.

Its delay of the critical path can be found to be 4.4 ns. The implementation has a total of 36 transistors.

Comparing two equivalent implementations, the second one, even though it has a higher number of gates, is apparently superior to the first one because of its smaller critical path delay and total area. Despite this result, the area and path delay are usually properties that need to be traded-off.

3.8   BLOCKING AND NON-BLOCKING ASSIGNMENTS

There are two kinds of procedural assignments: blocking and non-blocking. Blocking assignments (=) are order sensitive, and non-blocking assignments (<=) are order independent. Blocking assignments are executed sequentially in the order that they are listed in a procedural block. When they are executed, they have an immediate effect on the contents of the abstract **reg**, which must be carried out before the next assignment can be executed. Non-blocking assignments are executed concurrently by evaluating the expressions on the right-hand side of each statement in a procedural block before making the assignment to the left-hand-side abstract **reg**. As a result of the properties of non-blocking assignments, there is no interaction between assignments and the evaluations of expressions.

Name	Symbol	Function	Transistor Count	Delay (ns)
Buffer	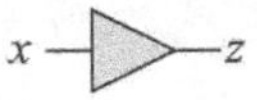 $x \longrightarrow z$	$z = x$	4	1.4
NOT	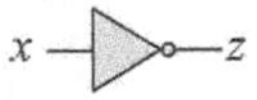 $x \longrightarrow z$	$z = \overline{x}$	2	0.7
AND	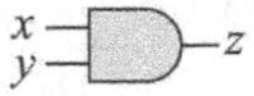 $\begin{array}{c}x\\y\end{array} \longrightarrow z$	$z = xy$	6	1.2
OR	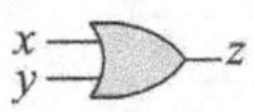 $\begin{array}{c}x\\y\end{array} \longrightarrow z$	$z = x + y$	6	1.2
NAND	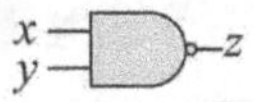 $\begin{array}{c}x\\y\end{array} \longrightarrow z$	$z = \overline{xy}$	4	1.0
NOR	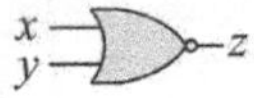 $\begin{array}{c}x\\y\end{array} \longrightarrow z$	$z = \overline{x + y}$	4	1.0
XOR	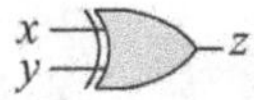 $\begin{array}{c}x\\y\end{array} \longrightarrow z$	$z = x \oplus y$	14	3.3
XNOR	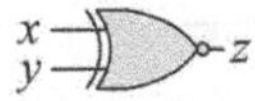 $\begin{array}{c}x\\y\end{array} \longrightarrow z$	$z = \overline{x \oplus y}$	12	3.5

Figure 3.16: Gate delays and transistor counts of several logic gates.

As can be seen in the example below, the blocking assignments in a begin-end block operate sequentially and hence are order sensitive. By contrast, non-blocking assignments are executed in parallel and are therefore independent of their order.

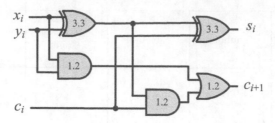

Figure 3.17: Schematic of a full adder. The numbers on the logic gates are the gate delays in ns.

Table 3.3: Longest path delays from each input to output.

Path	Longest delay (ns)
c_i to c_{i+1}	2.4
c_i to s_i	3.3
x_i and y_i to c_{i+1}	5.7
x_i and y_i to s_i	6.6

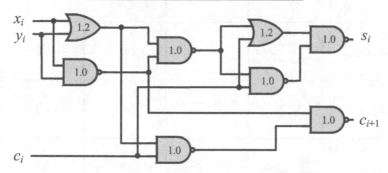

Figure 3.18: Schematic of another equivalent implementation of full adder.

```
1// Blocking assignment executes sequentially.
2initial begin
3   a=#12 1;
4   b=#3  0;
5   c=#2  3;
6end
7// Non-blocking assignment executes in parallel.
8initial begin
9   d<=#12 1;
10  e<=#3  0;
11  f<=#2  3;
12end
```

The difference between them is shown in the timing diagram in Figure 3.19.

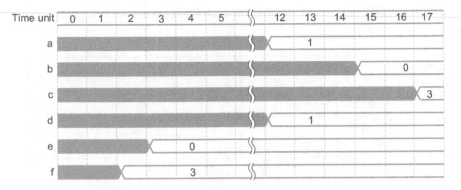

Figure 3.19: Comparison of blocking and non-blocking assignments.

Note: "<=" also means less than or equal for relational operators. To distinguish a relational operator from a non-blocking assignment, the relational operator can be interpreted as a comparative when it is found in logic statements, such as if-else, conditional operator, etc.

Figure 3.20 is another example of the differences between blocking and non-blocking assignments. The key information is displayed in the comments. Again, changing the order of the statements using the blocking assignment got a different result, while changing the order of the statements using the non-blocking assignment did not. So, the blocking assignment is order sensitive while the non-blocking assignment is order independent.

Blocking assignment	initial begin
	    a=1;
	    b=2;
	    a=b; // b=2 is used
	    b=a; // a=2 is used
	end
		initial begin
		    a=1;
		    b=2;
		    b=a; // a=1 is used
		    a=b; // b=1 is used
		end

Non-blocking assignment	initial begin
	    a=1;
	    b=2;
	    a<=b; // b=2 is used
	    b<=a; // a=1 is used
	end
		initial begin
		    a=1;
		    b=2;
		    b<=a; // a=1 is used
		    a<=b; // b=2 is used
		end

Figure 3.20: Comparison of blocking and non-blocking assignments: another example.

Combinational circuits are described by both blocking and non-blocking assignments in Figure 3.21.

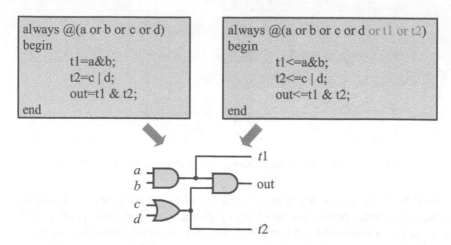

```
always @(a or b or c or d)          always @(a or b or c or d or t1 or t2)
begin                               begin
        t1=a&b;                             t1<=a&b;
        t2=c | d;                           t2<=c | d;
        out=t1 & t2;                        out<=t1 & t2;
end                                 end
```

Figure 3.21: Combinational circuits described by both blocking and non-blocking assignments.

In the example shown, we can intuitively grasp how a blocking assignment works in combinational circuits. For the always block with blocking assignments, the sensitivity list of the always block contains all the inputs, a, b, c, and d, of a combinational circuit. Each time the inputs change, the always block, and hence, the output out, must be reevaluated. The statements in an always block are sequentially executed. The up-to-date values of inputs are used to determine $t1$ and $t2$, and finally, new $t1$ and $t2$ are used to calculate out.

In an always block with non-blocking assignments, the statements are executed concurrently. Therefore, when the inputs that trigger the always block change, the out will use the old values of $t1$ and $t2$ because their new values are not yet available. To ensure the same behavior in a combinational circuit, internal signals of the circuit, $t1$ and $t2$, should also be put in the sensitivity list in addition to the circuitâĂŹs inputs. This will re-trigger (reentry) the always block each time the values of $t1$ and $t2$ are updated, enabling output out to finally be able to assess its new value. However, this model is relatively complex and can potentially be confusing, as the description of combinational circuits only uses the blocking assignment.

As another example, sequential circuits (triggered by keywords **posedge** or **negedge**) are described by both the blocking and non-blocking assignments in Figure 3.22.

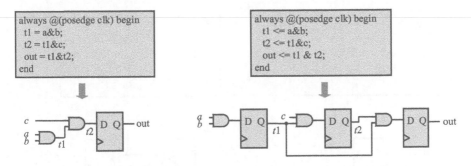

Figure 3.22: Sequential circuits described by both blocking and non-blocking assignments.

To understand what circuits these codes describe, we must analyze their behaviors. For the always block with blocking assignments, at every posedge of clk, three assignments are executed sequentially. Hence, $t1$ is updated using the values of a and b at posedge of clk, then $t2$ is updated using the new value of $t1$ and the value of c at posedge of clk. Finally, out is evaluated using the new values of $t1$ and $t2$. As can be seen, $t1$ and $t2$ are only used for temporary storage to conveniently partition a complex expression; they do not represent true hardware register outputs and might even be optimized away. Notably, the combinational circuit has been optimized in that out $= t1\&t2 = (a\&b)\&(t1\&c) = (a\&b)\&(a\&b\&c) = a\&b\&c = t1\&c = t2$.

For the always block with non-blocking assignments, at every posedge of clk, three assignments are concurrently executed: (1) $t1$ is updated by the values of a and b at posedge of clk, (2) concurrently $t2$ is updated using the old value (its new value is not available at this moment) of $t1$ and the value of c at posedge of clk, and (3) concurrently out is evaluated using the old values (their new values are not available at this moment) of $t1$ and $t2$.

As shown, blocking and non-blocking assignments describe quite different sequential circuits. Based on the behaviors of blocking and non-blocking assignments, they indicate one and three flip-flops, respectively. That is, when $t1$ and $t2$ are described using blocking assignments, they are combinational outputs rather than sequential outputs. Therefore, this model can be quite confusing so that the description of sequential circuits only uses the non-blocking assignment.

Yet another example is shown in Figure 3.23. As displayed above, it is clear that if we use blocking assignments to describe sequential circuits, the order of assignments produces different behaviors, and hence, different circuits. So, blocking assignment is order sensitive. If we change the assignments to non-blocking, the order of assignments does not affect the designated circuits. That is, non-blocking assignment is order independent.

To ensure synchronous operations in RTL design and a match between an HDL model and its synthesized circuit, non-blocking assignments must be used for all variables that are assigned values with an edge sensitive behavior, i.e., **always** clocked. The non-blocking behavior that appears in an edge sensitive always block

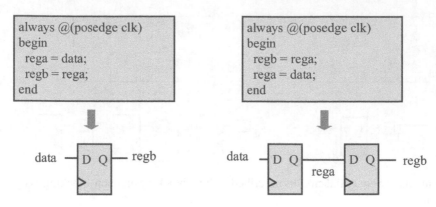

Figure 3.23: Sequential circuits described by blocking assignments using different orders.

models the behavior of the synchronous sequential circuit accurately. Moreover, non-blocking assignments store values until the end of the time slice, thereby avoiding simulation race conditions or ambiguous results.

In conclusion, the required procedure for describing combinational and sequential circuits demands that, you must know which signals are outputs of combinational circuits and which are outputs of sequential circuits. Most importantly, blocking and non-blocking assignments can be used to describe combinational and sequential circuits (including FFs and latches), respectively. Mixing blocking and non-blocking assignments in an always block, as shown below, is not allowed and must scrupulously be avoided.

```
1 // Avoid mixing blocking and non-blocking assignments
2 always @(posedge clk or negedge rst_n)
3   if(!rst_n) a=0; // Blocking assignment
4   else a<=b; // Non-blocking assignment
```

Finally, let us examine the combination of different assignments and delay controls, such as those shown in Figure 3.24. It can be seen that the inter-assignment delays and blocking assignments have higher priority than event triggers. Therefore, the always block can be triggered again until the non-blocking assignment with inter-assignment delay (signal b), blocking assignment with intra-assignment delay (signal c), and blocking assignment with inter-assignment delay (signal d) have been completed. It can be seen that reentrance is not allowed for blocking assignments and inter-assignment delays.

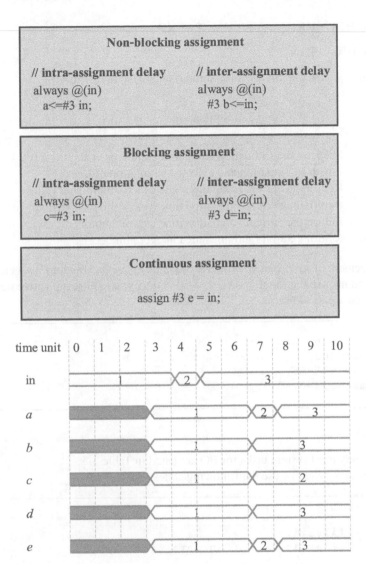

Figure 3.24: Combination of different assignments and delay controls.

It can be observed that the always block with the non-blocking assignment and intra-assignment delay (signal a) does not miss any events triggered by the input signal named in. Also, the continuous assignment with an inter-assignment delay does not miss any events triggered by the input signal in. Therefore, to model the output delay of an always block with sensitivity list of (posedge clk), we typically use the intra-assignment delay to model the clock-to-Q delays of sequential circuits. To model the output delay of a combinational circuit described using the continuous assignment, the inter-assignment delay is usually adopted.

3.9 SOME USEFUL SYSTEM TASKS

3.9.1 SIMULATION

The commonly used system tasks for simulation are listed in Table 3.4.

Table 3.4: Simulation system tasks.

Tasks	Description
$stop	Suspend the simulation and puts a simulator in an interactive mode
$finish	Finish a simulation and exits the simulation process
$time	Return the current simulation time as a 64-bit integer value
$stime	Return the current simulation time as a 32-bit unsigned integer value
$realtime	Return the current simulation time as a real number
$random	Return a 32-bit random signed integer number

The statement of a random system task modulus by s, i.e., $random %$s$, generates a random number in the range $[(-s+1)\sim(s-1)]$. If you require a positive number, you must add a pair of braces, i.e., { }, as follows.

```
1 integer a, b, c;
2 a=$random%60;         // -59<=a<=59
3 b={$random}%60;       // 0<=b<=59
4 c={$random}%60+40;    // 40<=c<=99
```

3.9.2 I/O

The commonly used system tasks for I/O are listed in Table 3.5.
To open a file, you can use the following codes.

```
1 // Method to open a file
2 integer file_id;
3 initial file_id=$fopen("in_data_file");
```

3.9.3 TIMING CHECK

Hardware registers have setup time and hold time requirements. Clock and reset pins have a minimum width requirement. They are shown in Figure 3.25.

Table 3.5: I/O system tasks.

Tasks	Description
$dumpfile	Specify which file is to be dumped.
$dumpvars	Specify which variables are to be dumped.
$dumpon	Enable dumping signals.
$dumpoff	Disable dumping signals.
$display	Display information.
$monitor	Display the values of monitored signals whenever they change.
$monitoron	Enable monitoring signals.
$monitoroff	Disable monitoring signals.
$strobe	Display the values of monitored signals on every time steps of the clock.
$write	Display information without a new line.
$fopen	Open a disk file for writing.
$fclose	Close a disk file.
$fdisplay	Display information in a file.
$fmonitor	Display the values of monitored signals whenever they change in a file.
$fstrobe	Display the values of monitored signals on every time steps of the clock in a file.
$fwrite	Display information without a new line in a file.
$readmemb	Read binary data.
$readmemh	Read hexadecimal data.

A timing check is performed using the specify block. The system tasks $setup, $hold, and $width can check the setup time, hold time, and signal width, respectively.

```
1 // Specify block for $setup, $hold, and $width
2 // timing checks
3 specify
4   $setup(data, posedge clock, 3);
5   $hold(posedge clock, data, 2);
6   $width(reset, 6);
7 endspecify
```

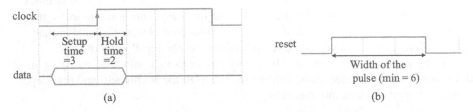

Figure 3.25: Timing checks: (a) setup time and hold time and (b) width.

Considering the setup time requirement, its impact can be written as:

$$\boxed{\text{critical path delay} + \text{setup time} < \text{clock period}}$$

This causes the clock period to increase, which lowers the clock rate. In such a case, we say that the registers are all clocked synchronously on each clock edge. The combinational circuits perform their operations in the interval between one clock edge and the next, a period called a clock cycle. The clocked synchronous timing design helps us ensure that operations are completed by combinational circuits before the time their results are clocked by the registers. This simplifies composition of a whole RTL design via pipelined (registered) stages.

Considering the hold time requirement, its impact can be written as:

$$\boxed{\text{path delay} > \text{hold time}}$$

A delay between flip-flops has a minimum value. Hold time requirements are often violated when flip-flops are connected back-to-back. To counteract this, buffers should be inserted into the paths which do not have a long enough delay. This will increase the chip area but will have no impact on the critical path or clock period because the delays of those critical paths are already too large.

To ensure the reliability of the chip, it is imperative that whatever operating condition it is in, the chip must be able to function well. Hence, the setup time requirement MUST be verified for the worst case operating condition using the maximum delay, while the hold time requirement MUST be verified in the best case operating condition using the minimum delay. Provided these timing constraints are met, it will then be possible to use the timing abstraction of synchronous designs. If a setup time error occurred during chip testing, it may still be possible to resolve the problem by extending the clock period or lowering the clock frequency. However, if the chip had a hold time error, it must be considered a fatal error, indicating that your chip may fail at some point.

The system task, $recovery, checks the recovery time from deassertion of an asynchronous control signal of sequential circuits, such as a reset, to next valid occurrence of a clock edge, as shown in Figure 3.26. The recovery time, t_{rec}, specifies the amount of time which must be provided for the deassertion of an asynchronous control signal to recover the normal function of clocked sequential circuits. The system task, $removal, checks the removal time of an asynchronous control signal of sequential circuits after a clock edge, as shown in Figure 3.26. Given that a clock edge has occurred, the removal time, t_{rem}, specifies the time relative to that particular clock edge which must be provided for the deassertion of an asynchronous control signal. When t_{rec}/t_{rem} for the deassertion of an asynchronous control signal is smaller than a clock period, t_{rec}/t_{rem} resembles the setup/hold time of the flip-flop input.

Timing information is annotated by the system task, $sdf_annotate, using an initial block, as demonstrated in the following. The SDF file is chip.sdf, and the scope at which to perform annotation is chip.

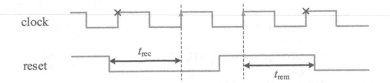

Figure 3.26: Recovery and removal time limits, where the reset signal is active high.

```
1 // Back annotate a SDF file for timing simulations.
2 initial
3   $sdf_annotate("chip.sdf", chip);
```

3.9.4 DATA CONVERSION

The commonly used system tasks for data conversion are listed in Table 3.6.

Table 3.6: Data conversion system tasks.

Tasks	Description
$realtobits	Convert a real number to a 64-bit representation
$bitstoreal	Convert the bit value to a real number
$rtoi	Convert a real-number to an integer value by truncation
$itor	Convert an integer to a real-number value

3.10 ADVANCED VERILOG SIMULATION

3.10.1 COMPILER DIRECTIVE

Directive is only intended to be used by a compiler; it is not an actual design function. We can direct conditional compilation (**'ifdef**), define text macros (**'define**), and hide a piece of codes (**'include**) in testbench as follows. The word size of in and the clock cycle of clk can simply be changed for various test patterns. Also, the conditional compilation can shape the Verilog codes in testbench for testing different conditions. The directive also allows you to include the entire contents of another Verilog file, say decode.v, during compilation.

```
1 // A testbench with compiler directives
2 'define WORD_SIZE 3
3 'define CLOCK_CYCLE 10
4 'define TEST_CONDITION1
5 module test_bench;
6 reg ['WORD_SIZE-1:0] in;
7 reg en;
```

```
 8 reg clk;
 9 `include decode.v
10 initial clk = 0;
11 always #`CLOCK_CYCLE/2 clk=~clk;
12 initial begin
13 `ifdef TEST_CONDITION1
14   en=1;
15 `else
16   en=0;
17 `endif
18 end
19 endmodule
```

The decode.v contains a piece of codes that you don't want to show in the testbench, such as the instantiation of the decoder module shown below.

```
1 // Verilog codes saved in decode.v
2 decoder dec(.y(out), .en(en), .x(in));
```

The decoder module is defined below.

```
1 // Dataflow description: decoder
2 module decoder(y, en, x);
3 output [7:0] y;
4 input en;
5 input [2:0] x;
6 assign y=en?1'b1<<x:8'h0;
7 endmodule
```

The text macro can also be defined using the simulation command option by "+define TEST_CONDITION1".

We can define a new macro using the (**`define**) directive. For example, the following defined macro, CLOG2, returns the ceiling function of the $\log_2(x)$, the logarithm to the base 2 of x.

```
1 // Defined macro
2 // Ceiling function of log2(x)
3 `define CLOG2(x) (x<=2)?1:(x<=4)?2:(x<=8)?3:(x<=16)?4:
4          (x<=32)?5:(x<=64)?6:(x<=128)?7:(x<=256)?8:
5          (x<=512)?9:(x<=1024)?10:(x<=2048)?11:-1;}
```

When depth= 1024, bit_number is 10.

```
1 wire depth=1024;
2 wire bit_number='CLOG2(depth);
```

If you are using Synopsys Design Compiler as your synthesis tool, you can control code segments that do or do not need to be translated by DC using "synopsys translate_on" and "synopsys translate_off", respectively. Such a handy control enables you to build behavioral codes or assertions into your design in a way that can monitor the design functionality, as follows.

```
1 // Behavioral codes not for synthesis
2 // synopsys translate_off
3 always @(rd_en or wr_en)
4    // Assertion for write and read at the same time
5    if(rd_en&&wr_en) begin
6      $display($stime, "Error!!");
7      $stop;
8    end
9 // synopsys translate_on
```

3.10.2 TIMING SIMULATION

Two kinds of timing simulation can be used with SDF: pre-sim and post-sim. To perform gate-level timing simulations, several steps must be followed.

- First, successfully synthesize your RTL codes, and then write out your gate-level netlist and SDF files.
- Use the system task $sdf_annotate in testbench to back annotate the timing information.
- Perform a gate-level timing simulation. For simulations with SDF back annotation, the min/typ/max delay used in the timing simulation is specified in the argument of the simulator command. For example, run Verilog through the following command. The Verilog files test.v is the testbench, chip.vg is the gate-level netlist of your design, and library.v is the technology simulation model.

> verilog test.v chip.vg −v library.v +typdelays (or +mindelays or +maxdelays).

Or, you can simulate using NC-Verilog as follows.

> ncverilog test.v chip.vg −v library.v +typdelays (or +mindelays or +maxdelays) +access+r.

If you do not want to check the timing during the RTL simulation, you can disable it by:

> verilog test.v chip.vg –v library.v +notimingchecks.

3.11   ADVANCED VERILOG FEATURES

3.11.1   ANSIC-C STYLE PORT DECLARATION

You can use ANSIC-C style declarations for module ports in Verilog 2001 as follows.

```
1 module module_v2001 #(parameter width=8)(
2 input rd_en, wr_en;
3 input [width-1:0] data_in;
4 );
5 ...
6 endmodule
```

In Verilog 1995, you must declare as follows.

```
1 module module_v1995(rd_en, wr_en, data_in);
2 input rd_en, wr_en;
3 input [width-1:0] data_in;
4 parameter width=8;
5 ...
6 endmodule
```

3.11.2   GENERATE STATEMENT

Verilog 2001 supports a generate statement that can produce an array of instances as follows. This is especially useful for a design with a variable and large number of instances. As shown below, the module has a parameterized number of 8 instances.

```
1 // Generate 1-D array architecture
2 module top #(parameter PE_NUM=8)(
3 input [PE_NUM-1:0] a, b;
4 output [PE_NUM-1:0] y;
5 );
6 genvar i;
7 generate
8   for(i=0;i<PE_NUM;i=i+1)
9     PE ProcessElement U(.a(a[i]), .b(b[i]), .y(y[i]));
10 endgenerate
11 endmodule
```

The I/O ports of module ProcessElement are defined below.

```
1 module ProcessElement (
2 input a, b;
3 output y;
4 );
5 ...
6 endmodule
```

As a result, 8 instances, PE[0].U, PE[1].U,..., PE[7].U, are produced with reference names, PE_0, PE_1,..., PE_7, respectively.

3.12   FURTHER READING

* David Money Harris and Sarah L. Harris, *Digital design and computer architecture*, 2nd Ed., Morgan Kaufmann, 2013.
* Donald E. Thomas and Philip R. Moorby, *The Verilog hardware description language*, 5th Ed., Kluwer Academic Publishers, 2002.
* John Michael Williams, *Digital VLSI design with Verilog: a textbook from Silicon Valley Polytechnic Institute*, 2nd Ed., Springer, 2014.
* Joseph Cavanagh, *Verilog HDL: digital design and modeling*, CRC Press, 2007.
* Joseph Cavanagh, *Computer arithmetic and Verilog HDL fundamentals*, CRC Press, 2010.
* M. J. S. Smith, *Application-specific integrated circuits*, Addison-Wesley, 1997.
* Ronald W. Mehler, *Digital integrated circuit design using Verilog and Systemverilog*, Elsevier, 2014.
* Samir Palnitkar, *Verilog HDL: a guide to digital design and synthesis, 2nd Ed.*, Pearson, 2011.
* Zainalabedin Navabi, *Verilog digital system design: RT level synthesis, testbench, and verification*, McGraw-Hill, 2005.

PROBLEMS

1. The following RTL design implements an accumulator that can add 16 8-bit inputs which are given one at a time. Assert a valid signal when the result is ready. (a) Find all of the bugs and fix them. (b) Verify the design using a functional simulation.

```
1 module acc(out_valid, sum, in_valid, in_data,
2             clk, reset);
3 output out_valid;
4 output [11:0] sum;
5 input in_valid;
6 input [7:0] in_data;
7 input clk, reset;
8 wire [11:0] sum;
9 wire [7:0] in_data;
10 wire [3:0] data_count;
11 initial begin
12    out_valid=0;
13    sum=0;
14    data_count=0;
15 end
16 always @(posedge clk)
17    if(in_valid) begin
18      data_count=data_count+1;
19      sum=sum+in_data;
20    end
21 always @(posedge clk)
22    if(in_valid&&data_count==15) out_valid=1'b1;
23    else out_valid=1'b0;
24 endmodule
```

2. Design a 4-to-1 multiplexer. The bit width of each input and output must be configurable or parameterized. Bit width has default value of 8 bits.

   a. Using an always block.
   b. Using a continuous assignment.

3. Design a 4-to-2 encoder using the case statement. The input $A[3:0]$ is a one-hot signal. That is, only one single bit can be 1 at a time. When A is 4'b0001, output $Y[1:0]$ is 2'd0; when A is 4'b0010, output $Y[1:0]$ is 2'd1, and so on. Since your conditions are not fully specified, you must use the default to specify other conditions. For the default condition, just output $Y[1:0]$ as 2'd0.

4. Design a 4-to-2 priority encoder using a casez or casex statement, together with a valid output to indicate the conditions that either bits of input A is logic 1. The truth table is displayed below, where X denotes the "don't care".

Table 3.7: Truth table of 4-to-2 priority encoder.

A[3]	A[2]	A[1]	A[0]	Y[1]	Y[0]	Valid
0	0	0	0	0	0	0
0	0	0	1	0	0	1
0	0	1	X	0	1	1
0	1	X	X	1	0	1
1	X	X	X	1	1	1

5. Design a 3-to-6 decoder without inferring latches.
6. Design the overflow detection for the following Verilog statement, where w is a 2-bit unsigned number.

```
1 x << w;
```

   a. Assume that x is a 3-bit unsigned number.
   b. Assume that x is a 3-bit signed number.
7. Plot the architecture of the following piece of code.

```
1 reg out;
2 always @(posedge clk) begin
3   if(sel)
4     out <= a;
5   else
6     out <= b;
7 end
```

8. Plot the architecture of the following piece of code.

```
1 reg [7:0] counter;
2 always @(posedge clk or negedge rst_n) begin
3   if (!rst_n)
4     counter <= 0;
5   else
6     counter <= counter + 1;
7 end
```

9. Plot the architecture of the following piece of code. Please note that this is a bad design that incurs a combinational loop.

```
1 reg [7:0] counter;
2 always @(*) begin
3   if (!rst_n)
```

```
4       counter=0;
5    else
6       counter=counter+1;
7 end
```

10. Considering the resource sharing, plot the architectures for the following RTL codes.

    a. RTL code 1: We assume that the adders are not shared.

    ```
    1 module noshare(z, v, w, x, k);
    2 output [3:0] z;
    3 input [2:0] k,v,w;
    4 input x;
    5 wire [3:0] y;
    6
    7 assign y=x?k+w:k+v;
    8 assign z=x?y+w:y+v;
    9 endmodule
    ```

    b. RTL code 2: We assume that the adders in the same always block can be shared.

    ```
    1 module share(z, v, w, k);
    2 output [3:0] z;
    3 input [2:0] k, v, w;
    4 input x;
    5 reg [3:0] y, z;
    6
    7 always @(x or k or v or w) begin
    8   if(x) y=k+w;
    9   else y=k+v;
    10 end
    11 always @(y or x or w or v) begin
    12   if(x) z=y+w;
    13   else z=y+v;
    14 end
    15 endmodule
    ```

11. A piece of Verilog codes is displayed below.

    ```
    1 integer i;
    2 for(i=0; i<=31; i=i+1) begin
    3   s[i]=a[i]^b[i]^carry;
    ```

```
4    carry=(a[i]&b[i])|(a[i]&carry)|(b[i]&carry);
5 end
```

a. Guess what the purpose of the codes is.
b. Unroll the for loop.
c. Plot the gate-level netlist of the for loop.

12. We want to sort four unsigned numbers, a, b, c, and d, and then output the maximum number. The module is shown below.

```verilog
1 module for_loop(out, a, b, c, d);
2 output [3:0] out;
3 input [3:0] a, b, c, d;
4 reg [3:0] temp[3:0];
5 reg [3:0] buffer, out;
6 integer i,j;
7 always @(a or b or c or d) begin
8    temp[0]=a;
9    temp[1]=b;
10   temp[2]=c;
11   temp[3]=d;
12   for(i=2;i>=0;i=i-1)
13     for(j=0;j<=i;j=j+1)
14       if(temp[j]>temp[j+1]) begin
15         buffer=temp[j+1];
16         temp[j+1]=temp[j];
17         temp[j]=buffer;
18       end
19   out=temp[3];
20 end
21 endmodule
```

a. How many comparisons are needed to sort 4 numbers?

b. How are sorting results arranged or assigned? That is, what is the maximum number, second highest number, and so on?

c. Plot the architecture of the module by unrolling for loops in terms of a comparison-and-swap unit, as shown below.

```verilog
1 function comp_swap(a, b);
2 input [3:0] a, b;
3 // Larger no is placed at the MSBs
4 if(a>b) comp_swap={b,a};
```

```
5 else comp_swap={a,b};
6 endfunction
```

d. Find the critical path in your architecture.
e. Write down your complete RTL code and verify it using Modelsim. Bit widths are programmable and assumed to be 3 bits. Write the testbench and prepare patterns to verify your design.
13. Modeling delay for the logic circuit in Figure 3.14.

   a. Use a lumped delay of 3 time units for all paths.
   b. Use a distributed delay to model a delay of 2 time units for both A and B to D, and a delay of 1 time unit for both D and C to E.
   c. Use a specify block to model a delay of 3 time units from A to E, and a delay of 4 time units from B to E, and a delay of 2 time units from C to E.
14. Modeling delay for the logic circuit in Figure 3.14.

   a. Describe the circuit using a continuous assignment. Then model a lumped delay of 3 time units for all paths.
   b. Describe the circuit using two always blocks with outputs D and E. Use the distributed delay to model a delay of 2 time units for both A and B to D, and a delay of 1 time unit for both D and C to E.
   c. Describe the circuit using two always blocks with outputs D and E. Use a specify block to model a delay of 3 time units from A to E, and a delay of 4 time units from B to E, and a delay of 2 time units from C to E.
15. Plot the inferred circuits.

   a. RTL code 1.

```
1 module rtl_1(regb, data, clk);
2 output regb;
3 input data, clk;
4 reg rega, regb;
5 always @(posedge clk) begin
6   rega=data;
7   regb=rega;
8 end
9 endmodule
```

   b. RTL code 2.

```
1 module rtl(regc, regd, data, clk);
2 output regc, regd;
3 input data, clk;
4 reg regc, regd;
5 always @(posedge clk) begin
```

```
6   regc <=data;
7   regd <=regc;
8 end
9 endmodule
```

16. Plot the inferred circuits.

   a. RTL code 1.

```
1 module latch_if2(out, en, A, B, C);
2 output out;
3 input en, A, B, C;
4 reg K, out;
5 always @(en or A or B or C)
6   if(en) begin
7     K<=!(A&B);
8     out<=!(K|C);
9   end
10 endmodule
```

   b. RTL code 2.

```
1 module latch_if3(out, en, A, B, C);
2 output out;
3 input en, A, B, C;
4 reg K, out;
5 always @(en or A or B or C)
6   if(en) begin
7     K=!(A&B);
8     out=!(K|C);
9   end
10 endmodule
```

17. Plot the inferred circuits.

   a. RTL code 1.

```
1 module test3(Clock, Data, YA, YB);
2 input Clock, Data;
3 output [3:0] YA;
4 reg [3:0] YA; reg [3:0] PA;
5 integer N;
6
7 always @(posedge Clock) begin
8   for(N=3;N>=1;N=N-1)
```

```
9       PA[N]<=PA[N-1];
10    PA[0]<=Data;
11    YA<=PA;
12 end
13 endmodule
```

b. RTL code 2.

```
1 module test1(Clock, Data, YA, YB);
2 input Clock, Data;
3 output [3:0] YA;
4 reg [3:0] YA, PA;
5 integer N;
6 always @(posedge Clock) begin
7    for(N=1;N<=3;N=N+1)
8            PA[N]=PA[N-1];
9    PA[0]=Data;
10    YA=PA;
11 end
12 endmodule
```

c. RTL code 3.

```
1 module test2(Clock, Data, YA, YB);
2 input Clock, Data;
3 output [3:0] YA;
4 reg [3:0] YA, PA;
5 integer N;
6 always @(posedge Clock) begin
7    for(N=3;N>=1;N=N-1)
8            PA[N]=PA[N-1];
9    PA[0]=Data;
10    YA=PA;
11 end
12 endmodule
```

18. There are six different design pieces below. Please plot their waveforms using the behaviors of blocking and non-blocking assignments. Then, verify your waveforms using simulation results. Signals a, b, c, and d are 5 bits; E is 1 bit; out is 7 bits; and e and f are 6 bits. What design pieces have the same functionality? Among them, identify those that obey the RTL coding guidelines.

a. RTL code 1.

```verilog
1 always @(posedge clk)
2   if(E)
3     out<=(a+b)+(c+d);
```

b. RTL code 2.

```verilog
1 always @(posedge clk) begin
2   e=a+b;
3   f=c+d;
4   if(E)
5     out<=e+f;
6 end
```

c. RTL code 3.

```verilog
1 always @(posedge clk) begin
2   e<=a+b;
3   f<=c+d;
4   if(E)
5     out<=e+f;
6 end
```

d. RTL code 4.

```verilog
1 always @(posedge clk) begin
2     e=a+b;
3     f=c+d;
4   if(E)
5     out=e+f;
6 end
```

e. RTL code 5.

```verilog
1 always @(posedge clk) begin
2   e<=a+b;
3   f<=c+d;
4   if(E)
5     out=e+f;
6 end
```

f. RTL code 6.

```
1 always @(a or b or c or d) begin
2   e=a+b;
3   f=c+d;
4 end
5 always @(posedge clk)
6   if(E)
7     out<=e+f;
```

19. Timing analysis: Assume that the clock is synchronous without any skew. The full adder, FA, is implemented using that in Figure 3.18. According to the specification, the input signals have an input delay of 2 time units. The output signals have an output delay of 3 time units. The flip-flops have setup time and hold time of 2.2 and 0.8 time units, respectively. (a) Please identify all paths and find their path delays in the RTL design. Notice that the registered output, result_r, and the non-registered output, result, are both the outputs of the module, adder. (b) Find the critical path and maximum allowable clock frequency.

```
1 module adder(result, result_r, op1, op2, clk, reset);
2 output [2:0] result, result_r;
3 input [1:0] op1, op2;
4 input clk, reset;
5
6 wire [2:0] result;
7 reg [2:0] result_r;
8
9 FA FA0(.s_out(result[0]), .c_out(carry),
10        .x_in(op1[0]), .y_in(op2[0]), .c_in(1'b0));
11 FA FA1(.s_out(result[1]), .c_out(result[2]),
12        .x_in(op1[1]), .y_in(op2[1]), .c_in(carry));
13
14 always @(posedge clk or posedge reset)
15   if (reset) result_r <=0;
16   else result_r <=result;
17
18 endmodule
19
20 module FA(s_out, c_out, x_in, y_in, c_in);
21 output s_out; // Sum
22 output c_out; // Carry out
23 input x_in; // Operand 1
24 input y_in; // Operand 2
25 input c_in; // Carry in
26 . . .
27 endmodule
```

20. What is the value of E in each HDL block, assuming that $R = 1$?

    a. RTL code 1.

```
1 R=R-1;
2 if (R==0) E=1;
3 else E=0;
```

    b. RTL code 2.

```
1 R<=R-1;
2 if (R==0) E<=1;
3 else E<=0;
```

21. Draw a block diagram of the following always block. Does the always block contain unnecessary codes? If yes, please remove them.

```
1 always @(posedge CLK) begin
2    if(sel1) R1<=R1+R2;
3    else if(sel2) R1<=R2+1;
4    else R1<=R1;
5 end
```

22. If the clock period of a design is 2 ns, the minimum width, recovery time, and removal time for the reset of sequential circuits in the design are 7, 5, and 9 ns, respectively. Please design the reset signal and an enable signal for the normal function that will obey the timing specifications.

4 Number Representation

Application-specific integrated circuits are used to process binary information. However, in many situations, integers without a fraction cannot meet our needs. For example, integers cannot distinguish a fraction, say 0.567, from 0.123. From the above reason, we will introduce the binary point, which is similar to the decimal point. Subsequently, the fixed-point binary numbers and their operations used in most ASIC designs will be introduced. To understand the fixed-point number representation, the conversion between binary and decimal values of fixed-point numbers is what we must know. Fixed-point number designs, including the bit width and precision (or resolution) design of fixed-point numbers, for digital signal processing applications are presented. Dynamic range of fixed-point numbers is the key to fixed-point design if we want to avoid the overflow. In other situations, we may want to represent data with a very large dynamic range. Hence, the floating-point binary numbers will be briefly introduced as well.

4.1 PRECISION AND RESOLUTION OF A NUMBER REPRESENTATION

In a digital system, we represent a number, x, as a bit string through a quantization function, $Q(\cdot)$. The absolute error of x is given by

$$e_a(x) = |Q(x) - x| \tag{4.1}$$

and the error percentage of x is

$$e_p(x) = \frac{e_a(x)}{|x|}. \tag{4.2}$$

The quality of a number representation is given by the precision (or accuracy), i.e., the maximum error over all inputs x within its range X. Thus, the absolute precision is given by

$$p_a = \max_{x \in X} e_a(x) \tag{4.3}$$

and the precision percentage is

$$p_p = \max_{x \in X} e_p(x). \tag{4.4}$$

Note that the error and precision percentages are not defined near $x = 0$.

When we want to represent numbers with a given absolute precision, fixed-point binary numbers are often used. By contrast, when a given precision percentage is required, floating-point numbers are more adequate.

DOI: 10.1201/9781003187196-4

For example, suppose we represent real numbers over the range $X = [0, 100]$ as 7-bit binary integers by representing each real number with the nearest integer. Picking the nearest integer to a real number is often referred to as rounding or truncation. Rounding may require an addition (or increment) while truncation does not. We would then represent 45.678 as 46 or 101110_2 using rounding, and the absolute error of representing this number by rounding is $e_a(45.678) = |45.678 - 46| = 0.322$. The absolute precision over the entire range can be found to be $p_a = 0.5$ since a value halfway between two integers, e.g., 45.500, has the maximum error whether it is rounded up or down. If the truncation is adopted, $e_a(45.678) = 0.678$ and $p_a = 1$.

We should clarify the difference between precision and resolution. The resolution of both the rounding and truncation representations discussed above is 1.0 because integers are uniformly spaced one unit apart. However, the precision of rounding is 0.5, and the precision of truncation is 1.0. Note that the smaller the precision is, the better the number representation is.

4.2 FIXED-POINT NUMBERS

4.2.1 REPRESENTATION

4.2.1.1 Binary to Decimal Number Conversion

A given number can be interpreted as several different values depending on where the binary point is assumed to be. To make design simpler, we generally use a fixed binary point throughout an algorithm.

An n-bit unsigned fixed-point binary number with p-bit integer and f-bit fraction is a representation of the binary number $\{\underbrace{a_{p-1}, a_{p-2}, ..., a_0}_{p} . \underbrace{a_{-1}, ..., a_{-f+1}, a_{-f}}_{f}\}$, where a single "." denotes the position of the binary point, $n = p + f$, p denotes the bit width of the integral part, and f denotes the bit width of the fractional part. The decimal value of the fixed-point binary number is given by

$$\frac{\sum_{i=0}^{n-1} a_{i-f} 2^i}{2^f} = \sum_{i=0}^{n-1} a_{i-f} 2^{i-f}. \tag{4.5}$$

As you can see, the first bit position to the right (left) of the binary point has a weight of $2^{-1} = 0.5$ ($2^0 = 1$), the second bit position to the right (left) of the binary point has a weight of $2^{-2} = 0.25$ ($2^1 = 2$), and so on. Additionally, the weights of all bits have positive values.

We use the format u($p.f$) to refer to the unsigned fixed-point binary number. Using this shorthand, the system with $n = 4$ and $p = 1$ is an u(1.3) fixed-point system. An example of u(1.2) fixed-point binary numbers and their decimal values is listed in Table 4.1. In this table, the integer values are the binary numbers without considering the binary point.

Table 4.1: Three-bit u(1.2) fixed-point binary numbers.

Binary	Integer	Decimal
3'b1.11	7	$7/4 = 1.75$
3'b1.10	6	$6/4 = 1.50$
3'b1.01	5	$5/4 = 1.25$
3'b1.00	4	$4/4 = 1.00$
3'b0.11	3	$3/4 = 0.75$
3'b0.10	2	$2/4 = 0.50$
3'b0.01	1	$1/4 = 0.25$
3'b0.00	0	$0/4 = 0.00$

Unfortunately, Verilog does not support the data type of fixed-point representation. To designate an unsigned fixed-point binary number, it can be declared as $a[(p-1) : -f]$ in Verilog. For example, an u(1.3) wire, $a[0 : -3]$, is declared as follows. The negative index clearly indicates the position of the binary point, and the number of bits to the left and right of the binary point. Even so, Verilog treats the variable $a[0 : -3]$ as integer. That is, if $a[0 : -3]$ =4'b1001, you will display it on a waveform or screen as 4'd9 (in decimal) instead of the real fixed-point number 1.125 (in decimal).

```
1// Unsigned fixed-point binary number declaration
2// The binary point is self-documented.
3wire [0:-3] a;              // u(1.3) fixed-point wire
```

Of course, you can also declare the u(1.3) wire as $a[3 : 0]$ below. However, the position of the binary point is not self-documented using this declaration. Notice that a number declared as $[0 : -3]$ and $[3 : 0]$ are interpreted by Verilog as the same value. It just has a negative index. The index range of $[0 : -3]$ is used to document the fixed-point number with 1-bit integral and 3-bit fractional parts.

```
1// Another unsigned fixed-point binary number declaration
2// The binary point is not self-documented.
3wire [3:0] a;              // u(1.3) fixed-point wire
```

If we add an additional sign bit to the left of the integral bits, we will refer to the n-bit signed fixed-point binary number with p-bit integer (including one bit allocated for the sign bit) and f-bit fraction, as a s($p.f$) format, where $n = p + f$. Like integers, we use 2's complement numbers in s($p.f$) systems. Similar to unsigned numbers, an n-bit signed fixed-point binary number is a representation where the value of the number $\{\underbrace{a_{p-1}, a_{p-2}, ..., a_0}_{p} . \underbrace{a_{-1}, ..., a_{-f+1}, a_{-f}}_{f}\}$ is given by

$$\frac{-a_{p-1}2^{n-1} + \sum_{i=0}^{n-2} a_{i-f}2^i}{2^f} \quad = \quad -a_{p-1}2^{n-1-f} + \sum_{i=0}^{n-2} a_{i-f}2^{i-f} \qquad (4.6)$$

where a_{p-1} is the sign bit. As you can see, similar to the unsigned numbers, the first bit position to the right (left) of the binary point has a weight of $2^{-1} = 0.5$ ($2^0 = 1$), the second bit position to the right (left) of the binary point has a weight of $2^{-2} = 0.25$ ($2^1 = 2$), and so on. However, the weight of the sign bit a_{p-1} is negative with a value of -2^{p-1}, and the weights of other bits still have positive values.

An example of s(1.2) fixed-point binary numbers and their decimal values is listed in Table 4.2. In this table, the integer values are the binary numbers without considering the binary point. It can be observed that when the sign bit a_{p-1} of a binary number is 1, its decimal value is negative.

Table 4.2: Three-bit s(1.2) fixed-point binary numbers.

Binary	Integer	Decimal
3'b0.11	+3	$+3/4 = +0.75$
3'b0.10	+2	$+2/4 = +0.50$
3'b0.01	+1	$+1/4 = +0.25$
3'b0.00	+0	$+0/4 = +0.00$
3'b1.11	−1	$-1/4 = -0.25$
3'b1.10	−2	$-2/4 = -0.50$
3'b1.01	−3	$-3/4 = -0.75$
3'b1.00	−4	$-4/4 = -1.00$

We can represent fixed-point numbers in Verilog using a multi-bit wire or register. When we use a multi-bit register for integers, we have consistently declared them with index values corresponding to the binary formats. Consequently, the signed fixed-point binary number can be declared as $a[(p-1) : -f]$ in Verilog. For example, a s(1.3) wire, $a[0 : -3]$, is declared as follows. The declaration specifies that there is 1-bit integer (including one sign bit) and 3-bit fraction in the number. Therefore, the number a is merely a signed fractional number.

```
1// Signed fixed-point binary number declaration
2// The binary point is self-documented.
3wire [0:-3] a;         // s(1.3) fixed-point wire
```

Example 4.1. Assuming that the binary point is four places from the right. What number is represented by the 8-bit unsigned u(4.4) fixed-point binary number, 01010010? That is, 0101.0010.

 Solution: The number is

$$0101.0010_2 = 2^2 + 2^0 + 2^{-3}$$
$$= 5.125.$$

Or, since the binary point is four places from the right, you can obtain the result from the integer by $82/16 = 5.125$.

□

Example 4.2. As you can see, the implied binary point is not specified in the hardware. The designer needs to consider an appropriate scaling factor to correctly interpret the result of the calculations. Assuming that the binary point is six places from the right. What number is represented by the 8-bit unsigned u(2.6) fixed-point binary number, 01010010, in the previous example? That is, 01.010010.

Solution: The number is

$$01.010010_2 = 2^0 + 2^{-2} + 2^{-5}$$
$$= 1.28125.$$

Or, since the binary point is two places left to that in the previous example, you can obtain the result directly from that in the previous example by $5.125/4 = 1.28125$.

☐

Example 4.3. Assuming that the binary point is four places from the right. What number is represented by the 6-bit signed s(2.4) fixed-point binary number, 101101? That is, 10.1101.

Solution: The number is

$$10.1101_2 = -2^1 + 2^{-1} + 2^{-2} + 2^{-4}$$
$$= -1.1875_{10}.$$

☐

The number of fractional bits, f, determines the resolution of a number system for both unsigned and signed fixed-point systems. The resolution, or the smallest interval we can distinguish, is $r = 2^{-f}$. In other words, the resolution is the distance between neighboring fixed-point numbers and is fixed. By contrast, the resolution of floating-point numbers is variable and is smaller toward 0 than away from 0. For example, our u(1.3) fixed-point system with $f = 3$ has a resolution of $2^{-3} = 1/8$, or 0.125. Each increment of the binary number changes the value represented by $1/8$. This applies for the signed fixed-point numbers.

For unsigned u($p.f$) fixed-point number a, the largest number we can represent is $2^p - r$ which is given by when $a_{p-1} = a_{p-2} = \ldots = a_{-f+1} = a_{-f} = 1$ because their weights are all positive. The smallest number is 0 when $a_{p-1} = a_{p-2} = \ldots = a_{-f+1} = a_{-f} = 0$. Consequently, an u($p.f$) fixed-point number a is in the following range,

$$0 \leq a \leq 2^p - r.$$

The dynamic range of n-bit unsigned integer b is

$$0 \leq b \leq 2^n - 1.$$

The dynamic range of the n-bit unsigned fixed-point number a can also be derived from the range of n-bit unsigned integer by multiply it with the resolution r as

$$0 = \frac{0}{2^f} \leq a \leq \frac{2^n - 1}{2^f} = r \times (2^n - 1) = 2^p - r.$$

For signed $s(p.f)$ fixed-point number a, the largest number we can represent is $2^{p-1} - r$ when $a_{p-1} = 0$ and $a_{p-2} = \ldots = a_{-f+1} = a_{-f} = 1$ because all of their weights are positive except that of the sign bit a_{p-1}. The smallest or most negative number is -2^{p-1} when $a_{p-1} = 1$ and $a_{p-2} = \ldots = a_{-f+1} = a_{-f} = 0$. Therefore, a $s(p.f)$ fixed-point number a is in the following range,

$$-2^{p-1} \leq a \leq 2^{p-1} - r.$$

The dynamic range of n-bit signed integer b is

$$-2^{n-1} \leq b \leq 2^{n-1} - 1.$$

The dynamic range of the n-bit unsigned fixed-point number a can also be derived from the range of n-bit unsigned integer by multiply it with the resolution r as

$$-2^{p-1} = \frac{-2^{n-1}}{2^f} \leq a \leq \frac{2^{n-1} - 1}{2^f} = r \times (2^{n-1} - 1) = 2^{p-1} - r.$$

The decimal value of a fixed-point binary number can be easily obtained from that without the binary point using the resolution. We can rewrite the value of an n-bit unsigned fixed-point binary number as

$$\frac{\sum_{i=0}^{n-1} a_{i-f} 2^i}{2^f} = 2^{-f} \sum_{i=0}^{n-1} a_{i-f} 2^i = r \underbrace{\sum_{i=0}^{n-1} a_{i-f} 2^i}_{\text{integer value}}. \tag{4.7}$$

Likewise, we can rewrite the value of an n-bit signed fixed-point binary number as

$$\frac{-a_{p-1} 2^{n-1} + \sum_{i=0}^{n-2} a_{i-f} 2^i}{2^f} = r \underbrace{\left(-a_{p-1} 2^{n-1} + \sum_{i=0}^{n-2} a_{i-f} 2^i \right)}_{\text{integer value}}. \tag{4.8}$$

Consequently, to convert a fixed-point binary number to its decimal value, we just

- Step 1: convert it to an integer,
- Step 2: multiply the result by r.

More examples are displayed in Table 4.3.

Table 4.3: Conversion of fixed-point binary numbers to decimal numbers.

Format	Binary	r	Integer	Decimal
u(4.4)	0111.0010	0.0625	114	7.125 (114/16)
s(2.4)	10.1101	0.0625	−19	−1.1875 (−19/16)
u(1.3)	1.001	0.125	9	1.125 (9/8)
s(2.3)	01.001	0.125	9	1.125 (9/8)
u(2.4)	10.1111	0.0625	47	2.9375 (47/16)

Example 4.4. Write a Verilog behavioral model to convert a s(2.3) fixed-point number to its decimal number.

Solution: To derive the decimal value of a fixed-point number a, we can declare a variable with **real** type to store the decimal representation of a fixed-point number by scaling the fixed-point number using the resolution of operands by $r = 2^{-f}$. In the following Verilog codes, the symbol, $**$, is the power operator. For example, $x**y$ means x to the power of y, i.e., x^y.

The system task, $itor, converts an **integer** (or **signed reg**) to a **real**-number value. The **signed** declaration will be introduced in the next chapter. The Verilog does not support a fixed-point data type, and hence, $a[p-1:-f]$ declared as **signed reg** is treated as an integer. For example, if fixed-point number $a[1:-3]$ is 10.101, $itor(a)$ will return -1.1×10^1 (-11) instead of $-11/8 = -1.375$ because $a[1:-3]$ and $a[4:0]$ are treated the same except that their indices are different. For $a[1:-3]$, bit 0 of it is called $a[-3]$, bit 1 of it is called $a[-2]$, and so on.

Therefore, the result of $itor needs to be scaled by the resolution $r = 2^{-3} = 1/8 = 0.125$ to obtain exact real value of the fixed-point number $a[1:-3]$, i.e., $-11/8 = -1.375$.

```
1 // Behavioral model converting fixed-point number to
2 // decimal number
3 // s(2.3) format
4 parameter n=5; parameter p=2; parameter f=3;
5 // Resolution
6 real r=1/(2**f);
7 wire signed [p-1:-f] a; // Original fixed-point version
8 real a_r; // Final real-value version
9 assign a_r=r*$itor(a); // Final or exact real value of a
```

□

4.2.1.2 Decimal to Binary Number Conversion

Conversely, to convert a decimal number to fixed-point binary number, the easiest approach is to

- Step 1: multiply the decimal number by $\frac{1}{r} = 2^f$,
- Step 2: round the resulting product to the nearest integer,
- Step 3: convert the resulting decimal integer to a binary integer,
- Step 4: multiply the binary integer by $r = 2^{-f}$ (in decimal), i.e., shift left the binary point by f bits.

Step 1 obtains the scaling version of the decimal number by dividing $r = 2^{-f}$ or multiplying it with $\frac{1}{r} = 2^f$, which right shifts the binary point of the binary representation of original decimal number by f positions. Step 2 obtains the integer value of the scaling version of the decimal number by rounding the scaling version of the decimal number to the nearest integer to reduce the conversion error. Step 3 just converts the integer value of the scaling version of the decimal number to a binary format, which is much simpler than directly converting a decimal number (with fraction part) to its fixed-point format. Step 4 scales the rounded integer to the fixed-point binary number by shifting the binary point of the binary format to the left by f positions.

The basic principle of the decimal number (with fraction) to fixed-point binary number conversion relies on the integer to binary number conversion. To this, it is therefore multiplied by $\frac{1}{r} = 2^f$ (Step 1) and then rounded to an integer (Step 2). The conversion of an integer to binary number is relatively simple (Step 3). For example, if an unsigned integer 87 is to be converted to binary number, it can be simply expressed by $87 = 64 + 16 + 4 + 2 + 1 = 2^6 + 2^4 + 2^2 + 2^1 + 2^0 = (1010111)_2$. Finally, it is scaled back to its (approximate) fixed-point binary number by multiplying the binary integer by $r = 2^{-f}$ (Step 4).

Suppose we want to convert 1.816 to our u(1.3) fixed-point format. We first multiply 1.816 by $2^f = 2^3 = 8$, giving 14.528. Then, we round 14.528 to integer 15. We then convert it to a binary integer 1111_2. Finally, we multiply it by $r = 2^{-f} = 1/8$ (in decimal) or shift left its binary point by $f = 3$ bits, giving 1.111_2, which represents 1.875. The absolute error, $e_a(1.816) = |1.816 - 1.875| = 0.059$. It can be shown that the precision is $r/2$, or 0.0625 in this case.

Example 4.5. Write a Verilog behavioral model to convert a (decimal) real number to the s(2.3) fixed-point format.

Solution: To derive the fixed-point format of a decimal number, we can declare a variable $a[p - 1, -f]$ with **signed reg** type to store the fixed-point representation of a decimal number by scaling the real number using the resolution of operands by $r = 2^{-f}$.

In the following Verilog codes, the system task, $rtoi, converts a **real** to an **integer** or **signed reg** value by "truncation". To round a decimal number, its fractional part of the scaled version, a_r_scaled_f, is obtained and compared to 0.5 to see if rounding is needed.

The Verilog does not support a fixed-point data type, and hence, $a[p - 1 : -f]$ declared as **signed reg** is treated as an integer. Therefore, the rounded (and scaled) result, a_r_round_i, is the final fixed-point version of the decimal number.

For your convenience, the real-value of the final fixed-point version, which is an integer or **signed reg**, is also obtained by scaling the fixed-point version using the resolution r.

```
1 // Behavioral model converting decimal number to
2 // fixed-point number
3 // s(2.3) format
4 parameter n=5; parameter p=2; parameter f=3;
5 // Resolution
6 real r=1/(2**f);
7 real a_r; // Original real-value number
```

```
 8// All parts of scaled real-value version
 9real a_r_scaled;
10// Integral part of scaled real-value version
11real a_r_scaled_i;
12// Fractional part of scaled real-value version
13real a_r_scaled_f;
14// Integral part of scaled and rounded real-value version
15real a_r_round_i;
16wire signed [p-1:-f] a; // Final fixed-point version
17real a_r_round; // Final real-value of fixed-point
18                        // version
19// All parts of scaled version
20assign a_r_scaled=a_r/r;
21// Integral part of scaled version
22assign a_r_scaled_i=$rtoi(a_r_scaled);
23// Fractional part of scaled version
24assign a_r_scaled_f=a_r_scaled-a_r_scaled_i;
25// Rounding
26assign a_r_round_i=(a_r_scaled_f>=0.5)?a_r_scaled_i+1:
27                                       a_r_scaled_i;
28assign a=a_r_round_i; // Final fixed-point version
29assign a_r_round=a*r; // Final real-value of fixed-point
30                        // version if needed
```

□

4.2.1.3 Digital Signal Processing Applications

Fixed-point representation allows us to use fractional numbers on low-cost integer hardware. Most importantly, the arithmetic operations of fixed-point representation are similar to those of integer representation. Hence, fixed-point numbers are popular in signal processing applications. In these applications, the range and precision of original data must be known. The bit width and the binary point can then be determined so that the full range of the data values is covered while eliminating (or minimizing) the possibility of the quantization error and overflow.

Typically, the values are scaled so they fall between -1 and 1. That is, they can be represented in a s($1.f$) format. For most signal processing applications, 16 bits suffice and a s(1.15) format is used. An advantage of the s(1.15) format is that the product z of the multiplication of two numbers, x and y, using s(1.15) format may require s(1.30) format, instead of s(2.30) format, provided that the maximum value of z, i.e., $+1$, can be ignored. That is, for $-1 \leq x \leq 1 - 2^{-15}$ and $-1 \leq y \leq 1 - 2^{-15}$, we have $-(1 - 2^{-15}) \leq z = xy \leq +1$. Only the maximum value of z in s(2.30) format, i.e., $+1$ (obtained by $x = y = -1$), cannot be represented by s(1.30) in the range $[-1, 1 - 2^{-30}]$. If x and y are uniformly distributed, the probability of $x = y = -1$ for s(1.30) format is $\frac{1}{2^{31}} \times \frac{1}{2^{31}} = \frac{1}{2^{62}} \approx 2.1684 \times 10^{-19}$, which is quite low.

To decide the fixed-point format, in addition to the dynamic range, its resolution should also be high enough. In the above example, the resolution of the adopted s(1.30) is $r = 2^{-30}$, which equals that of the ideal format, s(2.30).

To decide the fixed-number format of an application, we need to consider two main factors:

- The largest number that we need to represent in a given algorithm. This specifies how many bits must be used for the integral part.
- The tolerable precision or resolution of the algorithm. This determines the length of the fractional part.

Consider an example of representing a voltage between 0 and 5 V with 10 mV precision. To use the fewest number of bits to represent the voltage, it is clear that we will need 3 bits to the left of the binary point to represent the integral part, 5. To achieve 10 mV precision, if rounding is adopted, we will need $r = 20$ mV$= 0.02$ V resolution. Since $\lfloor \log_2 0.02 \rfloor \approx \lfloor -5.6439 \rfloor = -6$, we need 6 bits for the fractional part which gives us a resolution of $2^{-6} = 0.015625$ and a precision of $2^{-7} = 0.0078125$. Thus, an u(3.6) fixed-point format requires ten bits, which corresponds to the dynamic range $[0, 2^p - r]=[0, 2^3 - 2^{-6}]=[0, 7.984375]$ V.

An alternative representation would be to use a scaled number. If we scale this range by 20 mV, i.e., a count of 1 corresponds to 20 mV, we can use a 8-bit binary number ranging from 0 to 255, corresponding to $[0, 5.100]$ V, to cover the dynamic range. This number system has 10 mV precision with just 8 bits, i.e., u(8.0) fixed-point format. Compared to the previous u(3.6) fixed-point format, one bit is saved because the dynamic range of the scaled u(8.0) fixed-point format is less than that of u(3.6) fixed-point format.

Example 4.6. Write a Verilog module for a code converter that has an input representing an unsigned number in the range 0 to 24 with a precision of at least 0.01, and an output representing a signed number in the range -50 to 50 with a precision of at least 0.01.

Solution: For the input, we need 5 bits before the binary point, since $\lceil \log_2 24 \rceil = 5$. We need a precision that is smaller than 0.01, so that the required resolution is 0.02 for rounding. Since $\lfloor \log_2 0.02 \rfloor \approx \lfloor -5.6439 \rfloor = -6$, we need 6 bits for the fractional part which gives us a resolution of $2^{-6} = 0.015625$ and a precision of $2^{-7} = 0.0078125$. That is, the input is u(5.6) format.

For the output, $\lceil \log_2 50 \rceil = 6$, so we need 6 bits, plus one for the sign bit, giving 7 bits before the binary point. To give an output with a precision of at least 0.01, we also need 6 bits for the fractional part. That is, the output is s(7.6) format.

From above, we just need to extend the 5 integral bits of input with 2 zero bits to get the 7 integral bits of output. Two vacant bits are padded with 00 because the input is unsigned. Since we need the same output precision as the input, we need the same number of fractional bits, 6. Verilog codes are given below.

```
1// An example for converting u(5.6) to s(7.6) format
2module fixed_converter(out, in);
3output signed [6:-6] out; // s(7.6) fixed-point number
4input [4:-6] in; // u(5.6) fixed-point number
5assign out={2'b0, in};
6endmodule
```

□

4.2.2   OPERATIONS

4.2.2.1   Addition Operation

We can perform the basic operations on fixed-point binary numbers just as if they were integers. The position of the binary point must be kept in mind before/after the operation. For examples, adding two $u(p.f)$ fixed-point binary numbers gives a result of $u((p+1).f)$ fixed-point number. Therefore, 1 more bit is required if 2 numbers are added. An example is presented in Figure 4.1, where, to get rid of overflow, two $u(2.3)$ fixed-point binary numbers are added leading to the sum of $u(3.3)$ fixed-point format. Generally, if there are M numbers to be added, we should increase $\lceil \log_2(M) \rceil$ bits.

$$
\begin{array}{rr}
(+1.25) & 01.010\ (u(2.3)) \\
+\ (+3.625) & +\ 11.101\ (u(2.3)) \\
\hline
(+4.875) & 100.111\ (u(3.3))
\end{array}
$$

Figure 4.1: Adding two $u(2.3)$ fixed-point binary numbers. The sum requires one more bit which gives us $u(3.3)$ fixed-point format.

The Verilog codes can be written below.

```
1// An example for addition of fixed-point binary numbers
2// with the same format
3wire [1:-3] op1, op2; // u(2.3) fixed-point number
4wire [2:-3] sum; // u(3.3) fixed-point number
5assign sum=op1+op2; // Sign extension performed by
6                    // Verilog
```

To add two fixed-point numbers with different representations, it is necessary to align the binary points of the two numbers. This is most often achieved by converting both numbers to a fixed-point representation that has both p and f large enough to overlap both representations. For example, as shown below, consider adding the u(2.3) format number $A = 11.101$ to the u(4.2) format number $B = 1111.01$ without incurring an overflow. As shown in Figure 4.2, we first align the binary point of u(4.2) to u(4.3), and then add $Y = A + B = 11.101 + 1111.010$, which gives $Y = 10010.111$.

$$
\begin{array}{ll}
(+15.25) & 1111.010 \text{ (align u(4.2) to u(4.3))} \\
+\ (+\ 3.625) & +\quad 11.101 \text{ (u(2.3))} \\
\hline
(+18.875) & 10010.111 \text{ (u(5.3))}
\end{array}
$$

Figure 4.2: Adding u(2.3) number to the u(4.2) number. You need to align the binary point. The sum requires one more bit which gives us u(5.3) fixed-point format.

Generally, addition of $u(p_1.f_1)$ and $u(p_2.f_2)$ fixed-point numbers results in $u(p.f)$ fixed-point number, where $p = \max(p_1,p_2) + 1$ (one more bit is required), $f = \max(f_1,f_2)$, and $\max(A,B)$ returns the maximum number of A and B.

Verilog codes are given below. In addition to the alignment of binary point, we still need to sign extend the operands to the bit width of sum. Sign extension can expand the bit width of a number without affecting its value. For example, an u(2.3) number, 01010 (1.25 in decimal), can be changed to an u(5.3) number, **000**01010 (1.25 in decimal), without affecting its value. Similarly, a s(2.3) number, 11010 (-0.75 in decimal), can be changed to an s(5.3) number, **111**11010 (-0.75 in decimal), without affecting its value. Therefore, to expand the bit width of a number, its sign bit should be extended so that its original value can be maintained.

```
1 // An example for addition of fixed-point binary numbers
2 // with different formats
3 module fixed_add(Y, A, B);
4 output [4:-3] Y; // u(5.3) fixed-point number
5 input [1:-3] A;  // u(2.3) fixed-point number
6 input [3:-2] B;  // u(4.2) fixed-point number
7 wire [4:-3] A_ext, B_ext;
8 // Sign extend to bit width, 8, of sum
9 assign A_ext={3'b0, A};
10 // Sign extend to bit width, 8, of sum
11 // Need to align the binary point
12 assign B_ext={1'b0, B, 1'b0};
13 // u(5.3) fixed-point number
14 assign Y=A_ext+B_ext;
15 endmodule
```

4.2.2.2   Multiplication Operation

When we multiply two unsigned fixed-point numbers, the result needs total bits on both sides of the binary point of inputs. For example, if we multiply two u(2.3) fixed-point numbers, the result will be u(4.6) format, as that shown in Figure 4.3.

$$
\begin{array}{r}
(+1.25) \\
\times\ (+3.625) \\
\hline
(+4.53125)
\end{array}
\qquad
\begin{array}{r}
01.010\ (u(2.3)) \\
\times\ 11.101\ (u(2.3)) \\
\hline
01010 \\
00000 \\
01010 \\
01010 \\
01010 \\
\hline
100.100010\ (u(4.6))
\end{array}
$$

Figure 4.3: Multiplying two u(2.3) fixed-point binary numbers. The product requires the total bits of two operands, which gives us u(4.6) fixed-point format.

Generally, a multiplication with its operands of $u(p_1.f_1)$ and $u(p_2.f_2)$ (or $s(p_1.f_1)$ and $s(p_2.f_2)$) formats, its product is an $u(p_1 + p_2.f_1 + f_2)$ (or $s(p_1 + p_2.f_1 + f_2)$) fixed-point format without any overflow.

Therefore, the operands need to be sign extended to the bit number of product, as shown below.

```
1 // An example for multiplication of fixed-point binary
2 // numbers
3 module fixed_mul(Y, A, B);
4 output [3:-6] Y;  // u(4.6) fixed-point number
5 input [1:-3] A;   // u(2.3) fixed-point number
6 input [1:-3] B;   // u(2.3) fixed-point number
7 wire [6:-3] A_ext, B_ext;
8 // Sign extend to bit number, 10, of product
9 assign A_ext={5'b0, A};
10 // Sign extend to bit number, 10, of product
11 assign B_ext={5'b0, B};
12 // u(4.6) fixed-point number
13 assign Y=A_ext*B_ext;
14 endmodule
```

4.2.2.3 Signal Processing

Many signal processors scale numbers to a u(0.16) format for unsigned numbers or s(1.15) for signed numbers. Multiplying two u(0.16) numbers gives an u(0.32) number, and multiplying two s(1.15) numbers gives a s(1.30) number. To allow this operation to take place with no loss of precision, many popular signal processors have 40-bit accumulators. They accumulate up to 256 u(0.32) multiplication results, giving a sum in u(8.32) format. For signed numbers, the result is in s(9.30) format. In most cases, a result calculated using a high precision eventually must be scaled and rounded to the original precision. This sum is then usually scaled and rounded to get a final result back in u(0.16) format for unsigned numbers or s(1.15) for signed numbers.

Example 4.7. The inputs $x(n)$, coefficients h_m, $m = 0, 1, ..., 7$, and $y(n)$ of the eight-tap FIR filter in Figure 4.4 are all s(1.15) numbers. Determine the bit widths and fixed-point number formats of intermediate variables such that no quantization errors occur.

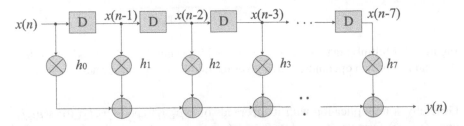

Figure 4.4: Eight-tap FIR filter.

Solution: The bit widths and fixed-point number formats of all signals are labeled in Figure 4.5. The block Q quantizes input using the truncation. Product of two s(1.15) numbers needs the s(1.30) format. Accumulation of 8 s(1.30) numbers requires the s(4.30) format, in which $\lceil \log_2(8) \rceil = 3$ more bits are added. Finally, the block Q quantizes input with s(4.30) format into s(1.15) format by dropping unnecessary bits using truncation without overflow detection.

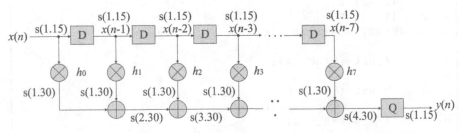

Figure 4.5: Bit width design of the eight-tap FIR filter.

□

Example 4.8. Write down the RTL codes of the eight-tap FIR filter.

Solution: After designing the fixed-point system, it is straightforward to write down its RTL codes as follows. In the Verilog codes, $x0$, $x1$,..., and $x7$ respectively represent $x(n-7)$, $x(n-6)$,..., and $x(n)$.

```
1 // RTL design of eight-tap FIR filter
2 module FIR(y, x, h0, h1, h2, h3, h4, h5, h6, h7, clk);
3 output signed [0:-15] y;
4 input signed [0:-15] x;
5 input signed [0:-15] h0, h1, h2, h3, h4, h5, h6, h7;
6 reg signed [0:-15] x0, x1, x2, x3, x4, x5, x6;
7 wire signed [0:-15] x7=x;
8 reg signed [3:-30] tmp_y;
9 always @(posedge clk) begin
10    x6<=x7; x5<=x6; x4<=x5; x3<=x4;
11    x2<=x3; x1<=x2; x0<=x1;
12 end
13 always @(*)
14    tmp_y=x7*h0+x6*h1+x5*h2+x4*h3+
15      x3*h4+x2*h5+x1*h6+x0*h7;
16 assign y=tmp_y[0:-15];
17 endmodule
```

□

To verify the digital design of the eight-tap FIR filter, a behavioral model of the eight-tap FIR filter using the real numbers are developed to check the results of fixed-point design. It must be emphasized here that the behavioral model as the gold design should do the same things as the fixed-point design, such as the quantization, so that they can perfectly match.

Verilog does not provide a data type for fixed-point numbers. To evaluate the value of the result of fixed-point number operation, we can declare a variable with **real** type to store the decimal representation of a fixed-point number by scaling the fixed-point number using the resolution of operands by $r = 2^{-15}$, as shown below. The scaling is required, since our actual interpretation of the variable is a fixed-point value with a fraction instead of an integer. Real variables are actually represented using floating-point format. Then, operations are performed on these real variables, as shown below, where $x0, x1,..., x7$ respectively represent $x(n-7), x(n-6),..., x(n)$.

In the Verilog codes, the **signed** declaration is very handy for the signed number arithmetic because sign extension can be automatically performed by Verilog and synthesis tool.

```
1 // Behavioral model of the eight-tap FIR filter
2 // Real number version
3 parameter p=1; parameter f=15; parameter n=p+f;
4 // Resolution of s(1.15)
5 real r=1/(2**f);
6 real x0_r, x1_r, x2_r, x3_r, x4_r, x5_r, x6_r, x7_r;
7 real h0_r, h1_r, h2_r, h3_r, h4_r, h5_r, h6_r, h7_r;
```

```verilog
 8 real tmp_y_r;
 9 // s(1.15) fixed-point number version
10 wire signed [p-1:-f] x0, x1, x2, x3, x4, x5, x6, x7;
11 wire signed [p-1:-f] h0, h1, h2, h3, h4, h5, h6, h7;
12 // Scaled by the resolution of x and h, r=2^(-15)
13 assign x0_r=$itor(x0)*r; assign x1_r=$itor(x1)*r;
14 assign x2_r=$itor(x2)*r; assign x3_r=$itor(x3)*r;
15 assign x4_r=$itor(x4)*r; assign x5_r=$itor(x5)*r;
16 assign x6_r=$itor(x6)*r; assign x7_r=$itor(x7)*r;
17 assign h0_r=$itor(h0)*r; assign h1_r=$itor(h1)*r;
18 assign h2_r=$itor(h2)*r; assign h3_r=$itor(h3)*r;
19 assign h4_r=$itor(h4)*r; assign h5_r=$itor(h5)*r;
20 assign h6_r=$itor(h6)*r; assign h7_r=$itor(h7)*r;
21 // FIR filter calculated using real numbers
22 assign tmp_y_r=x7_r*h0_r+x6_r*h1_r+x5_r*h2_r+x4_r*h3_r+
23     x3_r*h4_r+x2_r*h5_r+x1_r*h6_r+x0_r*h7_r;
```

Then, the quantization of real number also needs to be taken. It is performed by truncating the fixed-point number version of the FIR filter output from s(4.30) to s(1.15). The input of quantization is converted back to integer using the fixed-point format by scaling the input using its resolution, i.e., $r1 = 2^{-30}$. Finally, the quantized fixed-point number, y_i_q, is the gold result.

```verilog
 1 // Behavioral model of quantization
 2 // s(4.30) format
 3 parameter p1=4; parameter f1=30; parameter n1=p1+f1;
 4 // Resolution
 5 real r1=1/(2**f1);
 6 // Integer version of y
 7 wire [p1-1:-f1] tmp_y_i; // s(4.30) fixed-point number
 8                          // version
 9 // Gold result: integer version of quantized y
10 wire [p-1:-f] y_i_q; // s(1.15) fixed-point number
11                      // version
12 // Scaled by the resolution r1 of tmp_y_r
13 assign tmp_y_i=$rtoi(tmp_y_r/r1);
14 // Quantize y_i
15 assign y_i_q=tmp_y_i[p-1:-f];
```

4.3 FLOATING-POINT NUMBERS

Numbers with high dynamic range are often represented in floating-point format. In particular, a floating-point format is efficient for representing a number when we need a fixed precision percentage instead of absolute precision. Compared to fixed-point numbers, the position of the binary point for floating-point numbers may vary.

A floating-point number has two components: the exponent e and mantissa m. The value represented by a floating-point number is given by

$$v = m \times 2^{e-x} \tag{4.9}$$

where m is a binary fraction, e is a binary integer, and x is a bias on the exponent that is used to center the dynamic range. The mantissa, m, is a fraction which means that the binary point is on the left of the most significant bit (MSB) of m. The exponent, e, is an integer. If the bits of m are $\{m_{n-1}, ..., m_0\}$ and the bits of e are $\{e_{k-1}, ..., e_0\}$, the value of the floating-point number is given by

$$v = \sum_{i=0}^{n-1} m_i 2^{i-n} \times 2^{\sum_{i=0}^{k-1} e_i 2^k - x}. \tag{4.10}$$

We refer to a floating-point number system with an a-bit mantissa and a b-bit exponent as an aEb format. For example, a system with a 5-bit mantissa and a 3-bit exponent is a 5E3 system.

We will also use the "E" notation to write numbers. For example, the 5E3 number with a mantissa of 10110 and an exponent of 010 is 10110E010. Assuming zero bias, this number has a value of $v = \frac{22}{2^5} \times 2^2 = 22/32 \times 4 = 2.75$. Most floating-point number systems normalize the mantissa by shifting it left until either there is a 1 in the MSB of the mantissa or the exponent is 0. With normalized numbers, we can quickly check for equality by simply comparing two numbers bit-by-bit. If numbers are un-normalized, they must be normalized (or at least aligned) before they can be compared. Some number systems take another advantage of normalization by omitting the MSB of the mantissa, since it is almost always 1. Typically, when a floating-point number is stored, the exponent is stored to the left of the mantissa. For example, 10110E010 would be stored in eight bits as 01010110. Storing the exponent to the left allows integer comparison to work on floating-point numbers as long as numbers are normalized.

If we want to represent signed values, we typically add a sign bit to the left of the exponent. For example, in eight bits we can represent an S4E3 number which, from left to right, would contain a sign bit, a three-bit exponent, and then a four-bit mantissa (SEEEMMMM). In this representation, the bit string 11010110 represents $-6E5$ or (with zero bias) $\frac{-6}{2^4} \times 2^5 = -12$.

4.4   OTHER BINARY NUMBERS

The best-known methods of extending the binary numeral system to represent signed numbers are: signed magnitude, one's complement, and two's complement. For the signed magnitude number, a number's sign is represented with a sign bit: setting that bit (often the most significant bit) to 0 for a positive number or positive zero, and setting it to 1 for a negative number or negative zero. The remaining bits in the number indicate the magnitude (or absolute value).

4.5   FURTHER READING

- David Money Harris and Sarah L. Harris, *Digital design and computer architecture*, 2nd Ed., Morgan Kaufmann, 2013.
- Donald E. Thomas and Philip R. Moorby, *The Verilog hardware description language*, 5th Ed., Kluwer Academic Publishers, 2002.
- Joseph Cavanagh, *Computer arithmetic and Verilog HDL fundamentals*, CRC Press, 2010.
- M. Morris Mano and Michael D. Ciletti, *Digital design*, 4th Ed., Prentice Hall, 2006.
- Peter J. Ashenden, *Digital design: an embedded systems approach using Verilog*, Morgan Kaufmann Publishers, 2007.
- Stephen Brown and Zvonko Vranesic, *Fundamentals of digital logic with Verilog design*, McGraw-Hill, 2002.
- William J. Dally and R. Curtis Harting, *Digital design: a systems approach*, Cambridge University Press, 2012.

PROBLEMS

1. Convert decimal 67 to u(7.0) fixed-point binary format.
2. Convert decimal 0.375 to u(1.3) fixed-point binary format.
3. Convert decimal 67.75 to u(7.2) fixed-point binary format.
4. Convert u(5.2) unsigned fixed-point binary format, 10110.11, to decimal.
5. Convert the number 4.23 into each the following fix-point formats, and then convert it back to decimal. Obtain the absolute error and error percentage of each representation.

    a. u(4.1);
    b. s(5.2);
    c. s(5.5);

6. Designing a fixed-point system. The number ranges from 0 to 31 with a precision of 0.05.
7. Designing a floating-point system to represent a measurement of 1×10^{-6} to 1×10^7 with 2.5% precision. Represent the value 4.5 in this format.
8. Perform the following unsigned binary additions to produce 8-bit results. In each case, does the addition overflow or not?

    a. 00110010 + 10010100.
    b. 11110000 + 00110010.
    c. 11001100 + 10001111.

9. Write a Verilog code that adds four 12-bit unsigned binary numbers to produce a 12-bit result with overflow detection.
10. Perform the following unsigned binary subtractions to produce 8-bit results. In each case, does the subtraction overflows or not?

    a. 10111000 − 01010000.
    b. 01110000 − 00110010.
    c. 01111100 − 10000111.

11. What numbers are represented by the following unsigned u(4.3) fixed-point binary numbers, 1001001 and 0011110?
12. What is the range and precision of each of the following unsigned fixed-point representations?

    a. 12 bits, with $p = 5$ and $f = 7$.
    b. 10 bits, with $p = 0$ and $f = 10$.
    c. 8 bits, with $p = 8$ and $f = 0$.

13. How many integral and fractional bits would be required to represent numbers in the range from 0.0 to 12.0 with a precision of 0.002?
14. Assuming the signed s(5.3) fixed-point binary numbers. What decimal numbers are represented by the following binary numbers: 00101100 and 11111101?
15. How many integral and fractional bits would be required to represent numbers in the range from −5.0 to +5.0 with a precision of 0.01?
16. Prove that the sign extension does not affect the original value of a fixed-point number.

17. The architecture for 8-point decimation-in-time (DIT) fast Fourier transform (FFT) is shown in Figure 4.6. The complex inputs and outputs are parallel-in and parallel-out, respectively. That is, the input data in a block, $x[n]$, $n = 0, 1, , 7$, and output blocks, $X[k]$, $k = 0, 1, ..., 7$, are available in every clock cycle. The real and imaginary parts of all inputs, outputs, and twiddle factors $W_N^i = e^{-j2\pi i/N}$, $i = 0, 1, 2, 3$, are represented by $s(1,15)$ fixed-point numbers. Please design a pure combinational circuit for the feed-forward DIT FFT. Determine the bit widths of intermediate variables such that no quantization errors occur. The final outputs, $X[k]$, are quantized by the rounding such that they can be represented by $s(1,15)$ fixed-point numbers.

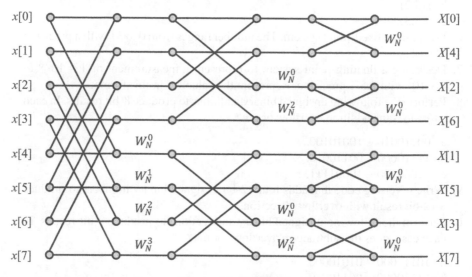

Figure 4.6: DIT FFT.

5 Combinational Circuits

Combinational and sequential logics are two essential components for the RTL design. A combinational circuit consists of logic gates whose outputs at any time are determined directly from the present combination of inputs without regard to previous inputs and/or outputs, as shown in Figure 5.1. Therefore, there is no notion of storage of information or dependence on values at previous times. There is no clock control as well. Many sophisticated logical functions are realized by combinational circuits.

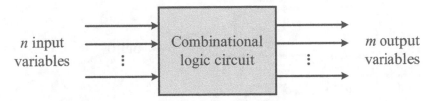

n input variables ⋮   Combinational logic circuit   ⋮ m output variables

Figure 5.1: Combinational circuits.

First, dataflow, behavioral, and structural descriptions of combinational circuits are presented in this chapter. Next, basic building blocks of combinational circuits, such as arithmetic and logic units, together with their RTL codes, are introduced. The logic units include multiplexer, demultiplexer, comparator, shifter and rotator, encoder, priority encoder, decoder, and bubble sorting, and arithmetic units consist of half adder, full adder, arithmetic logic unit, carry look-ahead adder, and complex multiplier. Finally, several design issues, including overflow detection, bit width design, and saturation arithmetic, are discussed thoroughly.

5.1 DATAFLOW DESCRIPTION

Continuous assignment is the most fundamental construct to describe a combinational logic. The continuous assignment is used to represent a combinational logic circuit that can be conveniently represented by an equation or Boolean equation. During simulations, continuous assignments execute whenever their expressions on the right-hand side change. As its name implies, the execution is immediate and its effect is that the output on the left-hand side of the expression is updated promptly once inputs change. Such a behavior is like that of the combinational circuit. For example,

```
1// Continuous assignment: simple combinational circuit
2assign out=(a&b)|c;
```

DOI: 10.1201/9781003187196-5

The bit-wise operators in the RTL codes represent straightforward logic gates shown in Figure 5.2.

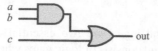

Figure 5.2: Logic gates for bit-wise operators.

In the Verilog codes, if a, b, c, and out are declared as 2-bit vectors with index $[1:0]$, the logic gates become that shown in Figure 5.3.

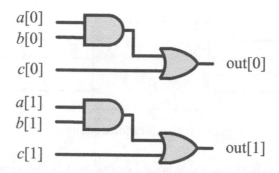

Figure 5.3: Logic gates for 2-bit bit-wise operators.

Arithmetic operators are interpreted in terms of arithmetic hardware blocks available to the tool. For example,

```
1 // Continuous assignment: full adder
2 assign {c_out, sum}=a+b+c_in;
```

Depending on the synthesis tool and design constraints, the arithmetic operator in the RTL codes may be implemented using logic gates shown in Figure 5.4.

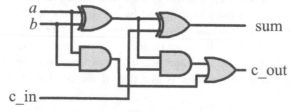

Figure 5.4: Logic gates of the full adder.

A 3-bit adder is described below. The sum of 3-bit number addition requires 4-bit, so that there exists no overflow.

```
1 // Continuous assignment: 3-bit adder
2 wire [2:0] a, b;
3 wire [3:0] sum;
4 assign sum=a+b;
```

The adder might be synthesized to the ripple-carry adder in Figure 5.5, where the full adder might also be implemented by the logic gates in Figure 5.4. About the ripple-carry adder, the carry in of the first full adder is tied to a constant 1'b0, the carry out of the first full adder, c_out[0], is connected to the carry in of the second full adder, and then the carry out of the second full adder, c_out[1], is connected to the carry in of the third full adder. As a result, the carry propagates from the least significant bit to the most significant bit just like a ripple in water. Consequently, such an adder is named the ripple-carry adder.

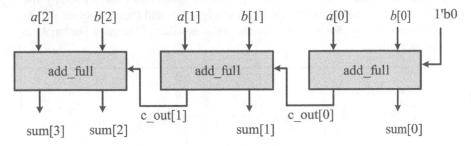

Figure 5.5: A 3-bit ripple-carry adder.

A conditional operator infers a multiplexer. For example,

```
1 // Continuous assignment: multiplexer
2 assign out=s?i1:i0;
```

The conditional operator in the RTL codes may be implemented using logic gates shown in Figure 5.6 or a multiplexer gate in a cell library.

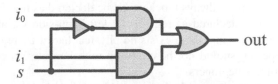

Figure 5.6: Logic gates for the conditional operator.

You can specify minimum, typical, and maximum values for the rising and falling delays in continuous assignments, as can be seen in the following. In this example, the (minimum : typical : maximum) delays for the rising delay are $(1 : 2 : 3)$, the (minimum : typical : maximum) delays for the falling delay are $(2 : 3 : 4)$, and the (minimum : typical : maximum) delays for the turn-off delay are $(3 : 4 : 5)$.

```
1// Modeling delays in continuous assignments
2// (minimum:typical:maximum) delays can be specified
3// for rising, falling, and turn-off delays.
4assign #(1:2:3, 2:3:4, 3:4:5) out=s?i1:i0;
```

5.2   BEHAVIORAL DESCRIPTION

The always statement is often used to describe the behavior of combinational circuits as well. The sensitivity list controls the way an always block executes. To describe a combinational circuit, the inputs of it should be specified in the sensitivity list. Whenever inputs change, the always block is triggered, and then its output will be evaluated immediately. Such a behavior also emulates that of the combinational circuit. For example,

```
1// Always block: full adder
2reg c_out, sum;
3always @(a or b or c_in)
4   {c_out, sum}=a+b+c_in;
```

To this, all inputs on the right-hand side (RHS) of expressions in a combinational circuit must appear in the sensitivity list of an always block. To prevent from inadvertently ignoring some inputs, you can use (*) to represent all inputs as follows.

```
1// Always block: full adder
2always @(*)
3   {c_out, sum}=a+b+c_in;
```

Moreover, according to the requirement of Verilog, those variables on the left-hand side (LHS) of expressions in always blocks must be declared as reg. It must be emphasized here that, even declared as reg for the left-hand-side variables, they are still combinational outputs, and there exists no physical hardware registers. Consequently, the datatype reg should not be confused with hardware registers. Such a misleading often bothers beginners.

The assignments in an always block for combinational circuits, which are executed sequentially, must be blocking.

```
1 // Always block: combinational circuit described
2 // using multiple blocking assignments
3 always @(a or b or c or d) begin
4   sum1=a+b;
5   sum2=c+d;
6   sum=sum1+sum2;
7 end
```

The calculation of sum is divided into sum1 and sum2. Therefore, sum1 and sum2 must be available before determining sum. This necessitates that the RTL codes should be executed in order using the blocking assignment.

Single if-else statement also infers a multiplexer. For example,

```
1 // Always block: multiplexer
2 always @(s or i0 or i1)
3   if(s) out=i1;
4   else out=i0;
```

However, multiple if-else-if statements do not synthesize to large multiplexers. They infer priority multiplexers. Besides, the case statement also can be used to infer a multiplexer. Large case statements may synthesize large multiplexers.

```
1 // Always block: large multiplexer
2 always @(s or i0 or i1 or i2 or i3)
3   case(s)
4     2'b00: out=i0;
5     2'b01: out=i1;
6     2'b10: out=i2;
7     2'b11: out=i3;
8   endcase
```

For loops are unrolled and can build a cascaded or parallel combinational logic. Therefore, the index of a for loop commonly declared as integer data type is dummy and dose not cost any hardware resources. For example, the (cascaded) 8-bit ripple-carry adder is displayed below.

```
1 // Always block: 8-bit ripple-carry adder described by a
2 // for loop
3 always @(a or b or c_in) begin
4   c=c_in;
```

```
5   for(i=0;i<=7;i=i+1)
6     {c, sum[i]}=a[i]+b[i]+c;
7   c_out=c;
8 end
```

In the preceding example, the variable c is used for all full adders, which is quite confusing. Moreover, it is also misleading that, for each full adder, c is a carry in (carry out of previous full adder) and carry out of current full adder. It's better to declare $c[i-1]$ and $c[i]$ as carry in and carry out of full adder i, respectively, as shown below. Such a description coincides with the physical connection of a multiple-bit adder.

```
1 // Always block: 8-bit ripple-carry adder described by a
2 // for loop using different carry in and carry out
3 always @(a or b or c_in) begin
4   c[-1]=c_in;
5   for(i=0;i<=7;i=i+1)
6     {c[i], sum[i]}=a[i]+b[i]+c[i-1];
7   c_out=c[7];
8 end
```

Another example, the parallel XOR gate is presented below.

```
1 // Always block: parallel XOR described by a for loop
2 always @(a or b)
3   for(i=0;i<=31;i=i+1)
4     s[i]=a[i]^b[i];
```

Functions are synthesized to combinational blocks with one output. For example,

```
1 // Function: a reusable combinational block
2 function [1:0] sum3;
3   input a, b, c_in;
4   sum3=a+b+c_in;
5 endfunction
```

Function contains procedural statements and is also a behavioral description. Function call is a simple combinational circuit which can be reused. Calling a function once essentially instantiates one combinational circuit. However, if the function was called in the if-else or case statement, only one combinational circuit may be introduced because the synthesis tool knows that only one function call in all mutually-exclusive case items is executed at a time, as shown below.

```
1// Calling a function using different case items
2// Resources are shared.
3wire [1:0] sel;
4wire [3:0] a, b, c;
5reg [1:0] out;
6always @(sel or a or b or c) begin
7   case(sel[1:0])
8   2'b00: out=sum3(a[0],b[0],c[0]);
9   2'b01: out=sum3(a[1],b[1],c[1]);
10  2'b10: out=sum3(a[2],b[2],c[2]);
11  default: out=sum3(a[3],b[3],c[3]);
12  endcase
13end
```

The synthesized circuit is presented in Figure 5.7. Therefore, the synthesis tool infers one circuit of sum3 and uses a multiplexer to select different inputs.

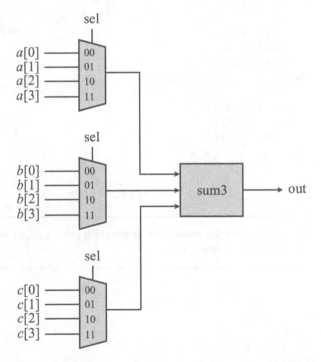

Figure 5.7: The number of function is optimized by selecting input operands.

Even so, it's still better to explicitly infer the multiplexer used to select different inputs, and one combinational circuit of sum3 as follows.

```
1// Selecting different inputs according to different
2// case items before calling a function
3wire [1:0] sel;
4wire [3:0] a, b, c;
5reg a_sel, b_sel, c_sel;
6wire [1:0] out;
7always @(sel or a or b or c) begin
8   case(sel[1:0])
9   2'b00: begin
10           a_sel=a[0];
11           b_sel=b[0];
12           c_sel=c[0];
13         end
14   2'b01: begin
15           a_sel=a[1];
16           b_sel=b[1];
17           c_sel=c[1];
18         end
19   2'b10: begin
20           a_sel=a[2];
21           b_sel=b[2];
22           c_sel=c[2];
23         end
24   default: begin
25           a_sel=a[3];
26           b_sel=b[3];
27           c_sel=c[3];
28         end
29   endcase
30end
31assign out=sum3(a_sel,b_sel,c_sel);
```

As another example, to find the maximum among 4 inputs, a, b, c, and d, three comparisons are required, as shown below.

```
1// Not balanced design
2always @(a or b or c or d) begin
3   if(a>=b) out1=a;
4   else out1=b;
5   if(out1>=c) out2=out1;
6   else out2=c;
7   if(out2>=d) out=out2;
8   else out=d;
9end
```

Another RTL codes with the same function are written below.

```
1 // Balanced design
2 always @(a or b or c or d) begin
3   if(a>=b) out1=a;
4   else out1=b;
5   if(c>=d) out2=c;
6   else out2=d;
7   if(out1>=out2) out=out1;
8   else out=out2;
9 end
```

Though the above two pieces of codes achieve the same functionality, they infer different structures as shown in Figure 5.8.

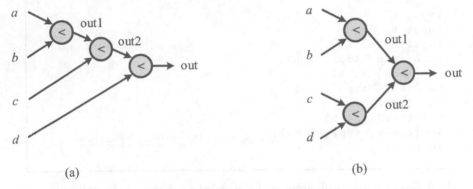

(a)   (b)

Figure 5.8: Different structures for finding the maximum of 4 inputs: (a) sequential comparison and (b) parallel comparison.

Regarding the critical path of two structures, it is clear that a balanced design is good for timing.

Only the (minimum : typical : maximum) delays of a single delay can be specified in procedural assignments. Therefore, the rising, falling, and turn-off delays must be the same. In the following example, if s is true, the (minimum : typical : maximum) delays of assigning $i1$ to out is $(1:2:3)$ time units; and if s is false, the (minimum : typical : maximum) delays of assigning $i0$ to out is $(2:3:4)$ time units.

```
1 // Modeling delays in always blocks
2 always @(s or i0 or i1)
3   if(s) #(1:2:3) out=i1;
4   else #(2:3:4) out=i0;
```

5.3   STRUCTURAL DESCRIPTION

Structural description for combinational circuits is quite simple and straightforward. It just intuitively describes the cell instances and connections among them based on the gate-level netlist. Verilog primitives are synthesizable. Therefore, it is a good practice to use Verilog primitives instead of instantiating logic cells in a cell library, which are not portable for different technology nodes. For example, we can use Verilog primitives to implement the full adder as follows. Notice that the instance names of Verilog primitives can be omitted.

```
1// Structural description: fill adder
2module fulladder (
3   output sum,
4   output c_out,
5   input a,
6   input b,
7   input c_in);
8   wire  tmp, tmp1, tmp2;
9   xor (tmp, a, b);
10  xor (sum, tmp, c_in);
11  and (tmp1, tmp, c_in);
12  and (tmp2, a, b);
13  or (c_out, tmp1, tmp2);
14endmodule
```

The delays of Verilog primitives can be modeled when they are instantiated.

```
1// Modeling delays of Verilog primitives
2or #(1:2:3, 2:3:4, 3:4:5) (c_out, tmp1, tmp2);
```

5.4   COMBINATIONAL LOOP

Combinational loop is not allowed. For example, the increment of a number is shown below.

```
1// Combinational loop
2always @(a)
3   a=a+1;
```

The always block infers the following combinational circuit with a feedback loop, as shown in Figure 5.9, where $\oplus$ represents an adder.

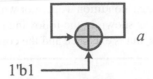

Figure 5.9: Combinational loop for the increment of a number.

Three serious problems exist in the combinational loop. 1) If *a* suddenly changes from one number to another, what result do you expect? The increment may perform once, twice, or more times within a given time interval. So, actually, the result will be unpredictable. 2) Timing loop is infinite. Timing analysis is impossible. 3) Your simulation will hang, because an infinite loop occurs.

A remedy to solve this problem can change the codes to those below.

```
1 // No combinational loop
2 always @(a)
3    b=a+1;
```

In Figure 5.10, a combinational loop does not exist, and *b* is the result of increment.

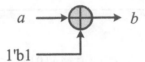

Figure 5.10: Increment without a combinational loop.

To avoid the combinational loop, you can also break the feedback path by using the sequential circuits, which can store or memorize the previous result.

```
1 // No combinational loop
2 always @(posedge clk)
3    a<=a+1;
```

This leads to the circuit in Figure 5.11.

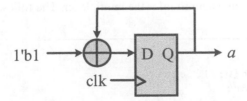

Figure 5.11: Breaking the combinational loop using sequential circuits.

Continuous assignment using a conditional operator with feedback may introduce
a combinational loop as well, as shown in the following example. When CS_b is 0
and WE_b is 1, data_out=data_out is executed and the combinational loop occurs.

```
1// Combinational loop produced by continuous assignment
2assign data_out=(CS_b==0)?
3                    ((WE_b==0)?data_in:data_out):
4                    1'bz;
```

If a careless combinational loop exists in a design, Design compiler (synthesis
tool) will automatically break feedback loops. Without disabling the combinational
feedback loop, the static timing analysis cannot resolve or analyze the path timing.

5.5   BASIC BUILDING BLOCKS OF COMBINATIONAL
CIRCUITS: LOGIC UNITS

5.5.1   MULTIPLEXER

For an n-to-1 multiplexer (or mux), there are $\lceil \log_2(n) \rceil$-bit select lines used to select
n multiplexer inputs. The structural, dataflow, and behavioral descriptions are given
below.

```
1// Structural description: multiplexer
2not (sel_inv, sel);
3and (and_out[0], sel_inv, mux_in[0]);
4and (and_out[1], sel, mux_in[1]);
5or (mux_out, and_out[0], and_out[1]);
6// Dataflow description: multiplexer
7assign mux_out1=sel?mux_in[1]:mux_in[0];
8// Behavioral description: multiplexer
9always @(sel or mux_in)
10   if(sel)
11     mux_out2=mux_in[1];
12   else
13     mux_out2=mux_in[0];
```

For logic circuits that are naturally described with a table, they can be designed
using a case or casex statement to infer the multiplexer. The following example describes a 8×16 table.

```
1// Behavioral description: 8x16 table
2reg [15:0] tab[0:7], out;
3wire [2:0] addr;
4always @(addr or tab)
```

```
 5    case(addr)
 6    3'd0:  out=tab[0];
 7    3'd1:  out=tab[1];
 8    3'd2:  out=tab[2];
 9    3'd3:  out=tab[3];
10    3'd4:  out=tab[4];
11    3'd5:  out=tab[5];
12    3'd6:  out=tab[6];
13    default:  out=tab[7];
14    endcase
```

5.5.2 DEMULTIPLEXER

The demultiplexer (or demux) is the reverse of the multiplexer. A demultiplexer is a component that takes a single input line and routes it to one of several output lines according to the select lines, which are used to select which output line to send the input. A demultiplexer is also called a data distributor. By setting the input to true, the demux behaves as a decoder.

The following example shows an 1-to-4 demultiplexer using 2 select lines (sel[1 : 0]) to determine which one of the 4 outputs (demux_out[3 : 0]) is routed from the input (demux_in). Its characteristics can be described using the truth table in Table 5.1.

Table 5.1: Truth table of demux_out.

sel[1]	sel[0]	demux_out[3]	demux_out[2]	demux_out[1]	demux_out[0]
0	0	0	0	0	demux_in
0	1	0	0	demux_in	0
1	0	0	demux_in	0	0
1	1	demux_in	0	0	0

The symbol and schematic of the demultiplexer are presented in Figure 5.12.

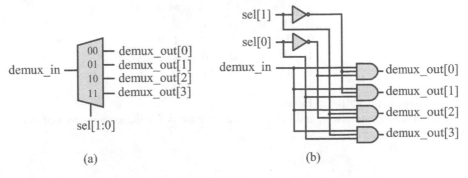

(a)   (b)

Figure 5.12: (a) Symbol. (b) Schematic of the demultiplexer.

The structural, dataflow, and behavioral descriptions of the 1-to-2 demultiplexer are given below.

```
1 // Structural description: demultiplexer
2 not (sel_inv, sel);
3 and (demux_out[0], sel_inv, demux_in);
4 and (demux_out[1], sel, demux_in);
5 // Dataflow description: demultiplexer
6 assign demux_out1[0]=~sel&demux_in;
7 assign demux_out1[1]=sel&demux_in;
8 // Behavioral description: demultiplexer
9 always @(sel or demux_in) begin
10    demux_out2=2'b00;
11    case(sel)
12    1'b0: demux_out2[0]=demux_in;
13    1'b1: demux_out2[1]=demux_in;
14    endcase
15 end
```

5.5.3 COMPARATOR

The truth table for the comparison of two 1-bit binary numbers is displayed in Table 5.2. Compared with b, the comparator determines whether a is greater than, less than, equal, or not equal to it using outputs $y1$, $y2$, $y3$, and $y4$, respectively. Notably, $y4 = a \oplus b = a \cdot \bar{b} + \bar{a} \cdot b$ can be used to decide whether 2 bits are different, where $\oplus$, $\cdot$, $(\bar{\cdot})$, and $+$ denote the bitwise XOR, AND, NOT, and OR operators, respectively. Similarly, $y3 = \overline{a \oplus b} = \bar{a} \cdot \bar{b} + a \cdot b$ can be used to decide whether 2 bits are the same. In this book, $\oplus$ symbol in a Boolean equation represents the bitwise XOR; otherwise, it represents an adder.

Table 5.2: Truth table of the comparator.

a	b	$y1$	$y2$	$y3$	$y4$
0	0	0	0	1	0
0	1	0	1	0	1
1	0	1	0	0	1
1	1	0	0	1	0

Its schematic is presented in Figure 5.13.

The structural, dataflow, and behavioral descriptions for the comparators of two 1-bit numbers are given below.

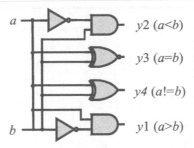

Figure 5.13: Schematic of the comparator.

```
1// Structural description: comparators
2not (b_inv, b);
3and (y1, b_inv, a);
4not (a_inv, a);
5and (y2, a_inv, b);
6xnor (y3, a, b);
7xor (y4, a, b);
8// Dataflow description: comparators
9assign y1_1=a>b;
10assign y2_1=a<b;
11assign y3_1=a==b;
12assign y4_1=a!=b;
13// Behavioral description: comparators
14always @(a or b) begin
15   if(a>b) y1_2=1'b1;
16   else y1_2=1'b0;
17   if(a<b) y2_2=1'b1;
18   else y2_2=1'b0;
19   if(a==b) y3_2=1'b1;
20   else y3_2=1'b0;
21   if(a!=b) y4_2=1'b1;
22   else y4_2=1'b0;
23end
```

5.5.4 SHIFTER AND ROTATOR

The shift operators $\ll$ and $\gg$ shift your input and pad with zeros. Left shift and right shift do not necessitate any digital circuits. Instead, only wiring is needed. For example, $a[2:0] = b[2:0] \ll 1$ equals connecting $a[0]$ with logic 0, $a[1]$ with $b[0]$, and $a[2]$ with $b[1]$. The structural, dataflow, and behavioral descriptions of the shifter are given below.

```
1 // Structural description: shifter
2 assign a[0]=1'b0;
3 buf (a[1], b[0]);
4 buf (a[2], b[1]);
5 // Dataflow description: shifter
6 assign a1[2:0]=b[2:0]<<1;
7 // Behavioral description: shifter
8 always @(b)
9    a2[2:0]=b[2:0]<<1;
```

The left rotator and right rotator rotate your input circularly. The left rotator by 1 bit simply connects $a[0]$ with $b[2]$, $a[1]$ with $b[0]$, and $a[2]$ with $b[1]$, as shown below.

```
1 // Structural description: rotator
2 buf (a[0], b[2]);
3 buf (a[1], b[0]);
4 buf (a[2], b[1]);
5 // Dataflow description: rotator
6 assign a1[2:0]={b[1:0],b[2]};
7 // Behavioral description: rotator
8 always @(b) begin
9    {carry, a[2:0]}=b[2:0]<<1;
10   a2[0]=carry;
11 end
```

If we write the Verilog codes below, where b is a variable, we got the barrel shifter, which has a layer corresponding to each bit-of-shift.

```
1 // Dataflow description: barrel shifter
2 assign y=a<<b;
```

Consequently, an 8-bit barrel shifter needs 3 bits to indicate how many bits to shift, and hence 3 layers of multiplexers, as shown in Figure 5.14.

5.5.5 ENCODER

The truth table for the 4-to-2 encoder is displayed in Table 5.3. When $\{a,b,c,d\}=$ 0001, the output encodes it using $y = 00$, and $\{a,b,c,d\} = 0010$, the output encodes it using $y = 01$, and so on.

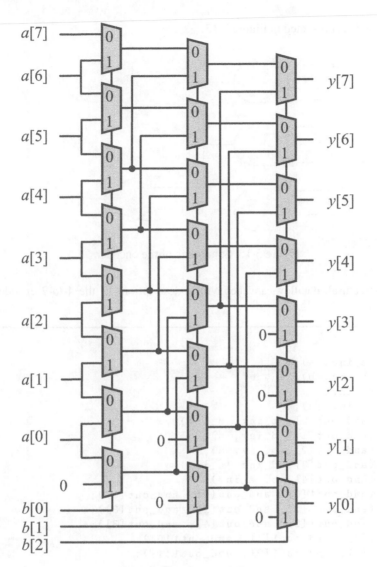

Figure 5.14: Barrel shifter.

Table 5.3: Truth table of the encoder.

a	b	c	d	y[1:0]
0	0	0	1	00
0	0	1	0	01
0	1	0	0	10
1	0	0	0	11

Its schematic is presented in Figure 5.15.

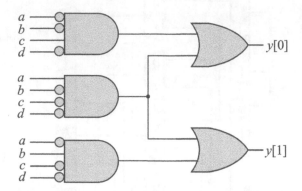

Figure 5.15: Schematic of the encoder.

The structural, dataflow, and behavioral descriptions of the 4-to-2 encoder are given below.

```
1 // Structural description: encoder
2 not (a_inv, a);
3 not (b_inv, b);
4 not (c_inv, c);
5 not (d_inv, d);
6 and (and_out[0], b_inv, a_inv);
7 and (and_out[1], d_inv, c);
8 and (and_out[2], b_inv, a);
9 and (and_out[3], d_inv, c_inv);
10 and (and_out[4], b, a_inv);
11 and (and_out1[0], and_out[0], and_out[1]);
12 and (and_out1[1], and_out[2], and_out[3]);
13 and (and_out1[2], and_out[4], and_out[3]);
14 or (y[0], and_out1[1], and_out1[0]);
15 or (y[1], and_out1[2], and_out1[1]);
16 // Dataflow description: encoder
17 assign all={a, b, c, d};
18 assign y1[0]=(all==4'b0010)|(all==4'b1000);
19 assign y1[1]=(all==4'b0100)|(all==4'b1000);
20 // Behavioral description: encoder
21 always @(all)
22   case(all)
23   4'b0001: y2=2'b00;
24   4'b0010: y2=2'b01;
25   4'b0100: y2=2'b10;
26   4'b1000: y2=2'b11;
```

```
27  default: y2=2'b00;
28  endcase
```

5.5.6 PRIORITY ENCODER

The truth table for the 4-to-2 priority encoder is displayed in Table 5.4.

Table 5.4: Truth table of 4-to-2 priority encoder.

d	c	b	a	$y[1]$	$y[0]$
0	0	0	0	0	0
0	0	0	1	0	0
0	0	1	x	0	1
0	1	x	x	1	0
1	x	x	x	1	1

Its schematic is presented in Figure 5.16. Notably, according to the Karnaugh map, the output y does not depend on input a.

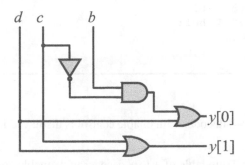

Figure 5.16: Schematic of the priority encoder.

The structural, dataflow, and behavioral descriptions of the 4-to-2 priority encoder are given below.

```
1// Structural description: priority encoder
2not (c_inv, c);
3and (and_out, c_inv, b);
4or (y[0], d, and_out);
5or (y[1], c, d);
6// Dataflow description: priority encoder
7assign all={d, c, b, a};
8assign y1[0]=(all[1]&~all[2])|(all[3]);
9assign y1[1]=(all[2])|(all[3]);
10// Behavioral description: priority encoder
```

```
11 always @(all) begin
12   casex(all)
13   4'b0000:  y2=2'b00;
14   4'b0001:  y2=2'b00;
15   4'b001x:  y2=2'b01;
16   4'b01xx:  y2=2'b10;
17   4'b1xxx:  y2=2'b11;
18   default:  y2=2'b00;
19   endcase
20 end
```

We present another behavioral description of the priority encoder using the if-else-if statement below. As presented, the decoder has priority for d. Also, it's apparent that the output $y3$ is not related to a.

```
1 // Behavioral description #1: priority encoder
2 always @(*) begin
3   if(d) y3=2'b11;
4   else if(c) y3=2'b10;
5   else if(b) y3=2'b01;
6   else y3=2'b00;
7 end
```

5.5.7 DECODER

The truth table of 3-to-8 decoder with enable control is displayed in Table 5.5.

Table 5.5: Truth table of 3-to-8 decoder with enable control.

e	$x[2]$	$x[1]$	$x[0]$	$y[7]$	$y[6]$	$y[5]$	$y[4]$	$y[3]$	$y[2]$	$y[1]$	$y[0]$
0	X	X	X	0	0	0	0	0	0	0	0
1	0	0	0	0	0	0	0	0	0	0	1
1	0	0	1	0	0	0	0	0	0	1	0
1	0	1	0	0	0	0	0	0	1	0	0
1	0	1	1	0	0	0	0	1	0	0	0
1	1	0	0	0	0	0	1	0	0	0	0
1	1	0	1	0	0	1	0	0	0	0	0
1	1	1	0	0	1	0	0	0	0	0	0
1	1	1	1	1	0	0	0	0	0	0	0

Its gate-level netlist is presented in Figure 5.17.

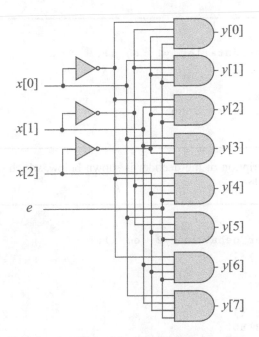

Figure 5.17: Gate-level netlist of the 3-to-8 decoder with enable control.

The structural description of the decoder is shown below.

```
1 // Structural description: decoder
2 module decoder_struct (y, e, x);
3 output [7:0] y;
4 input e;
5 input [2:0] x;
6 wire [7:0] y;
7 wire tmp0, tmp1, tmp2;
8 not u0(tmp0, x[0]);
9 not u1(tmp1, x[1]);
10 not u2(tmp2, x[2]);
11 and u3(y[0], e, tmp0, tmp1, tmp2);
12 and u4(y[1], e, x[0], tmp1, tmp2);
13 and u5(y[2], e, tmp0, x[1], tmp2);
14 and u6(y[3], e, x[0], x[1], tmp2);
15 and u7(y[4], e, tmp0, tmp1, x[2]);
16 and u8(y[5], e, x[0], tmp1, x[2]);
17 and u9(y[6], e, tmp0, x[1], x[2]);
18 and u10(y[7], e, x[0], x[1], x[2]);
19 endmodule
```

The dataflow description of the decoder is shown below.

```
1// Dataflow description: decoder
2module decoder_dataflow(y1, e, x);
3output [7:0] y1;
4input e;
5input [2:0] x;
6assign y1=e?1'b1<<x:8'h0;
7endmodule
```

The behavioral description of the decoder is shown below, which directly realizes
the logic of truth table.

```
1// Behavioral description: decoder
2module decoder_behavior(y2, e, x);
3output [7:0] y2;
4input    e;
5input [2:0] x;
6reg [7:0] y2;
7always @(e or x)
8   if(!e) y2=8'h00;
9   else
10    case(x)
11    3'b000: y2 = 8'h01;
12    3'b001: y2 = 8'h02;
13    3'b010: y2 = 8'h04;
14    3'b011: y2 = 8'h08;
15    3'b100: y2 = 8'h10;
16    3'b101: y2 = 8'h20;
17    3'b110: y2 = 8'h40;
18    default: y2 = 8'h80; // 3'b111
19    endcase
20endmodule
```

The hierarchical design of the 3-to-8 decoder based on the 2-to-4 decoder is shown
in Figure 5.18.

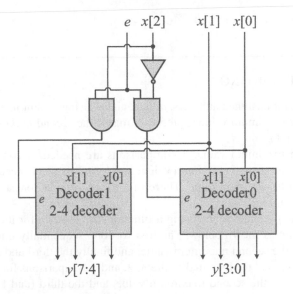

Figure 5.18: Hierarchical design of the 3-to-8 decoder.

Its RTL codes are written below.

```
1// Structural description: bottom-up design of
2// 3-to-8 decoder
3module decode_3_8(e, x, y);
4output [7:0] y;
5input e;
6input [2:0] x;
7wire e1, g1, g2;
8not u0(e1, x[2]);
9and u1(g1, e, x[2]);
10and u2(g2, e, e1);
11decoder_2_4 u0(y[7:4], g1, x[1:0]);
12decoder_2_4 u1(y[3:0], g2, x[1:0]);
13endmodule
```

In the above module, the 2-to-4 decoder is defined below.

```
1// Dataflow description: 2-to-4 decoder
2module decoder_2_4(y, e, x);
3output [3:0] y;
4input e;
5input [1:0] x;
```

```
6 assign y=e?1'b1<<x:4'h0;
7 endmodule
```

5.5.8 BUBBLE SORTING

We want to sort four unsigned numbers, *a*, *b*, *c*, and *d*, using a combinational circuit. After sorting, the maximum value is stored in max1, the second maximum value is stored in max2, and so on.

To decide the maximum value, 3 comparisons are needed; 2 comparisons are needed to decide the second maximum value; and 1 comparison is needed to decide the third and fourth maximum value. Therefore, total 6 comparisons are required to sort 4 unsigned numbers.

The sorting circuit is described using a function. We use two for loops to implement the algorithm as shown below. The first for loop sequentially finds the maximum value, then the second maximum value, and finally the third and fourth maximum value. The second for loop makes the 3, 2, and 1 comparisons for determining the maximum value, the second maximum value, and the third (and fourth) maximum value, respectively.

```
1 // Combinational circuit of bubble sorting
2 wire [7:0] max1, max2, max3, max4;
3 assign {max1, max2, max3, max4}=sort(a, b, c, d);
4 function [31:0] sort(a, b, c, d);
5 input [7:0] a, b, c, d;
6 reg [7:0] temp[0:3];
7 reg [7:0] buffer;
8 integer i,j;
9 begin
10 // Store sorted numbers into a 2-D array,
11 // so that 2-D array can be indexed by for loops.
12    temp[3]=a;
13    temp[2]=b;
14    temp[1]=c;
15    temp[0]=d;
16    for(i=2;i>=0;i=i-1)
17      for(j=0;j<=i;j=j+1)
18        if(temp[j]>temp[j+1]) begin
19          // Swapping is needed.
20          buffer=temp[j+1];
21          temp[j+1]=temp[j];
22          temp[j]=buffer;
23        end
24    sort={temp[3],temp[2],temp[1],temp[0]};
25 end
26 endfunction
```

The basic unit used to swap 2 numbers, say x and y, is the statements in the begin-end pair of the if statement, and its schematic is displayed below,

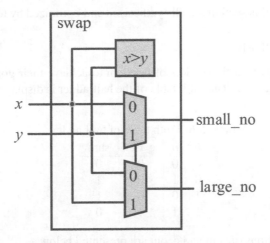

Figure 5.19: Basic unit of swapping 2 numbers.

The overall architecture of bubble sorting circuit is presented below, and the indices, i/j, of the first/second for loops are displayed. As shown, the critical path of the bubble sorting consists of 5 swapping units, which grows linearly with the number of sorting numbers.

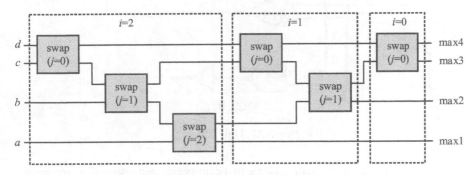

Figure 5.20: Architecture of bubble sorting circuit.

5.6 BASIC BUILDING BLOCKS OF COMBINATIONAL CIRCUITS: ARITHMETIC UNITS

The RTL codes in this section are all synthesized and optimized by tools.

5.6.1 HALF ADDER

The RTL design gives designers lots of freedom to achieve their goals. We use the half adder as an example. The truth table of the half adder is displayed in Table 5.6.

Table 5.6: Truth table of half adder.

b	a	c_out	sum
0	0	0	0
0	1	0	1
1	0	0	1
1	1	1	0

The Boolean equations of sum and c_out are presented below.

$$sum = a \oplus b$$
$$c\_out = a \cdot b \tag{5.1}$$

We got the schematic design.

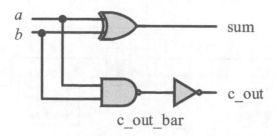

c_out_bar

Figure 5.21: Half adder.

The functionality of the half adder can be implemented using the structural description.

```
1 // Structural description: half adder
2 module add_half(sum, c_out, a, b);
3 output sum, c_out;
4 input a, b;
5 wire c_out_bar;
6 xor u0(sum, a, b);
7 nand u1(c_out_bar, a, b);
```

```
8 not u2(c_out, c_out_bar);
9 endmodule
```

The functionality of the half adder can also be implemented using the dataflow description.

```
1 // Dataflow description: half adder
2 module add_half(sum, c_out, a, b);
3 output sum, c_out;
4 input a, b;
5 assign {c_out, sum}=a+b;
6 endmodule
```

Or, the behavioral description #1

```
1 // Behavioral description: half adder #1
2 module add_half(sum, c_out, a, b);
3 output sum, c_out;
4 input a, b;
5 reg sum, c_out;
6 always @(a or b) begin
7   sum=a^b;
8   c_out=a&b;
9 end
10 endmodule
```

Another behavioral description #2 is displayed below, which directly implements the function based on its truth table.

```
1 // Behavioral description: half adder #2
2 module add_half(sum, c_out, a, b);
3 output sum, c_out;
4 input a, b;
5 reg sum, c_out;
6 always @(a or b) begin
7   case({a,b})
8   2'b00: begin
9           sum = 0; c_out = 0;
10          end
11  2'b01: begin
12          sum = 1; c_out = 0;
13          end
14  2'b10: begin
15          sum = 1; c_out = 0;
```

```
16              end
17    default:begin  // 2'b11
18                   sum = 0; c_out = 1;
19              end
20    endcase
21 end
22 endmodule
```

5.6.2 FULL ADDER

We then use the full adder as another example. The truth table of the full adder is displayed in Table 5.7.

Table 5.7: Truth table of the full adder.

a	b	c_in	c_out	sum
0	0	0	0	0
0	1	0	0	1
1	0	0	0	1
1	1	0	1	0
0	0	1	0	1
0	1	1	1	0
1	0	1	1	0
1	1	1	1	1

The Boolean equation can be shown to be the following.

$$\begin{aligned} \text{sum} &= (a \oplus b) \oplus \text{c\_in}, \\ \text{c\_out} &= a \cdot b + (a \oplus b) \cdot \text{c\_in} \end{aligned} \tag{5.2}$$

The functionality of the full adder can be implemented using the dataflow description.

```
1 // Dataflow description: full adder
2 module add_full(sum, c_out, a, b, c_in);
3 output sum, c_out;
4 input a, b, c_in;
5 reg sum, c_out;
6
7 assign {c_out, sum}=a+b+c_in;
8 // You can try the behavioral description,
9 // which realizes the boolean equation.
10 /*always @(a or b or c_in) begin
11      sum=(a^b)^c_in;
12      c_out=(a&b)|((a^b)&c_in);
```

```
13    end*/
14 endmodule
```

Or, you can use the module add_half to build up the bottom-up design, as shown in Figure 5.22.

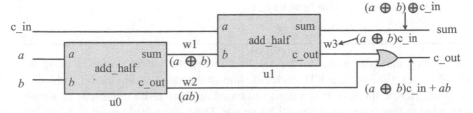

Figure 5.22: Bottom-up full adder design.

The RTL codes are

```
1 // Structural description: bottom-up design of full adder
2 module add_full(sum, c_out, a, b, c_in);
3 output sum, c_out;
4 input a, b, c_in;
5 wire w1, w2, w3;
6
7 add_half u0(w1, w2, a, b); // In-order port mapping
8 add_half u1(sum, w3, c_in, w1);
9 or u2(c_out, w2, w3);
10 endmodule
```

We then design a 4-bit adder, as shown in Figure 5.23.

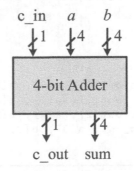

Figure 5.23: 4-bit adder.

Its RTL codes can be simply written as

```
1// Dataflow description: full adder
2module adder_4_RTL(sum, c_out, a, b, c_in);
3output [3:0] sum;
4output c_out;
5input [3:0] a, b;
6input c_in;
7assign {c_out, sum}=a+b+c_in;
8endmodule
```

Comparing the 4-bit adder to the previous (1-bit) full adder designed using the dataflow description, their RTL codes are almost the same except the bit width declaration. Hence, the RTL codes designed based on the one-bit scalar can be simply extended to that based on the multi-bit vector. The synthesized circuit is dependent on the tool you use (might be ripple-carry adder, carry-lookahead, or other adders).

Of course, you can build up the bottom-up design of the 4-bit adder, as shown in Figure 5.24.

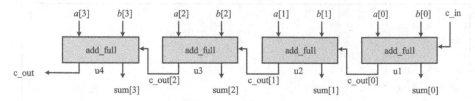

Figure 5.24: Bottom-up 4-bit adder.

This structure is a ripple-carry adder with the following RTL codes.

```
1// Structural description: bottom-up design of full adder
2module add_rca_4(sum, c_out, a, b, c_in);
3output [3:0] sum;
4output c_out;
5input [3:0] a, b;
6input c_in;
7wire [2:0] c_out;
8add_full u1(sum[0], c_out[0], a[0], b[0], c_in);
9add_full u2(sum[1], c_out[1], a[1], b[1], c_out[0]);
10add_full u3(sum[2], c_out[2], a[2], b[2], c_out[1]);
11add_full u4(sum[3], c_out, a[3], b[3], c_out[2]);
12endmodule
```

5.6.3 SIGNED ARITHMETIC

Before introducing signed arithmetic operations, we present the 1's complement number here. For an n-bit binary number, $x = \{x_{n-1}, x_{n-2}, ..., x_0\}$, its 1's complement number $y = \{y_{n-1}, y_{n-2}, ..., y_0\}$ satisfies

$$x + y = 2^n - 1. \tag{5.3}$$

For example, the 1's complement number y of 4-bit binary number $x = 0001_2$ is $y = 1110_2$ because $0001_2 \ (1_{10}) + 1110_2 \ (14_{10}) = 2^4 - 1 = 15 \ (1111_2 = 15_{10})$. Alternatively, you can obtain the 1's complement number of x by "inverting every bits of x". For example, after inverting every bits of x, you got 1110_2. The one's-complement number system encodes 1's complement of x as its negative number in a binary number representation. Therefore, in an one's-complement number system, the 1's complement number $y = 1110_2$ of $x = 0001_2$ is treated as -1_{10} instead of $+14_{10}$.

There are three popular signed number representations for a 4-bit integer, $\{x_3 x_2 x_1 x_0\}$, as shown in Table 5.8, within which x_3 is the sign bit. There are two zeros for the signed-magnitude and 1's complement representations.

Table 5.8: Signed number representation.

$x_3 x_2 x_1 x_0$	Signed-magnitude	1's complement	2's complement
0111	+7	+7	+7
0110	+6	+6	+6
0101	+5	+5	+5
0100	+4	+4	+4
0011	+3	+3	+3
0010	+2	+2	+2
0001	+1	+1	+1
0000	+0	+0	+0
1000	-0	-7	-8
1001	-1	-6	-7
1010	-2	-5	-6
1011	-3	-4	-5
1100	-4	-3	-4
1101	-5	-2	-3
1110	-6	-1	-2
1111	-7	-0	-1

The properties of different representations are summarized below.

- Signed-magnitude representation: easy to understand but not suitable for use in computers. You need to process the sign bits and magnitudes separately.
- 1's complement representation: converting between negative and positive numbers by simply complementing each bit.

- 2's complement representation: converting between negative and positive numbers by simply adding 1 to its 1's complement. An n-bit unsigned number x can represent values in the range: $0 \leq x \leq 2^n - 1$. An n-bit signed number x can represent values in the range: $-2^{n-1} \leq x \leq 2^{n-1} - 1$.

Addition of positive numbers is the same for three representations, but different when operands have opposite signs. Under the condition that there is no overflow, the differences among them are listed below.

- Addition of signed-magnitude: it is necessary to subtract smaller number from larger one. This means that comparator and subtractor are needed.
- Addition of 1's complement: a negative number is generated simply. Correction is needed when there is a carry, as shown in Figure 5.25.
- Addition of 2's complement: correction is not needed by simply ignoring the carry, as shown in Figure 5.25.

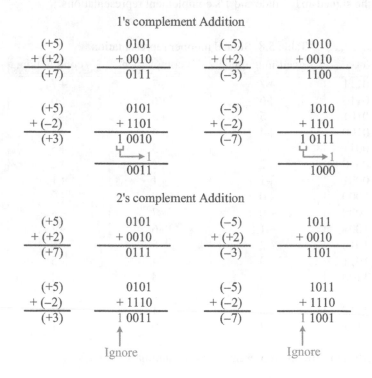

Figure 5.25: Additions of 1's complement and 2's complement.

5.6.3.1 Fundamentals of Addition and Subtraction Using 2's Complement

Subtraction of 2's complement is done by finding the 2's complement of the subtrahend and then performing the addition, as shown in Figure 5.26.

$$
\begin{array}{rcl}
(+5) & \quad 0101 & \quad 0101 \\
-\ (+2) & \quad -\ 0010 & \quad +\ 1110 \\
\hline
(+3) & & \quad 1\ 0011 \\
\end{array}
$$

$\uparrow$
Ignore

$$
\begin{array}{rcl}
(-5) & \quad 1011 & \quad 1011 \\
-\ (+2) & \quad -\ 0010 & \quad +\ 1110 \\
\hline
(-7) & & \quad 1\ 1001 \\
\end{array}
$$

$\uparrow$
Ignore

$$
\begin{array}{rcl}
(+5) & \quad 0101 & \quad 0101 \\
-\ (-2) & \quad -\ 1110 & \quad +\ 0010 \\
\hline
(+7) & & \quad 0111 \\
\end{array}
$$

$$
\begin{array}{rcl}
(-5) & \quad 1011 & \quad 1011 \\
-\ (-2) & \quad -\ 1110 & \quad +\ 0010 \\
\hline
(-3) & & \quad 1101 \\
\end{array}
$$

Figure 5.26: Subtraction of 2's complement.

Adding 1 in the least-significant bit position of an adder can be done by setting the carry-in bit to 1. Hence, no extra hardware is needed for the 2's complement conversion of subtraction. Correction is not needed by simply ignoring the carry-out bit, as shown in Figure 5.27, where $\overline{\text{Add}}/\text{Sub}$ control is a control signal indicates addition (logic 0) or subtraction (logic 1) operation. When $\overline{\text{Add}}/\text{Sub}$ control is logic 0, the output of XOR gates is $y = \{y_{n-1}, ..., y_1, y_0\}$, and the carry-in $c_{-1} = 0$. When $\overline{\text{Add}}/\text{Sub}$ control is logic 1, the output of XOR gates is the 1's complement of y, i.e., $\{\overline{y_{n-1}}, ..., \overline{y_1}, \overline{y_0}\}$, and the carry-in $c_{-1} = 1$. Therefore, when $\overline{\text{Add}}/\text{Sub}$ control is logic 0, "$x = \{x_{n-1}, ..., x_1, x_0\}$ adds y" is performed; when $\overline{\text{Add}}/\text{Sub}$ control is logic 1, "x adds the 2's complement of y", which results in subtracting y from x. In the sequel, the same adder circuit can be shared for both addition and subtraction with no extra hardware except the XOR gates.

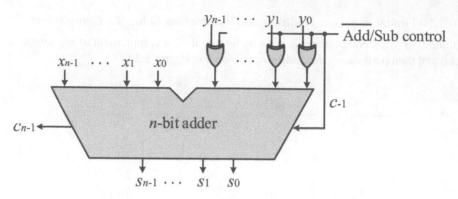

Figure 5.27: Addition and subtraction of 2's complement.

If n bits are used to represent signed numbers, then the result must be in the range -2^{n-1} to $2^{n-1} - 1$. Otherwise, overflow occurs. Hence, overflow happens when the result can not be represented because the value is too large or too small. Intuitively, overflow occurs only when inputs x and y have the same sign. One way to detect overflow is to check the sign bit of the sum. If the sign bit of the sum does not match the sign bits of x and y, then there's overflow. More specifically, its Boolean can be written as

$$\text{overflow} = x_{n-1} \cdot y_{n-1} \cdot \overline{s_{n-1}} + \overline{x_{n-1}} \cdot \overline{y_{n-1}} \cdot s_{n-1}. \tag{5.4}$$

The following table illustrates the sum of 2 3-bit signed numbers for detecting the overflow using (5.4). For simplicity, the subtrahend, $y_2 y_1 y_0 = 001$ (+1), is fixed. The results of other subtrahends can be similarly shown and omitted here.

Table 5.9: Examples for the overflow detection of sum of 2 3-bit signed numbers using Equation (5.4).

$x_2 x_1 x_0$	$y_2 y_1 y_0$	c_2	$s_2 s_1 s_0$	Overflow
011 (+3)	001 (+1)	0	100 (−4)	1
010 (+2)	001 (+1)	0	011 (+3)	0
001 (+1)	001 (+1)	0	010 (+2)	0
000 (+0)	001 (+1)	0	001 (+1)	0
100 (−4)	001 (+1)	0	101 (−3)	0
101 (−3)	001 (+1)	0	110 (−2)	0
110 (−2)	001 (+1)	0	111 (−1)	0
111 (−1)	001 (+1)	1	000 (+0)	0

Another way to detect the overflow is displayed in Figure 5.28.

$$c_3c_2c_1c_0$$

Overflow: $[0\ 1\!]1\ 0$

$(+7)$ $0\ 1\ 1\ 1$

$+\ (+2)$ $+\ 0\ 0\ 1\ 0$

$(+9)$ $1\ 0\ 0\ 1$

$$c_3c_2c_1c_0$$
$$0\ 0\ 0\ 0$$

(-7) $1\ 0\ 0\ 1$

$+\ (+2)$ $+\ 0\ 0\ 1\ 0$

(-5) $1\ 0\ 1\ 1$

$$c_3c_2c_1c_0$$
$$1\ 1\ 1\ 0$$

$(+7)$ $0\ 1\ 1\ 1$

$+\ (-2)$ $+\ 1\ 1\ 1\ 0$

$(+5)$ $1\ 0\ 1\ 0\ 1$

$$c_3c_2c_1c_0$$

Overflow: $[1\ 0\!]0\ 0$

(-7) $1\ 0\ 0\ 1$

$+\ (-2)$ $+\ 1\ 1\ 1\ 0$

(-9) $1\ 0\ 1\ 1\ 1$

Figure 5.28: Another way to detect the overflow of 2's complement for addition and subtraction of 3-bit signed integer.

In the examples, when the carry outs of the 3rd and 4th full adders differ, overflow occurs. That is, Overflow$= c_3 \cdot \overline{c_2} + \overline{c_3} \cdot c_2 = c_3 \oplus c_2$. Generally, for n-bit numbers,

$$\text{overflow} = c_{n-1} \oplus c_{n-2}. \tag{5.5}$$

How to interpret this result? There are two distinctive cases, as displayed below. Let's look at the left-most full adder, FA_{n-1}, as displayed in Figure 5.29. Case 1: 0 carried in, and 1 carried out. If a 0 is carried in, then the only way that 1 can be carried out is if $x_{n-1} = 1$ and $y_{n-1} = 1$. That way, the sum s_{n-1} is 0, and the carry out is 1. This is the case when you add two negative numbers, but the result is positive. Case 2: 1 carried in, and 0 carried out. The only way 0 can be carried out if there's a 1 carried in is if $x_{n-1} = 0$ and $y_{n-1} = 0$. In that case, 0 is carried out, and the sum s_{n-1} is 1. This is the case when you add two positive numbers and get a negative result.

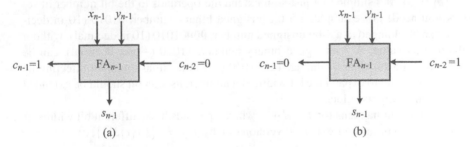

Figure 5.29: Yet another way to detect the overflow.

5.6.3.2 Addition and Subtraction in 2's Complement Using Verilog

Attention should be paid to operations when the result has more bits than the operands or when you are using different bit-width operands, as shown below.

```
1 // Result has more bits than the operands
2 wire [2:0] a, b;
3 wire [3:0] c;
4 assign c=a+b;
5 // Different bit-width operands
6 wire [7:0] d;
7 wire [3:0] e;
8 wire [7:0] f;
9 assign f=d+e;
```

In the piece of codes, if a and b are unsigned numbers, no problem happens, because 0s will be padded to the MSB of operands. But if a and b are signed numbers, padding 0s on the left makes a and b 4-bit vectors, but the result will be incorrect. However, if padding is performing by the sign extension, we can obtain the correct result.

$$
\begin{array}{r}
0\ 0\ 1\ 0 \quad (+2) \\
+ \quad 0\ 1\ 0\ 1 \quad (-3) \\
\hline
0\ 1\ 1\ 1 \quad (+7)
\end{array}
\quad \longrightarrow \quad \text{incorrect}
$$

$$
\begin{array}{r}
0\ 0\ 1\ 0 \quad (+2) \\
+ \quad 1\ 1\ 0\ 1 \quad (-3) \\
\hline
1\ 1\ 1\ 1 \quad (-1)
\end{array}
\quad \longrightarrow \quad \text{correct}
$$

Figure 5.30: Potential errors in 2's complement operation using Verilog.

Consequently, it is necessary to use a sign-extended version of a and b by $c=\{a[2], a\}+\{b[2], b\}$. It's simple that just sign extend the operands to the bit number of results you need! For example, a 5-bit unsigned binary number, 01010 (10 in decimal), can be changed to a 8-bit unsigned number, **000**01010 (10 in decimal), without affecting its value. A 5-bit signed binary number, 11010 (-6 in decimal), can be changed to a 8-bit signed number, **111**11010 (-6 in decimal), without affecting its value. Therefore, to expand the bit width of a number, its sign bit should be extended without changing its value.

Similar result happens for $f = d + e$, where operands have different bit widths. It is necessary to use a sign-extended version of e by $f = d + \{\{4\{e[3]\}\}, e\}$.

If you do not want to perform the sign extension manually, you can try signed declaration in Verilog-2001. It's very convenient that synthesis tools can now synthesize and optimize the signed number arithmetics automatically.

```
1// Sign extension is done by signed declaration
2wire signed [2:0] a, b;
3wire signed [3:0] c;
4wire signed [7:0] d;
5wire signed [3:0] e;
6wire signed [7:0] f;
7assign c=a+b;
8assign f=d+e;
```

You can also use signed system task in Verilog-2001.

```
1// Sign extension is done by signed task
2wire signed [2:0] a, b;
3wire signed [3:0] c;
4wire signed [7:0] d;
5wire signed [3:0] e;
6wire signed [7:0] f;
7c=$signed(a)+$signed(b);
8f=$signed(d)+$signed(e);
```

Input and output ports can also be declared as "signed" ports as follows.

```
1// Signed port declaration
2input signed [2:0] a, b;
3output signed [3:0] c;
```

In addition to sign extension, addition of signed fixed-point numbers also requires to align the binary points of operands. After that, you can still use signed declaration without manual sign extension. As shown in following Verilog codes, a s(2.3) fixed-point number is added to a s(4.2) fixed-point number. The binary point of s(4.2) must first be aligned to that of s(2.3), i.e., s(4.3) is derived. After that, the adder can be inferred using the signed declaration.

```
1// Addition of signed fixed-point numbers
2module fixed_add_signed(y, a, b);
3output signed [4:-3] y; // s(5.3) fixed-point number
4input signed [1:-3] a;  // s(2.3) fixed-point number
5input signed [3:-2] b;  // s(4.2) fixed-point number
6wire signed [3:-3] b_align;  // s(4.3) fixed-point number
```

```
7// Only need to align the binary point
8assign b_align={b, 1'b0};
9// s(5.3) fixed-point number
10assign y=a+b_align;
11endmodule
```

In conclusion, it is the most convenient to infer a signed number adder and subtractor in hardware using the signed number declaration. Just declare the original number of bits in operands and the required number of bits in results. Tools will take care of the sign extension. You do not have to manually sign extend the operands nor do you need to implement them in gate level. That is, we only describe the behavior of adder/subtractor in RTL. Details are left to synthesis. However, the binary point of fixed-point numbers should still be aligned.

5.6.3.3   Multiplication in 2's Complement Using Verilog

If you do the signed multiplication, you can also manually sign extend the operands. In the following example, you describe a 10 bits × 10 bits unsigned multiplier. Fortunately, unnecessary bits will be optimized and removed by synthesis tools.

```
1// Multiplication of unsigned numbers
2wire [4:0] a, b;
3wire [9:0] c;
4assign c={{5{a[4]}},a}*{{5{b[4]}},b};
```

You can also try signed declaration in Verilog-2001.

```
1// Multiplication of signed numbers
2// Sign extension is done by signed declaration
3wire signed [4:0] a, b;
4wire signed [9:0] c;
5// 5 bits x 5 bits signed multiplier will be synthesized
6assign c=a*b;
```

Or, try the signed system task in Verilog-2001.

```
1// Multiplication of signed numbers
2// Sign extension is done by signed task
3wire [4:0] a, b;
4wire [9:0] c;
5// 5 bits x 5 bits signed multiplier will be synthesized
6assign c=$signed(a)*$signed(b);
```

For the multiplication of signed fixed-point numbers, the alignment of binary points is not needed. Hence, you can use signed declaration without manual sign extension, as shown below.

```
1// Multiplication of signed fixed-point numbers
2module fixed_mul_signed(y, a, b);
3output signed [5:-5] y; // s(6.5) fixed-point number
4input signed [1:-3] a;  // s(2.3) fixed-point number
5input signed [3:-2] b;  // s(4.2) fixed-point number
6// s(6.5) fixed-point number
7assign y=a*b;
8endmodule
```

In conclusion, it is the most convenient to infer a signed number multiplier in hardware using the signed number declaration. That is, we only describe the behavior of multiplier in RTL. Details (or sign extension) are left to synthesis.

5.6.3.4   Bit Width Design

To prevent overflow in the addition $z = x + y$, if a 3-bit unsigned number plus a 3-bit unsigned number, result should have 4 bits because $0 \leq x \leq 7$ and $0 \leq y \leq 7$, leading to $0 \leq z \leq 14$, which can be completely represented by a 4-bit unsigned number. The RTL codes are written as follows.

```
1// Addition of unsigned numbers
2// Padding with 0 is done by tool
3wire [2:0] x, y;
4wire [3:0] z;
5assign z=x+y;
```

Similarly, if a 3-bit signed number plus a 3-bit signed number, result should have 4 bits. The RTL codes are written as follows because $-4 \leq x \leq 3$ and $-4 \leq y \leq 3$. This yields $-8 \leq z \leq 6$, which can be represented by a 4-bit signed number.

```
1// Addition of signed numbers
2// Padding using sign extension is done by tool
3wire signed [2:0] x, y;
4wire signed [3:0] z;
5assign z=x+y;
```

If a 3-bit unsigned number multiplies a 3-bit unsigned number, result should have 6 bits. The RTL codes are written as follows. Because $0 \leq x \leq 7$ and $0 \leq y \leq 7$, this yields $0 \leq z \leq 49$, which can be represented by a 6-bit unsigned number.

```
1// Multiplication of unsigned numbers
2// Padding with 0 is done by tool
3wire [2:0] x, y;
4wire [5:0] z;
5assign z=x*y;
```

If a 3-bit signed number multiplies a 3-bit signed number, result should have 6 bits. The RTL codes are written as follows. Because $-4 \leq x \leq 3$ and $-4 \leq y \leq 3$, this yields $-12 \leq z \leq 16$, which can be represented by a 6-bit signed number.

```
1// Multiplication of signed numbers
2// Padding using sign extension is done by tool
3wire signed [2:0] x, y;
4wire signed [5:0] z;
5assign z=x*y;
```

From above, if a 3-bit signed number multiplies a 3-bit signed number, result x should have 6 bits. It the results are then accumulated 8 times, the accumulator output y needs $6 + 3 = 9$ bits (rather than $6 + 7 = 13$ bits). This can be explained in Figure 5.31.

5.6.3.5   More on Overflow Detection

Two's complement numbers can be represented using a circle in Figure 5.32. Moreover, addition and subtraction can be derived by clockwise and counterclockwise rotation, respectively. For example, for a 4-bit signed integer, if you add 1 (0001_2) to 7 (0111_2), you get -8 (1000_2) (overflow happens). Then, if you add -1 (1111_2) to the result (-8 or (1000_2)), you will get 7 (0111_2) again. Therefore, an advantage of 2's complement lies in that its overflow is gracefully treated.

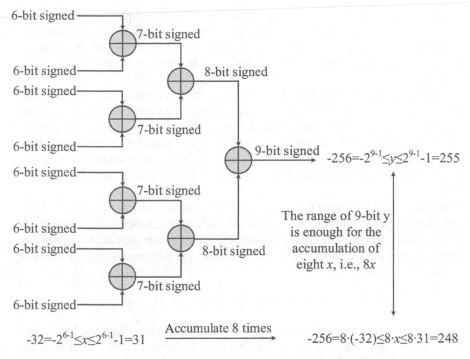

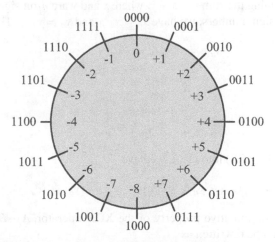

Figure 5.31: Bit width for the accumulation of 8 multiplication results produced by 3-bit signed number multiplication.

Figure 5.32: Representation of 4-bit signed integer using a circle.

Overflow is usually an error condition. Adders perform modulo arithmetic on an overflow condition. For example, if $a = 111_2$ and $b = 010_2$ are 3-bit unsigned numbers, $a+b$ gives 001_2 ($7_{10}+2_{10}=1_{10}$ (mod 8_{10})). Even 2' complement arithmetic is graceful, i.e., final result can be correct if temporary overflow happens provided that the final result is guaranteed without an overflow. However, if the final result has an overflow, a large error may exist. From the above example, the result changes from 9_{10} to 1_{10}.

Therefore, it is typically desirable to have a saturation adder, producing a result between $2^{n-1}-1$ and -2^{n-1} for n-bit signed number in this case on an overflow condition rather than producing a modular result. To eliminate such a large error of arithmetic operations, the saturation arithmetic, within which all operations such as addition and multiplication are limited to a fixed range between a minimum and maximum value, is usually adopted. The saturation arithmetic necessitates the overflow detection.

Overflow detection using carry outs in (5.5) is simple and requires only an XOR gate. However, carry outs are not readily available using the behavioral description of arithmetic operator, i.e., "+" in Verilog. Therefore, rather than detecting the difference between carry outs in (5.5), we can detect the difference between sum bits for overflow as follows,

$$\text{overflow} = s_n \oplus s_{n-1} \tag{5.6}$$

where s_n and s_{n-1} are sign bits of the sum of the sign-extended addition before and after dropping out one bit, respectively, and $\oplus$ is the bitwise XOR. Intuitively, the detector output an overflow event when s_n is different with s_{n-1}, i.e., the sign bits are different.

It can be proved that the detectors in (5.5) and (5.6) are equivalent. Due to sign extension for obtaining the sum $s = x + y$, where x and y are n-bit sign numbers, and s is an $(n+1)$-bit sign numbers, we have $x_n = x_{n-1}$ and $y_n = y_{n-1}$. Therefore,

$$\begin{aligned} s_n &= x_n \oplus y_n \oplus c_{n-1} \\ &= x_{n-1} \oplus y_{n-1} \oplus c_{n-1} \end{aligned} \tag{5.7}$$

and

$$s_{n-1} = x_{n-1} \oplus y_{n-1} \oplus c_{n-2}. \tag{5.8}$$

Substituting (5.7) and (5.8) into (5.6), we have

$$\text{overflow} = (x_{n-1} \oplus y_{n-1} \oplus c_{n-1}) \oplus (x_{n-1} \oplus y_{n-1} \oplus c_{n-2}). \tag{5.9}$$

According to the commutative property of the XOR operator, $A \oplus B = B \oplus A$, and $A \oplus A = 0$, (5.9) can be rewritten as

$$\begin{aligned} \text{overflow} &= (x_{n-1} \oplus y_{n-1}) \oplus (x_{n-1} \oplus y_{n-1})(\oplus c_{n-1} \oplus c_{n-2}) \\ &= c_{n-1} \oplus c_{n-2}. \end{aligned} \tag{5.10}$$

The proof follows.

The following table illustrates the sum of 2 3-bit signed numbers for detecting the overflow using (5.6), which is the same as that using (5.4) in Table 5.9. For simplicity, the subtrahend, $y_2 y_1 y_0 = 001$ (+1), is fixed. The results of other subtrahends can be similarly shown and omitted here.

Table 5.10: Examples for the overflow detection of sum of 2 3-bit signed numbers using Equation (5.6).

$x_2 x_1 x_0$	$y_2 y_1 y_0$	s_3	$s_2 s_1 s_0$	Overflow
011 (+3)	001 (+1)	0	100 (−4)	1
010 (+2)	001 (+1)	0	011 (+3)	0
001 (+1)	001 (+1)	0	010 (+2)	0
000 (+0)	001 (+1)	0	001 (+1)	0
100 (−4)	001 (+1)	1	101 (−3)	0
101 (−3)	001 (+1)	1	110 (−2)	0
110 (−2)	001 (+1)	1	111 (−1)	0
111 (−1)	001 (+1)	0	000 (+0)	0

The overflow detection in (5.6) can be generalized for dropping more than one bits in other arithmetic operators, e.g., multiplication. This becomes a quantization problem. That is, if the original result s of an arithmetic operation without overflow has m bits and it is desired to be truncated by p bits, $p \geq 1$, so that $s_{m-1}, s_{m-2}, ..., s_{m-p}$ are dropped, and s_{m-p-1} is the new sign bit of the truncated result, as shown below,

$$\underbrace{\{s_{m-1}, s_{m-2}, ..., s_{m-p},}_{\text{dropped}} \underbrace{s_{m-p-1}, ..., s_1, s_0\}}_{\text{kept}}.$$

The overflow probably happens and it can be detected by the Boolean equation as

$$\text{Overflow} = s_{m-1} \oplus s_{m-2} + s_{m-1} \oplus s_{m-3} + ... + s_{m-1} \oplus s_{m-p-1}. \tag{5.11}$$

To get rid of the overflow, the dropped bits must be unnecessary sign bits such that $s_{m-1}, s_{m-2}, ...,$ and s_{m-p-1} are the same. In other words, if the sign bit s_{m-1} of the original result does not agree with those dropped sign bits, $s_{m-2}, ..., s_{m-p}$ and the remaining sign bit s_{m-p-1}, the overflow occurs.

We often need to separately detect the "positive" and "negative" overflows for the saturation arithmetic. The positive (negative) overflow is such that the original result s is larger (smaller) than the maximum positive (minimum negative) number that the quantized result can represent. The detection of positive overflow can thus be expressed by the Boolean equation as

$$\begin{aligned} \text{Positive overflow} &= \overline{s_{m-1}} \cdot s_{m-2} + \overline{s_{m-1}} \cdot s_{m-3} + \cdots + \overline{s_{m-1}} \cdot s_{m-p-1} \\ &= \overline{s_{m-1}} \cdot (s_{m-2} + s_{m-3} + \cdots + s_{m-p-1}). \end{aligned} \tag{5.12}$$

That is, when s is positive ($s_{m-1} = 0$), but any bits of s_{m-2}, s_{m-3},..., or s_{m-p-1} are negative (logic 1), positive overflow occurs. The detection of negative overflow can similarly be expressed by the Boolean equation as

$$\text{Negative overflow} = s_{m-1} \cdot (\overline{s_{m-2}} + \overline{s_{m-3}} + \cdots + \overline{s_{m-p-1}}). \tag{5.13}$$

That is, when s is negative ($s_{m-1} = 1$), but any bits of s_{m-2}, s_{m-3},..., or s_{m-p-1} are positive (logic 0), negative overflow occurs.

The following table illustrates the overflow detection for truncating a 5-bit sign number s to a 3-bit sign number z. Those truncated bits are $\{s_4, s_3, s_2\}$. The detection of positive and negative overflow can be written by the Boolean equations as

$$\text{Positive overflow} = \overline{s_4} \cdot (s_3 + s_2) \tag{5.14}$$

and

$$\text{Negative overflow} = s_4 \cdot (\overline{s_3} + \overline{s_2}), \tag{5.15}$$

respectively.

Table 5.11: Overflow detection for truncating a 5-bit sign number s to a 3-bit sign number z.

$s_4 s_3 s_2 s_1 s_0$	$z_2 z_1 z_0$	Overflow
01111 (+15)	111 (−1)	1 (positive)
01110 (+14)	110 (−2)	1 (positive)
01101 (+13)	101 (−3)	1 (positive)
01100 (+12)	100 (−4)	1 (positive)
01011 (+11)	011 (+3)	1 (positive)
01010 (+10)	010 (+2)	1 (positive)
01001 (+9)	001 (+1)	1 (positive)
01000 (+8)	000 (+0)	1 (positive)
00111 (+7)	111 (−1)	1 (positive)
00110 (+6)	110 (−2)	1 (positive)
00101 (+5)	101 (−3)	1 (positive)
00100 (+4)	100 (−4)	1 (positive)
00011 (+3)	011 (+3)	0
00010 (+2)	010 (+2)	0
00001 (+1)	001 (+1)	0
00000 (+0)	000 (+0)	0
10000 (−16)	000 (+0)	1 (negative)
10001 (−15)	001 (+1)	1 (negative)
10010 (−14)	010 (+2)	1 (negative)
10011 (−13)	011 (+3)	1 (negative)
10100 (−12)	100 (−4)	1 (negative)
10101 (−11)	101 (−3)	1 (negative)
10110 (−10)	110 (−2)	1 (negative)

10111 (−9)	111 (−1)	1 (negative)
11000 (−8)	000 (+0)	1 (negative)
11001 (−7)	001 (+1)	1 (negative)
11010 (−6)	010 (+2)	1 (negative)
11011 (−5)	011 (+3)	1 (negative)
11100 (−4)	100 (−4)	0
11101 (−3)	101 (−3)	0
11110 (−2)	110 (−2)	0
11111 (−1)	111 (−1)	0

The saturation adder of n-bit unsigned numbers is much simpler than that of signed numbers by investigating the last carry out of the $(n-1)$-th full adder, which is s_n and available using the arithmetic operator "+" in Verilog. You can use n-bit adder and an n-bit multiplexer to generate the final result, sum_q, as shown below.

```
1// Overflow detection using sum of unsigned numbers
2// Drop one bit
3wire [2:0] x, y;
4wire [2:0] sum_q; // Quantized sum
5wire [3:0] sum; // Original sum
6assign sum=x+y;
7// Select the max output when overflow occurs
8assign sum_q=sum[3]?3'b111:sum[2:0];
```

Generally, if we want to truncate an m-bit unsigned arithmetic result, s, by p bits, $p \geq 1$, so that $s_{m-1}, s_{m-2}, ..., s_{m-p}$ are dropped, and s_{m-p-1} is the new sign bit of the truncated result. The overflow probably happens and it can be detected by the Boolean equation as

$$\text{Overflow} = s_{m-1} + s_{m-2} + \cdots + s_{m-p}. \tag{5.16}$$

That is, any truncated bits that have logic 1 lead to the overflow.

```
1// Overflow detection using sum of unsigned numbers
2// Drop three bit
3wire [7:0] x, y;
4wire [5:0] sum_q; // Quantized sum
5wire [8:0] sum; // Original sum
6assign sum=x+y;
7// Select the max output when overflow occurs
8assign sum_q=|sum[8:6]?6'b11_1111:sum[5:0];
```

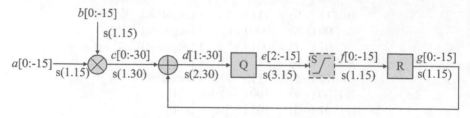

Figure 5.33: A multiply-and-accumulate circuit.

5.6.3.6 Bit Width Design of Digital Signal Processing System

The fixed-point number representation and its declaration in Verilog can be summarized in Table 5.13.

Table 5.13: Fixed-point number representation and its declaration.

Representation	Verilog Declaration	Example
u($p.f$)	$a[(p-1):-f]$	u(8.8)$\rightarrow$ a[7 : -8]
s($p.f$)	$a[(p-1):-f]$	s(8.8)$\rightarrow$ a[7 : -8]

The meaning of the declaration $a[(p-1):-f]$ for both unsigned and signed number is $\{\underbrace{a_{p-1}, a_{p-2}, ..., a_0}_{p} . \underbrace{a_{-1}, ..., a_{-f+1}, a_{-f}}_{f}\}$, where p and f denote the numbers of integer and fraction bits, respectively, and "." denotes the binary point. However, a_{p-1} is the sign bit of a signed number.

If we want to design the bit width of the digital signal processing system in Figure 5.33, the fixed-point number representation and its declaration are labeled in the block diagram. Notice that, to save one bit of the product, the product c is represented by s(1.30). The block Q quantizes the number using the rounding. The block S clamps or saturates the result on an overflow to minimize the error. The block R denotes the register.

Addition of fixed-point numbers must align their binary points. Therefore, 15 zeros are padded in the LSBs of g[0 : -15] (in s(1.15) format) to make it become s(1.30) format. Besides, the manual sign extension is needed if the number of bits of a sliced operand, which will be treated as an unsigned number, is not enough for an arithmetic operation. Moreover, the most positive value of f with s(1.15) format is $0111\_1111\_1111\_1111_2$ or 16'h7fff, and the most negative value of f with s(1.15) format is $1000\_0000\_0000\_0000_2$ or 16'h8000. According to the fixed-point design in Figure 5.33, the RTL model is described below.

```
1// DSP system: multiply-and-accumulate circuit
2wire signed [0:-15] a, b, f;
3wire signed [0:-30] c;
4wire signed [1:-30] d;
```

```
 5 wire signed [2:-15] e;
 6 reg signed [0:-15] g;
 7 assign c=a*b;
 8 // Alignment for g to be s(1.30) is needed.
 9 assign d=c+{g,15'b0};
10 // Manual sign extension is needed because slice of d
11 // will be treated as unsigned number
12 assign e={d[1],d[1:-15]}+d[-16];
13 // Overflow detection: of_pos is positive overflow
14 assign of_pos=~e[2]&(e[1]|e[0]);
15 // Overflow detection: of_neg is negative overflow
16 assign of_neg=e[2]&(~e[1]|~e[0]);
17 // Saturation operation
18 assign f=of_pos?16'h7fff:
19           (of_neg?16'h8000:e[0:-15]);
20 always @(posedge clk)
21   g<=f;
```

5.6.4   ARITHMETIC LOGIC UNIT

The arithmetic logic unit (ALU) is a building block for central-processing unit (CPU). We want to design an ALU with the functions, as shown in Table 5.14.

Table 5.14: Functions of an ALU.

sel	Operation	Function	Implementation
0000	$y = a$	Transfer a	Arithmetic Unit
0001	$y = a+1$	Increment a	Arithmetic Unit
0010	$y = a+b$	Addition	Arithmetic Unit
0011	$y = b+1$	Increment b	Arithmetic Unit
0100	$y = a+\bar{b}$	a plus 1's complement of b	Arithmetic Unit
0101	$y = a-b$	Subtraction	Arithmetic Unit
0110	$y = a-1$	Decrement a	Arithmetic Unit
0111	$y = b$	Transfer b	Arithmetic Unit
1000	$y = a\&b$	Logic AND	Logic Unit
1001	$y = a|b$	Logic OR	Logic Unit
1010	$y = a^{\wedge}b$	Logic XOR	Logic Unit
1011	$y = \bar{a}$	Complement a	Logic Unit
1100	$y = \bar{b}$	Complement b	Logic Unit
1101	$y = a \gg 1$	Shift right a	Logic Unit
1110	$y = a \ll 1$	Shift left a	Logic Unit
1111	$y = 0$	Transfer 0	Logic Unit

The RTL codes can be written as follows.

```
 1// Module of arithmetic logic unit
 2module alu(y, sel, a, b);
 3output [7:0] y;
 4input  [3:0] sel;
 5input  [7:0] a, b;
 6reg    [7:0] y;
 7always @(sel or a or b)
 8  case(sel)
 9  4'b0000:y=a;
10  4'b0001:y=a+1;
11  4'b0010:y=a+b;
12  4'b0011:y=b+1;
13  4'b0100:y=a+~b;
14  4'b0101:y=a+~b+1;
15  4'b0110:y=a-1;
16  4'b0111:y=b;
17  4'b1000:y=a&b;
18  4'b1001:y=a|b;
19  4'b1010:y=a^b;
20  4'b1011:y=~a;
21  4'b1100:y=~b;
22  4'b1101:y=a>>1;
23  4'b1110:y=a<<1;
24  4'b1111:y=0;
25  default:y=8'bX;
26  endcase
27endmodule
```

5.6.5 CARRY LOOK-AHEAD ADDER

The carry look-ahead adder (CLA) is a fast adder we often use. Considering the circuit of the full adder, we define the carry generate, g_i, and the carry propagate, p_i, of the i-th stage as

$$
\begin{aligned}
p_i &= a_i \oplus b_i, \\
g_i &= a_i \cdot b_i,
\end{aligned}
$$

where a_i and b_i are operands of the adder. Notably, p_i and g_i are not related to carry in of the i-th stage, c_{i-1}. According to the Boolean equation of the full adder,

$$
\begin{aligned}
s_i &= (a_i \oplus b_i) \oplus c_{i-1}, \\
c_i &= a_i \cdot b_i + (a_i \oplus b_i) \cdot c_{i-1},
\end{aligned}
$$

the output sum, s_i, and carry, c_i, of the i-th stage can be expressed as

$$
\begin{aligned}
s_i &= p_i \oplus c_{i-1}, \\
c_i &= g_i + p_i \cdot c_{i-1}.
\end{aligned} \tag{5.17}
$$

As shown, the carry generate g_i produces a carry c_i of 1 when both a_i and b_i are 1, and the carry propagate p_i determines whether a carry into stage i, i.e., c_{i-1}, will propagate into stage $(i+1)$ by c_i.

The carry out c_i in Equation 5.17 is an iterative equation. We now write the carry output c_i of each stage, $i = 0, 1, ...$, and substitute c_{i-1} from the previous stage until reaching the input carry c_{-1}:

$$
\begin{aligned}
c_0 &= g_0 + p_0 \cdot c_{-1}, \\
c_1 &= g_1 + p_1 \cdot c_0 = g_1 + p_1 \cdot g_0 + p_1 \cdot p_0 \cdot c_{-1}, \\
c_2 &= g_2 + p_2 \cdot c_1 = g_2 + p_2 \cdot g_1 + p_2 \cdot p_1 \cdot g_0 + p_2 \cdot p_1 \cdot p_0 \cdot c_{-1}.
\end{aligned}
$$

...

The process can continue until all carries have been expressed by g_i, p_i, and c_{-1}. As presented, c_i now depends on g_j and p_j, $j = i, i-1, ..., 0$, and c_{-1}, and is not related to c_{i-1}. The carry of CLA needs not to propagate like that of carry-ripple adder. Therefore, the CLA is faster than the traditional carry-ripple adder. However, expanding the iterative equation in Equation 5.17 makes the common term, c_{i-1}, cannot be shared for c_i and subsequent carry outs. Hence, the circuit area of the CLA is larger than that of carry-ripple adder.

Similarly, the output sum s_i can also be expanded and expressed using g_i, p_i, and c_{-1} below.

$$
\begin{aligned}
s_0 &= p_0 \oplus c_{-1}, \\
s_1 &= p_1 \oplus c_0 = p_1 \oplus (g_0 + p_0 \cdot c_{-1}), \\
s_2 &= p_2 \oplus c_1 = p_2 \oplus (g_1 + p_1 \cdot g_0 + p_1 \cdot p_0 \cdot c_{-1}).
\end{aligned}
$$

...

The schematic of the CLA is presented in Figure 5.34. The CLA can add in less time than carry-ripple adder because c_3 does not have to wait for c_2 and c_1 to propagate. Compared to the carry-ripple adder in Figure 5.5 and the full adder in Figure 5.4, the gain in speed of operation is achieved at the expense of additional hardware complexity.

5.6.6 COMPLEX MULTIPLIER

Multiplying two complex numbers $x = a + bj$ and $y = c + dj$ gives

$$
z = x \times y = (a + bj) \times (c + dj) = (ac - bd) + (bc + da)j \tag{5.18}
$$

where $j = \sqrt{-1}$. Producing the real and imaginary parts of the product requires four multiplications and two additions, as shown in Figure 5.35, where a, b, c, and d are represented by s(1.15). The block Q quantizes the number using the rounding.

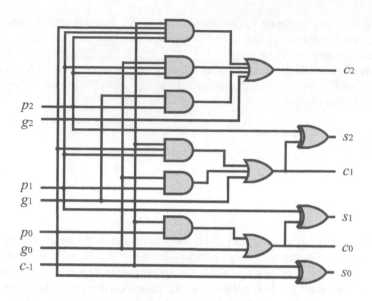

Figure 5.34: Schematic of the CLA.

The block S clamps or saturates the result on an overflow to minimize the error. Note that it is also possible to build this circuit using three multipliers for obtaining ad, bc, and $(a-b)(c+d)$, but we focus on the intuitive implementation with four multipliers here.

Our complex multiplier uses an signed s(1.15) fixed-point format, which is common in many signal processing tasks. To avoid incurring an overflow error or losing precision until after the final summation, we keep intermediate values at full bit width. For a signed s(p.f) fixed-point number a, its dynamic range is $-2^{p-1} \le a \le 2^{p-1} - r$, where $r = 2^{-f}$. For example, the dynamic range of a signed s(1.15) fixed-point number is $-1 \le a \le 1 - 2^{-15}$. Multiplying two s(1.15) numbers, a and b, gives a dynamic range of $-(1 - 2^{-15}) \le ab \le 1$, which requires a signed s(2.30) fixed-point number c with dynamic range of $-2 \le c \le 2 - 2^{-30}$. However, if the maximum value 1 of ab, which is obtained by $a = -1$ and $b = -1$, can be ignored, a signed s(1.30) fixed-point number d suffices and it has a dynamic range of $-1 \le d \le 1 - 2^{-30}$. Doing so can save one bit in the product of two signed fixed-point numbers.

Then, adding two of these products with signed s(1.30) format gives an s(2.30) result. We then quantize the s(2.30) result, i.e., the real part s_rnd_r and the imaginary part s_rnd_i, using the rounding to s(3.15). The final stage, i.e., limiter, checks overflow to saturate the s(3.15) result back to an s(1.15) number.

A positive overflow of s_rnd_r has occurred when the sign bit of s_rnd_r[17] is 0 (positive), but it does not agree with that of s_rnd_r[16] (negative) or s_rnd_r[15] (negative). For example, if a 4-bit signed number, a, in Table 5.8 is to be truncated to

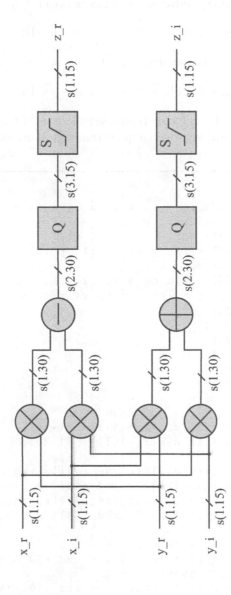

Figure 5.35: Complex multiplier, where x_r, x_i, y_r, y_i, z_r, and z_i are real part (a) of x, imaginary part (b) of x, real part (c) of y, imaginary part (d) of y, real part of z, and imaginary part of z, respectively.

a 3-bit signed number, the 4-bit numbers 4'b0100, 4'b0101, 4'b0110, and 4'b0111 are larger than the maximum positive value, 3'b011, that a 3-bit signed number can represent. In these cases, a positive overflow occurs, which can be detected using $a[3]$ and $a[2]$ by $\overline{a[3]} \cdot a[2]$. Generally, if an m-bit signed number a is desired to be truncated by p bits, $p \geq 1$, the positive overflow can be detected by

$$\overline{a[m-1]} \cdot (a[m-2] + a[m-3] + \cdots + a[m-p-1]). \tag{5.19}$$

The negative overflow of a can be similarly detected by

$$a[m-1] \cdot (\overline{a[m-2]} + \overline{a[m-3]} + \cdots + \overline{a[m-p-1]}). \tag{5.20}$$

The overflow detection of s_rnd_i can be similarly performed. Our complex multiplier uses the saturation arithmetic to clamp the result on an overflow to minimize the error.

```verilog
// Module of complex multiplier
module complex_mul(z_r, z_i, x_r, x_i, y_r, y_i);
output signed [0:-15] z_r, z_i;               // s(1.15)
input signed [0:-15] x_r, x_i, y_r, y_i;      // s(1.15)
wire signed [0:-30] p_r1, p_r2, p_i1, p_i2;   // s(1.30)
wire signed [1:-30] s_r, s_i;                 // s(2.30)
wire signed [2:-15] s_rnd_r, s_rnd_i;         // s(3.15)
wire of_pos_r, of_neg_r, of_pos_i, of_neg_i;
assign p_r1=x_r*y_r;
assign p_r2=x_i*y_i;
assign p_i1=x_i*y_r;
assign p_i2=x_r*y_i;
assign s_r=p_r1-p_r2;
assign s_i=p_i1+p_i2;
// Quantization: Manual sign extension because s_r[1:-15]
// will be treated as an unsigned number.
assign s_rnd_r={s_r[1],s_r[1:-15]}+s_r[-16];
assign s_rnd_i={s_i[1],s_i[1:-15]}+s_i[-16];
// Check overflow
assign of_pos_r=~s_rnd_r[2]&(s_rnd_r[1]|s_rnd_r[0]);
assign of_neg_r=s_rnd_r[2]&(~s_rnd_r[1]|~s_rnd_r[0]);
assign of_pos_i=~s_rnd_i[2]&(s_rnd_i[1]|s_rnd_i[0]);
assign of_neg_i=s_rnd_i[2]&(~s_rnd_i[1]|~s_rnd_i[0]);
// Output of Limiter
assign z_r=of_pos_r? 16'h7fff : (
                of_neg_r? 16'h8000 : s_rnd_r[0:-15]);
assign z_i=of_pos_i? 16'h7fff : (
                of_neg_i? 16'h8000 : s_rnd_i[0:-15]);
endmodule
```

5.6.7 MORE ON SIZING AND SIGNING

Regarding assignment of signed and unsigned numbers, constant decimal numbers (e.g., −12) are treated as signed numbers. But constant based numbers (with or without size) (e.g., −12) are treated as unsigned numbers. For example,

```
// Example: based numbers are treated as unsigned numbers
reg [7:0] a;
integer int32;
initial begin
  a=-4'd6;
  int32=-4'd6;
end
```

In the first assignment, 4-bit unsigned number (1010_2) is assigned to a 8-bit unsigned number, $−4'd6$ is zero extended as 0000_1010_2, which is a potential problem. In the second assignment, 4-bit unsigned number (1010_2) is assigned to a 32-bit signed number, $−4'd6$ is sign extended as $1111\_..._1111\_1010_2$, which is fine for signed-magnitude representation, but is still not good for 2's complement representation. This is quite confusing. Hence, do not use base when you refer to a negative number.

In another example,

```
// Example #1: RHS is sign extended or truncated and
// then assigned to LHS
reg [3:0] a, b;
reg [15:0] c;
initial begin
  a=-1;
  b=8;
  c=8;
  #10 b=b+a;
  #10 c=c+a;
end
```

Firstly, assign $−1_{10}$ to a 4-bit unsigned reg, a, which gives a 4-bit 2's complement of $−1_{10}$, which is 1111_2. So, a is 1111_2. Secondly, assign 8 to a 4-bit unsigned reg, b. So, b is 1000_2. Thirdly, assign 8 to a 16-bit unsigned reg, c. So, c is $0000\_0000\_0000\_1000_2$. Fourthly, 4-bit unsigned a and 4-bit unsigned b are added, the result is assigned to 4-bit unsigned b. The addition result is 1_0111_2, which is truncated to 0111_2 and then assigned to b. Finally, 16-bit unsigned c and 4-bit unsigned a are added, the result is assigned to 16-bit unsigned c. The 4-bit unsigned a is padded to $0000\_0000\_0000\_1111_2$. So, the addition result is $0000\_0000\_0001\_0111_2$, which is then assigned to c.

In another example,

```
1// Example #2: RHS is sign extended or truncated and
2// then assigned to LHS
3reg [3:0] a;
4integer b; // 32-bit signed number
5initial begin
6   b=32'hffff_fff0;
7   #10 a=b+1;
8end
```

Firstly, b is a 32-bit signed number. So, b is assigned $ffff\_fff0_{16}$, which is -16_{10} in 2's complement. Then, $-16_{10} + 1$ results in -15_{10}, or $ffff\_fff1_{16}$. So, the addition result is truncated to 0001_2 and assigned to a.

In summary, there are several steps to evaluate an expression.

Step 1: determine the sign of RHS.

- If all RHS operands are signed, the result is signed, regardless of operator.
- If any RHS operand is unsigned, the result is unsigned.
- If RHS operands are constant decimal numbers (e.g., -12), they are treated as signed numbers. But constant based numbers (e.g., -12) are unsigned.

Step 2: evaluate the RHS expression, producing a result of the type (i.e., sign) found in Step 1. The result has a size of the largest RHS operand.

Step 3: assign RHS to LHS according to the size of the LHS.

- If the bit width of RHS is smaller than LHS and the result of RHS is signed, signed number is sign extended.
- If the bit width of RHS is smaller than LHS and the result of RHS is unsigned, unsigned number is zero extended.
- If the bit width of RHS is larger than LHS, RHS is truncated.

5.7   FURTHER READING

- David Money Harris and Sarah L. Harris, *Digital design and computer architecture*, 2nd Ed., Morgan Kaufmann, 2013.
- Donald E. Thomas and Philip R. Moorby, *The Verilog hardware description language*, 5th Ed., Kluwer Academic Publishers, 2002.
- John F. Wakerly, *Digital design: principles and practices*, 5th Ed., Prentice Hall, 2018.
- Joseph Cavanagh, *Computer arithmetic and Verilog HDL fundamentals*, CRC Press, 2010.
- M. Morris Mano and Michael D. Ciletti, *Digital design*, 4th Ed., Prentice Hall, 2006.
- Michael D. Ciletti, *Advanced digital design with the Verilog HDL*, 2nd Ed., Prentice Hall, 2010.

- Peter J. Ashenden, *Digital design: an embedded systems approach using Verilog*, Morgan Kaufmann Publishers, 2007.
- Samir Palnitkar, *Verilog HDL: a guide to digital design and synthesis, 2nd Ed.*, Pearson, 2011.
- Stephen Brown and Zvonko Vranesic, *Fundamentals of digital logic with Verilog design*, McGraw-Hill, 2002.
- Stine, James E., *Digital computer arithmetic datapath design using Verilog HDL*, Kluwer Academic Publishers, 2004.
- Vaibbhav Taraate, *Digital logic design using Verilog: coding and RTL synthesis*, Springer, 2016.
- William J. Dally and R. Curtis Harting, *Digital design: a systems approach*, Cambridge University Press, 2012.
- Zainalabedin Navabi, *Verilog digital system design: RT level synthesis, testbench, and verification*, McGraw-Hill, 2005.

PROBLEMS

1. Design the combinational shifter with the function table in Table 5.15.

Table 5.15: Combinational shifter.

Sel	Operation	Function
0	$Y = A$	No shift
1	$Y = A \ll 1$	Shift left
2	$Y = A \gg 1$	Shift right
3	$Y = 0$	Zero output

2. Detect the overflow for the 3-bit result of unsigned addition and subtraction of 3-bit operands.

3. Plot the architecture of the barrel shifter realized by the RTL code, $A[7:0] \gg B[2:0]$.

4. Plot the architecture of the RTL codes.

```
1 wire [4:0] a, b;
2 reg [4:0] c;
3 integer i;
4 always @(*)
5   for(i=0;i<5;i=i+1)
6     c[i]=a[i]|b[4-i];
```

5. Plot the architecture of the RTL codes.

```
1 wire a, b, c;
2 reg d, e;
3 always @(*) begin
4   d=(a&b)&(a|c);
5   e=c^d;
6 end
```

6. Detect the overflow for the 3-bit result of signed addition and subtraction of 3-bit operands.

7. Prove that the sign extension does not affect the original value of both signed and unsigned integer numbers.

8. We are familiar with addition using signed-magnitude representation. However, it is most convenient to implement addition using 2's complement representation. If we want to design a circuit for calculating

$$Y = A + B - C \tag{5.21}$$

where A, B, and C are 3-bit signed-magnitude numbers. A kind of feasible implementation can use the block diagram in Figure 5.36.

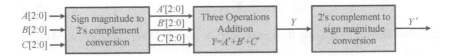

Figure 5.36: Signed-magnitude operation.

a. The first block converts one signed-magnitude number to one 2's complement number. To design the first block, i.e., signed-magnitude to 2's complement conversion, write down the one-to-one relation between signed-magnitude and 2's complement representations. Based on the relation, write down your RTL code based on a lookup table. Since the conversion should be instantiated 3 times, please design the first block using a module.

b. A possible implementation of the second block is shown in Figure 5.37. To prevent overflow, what's the bit width of Y? Write down your RTL code in a module. You are not allowed to use the "signed" declaration. Remember to do sign extension before the addition.

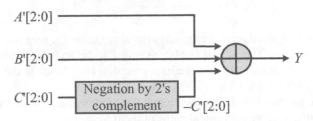

Figure 5.37: Three-number 2's complement addition.

c. The third block is the "reverse process" of the first block. Based on the relation of signed-magnitude and 2's complement representations, write down your RTL code in a module.

d. Write down your RTL code of the top module by instantiating above 3 modules.

e. Can you reduce the area of the design by combining the conversion of $C[2:0]$ in the first block and negating $C[2:0]$ in the second block?

f. Rewrite (a) using a function.

g. Can you design a smaller signed-magnitude to 2's complement conversion circuit using an adder instead of lookup table in item a. of this problem? What's the advantage of your new design?

9. a. Using the Boolean algebra to prove that

$$c_{n-1} \cdot \overline{c_{n-2}} = x_{n-1} \cdot y_{n-1} \cdot \overline{s_{n-1}} \qquad (5.22)$$

where c_{n-1} and c_{n-2} are carry outs in (5.4).

b. Similarly, using the Boolean algebra to prove that

$$\overline{c_{n-1}} \cdot c_{n-2} = \overline{x_{n-1}} \cdot \overline{y_{n-1}} \cdot s_{n-1}. \tag{5.23}$$

c. From above, prove that the overflow detectors in (5.4) and (5.5) are equivalent.

10. Design a 6-bit signed-magnitude comparator.
11. Plot the architecture of the ALU in Table 5.14.
12. Prove that the multiplication of two n-bit numbers gives a product of width less than or equal to $2n$ bits.
13. Prove that the additon of one n-bit number and one m-bit number gives a sum of width less than or equal to $n + m$ bits.
14. Write an RTL behavioral description for adding two 8-bit signed numbers in signed-magnitude representation and verify it.
15. Please redesign the module complex_mul such that the maximum value 1 of the product of two s(1.15) numbers cannot be ignored.
16. An approximation for finding the square root of a number about 1 can be found by computing its Taylor series as

$$\sqrt{x} \approx x + \frac{(x-1)^2}{2} + \frac{(x-1)^3}{6}. \tag{5.24}$$

Design a Verilog module that computes the approximate square root of x using the u(1.8) format. The output is also assumed to be an u(1.8) number. Your design must not suffer any intermediate precision loss. What is the worst case error for all x between 0.5 and 1.5?

17. Plot the architectures of the following two RTL codes using 2-to-1 multiplexers. Subsequently, analyze the critical paths of them.
RTL codes 1:

```
1 always @(*)
2   if(sel==2'b00) out=a;
3   else if(sel==2'b01) out=b;
4   else if(sel==2'b10) out=c;
5   else out=d;
```

RTL codes 2:

```
1 always @(*)
2   case(sel)
3   2'b00: out=a;
4   2'b01: out=b;
5   2'b10: out=c;
6   default: out=d;
7   endcase
```

18. An approximation for finding the reciprocal of a number between 0.3 and 0.8 is given by

$$\frac{1}{x} \approx 1 + (1-x) + (1-x)^2 + (1-x)^3. \tag{5.25}$$

a. Plot the error of this approximation for $0.3 \leq x \leq 0.8$.
b. Plot the architecture of the approximation circuit.
c. Design the Verilog module for x using the u(0.4) format. Your design must not suffer any intermediate precision loss.

19. Design a circuit implementing a 8-bit signed magnitude comparator.
20. Design a serial adder of s(1.4) signed numbers.
21. Design a serial multiplier of s(1.4) signed numbers.
22. Design a serial divider of s(1.4) signed numbers.
23. Please design a circuit used to decode whether the sums of all elements in every rows and columns of a 4×4 matrix, as presented below, can be divided exactly by 2, where $a_{ij} \in \{0,1\}, i,j = 0,1,2,3$.

$$\begin{bmatrix} a_{00} & a_{01} & a_{02} & a_{03} \\ a_{10} & a_{11} & a_{12} & a_{13} \\ a_{20} & a_{21} & a_{22} & a_{23} \\ a_{30} & a_{31} & a_{32} & a_{33} \end{bmatrix} \tag{5.26}$$

The interface of the decoder is displayed below. When all sums of elements in every rows and columns are divisible by 2, the output $r[1:0]=2\text{'b00}$; when there is only one single element causing one row and one column not to be divisible by 2, the output $r[1:0]=2\text{'b01}$; otherwise, the output $r[1:0]=2\text{'b10}$. Besides, when $r[1:0]=2\text{'b01}$, output the row and column indices, i.e., row$[1:0]$ and col$[1:0]$, respectively, of the element causing the sums not to be divisible by 2; when $r[1:0] \neq 2\text{'b01}$, row$[1:0]$ and col$[1:0]$ are "don't care".

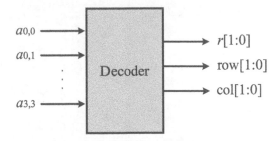

Figure 5.38: Interface of the decoder.

a. Design a module, called add4, that can sum four elements in a row or column.
b. Write the RTL codes that can decide if the output of an add4 is divisible exactly by 2.

c. Instantiate add4 8 times. Based on the decision results of every rows and columns, output $r[1:0]$, $row[1:0]$, and $col[1:0]$.

24. For the half adder circuit in Figure 5.21, complete the timing diagrams with respect to the following timing models.

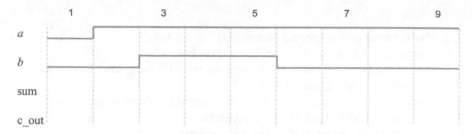

Figure 5.39: Waveform of the half adder.

a. Gate delays of XOR, NAND, and NOT gates are 2.5, 1.5, 0.5 time units, respectively.

b. In the typical-case operating condition, rising time delays of XOR, NAND, and NOT gates are 2.5, 1.5, 0.5 time units, respectively. Falling time delays of XOR, NAND, and NOT gates are 2.2, 1.2, 0.4 time units, respectively.

c. In the worst-case operating condition, all delays are 1.6 times those in the typical-case operating condition.

25. Redesign the fixed-point addition in Section 4.2.2 using the signed declaration.

26. Redesign the fixed-point multiplication in Section 4.2.2 using the signed declaration.

6 Sequential Circuits

Versatile and highly complicated functions have been achieved through sequential circuits. This chapter introduces two sequential circuits, such as asynchronous latch and synchronous flip-flop. The rationales for timing constraints, including the requirements of setup time, hold time, and clock-to-Q delay, of flip-flops are illustrated in details. We then give examples of behavioral and structural descriptions of sequential circuits. Basic but essential building blocks of sequential circuits, such as registers, shift registers, register files, state machines, (synchronous and asynchronous) counters, and FIFO buffer (or queue), are presented, together with their RTL codes. Finally, the way to solve the race condition in Verilog codes is briefly described.

6.1 INTRODUCTION TO SEQUENTIAL CIRCUITS

Combinatorial circuits are important because they can implement the main functions in digital systems. However, almost all digital systems are sequential. In other words, they more or less contain storage units, allowing output to be determined by both current and previous inputs. For example, we often need to know the current state of the system to determine the state of the system in the future.

There are two kinds of sequential circuits: asynchronous (latch) and synchronous (flip-flop). Latch may change their output states whenever a change in inputs occurs. By contrast, flip-flops can change their states only at fixed points of time (specified by the clock signal). Modern digital circuits are synchronous circuits using synchronous flip-flops, which are easy to design and tool-assisted. Latches should be used only when smaller area (about half of a flip-flop) and less power than flip-flops are required. However, flip-flop based design is preferred to latch based design because flip-flop based design has a fair area and timing, and easier static timing analysis and design for test (scan test).

Synchronous storage components store data and perform some simple operations. They can be applied to registers, counters, register files, memories, queues, and stacks. Synchronous sequential circuit operates on the edges of a clock, which is periodic signal, as shown in Figure 6.1.

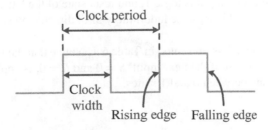

Figure 6.1: Periodic clock waveform.

DOI: 10.1201/9781003187196-6

Clock period (usually measured in micro or nanoseconds) is the time between successive transitions in the same direction (positive or negative edge). Clock frequency (measured in MHz or GHz) is the reciprocal of clock period. Clock width is the time interval during which clock is equal to logic 1. Duty cycle is the ratio of the clock width to clock period. The 50% duty cycle is good for a clock waveform. Though a clock waveform with a non-50% duty cycle is applicable for a digital circuit provided that the clock width conforms to the device specification, attention should be paid when the design is complicated that there exists signals across clock domains or with a mixture of positive and negative edges. Clock signal is active high if the changes occur at the rising edge (for flip-flops) or during the clock width (for latches). Otherwise, it is active low.

6.1.1   LATCH

Recall that the output of a combinational circuit depends only on its current inputs. Also, combinational circuits are acyclic. If we add a feedback path to a combinational circuit, the circuit might become sequential, which allows the circuit to store information of its past inputs. That is, the output of a sequential circuit can depend not only on its current inputs, but also rely on its previous inputs. The information stored on the feedback signals are referred to as the state of a sequential circuit.

Latches are level-sensitive sequential circuits since they respond to input changes during clock width, as shown in Figure 6.2. Consequently, a latch may change many times during a clock width. Latches are difficult to work with for this reason.

Clock width

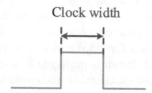

Figure 6.2: Latches respond to clock width.

All latches are constructed from the SR (set-reset) latch consisting of NOR gates introduced here, as shown in Figure 6.3, where $\overline{(\cdot)}$ denotes the bitwise NOT operation. Set state of the latch output is logic 1, and reset state of the latch output is logic 0. A latch can maintain a binary state indefinitely until directed by an input signal to switch states.

The truth table of a latch is presented in Table 6.1. Notice that the input, $S = 1$ and $R = 1$, is forbidden because if the next input, $S = 0$ and $R = 0$, is applied, the output $Q(t+1)$ may oscillate between 0 and 1 states.

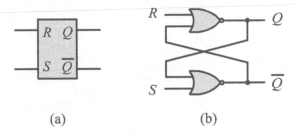

Figure 6.3: SR latch: (a) symbol and (b) schematic.

Table 6.1: Truth table of latch.

S	R	$Q(t+1)$	$\overline{Q(t+1)}$
1	0	1	0
0	1	0	1
0	0	$Q(t)$	$\overline{Q(t)}$
1	1	Unpredictable	Unpredictable

It can be shown that, according to Figure 6.3(b), the output

$$Q(t+1) = R \cdot (S + Q(t)), \qquad (6.1)$$

and its complement

$$\overline{Q(t+1)} = \overline{S} \cdot (R + \overline{Q(t)}), \qquad (6.2)$$

are fed back to the inputs as state variables, where $\cdot$ and $+$ denote the bitwise AND and OR operations, respectively. The equation clearly tells us how to derive the new state of $Q(t+1)$ as a function of the input and its old state $Q(t)$. From the equations, it is easy to see that if $R = 1$ and $S = 0$, the $Q(t+1)$ is reset and $\overline{Q(t+1)}$ is set which is a stable state; if $S = 1$ and $R = 0$, $Q(t+1)$ is set and $\overline{Q(t+1)}$ is reset which is also a stable state; if $S = 0$ and $R = 0$, the $Q(t+1) = Q(t)$ and $\overline{Q(t+1)} = \overline{Q(t)}$ which stay in whatever states they were in. This is still a stable state; if $R = 1$ and $S = 1$, $Q(t+1) = 0$ and $\overline{Q(t+1)} = 0$, which is an unstable state. If then $R = 0$ and $S = 0$, $Q(t+1)$ and $\overline{Q(t+1)}$ may oscillate between 0 and 1.

Figure 6.4 presents the SR latch with enable control. To this, first, the NOR-gate SR latch is converted to the NAND-gate implementation. Second, u1 and u4 are merged. So are u2 and u3. Third, an enable signal, E, is added. When $E = 1$, the SR latch works as it was. When $E = 0$, the SR latch stays in whatever states they were in.

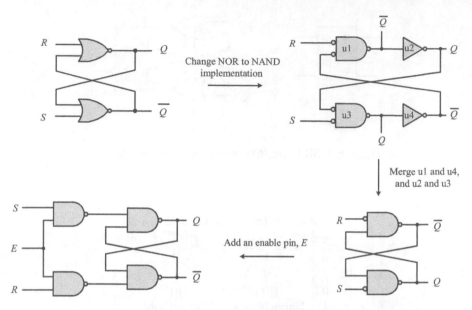

Figure 6.4: SR latch with enable control implemented by NAND gates.

Its functional table is displayed in Table 6.2.

Table 6.2: Functional table of SR latch with enable control.

E	S	R	$Q(t+1)$
0	X	X	$Q(t)$
1	0	0	$Q(t)$
1	0	1	0
1	1	0	1
1	1	1	Unpredictable

However, the indeterminate state still makes the SR latch difficult to use. To eliminate the undesirable condition of the indeterminate state in the SR latch, the D latch (transparent latch) in Figure 6.5(a) is designed, where S and R pins of SR latch are connected so that S is directly tied to D pin and R pin is tied to the inverse of D pin, as shown in Figure 6.5(b).

Its functional table is displayed in Table 6.3.

Table 6.3: Functional table of D latch.

E	D	$Q(t+1)$
0	X	$Q(t)$
1	0	0
1	1	1

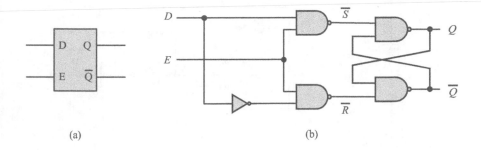

(a)   (b)

Figure 6.5: D latch: (a) circuit symbol and (b) schematic.

Its function is simple. When $E = 1$, output Q is D; otherwise, no change is allowed to Q. Therefore, the state Q of D latch can continuously change during the interval that E is true, so D latch is level triggered (or level-sensitive). D latch is also called transparent latch that, during $E = 1$, the latch behaves like that it is transparent because output Q is always D.

The level-triggered latch has the instability problem, as shown in Figure 6.6. Since the time interval of logic 1 for the enable pin remains for a duration, the feedback path may cause instability problem. That is, multiple transitions might happen during logic 1 level of the enable pin. Rather, for the edge-triggered flip-flops, the state transition happens only at the edge of clock pin. So, they eliminate the multiple-transition problem.

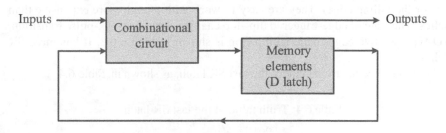

Figure 6.6: Problem of D latch.

The D-latches introduced before use static CMOS gates. CMOS technology, however, also permits us to construct a D-latch, as shown in Figure 6.7(b), with a transmission gate, a tristate inverter, and inverters. The tristate inverter is equivalent to an inverter followed by a transmission gate in Figure 6.7(a), where, when $E = 1$, the output $Y = \overline{A}$ by turning on both NMOS and PMOS in the transmission gate; when $E = 0$, the output Y is in tristate by turning off NMOS and PMOS, such that Y is isolated from A. Most CMOS latches use transmission gates in this style because this results in a latch that is both smaller and faster than the static CMOS gates. Compared to the static CMOS D-latch gate in Figure 6.5(b) with 18 transistors, the D-latch using the transmission gate requires only 12 transistors.

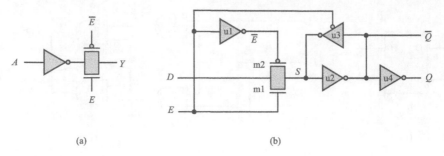

(a)   (b)

Figure 6.7: (a) Tristate inverter. (b) CMOS D-latch using transmission gate and tristate inverter.

When enable E is high (and $\overline{E}$ is low), the transmission gate formed by NMOS m1 and PMOS m2 is on, allowing the value on input D to pass to storage node S. Output Q follows storage node S buffered by inverter u2 and u4. Thus, when E is high, the output Q follows input D. When enable E goes low, the transmission gate formed by m1 and m2 turns off isolating storage node S from the input. At this time, the input is sampled onto the storage node. Concurrently, tristate inverter u3 turns on, closing a storage loop from S back to itself through two inverters, u2 and u3. This feedback loop reenforces the stored value, allowing it to be retained indefinitely.

6.1.2   FLIP-FLOP

Flip-flops respond to input changes only during the change in clock signal (the rising edge or the falling edge). They are easy to work with though more expensive than latches. The state of edge-triggered flip-flop changes during a clock-pulse transition. A D-type positive-edge-triggered flip-flop is shown in Figure 6.8. It has three SR latches.

We will utilize the truth table of the last SR latch, as shown in Table 6.4.

Table 6.4: Truth table of the last SR latch.

$\overline{S}$	$\overline{R}$	$Q(t+1)$
0	1	1
1	0	0
1	1	$Q(t)$
0	0	Unpredictable

The functionality of D-type flip-flop is described in Figure 6.9. In addition to signal waveform, its corresponding signal values with an emphasis on their transitions are labeled in the schematic for your easy convenience. Notably, the unpredictable condition of $\overline{S} = \overline{R} = 0$ does not happen.

In summary, the waveform tells us that

- when clk=0, $(\overline{S},\overline{R}) = (1,1)$, so there is no state change according to the truth table of the last SR latch.

- when clk=↑ (rising edge), the state changes once.
- when clk=1, the state holds its old value.

Hence, edge-triggered flip-flops eliminate the feedback problems in sequential circuits by allowing all flip-flops to make their transition at the same time or positive edge of clock, which leads to the synchronous design. Consequently, all flip-flops must make their transitions concurrently. This is an important property of synchronous digital design.

In Figure 6.10(a), a combinational loop is introduced. By contrast, the flip-flop with feedback does not induce the loop problem, as shown in Figure 6.10(b). In the circuit with flip-flop, there are two paths that may affect the D input of D flip-flop. To guarantee a normal function, the D input just has to be ready before the rising edge of clock in every clock cycles. Remember that $a = a + c$ in C codes may be translated into Assembly language like this, r0 = r0 + r1, where r0 and r1 registers store the variables of a and c, respectively. They indeed operate on registers like that in Figure 6.10(b).

Continuous assignment using a conditional operator with feedback will synthesize into a latch, as shown in the following example. When CS_b is 0 and WE_b is 1, data_out=data_out is executed. Synthesis tools infer the behavioral of a latch, because data_out holds its content in this case and timing loop must be broken.

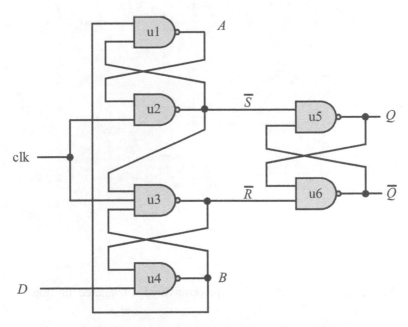

Figure 6.8: D-type positive-edge-triggered flip-flop.

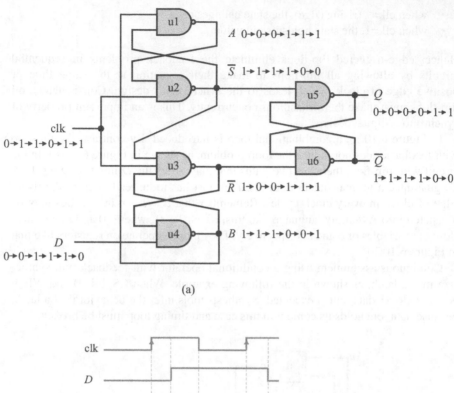

(a)

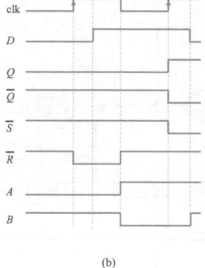

(b)

Figure 6.9: Functionality of D-type positive-edge-triggered flip-flop.

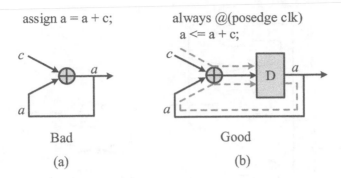

$$\text{assign } a = a + c;$$

$$\text{always @(posedge clk)}$$
$$a <= a + c;$$

Bad   Good

(a)   (b)

Figure 6.10: (a) Combinational loop. (b) Feedback of flip-flop output is not a problem.

```
1 // Combinational loop produced by continuous assignment
2 assign data_out=(CS_b==0)?
3                       ((WE_b==0)?data_in:data_out):
4                       1'bz;
```

In a short summary, combinational loop should be avoided in any cascs. Moreover, flip-flops do not introduce any combinational loops.

6.1.3   SETUP AND HOLD TIMES OF FLIP-FLOPS

Considering physical gate delays, an positive edge-triggered flip-flop has setup and hold times requirement. The setup time is defined as that D input must be maintained at a constant value prior to the application of the positive-edge clock pulse. As shown in Figure 6.11, to ensure a successful 0 to 1 transition in Q output at a rising edge of clk (the 3rd transition), the input D must transits from 0 to 1 (the 2nd transition) before the rising edge. Therefore, the signal marked by the dashed arrow must be stable (caused by 0 to 1 transition of D) before the rising edge of clk. Hence, the rising setup time for 0 to 1 transition in Q is the propagation delay through gates u4 and u1. Additionally, the clock-to-Q delay, t_{CQ}, is the delay for the Q output to reflect the D input after the rising edge of clk. The path marked by the solid arrow represents the rising clock-to-Q delays. Therefore, the rising clock-to-Q delay is the propagation delay through gates u2 and u5.

Similarly, the falling setup time for 1 to 0 transition in Q is the propagation delay through gate u4 (marked by the dashed arrow), and the falling clock-to-Q delay is the propagation delay through gates u3, u6, and u5 (marked by the solid arrow).

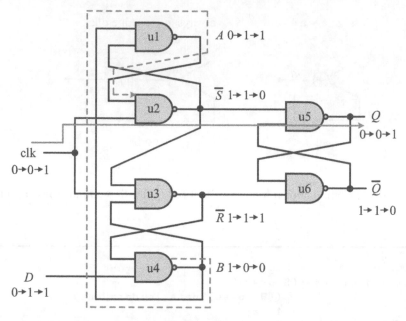

Figure 6.11: Rising setup and clock-to-Q delay times requirement. Signal values with an emphasis on their transitions for 0 to 1 transition in Q are labeled in the schematic.

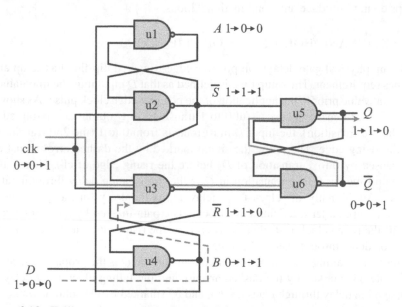

Figure 6.12: Falling setup and clock-to-Q delay times requirement. Signal values with an emphasis on their transitions for 1 to 0 transition in Q are labeled in the schematic.

Moreover, the hold time is defined as that D input must not change after the application of the positive-edge clock pulse (the 2nd transition). As shown in Figure 6.13, the signal marked by the dashed arrow must be stable before the change of D (the 3rd transition). Therefore, it is the propagation delay of gate u3, i.e., clock to the internal latch.

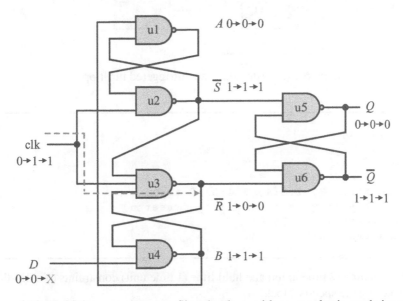

Figure 6.13: Hold time requirement. Signal values with an emphasis on their transitions are labeled in the schematic.

The clock-to-Q delay, t_{CQ}, is defined as the delay that it takes for the register output to be in a stable state after a clock edge occurs. We can use the intra assignment delay to model clock-to-Q delay, as shown below, where a clock-to-Q delay of 1 time unit is added. The delay will be removed during synthesis. It can be used to distinguish the events of clock rising edges and those for the evaluation of the outputs of sequential circuits. In this example, at rising edges of clk, D input (or $A + B$) of flip-flops is evaluated. Then, the result is delayed and finally assigned to Q after 1 time unit.

```
1// Modeling clock-to-Q delay
2 always @(posedge clk or negedge reset_n)
3   if(!reset_n) Q<=#1 0;
4   else Q<=#1 A+B;
```

Only the (minimum : typical : maximum) delays of a single delay can be specified in procedural assignments. Therefore, the rising, falling, and turn-off delays must be the same. To distinguish the rising and falling delays, the continuous assignment is used as follows. In the following example, Q models the real output of the flip-flops. The (minimum : typical : maximum) delays of rising, falling, and turn-off delays are $(1:2:3)$, $(2:3:4)$, and $(3:4:5)$, respectively.

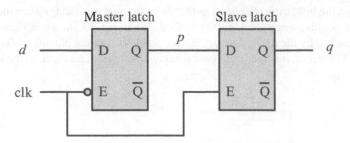

Figure 6.14: Master-slave edge-triggered flip-flop.

```
1// Modeling rising, falling, and turn-off clock-to-Q
2// delays
3// The (minimum:typical:maximum) delays of them are also
4// differentiated.
5assign #(1:2:3, 2:3:4, 3:4:5) Q=tmpQ;
6always @(posedge clk or negedge reset_n)
7  if(!reset_n) tmpQ <=0;
8  else tmpQ <=A+B;
```

The setup time (2 time units) and hold time (1 time unit) constraints of a flip-flop are checked by the specify block.

```
1// Specify block for setup and hold time check of FF
2specify
3  $setup(D, posedge clk, 2);
4  $hold(posedge clk, D, 1);
5endspecify
```

6.1.4 MASTER-SLAVE FLIP-FLOP

Another popular edge-triggered flip-flop with two D-latches uses the master-slave structure in Figure 6.14. When clk is low, the master latch is enabled, but the input d cannot directly influence output q because the slave latch is disabled. Therefore, the slave latch blocks the input so that the problem of the transparency of D-latches is resolved.

At the clock rising edge, the master latch changes from being enabled to disabled, while the slave latch changes from being disabled to enabled and becomes transparent. Therefore, the input d is captured by the master latch as p, which then drives the output q.

The timing diagram of the master-slave edge-triggered flip-flop is displayed in Figure 6.15. As presented, the master-slave flip-flop is actually edge-triggered.

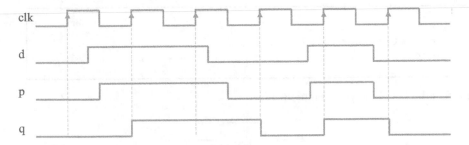

Figure 6.15: Timing diagram of the master-slave edge-triggered flip-flop.

6.1.5   LATCH VS. FLIP-FLOP

The difference between latch and flip-flop is displayed in Figures 6.16(a) and 6.16(b), respectively. As presented, the latch output changes multiple times whenever its enable signal (connected with clk) is high. Instead, the flip-flop toggles once only at the positive or negative edge of clk.

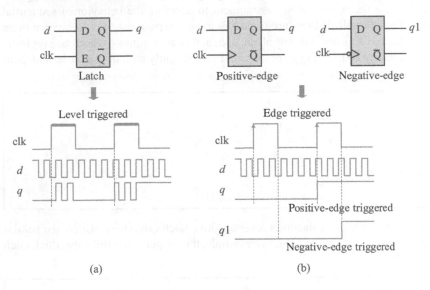

Figure 6.16: (a) Level-triggered latch and (b) edge-triggered flip-flop.

6.2   BEHAVIORAL DESCRIPTION

Always statement can infer both sequential and combinational logic circuits. For example, the positive edge-triggered D flip-flops (D-FFs) are inferred by the posedge in the sensitivity list.

```
1 // Positive edge-triggered flip-flops inference
2 always @(posedge clk)
3     q<=d;
```

It infers the D-FF shown in Figure 6.17.

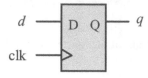

Figure 6.17: D-FF inferred by the always statement.

At every positive edge of clk, q is set as d. Therefore, when the input d changes, the registered output q reflects (and memorizes) the result of d at the next rising edge of clk. If we change the posedge to negedge, we get the negative edge-triggered D-FF. We use the non-blocking assignment to describe the behavior of sequential circuits. For example, if there are three FFs to be inferred, they can be written in an always block as follows. The variables, a, b, and c, are outputs of hardware registers implemented by D-FFs. They are executed concurrently and, hence, order independent.

```
1 // Flip-flops inference using non-blocking assignment
2 always @(posedge clk) begin
3     a<=d+e;
4     b<=f+g;
5     c<=h+i;
6 end
```

The always block can also infer level sensitive latch using the sensitive list similar to that of a combinational circuit. For example, the output is not fully specified, latch is inferred.

```
1 // Latches inference using incomplete if-else pair
2 always @(clk or d)
3     if(clk) q<=d;
```

The positive edge-triggered D-FF with asynchronous active-low reset, reset_n, is written as follows.

```
1// Flip-flops inference with asynchronous
2// active-low reset
3always @(posedge clk or negedge reset_n)
4    if(!reset_n) q<=0;
5    else q<=d;
```

There are two functions mixed in the always block: reset and normal functions. The reset is asynchronous because it is put in the sensitivity list. That is, whenever the negative edge (negedge) of reset_n happens, the output q of FF is cleared (assigned logic 0) because the reset_n= 0 and has the highest priority than normal function (assigned d). Hence, the FF responds to asynchronous reset immediately. Otherwise, the normal function takes action. The above RTL codes exactly describe the behavioral of an edge-triggered D-FF with asynchronous reset in Figure 6.18. The timing diagram is also presented.

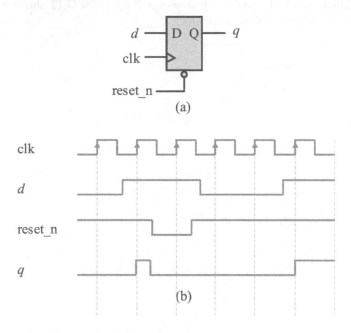

(a)

(b)

Figure 6.18: D-FF with asynchronous reset: (a) schematic and (b) timing diagram.

Typically, the power-on-reset (POR) and hardware reset (asserted by the reset push button) are applied using the asynchronous reset, while normal function uses the synchronous reset to reset (or clear) a block or a portion of the digital circuits. Specifically, for active-low POR and hardware reset, they are AND-ed to generate the asynchronous reset, as shown below. The POR can be generated by the voltage regulator once the supply voltage is stable.

```
1// Combine power-on-reset and hardware reset
2assign reset_n=reset_n_por & reset_n_hard;
```

The positive edge-triggered D-FF with synchronous reset is written below.

```
1// Flip-flops inference with synchronous reset
2always @(posedge clk)
3   if(!reset_n) q<=0;
4   else q<=d;
```

At every posedge of clk, if reset_n is 0, then reset D flip-flop; if reset_n is 1, then $q = d$. Reset happens synchronously to the edge of clk, so this is called synchronous reset. The normal function is performed when reset_n is not asserted. The synchronous reset works like the select signal of a multiplexer. It infers the D-FF shown in Figure 6.19. The timing diagram is also presented.

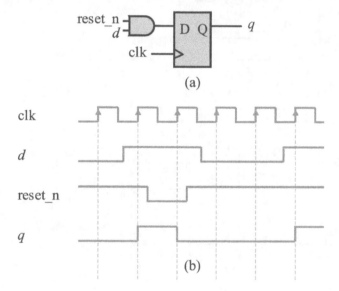

Figure 6.19: D-FF with synchronous reset: (a) schematic and (b) timing diagram.

There are two typical ways to describe the outputs of sequential circuits.

Method 1: one always block combining both combinational and sequential circuits.

```
1// Combine the description of both combinational and
2// sequential logics in an always block.
```

```
3 always @(posedge clk or negedge reset_n)
4   if (!reset_n) q<=4'd0;
5   else q<=a+b;
```

Method 2: two always blocks separately describing combinational and sequential circuits. Doing so emphasizes the roles of combinational and sequential circuits, particularly when the next state of FFs, i.e., the output of a combinational circuit, is required for some logic function.

```
1 // Separate the description of combinational and
2 // sequential logics into two always blocks.
3 // Combinational circuits
4 always @(a or b)
5   d=a+b;
6 // Sequential circuits
7 always @(posedge clk or negedge reset_n)
8   if (!reset_n) q<=4'd0;
9   else q<=d;
```

6.3 STRUCTURAL DESCRIPTION

By feeding back the output $\overline{Q}$ to the input terminal D, a frequency divider-by-2 is obtained and shown below, where DFF denotes the D-type flip-flop gate in a cell library. The clock divider works by toggling the output Q (signal clock_div2) at every positive edge of clock. It can be seen that, by drawing the timing diagram (omitted here), the output pulses at Q have a frequency that is exactly one half that of the input clock.

```
1 // Instantiate a flip-flop for the frequency divider.
2 DFF u0(.D(clock_div2_inv), .Q(clock_div2),
3        .QN(clock_div2_inv), .CLK(clock));
```

6.4 BASIC BUILDING BLOCKS OF SEQUENTIAL CIRCUITS

A circuit with sequential gates, such as flip-flops, is considered a sequential circuit even in the absence of combinational gates.

6.4.1 REGISTERS

An n-bit register is a group of n binary sequential cells (or flip-flops). A binary sequential cell can store one bit of information, or two states: 0 (reset) and 1 (set) state. The state of a register is an n-tuple of 1's and 0's. The registers with synchronous enable or load are presented below.

```
1// D-FFs with synchronous enable
2module dff_en(q, enable, d, clk);
3output [3:0] q;
4input clk, enable;
5input [3:0] d;
6reg [3:0] q;
7always @(posedge clk)
8   if(enable) q<=d;
9endmodule
```

The module infers the registers shown in Figure 6.20.

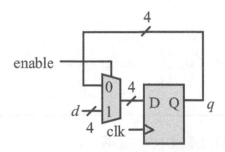

Figure 6.20: D-FF with enable or load.

6.4.2   SHIFT REGISTERS

A register capable of shifting the binary information held in each cell to its neighboring cell is called a shift register. This is also called the serial-in to serial-out (SISO) shifter. The shifting direction can be right- or left-shift. The logical configuration of a shift register consists of a chain of flip-flops in cascade, as shown in Figure 6.21. The output of one flip-flop is connected to the input of the next flip-flop. Every clock pulse activates the shifting of data from one stage to the next.

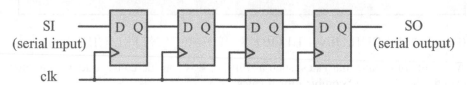

Figure 6.21: A four-bit shift register.

A digital system is said to operate in serial mode when information is transferred or manipulated one bit at a time. Information is transferred one bit at a time by shifting the bits out of the source register and into the destination register. Serial mode can save the pin counts and wiring complexity. In contrast, the parallel transfer mode transfers all the bits of the register at the same time to achieve a high bit rate of data transmission.

A serial transfer is demonstrated in Figure 6.22. The transmitter/receiver converts a parallel/serial input to serial/parallel output.

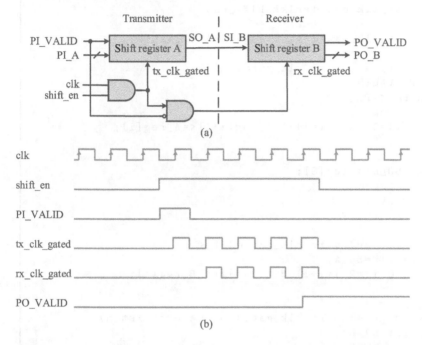

(a)

(b)

Figure 6.22: A serial transfer mode with shift control: (a) block diagram and (b) timing diagram of gated clock.

We assume that the parallel input and output are 4 bits. When PI_VALID is true, the input PI_A is loaded into register A. When PO_VALID is true, the output PO_B is output from register B. The serial output (SO) of register A is connected to the serial input (SI) of register B. That is, registers A and B are transferred in parallel-in to serial-out (PISO) and serial-in to parallel-out (SIPO) modes, respectively.

The shift control input (shift_en) determines when and how many times the register A are loaded or shifted. This is done with an AND gate that allows clock pulses to pass into the clock terminals of registers only when the shift control signal is high. Gating the clock signal is called clock gating. This practice may be problematic because it may influence the clock path of the circuit so that glitches may be produced on the tx_clk_gated signal. The functionality of the shift register can fail owing to extra edges on the tx_clk_gated signal. Therefore, the control signal, shift_en, should be carefully designed so that no glitch can be produced in the gated clock.

The signal, rx_clk_gated, determines how many times the register B are shifted. When a complete word has been shifted in, the signal PO_VALID becomes true.

The RTL codes are written below.

```
1 //****************
2 //* Transmitter
3 //****************
4 // Generate gated clock
5 assign tx_clk_gated=clk&shift_en;
6 // Generate gated clock
7 assign rx_clk_gated=tx_clk_gated&~PI_VALID;
8 // Shift register A
9 always @(posedge tx_clk_gated) begin
10   if(PI_VALID)
11     A_reg<=PI_A;
12   else begin
13     for(i=0:i<=2;i=i+1) A_reg[i+1]<=A_reg[i];
14   end
15 end
16 assign SO_A=A_reg[3];
17 //****************
18 //* Receiver
19 //****************
20 // Shift register B
21 always @(posedge rx_clk_gated) begin
22   B_reg[0]<=SO_A;
23   for(i=0:i<=2;i=i+1) B_reg[i+1]<=B_reg[i];
24 end
25 // Counter is used to generate PO_VALID
26 always @(posedge rx_clk_gated or negedge rst_n)
27   if(!rst_n) begin
28     counter <=0;
29     PO_VALID <=0;
30   end
31   else begin
32     if(counter==3) begin
33       counter <=0;
34       PO_VALID <=1'b1;
35     end
36     else begin
37       counter <=counter+1'b1;
38       PO_VALID <=1'b0;
39     end
40   end
41 assign PO_B=B_reg;
```

6.4.3 REGISTER FILES

A register file is an array of registers in a central processing unit. It can store intermediate results of the CPU, such as arithmetic logic unit & memory management
unit. Though registers can be implemented using a bank of flip-flop registers, static

random-access memory (SRAM)-based full-custom register files require less area and power. Such SRAM-based register files have dedicated read and write ports, whereas ordinary SRAMs usually have a port that can be read or write. In contrast to the transparent caches, the register file is visible to the programmer.

Due to the limitation of chip area, past microprocessors had only few registers. Nowadays, microprocessors have room for a large number of registers. The number of registers is merely limited by the operand fields, time spent for withdrawing and depositing program registers on an interrupt or context switching.

The performance of the processor is directly proportional to the access speed of a register file. Therefore, the register file available to the microprocessor is typically implemented by the fastest memory. Moreover, the overall performance of CPUs is usually limited by the speed of the read operation of the register file. Hence, at least 1 write port and 2 read ports need to accommodate a single ALU with 2-operand instructions. For example, the addition operation, r3 = r2 + r1, requires 2 reads of registers r1 and r2 and 1 write of register r3.

The behavioral model of a 256 × 32-bit register file is written below. The write port is implemented using a decoder with enable control, while read ports are implemented using multiplexers.

```
1 // SRAM-based register files
2 module reg_files(ren1, raddr1, dout1, ren2, raddr2,
3                  dout2, wen, waddr, din, clk);
4 output [31:0] dout1, dout2;
5 input ren1, ren2, wen;
6 input [7:0] raddr1, raddr2, waddr;
7 input [31:0] din;
8 input clk;
9 reg [31:0] mem[0:255], tempQ1, tempQ2, dout1, dout2;
10 always @(posedge clk) // One write port
11   if(wen) mem[waddr]<=din;
12 always @(ren1 or raddr1) // Read port 1
13   if(ren1) tempQ1=mem[raddr1];
14   else tempQ1=8'hzz;
15 always @(posedge clk)
16   dout1<=tempQ1;
17 always @(ren2 or raddr2) // Read port 2
18   if(ren2) tempQ2=mem[raddr2];
19   else tempQ2=8'hzz;
20 always @(posedge clk)
21   dout2<=tempQ2;
22 endmodule
```

6.4.4   STATE MACHINE

The finite state machine (FSM) is usually used to generate the control sequence (or signal) that governs the operation of datapath units. The Mealy FSM, shown in Figure 6.23, has its outputs depending on inputs and current state. By contrast, the outputs of Moor state machine depend only on the current state.

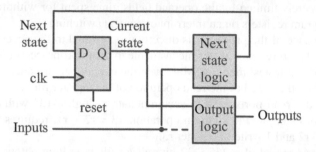

Figure 6.23: Finite state machine.

6.4.4.1   State Reduction

Since m flip-flops produce 2^m states, a reduction in the number of states may result in a fewer number of flip-flops. We start with a state transition diagram shown in Figure 6.24. There are 7 states, a, b, c, d, e, f, g, in the state diagram. The states marked inside the circles are denoted by letter symbols instead of their binary values, which can be assigned using different coding techniques described in the next section.

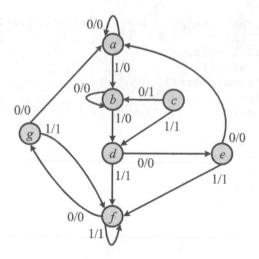

Figure 6.24: State diagram.

Next, it is more convenient to apply the state table for the state reduction shown in Figure 6.25, where x is the single bit input. Two states are said to be equivalent if, they depend on the same input, give exactly the same output, and transits to the same state or equivalent state. When two states are equivalent, such as g and e, and d and f, one of them can be removed without altering the input-output relationships. The state diagram for the reduced table shown in Figure 6.25 finally consists of only five states. In this example, even the number of flip-flops is not reduced, the combinational logic still lowers due to a fewer number of states.

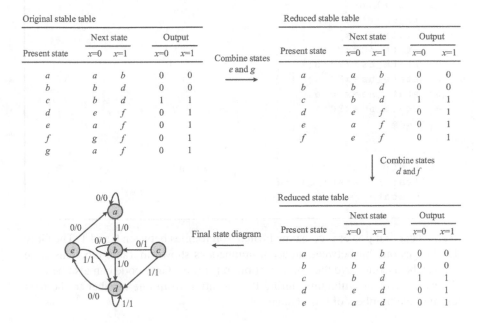

Original stable table

Present state	Next state $x=0$	$x=1$	Output $x=0$	$x=1$
a	a	b	0	0
b	b	d	0	0
c	b	d	1	1
d	e	f	0	1
e	a	f	0	1
f	g	f	0	1
g	a	f	0	1

Combine states e and g →

Reduced stable table

Present state	Next state $x=0$	$x=1$	Output $x=0$	$x=1$
a	a	b	0	0
b	b	d	0	0
c	b	d	1	1
d	e	f	0	1
e	a	f	0	1
f	e	f	0	1

Combine states d and f ↓

Reduced state table

Present state	Next state $x=0$	$x=1$	Output $x=0$	$x=1$
a	a	b	0	0
b	b	d	0	0
c	b	d	1	1
d	e	d	0	1
e	a	d	0	1

Final state diagram ←

Figure 6.25: State table reduction.

6.4.4.2 State Assignment

To design a physical sequential circuit, it is necessary to assign unique coded binary values to its states. For a circuit with m states, the code must contain n bits, where $2^n \geq m$. The simplest way to code five states is to use the first five integers in binary counting order, as shown in Table 6.5.

Table 6.5: Three possible binary state assignments.

State	Binary code	Gray code	One-hot code
a	000	000	00001
b	001	001	00010
c	010	011	00100
d	011	010	01000
e	100	110	10000

The state machine of the traditional binary encoding is presented below.

```
1// State machine: traditional binary encoding
2reg [2:0] state_ns, state_cs;
3parameter a=3'b000; parameter b=3'b001;
4parameter c=3'b010; parameter d=3'b011;
5parameter e=3'b100;
6// Combinational logic
7always @(*) begin
8   state_ns=state_cs;
9   case(state_cs)
10  a: state_ns=x?b:a;
11  b: state_ns=x?d:b;
12  c: state_ns=x?d:b;
13  d: state_ns=x?d:e;
14  e: state_ns=x?d:a;
15  endcase
16 end
17// Sequential logic
18always @(posedge clk or negedge rst_n)
19  if(!rst_n) state_cs <=a;
20  else state_cs <=state_ns;
```

Remember that power is consumed when a bit toggles between 0 and 1. The Gray code changes one bit between adjacent numbers as shown in Table 6.6. This code group can be used to save the number of bit transitions. Gray code can also be used to detect an error or ambiguity during the transition from one number to the next when multiple numbers of bits change.

Table 6.6: Gray code.

Gray code	Decimal equivalent
000	0
001	1
011	2
010	3
110	4
111	5
101	6
100	7

The state machine of the Gray encoding is presented below. Since the RTL codes are the same as those of the traditional binary encoding, they are omitted here except the parameter definition.

```
1// State machine: Gray encoding
2parameter a=3'b000; parameter b=3'b001;
3parameter c=3'b011; parameter d=3'b010;
4parameter e=3'b110;
```

Another possible assignment often used in the design of state machines to control datapath units is the one-hot assignment, which can reduce the critical path potential in datapath units because the decoder of the state machine can be eliminated. The state machine of the one-hot encoding is presented below. For example, if we want to determine whether the state state_cs is state a by the Verilog code "state_cs==a", it will be optimized by simply "state_cs[0]==1'b1", and the decoder is not needed. Therefore, the one-hot encoding can achieve a faster circuit because combinational circuits of decoders are not required to generate the control signals resulted from FSM. However, more registers, which equals the number of states instead of $\lceil \log_2(\cdot) \rceil$ of it, are needed for the one-hot encoding.

```
1// State machine: one-hot encoding
2reg [4:0] state_ns, state_cs;
3parameter a=5'b00001; parameter b=5'b00010;
4parameter c=5'b00100; parameter d=5'b01000;
5parameter e=5'b10000;
```

6.4.5   COUNTER

A counter is essentially a register that goes through a predetermined sequence of binary states. The gates in the counter are connected in such a way as to generate the specified sequence of states.

6.4.5.1   Synchronous Counter

All flip-flops in a synchronous counter receive the same clock pulse and so change state simultaneously. A synchronous counter is written as below. The counter has a synchronous reset and counts from 0,1,...,7 then to 0 when enable==1'b1.

```
1// Synchronous counter
2module counter1(out, enable, clk, reset);
3output [2:0] out;
4input enable, clk, reset;
5reg [2:0] out;
6always @(posedge clk) begin
7   if(reset) // Synchronous reset
8      out<=3'b0;
9   else if(enable==1'b1)
10      out<=out+1'b1;
```

```
11 end
12 endmodule
```

The RTL codes describe the structure in Figure 6.26.

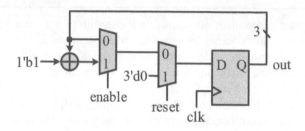

Figure 6.26: Synchronous counter.

If the counter counts till 3'd5, the comparison to 3'd5 is required as follows.

```
1 // Synchronous counter
2 module counter1(out, enable, clk, reset);
3 output [2:0] out;
4 input enable, clk, reset;
5 reg [2:0] out;
6 always @(posedge clk) begin
7   if(reset) // Synchronous reset
8      out<=3'b0;
9   else if(enable==1'b1) begin
10     if(out==3'd5) out<=3'b0;
11     else out<=out+1'b1;
12  end
13 end
14 endmodule
```

Example 6.1. A digital alarm clock needs to generate a periodic signal at a frequency of approximately 500 Hz to drive the speaker for the alarm tone. Use a counter to divide the system's master clock signal with a frequency of 1 MHz to derive the 500 Hz alarm tone.

Solution: The RTL codes of the alarm tone is presented below. The counter ticks every positive edge of master clock until it reaches 1000. When the counter is 1000, the alarm tone toggles. Consequently, the frequency of the alarm tone is 1/2000 that of the master clock, i.e., 1 MHz $\times$ 1/2000 = 500 Hz.

```
1 // Alarm generated by a counter
2 reg [9:0] counter;
```

```
3 always @(posedge master_clock or negedge rst_n)
4   if(!rst_n) begin
5     counter <=0;
6     alarm_tone <=0;
7   end
8   else if(counter ==10'd999) begin
9     counter <=0;
10    alarm_tone <=~alarm_tone;
11  end
12  else
13    counter <=counter+1'b1;
```

□

6.4.5.2   Asynchronous Counter

Asynchronous counter is also called a ripple counter. Flip-flops transitions ripple
through from one flip-flop to the next in sequence until all flip-flops reach a new stable value (state). Each single flip-flop stage divides the frequency of its input signal
by two. An asynchronous count-down counter is written below. The asynchronous
counter is also called the ripple counter.

```
1 // Asynchronous counter: period of 16
2 module CNT_ASYNC_CLK_DIV16(clk,rst_n,Y);
3 input clk, rst_n; output Y;
4 reg div2, div4, div8, div16, Y;
5 always @(posedge clk or negedge rst_n) // Divide by 2
6   if(!rst_n) div2=0;
7   else div2=~div2;
8 always @(posedge div2 or negedge rst_n) // Divide by 4
9   if(!rst_n) div4=0;
10  else div4=~div4;
11 always @(posedge div4 or negedge rst_n) // Divide by 8
12  if(!rst_n) div8=0;
13  else div8=~div8;
14 always @(posedge div8 or negedge rst_n) // Divide by 16
15  if(!rst_n) div16=0;
16  else div16=~div16;
17 // Synchronous output
18 always @(posedge clk or negedge rst_n)
19  if(!rst_n) Y=0;
20  else Y=div16;
21 endmodule
```

The RTL codes describe the structure in Figure 6.27.

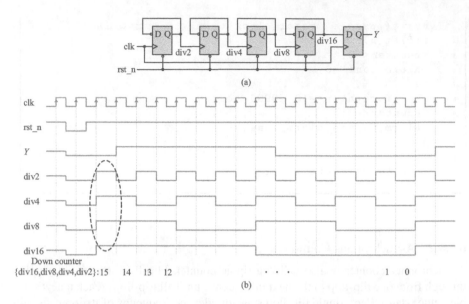

Figure 6.27: Asynchronous counter: (a) architecture and (b) timing diagram.

The purpose of register Y at the last stage is to synchronize the output Y to clk. Each single flip-flop stage divides the frequency of its input signal by two. So, the asynchronous counter can also be used for the frequency divider. This circuit divides the clock frequency by 16, and it can be used for a clock divider.

The main advantages of a ripple counter are that it uses much less circuitry in its implementation (since an increment is not required) and that it consumes less power. However, an important timing issue arises from the fact that the flip-flops in a ripple counter are not all clocked together. Each flip-flop has a propagation delay between a rising edge occurring on its clock input and the outputs changing values. Since each flip-flop is clocked from the output of the previous flip-flop, the propagation delays accumulate. The length of the counter should be considered. For longer counters, there are more flip-flops through which changes have to propagate. The accumulated delay may exceed the clock period. For shorter counters, the delay may be acceptable.

The following RTL codes describe a clock divider divided by 13, instead of power of 2, using an asynchronous (ripple) counter.

```
1// Asynchronous counter: period of 13
2module CNT_ASYNC_CLK_DIV13(clk,rst_n,Y);
3input clk, rst_n;   output Y;
4reg div2, div4, div8, div16, Y, clear;
5wire div2_b, div4_b, div8_b, div16_b;
6wire [3:0] counter;
```

```
 7 always @(posedge clk or negedge rst_n
 8          or posedge clear)
 9   if(!rst_n) div2<=0;
10   else if(clear) div2<=0;
11   else div2<=~div2;
12 assign div2_b=!div2;
13 always @(posedge div2 or negedge
14          rst_n or posedge clear)
15   if(!rst_n) div4<=0;
16   else if(clear) div4<=0;
17   else div4<=~div4;
18 assign div4_b =!div4;
19 always @(posedge div4 or negedge
20          rst_n or posedge clear)
21   if(!rst_n) div8<=0;
22   else if(clear) div8<=0;
23   else div8<=~div8;
24 assign div8_b=~div8;
25 always @(posedge div8 or negedge
26          rst_n or posedge clear)
27   if(!rst_n) div16<=0;
28   else if(clear) div16<=0;
29   else div16<=~div16;
30 assign div16_b=~div16;
31 assign counter={div16_b , div8_b , div4_b , div2_b};
32 always @(posedge clk or negedge rst_n)
33   if(!rst_n) Y<=0;
34   else if(counter==11)
35        Y<=1;
36   else Y<=0;
37 always @(div16_b or div8_b or div4_b or div2_b)
38   if(counter==12)
39     clear=1;
40   else clear=0;
41 endmodule
```

The RTL simulation derives the waveform in Figure 6.28.

However, the clear signal is a combinational output which may have glitches causing errors in the clear function. It's better to change it to a registered output, as shown below. Two places have been modified: 1. The output Y advances 1 clock cycle; however, its period is still 13. 2. The clear signal is a registered output by simply latching Y at the falling edge of clk. Consequently, there is no glitches on the clear signal. Notably, mixing posedge and negedge of clocks in sequential circuits is not encouraged, and it may be problematic for chip testing and should be carefully treated.

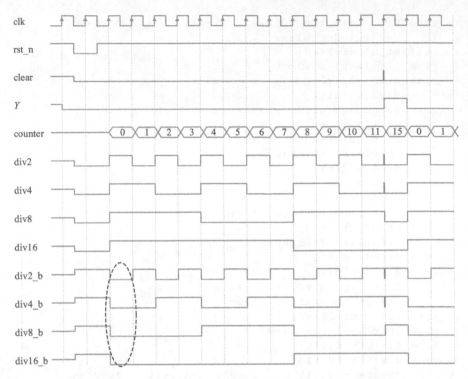

Figure 6.28: Asynchronous count-up counter counts 13 cycles cyclically.

```verilog
// Asynchronous counter: period of 13
module CNT_ASYNC_CLK_DIV13(clk,rst_n,Y);
input clk, rst_n;  output Y;
reg div2, div4, div8, div16, Y, clear;
wire div2_b, div4_b, div8_b, div16_b;
wire [3:0] counter;
always @(posedge clk or negedge rst_n
        or posedge clear)
  if(!rst_n) div2<=0;
  else if(clear) div2<=0;
  else div2<=~div2;
assign div2_b=!div2;
always @(posedge div2 or negedge
        rst_n or posedge clear)
  if(!rst_n) div4<=0;
  else if(clear) div4<=0;
  else div4<=~div4;
assign div4_b =!div4;
```

```
19 always @(posedge div4 or negedge
20         rst_n or posedge clear)
21   if(!rst_n) div8<=0;
22   else if(clear) div8<=0;
23   else div8<=~div8;
24 assign div8_b=~div8;
25 always @(posedge div8 or negedge
26         rst_n or posedge clear)
27   if(!rst_n) div16<=0;
28   else if(clear) div16<=0;
29   else div16<=~div16;
30 assign div16_b=~div16;
31 assign counter={div16_b , div8_b , div4_b , div2_b};
32 always @(posedge clk or negedge rst_n)
33   if(!rst_n) Y<=0;
34   else if(counter==10)
35       Y<=1;
36   else Y<=0;
37 always @(negedge clk or negedge rst_n)
38   if(!rst_n) clear<=0;
39   else clear<=Y;
40 endmodule
```

The RTL simulation derives the waveform in Figure 6.29.

6.4.6   FIFO

As shown in Figure 6.30, the first-in-first-out (FIFO) buffer can be used to store elements (or data) when the service is temporarily unavailable. One new element can arrive at a time, and one element can be served and then depart at a time as well. The terms FIFO buffer and queue are interchangeable. FIFO is a common term in hardware, while queue is more common in most programming languages. Queue and stack terms refer to FIFO and last-in-first-out (LIFO) buffers, respectively.

FIFO finds its applications in many areas of hardware design, such as queue or synchronizer. A FIFO is typically implemented using a circular buffer structure, as shown below.

We want to design a 10×8 FIFO whose memory is realized using flip-flops. The I/O interface of the FIFO is presented in Table 6.7. There are a read port and a write port.

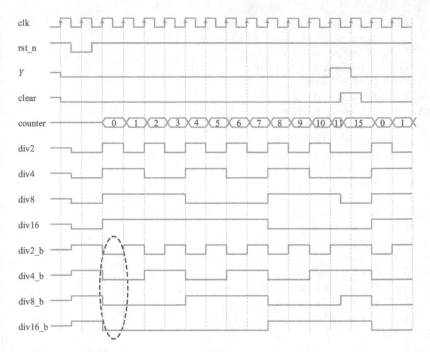

Figure 6.29: Asynchronous count-up counter counts 13 cycles cyclically without glitches on the clear signal.

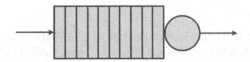

Figure 6.30: FIFO buffer with a depth of 10 elements.

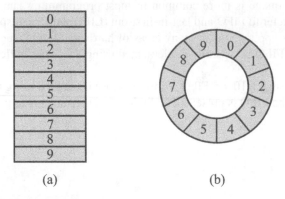

Figure 6.31: FIFO memory with a depth (or address space) of 10 elements: (a) physical structure and (b) logical circular buffer structure.

Table 6.7: I/O interface.

Signal name	I/O	Description
clk	I	System clock
rst_n	I	Active-low reset signal
fifo_full	O	FIFO full indication
fifo_wr	I	FIFO write enable of write port
fifo_wdata	I	FIFO write data of write port
fifo_notempty	O	FIFO non-empty indication
fifo_rd	I	FIFO read enable of read port
fifo_rdata	O	FIFO read data of read port

As presented in Figure 6.32, the FIFO write (or read) pointer, wr_ptr (or rd_ptr), is the address a new element will be written (or read). Besides read pointer, rd_ptr, and write pointer, wr_ptr, the queue length is counted by queue_length so that all entries of the fifo memory can be fully utilized.

As shown below, the FIFO buffer is a parameterized design. The parameter DEPTH_BITS is the ceiling function of the $\log_2$(DEPTH) defined by the macro, CLOG2, in Chapter 3, where $\log_2(x)$ denotes the logarithm to the base 2 of x. When the FIFO write (or read) enable, fifo_wr (or fifo_rd), is asserted, an element is written (or read) into (or from) the fifo memory indexed by the wr_ptr (or rd_ptr), and the wr_ptr (or rd_ptr) automatically increments. The fifo memory is implemented as a circular buffer. Therefore, when wr_ptr (or rd_ptr) reaches the end of the fifo memory, i.e., 9, it goes back to address 0. When fifo_wr is asserted and fifo_rd is not, the queue_length increments; when fifo_rd is asserted and fifo_wr is not, the queue_length decrements; otherwise, the queue_length keeps its value because, in this situation, either both fifo_wr and fifo_rd are not asserted or both fifo_wr and fifo_rd are asserted.

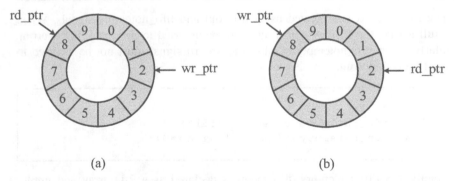

(a)   (b)

Figure 6.32: The FIFO memory is indexed by write and read pointers. (a) When wr_ptr= 2 and rd_ptr= 8, queue_length= 4. (b) When wr_ptr= 8 and rd_ptr= 2, queue_length= 6.

```
1 // FIFO write pointer, read pointer, and queue length
2 parameter DEPTH=10; parameter BITS=8;
3 parameter DEPTH_BITS='CLOG2(DEPTH);
4 reg [DEPTH_BITS-1:0] wr_ptr, rd_ptr;
5 reg [DEPTH_BITS-1:0] queue_length;
6 // FIFO write pointer
7 always @(posedge clk or negedge rst_n)
8   if(!rst_n)
9     wr_ptr <= 0;
10  else if(fifo_wr && wr_ptr==DEPTH-1)
11    wr_ptr <= 0;
12  else if(fifo_wr)
13    wr_ptr <= wr_ptr+1'b1;
14 // FIFO read pointer
15 always @(posedge clk or negedge rst_n)
16  if(!rst_n)
17    rd_ptr <= 0;
18  else if(fifo_rd && rd_ptr==DEPTH-1)
19    rd_ptr <= 0;
20  else if(fifo_rd)
21    rd_ptr <= rd_ptr+1'b1;
22 // FIFO length, so that all entries can be fully utilized
23 always @(posedge clk or negedge rst_n)
24  if(!rst_n)
25    queue_length <= 0;
26  else if(fifo_wr && !fifo_rd)
27    queue_length <= queue_length+1'b1;
28  else if(fifo_rd && !fifo_wr)
29    queue_length <= queue_length-1'b1;
```

The FIFO status is indicated using fifo_full and fifo_notempty signals. When fifo_full is true, the fifo_wr signal must not be asserted to prevent FIFO overrun. Similarly, when fifo_notempty is false, the fifo_rd signal must not be asserted to prevent FIFO underrun.

```
1 // FIFO status
2 assign fifo_full=queue_length==DEPTH;
3 assign fifo_notempty=~(queue_length==0);
```

Finally, the FIFO memory, fifo_mem, is declared as a 2-D array and implemented using flip-flops. At rising edge of clk, if fifo_wr is asserted, the write data, fifo_wdata, is written into fifo_mem indexed by the write pointer, wr_ptr. The read data, fifo_rdata, is output through a combinational circuit of multiplexer indexed by the read pointer, rd_ptr.

```
1// FIFO write port and read port
2reg [BITS-1:0] fifo_rdata;
3reg [BITS-1:0] fifo_mem[0:DEPTH-1];
4// FIFO controller
5// FIFO write operation
6always @(posedge clk)
7  if(fifo_wr) fifo_mem[wr_ptr] <= fifo_wdata;
8// FIFO read operation
9always @(*)
10  fifo_rdata=fifo_mem[rd_ptr];
```

Another popular FIFO controller is realized using only read and write point-ers without the queue_length counter. When the FIFO is full, wr_ptr and rd_ptr are the same. Therefore, anther way to detect the FIFO full status is to see if wr_ptr==rd_ptr. However, when the FIFO is empty, wr_ptr and rd_ptr are also the same. To differentiate the FIFO full status from the FIFO empty status, the FIFO full is asserted when the next write pointer equals the current read pointer. That is, the FIFO full is asserted when rd_ptr==wr_ptr+1 or when rd_ptr is 0 and wr_ptr is 9 (end of the physical structure). In the sequel, doing so intends to leave one element unoccupied, and a buffer space is wasted.

6.4.7 PROBLEMS WHEN INTERACTING WITH SIGNALS FROM DIFFERENT PROCEDURAL BLOCKS

The Verilog HDL is used to model concurrent hardware components. Therefore, it is essential that the users can understand what execution order is guaranteed and what else are indeterministic (not specified by IEEE standard). The Verilog event queue is logistically separated into five sequential regions.

- Active events: events that occur at the same simulation time can be pro-cessed in any order. For example, the blocking and continuous assignments, and evaluation of non-blocking assignments.
- Inactive events: events that occur at the same simulation time but should be processed after all active events have been processed. For example, an explicit zero-delay assignment, such as #0 y = x, will be processed after all active events at the same simulation time are processed.
- Non-blocking assign update events: events that have been evaluated at some (previous) simulation time but should be assigned after all active and inactive events have been processed. For example, the assignment of non-blocking assignment statements.
- Monitor events: events that shall be processed after all active, inactive, and non-blocking assign update events have been processed. For example, the $monitor and $strobe system tasks.
- Future events: events that occur at some future simulation time. Future events are divided into future inactive and future non-blocking assign up-date events.

When an event is performed, it may trigger additional events. For example, a non-blocking assign update or an active event can trigger an active event (described using an always block or continuous assignment). Activity between non-blocking assign update (or active) events and active events at the current simulation time continues to iterate until all events in the event queue have been executed.

Remember that a non-blocking assignment is performed in two steps. First, the expression of right-hand-side variables is evaluated and stored in a temporary storage. Second, the result of temporary storage is assigned to the left-hand-side variable, which will be scheduled as a non-blocking assign update or future non-blocking assign update event that is written into its corresponding queue region depending on the delay control.

The freedom to choose an arbitrary order of processing active events is the core source of nondeterminism in Verilog simulators. For example, if the input x for the state machine of the traditional binary encoding in Section 6.4.4.2 is generated from an initial block presented below.

```
1 initial begin
2   #1 wait(!rst_n); // Wait for assertion of reset
3   wait(rst_n); // Wait for de-assertion of reset
4   @(posedge clk) x=1; // Assert x for one cycle
5   @(posedge clk) x=0;
6 end
```

However, the race condition might occur leading to different results when the order of statement execution, or specifically, the order of active events, is changed. In Figure 6.33, we assume that, at the third rising edge of clk, three active events may be scheduled by the Verilog simulator using the sequence: $x = 1$, update state_ns due to change of x, and evaluation of state_cs. That is, first, 1 will be assigned to x; then the always block of the state machine for determining its (combinational) next state will be triggered (causing state_ns to be state b), finally, state b will be assigned to temporary storage of the non-blocking assignment of state_cs.

After processing active events, the non-blocking assign update event causes state_cs to be state b of temporary storage. The change of state_cs causes an additional active event that triggers the update of state_ns due to change of state_cs, which causes state_ns to become state d when x is 1. Similar events happen at the fourth edge of clk except that an additional active event is not triggered because state_cs does not change its value after the non-blocking assign update event.

It's apparent that the interaction between signals generated by blocking (initial blocks in testbench) and non-blocking (always blocks triggered by posedge clk in RTL codes) assignments may produce a wrong result, as displayed in Figure 6.33. To solve the race condition, we can either assign the primary input x at a time instance other than clock edges or try to use non-blocking assignments in testbench.

The following example assigns the primary input x at a time instance of 1 time unit after the clock edges.

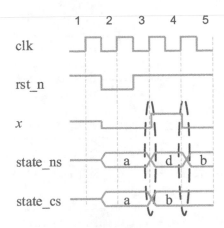

Figure 6.33: Wrong waveform due to the race condition.

```
1 initial begin
2   #1 wait(!rst_n); // Wait for assertion of reset
3   wait(rst_n); // Wait for de-assertion of reset
4   @(posedge clk) #1 x=1; // Assert x for one cycle
5   @(posedge clk) #1 x=0;
6 end
```

The following example produces input *x* using non-blocking assignments.

```
1 initial begin
2   #1 wait(!rst_n); // Wait for assertion of reset
3   wait(rst_n); // Wait for de-assertion of reset
4   @(posedge clk) x<=1; // Assert x for one cycle
5   @(posedge clk) x<=0;
6 end
```

Either way produces the correct waveform presented in Figure 6.34.

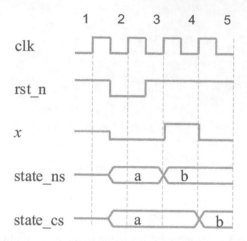

Figure 6.34: Correct waveform without the race condition.

6.5   FURTHER READING

- David Money Harris and Sarah L. Harris, *Digital design and computer architecture*, 2nd Ed., Morgan Kaufmann, 2013.
- Donald E. Thomas and Philip R. Moorby, *The Verilog hardware description language*, 5th Ed., Kluwer Academic Publishers, 2002.
- John F. Wakerly, *Digital design: principles and practices*, 5th Ed., Prentice Hall, 2018.
- John Michael Williams, *Digital VLSI design with Verilog: a textbook from Silicon Valley Polytechnic Institute*, 2nd Ed., Springer, 2014.
- Joseph Cavanagh, *Computer arithmetic and Verilog HDL fundamentals*, CRC Press, 2010.
- M. Morris Mano and Michael D. Ciletti, *Digital design*, 4th Ed., Prentice Hall, 2006.
- Michael D. Ciletti, *Advanced digital design with the Verilog HDL*, 2nd Ed., Prentice Hall, 2010.
- Peter J. Ashenden, *Digital design: an embedded systems approach using Verilog*, Morgan Kaufmann Publishers, 2007.
- Samir Palnitkar, *Verilog HDL: a guide to digital design and synthesis, 2nd Ed.*, Pearson, 2011.
- Stephen Brown and Zvonko Vranesic, *Fundamentals of digital logic with Verilog design*, McGraw-Hill, 2002.
- Vaibbhav Taraate, *Digital logic design using Verilog: coding and RTL synthesis*, Springer, 2016.
- William J. Dally and R. Curtis Harting, *Digital design: a systems approach*, Cambridge University Press, 2012.
- Zainalabedin Navabi, *Verilog digital system design: RT level synthesis, testbench, and verification*, McGraw-Hill, 2005.

PROBLEMS

1. Redesign the bubble sorting problem using only one processing element (PE), i.e., comparison-and-swap unit, and a suitable state machine.

   a. Plot datapath of your architecture.
   b. Specify the critical path in your design.
   c. Write down your complete RTL codes (including FSM) and verify it. The bit width is programmable using the parameterized design and it is assumed to be 3 bits.

2. Design a state machine that can detect the bit sequence "1011". For example, if input is "0011_1011_0110", the output is "0000_0001_0010".

3. Plot the architecture of the following RTL codes.

```
1 wire a, b, c;
2 reg d, e, f;
3 always @(posedge clk) begin
4   d<=a^b;
5   e<=c|d;
6   f<=d&e;
7 end
```

4. Write down the RTL codes for the 1-bit D-FF with asynchronous set.
5. Write down the RTL codes for the 1-bit D-FF with synchronous set.
6. Write down the RTL codes for the 1-bit D-FF with synchronous enable, as shown in Figure 6.35. That is, when enable is true, x is assigned to y.

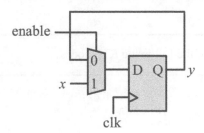

enable

x

clk

y

Figure 6.35: D-FF with synchronous enable.

7. Write down the RTL codes for the 1-bit D-FF with synchronous load, as shown in Figure 6.36. That is, when load_en is true, load_data is assigned to y; otherwise, x is assigned to y.

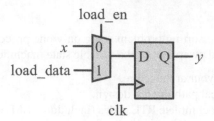

Figure 6.36: D-FF with synchronous load.

8. Change the above 1-bit D-FF to 8-bit D-FFs.
9. Plot the schematics of the following RTL codes.

```
1 module code3(Sel, A, B1, B2);
2 input Sel; input [1:0] A;
3 output [1:0] B1, B2; reg [1:0] B1, B2;
4 always @(Sel or A)
5   if(Sel)
6     if(A==1) begin
7       B1=0; B2=0;
8     end
9     else begin
10        B1=1; B2=1;
11      end
12   else begin
13     B1=2; B2=2;
14   end
15 endmodule
```

10. Plot the schematics of the following RTL codes.

```
1 module code4(Sel, A, B1, B2);
2 input Sel; input [1:0] A;
3 output [1:0] B1, B2;
4 reg [1:0] B1, B2;
5 always @(Sel or A)
6   if(Sel)
7     if(A==1) begin
8       B1=0; B2=0;
9     end
10     else
11        B1=1;
12   else begin
13     B1=2; B2=2;
```

```
14  end
15 endmodule
```

11. Plot the schematic of the following RTL codes.

```
1 module code2(Sel, A, B1, B2);
2 input Sel; input [1:0] A;
3 output [1:0] B1, B2;
4 reg [1:0] B1, B2;
5 always @(Sel or A)
6   if(Sel)
7     if(A==1) begin
8       B1=0;
9       B2=0;
10    end
11    else begin
12      B1=1;
13      B2=1;
14    end
15 endmodule
```

12. Plot the schematic of the following RTL codes.

```
1 module code1(Sel, A, B1, B2);
2 input Sel; input [1:0] A;
3 output [1:0] B1, B2;
4 reg [1:0] B1, B2;
5 always @(Sel or A) begin
6   if(Sel) begin
7     if(A==1) begin
8       B1=0; B2=0;
9     end
10    else B1=1;
11  end
12 end
13 endmodule
```

13. Redesign the synchronous counter.

   a. With the load function as shown below, which has a lower priority than Reset but higher than Enable.

```
1 if (Load)
2   Out=Data_In;
```

b. With the control pin, up_down, to control the counter to count up or count down.

c. With the control pin, count_mode, to control the counter to count with an increment or decrement by 1 or 2.

14. Redesign the asynchronous count-down counter as count-up counter.

15. Redesign the asynchronous count-up counter from 0 to 12, such that the clear signal is a registered output.

16. A counter can be used for the timer. Please use a 1 MHz clock to generate a pulse every 1 ms.

17. Design a pseudo-random binary sequence (PRBS) generator, as shown in Figure 6.37.

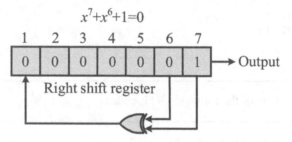

Figure 6.37: A 7-bit **PRBS** sequence generator.

18. Design a left- or right-shift 8-bit register (controlled by signal left_shift_en and right_shift_en) that can be loaded a 8-bit value by port, load_value[7:0] (loaded and enabled by load_en).

19. Clock divider problem: it is simple to derive a divide-by-N clock with non 50% duty cycle, where N is an integer. If N is an even number, it is intuitive to obtain the derived clock by using the ripple clock. Since clock is a very important signal, you should guarantee that the derived clock is glitch-free.

    a. Design the clock divider for $N = 2$ using ripple and non-ripple clocks.

    b. Design the clock divider for $N = 5$ using ripple and non-ripple clock. Notice that, for ripple clock, the clear signal should be the flip-flop output, i.e., glitch-free.

    c. Design the clock divider for $N = 1.5$ using non-ripple clock. A fractional clock divider, for $N = 1.5, 2.5, 3.5$, etc., is not supposed to be obtained directly using the output of a single flip-flop. In contrast, you can only obtain it using a combinational circuit with inputs from several flip-flops. The duty cycle of derived clock needs not be 50%. Hint: You can use the combination of two counters, each having two bits and counting with sequence 2'b00, 2'b01,

2'b11, 2'b00, 2'b01,..., etc., i.e., they count three times and then reset. The intent of the sequence is to avoid unnecessary glitch. These two counters are triggered by positive edge and negative edge of clock, respectively.

20. Design a register file with 32 64-bit registers using flip-flops with 4 read ports and 2 write ports.

21. Design the FIFO without the queue_length indicator. In this design, use the rd_ptr and wr_ptr to determine the fifo_full and fifo_notempty statuses. To accurately indicate the status of queue, an entry of the FIFO could be wasted. What are the pros and cons of this design compared to that using the queue_length indicator?

22. Design the stack by modifying the FIFO module. A stack has only a write pointer, wr_ptr. Its read pointer is implicitly pointed to by wr_ptr−1.

23. A flip-flop has a clock-to-Q delay, t_{CQ}, of 1-ns delay. What is the delay in a 10-bit binary ripple counter that uses this type of flip-flop? What is the maximum frequency the counter can operate on?

24. a. Design a counter with the following repeated binary sequence: 0, 1, 2, 3, 4, 5.

    b. Design a counter with the following repeated binary sequence: 0, 1, 4, 6.

    c. Design a 8-bit counter with the following repeated binary sequence: 1, 2, 1, 4, 1, 8, 1, 16, 1, 32, 1, 64, 1, 128.

25. Write a testbench to verify the 10-bit ripple counter.

26. Redesign the edge-triggered flip-flop using the NOR-gate implementation.

27. Please redesign the clock divider divided by 13 such that the clear signal is a registered output.

28. Write a testbench to verify the 4-bit shift register.

29. We can use two D-latches to establish a flip-flop, as shown in Figure 6.38. We call it master-slave D flip-flop. The first latch, called the master latch, passes input d to x (the master is transparent) and output q is not affected by x when clk is low. When clk goes high, d is sampled to x which is then passed to output q (the slave is transparent). When clk goes low, x is sampled to q. The slave holds the value of q when the clock is low.

    The gate-level schematic of a master-slave D flip-flop is shown in Figure 6.39.

    a. Verify its functionality using the waveform in Figure 6.38(b).

    b. The t_S (setup time) is just the setup time of the master latch. Determine the rising setup time of flip-flop.

    c. For correct operation of the master-slave flip-flop, it is critical that the output of the master does not change until t_H (hold time) after the slave clock falls. Determine the hold time of flip-flop.

    d. Determine its rising clock-to-Q delay time, t_{CQ}.

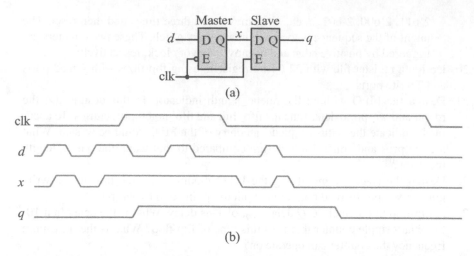

(a)

(b)

Figure 6.38: A master-slave D flip-flop is constructed from two latches.

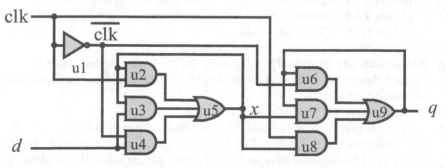

Figure 6.39: The gate-level schematic of a master-slave D flip-flop.

30. Repeat the above problem for the master-slave flip-flop shown in Figure 6.40.

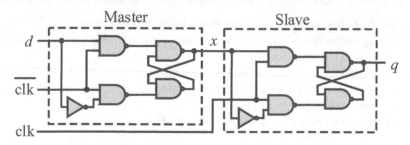

Figure 6.40: Another master-slave D flip-flop.

31. Similar to the previous problem, we can calculate the timing constraints of the CMOS master-slave flip-flop constructed from two CMOS latches, as shown in

Figure 6.41. The CMOS master-slave flip-flop can be derived by substituting the CMOS D-latch in Figure 6.7(b) into the master-slave flip-flop in Figure 6.14.

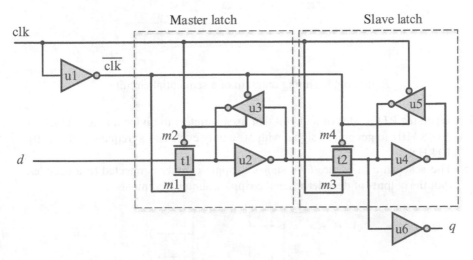

Figure 6.41: A CMOS master-slave flip-flop constructed from two CMOS latches.

    a. Determine its rising setup time.
    b. Determine its hold time.
    c. Determine its rising clock-to-Q delay time.
32. Complete the timing diagram, showing the operation of a rising-edge triggered D flip-flop.

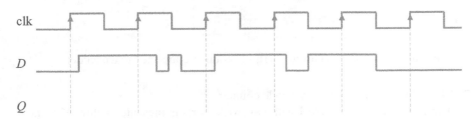

Figure 6.42: Timing diagram of a D flip-flop.

33. Develop a sequential circuit with a single data input D and a single output Q. The output is high when the input value in the current clock cycle is different from the input value in the previous clock cycle, as shown in Figure 6.43.
34. Write the RTL codes of a circuit for a free-running counter that counts 30 clock cycles and produce a control signal that is 1 during every 4th, 18th, and 21th cycle.

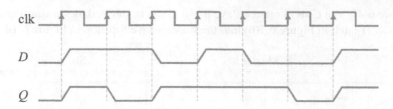

Figure 6.43: Timing diagram of a sequential circuit.

35. Write the RTL codes of a circuit that uses counters to divide a master clock of 20.48 MHz to generate a signal with 50% duty cycle and a frequency of exactly 10 kHz.

36. The schematic in Figure 6.44 shows a ripple counter connected to a decoder. Plot the outputs of decoder when the ripple counter increments.

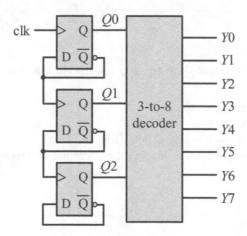

Figure 6.44: An (asynchronous) ripple counter connected to a decoder.

37. Please implement a 4-bit Gray code counter.

38. The RTL code of an SRAM with two write ports is presented below. Plot the circuit architecture that it describes.

```
1 always @(wen1 or wen2 or addr1 or
2           addr2 or din1 or din2)
3 begin
4   if(wen1) mem[addr1]<=din1;
5   if(wen2) mem[addr2]<=din2;
6 end
```

39. Write the Verilog codes of the eight-tap FIR filter in Example 4.7.

7 Digital System Designs

Several important system-level hardware design issues, including the pipelining and parallelism techniques, FIFO and its use for buffering data, arbiter, interconnect, and memory system, will be presented in this chapter. To derive an efficient and robust design, we suggest that readers should plot the architecture and timing diagrams of the designs before writing their RTL codes. Several examples following this guideline are exemplified, such as complex multiplier, two additions, and FIR filter. The architectural diagram lets you understand what components are required in the design, and the timing diagram governs the operating sequence of the design and, if necessary, enables you to fine tune the system performance. Finally, a digital design of Huffman encoding is illustrated from the algorithm design aspect to its RTL code.

7.1 SYSTEM-LEVEL DESIGN: MOVING FROM THE VIRTUAL TO THE REAL

A complete system usually consists of hardware and software. For a system with hardware/software co-design, once functionality has been categorized as either hardware or software, development for each can proceed concurrently, as shown in Figure 7.1.

A general representation of a part of digital hardware design can be seen in Figure 7.2. Sequential circuits contain memory elements. The outputs can depend on inputs, sequential circuits, or both.

A digital system is a sequential logic system constructed with sequential and combinational logic gates. Because of its importance and complexity, it is most comprehensively written using the RTL. The RTL is commonly used to represent a combination of dataflow modeling and behavioral modeling. There are three kinds of RTL descriptions: behavioral (always block), dataflow, and structural. Verilog is a hardware description language which supports both high-level RTL descriptions using behavioral (always block) and dataflow constructs and low-level RTL descriptions which contain the structural construct. Different RTL descriptions can also be mixed and combined when useful or necessary.

In the following, we will emphasize the relation between Verilog constructs and their logic gate representation because, to be really proficient in RTL design, it is critical that the designer views the problems and issues from the perspective of hardware (circuit centric) rather than with a primary focus on software (Verilog centric). RTL describes how data are transformed as they are passed from one register to another. The transformation of the data is performed by the combinational logic that exists between the registers. When describing combinational logic using always blocks, it is crucial that sensitivity lists are complete. Continuous assignments are a valid way of describing designs for RTL synthesis tools. If you want to design a workable circuit

DOI: 10.1201/9781003187196-7

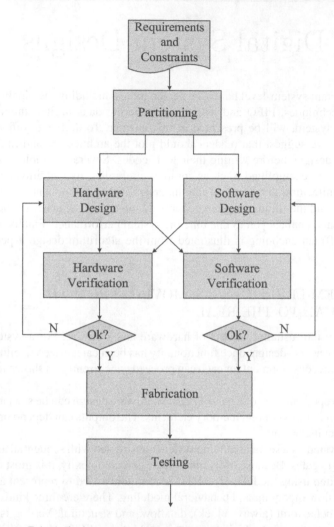

Figure 7.1: A design methodology for hardware/software co-design.

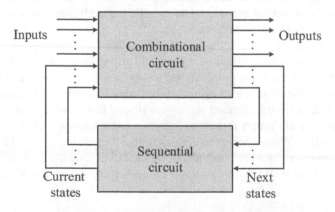

Figure 7.2: Synchronous digital design.

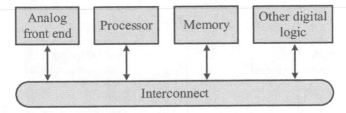

Figure 7.3: A modern digital system. An abstract interconnect provides connections between a number of clients.

that meets your specifications, you must also guarantee the timing of your circuits. RTL is ideal for this because its descriptions are a natural fit for the type of pipeline design that inserts additional registers into a critical path to reduce its depth.

Module instances are also examples of synthesizable RTL statements. However, one reason for using synthesis technology is to take advantage of its ability to describe the design at a higher level of abstraction than is possible when using a collection of module instances or low-level binary operators in a continuous assignment. The most satisfactory approach is to describe what the design does and trust the synthesis tool to make all of the correct decisions regarding how the design is implemented. This is the first step on the road to successful high-level design.

As mentioned, RTL design contains behavioral (always block), dataflow (continuous assignment), and structural descriptions. Ideally, the output of a system can be completely specified using a state table. However, the state table for a large digital system can become huge and unwieldy due to the enormous number of potential states of current and previous inputs. To overcome this problem, digital systems are usually designed using a modular approach: the system is partitioned into modular subsystems, as shown in Figure 7.3, each of which performs some function. Data are then exchanged using an interconnect, such as a bus. The problem remains to partition the system at a level in which the design becomes manageable. Once it has been successfully done, the rest of the task becomes much simpler and relatively straightforward. Establishing a stable, workable system-level design is one of the most interesting and challenging aspects of digital design.

The digital design process begins with a specification, as shown in Figure 7.4. Major steps are listed and described below.

- **Specification**: the most important step for designing a system is defining and clearly specifying what you are going to build.
- **Partitioning**: once the system has been specified, it must be divided into manageable subsystems or modules. This can be thought of as a divide-and-conquer process in which a potentially overwhelmingly large and complex overall system is divided into manageable subsystems which can then be designed separately. As can easily be imagined, a lot can go wrong if any errors are made at this point. To ensure that things go smoothly, it is particularly important that the interfaces between subsystems be described in ade-

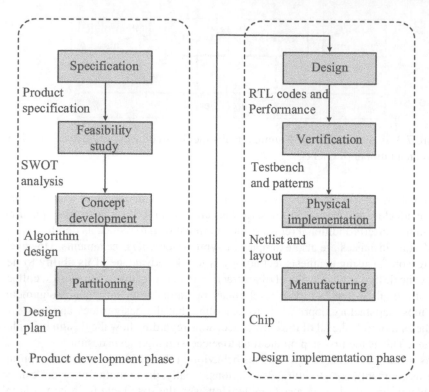

Figure 7.4: Design process.

quate detail. When interface specifications are clearly written, it is possible for individual modules to be developed and verified independently. The interface should allow modules to be modified without adversely affecting the overall system.

- **Design**
  - **Timing design**: early in the design of a system, it is important to describe the timing and sequencing of operations. In particular, as data flow between modules, the sequencing of which module executes a particular task in a specific cycle must be precisely established to ensure that the required data come together at the correct place and time. This timing design also drives the performance tuning step described below.
  - **Module design**: once the above steps have been worked out, the individual modules can be designed and verified independently. Often, the exact performance and timing (e.g., throughput, latency, or pipeline depth) of a module cannot be known exactly until after the module design is complete. A good system design is one in which the partitioned modules can be integrated into a working system without excessive reworking and debugging.

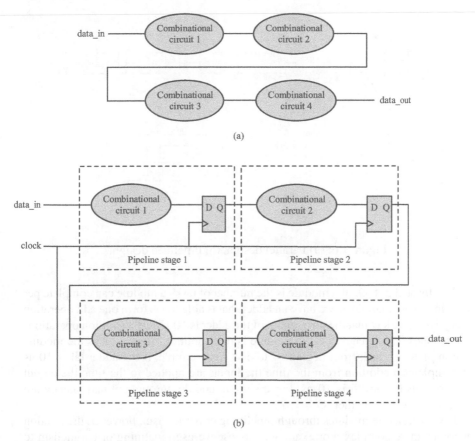

Figure 7.5: (a) A combinational circuit composed of 4 subcircuits. (b) Four pipeline stages containing each subcircuit.

- **Performance tuning**: once the performance of each module has been characterized (or at least estimated), the system can be analyzed to see if it meets its performance specification. If a system falls short of a performance goal, the performance might be tuned by increasing parallelism.

7.1.1 PIPELINED DESIGN

Pipeline in a digital system somewhat resembles an assembly line for a process such as putting together a car. An example is shown in Figure 7.5. In Figure 7.5(a), an overall task (a combinational circuit) is broken into 4 subtasks (4 combinational circuits). In Figure 7.5(b), sequential circuits are added after each subcircuits. A sequential circuit is similar to the station along an assembly line. We then have a separate unit, called a pipeline stage, which performs each subtask in Figure 7.5(b). The stages are tied together in a linear manner so that the output of each unit becomes the input of the subsequent unit similar to stations along an assembly line.

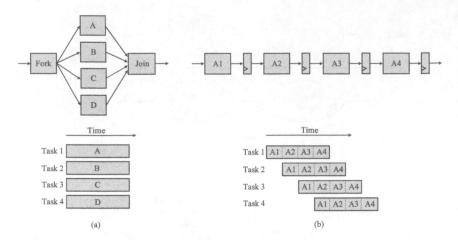

Figure 7.6: (a) Parallel design. (b) Pipelined design.

The throughput, Θ, of a module is the number of tasks a module can complete per unit time. For example, if we have an adder that is able to perform one add operation every 10 ns, we say that the throughput of the adder is 100 MOPS (million operations per second). The latency, T, of a module is the amount of time it takes the module to complete one task from beginning to end. For example, if the adder takes 10 ns to complete an addition from the time the inputs are applied to the time the output is stable, its latency T is 10 ns. For a simple module, throughput and latency are reciprocals of one another: $\Theta = 1/T$.

If we accelerate modules through pipelining or parallelism, however, the relation becomes more complex. For example, suppose we use pipelining or parallelism to increase the throughput of a module, in which $T = 10$ ns, $\Theta = 100$ MOPS, by a factor of 4. If we are using a parallel design, we could build four copies of our module, as shown in Figure 7.6(a). Modules A–D are identical copies of our original module. The fork block distributes tasks to the four modules, and the join block combines the outcomes. Using such a structure, we can start four tasks in parallel. Our latency is still $T = 10$ ns because it still takes 10 ns to complete one task. Our throughput, however, has been increased to $\Theta = 400$ MOPS since we are able to solve four tasks every 10 ns.

An alternative method of increasing throughput is to pipeline a single copy of the module, as shown in Figure 7.6(b). Here, we have taken a single module, A, and divided it into four subtasks, A1, ..., A4. For this example, we assume that we are able to partition the tasks evenly so that the delay of each of the four submodules, Ai, $i = 1,2,3,4$, is $T_{Ai} = 2.5$ ns. When pipeline registers are between stages, they hold the result of the preceding submodule, freeing that submodule to begin working on the next task. Thus, as shown, this pipeline can operate on four tasks at once in a staggered fashion. As soon as submodule A1 finishes work on problem Task1, it starts working on Task2, while Task2 continues work on Task1. Each task continues

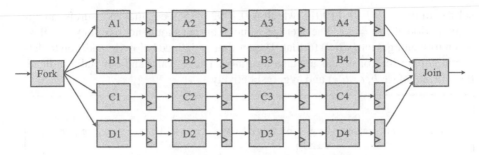

Figure 7.7: A design combining parallelism and pipelining techniques.

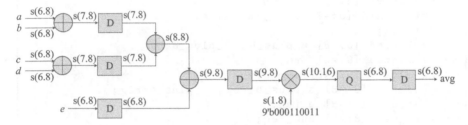

Figure 7.8: Pipelined design for computing the average value of five inputs, a, b, c, d, and e.

down the pipeline, advancing one stage each clock cycle, until it is completed by module A4. If we ignore register overhead, our latency is still $T = 2.5$ ns $\times$ 4 stages $=$ 10 ns and our throughput has been increased to 400 MOPS. The system completes a task every 2.5 ns.

The throughput can be further enhanced by combining the parallelism and pipelining techniques, as shown below. Independent tasks can be fed into modules A, B, C, and D in every clock cycle. The submodules A_i, B_i, C_i, and D_i, $i = 1, 2, 3, 4$, complete each subtask in one cycle. Hence, the overall throughput can now achieve $4 \times 400 = 1600$ MOPS.

Example 7.1. Design a Verilog model for a pipelined circuit that computes the average value of five inputs, a, b, c, d, and e, as that shown in Figure 7.8. The pipeline consists of three stages. The first stage separately adds values of a and b, and c and d and then register the results. Because the value of e must also be registered, the second stage adds the stored value of e and the sums calculated in the first stage. Finally, in the third stage the results are divided by 5. The inputs and output are all signed numbers with fixed-point format s(6.8). Please design the circuit such that there is no overflow in the intermediate results. For your convenience, the fixed-point number formats are also presented in the figure, where block Q quantizes a number using the truncation and D denotes the D-type flip-flop.

Solution: Since a multiplication is generally simpler than division, we express the division by 5 as a multiplication by 1/5 using approximately the binary fixed-point s(1.8) number as 9'b000110011, which is 0.19921875 in decimal and, surely, an approximation of $1/5 = 0.2$. The average value of output should not have any overflow when truncating it into s(6.8) format. The module is defined below. In addition to datapath, simple control signals are also designed. The in_valid and out_valid indicate the validity of (a, b, c, d, e) and avg, respectively.

```verilog
1 // A module for computing average value of five inputs
2 module avg_value(avg, out_valid, in_valid, a, b, c, d, e,
3                  clk);
4 output signed [5:-8] avg;
5 output out_valid;
6 input in_valid;
7 input signed [5:-8] a, b, c, d, e;
8 input clk;
9 wire signed [6:-8] a_plus_b, c_plus_d;
10 wire signed [8:-8] sum;
11 wire signed [9:-16] sum_div_5;
12 reg signed [6:-8] a_plus_b_reg, c_plus_d_reg;
13 reg signed [5:-8] e_reg;
14 reg signed [8:-8] sum_reg;
15 reg signed [5:-8] avg;
16 reg in_valid_r, in_valid_rr, in_valid_rrr;
17 parameter const_1over5=9'b000110011;
18 assign a_plus_b=a+b;
19 assign c_plus_d=c+d;
20 assign sum=a_plus_b_reg+c_plus_d_reg+e_reg;
21 assign sum_div_5=sum_reg*const_1over5;
22 assign out_valid=in_valid_rrr;
23 always @(posedge clk) begin // Pipelining in_valid
24   in_valid_r<=in_valid;
25   in_valid_rr<=in_valid_r;
26   in_valid_rrr<=in_valid_rr;
27 end
28 always @(posedge clk)
29   if(in_valid) begin // Pipeline register 1
30     a_plus_b_reg<=a_plus_b;
31     c_plus_d_reg<=c_plus_d;
32     e_reg<=e;
33   end
34 always @(posedge clk)
35   if(in_valid_r)
36     sum_reg<=sum; // Pipeline register 2
37 always @(posedge clk)
38   if(in_valid_rr) // Pipeline register 3
39     avg <= sum_div_5[5:-8];
40 endmodule
```

□

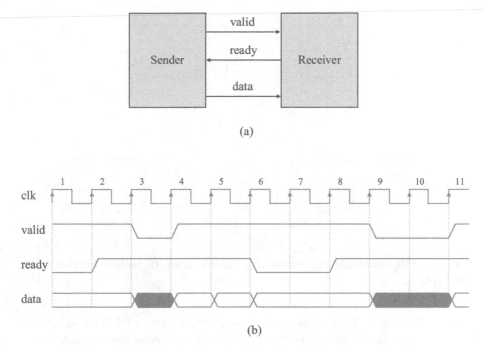

(a)

(b)

Figure 7.9: (a) Interface for the flow-controlled timing. (b) Timing diagram.

7.1.2   FIFO FOR BUFFERING DATA

The interfaces between modules can be either always-valid or flow-controlled. Flow-controlled timing uses a handshaking mechanism through signals, usually called "valid" and "ready", to sequence the transfer of data over the interface, as shown in Figure 7.9. As the names imply, a datum is passed between two modules only when the sender indicates that the datum is "valid" and the receiver indicates that it is "ready" to receive it. Once the transfer has been made, the process moves on to the next one. If either ready or valid signal is not asserted, no transfer takes place. Therefore, the transfer will stop if the receiver is busy or there is no new data available for the receiver.

The delay (or execution time) of a pipeline stage needs not always be constant. However, the upstream stages will be stalled each time a downstream stage takes an excessive amount of time to process one subtask, as shown in Figure 7.10(a). By inserting FIFO buffers between pipelined stages, as shown in Figure 7.10(b), variation in throughput can be eliminated. An upstream pipelined stage inserts results into the tail of the queue unless it is full, whereas the downstream stage takes a subtask instance from the head of the queue unless it is empty. The depth of FIFO depends on the variation in the execution time of the downstream stage. This can achieve a throughput dependent only on the average throughput of each stage. Specifically, the overall throughput can achieve the ideal one, i.e., the minimum average throughput among all stages.

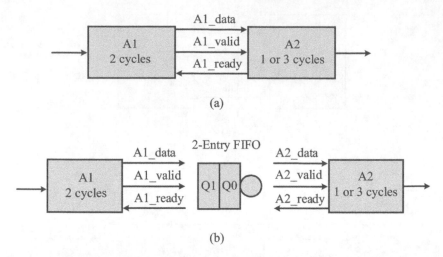

(a)

(b)

Figure 7.10: Pipeline under the condition of variable delay: (a) without FIFO and (b) with FIFO.

The scheduling and timing diagram of the pipeline without FIFO are shown in Figures 7.11(a) and 7.11(b), respectively. The numbers in parenthesis represent the task identifications (IDs). As displayed, it takes 16 cycles to finish total 6 tasks in this case.

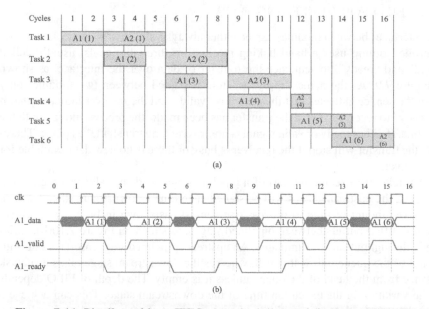

Figure 7.11: Pipeline without FIFO: (a) scheduling and (b) timing diagram.

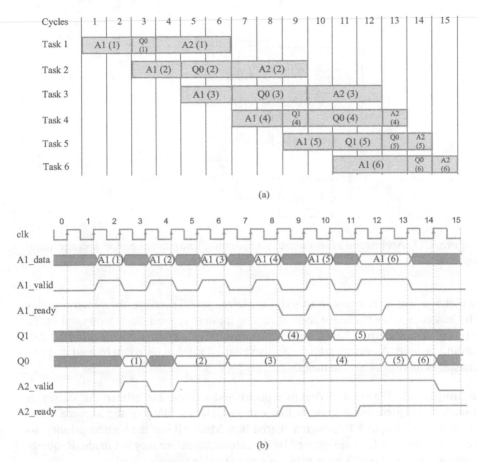

(a)

(b)

Figure 7.12: Pipeline with FIFO: (a) scheduling and (b) timing diagram.

The scheduling and timing diagram of the pipeline with FIFO are shown in Figures 7.12(a) and 7.12(b), respectively. As displayed, the pipeline stage A1 of the pipeline with FIFO has no stalling issues and A2 always has data to process. Besides, A1 and A2 can operate at their full speeds because the FIFO can temporarily buffer data from A1 and provide date to A2 when needed. Hence, the processing proceeds smoothly and the overall time to complete 6 tasks is 15 cycles and reduced.

7.1.3   ARBITER

Sometimes, a resource (bus or slave) may be shared between modules. In such cases, an arbiter is used to prevent more than one master from occupying the resource at any given time. At each resource cycle, if the master needs the resource, it sends a request signal. The arbiter will grant the resource to only one master. A master

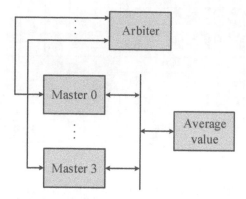

Figure 7.13: Architecture for 4 masters requesting one slave, i.e., the average value module.

which receives no response must wait for a later cycle. Therefore, the arbiter resolves the bus contention whenever more than one masters request the bus ownership. To prevent a master from being starved, a fair arbiter, such as a round-robin arbiter, should be used. A priority arbiter can also be used if it has been determined that one master is more critical than the others.

Example 7.2. We want to design a prioritized round-robin arbiter. As shown in Figure 7.13, there are 4 masters that can request one slave of the average value module in Example 7.1 through a shared bus. Master 0 has the highest priority, so requests from master 0 are granted by the arbiter whenever they are made. Requests from masters 1, 2, and 3 are granted in a round-robin manner.

Solution: The arbiter is implemented using a state machine and designed as described below. At each state, the request of master 0 is checked and given precedence. Remaining requests are examined in a round-robin manner. We assume that the next master can be granted only when the previous master de-asserts its request.

```
1// Arbiter of 4 masters
2// Master 0 has the highest priority.
3module arbiter(gnt, req, clk, rst_n);
4output [3:0] gnt; // Grant
5input [3:0] req; // Request
6input clk;
7input rst_n;
8reg [3:0] gnt;
9reg [2:0] state_ns, state_cs;
10parameter ST_IDLE=3'b000; parameter ST_M0=3'b001;
11parameter ST_M1=3'b011; parameter ST_M2=3'b010;
```

```
12 parameter ST_M3=3'b100;
13 always @(*) begin
14   state_ns=state_cs;
15   case(state_cs)
16   ST_IDLE: state_ns=req[0]?ST_M0:
17             (req[1]?ST_M1:
18             (req[2]?ST_M2:
19             (req[3]?ST_M3:ST_IDLE)));
20   ST_M0: state_ns=~req[0]&req[1]?ST_M1:
21             (~req[0]&req[2]?ST_M2:
22             (~req[0]&req[3]?ST_M3:
23             (req[0]?ST_M0:ST_IDLE)));
24   ST_M1: state_ns=~req[1]&req[0]?ST_M0 :
25             (~req[1]&req[2]?ST_M2:
26             (~req[1]&req[3]?ST_M3:
27             (req[1]?ST_M1:ST_IDLE)));
28   ST_M2: state_ns=~req[2]&req[0]?ST_M0 :
29             (~req[2]&req[3]?ST_M3:
30             (~req[2]&req[1]?ST_M1:
31             (req[2]?ST_M2:ST_IDLE)));
32   ST_M3: state_ns=~req[3]&req[0]?ST_M0 :
33             (~req[3]&req[1]?ST_M1:
34             (~req[3]&req[2]?ST_M2:
35             (req[3]?ST_M3:ST_IDLE)));
36   endcase
37 end
38 always @(posedge clk or posedge reset)
39   if(reset) state_cs<=ST_IDLE;
40   else state_cs<=state_ns;
41 always @(posedge clk or posedge reset)
42   if(reset) gnt<=4'b0000;
43   else case(state_ns)
44         ST_IDLE:gnt<=4'b0000;
45         ST_M0:gnt<=4'b0001;
46         ST_M1:gnt<=4'b0010;
47         ST_M2:gnt<=4'b0100;
48         ST_M3:gnt<=4'b1000;
49       endcase
50 endmodule
```

□

7.1.4 INTERCONNECT

Simple modules are connected with direct point-to-point connections, while a large
and complex system can be more flexibly organized using an interconnect, such as

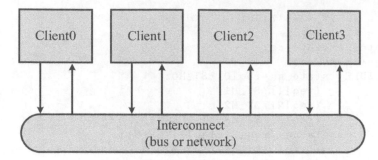

Figure 7.14: An abstract interconnect provides connections between 4 clients. The source client can initiate a transaction or transfer a packet containing the address or identification of the destination client.

a bus or a network, as shown in Figure 7.14. The links may be parallel or serialized. The flow control mechanism is often required to back pressure the clients when a contention occurs. The interconnect may or may not permit multiple simultaneous operations. To achieve a high throughput, an interconnect that supports multiple concurrent transactions is required under the situation without any conflicts.

A transaction may be fulfilled using a packet format, including, at minimum, a destination device address D and a payload P of arbitrary length. Because the interconnect has been addressed, any client i can communicate with any client j while requiring only a single pair of unidirectional links for input and output to each client module. A packet (D, P) sent from i to j, i.e., $D = j$, may result in j sending a response or reply packet (S, Q), i.e., $S = i$, with payload Q back to i. The payload may contain a request type (e.g., read or write), a (memory-mapped) address in D, and data or other arguments for a remote operation.

7.1.4.1   Buses

A bus interconnect, such as the one shown in Figure 7.15, is a general-purpose interconnect which is widely used in applications that have modest performance requirements. We use the term bus to refer to the collection of signals that form the interconnect. A bus has the advantages of simplicity, a broadcast nature, and the ability to serialize and order all transactions. The major disadvantage of a bus is its performance: it can only allow one transaction to be sent at a time. There are two masters and two slaves in the system. The master granted by the arbiter connects to the slave it requests as if they communicate using a point-to-point connection. The signals from the master/slave are selected by the multiplexer u0/u3 and subsequently routed to the slave/master by the demultiplexer u1/u2. If there is only a slave, the demultiplexer u1 and the multiplexer u3 might be saved.

A bus interface can convert the module's valid-ready flow control to bus arbitration, as shown in Figure 7.16, where detailed interface signals are displayed. Each module's connection to the interface may include device address, data, and read-

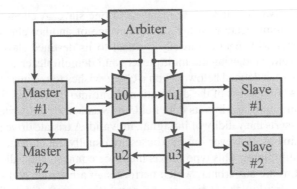

Figure 7.15: Bus constructed by multiplexers and demultiplexers.

/write signals. In Figure 7.16, we assume that there are 4 clients. Notably, the demultiplexers for s_rw, s_wdata0,..., s_wdata3, and m_rdata0,..., m_rdata3 can be saved because s_rw and s_wdata for a destined slave can be indicated by s_valid. Similarly, m_rdata for a destined master can be indicated by s_ready.

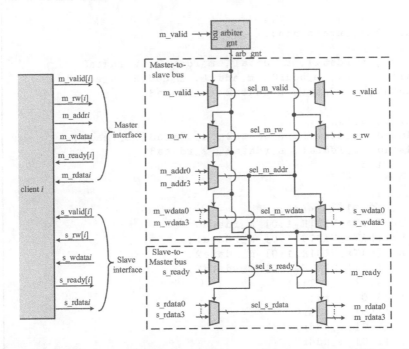

Figure 7.16: Modules connected to the bus interconnect. A source module arbitrates for access to the bus and then drives its transaction onto the bus. The destined client receives or transmits the data to the source client depending upon whether it performs a write or read transaction.

Each client has two interfaces, one master and one slave. A client uses its master interface to communicate with the slave interface of another client on the bus. The granted master will seem to directly connect to its destined slave through the interconnect implemented using the multiplexers and demultiplexers.

The bus protocol is defined below. When a client wishes to begin a transaction on the bus, it inserts the address of the destination client into its address field, m_addr, the data to be communicated into its data field, m_wdata, the read/write control signal, m_rw, and asserts the validity of its signal, m_valid. A tristate drive is sometimes used in an off-chip bus. However, on-chip buses are usually implemented by the multiplexer and demultiplexer. This type of bus interface connects the valid signal from the source client to the bus arbiter, which performs an arbitration and sends a grant signal, arb_gnt, to multiplex the signals of a requesting master, including m_valid, m_rw, m_addr, and m_wdata. The multiplexed m_valid, m_rw, and m_wdata are demultiplexed to the corresponding slave through the multiplexed deviceâĂŹs address, m_addr. Similarly, the slave signals, s_ready and s_rdata, are multiplexed by the multiplexed device address, m_addr, and then demultiplexed through the arb_gnt to the corresponding master, including the signals m_ready and m_rdata.

The Verilog codes for a bus interconnect of 4 clients are shown below.

```verilog
1// Interconnect of 4 clients
2module bus_interconnect(
3// Master interface
4m_ready, m_rdata0, m_rdata1, m_rdata2, m_rdata3,
5m_valid, m_rw, m_addr0, m_addr1, m_addr2, m_addr3,
6m_wdata0, m_wdata1, m_wdata2, m_wdata3,
7// Slave interface
8s_valid, s_rw,
9s_wdata0, s_wdata1, s_wdata2, s_wdata3, s_ready,
10s_rdata0, s_rdata1, s_rdata2, s_rdata3,
11clk, rst_n
12);
13// Master interface
14output [3:0] m_ready; //
15output [DATA_WIDTH-1:0] m_rdata0; //
16output [DATA_WIDTH-1:0] m_rdata1; //
17output [DATA_WIDTH-1:0] m_rdata2; //
18output [DATA_WIDTH-1:0] m_rdata3; //
19input [3:0] m_valid; //
20input [3:0] m_rw; //
21input [1:0] m_addr0; //
22input [1:0] m_addr1; //
23input [1:0] m_addr2; //
24input [1:0] m_addr3; //
25input [DATA_WIDTH-1:0] m_wdata0; //
26input [DATA_WIDTH-1:0] m_wdata1; //
```

```verilog
27 input [DATA_WIDTH-1:0] m_wdata2; //
28 input [DATA_WIDTH-1:0] m_wdata3; //
29 // Slave interface
30 output [3:0] s_valid; //
31 output [3:0] s_rw; //
32 output [DATA_WIDTH-1:0] s_wdata0; //
33 output [DATA_WIDTH-1:0] s_wdata1; //
34 output [DATA_WIDTH-1:0] s_wdata2; //
35 output [DATA_WIDTH-1:0] s_wdata3; //
36 input [3:0] s_ready; //
37 input [DATA_WIDTH-1:0] s_rdata0; //
38 input [DATA_WIDTH-1:0] s_rdata1; //
39 input [DATA_WIDTH-1:0] s_rdata2; //
40 input [DATA_WIDTH-1:0] s_rdata3; //
41 input clk, rst_n;
42 wire [3:0] arb_gnt;
43 parameter DATA_WIDTH=16;
44 // Arbiter interface
45 arbiter arb(.gnt(arb_gnt), .req(m_valid), .clk(clk),
46             .rst_n(rst_n));
47 // Mux and demux interface
48 mux_demux mux_demux(
49 // Master interface
50 .m_ready(m_ready), .m_rdata0(m_rdata0),
51 .m_rdata1(m_rdata1), .m_rdata2(m_rdata2),
52 .m_rdata3(m_rdata3),
53 .gnt(arb_gnt), .m_valid(m_valid), .m_rw(m_rw),
54 .m_addr0(m_addr0), .m_addr1(m_addr1), .m_addr2(m_addr2),
55 .m_addr3(m_addr3),
56 .m_wdata0(m_wdata0), .m_wdata1(m_wdata1),
57 .m_wdata2(m_wdata2), .m_wdata3(m_wdata3),
58 // Slave interface
59 .s_valid(s_valid), .s_rw(s_rw), .s_wdata0(s_wdata0),
60 .s_wdata1(s_wdata1), .s_wdata2(s_wdata2),
61 .s_wdata3(s_wdata3), .s_ready(s_ready),
62 .s_rdata0(s_rdata0), .s_rdata1(s_rdata1),
63 .s_rdata2(s_rdata2), s_rdata3(s_rdata3)
64 );
65 endmodule
```

A module for the multiplexers and demultiplexers is presented below.

```verilog
1 // Multiplexers and demultiplexers
2 module mux_demux(
3 // Master interface
4 m_ready, m_rdata0, m_rdata1, m_rdata2, m_rdata3,
5 gnt, m_valid, m_rw,
6 m_addr0, m_addr1, m_addr2, m_addr3,
7 m_wdata0, m_wdata1, m_wdata2, m_wdata3,
8 // Slave interface
9 s_valid, s_rw, s_wdata0, s_wdata1, s_wdata2,
10 s_wdata3, s_ready, s_rdata0, s_rdata1,
11 s_rdata2, s_rdata3
12 );
13 // Master interface
14 output [3:0] m_ready;
15 output [DATA_WIDTH-1:0] m_rdata0, m_rdata1,
16                         m_rdata2, m_rdata3;
17 input [3:0] gnt; // Grant
18 input [3:0] m_valid, m_rw, ;
19 input [1:0] m_addr0, m_addr1, m_addr2, m_addr3;
20 input [DATA_WIDTH-1:0] m_wdata0, m_wdata1,
21                        m_wdata2, m_wdata3;
22 // Slave interface
23 output [3:0] s_valid, s_rw;
24 output [DATA_WIDTH-1:0] s_wdata0, s_wdata1,
25                         s_wdata2, s_wdata3;
26 input [3:0] s_ready;
27 input [DATA_WIDTH-1:0] s_rdata0, s_rdata1,
28                        s_rdata2, s_rdata3;
29 reg sel_m_valid;
30 reg sel_m_rw;
31 reg [1:0] sel_m_addr;
32 reg [DATA_WIDTH-1:0] sel_m_wdata;
33 reg [3:0] m_ready;
34 reg [DATA_WIDTH-1:0] m_rdata0;
35 reg [DATA_WIDTH-1:0] m_rdata1;
36 reg [DATA_WIDTH-1:0] m_rdata2;
37 reg [DATA_WIDTH-1:0] m_rdata3;
38 reg [3:0] s_valid;
39 reg [3:0] s_rw;
40 reg [DATA_WIDTH-1:0] s_wdata0;
41 reg [DATA_WIDTH-1:0] s_wdata1;
42 reg [DATA_WIDTH-1:0] s_wdata2;
43 reg [DATA_WIDTH-1:0] s_wdata3;
44 reg sel_s_ready;
45 reg [DATA_WIDTH-1:0] sel_s_rdata;
```

```
46 parameter DATA_WIDTH=16;
47 // mux & demux
48 always @(*)
49   case(gnt)
50   4'b0001: begin
51               sel_m_valid=m_valid[0];
52               sel_m_rw=m_rw[0];
53               sel_m_addr=m_addr0;
54               sel_m_wdata=m_wdata0;
55               m_ready={1'b0,1'b0,1'b0,sel_s_ready};
56               m_rdata0=sel_s_rdata;
57               m_rdata1={DATA_WIDTH{1'b0}};
58               m_rdata2={DATA_WIDTH{1'b0}};
59               m_rdata3={DATA_WIDTH{1'b0}};
60            end
61   4'b0010: begin
62               sel_m_valid=m_valid[1];
63               sel_m_rw=m_rw[1];
64               sel_m_addr=m_addr1;
65               sel_m_wdata=m_wdata1;
66               m_ready={1'b0,1'b0,sel_s_ready,1'b0};
67               m_rdata0={DATA_WIDTH{1'b0}};
68               m_rdata1=sel_s_rdata;
69               m_rdata2={DATA_WIDTH{1'b0}};
70               m_rdata3={DATA_WIDTH{1'b0}};
71            end
72   4'b0100: begin
73               sel_m_valid=m_valid[2];
74               sel_m_rw=m_rw[2];
75               sel_m_addr=m_addr2;
76               sel_m_wdata=m_wdata2;
77               m_ready={1'b0,sel_s_ready,1'b0,1'b0};
78               m_rdata0={DATA_WIDTH{1'b0}};
79               m_rdata1={DATA_WIDTH{1'b0}};
80               m_rdata2=sel_s_rdata;
81               m_rdata3={DATA_WIDTH{1'b0}};
82            end
83   default: begin // Also for 4'b1000
84               sel_m_valid=m_valid[3];
85               sel_m_rw=m_rw[3];
86               sel_m_addr=m_addr3;
87               sel_m_wdata=m_wdata3;
88               m_ready={sel_s_ready,1'b0,1'b0,1'b0};
89               m_rdata0={DATA_WIDTH{1'b0}};
90               m_rdata1={DATA_WIDTH{1'b0}};
91               m_rdata2={DATA_WIDTH{1'b0}};
92               m_rdata3=sel_s_rdata;
```

```verilog
93                 end
94    endcase
95 always @(*)
96    case(sel_m_addr)
97    2'b00: begin
98                 sel_s_ready=s_ready[0];
99                 sel_s_rdata=s_rdata0;
100                s_valid={1'b0,1'b0,1'b0,sel_m_valid};
101                s_rw={1'b0,1'b0,1'b0,sel_m_rw};
102                s_wdata0=sel_m_wdata;
103                s_wdata1={DATA_WIDTH{1'b0}};
104                s_wdata2={DATA_WIDTH{1'b0}};
105                s_wdata3={DATA_WIDTH{1'b0}};
106          end
107    2'b01: begin
108                sel_s_ready=s_ready[1];
109                sel_s_rdata=s_rdata1;
110                s_valid={1'b0,1'b0,sel_m_valid,1'b0};
111                s_rw={1'b0,1'b0,sel_m_rw,1'b0};
112                s_wdata0={DATA_WIDTH{1'b0}};
113                s_wdata1=sel_m_wdata;
114                s_wdata2={DATA_WIDTH{1'b0}};
115                s_wdata3={DATA_WIDTH{1'b0}};
116          end
117    2'b10: begin
118                sel_s_ready=s_ready[2];
119                sel_s_rdata=s_rdata2;
120                s_valid={1'b0,sel_m_valid,1'b0,1'b0};
121                s_rw={1'b0,sel_m_rw,1'b0,1'b0};
122                s_wdata0={DATA_WIDTH{1'b0}};
123                s_wdata1={DATA_WIDTH{1'b0}};
124                s_wdata2=sel_m_wdata;
125                s_wdata3={DATA_WIDTH{1'b0}};
126          end
127    default: begin
128                sel_s_ready=s_ready[3];
129                sel_s_rdata=s_rdata3;
130                s_valid={sel_m_valid,1'b0,1'b0,1'b0};
131                s_rw={sel_m_rw,1'b0,1'b0,1'b0};
132                s_wdata0={DATA_WIDTH{1'b0}};
133                s_wdata1={DATA_WIDTH{1'b0}};
134                s_wdata2={DATA_WIDTH{1'b0}};
135                s_wdata3=sel_m_wdata;
136          end
137    endcase
138 endmodule
```

Example 7.3. Please design the bus used in Figure 7.13 and integrate arbiter and avg_value modules.

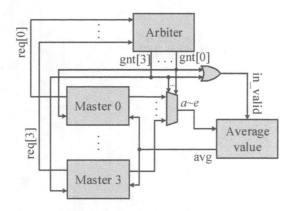

Figure 7.17: Detailed bus interface.

Solution: The bus is implemented using multiplexers for selecting input signals, a, b, c, d, and e, of the avg_value module, as that shown in Figure 7.17. The gnt signal produced by the arbiter is used for both select signals of multiplexers and OR-ed to generate the in_valid signal of the avg_value module. Since there is only a slave module, the demultiplexers of the master-to-slave bus and multiplexers of the slave-to-master bus are saved. Besides, the gnt signal can be used to the indicator of the bus or slave owner, and the demultiplexers of the slave-to-master bus are also omitted. Therefore, the output signal, avg, of the avg_value module is broadcast to all masters. The output signal, out_valid, of the avg_value module is not used. Owing to the 3-stage pipeline of the avg_value module, the master obtains the output result, avg, 3 cycles later after it is granted.

Assuming that masters 0 and 1 send their requests to the arbiter at the same time but other masters (not shown) don't. The timing diagram is demonstrated in Figure 7.18. When gnt[i] of mater i is true, mater i is the bus (or slave) owner and a data output is valid after 3 cycles. The output data lasts for 2 cycles due to handshaking overhead when the master is granted; hence, any avg signals in these 2 cycles can be used. As displayed, the throughput is quite low if the request signal, req, de-asserts 3 cycles later after it is granted. Therefore, the master will occupy the bus (indicated by the grant signal) by 5 cycles due to the pipelined architecture of avg_value module. □

A split transaction is sometimes used to enhance bus performance in a way that allows the reply (or ready signal) to be transmitted later, after the bus request. Doing so enables the arbiter to give access to another master without occupying the bus by a master when waiting for the response of a slave. This can be particularly useful for a device with long access latency, such as a slow or pipelined device.

Example 7.4. Please modify the bus protocol in Example 7.3 using the split transaction to enhance the throughput.

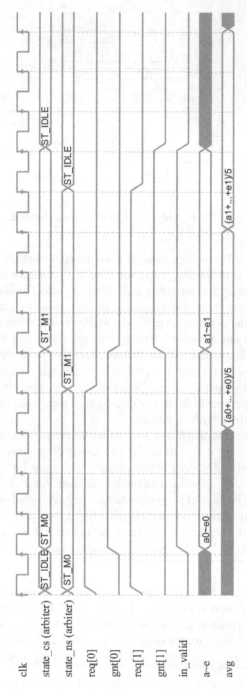

Figure 7.18: Timing diagram of bus protocol 1.

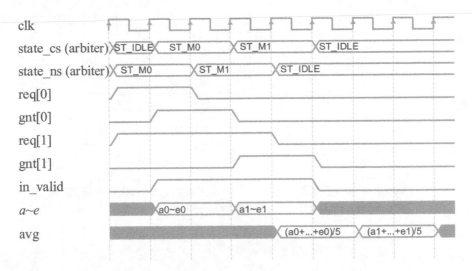

Figure 7.19: Timing diagram of bus protocol 2.

Solution: Assuming that masters 0 and 1 send their requests to the arbiter at the same time but other masters (not shown) don't. The request signal de-asserts after receiving its grant signal instead of waiting for its avg result. Due to the split trans-action, when the output data is valid, the master's grant signal has already gone low. The timing diagram is demonstrated in Figure 7.19. As displayed, a master now occupies the bus by 2 cycles. The avg signal destined to mater i lasts for 2 cycles due to handshaking overhead; hence, any avg signals in these 2 cycles can be used. To receive the first output data for a master, the master must wait 3 cycles after it is granted.

□

Example 7.5. Please modify the bus protocol in Example 7.4 using the split trans-action to further enhance the throughput.

Solution: We design a new request signal, req_i, used by the state machine of the arbiter, as shown below. When gnt[i] is true, it will mask req[i] and the internal request req_i[i] used by the state machine will become false. Consequently, the bus can be handed over to the next master earlier than before.

```
1// Internal requests used by arbiter
2assign req_i[0]=req[0]&~gnt[0];
3assign req_i[1]=req[0]&~gnt[1];
4assign req_i[2]=req[0]&~gnt[2];
5assign req_i[3]=req[0]&~gnt[3];
```

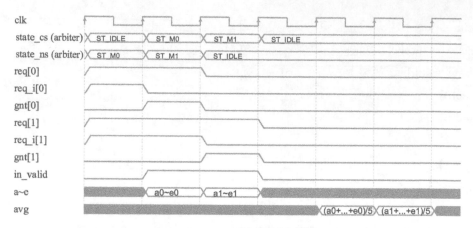

Figure 7.20: Timing diagram of bus protocol 3.

The timing diagram is demonstrated in Figure 7.20. Due to the split transaction, when output data is ready, the master's grant signal has already gone low. As displayed, a master now occupies the bus by 1 cycle because the request signal used by the state machine of the arbiter shortens by qualifying the grant signal. The pipelined avg_value module now can process input data of masters at its maximum speed. To receive the first output data for a master, the master must wait 3 cycles after it is granted.

□

7.1.4.2 Crossbar Switches

When an interconnect with a higher performance than a bus is required, and a small or moderate number of clients is connected, a crossbar (or cross-point) switch is often a good solution, as shown in Figure 7.21. Similar to the bus interconnect, the master provides valid, read/write, device address, and data output signals, while signals indicating readiness and data input are given by the slave. If there are m transmitting (Tx) masters and n receiving (Rx) slaves, the arbiter considers all m sending requests and generates a set of grants for those non-conflicting requests and routes the master's and slave's signals to its corresponding slave and master, respectively. For example, if master i's request to send a transaction to slave j is granted, the connection between them is established so they can communicate as if using a direct point-to-point connection. Each row of the request matrix can have at most a single 1 because each master can request no more than one slave at a time. In such an array, there are n arbiters, one for each column (or slave). To avoid conflicts, each slave is assigned to only a single master.

Verilog code for a 4×4 crossbar switch is shown below. The arbiter in this example always gives priority to client 0. Like the bus, the arbitration is pipelined one cycle ahead of data communication. At most, each master can access one

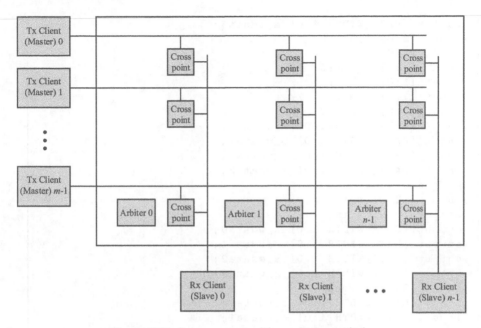

Figure 7.21: Interconnect with a crossbar switch.

non-conflicting slave such that the performance can be enhanced fourfold. The modules, arbiter and mux_demux, reuse those defined in the previous sections. The throughput of a crossbar can be increased by providing a buffer at the crosspoint, which decouples input and output scheduling.

```verilog
// Module of crossbar switches
module crossbar_interconnect(
// Master interface
m_ready, m_rdata0, m_rdata1, m_rdata2, m_rdata3,
m_valid, m_rw, m_addr0, m_addr1, m_addr2, m_addr3,
m_wdata0, m_wdata1, m_wdata2, m_wdata3,
// Slave interface
s_valid, s_rw,
s_wdata0, s_wdata1, s_wdata2, s_wdata3, s_ready,
s_rdata0, s_rdata1, s_rdata2, s_rdata3,
clk, rst_n
);
// Master interface
output [3:0] m_ready; //
output [DATA_WIDTH-1:0] m_rdata0; //
output [DATA_WIDTH-1:0] m_rdata1; //
output [DATA_WIDTH-1:0] m_rdata2; //
```

```
18 output [DATA_WIDTH-1:0] m_rdata3; //
19 input  [3:0] m_valid; //
20 input  [3:0] m_rw; //
21 input  [1:0] m_addr0; //
22 input  [1:0] m_addr1; //
23 input  [1:0] m_addr2; //
24 input  [1:0] m_addr3; //
25 input  [DATA_WIDTH-1:0] m_wdata0; //
26 input  [DATA_WIDTH-1:0] m_wdata1; //
27 input  [DATA_WIDTH-1:0] m_wdata2; //
28 input  [DATA_WIDTH-1:0] m_wdata3; //
29 // Slave interface
30 output [3:0] s_valid; //
31 output [3:0] s_rw; //
32 output [DATA_WIDTH-1:0] s_wdata0; //
33 output [DATA_WIDTH-1:0] s_wdata1; //
34 output [DATA_WIDTH-1:0] s_wdata2; //
35 output [DATA_WIDTH-1:0] s_wdata3; //
36 input  [3:0] s_ready; //
37 input  [DATA_WIDTH-1:0] s_rdata0; //
38 input  [DATA_WIDTH-1:0] s_rdata1; //
39 input  [DATA_WIDTH-1:0] s_rdata2; //
40 input  [DATA_WIDTH-1:0] s_rdata3; //
41 input  clk, rst_n;
42 // Slave 0
43 wire [3:0] m_ready_s0; //
44 wire [DATA_WIDTH-1:0] m_rdata0_s0; //
45 wire [DATA_WIDTH-1:0] m_rdata1_s0; //
46 wire [DATA_WIDTH-1:0] m_rdata2_s0; //
47 wire [DATA_WIDTH-1:0] m_rdata3_s0; //
48 wire [3:0] m_valid_s0; //
49 wire [3:0] s_valid_s0; //
50 wire [3:0] s_rw_s0; //
51 wire [DATA_WIDTH-1:0] s_wdata0_s0; //
52 wire [DATA_WIDTH-1:0] s_wdata1_s0; //
53 wire [DATA_WIDTH-1:0] s_wdata2_s0; //
54 wire [DATA_WIDTH-1:0] s_wdata3_s0; //
55 // Slave 1
56 wire [3:0] m_ready_s1; //
57 wire [DATA_WIDTH-1:0] m_rdata0_s1; //
58 wire [DATA_WIDTH-1:0] m_rdata1_s1; //
59 wire [DATA_WIDTH-1:0] m_rdata2_s1; //
60 wire [DATA_WIDTH-1:0] m_rdata3_s1; //
61 wire [3:0] m_valid_s1; //
62 wire [3:0] s_valid_s1; //
63 wire [3:0] s_rw_s1; //
64 wire [DATA_WIDTH-1:0] s_wdata0_s1; //
```

```verilog
65 wire [DATA_WIDTH-1:0] s_wdata1_s1; //
66 wire [DATA_WIDTH-1:0] s_wdata2_s1; //
67 wire [DATA_WIDTH-1:0] s_wdata3_s1; //
68 // Slave 2
69 wire [3:0] m_ready_s2; //
70 wire [DATA_WIDTH-1:0] m_rdata0_s2; //
71 wire [DATA_WIDTH-1:0] m_rdata1_s2; //
72 wire [DATA_WIDTH-1:0] m_rdata2_s2; //
73 wire [DATA_WIDTH-1:0] m_rdata3_s2; //
74 wire [3:0] m_valid_s2; //
75 wire [3:0] s_valid_s2; //
76 wire [3:0] s_rw_s2; //
77 wire [DATA_WIDTH-1:0] s_wdata0_s2; //
78 wire [DATA_WIDTH-1:0] s_wdata1_s2; //
79 wire [DATA_WIDTH-1:0] s_wdata2_s2; //
80 wire [DATA_WIDTH-1:0] s_wdata3_s2; //
81 // Slave 3
82 wire [3:0] m_ready_s3; //
83 wire [DATA_WIDTH-1:0] m_rdata0_s3; //
84 wire [DATA_WIDTH-1:0] m_rdata1_s3; //
85 wire [DATA_WIDTH-1:0] m_rdata2_s3; //
86 wire [DATA_WIDTH-1:0] m_rdata3_s3; //
87 wire [3:0] m_valid_s3; //
88 wire [3:0] s_valid_s3; //
89 wire [3:0] s_rw_s3; //
90 wire [DATA_WIDTH-1:0] s_wdata0_s3; //
91 wire [DATA_WIDTH-1:0] s_wdata1_s3; //
92 wire [DATA_WIDTH-1:0] s_wdata2_s3; //
93 wire [DATA_WIDTH-1:0] s_wdata3_s3; //
94 wire [3:0] arb_gnt_s0;
95 wire [3:0] arb_gnt_s1;
96 wire [3:0] arb_gnt_s2;
97 wire [3:0] arb_gnt_s3;
98 parameter DATA_WIDTH=16;
99 // Arbiter interface
100 // Request matrix
101 assign m_valid_s0={m_valid[3] & (m_addr3==2'd0),
102                    m_valid[2] & (m_addr2==2'd0),
103                    m_valid[1] & (m_addr1==2'd0),
104                    m_valid[0] & (m_addr0==2'd0)};
105 assign m_valid_s1={m_valid[3] & (m_addr3==2'd1),
106                    m_valid[2] & (m_addr2==2'd1),
107                    m_valid[1] & (m_addr1==2'd1),
108                    m_valid[0] & (m_addr0==2'd1)};
109 assign m_valid_s2={m_valid[3] & (m_addr3==2'd2),
110                    m_valid[2] & (m_addr2==2'd2),
111                    m_valid[1] & (m_addr1==2'd2),
```

```
112                        m_valid[0] & (m_addr0==2'd2)};
113 assign m_valid_s3={m_valid[3] & (m_addr3==2'd3),
114                    m_valid[2] & (m_addr2==2'd3),
115                    m_valid[1] & (m_addr1==2'd3),
116                    m_valid[0] & (m_addr0==2'd3)};
117 arbiter arb0(.gnt(arb_gnt_s0), .req(m_valid_s0),
118          .clk(clk), .rst_n(rst_n));
119 arbiter arb1(.gnt(arb_gnt_s1), .req(m_valid_s1),
120          .clk(clk), .rst_n(rst_n));
121 arbiter arb2(.gnt(arb_gnt_s2), .req(m_valid_s2),
122          .clk(clk), .rst_n(rst_n));
123 arbiter arb3(.gnt(arb_gnt_s3), .req(m_valid_s3),
124          .clk(clk), .rst_n(rst_n));
125 // mux and demux interface
126 assign m_ready=m_ready_s0|m_ready_s1|m_ready_s2|
127                m_ready_s3;
128 assign m_rdata0=m_rdata0_s0|m_rdata0_s1|
129                 m_rdata0_s2|m_rdata0_s3;
130 assign m_rdata1=m_rdata1_s0|m_rdata1_s1|
131                 m_rdata1_s2|m_rdata1_s3;
132 assign m_rdata2=m_rdata2_s0|m_rdata2_s1|
133                 m_rdata2_s2|m_rdata2_s3;
134 assign m_rdata3=m_rdata3_s0|m_rdata3_s1|
135                 m_rdata3_s2|m_rdata3_s3;
136 assign s_valid=s_valid_s0|s_valid_s1|s_valid_s2|
137                s_valid_s3;
138 assign s_rw=s_rw_s0|s_rw_s1|s_rw_s2|s_rw_s3;
139 assign s_wdata0=s_wdata0_s0|s_wdata0_s1|
140                 s_wdata0_s2|s_wdata0_s3;
141 assign s_wdata1=s_wdata1_s0|s_wdata1_s1|
142                 s_wdata1_s2|s_wdata1_s3;
143 assign s_wdata2=s_wdata2_s0|s_wdata2_s1|
144                 s_wdata2_s2|s_wdata2_s3;
145 assign s_wdata3=s_wdata3_s0|s_wdata3_s1|
146                 s_wdata3_s2|s_wdata3_s3;
147 // mux and demux interface of slave 0
148 mux_demux mux_demux_s0(
149 // Master interface
150 .m_ready(m_ready_s0), .m_rdata0(m_rdata0_s0),
151 .m_rdata1(m_rdata1_s0), .m_rdata2(m_rdata2_s0),
152 .m_rdata3(m_rdata3_s0),
153 .gnt(arb_gnt_s0), .m_valid(m_valid_s0), .m_rw(m_rw),
154 .m_addr0(m_addr0), .m_addr1(m_addr1), .m_addr2(m_addr2),
155 .m_addr3(m_addr3),
156 .m_wdata0(m_wdata0), .m_wdata1(m_wdata1),
157 .m_wdata2(m_wdata2), .m_wdata3(m_wdata3),
158 // Slave interface
```

```
159 .s_valid(s_valid_s0), .s_rw(s_rw_s0),
160 .s_wdata0(s_wdata0_s0),
161 .s_wdata1(s_wdata1_s0), .s_wdata2(s_wdata2_s0),
162 .s_wdata3(s_wdata3_s0), .s_ready(s_ready),
163 .s_rdata0(s_rdata0), .s_rdata1(s_rdata1),
164 .s_rdata2(s_rdata2), .s_rdata3(s_rdata3)
165 );
166 // mux and demux interface of slave 1
167 mux_demux mux_demux_s1 (
168 // Master interface
169 .m_ready(m_ready_s1), .m_rdata0(m_rdata0_s1),
170 .m_rdata1(m_rdata1_s1), .m_rdata2(m_rdata2_s1),
171 .m_rdata3(m_rdata3_s1),
172 .gnt(arb_gnt_s1), .m_valid(m_valid_s1), .m_rw(m_rw),
173 .m_addr0(m_addr0), .m_addr1(m_addr1), .m_addr2(m_addr2),
174 .m_addr3(m_addr3),
175 .m_wdata0(m_wdata0), .m_wdata1(m_wdata1),
176 .m_wdata2(m_wdata2), .m_wdata3(m_wdata3),
177 // Slave interface
178 .s_valid(s_valid_s1), .s_rw(s_rw_s1),
179 .s_wdata0(s_wdata0_s1),
180 .s_wdata1(s_wdata1_s1), .s_wdata2(s_wdata2_s1),
181 .s_wdata3(s_wdata3_s1), .s_ready(s_ready),
182 .s_rdata0(s_rdata0), .s_rdata1(s_rdata1),
183 .s_rdata2(s_rdata2), .s_rdata3(s_rdata3)
184 );
185 // mux and demux interface of slave 2
186 mux_demux mux_demux_s2 (
187 // Master interface
188 .m_ready(m_ready_s2), .m_rdata0(m_rdata0_s2),
189 .m_rdata1(m_rdata1_s2), .m_rdata2(m_rdata2_s2),
190 .m_rdata3(m_rdata3_s2),
191 .gnt(arb_gnt_s2), .m_valid(m_valid_s2), .m_rw(m_rw),
192 .m_addr0(m_addr0), .m_addr1(m_addr1), .m_addr2(m_addr2),
193 .m_addr3(m_addr3),
194 .m_wdata0(m_wdata0), .m_wdata1(m_wdata1),
195 .m_wdata2(m_wdata2), .m_wdata3(m_wdata3),
196 // Slave interface
197 .s_valid(s_valid_s2), .s_rw(s_rw_s2),
198 .s_wdata0(s_wdata0_s2),
199 .s_wdata1(s_wdata1_s2), .s_wdata2(s_wdata2_s2),
200 .s_wdata3(s_wdata3_s2), .s_ready(s_ready),
201 .s_rdata0(s_rdata0), .s_rdata1(s_rdata1),
202 .s_rdata2(s_rdata2), .s_rdata3(s_rdata3)
203 );
204 // mux and demux interface of slave 3
205 mux_demux mux_demux_s3 (
```

```
206 // Master interface
207 .m_ready(m_ready_s3), .m_rdata0(m_rdata0_s3),
208 .m_rdata1(m_rdata1_s3), .m_rdata2(m_rdata2_s3),
209 .m_rdata3(m_rdata3_s3),
210 .gnt(arb_gnt_s3), .m_valid(m_valid_s3), .m_rw(m_rw),
211 .m_addr0(m_addr0), .m_addr1(m_addr1), .m_addr2(m_addr2),
212 .m_addr3(m_addr3),
213 .m_wdata0(m_wdata0), .m_wdata1(m_wdata1),
214 .m_wdata2(m_wdata2), .m_wdata3(m_wdata3),
215 // Slave interface
216 .s_valid(s_valid_s3), .s_rw(s_rw_s3),
217 .s_wdata0(s_wdata0_s3),
218 .s_wdata1(s_wdata1_s3), .s_wdata2(s_wdata2_s3),
219 .s_wdata3(s_wdata3_s3), .s_ready(s_ready),
220 .s_rdata0(s_rdata0), .s_rdata1(s_rdata1),
221 .s_rdata2(s_rdata2), .s_rdata3(s_rdata3)
222 );
223 endmodule
```

7.1.4.3   Interconnect Networks

When a large (more than 16) clients must be connected, an interconnect network is usually required to enable communication between the clients. An interconnect network consists of a set of routers connected by channels and is characterized by a topology, a routing algorithm, and a flow control mechanism. Figure 7.22 shows an interconnect network that connects 18 clients using a two-dimensional 3×3 mesh topology with 2 clients per router. The network has 9 routers, each of which has up to 6 bi-directional ports or 12 uni-directional channels. The routing algorithm specifies a path through this network which goes from a source client to a destination client. One possible routing algorithm for this network requires a path that travels first in the x-dimension to the destination column and then switches to the y-dimension where it proceeds to the destination row, and finally to the designated client port.

The flow control in an interconnect network, as opposed to that of an interface, deals with the allocation of channels and buffers to packets as they traverse the network. Each channel and buffer is allocated to a particular packet for an interval of time, after which, it is reallocated to a different packet. So far, we have assumed the entire packet is delivered in parallel in a single clock cycle. However, as with the other interconnects, an interconnect network can be serialized so that a packet is delivered over several cycles across a narrow interface. In a serialized network, the flow control can either be performed at the level of the whole packet, in which case routers must have buffers large enough to hold whole packets, or at the level of flow-control digit, or flit, the amount of information that can be delivered in one clock cycle. Packet-level flow control is similar to frame-level flow control, while flit-level flow control is similar to the valid-ready flow control of an interface.

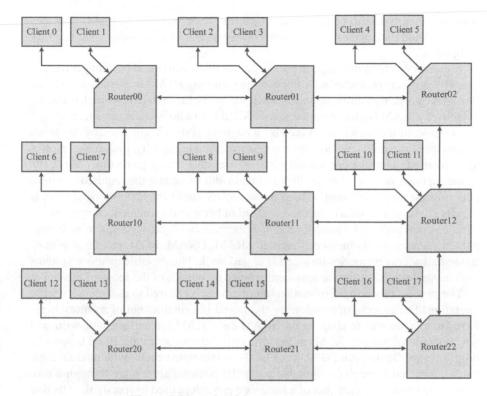

Figure 7.22: A 3 × 3 interconnect network.

7.2   SYSTEM-LEVEL DESIGN: MEMORY SYSTEM

Memory is widely used in digital systems for many different purposes. In a processor, DRAM chips are used for main memory, while SRAM arrays are used to implement caches and other internal storage. In an Internet router, memory is used for packet buffer and routing tables. In a cellphone, memory can be used to buffer video and audio streaming data.

Memory is characterized by three key parameters: capacity, latency, and throughput. Capacity is the amount of data that can be stored, latency is the amount of time required to access the stored data, and throughput is the amount of access that can occur in a time unit. The advantage of DRAM is the structural simplicity of its memory cells: only one transistor and one tiny capacitor are required per bit, compared to six transistors in SRAM. This allows DRAM to reach a very high density that makes it much cheaper per bit. The capacitor can either be charged or discharged to represent either of the two states, 0 or 1, of a bit. However, the electric charge on the capacitor eventually leaks away, so without refreshing, the data on the chip is soon lost. To prevent this, DRAM requires an external memory refresh circuit which periodically rewrites the data in the capacitors, restoring them to their original states. This refresh process is the defining characteristic of DRAM, in contrast to SRAM, which does not require data to be refreshed. The term "static" (the S of SRAM) indicates that the stored data persists indefinitely so long as power is applied to the memory component.

A memory system in a large digital system is often composed of multiple memories with different characteristics. For example, on-chip SRAM is characterized by its low latency and high throughput, while DRAM is characterized by its high capacity. Moreover, DRAM is often external to an ASIC due to a different process technology. The number of memories used to realize a memory system is governed by its capacity and throughput. If a memory does not have sufficient capacity, multiple memories must be used, with just one memory being accessible at any given time. Similarly, if one memory does not have sufficient bandwidth to sustain the required throughput, multiple memories must be used in parallel. Notably, the memory bandwidth is usually expressed in units of bits/sec, instead of hertz in communication systems.

The access policy of a memory can be either random access or sequential. Examples of random-access memories include SRAM, DRAM, ROM, etc. Examples of sequential access memories include FIFO and stack. Non-volatile memory systems such as storage disks used for persistent storage lie outside of the scope of this book.

The process of storing information into memory is referred to as a memory write operation. The process of transferring the stored information out of memory is referred to as a memory read operation. SRAM and DRAM can perform both write and read operations, whereas ROM can perform only the read operation. ROM is part of a programmable logic device (PLD). A PLD is an integrated circuit with internal logic gates connected through configurable paths. Its contents are written through a programming process and are part of a hardware procedure used to specify the bits that are inserted into the hardware configuration of the device. The programming of ROM determines the fuses which are to be connected or disconnected. Other PLDs include programmable logic array (PLA), programmable array logic (PAL), and FPGA.

7.2.1 STATIC RANDOM-ACCESS MEMORY

On-chip SRAM arrays are useful for building small, fast, or dedicated memories integrated near the logic that produces and consumes the data they store. Typically, the total capacity of an SRAM array that can be realized on one chip is small compared to even a single DRAM chip. However, on-chip SRAM can be accessed in a single clock cycle compared to several tens of cycles required for an off-chip DRAM. By operating many SRAM arrays in parallel, a very high aggregate bandwidth can be achieved.

An SRAM interface consists of a read/write enable signal, an address, a data output, and a data input. An SRAM can have more than one port. Although the majority of SRAMs have a single port because the cost increases as the square of the number of ports, dual-port SRAMs with one read and one write port are not uncommon. Most SRAMs operate synchronously based on a clock, as shown in Figure 7.23. We call it synchronous SRAM (SSRAM). In this example, the data d0 is written into the address of 8 at cycle 0. The data at this same address is then read at cycle 1. According to the clock, the read/write enable (ren/wen), read/write address (raddr/waddr),

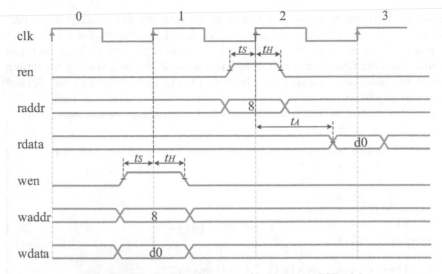

Figure 7.23: Timing diagram of a dual-port SSRAM.

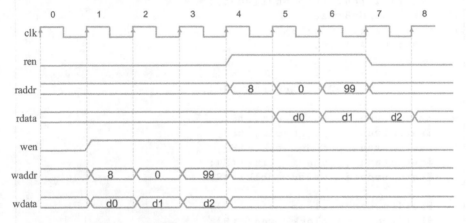

Figure 7.24: Timing diagram of a burst read and write.

and write data (wdata) have setup time (t_S) and hold time (t_H) constraints. The read data (rdata) signal has access time (t_A) constraint. A single SSRAM array typically operates in one clock cycle.

An SSRAM can be burst read and written. Every cycle, the address (and data for a write access) can change to a new and random one without incurring any interruption or overhead, as shown in Figure 7.24.

Example 7.6. The behavior model of a 512×16 single-port SSRAM is written below, where rdata, cen, wen, ren, addr, and wdata are read data, chip enable, write enable, read enable, address, and data input, respectively. The SSRAM is on-chip so that read (rdata) and write (wdata) data buses are separate. For off-chip single-port SSRAMs, read and write data buses are usually shared, i.e., bidirectional, to save the pin counts. If cen and ren are true, the read operation is performed; if cen and wen are true, the write operation is performed. The delayed assignment using the timing control, $\#t_A$, models the access time. The setup time t_S and hold time t_H are checked using a specify block.

```verilog
// SSRAM behavior model
module SSRAM(rdata, clk, cen, wen, ren, addr, wdata);
output [7:0] rdata;
input clk, cen, wen, ren;
input [15:0] addr;
input [7:0]  wdata;
reg [7:0] mem[0:65535], tempQ, rdata;
parameter tA=3;
always @(posedge clk)
  if(cen & wen) mem[addr]<=wdata[7:0];
always @(addr or ren or cen)
  if(cen & ren) tempQ=mem[addr];
  else tempQ=8'hzz;
always @(posedge clk)
  rdata<=#tA tempQ;
specify
  // Parameters of setup time & hold time requirement
  specparam tS=2; specparam tH=1;
  // Setup time check
  $setup(cen, posedge clk, tS);
  $setup(wen, posedge clk, tS);
  $setup(ren, posedge clk, tS);
  $setup(addr, posedge clk, tS);
  $setup(wdata, posedge clk, tS);
  // Hold time check
  $hold(posedge clock, cen, tH);
  $hold(posedge clock, wen, tH);
  $hold(posedge clock, ren, tH);
  $hold(posedge clock, addr, tH);
  $hold(posedge clock, wdata, tH);
endspecify
endmodule
```

□

SRAMs are organized as arrays of cells with row decoders and column multiplexers. Depending on the multiplexing factor, various SRAMs with different numbers of entries and bit widths can be realized. If we need a RAM with a larger capacity or higher bandwidth, we can combine multiple RAM arrays via bit-slicing or banking. The bit-slicing technique can be used to design a memory system with a capacity of

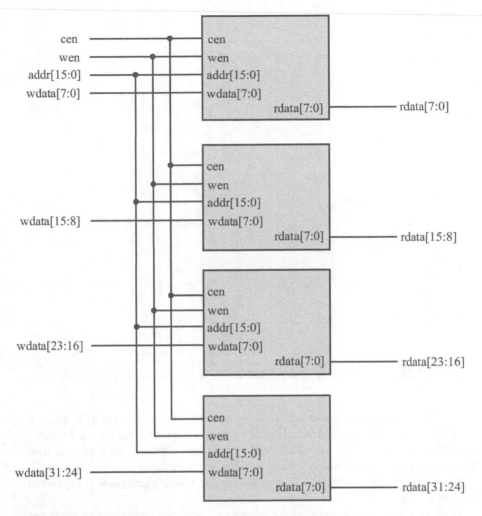

Figure 7.25: Connection of memory components in parallel to form a memory system with broader data width, and hence, bandwidth.

64 K×32-bit using four 64 K×8-bit memories to broaden the data width, as shown in Figure 7.25. All 4 memory arrays are all accessed in parallel at a time. If cen is true and wen is false, the read operation is performed; if cen and wen are true, the write operation is performed.

The memory space of the RAM arrays using the bit-slicing technique is organized in Figure 7.26.

We can also adopt the banking technique to design a 64 K×32-bit memory system using four 16 K×32-bit components to increase the capacity, as shown in Figure 7.27. A decoder with enable control and a multiplexer are required. When

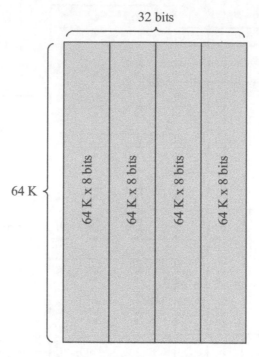

Figure 7.26: Memory space of the RAM arrays using the bit-slicing technique.

addr[15:14] is 00, the first memory array (counted from top to bottom) is enabled via the decoder and its rdata is selected via the multiplexer, and so on. Notably, addr[15:14] used to select the rdata[31:0] needs to be pipelined because read data are commonly available one cycle later than the read command.

The memory space of the RAM arrays using the banking technique is organized in Figure 7.28.

Both configurations have the same capacity (2 Mb) and bandwidth (4 bytes per cycle). In a bit-sliced memory, all memory arrays must be accessed to complete an operation, since each provides a portion of the final result. In a banked memory, however, only one array needs to be accessed such that power can be saved. However, extra decoder and multiplexer are required using a banked memory.

We can simplify the connection of memory components to form a larger memory system by using a tristate buffer for each of the data outputs, as shown in Figure 7.29. To drive the output, the enable signal must be true. If the enable signal is false, the input of the tristate buffer is effectively isolated from its output and, of course, the component the output is connected to as well. If we use memory components with tristate data outputs to construct a larger memory system, the output multiplexers, such as the one shown in Figure 7.27, can be omitted.

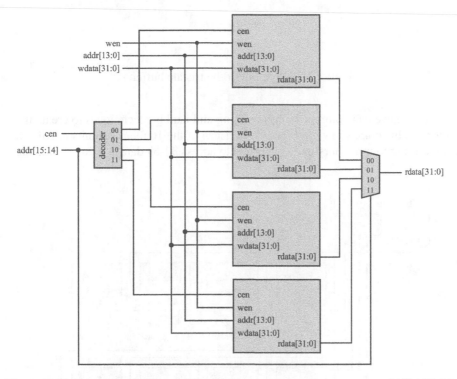

Figure 7.27: Connection of four 16 K×32-bit components to construct a 64 K×32-bit memory system with a larger capacity.

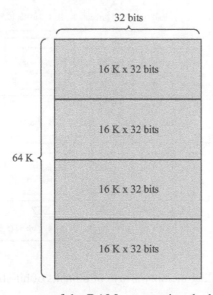

Figure 7.28: Memory space of the RAM arrays using the banking technique.

Figure 7.29: Symbol of the tristate buffer.

Therefore, we can combine both bit-slicing and banking techniques to create the memory architecture shown in Figure 7.30. Each of the 16 memory units is 16K×8 bits, requiring four memory units (one row) to access 32-bit data at a time, while the

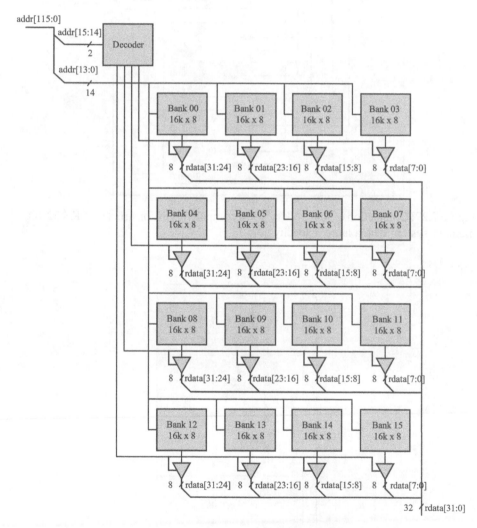

Figure 7.30: Tiling memory arrays into banks of bit-sliced arrays.

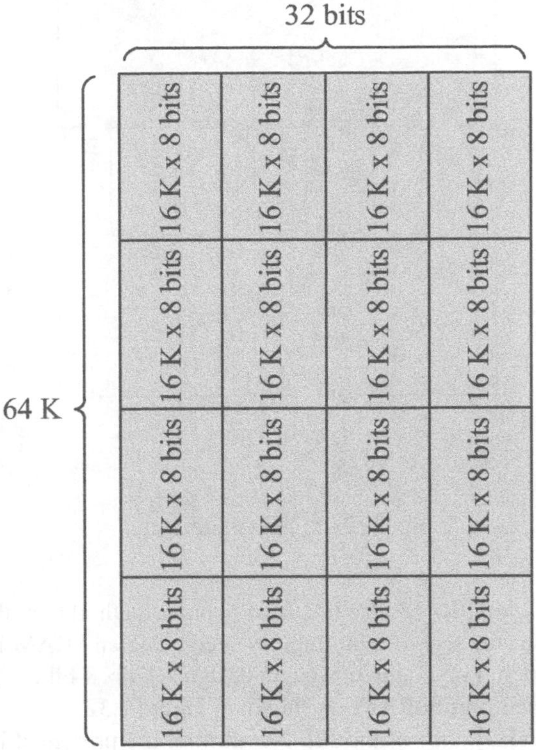

32 bits

Figure 7.31: Memory space of the RAM arrays using both bit-slicing and banking techniques.

other 12 units remain idle to save power. In this manner, the clock speed can also be increased owing to the smaller size of SRAM chips. Four rows, known as banks, are needed to give the required memory capacity of 2 Mb. Only the read data bus is displayed in Figure 7.30. The selected bank (by the decoder) will drive the data bus, while other non-selected banks will stay in tristate so that they cannot affect the read data of a selected bank.

The memory space of the RAM arrays using both bit-slicing and banking techniques is organized in Figure 7.31.

Allowing multiple requests to access multiple banks simultaneously with an arbitrated crossbar increases the aggregate memory bandwidth from one word per cycle to $\min(N, M)$ words per cycle, where M is the number of requesters and N is the number of interleaved banks. Each of the multiple instances of memory access for each bank is decoded based on its memory address. This enables multiple requests to be granted every cycle. Of course, these banks can be further bit-sliced and/or banked, however, if two requests require access to the same bank at the same time, a conflict occurs and one request must be postponed.

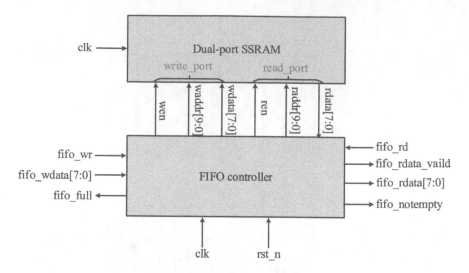

Figure 7.32: FIFO interface.

Example 7.7. On-chip SRAMs are the most popular method to realize a large data storage because the area size of a bit implemented using an SRAM is much smaller than that of a flip-flop. For example, we can design a 1 K×8-bit FIFO using a FIFO controller with a dual-port SSRAM, as shown in Figure 7.32.

Solution: The RTL codes of the FIFO controller are presented below. For simplicity, one port of the SSRAM is dedicated to the write access, while another is dedicated to the read access. To get rid of any possible timing issues, the output signals, including wen, waddr, wdata, ren, and raddr, of memory interface are registered outputs, and input signal, rdata, is directly latched by flip-flops without going through a combinational circuits. An output signal, fifo_rdata_valid, of the fifo read interface is added to indicate the validity of fifo_rdata.

The SSRAM interface typically has the hold time constraints, including wen, waddr, wdata, ren, and raddr signals. Hold time violations will be fixed during the synthesis stage by inserting buffers on those timing paths.

```
1// Large FIFO buffer implemented using SSRAM
2module fifo_ctrl(
3// FIFO interface
4fifo_full , fifo_wr , fifo_wdata ,
5fifo_notempty , fifo_rdata_valid , fifo_rdata , fifo_rd ,
6// SSRAM interface
7wen , waddr , wdata ,
8ren , raddr , rdata ,
9clk , rst_n
10);
```

```verilog
11 // FIFO interface
12 output fifo_full; //
13 input fifo_wr; //
14 input [7:0] fifo_wdata; //
15 output fifo_notempty; //
16 output fifo_rdata_valid; //
17 output [7:0] fifo_rdata; //
18 input fifo_rd; //
19 // SSRAM interface
20 output wen; //
21 output [9:0] waddr;
22 output [7:0] wdata;
23 output ren; //
24 output [9:0] raddr;
25 input [7:0] rdata;
26 input clk, rst_n;
27 reg [9:0] wr_ptr, rd_ptr;
28 reg [10:0] queue_length;
29 reg fifo_rd_r, fifo_rd_rr;
30 reg [7:0] fifo_rdata;
31 // FIFO controller
32 assign fifo_full=queue_length==11'd1024;
33 assign fifo_notempty=~(queue_length==11'd0);
34 always @(posedge clk or negedge rst_n)
35   if(!rst_n)
36     wr_ptr<=0;
37   else if(fifo_wr)
38     wr_ptr<=wr_ptr+1'b1;
39 always @(posedge clk or negedge rst_n)
40   if(!rst_n)
41     rd_ptr<=0;
42   else if(fifo_rd)
43     rd_ptr<=rd_ptr+1'b1;
44 always @(posedge clk or negedge rst_n)
45   if(!rst_n)
46     queue_length<=0;
47   else if(fifo_wr&&!fifo_rd)
48     queue_length<=queue_length+1'b1;
49   else if(fifo_rd&&!fifo_wr)
50     queue_length<=queue_length-1'b1;
51 // SSRAM controller, write port
52 assign wen=fifo_wr;
53 assign waddr=wr_ptr;
54 assign wdata=fifo_wdata;
55 // SSRAM controller, read port
56 assign ren=fifo_rd;
57 assign raddr=rd_ptr;
```

```
58 assign fifo_rdata_valid=fifo_rd_rr;
59 always @(posedge clk or negedge rst_n)
60   if(!rst_n) begin
61     fifo_rd_r <=1'b0;
62     fifo_rd_rr<=1'b0;
63   end
64   else begin
65     fifo_rd_r <=fifo_rd;
66     fifo_rd_rr<=fifo_rd_r;
67   end
68 always @(posedge clk)
69   if(fifo_rd_r) fifo_rdata<=rdata;
70 endmodule
```

□

7.2.1.1 More on Bidirectional Bus

To construct a bidirectional bus to save the pin counts of an off-chip memory, we simply connect the data outputs of the memory components together. When a read operation is performed, only the data output for the selected memory component is enabled. The outputs for all of the disabled components remain in a high-impedance state. A bidirectional bus with tristate data outputs is shown in Figure 7.33. The designer must ensure that only one component can drive the bidirectional bus at a time. That is, only one instance of either enable1, enable2, or enable3 can be true at any given time. Also, to prevent bus conflicts, a turn around period for the next driver is typically required after disabling the previous bus driver or owner.

The bidirectional bus, named bus, can be modeled using the following primitives. In which, the bidirectional bus is a tristate signal. It is therefore declared using the **tri** data type.

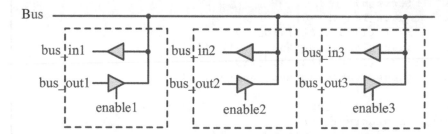

Figure 7.33: Bidirectional data bus.

```
1// Bidirectional bus using Verilog primitives
2tri bus;
3bufif1 u1(bus, bus_out1, enable1);
4bufif1 u2(bus, bus_out2, enable2);
5bufif1 u3(bus, bus_out3, enable3);
6buf u4(bus_in1, bus);
7buf u5(bus_in2, bus);
8buf u6(bus_in3, bus);
```

Continuous assignments can also be used.

```
1// Bidirectional bus using continuous assignments
2tri bus;
3assign bus=enable1?bus_out1:1'bz;
4assign bus=enable2?bus_out2:1'bz;
5assign bus=enable3?bus_out3:1'bz;
6assign bus_in1=bus;
7assign bus_in2=bus;
8assign bus_in3=bus;
```

Either approach allows an expanded memory with bidirectional data bus to be constructed, such as the one shown in Figure 7.34. The data bus, data[31:0], is a bidirectional bus. For memory components implemented as separate ICs for use on PCBs, the use of bidirectional connections results in significant cost savings, since fewer package pins and interconnection wires are required.

However, if a port with a bidirectional data bus is used for both read and write accesses, attention should be paid to a write after read (WAR) access. In Figure 7.35, at every rising edge of clk, when wen is 1/0, a write/read access is performed. As presented, a memory conflict of the data bus happens at cycle 2 because a write command is issued at that cycle, and concurrently read data is available.

7.2.1.2 Asynchronous SRAM

One of the oldest and simplest forms of memory is asynchronous SRAM, as shown in Figure 7.36. It is asynchronous because the memory does not rely on a clock for its timing. SRAM is volatile, meaning that it requires power to maintain the stored data, and loses the data if power is removed.

The timing of an off-chip asynchronous SRAM for write and read operations is shown in Figure 7.37, where addr, $\overline{cen}$, $\overline{wen}$, $\overline{ren}$, and data are address, chip enable (active low), write enable (active low), read enable (active low), and (bidirectional) data signals. The data are written at the positive edge of $\overline{wen}$ and have setup (t_S) and hold-time (t_H) constraints. The data are output at the negative edge of $\overline{ren}$ and available after a delay (or access time) of t_A. The control signals, write and read enables, have signal width constraints, t_W. If the clock period of logic circuits used

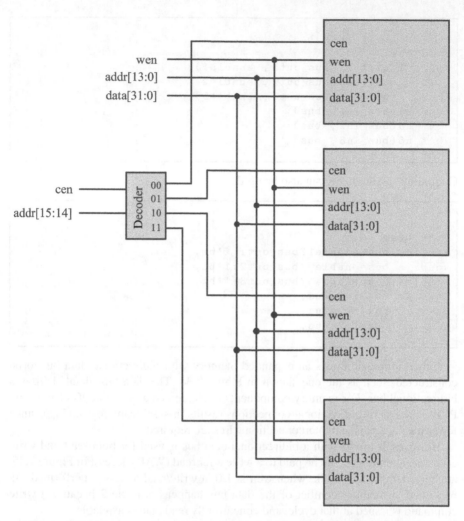

Figure 7.34: A memory system constructed with a bidirectional data bus.

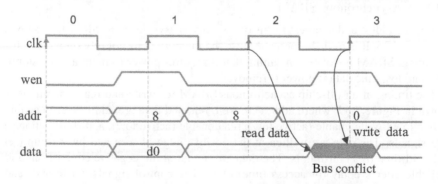

Figure 7.35: Memory conflict for a write after read access.

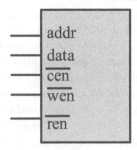

Figure 7.36: Interface of an asynchronous SRAM.

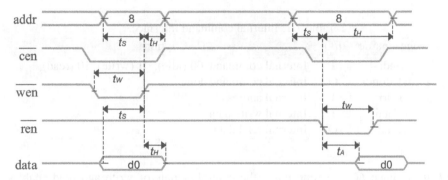

Figure 7.37: Timing for write and read operations in an asynchronous SRAM.

to generate signals of memory interface is smaller than the timing constraints, the signals should be lengthened to meet the specification.

Example 7.8. We want to design a controller in Figure 7.38 for an off-chip 1024×32 bits asynchronous SRAM. Therefore, the data signal is a bidirectional bus to save the pin counts. For simplicity, the chip enable ties to low so that the asynchronous

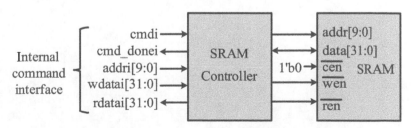

Figure 7.38: Interface of the asynchronous SRAM controller.

SRAM is always enabled. Assuming that $t_S = 5$, $t_H = 2$, $t_A = 7$, and $t_W = 5$ time units in Figure 7.37. The clock period of SRAM controller is 3 time units. Please design the SRAM controller such that the SRAM interface timing can be ensured.

The internal command interface of the asynchronous SRAM controller is presented in Table 7.1. When internal command cmdi=2'b00, no command is issued. When internal command cmdi=2'b01, the write command is issued, and addri, wdatai, and cmd_donei are address, write data, and command done, respectively. When internal command cmdi=2'b10, the read command is issued, and addri, rdatai, and cmd_donei are address, read data, and command done, respectively. For the read command, the command done signal, cmd_donei, also indicates the validity of read data. After an internal command has been done, the next new command can be issued.

Table 7.1: Internal command interface.

Signal name	I/O	Description
cmdi	I	Internal command: 00 (idle), 01 (write), 10 (read)
cmd_donei	O	Internal command done
addri	I	Internal address
wdatai	I	Internal write data
rdatai	O	Internal read data

Solution: Since $t_W = 5$ time units, the control signals of write and read enables should last for 2 clock cycles of asynchronous SRAM controller. Similarly, the setup time $t_S = 5$ and hold time $t_H = 2$ require 2 and 1 clock cycles, respectively. The timing diagram is presented in Figure 7.39. The state machine used to generate the control sequence is also presented.

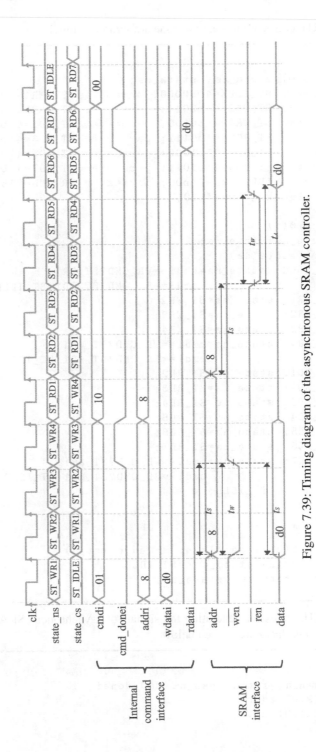

Figure 7.39: Timing diagram of the asynchronous SRAM controller.

The RTL codes of the state machine are written below.

```
1 // State machine: asynchronous SRAM controller
2 reg [3:0] state_ns, state_cs;
3 parameter ST_IDLE=4'b0000; parameter ST_WR1=4'b0001;
4 parameter ST_WR2=4'b0011; parameter ST_WR3=4'b0010;
5 parameter ST_WR4=4'b0100; parameter ST_RD1=4'b0101;
6 parameter ST_RD2=4'b0111; parameter ST_RD3=4'b0110;
7 parameter ST_RD4=4'b1000; parameter ST_RD5=4'b1001;
8 parameter ST_RD6=4'b1011; parameter ST_RD7=4'b1010;
9 parameter IDLE_CMD=2'b00; parameter WR_CMD=2'b01;
10 parameter RD_CMD=2'b10;
11 // Combinational logic
12 always @(*) begin
13   state_ns=state_cs;
14   case(state_cs)
15   ST_IDLE: state_ns=cmdi==WR_CMD?ST_WR1:
16                     cmdi==RD_CMD?ST_RD1:ST_IDLE;
17   ST_WR1: state_ns=ST_WR2;
18   ST_WR2: state_ns=ST_WR3;
19   ST_WR3: state_ns=ST_WR4;
20   ST_WR4: state_ns=cmdi==WR_CMD?ST_WR1:
21                    cmdi==RD_CMD?ST_RD1:ST_IDLE;
22   ST_RD1: state_ns=ST_RD2;
23   ST_RD2: state_ns=ST_RD3;
24   ST_RD3: state_ns=ST_RD4;
25   ST_RD4: state_ns=ST_RD5;
26   ST_RD5: state_ns=ST_RD6;
27   ST_RD6: state_ns=ST_RD7;
28   ST_RD7: state_ns=cmdi==WR_CMD?ST_WR1:
29                    cmdi==RD_CMD?ST_RD1:ST_IDLE;
30   default: ST_IDLE;
31   endcase
32 end
33 // Sequential logic
34 always @(posedge clk or negedge rst_n)
35   if(!rst_n) state_cs<=ST_IDLE;
36   else state_cs<=state_ns;
```

The RTL codes for generating the signals of asynchronous SRAM and internal command interfaces are written below.

```
1 // Interface signals: asynchronous SRAM controller
2 reg wen_n, ren_n, oen_n, cmd_donei;
3 reg [9:0] addr;
4 tri [31:0] data;
```

```
 5 reg [31:0] datai;
 6 reg [31:0] rdatai;
 7 // asynchronous SRAM interface
 8 always @(posedge clk or negedge rst_n)
 9   if(!rst_n) wen_n<=1;
10   else if(state_ns==ST_WR1) wen_n<=0;
11   else if(state_ns==ST_WR3) wen_n<=1;
12 always @(posedge clk or negedge rst_n)
13   if(!rst_n) oen_n<=1;
14   else if(state_ns==ST_WR1) oen_n<=0;
15   else if(state_ns==ST_WR4) oen_n<=1;
16 always @(posedge clk)
17   if(state_ns==ST_WR1|state_ns==ST_RD1) addr<=addri;
18 always @(posedge clk)
19   if(state_ns==ST_WR1) datai<=wdatai;
20 // bidirectional bus
21 assign data=~oen_n?datai:32'bz;
22 always @(posedge clk or negedge rst_n)
23   if(!rst_n) ren_n<=1;
24   else if(state_ns==ST_RD3) ren_n<=0;
25   else if(state_ns==ST_RD5) ren_n<=1;
26 // Internal command interface
27 always @(posedge clk)
28   if(state_ns==ST_RD6) rdatai<=data;
29 always @(posedge clk or negedge rst_n)
30   if(!rst_n) cmd_donei <=0;
31   else if(state_ns==ST_WR3|state_ns==ST_RD6)
32           cmd_donei <=1;
33   else cmd_donei <=1;
```

□

7.2.2 READ-ONLY MEMORY

The memory that we have looked at so far can both read and write (or update) the stored data arbitrarily. In contrast, a read-only memory, or ROM, can only read the data. This is useful in cases where the data is fixed, so there is no need to update it. The data is either incorporated into the circuit during its manufacture, or is programmed into the ROM subsequently.

A simple ROM is a combinational circuit that maps an input address to an output data with constant value. We could specify the ROM contents in tabular form, with a row for each address and an entry showing the data value for that address. Such a table is essentially a truth table, so we could, in principle, implement the mapping using a combinational circuit. However, ROM circuit structures are generally much denser than arbitrary logic-based circuits, since each ROM cell needs at most one transistor.

Example 7.9. Design a combinational circuit for Table 7.2.

Table 7.2: 512×16 Table implemented using a combinational circuit.

addr[8:0]	rdata[15:0]
0	0123
1	4567
2	89AB
3	CDEF
...	...

Solution: The RTL codes of the table are presented below.

```verilog
1 // A module implementing a table lookup
2 module table(
3 rdata,
4 addr,
5 );
6 output [15:0] rdata;
7 input [8:0] addr;
8 reg [15:0] rdata;
9 always @(*)
10   case(addr)
11   9'd0:rdata=16'h0123;
12   9'd1:rdata=16'h4567;
13   9'd2:rdata=16'h89AB;
14   9'd3:rdata=16'hCDEF;
15   ...
16   default:rdata=16'h0123;
17   endcase
18 endmodule
```

□

The behavior model of a 512×16 ROM is written below. We use the $readmemh or $readmemb system task to load the memory content.

```verilog
1 // ROM behavior model
2 module ROM(rdata1, ren, addr, clk);
3 output [15:0] rdata1;
4 input ren;
5 input [8:0] addr;
6 input clk;
7 reg [15:0] data_array[0:511];
8 reg [15:0] rdata1;
9 initial $readmemh("rom.data", data_array);
10 parameter tA=3;
```

```
11 always @(posedge clk)
12   if(ren) rdata1 <=#tA data_array[addr];
13 endmodule
```

The $readmemh system task expects the content of the named file to be a sequence of hexadecimal numbers, separated by spaces or line breaks. Thus, the file rom.data specified in the above example could contain the data:

```
1 // ROM data
2 0123 4567 89AB CDEF
3 1009 266A 3115 5435
4 ...
```

Values are read from the file, rom.data, into successive elements of the variable, data_array, until either the end of the file reached or all elements of the variable are loaded. Similarly, $readmemb expects the file to contain a sequence of binary numbers.

The timing diagram of a table implemented using a combinational circuit and ROM is displayed in Figure 7.40. The table implemented by combinational circuits typically does not need the read enable, ren, and its output, rdata, is selected through a combinational logic of multiplexer. By contrast, The table implemented by ROM usually requires an access time, t_A, to obtain the read data, rdata1. Therefore, their outputs are available in different clock cycles.

The contents of ROMs should not need to be changed over the lifetime of the product. ROMs tend to be used for applications in which the number of manufactured parts is high. For some applications, it might be preferable to occasionally be able to update the ROM contents, especially for low-volume production. To accomplish this, a programmable ROM (PROM), an off-the-shelf chip with no contents stored in its memory cells, can be used. The memory contents of PROM are programmed into the cells after manufacturing, either using a special programming device before

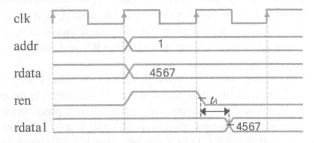

Figure 7.40: Timing diagram of a table implemented using a combinational circuit and ROM.

the chip is inserted into the system, or using special programming circuits when the chip has already been installed.

PROMs come in a number of forms. Early PROMs used fusible links to program the memory cells. Once a link was fused, it could not be replaced, so programming could only be done once. These devices are now largely obsolete. They were replaced by PROMs that could be erased, either with ultraviolet light (so called EPROMs), or electrically using a higher voltage than a normal one (so-called electrically erasable PROMs, or EEPROMs).

7.3   ARCHITECTURE DESIGN AND TIMING DIAGRAM

The logic design of a digital system can be divided into two distinct parts: datapath unit and control unit (or control path). The datapath unit is concerned with the design of the digital circuits that perform the data-processing operations so as to manipulate data in registers that adhere to the system's requirements. The datapath contains the combinational circuits that implement the basic operations and the registers that store intermediate results. The control path is concerned with the design of the control circuits that govern the sequence in which the various data-processing operations are performed. The control unit ensures that the control signals are activated in the right order and at the right times to enable the datapath to perform the required operations as the data flow through it. In many cases, the control path makes use of status signals generated by the datapath.

Therefore, all binary information stored in a digital system can be classified as either data or control information. Data are discrete signals that are manipulated by performing arithmetic and/or logic operations. These operations are implemented by digital components, such as adders, decoders, and multiplexers. Control information provides signals that coordinate and execute the various operations in the data section in order to accomplish the desired data-processing tasks. Control information is best implemented by a state machine.

A hierarchical top-down design approach is represented in Figure 7.41. The architecture design is a divide-and-conquer process which is executed until the whole design becomes manageable. For the architecture of RTL designs, flip-flops should be explicitly determined and plotted so that the critical path can be clearly identified or analyzed. Therefore, if you are a (fresh) designer, it is strongly recommended that you should plot the architectural diagram of, at least, the datapath unit. Doing so can clearly understand what components are included and where a potential critical path is in a design.

In addition to physical timing specification, such as the setup time and hold time constraints of flip-flops, a timing diagram can clearly demonstrate the relation between inputs and outputs, and the sequence of operations of a pipelined RTL design. Therefore, it is also strongly recommended to plot the timing diagram of the design before writing its RTL codes. Doing this can clearly understand the evolution of signals over time so that right things can be performed at the right times. If a performance issue raises, some pipeline stages might need to be adjusted.

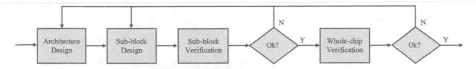

Figure 7.41: Hierarchical design and verification.

Example 7.10. There are 2 ways of implementing addition of 4 numbers, a, b, c, and d, as shown below, where $y1$ is a purely combinational output and $y2$ has 2 pipeline stages in it. The input data are fed into the design like streaming data; and hence, only datapath is required and control unit is not needed. Please plot their architecture and timing diagrams.

```
1// Two approaches for addition of 4 numbers
2// Approach 1: purely combinational output
3assign y1=(a+b)+(c+d);
4// Approach 2: 2 pipeline stages
5always @(posedge clk) begin
6    sum_ab<=a+b;
7    sum_cd<=c+d;
8    y2<=sum_ab+sum_cd;
9end
```

Solution: Their architecture and timing diagrams are displayed in Figure 7.42(a) and 7.42(b), respectively. As presented in Figure 7.42(a), the components of $y1$ requires 3 adders, whereas $y2$ requires 3 adders and 3 more registers. Additionally, the critical paths of $y1$ and $y2$ have two and one adders, respectively. About the timing in 7.42(b), the result $y1$ is available at the same cycle whenever a, b, c, and d are provided. Rather, $y2$ is available 2 cycles after giving a, b, c, and d.

However, if inputs are continuously fed into the circuits, one output is available on both $y1$ and $y2$ in every cycle; and therefore, they achieve the same throughput under the situation of the same clock period. Since the critical path of $y2$ is half that of $y1$, the maximum clock frequency of $y2$ can ideally be twice that of $y1$. Consequently, the throughput of $y2$ is twice that of $y1$ at their maximum clock frequencies as well.

From above, the architecture and timing diagrams can give us insights on choosing the most suitable design in terms of area, speed, and even power consumption. Most importantly, the performance can be assessed in an earlier design stage.

□

7.3.1 COMPLEX MULTIPLIER

One of the most challenging tasks in digital design is designing a datapath and corresponding control unit such that they satisfy the given requirements and constraints.

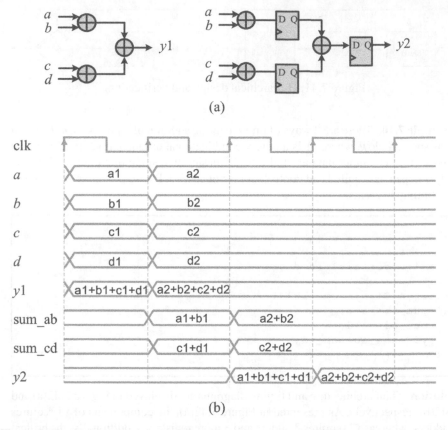

(a)

(b)

Figure 7.42: (a) Architecture and (b) timing diagrams of addition of 4 numbers with and without pipeline.

There are usually many alternative datapaths capable of meeting the functional requirements of the system, but some will have advantages over others. Choosing among them usually involves a tradeoff between area and performance.

We demonstrate another example of the complex multiplier designed using the architecture and timing diagrams here.

Example 7.11. The design of a module, including the datapath and control unit, to perform a complex multiplication of two complex numbers, is shown in Figure 7.43. The operands and product are all in Cartesian form. The real and imaginary parts of the operands are represented as 16-bit signed $s(4.12)$ fixed-point binary numbers. The real and imaginary parts of the product are represented as 32-bit signed $s(8.24)$ fixed-point binary numbers.

Solution: The complex multiplication is sequenced by the timing diagram in Figure 7.44.

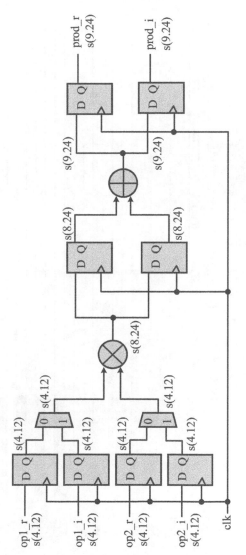

Figure 7.43: Datapath of a complex multiplier.

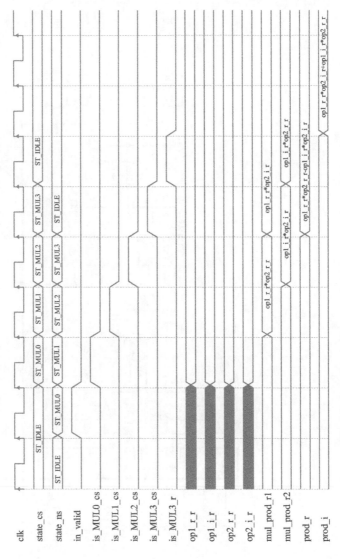

Figure 7.44: Timing diagram of a complex multiplier.

The RTL codes are presented below. There are two complex operands, op1$= a =$ $a_r + ja_i$ and op2$= b = b_r + jb_i$, where $j = \sqrt{-1}$, and the result is the output signal, prod$= a \times b = a_r b_r - a_i b_i + j(a_r b_i + a_i b_r)$. The real and imaginary parts are indicated by the suffix r and i, respectively. Consequently, the real and imaginary parts of the result, prod, both require two real multiplications and one real addition/subtraction. Notably, the real/imaginary parts of op1, i.e., a_r/a_i, are represented by the signals, op1_r/op1_i, and the real/imaginary parts of op2, i.e., b_r/b_i, are represented by the signals, op2_r/op2_i in Figure 7.43.

After plotting the architectural diagram and deriving the fixed-point design, the datapath unit design is quite straightforward. To guarantee that right operations are taken at right times, we use a state machine as the control unit to govern the operation sequence and generate corresponding control signals.

```
1 // Module of complex multiplier including datapath and
2 // control unit
3 module comp_mul(out_valid, prod_r, prod_i,
4                 in_valid, op1_r, op1_i,
5                 op2_r, op2_i, clk, rst_n);
6 output out_valid;
7 output signed [8:-24] prod_r, prod_i;
8 input in_valid;
9 input signed [3:-12] op1_r, op1_i, op2_r, op2_i;
10 input clk, rst_n;
11 reg [2:0] state_ns, state_cs;
12 wire is_MUL0_cs, is_MUL1_cs, is_MUL2_cs, is_MUL3_cs;
13 reg is_MUL3_cs_r;
14 reg signed [3:-12] op1_r1, op1_i1, op2_r1, op2_i1;
15 wire signed [3:-12] mul_op1, mul_op2;
16 wire signed [7:-24] mul_prod, mul_prod_r1, mul_prod_r2;
17 wire signed [7:-24] sum_op1, sum_op2;
18 wire signed [8:-24] sum;
19 reg signed [8:-24] prod_r, prod_i;
20 // Control unit
21 parameter ST_IDLE=3'b000; parameter ST_MUL0=3'b001;
22 parameter ST_MUL1=3'b011; parameter ST_MUL2=3'b010;
23 parameter ST_MUL3=3'b100;
24 assign is_MUL0_cs=state_cs==ST_MUL0;
25 assign is_MUL1_cs=state_cs==ST_MUL1;
26 assign is_MUL2_cs=state_cs==ST_MUL2;
27 assign is_MUL3_cs=state_cs==ST_MUL3;
28 always @(*) begin
29   state_ns=state_cs;
30   case(state_cs)
31   ST_IDLE:state_ns=in_valid?ST_MUL0:ST_IDLE;
32   ST_MUL0:state_ns=ST_MUL1;
33   ST_MUL1:state_ns=ST_MUL2;
```

```
34  ST_MUL2:state_ns=ST_MUL3;
35  ST_MUL3:state_ns=ST_IDLE;
36  endcase
37 end
38 always @(posedge clk or negedge rst_n)
39  if(!rst_n) state_cs<=ST_IDLE;
40  else state_cs<=state_ns;
41 always @(posedge clk or negedge rst_n)
42  if(!rst_n) is_MUL3_cs_r<=1'b0;
43  else is_MUL3_cs_r<=is_MUL3_cs;
44 // Datapath
45 always @(posedge clk)
46  if(in_valid) begin
47    op1_r_r<=op1_r;
48    op1_i_r<=op1_i;
49    op2_r_r<=op2_r;
50    op2_i_r<=op2_i;
51  end
52 assign mul_op1=(is_MUL0_cs|is_MUL2_cs)?op1_r_r:op1_i_r;
53 assign mul_op2=(is_MUL0_cs|is_MUL3_cs)?op2_r_r:op2_i_r;
54 assign mul_prod=mul_op1*mul_op1;
55 always @(posedge clk)
56  if(is_MUL0_cs|is_MUL2_cs) begin
57    mul_prod_r1<=mul_prod;
58  end
59 always @(posedge clk)
60  if(is_MUL1_cs|is_MUL3_cs)
61    mul_prod_r2<=mul_prod;
62 assign sum_op1=mul_prod_r1;
63 assign sum_op2=is_MUL2_cs?-mul_prod_r2:mul_prod_r2;
64 assign sum=sum_op1+sum_op2;
65 always @(posedge clk)
66  if(is_MUL2_cs) prod_r<=sum;
67 always @(posedge clk)
68  if(is_MUL3_cs_r) prod_i<=sum;
69 endmodule
```

□

7.3.2 TWO ADDITIONS

There are two kinds of datapaths used to implement two additions, as shown in Figure 7.45. The bit width design is also displayed.

Notice that, for the folded design, the register stores the 9-bit result of $a + b$. Consequently, b needs to be sign extended to 9 bits owing to the bit width of 9 bits for the addition result of $a + b$. At first glance, the intuitive implementation using

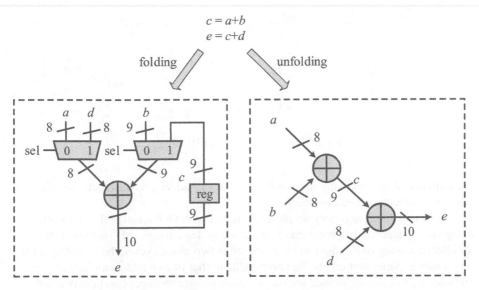

Figure 7.45: Unfolding and folding architecture of datapath for two additions.

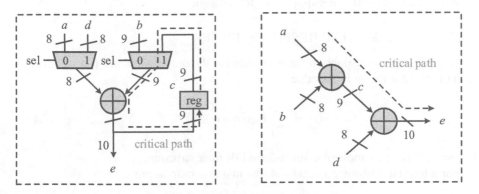

Figure 7.46: Critical path analysis.

two adders seems to have a higher resource cost (two adders) and higher speed (one result per clock cycle). By contrast, the folding one using one adder seems to have a lower resource cost (one adder, ignoring the cost of multiplexers) and lower speed (one result in two clock cycles).

However, a closer examination of the critical paths gives us a different view, as shown in Figure 7.46.

The implementation using two adders has a longer critical path, so its clock period is longer and clock rate is slower. By contrast, the other implementation method, using one adder, has a shorter critical path, so its clock period is shorter and clock rate is faster. If the delay of multiplexers (and a little bit wider adder) can be ignored,

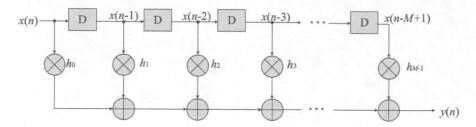

Figure 7.47: Direct-form FIR filter.

the critical path delay of one adder is half that of two adders, so the clock rate of one adder implementation can be doubled.

The timing diagram is very simple and omitted here. One result of the architecture using two adders can be produced in one clock cycle. Though only one result of the architecture using one adder can be produced in two clock cycles, the throughput of one adder implementation can be comparable to that of two adder implementation, but with the benefit, mentioned above, of having a lower resource cost than two adder implementation. Hence, which architecture is better for any specific case should be carefully analyzed before deciding on its RTL design.

7.3.3 FINITE IMPULSE RESPONSE FILTER

For a finite impulse response filter, each value of the output sequence is a weighted sum of the most recent input values as

$$y(n) = \sum_{m=0}^{M-1} h_m x(n-m). \tag{7.1}$$

Figure 7.47 is an example of a direct-form FIR filter structure.

For a four-tap FIR filter, i.e., $M = 4$, the first four outputs are

$$\begin{cases} y(0) = h_0 x(0) + h_1 x(-1) + h_2 x(-2) + h_3 x(-3) \\ y(1) = h_0 x(1) + h_1 x(0) + h_2 x(-1) + h_3 x(-2) \\ y(2) = h_0 x(2) + h_1 x(1) + h_2 x(0) + h_3 x(-1) \\ y(3) = h_0 x(3) + h_1 x(2) + h_2 x(1) + h_3 x(0) \end{cases} \tag{7.2}$$

Notice that $x(n) = 0, \forall n < 0$.

Here, several architectures are presented to realize the FIR filter.

The first architecture, FIR 1, is displayed in Figure 7.48, where $x0$, $x1$, $x2$, $x3$, and y represent $x(n-3)$, $x(n-2)$, $x(n-1)$, $x(n)$, and $y(n)$, respectively. We assume the tap number is 4. The bit widths of inputs and taps are 8 and 3 bits, respectively. Notice that the 4 inputs should be available at once. The critical path is one multiplier plus two adders. The area complexity of the circuit is 4 multipliers and 3 adders.

The RTL codes are written below.

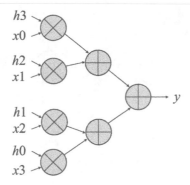

Figure 7.48: FIR filter 1.

```
1 // FIR 1
2 module fir1(y, x0, x1, x2, x3, h0, h1, h2, h3);
3 output [12:0] y;
4 input [7:0] x0, x1, x2, x3;
5 input [2:0] h0, h1, h2, h3;
6 reg [12:0] y;
7 always @(*)
8   y=h0*x3+h1*x2+h2*x1+h3*x0;
9 endmodule
```

Another factor to keep in mind when deciding upon implementation is that the output is a registered one, so the critical path of this module does not influence those using the filter output, as shown in FIR 2 below.

```
1 // FIR 2
2 module fir2(y, x0, x1, x2, x3, h0, h1, h2, h3, clk);
3 output [12:0] y;
4 input [7:0] x0, x1, x2, x3;
5 input [2:0] h0, h1, h2, h3;
6 input clk;
7 reg [12:0] y;
8 always @(posedge clk)
9   y<=h0*x3+h1*x2+h2*x1+h3*x0;
10 endmodule
```

The direct-form FIR filter can be constructed by inserting more registers such that one item of input data enters the filter every clock cycle, which is more suitable for limited memory access and pin number reduction, as shown in Figure 7.49, where ports x and y are $x(n)$ and $y(n)$, respectively. The critical path is one multiplier as

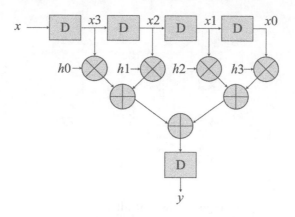

Figure 7.49: FIR filter 3.

well as two adders. The area complexity of the circuit is 4 multipliers, 3 adders, and 5 registers.

RTL codes of FIR 3 are written below. It should be noted that correct results start after the 5th clock. After that, one output is available per clock cycle.

```
1 // FIR 3
2 module fir3(y, x, h0, h1, h2, h3, clk);
3 output [12:0] y;
4 input [7:0] x;
5 input [2:0] h0, h1, h2, h3;
6 input clk;
7 reg [12:0] y;
8 reg [7:0] x0, x1, x2, x3;
9 always @(posedge clk) begin
10    x3 <= x;
11    x2 <= x3;
12    x1 <= x2;
13    x0 <= x1;
14    y <= (h0*x3+h1*x2)+(h2*x1+h3*x0);
15 end
16 endmodule
```

If we further pipeline the filter, the critical path is further shortened, as shown in Figure 7.50. Since the complexity of a multiplier is typically much higher than that of an adder (provided that the coefficients have a non-negligible number of bits), the critical path is one multiplier. The area complexity of the circuit is 4 multipliers, 3 adders, and 9 registers.

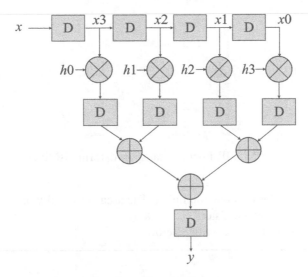

Figure 7.50: FIR filter 4.

The RTL codes of FIR 4 are written below.

```
1 // FIR 4
2 module fir4(y, x, h0, h1, h2, h3, clk);
3 output [12:0] y;
4 input [7:0] x;
5 input [2:0] h0, h1, h2, h3;
6 input clk;
7 reg [12:0] y;
8 reg [7:0] x0, x1, x2, x3;
9 reg [10:0] y0, y1, y2, y3;
10 always @(posedge clk) begin
11   x3<=x;
12   x2<=x3;
13   x1<=x2;
14   x0<=x1;
15   y3<=h0*x3;
16   y2<=h1*x2;
17   y1<=h2*x1;
18   y0<=h3*x0;
19   y<=(y3+y2)+(y1+y0);
20 end
21 endmodule
```

Another equivalent FIR filter structure uses a transposed form that can be constructed from the direct-form FIR filter by exchanging the input and output and inverting the direction of the signal flow, as shown in Figure 7.51. The critical path

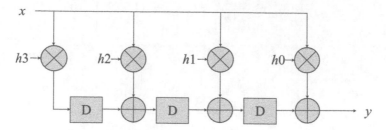

Figure 7.51: FIR filter 5. Transposed-form FIR filter.

now becomes one adder plus one multiplier. The area complexity of the circuit is 4
multipliers, 3 adders, and 3 registers.

The RTL codes of FIR 5 are written below.

```
1 // FIR 5
2 module fir5(y, x, h0, h1, h2, h3, clk);
3 output [12:0] y;
4 input [7:0] x;
5 input [2:0] h0, h1, h2, h3;
6 input clk;
7 reg [10:0] y3;
8 reg [11:0] y2;
9 reg [12:0] y1;
10 reg [12:0] y0;
11 reg [10:0] y3_r;
12 reg [11:0] y2_r;
13 reg [12:0] y1_r;
14 assign y=y0;
15 always @(*) begin
16    y3=h3*x;
17    y2=h2*x+y3_r;
18    y1=h1*x+y2_r;
19    y0=h0*x+y1_r;
20 end
21 always @(posedge clk) begin
22    y3_r<=y3;
23    y2_r<=y2;
24    y1_r<=y1;
25 end
26 endmodule
```

Table 7.3: Summary of different architectures of FIR filter.

FIR filter	Critical path	Area
1	$1 \otimes + 2 \oplus$	$4 \otimes + 3 \oplus$
2	$1 \otimes + 2 \oplus$	$4 \otimes + 3 \oplus + 1\,R$
3	$1 \otimes + 2 \oplus$	$4 \otimes + 3 \oplus + 5\,R$
4	$1 \otimes$	$4 \otimes + 3 \oplus + 9\,R$
5	$1 \otimes + 1 \oplus$	$4 \otimes + 3 \oplus + 3\,R$

The results of different architectures of the FIR filter are summarized in Table 7.3, where $\otimes$, $\oplus$, and R represent the multiplier, adder, and register, respectively. When the number of coefficient taps increases, the advantages of FIR 5 will become clear that it has a fixed and the (almost) shortest critical path as well as the (almost) smallest area.

In this section, several architectures which can be used to implement the FIR filter have been demonstrated, each with its own specific pros and cons. Designers must take a number of factors into consideration and carefully explore, analyze, and optimize different architectures before writing their RTL codes.

7.4   DIGITAL DESIGN OF HUFFMAN CODING

At the end of this chapter, we demonstrate a complete digital design. Huffman coding is a kind of variable-length encoding first created by David Albert Huffman in 1952. To reduce the memory requirement of all symbols, the symbols are encoded according to their probability of occurrence. Shorter codes are given to symbols with higher probability of occurrence, and vice versa. The net result is data compression; that is, the codes of symbols are generated by fewer bits than would be required if all symbols were encoded with the same number of bits. Huffman code is also called an entropy code. To be able to distinguish short bit strings from the first parts of longer bit strings, no longer bit string can use a prefix that resembles a shorter bit string.

The Huffman code is illustrated below. It is critical that the probability of occurrence of each symbol is known in advance. Knowing the probability of occurrence of each symbol, the Huffman coding is exemplified below. Suppose that we have 5 symbols, A_i, $i = 1, 2, ..., 5$, to be encoded, and their probabilities of occurrence, $P(A_i)$, are shown in Table 7.4.

Table 7.4: Probability of occurrence of each symbol.

Symbol	$P(A_i)$
A_1	0.09
A_2	0.02
A_3	0.51
A_4	0.13
A_5	0.25

Huffman codes are generated in three stages: initialization, combination, and splitting. The initialization stage counts the numbers of occurrence of all symbols (to determine the probability of occurrence), and then sorts the symbols according to their projected frequency, as shown in Table 7.5.

Table 7.5: Initialization stage after sorting the probability of occurrence.

$P(A_i)$	Symbol
0.51	A_3
0.25	A_5
0.13	A_4
0.09	A_1
0.02	A_2

The combination stage merges the two symbols in Huffman table with the lowest probabilities of occurrence and adds their probabilities of occurrence, and then sorts the remaining probabilities of occurrence again, as shown in Figure 7.52. The tree structure used for the splitting stage introduced later is also displayed. In the merged symbol set, the symbol, A_2, which has a lower probability of occurrence, is put onto the left subtree, while the symbol, A_1, with a higher probability of occurrence, is put onto the right subtree. The sum of the probabilities of occurrence of A_1 and A_2 is 0.11.

Similarly, the second round of the combination stage is displayed in Figure 7.53.

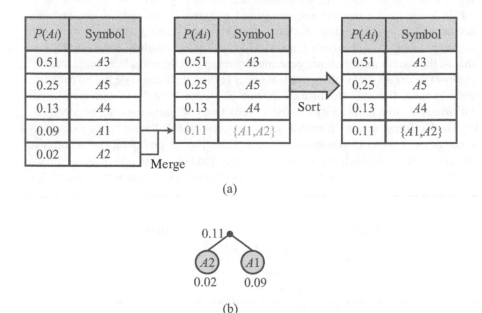

(a)

(b)

Figure 7.52: The first round of the combination stage: (a) table and (b) tree.

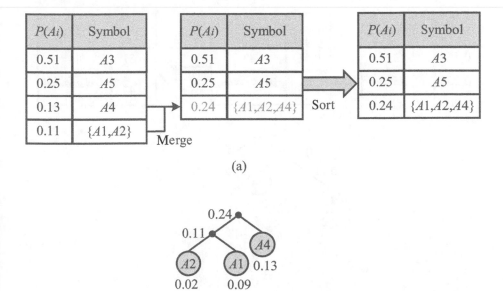

(a)

(b)

Figure 7.53: The second round of the combination stage: (a) table and (b) tree.

In the newly merged symbol set, the previously merged symbol set, $\{A_1,A_2\}$, with a lower probability of occurrence is put onto the left subtree, while the symbol, A_4, which indicates a higher probability of occurrence is put onto the right subtree.

The third and the fourth (final) rounds of the combination stage are presented in Figure 7.54. After the fourth round, the combination stage has completed.

An overview of the Huffman table is presented in Figure 7.55.

The last stage is the splitting stage, which is used to encode the symbols into the tree structure, as shown in Figure 7.56. Here, the symbol $A3$ has a higher probability of occurrence than the symbol set $\{A1,A2,A4,A5\}$, so it is assigned bit 0, while the symbol set $\{A1,A2,A4,A5\}$ is assigned bit 1. This means that when reading the MSB of a code with bit 0, it must be the symbol $A3$. However, when reading the MSB of a code with bit 1, it could be any one of the symbols in $\{A1,A2,A4,A5\}$. Therefore, extra bits must be used for decoding so that the correct symbol can be selected. The process continues until all symbols have been assigned a unique code, as displayed in Figure 7.56.

The final Huffman codes are shown in Table 7.6.

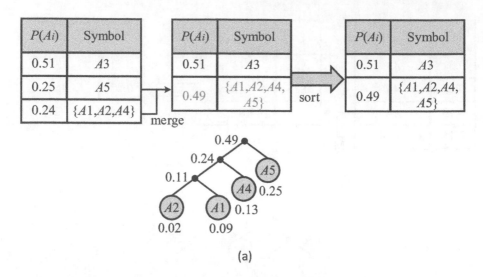

(a)

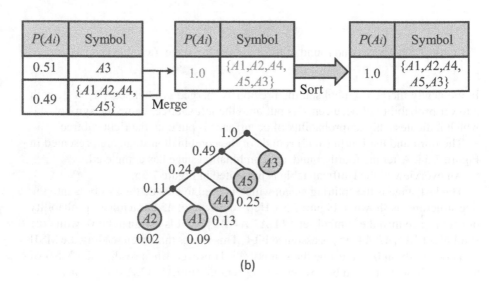

(b)

Figure 7.54: (a) The third and (b) the fourth (final) rounds of the combination stage.

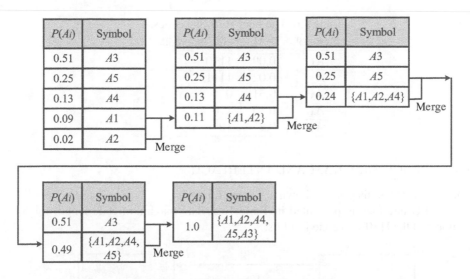

Figure 7.55: Complete Huffman table.

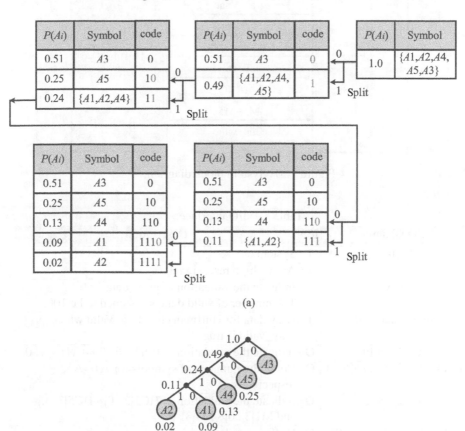

(a)

(b)

Figure 7.56: The splitting stage: (a) table and (b) tree.

Table 7.6: The final Huffman codes.

Symbol	$P(A_i)$	Huffman code
A_1	0.09	1110
A_2	0.02	1111
A_3	0.51	0
A_4	0.13	110
A_5	0.25	10

7.4.1 BLOCK DIAGRAM AND INTERFACE

The system block diagram is shown in Figure 7.57.

The I/O interface is presented in Table 10.1. The maximum code length for 5 symbols of the Huffman code is 4 bits.

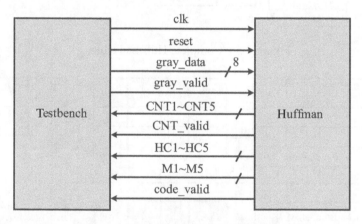

Figure 7.57: System block diagram.

Table 7.7: I/O interface.

Signal name	I/O	Description
clk	I	System clock.
reset	I	Active-high reset signal.
gray_valid	I	Indicate the validation of gray_data[7 : 0]. The number of valid data is assumed to be 100.
gray_data[7 : 0]	I	Gray data for Huffman encoding. Valid when gray_valid is true.
CNT_valid	O	Indicate the validation of CNT1[6 : 0]~CNT5[6 : 0].
CNT1[6 : 0]~CNT5[6 : 0]	O	Count the numbers of symbols for A1~A5, respectively.
code_valid	O	Indicate the validation of HC1[3 : 0]~HC5[3 : 0] and M1[3 : 0]~M5[3 : 0].
HC1[3 : 0]~HC5[3 : 0]	O	Huffman codes of A1~A5, respectively.
M1[3 : 0]~M5[3 : 0]	O	Bit-valid masks for Huffman codes of A1~A5, respectively.

Huffman coding is a variable length encoder, which uses masks to indicate code length. For example, if the binary Huffman code of $A5$ is 10, then $HC5 = XX10$ and $M5 = 0011$, which indicates the least significant two bits of the code, $HC5$, are valid, while the most significant two bits are "don't care".

7.4.2   ALGORITHM DESIGN

To implement the Huffman coding, a state machine like the one shown in Figure 7.58 is used to indicate the counting, sorting, and merging tasks, while the splitting task is not explicitly needed. In this example, we assume there are 5 symbols which need to be encoded and the total number of occurrences is 100. Two symbol sets with the two lowest numbers of occurrence are then merged, one by one. Consequently, there will be 4 merging states through which all 5 symbols (5 original sets with one symbol in each) will eventually be merged into one final set.

It should be noted that the number of occurrences, rather than the probability of occurrence is used to determine how symbols will be encoded. The initialization stage includes states, ST_CNT and ST_SORT1. The state ST_CNT calculates the number of occurrences, sym_cnt[i], for the i-th symbol, and then the state ST_SORT1 sorts the numbers of occurrences. An additional variable, sym_bmap[i], records the bit mapping of the i-th symbol (set). After sorting, the sym_cnt[0] stores the maximum number of occurrences and sym_bmap[0] stores its corresponding symbol set, sym_cnt[1] stores the second maximum number of occurrences and sym_bmap[1] stores its symbol set, and so on.

During the combination stage, which includes ST_MERG1, ST_SORT2, ST_MERG2, ST_SORT3, ST_MERG3, ST_SORT4, and ST_MERG4 states, the Huffman table is constructed, together with the Huffman codes. Therefore, there is no explicit splitting stage. In the combination stage, sym_cnt and sym_bmap represent the number of occurrences and the bit mapping of a symbol set, respectively, and sym_code and sym_mask represent the Huffman symbol code and symbol mask, respectively.

In the merging state, the two symbol sets with the two lowest numbers of occurrences are merged. Their numbers of occurrences are added and their bit mappings are OR-ed to record (or merge) all the symbols they contain. Concurrently, among these two symbol sets, the Huffman symbol codes, sym_code, of all symbols belonging to the symbol set with the lowest number of occurrences are prepended bit 1 at

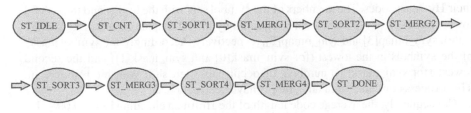

Figure 7.58: State machine.

the position left to the left-most bit 1 of the symbol masks sym_mask. Similarly, the Huffman codes of all symbols belonging to the symbol set with the second lowest number of occurrences are prepended bit 0. The members of the i-th symbol set are indicated by its bit mapping, sym_bmap[i]. The position to the left of the left-most bit 1 of the symbol mask sym_mask can be determined by adding all the bits of the symbol mask. In addition, to derive a new symbol mask, the symbol masks of the symbols in the lowest two symbol sets left shift with bit 1 shifted in.

In the sorting state, the numbers of occurrences for all alive symbol sets are sorted just like the state ST_SORT1, which enables the same sorting circuit to be shared. The merging and sorting states interleave until only one symbol set remains. Finally, the state ST_DONE outputs the Huffman codes and their masks.

Figure 7.59 is an example, as that shown in Table 7.4, of the Huffman encoding performed by the proposed algorithm. In the state, ST_CNT, the numbers of occurrences of the 5 symbols are counted and the sym_bmap is initialized for each symbol, 1 at bit 0 for $A1$, 1 at bit 1 for $A2$, etc.

In the state, ST_SORT1, the symbols are sorted according to the numbers of times they occur, i.e., sym_cnt. The bit mappings of them, sym_bmap, are also reordered accordingly. In the state, ST_MERG1, the two symbol sets, $\{A1\}$ and $\{A2\}$, which have the two lowest numbers of occurrences, are merged. A new symbol set, $\{A1, A2\}$, is then formed and its number of occurrences is calculated by adding all the occurrences of $A1$ and $A2$. Simultaneously, the symbol sets, $\{A2\}$ and $\{A1\}$, with the lowest and the second lowest numbers of occurrences are respectively prepended bits 1 and 0 to their Huffman codes, sym_code2 and sym_code1. The members of the symbol sets with the lowest and the second lowest numbers of occurrences are indicated by the bit mappings (after ST_SORT1 state), sym_bmap[4] and sym_bmap[3], respectively. Accordingly, the symbol masks of the symbols in the lowest (for sym_mask[1]) and the second lowest (for sym_mask[0]) numbers of occurrences left shift with bit 1 shifted in.

In the state, ST_SORT2, the symbols are sorted again according to the new sym_cnt's. The bit mappings of them, sym_bmap, are also reordered accordingly. In the state, ST_MERG2, the two symbol sets, $\{A1,A2\}$ and $\{A4\}$, which have the two lowest numbers of occurrences, are merged. A new symbol set, $\{A1, A2, A4\}$, is then formed and its number of occurrences is calculated by adding all the occurrences of $\{A1,A2\}$ and $\{A4\}$. Simultaneously, the symbol sets, $\{A1,A2\}$ and $\{A4\}$, with the lowest and the second lowest numbers of occurrences are respectively prepended bits 1 (for sym_code2 and sym_code1) and 0 (for sym_code4) to their Huffman codes. The members of the symbol sets with the lowest and the second lowest numbers of occurrences are indicated by the bit mappings (after ST_SORT2 state), sym_bmap[3] and sym_bmap[2], respectively. Accordingly, the symbol masks of the symbols in the lowest (for sym_mask[0] and sym_mask[1]) and the second lowest (for sym_mask[3]) numbers of occurrences left shift with bit 1 shifted in. This process continues until all symbols have been encoded.

Consequently, the average code length of the Huffman encoding is $4 \times 0.09 + 4 \times 0.02 + 1 \times 0.51 + 3 \times 0.13 + 2 \times 0.25 = 1.84$ bits. In comparison to a system which

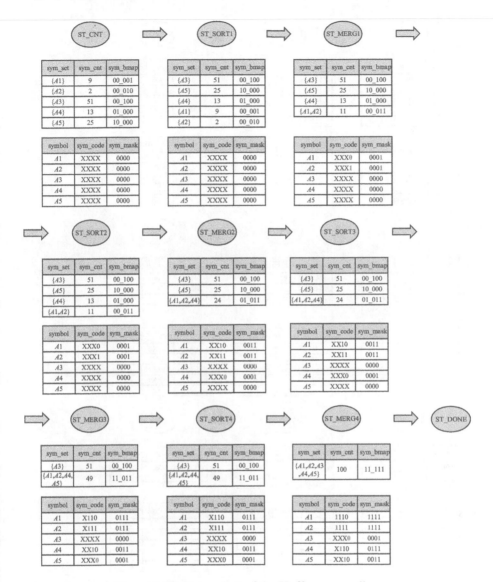

Figure 7.59: Example 1 of the Huffman encoding.

does not use Huffman encoding, which requires 3 bits for every 5 symbols, the saved bit width when using the Huffman code for each symbol is $3 - 1.84 = 1.16$ bits.

Figure 7.60 presents another example. The average code length of the Huffman encoding is $2 \times 0.2 + 3 \times 0.2 + 3 \times 0.2 + 2 \times 0.2 + 2 \times 0.2 = 2.4$ bits. Compared to that without the Huffman encoding, the saved bit width for the Huffman code of each symbol is $3 - 2.4 = 0.6$ bits.

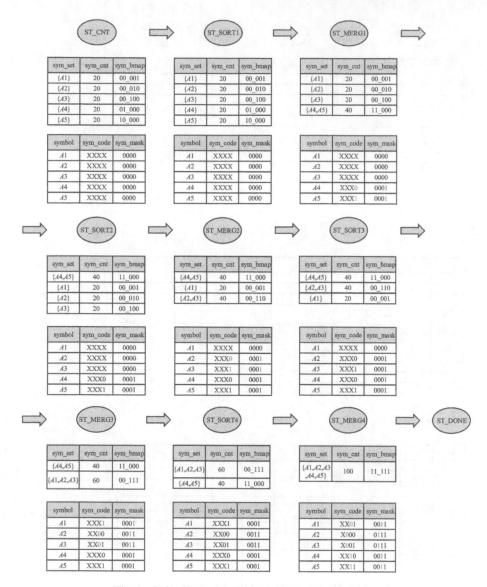

Figure 7.60: Example 2 of the Huffman encoding.

7.4.3   RTL DESIGN

The timing diagram that governs the Huffman encoding of Example 1 is presented in Figure 7.61.

The RTL codes of the state machine are illustrated below.

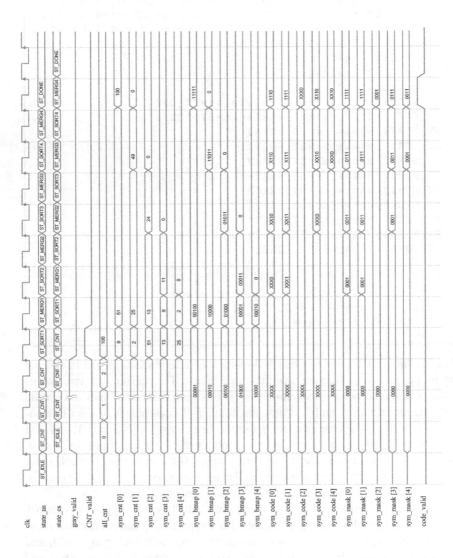

Figure 7.61: Timing diagram of the Huffman encoding.

```
1// State machine
2reg [3:0] state_ns, state_cs;
3parameter ST_IDLE =4'b0000; parameter ST_CNT  =4'b0001;
4parameter ST_SORT1=4'b0011; parameter ST_MERG1=4'b0010;
5parameter ST_SORT2=4'b0110; parameter ST_MERG2=4'b0111;
6parameter ST_SORT3=4'b0101; parameter ST_MERG3=4'b0100;
7parameter ST_SORT4=4'b1100; parameter ST_MERG4=4'b1101;
8parameter ST_DONE =4'b1111;
9always @(*) begin
10    state_ns=state_cs;
11    case(state_cs)
12    ST_IDLE:if(gray_valid) state_ns=ST_CNT;
13    ST_CNT:if(CNT_valid) state_ns=ST_SORT1;
14    ST_SORT1:state_ns=ST_MERG1;
15    ST_MERG1:state_ns=ST_SORT2;
16    ST_SORT2:state_ns=ST_MERG2;
17    ST_MERG2:state_ns=ST_SORT3;
18    ST_SORT3:state_ns=ST_MERG3;
19    ST_MERG3:state_ns=ST_SORT4;
20    ST_SORT4:state_ns=ST_MERG4;
21    ST_MERG4:state_ns=ST_DONE;
22    ST_DONE:state_ns=ST_IDLE;
23    endcase
24end
25always @(posedge clk or posedge reset)
26    if(reset) state_cs<=ST_IDLE;
27    else state_cs<=state_ns;
```

The remaining RTL codes when following the state machine precepts and the using proposed timing diagram are illustrated below. The register, all_cnt, counts the total number of occurrences until 8'd100 has been reached. When gray_valid is true, the register, sym_cnt[i], counts the number of occurrences of the i-th symbol. In ST_SORT1 state, the original symbol counts, sym_cnt[i], $i = 0, 1, ..., 4$, are sorted and the sorted results, sort_sym_cnt, obtained by the function, sort_result, are stored in sym_cnt again. Therefore, sym_cnt[0] has the maximum symbol count, sym_cnt[1] has the second maximum symbol count, and so on. In other sorting states, sym_cnt latches the sorting results of the merged numbers of occurrences.

To find the maximum value of 5 numbers, sym_cnt[4], sym_cnt[3],...,sym_cnt[0], the function sort_result compares sym_cnt[4] and sym_cnt[3], and places their maximum in sym_cnt[3]; then sort_result compares sym_cnt[3] and sym_cnt[2], and places their maximum in sym_cnt[2]; then sort_result compares sym_cnt[2] and sym_cnt[1], and places their maximum in sym_cnt[1]; finally, sort_result compares sym_cnt[1] and sym_cnt[0], and places their maximum in sym_cnt[0]. Therefore, the final maximum value is stored in sym_cnt[0]. To find the maximum value of remaining 4 numbers, sym_cnt[4], sym_cnt[3],...,sym_cnt[1], similar procedures are performed and the second maximum value is stored in sym_cnt[1], and so on.

```
1 reg [6:0] all_cnt;        // Max 100
2 reg [6:0] sym_cnt[0:4]; // Max 100 even for merging
3 wire CNT_valid;
4 wire [6:0] CNT1, CNT2, CNT3, CNT4, CNT5;
5 integer i;
6 parameter SYM0_PAT=8'h01; parameter SYM1_PAT=8'h02;
7 parameter SYM2_PAT=8'h03; parameter SYM3_PAT=8'h04;
8 parameter SYM4_PAT=8'h05;
9 assign CNT_valid=all_cnt==8'd100;
10 always @(posedge clk or posedge reset)
11   if(reset)
12     all_cnt<=0;
13   else if(gray_valid)
14     all_cnt<=all_cnt+1'b1;
15   else if(CNT_valid)
16     all_cnt<=0;
17 assign CNT1=sym_cnt[0]; assign CNT2=sym_cnt[1];
18 assign CNT3=sym_cnt[2]; assign CNT4=sym_cnt[3];
19 assign CNT5=sym_cnt[4];
20 always @(posedge clk or posedge reset)
21   if(reset)
22     for(i=0;i<=4;i=i+1)
23       sym_cnt[i]=0;
24   else if(gray_valid)
25         case(gray_data)
26         SYM0_PAT: // Incrementer can be shared
27           sym_cnt[0]<=sym_cnt[0]+1'b1;
28         SYM1_PAT: // Incrementer can be shared
29           sym_cnt[1]<=sym_cnt[1]+1'b1;
30         SYM2_PAT: // Incrementer can be shared
31           sym_cnt[2]<=sym_cnt[2]+1'b1;
32         SYM3_PAT: // Incrementer can be shared
33           sym_cnt[3]<=sym_cnt[3]+1'b1;
34         SYM4_PAT: // Incrementer can be shared
35           sym_cnt[4]<=sym_cnt[4]+1'b1;
36         endcase
37   else
38     case(state_ns)
39     ST_SORT1,ST_SORT2,ST_SORT3,ST_SORT4:
40             for(i=0;i<=4;i=i+1)
41               sym_cnt[i]<=sort_sym_cnt[i];
42     ST_MERG1: begin
43             // Adder can be shared
44             sym_cnt[3]<=sym_cnt[3]+sym_cnt[4];
45             sym_cnt[4]<=0;
46           end
```

```
47      ST_MERG2 : begin
48                   // Adder can be shared
49                   sym_cnt [2] <= sym_cnt [2] + sym_cnt [3];
50                   sym_cnt [3] <= 0;
51              end
52      ST_MERG3 : begin
53                   // Adder can be shared
54                   sym_cnt [1] <= sym_cnt [1] + sym_cnt [2];
55                   sym_cnt [2] <= 0;
56              end
57      ST_MERG4 : begin
58                   // Adder can be shared
59                   sym_cnt [0] <= sym_cnt [0] + sym_cnt [1];
60                   sym_cnt [1] <= 0;
61              end
62      endcase
63 function [59:0] sort_result; // Function call definition
64   input [6:0] sym_cnt0 , sym_cnt1 , sym_cnt2 , sym_cnt3 ,
65                sym_cnt4;
66   input [4:0] sym_bmap0 , sym_bmap1 , sym_bmap2 , sym_bmap3 ,
67                sym_bmap4;
68   reg [6:0] sort_sym_cnt [0:4];
69   reg [4:0] sort_bmap [0:4];
70   reg [6:0] tmp_cnt;
71   reg [4:0] tmp_map;
72   integer i, j;
73   begin
74     sort_sym_cnt [0] = sym_cnt0; sort_sym_cnt [1] = sym_cnt1;
75     sort_sym_cnt [2] = sym_cnt2; sort_sym_cnt [3] = sym_cnt3;
76     sort_sym_cnt [4] = sym_cnt4;
77     sort_sym_bmap [0] = sym_bmap0;
78     sort_sym_bmap [1] = sym_bmap1;
79     sort_sym_bmap [2] = sym_bmap2;
80     sort_sym_bmap [3] = sym_bmap3;
81     sort_sym_bmap [4] = sym_bmap4;
82     for (i=3; i>=0; i=i-1)
83       for (j=3; j>=3-i; j=j-1)
84         if (sort_sym_cnt [j+1] > sort_sym_cnt [j]) begin
85           tmp_cnt = sort_sym_cnt [j]; // Sym count swapped
86           sort_sym_cnt [j] = sort_sym_cnt [j+1];
87           sort_sym_cnt [j+1] = tmp_cnt;
88           tmp_map = sort_sym_bmap [j]; // Bitmap swapped
89           sort_sym_bmap [j] = sort_sym_bmap [j+1];
90           sort_sym_bmap [j+1] = tmp_map;
91         end
92     sort_result = {sort_sym_bmap [0], sort_sym_bmap [1],
93       sort_sym_bmap [2], sort_sym_bmap [3], sort_sym_bmap [4],
```

```
94      sort_sym_cnt [0] , sort_sym_cnt [1] ,
95      sort_sym_cnt [2] , sort_sym_cnt [3] , sort_sym_cnt [4]};
96   end
97 endfunction
```

The sorting states, ST_SORT1, ST_SORT2, ST_SORT3, and ST_SORT4, sort the remaining 5, 4, 3, and 2 symbol sets, respectively. In the sorting states, the bit mapping, sym_bmap, of each symbol set is determined according to the sorting results. That is, if symbol counts are swapped, corresponding bit mappings are swapped accordingly.

During the merging states, ST_MERG1, ST_MERG2, ST_MERG3, and ST_MERG4, the symbol sets with the two lowest numbers of occurrence are merged by adding their number of occurrences and OR-ing their bit maps. Notice that, in the RTL codes, integer variables in different always blocks should be designated as different variables; otherwise, local variables of a named block can also be used.

```
1 reg  [4:0]  sym_bmap [0:4] ;
2 wire  [6:0]  sort_sym_cnt [0:4] ;
3 wire  [4:0]  sort_sym_bmap [0:4] ;
4 integer  i1;
5 assign
6 {sort_sym_bmap [0] , sort_sym_bmap [1] , sort_sym_bmap [2] ,
7 sort_sym_bmap [3] , sort_sym_bmap [4] ,
8 sort_sym_cnt [0] , sort_sym_cnt [1] , sort_sym_cnt [2] ,
9 sort_sym_cnt [3] , sort_sym_cnt [4]}=
10               sort_result (sym_cnt , sym_bmap);
11 always  @(posedge  clk  or  posedge  reset)
12   if (reset)
13     for (i1=0; i1<=4; i1=i1+1)
14       sym_bmap [i1] <=1'b1 <<i1 ;
15   else
16     case (state_ns)
17     ST_SORT1 , ST_SORT2 , ST_SORT3 , ST_SORT4 :
18               for (i1=0; i1<=4; i1=i1+1)
19                 sym_bmap [i1] <=sort_sym_bmap [i1] ;
20     ST_MERG1 : begin
21                 sym_bmap [3] <=sym_bmap [3] | sym_bmap [4] ;
22                 sym_bmap [4] <=0;
23               end
24     ST_MERG2 : begin
25                 sym_bmap [2] <=sym_bmap [2] | sym_bmap [3] ;
26                 sym_bmap [3] <=0;
27               end
28     ST_MERG3 : begin
29                 sym_bmap [1] <=sym_bmap [1] | sym_bmap [2] ;
```

```
30                      sym_bmap [2] <=0;
31                  end
32      ST_MERG4:  begin
33                      sym_bmap [0] <= sym_bmap [0] | sym_bmap [1] ;
34                      sym_bmap [1] <=0;
35                  end
36      endcase
```

The Huffman codes, sym_code, of all symbols belonging to the symbol set with the lowest number of occurrences are prepended 1 at the bit location to the left of the mask, sym_mask, while the Huffman codes, sym_code, of all symbols belonging to the symbol set with the second lowest number of occurrences are prepended 0 at the same bit location. The bit location that is to the left of the first bit with logic 1 of the mask can be calculated by adding all the bits in the mask, sym_mask. The mask, sym_mask, then shifts left with one additional 1 shifted in.

```
1 // 4 bits suffice for the longest code
2 reg [3:0] sym_code [0:4] , sym_mask [0:4] ;
3 // First zero location of each symbol
4 reg [1:0] sym_mask_0_loc [0:4] ;
5 wire [3:0] HC1, HC2, HC3, HC4, HC5 ;
6 wire [3:0] M1, M2, M3, M4, M5 ;
7 integer i2, i3 ;
8 assign {HC1, HC2, HC3, HC4, HC5}=
9         {sym_code [0] , sym_code [1] , sym_code [2] ,
10        sym_code [3] , sym_code [4] };
11 assign {M1, M2, M3, M4, M5}={sym_mask [0] , sym_mask [1] ,
12        sym_mask [2] , sym_mask [3] , sym_mask [4] };
13 always @(posedge clk or posedge reset)
14   if (reset)
15     for (i2=0; i2 <=4; i2=i2+1)
16       sym_mask [i2] <=0;
17   else
18     case (state_ns)
19     ST_MERG1: for (i2=0; i2 <=4; i2=i2+1) begin
20                 if (sym_bmap [4] [i2]==1'b1) begin
21                   sym_code [i2] [sym_mask_0_loc [i2]] <=1'b1;
22                   sym_mask [i2] <={sym_mask [i2] [2:0] ,1'b1};
23                 end
24                 if (sym_bmap [3] [i2]==1'b1) begin
25                   sym_code [i2] [sym_mask_0_loc [i2]] <=1'b0;
26                   sym_mask [i2] <={sym_mask [i2] [2:0] ,1'b1};
27                 end
28               end
29     ST_MERG2: for (i2=0; i2 <=4; i2=i2+1) begin
```

```
30              if(sym_bmap[3][i2]==1'b1) begin
31                  sym_code[i2][sym_mask_0_loc[i2]]<=1'b1;
32                  sym_mask[i2]<={sym_mask[i2][2:0],1'b1};
33              end
34              if(sym_bmap[2][i2]==1'b1) begin
35                  sym_code[i2][sym_mask_0_loc[i2]]<=1'b0;
36                  sym_mask[i2]<={sym_mask[i2][2:0],1'b1};
37              end
38          end
39  ST_MERG3:  for(i2=0;i2<=4;i2=i2+1) begin
40              if(sym_bmap[2][i2]==1'b1) begin
41                  sym_code[i2][sym_mask_0_loc[i2]]
42                    <=1'b1;
43                  sym_mask[i2]
44                    <={sym_mask[i2][2:0],1'b1};
45              end
46              if(sym_bmap[1][i2]==1'b1) begin
47                  sym_code[i2][sym_mask_0_loc[i2]]
48                    <=1'b0;
49                  sym_mask[i2]
50                    <={sym_mask[i2][2:0],1'b1};
51              end
52          end
53  ST_MERG4:  for(i2=0;i2<=4;i2=i2+1) begin
54              if(sym_bmap[1][i2]==1'b1) begin
55                  sym_code[i2][sym_mask_0_loc[i2]]
56                    <=1'b1;
57                  sym_mask[i2]
58                    <={sym_mask[i2][2:0],1'b1};
59              end
60              if(sym_bmap[0][i2]==1'b1) begin
61                  sym_code[i2][sym_mask_0_loc[i2]]
62                    <=1'b0;
63                  sym_mask[i2]
64                    <={sym_mask[i2][2:0],1'b1};
65              end
66          end
67     endcase
68 always @(*)
69   for(i3=0;i3<=4;i3=i3+1)
70     sym_mask_0_loc[i3]=sum_bits(sym_mask[i3][2:0]);
71 function [1:0] sum_bits; // Function call definition
72   input [2:0] val;
73   sum_bits=val[0]+val[1]+val[2];
74 endfunction
```

Finally, code_valid is asserted when the current state, state_cs, equals
ST_DONE.

```
1// Generation of code_valid signal by combinational
2// circuit
3wire code_valid;
4assign code_valid=state_cs==ST_DONE;
```

It's better to have a registered output as follows if timing is a major concern.

```
1// Generation of code_valid signal by sequential circuit
2reg code_valid;
3always @(posedge clk or posedge reset)
4  if(reset) code_valid<=0;
5  else if(state_ns==ST_DONE) code_valid<=1;
6  else code_valid<=0;
```

7.5   FURTHER READING

- David Money Harris and Sarah L. Harris, *Digital design and computer architecture*, 2nd Ed., Morgan Kaufmann, 2013.
- John F. Wakerly, *Digital design: principles and practices*, 5th Ed., Prentice Hall, 2018.
- Mark Gordon Arnold, *Verilog digital computer design: algorithms into hardware*, Prentice Hall, 1999.
- Michael D. Ciletti, *Advanced digital design with the Verilog HDL*, 2nd Ed., Prentice Hall, 2010.
- Peter J. Ashenden, *Digital design: an embedded systems approach using Verilog*, Morgan Kaufmann Publishers, 2007.
- Stephen Brown and Zvonko Vranesic, *Fundamentals of digital logic with Verilog design*, McGraw-Hill, 2002.
- William J. Dally and R. Curtis Harting, *Digital design: a systems approach*, Cambridge University Press, 2012.

PROBLEMS

1. Develop the testbench of Example 7.1 and a behavior model as a gold result to verify the design output.
2. In Example 7.2, whenever the current state stays in the ST_M0 state, the arbiter will check the requests of master 1, master 2, and then, master 3. Hence, the arbitration is not truly equal to masters 1, 2, and 3 in this state because master 0 always has the highest priority. It is best to redesign the arbiter such that a truly fair arbiter can be obtained.
3. Write the Verilog codes for an arbiter that takes four high-priority requests and four low-priority requests and outputs the eight grant signals.

   a. Write a baseline module that low-priority requests can be starved.
   b. Write a module that after 4 cycles of granting high-priority requests will grant a low-priority request. A static tie-breaking scheme for requests with equal priority is adopted.
   c. Modify the above module to implement a round-robin way for breaking ties within a class with the same priority. That is, among four requests with the same priority, each request will be granted sequentially. For example, request 0 has the highest priority until it has been granted, after which request 1 will have the highest priority, etc.
4. Implement a system with master, slave, and arbiter.

   a. Please write a master module that can send a request for calculating the average of 5 numbers with fixed-point number format s(6.8).
   b. Instantiate 4 masters and master 0 has the highest priority. The slave and arbiter use the designs in Examples 7.1 and 7.2, respectively.
   c. Analyze the throughput of your system. Improve the throughput by modifying the handshake protocol and designs if necessary so that the pipelined slave can be fully utilized in every cycle.
   d. Verify the above designs by simulations.
5. Modify the module of the average of 5 numbers, avg_value, by moving the two additions to the first pipeline stage so that the second pipeline stage has only one addition. Identify advantages of the new design, and then verify your design. Then develop a behavioral model for the module of the average of 5 numbers, avg_value, as the gold result to verify the result of avg_value module.
6. The memory units that follow are specified by the number of words multiplied by the number of bits per word. How many address lines and input-output data lines will be needed in each case?

   a. 8K×16 bits,
   b. 2G×8 bits,
   c. 16M×32 bits,
   d. 256K×164 bits.
7. Implement a 8 × 16 ROM using a case statement.
8. For the RAM module in Example 7.6,

  a. add the access time, 1.2 time units, of rdata, i.e., the time required for the
     rising edge of the clock to output the available data.
  b. add the setup time check for 1 time unit and hold time check of 0.2 time units
     for all input ports of RAM, including cen, wen, ren, addr, and wdata.
  c. write a testbench to verify the above timing constraints.
9. Model a 256×16 bits single-port memory array with 4 signals: data bus,
   data[15 : 0], address bus, addr[7 : 0], active-low output enable, ren, and active-
   low write enable, wen. The memory stores data[15 : 0] on the falling edge of the
   wen. The memory should drive the data bus whenever ren is low.
10. For the ROM module in Section 7.2.2,

  a. add the access time, 1.2 time units, of data, rdata, i.e., the time required for
     the rising edge of the clock to output the available data.
  b. add the setup time check for 1 time unit and hold time check of 0.2 time units
     for all input ports of ROM, including ren and addr.
  c. write a testbench to verify the above timing constraints.
11. Write a Verilog model which can implement the following:

  a. A memory of eight bit-sliced arrays, each with $1K \times 16$ bits.
  b. A memory of 16 banked arrays, each with 512×128 bits. Only the necessary
     bank should be activated.
12. Please design a 50-entry FIFO. Each entry must have 16 bits.

  a. Using dual-port SSRAM.
  b. Using single-port SSRAM.
  c. Please redesign the FIFO using flip-flops. What are the pros and cons for the
     implementations using either SSRAM or flip-flops?
13. Please design an interleaved memory system in which $M = 8$ requesters and
    $N = 4$ memory banks by modifying the crossbar interconnect. Each memory
    bank must have $16 K \times 32$ bits.
14. Design a filter that can detect the bit sequence "1011". For example, if the input
    is "0011_1011_0110", the output will be "0000_0001_0010".
15. Design a filter that can detect the bit sequence "1011" and its inverse
    "0100". For example, if the input is "0100_1011_0110", the output will be
    "0001_0001_0010".
16. Design two filters that can detect the bit sequence "1011" and "1101". For exam-
    ple, if the input is "0011_1011_0110", the output will be "0000_0011_0110".
17. Design a module that can add 3 numbers, as shown in Figure 7.62. Two adders
    must be implemented to produce one result at a time. Inputs a, b, and e are
    signed numbers. No overflow is allowed. We must have flip-flopped (or regis-
    tered) output. Datapath typically does not need to be reset. Please add control
    signals in_valid and out_valid to start the operation and indicate the valid result,
    respectively.

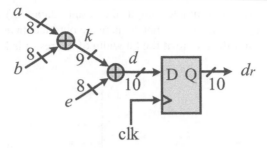

Figure 7.62: Three-number addition using two adders.

18. Design another module that can add 3 numbers, as shown in Figure 7.63. One adder must be implemented to produce one result every 2 cycles. Inputs a, b, and e are signed numbers. No overflow is allowed. We must have flip-flopped (or registered) output. Datapath typically does not need to be reset. Please add control signals in_valid and out_valid to start the operation and indicate the valid result, respectively.

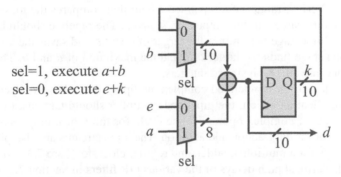

Figure 7.63: Three-number addition using one adder.

19. Develop a sequential circuit that has a single-bit data input S, and produces an output Y. The output is 1 whenever S has the same value over three successive clock cycles; otherwise, output is 0.

20. Use a state machine to design a divide-by-3 pulse width reducer with a single input in and a single output out. The output is asserted once after every three (nonconsecutive) cycles that the input has been asserted.

21. Write a Verilog model of a circuit that calculates the average of four 16-bit 2's complement signed numbers, without checking for overflow.

22. Design an arithmetic unit to implement 1) when cmd is 0, accumulation of 4 8-bit unsigned numbers, and 2) when cmd is 1, multiplication of two 8-bit unsigned numbers. When cmd_valid and data_in_valid are asserted (true), cmd and data_in are valid, respectively. After the command is issued, corresponding operands are input one at a time. For cmd 0/1, four/two operands take four/two

cycles to input. When complete, output the result (data_out) and indicate it through data_out_valid. Both commands share the output data bus data_out. Pad zeros at the most significant bits if the bit width of the result is less than 16 bits.

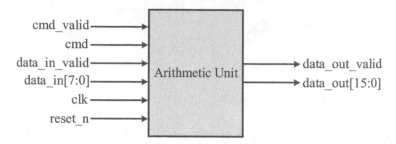

Figure 7.64: Arithmetic unit.

23. Develop a testbench model for a sequential multiplier. Verify that the results computed by the multiplier are the same as those produced using multiplication with real numbers.

24. Develop a Verilog model of a pipelined circuit that compares the maximum of corresponding values in three inputs, a, b, and c. The pipeline should have two stages: the first stage determines the larger of a and b and saves the value of c; the second stage finds the larger of c and the maximum of a and b. The inputs and outputs are all 14-bit signed integers.

25. Draw a datapath for a pipelined complex multiplier that takes five cycles to do each multiplication action; the pipelined multiplier should take just two cycles for each pair of complex operands: one cycle for the four multiplications and one cycle for the subtraction and addition. The input streams are also pipelined.

26. If the delays for a multiplier, adder, and register clock-to-Q are 7.3, 2.6, and 1.2 ns, find the critical path delays of the various FIR filters in Section 7.3.3.

27. Typically, the coefficients of FIR filters are symmetric. If the coefficients of fir1 are $h_3 = h_0$ and $h_2 = h_1$, redesign the fir1 by minimizing its area.

28. Redesign the FIR filter 5 by inserting a new pipeline such that its critical path has only one multiplier. Compare your design to FIR filter 4.

29. If we want to save the cost of a FIR filter, the folding technique in Figure 7.65 can be adopted to design a single processing element FIR filter. As displayed, the multiply-accumulate (MAC) operation is fundamental for DSP. Please write down its RTL codes.

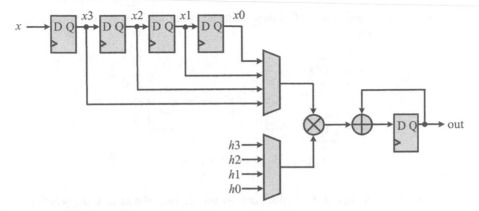

Figure 7.65: FIR filter using single processing element.

30. Design a 4-bit SISO shifter as shown in Figure 7.66. This module must be serial in, serial out. Clear signal is asynchronous. An output valid indicator is needed.

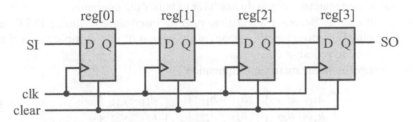

Figure 7.66: SISO shifter.

31. Design a 4-bit SIPO shifter as shown in Figure 7.67. This module is a serial in, parallel out. Clear signal is asynchronous. An output valid indicator is needed.

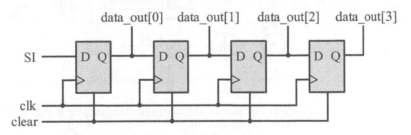

Figure 7.67: SIPO shifter.

32. Design a 4-bit PISO shifter. This module must be parallel in, serial out. Clear signal is asynchronous. The data input should arrive at most every 4 clock cycles. An output valid indicator is needed.
33. MAC design.

a. We want to design a MAC whose datapath is the same as that demonstrated in Figure 7.68.

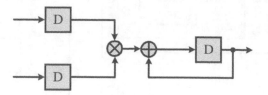

Figure 7.68: MAC design.

The two operands of the multiplier may not arrive at the same time, which is indicated by control signals in_valid0 and in_valid1 (not shown in the figure). The bit widths of the integer operands are 16-bit. When both operands have arrived, the MAC operation is performed. After 16 MACs are done, the result is output and the out_valid signal (not shown in the figure) asserts. Please design the circuit without overflow. Note that the two operands arrive in a one-to-one manner, so you do not have to buffer the operands.

b. If you want to decrease the critical path by inserting a re-timing D-FF (introducing one more pipeline stage) at the output of the multiplier, it will be necessary to redesign the circuit.

34. Please implement the matrix multiplication

$$\begin{bmatrix} a_{11} & a_{12} \\ a_{21} & a_{22} \end{bmatrix} \begin{bmatrix} b_{11} & b_{12} \\ b_{21} & b_{22} \end{bmatrix} = \begin{bmatrix} c_{11} & c_{12} \\ c_{21} & c_{22} \end{bmatrix} \quad (7.3)$$

using the processing element of a systolic array in Figure 7.69. Determine the bit width by yourself.

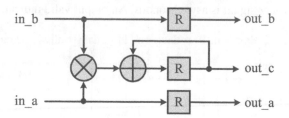

Figure 7.69: Processing element of the matrix multiplication, where R denotes the register.

35. Suppose a system includes a data source that provides a stream of 16-bit data values and a processing unit that operates on the stream, as shown in Figure 7.70. The source provides successive values at irregular intervals, sometimes faster than they can be processed, and sometimes slower. It has a valid output that is 1 during a clock cycle when a data item is available. The processing unit

has a "start" control input to initiate processing and a "done" output that is set to 1 for a cycle when a data item is processed. Show how the source and processing unit can be connected using the FIFO, including any control sequences required. Assume that if the FIFO is full when a new data item is provided by the source, the data item is dropped from the stream.

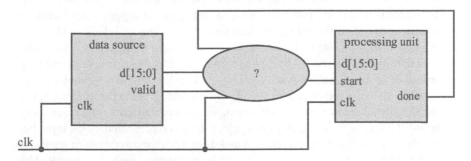

Figure 7.70: FIFO as a data buffer for 2 blocks.

36. Please design a 64-entry stack using dual-port SSRAM. The stack only has a write pointer that specifies the write address, and the value of the write pointer minus one indicates the read address. Initially, the pointer addresses the bottom (address 0) of the stack. The pointer increases or decreases by one automatically upon the write or read operation, respectively.

37. Please redesign the complex multiplier in Example 7.11 by

    a. two real multipliers,
    b. four real multipliers.

38. Please redesign the complex multiplier in Example 7.11 for a complex multiplication of a complex number and a complex conjugation of another number. That is, if op1$= a = a_r + ja_i$ and op2$= b = b_r + jb_i$, the result is prod$= a \times b^* = a_r b_r + a_i b_i + j(-a_r b_i + a_i b_r)$.

39. Please design the datapath and control unit for two kinds of implementations of two additions, as displayed in Figure 7.45.

40. Please redesign the complex multiplier in Example 7.11 using 3 real multiplications. That is, if op1$= a = a_r + ja_i$ and op2$= b = b_r + jb_i$, the result is prod $= (\text{prod1} - \text{prod2}) + j(\text{prod3} - \text{prod2} - \text{prod1})$, where prod1$= a_r b_r$, prod2$= a_i b_i$, and prod3$= (a_r + a_i)(b_r + b_i)$.

41. Please redesign the FIR filter 1 using single processing element of MAC and the coefficients in Table 7.2. In this design, one valid output should be produced every 4 clock cycles.

42. Please redesign the Huffman encoder for 8 symbols, with 128 as the total number of occurrences.

43. Please design the Huffman decoder based upon the Huffman code in Table 7.4.

44. Design the Huffman code generator using the table lookup (TLU) based on the Huffman coding illustrated in this Chapter.

45. Design the Huffman decoder using the TLU based on the Huffman coding illustrated in this Chapter.

46. Rewrite the Verilog codes of Huffman encoder using the named block for all **for** loops.

47. Design a save-our-soul (SOS) detector of Morse code using a FSM. Morse code is a method used in telecommunication to encode text characters, like alphabet, numbers, and a few punctuation marks, using on/off signals as standardized sequences of two different signal durations, called dots and dashes. The SOS encoded in Morse code is three dots (S), a space, three dashes (O), a space, and three dots again (the second S). In a symbol, a dot and dash are a short and long periods of an on signal, respectively. Dots and dashes within a symbol are separated by short periods of an off signal, while symbols are separated by a space encoding by a long period of an off signal. We assume that a dot is represented by the input being high for exactly one cycle, a dash is represented by the input being high for exactly three cycles, dots and dashes within a symbol are separated by the input being low for exactly one cycle, and that a space is represented by the input being low for three or more cycles. Note that the input going either high or low for exactly two cycles is an illegal condition. When an illegal condition happens, previously detected characters must be dropped and ignored. With this set of definitions, one legal SOS string is 10101000111011101110010101000.

48. The architecture for 8-point DIT-FFT is shown in Figure 7.71. The complex inputs and outputs are parallel-in and parallel-out, respectively. Please design a pipelined FFT such that consecutive blocks can be input continuously. That is, the input data in a block, $x[n]$, $n = 0, 1, , 7$, and output blocks, $X[k]$, $k = 0, 1, ..., 7$,

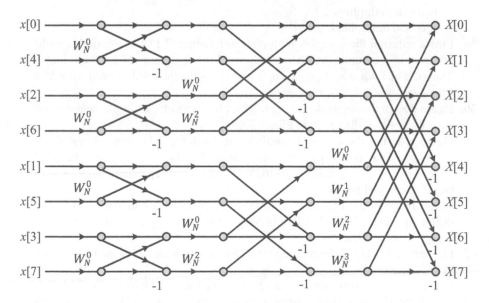

Figure 7.71: DIT FFT.

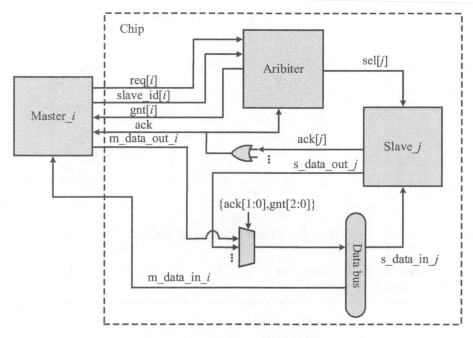

Figure 7.72: Simple SoC.

are available in every clock cycle. Input data $x[n]$ and twiddle factors $W_N^i = e^{-j2\pi i/N}$, $i = 0, 1, 2, 3$, are all 8-bit numbers. Determine the bit widths of inter-mediate variables such that no quantization errors occur. Your design must be correct for all kinds of random input.

49. A block diagram is shown in Figure 7.72. Please finish the design named chip. The masters are behavioral models, which will be provided together with the testbench. There are three masters, two slaves (MAC and FFT accelerators), and one arbiter in the system-on-a-chip (SoC). The data bus, arbitrated by the arbiter, is shared among all masters and slaves. The timing diagram and interface protocol are shown in Figure 7.73. The master i, $i = 0$, 1, 2, requests the data bus and slave j, $j = 0$, 1, by the signals, req[i] and slave_id[i], respectively, to the arbiter. If slave_id[i]= j, once granted by the arbiter via the signal, gnt[i], the master can send data via the signal, m_data_out_i, to slave j via the data bus. Meanwhile, the slave j will be selected by the signal, sel[j], to receive data. After the slave finishes receiving data, the operation will start immediately. After the operation is done, the signal ack[j] will be asserted until the data has been transferred to the master i via the signal, s_data_out_j. After the deassertion of ack[j], req[i], gnt[i], and sel[j] will de-assert, too, after which the next master will be granted and the above handshake protocol will repeat again.

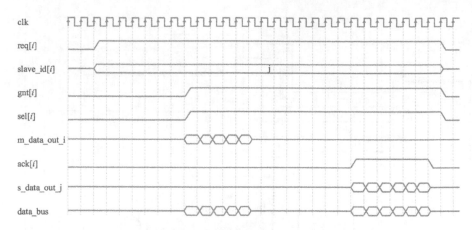

Figure 7.73: Timing diagram of SoC.

a. Please design an arbiter with
   – Round-robin arbitration

```verilog
1 parameter IDLE=2'b00;
2 parameter M0=2'b01;
3 parameter M1=2'b10;
4 parameter M2=2'b11;
5 always @(*)
6 begin
7 state_ns=state_cs;
8 case(state_cs)
9   IDLE:        if(req[0])
10                   state_ns=M0;
11        else   if(req[1])
12                   state_ns=M1;
13        else   if(req[2])
14                   state_ns=M2;
15  M0:          if(cmd_done & req[1])
16                   state_ns=M1;
17        else   if(cmd_done & req[2])
18                   state_ns=M2;
19        else   if(cmd_done)
20                   state_ns=IDLE;
21  M1:          if(cmd_done & req[2])
22                   state_ns=M2;
23        else   if(cmd_done & req[0])
24                   state_ns=M0;
25        else   if(cmd_done)
26                   state_ns=IDLE;
27  M2:          if(cmd_done & req[0])
```

```
28                          state_ns=M0;
29          else   if(cmd_done & req[1])
30                          state_ns=M1;
31          else   if(cmd_done)
32                          state_ns=IDLE;
33 endcase
34 end
35 always @(posedge clk or negedge rst_n)
36   if(!rst_n) state_cs <= IDLE;
37   else state_cs <= state_ns;
38 assign cmd_done=~ack & ack_r;
39 always @(posedge clk)
40   ack_r <= ack;
```

- Prioritized arbitration with master 0 (M0), master 1 (M1), and master 2 (M2) exhibiting the highest, second highest, and lowest priorities.

```
1 // Only the next state transition is shown here.
2 // Other parts are the same as those of round-
3 // robin arbitration.
4 always @(*)
5 begin
6 state_ns=state_cs;
7 case(state_cs)
8   IDLE:       if(req[0])
9                          state_ns=M0;
10          else   if(req[1])
11                          state_ns=M1;
12          else   if(req[2])
13                          state_ns=M2;
14  M0:         if(cmd_done & req[1])
15                          state_ns=M1;
16          else   if(cmd_done & req[2])
17                          state_ns=M2;
18          else   if(cmd_done)
19                          state_ns=IDLE;
20  M1:         if(cmd_done & req[0])
21                          state_ns=M0;
22          else   if(cmd_done & req[2])
23                          state_ns=M2;
24          else   if(cmd_done)
25                          state_ns=IDLE;
26  M2:         if(cmd_done & req[0])
27                          state_ns=M0;
28          else   if(cmd_done & req[1])
29                          state_ns=M1;
```

```
30          else  if(cmd_done)
31                    state_ns=IDLE;
32 endcase
33 end
```

b. Please design the interface of slaves conforming to the above handshake protocol.

c. Integrate the whole chip using some glue logics shown in the block diagram.

```
1 casex({ack[1:0], gnt[2:0]})
2   5'b1x_xxx: data_bus=s_data_out_1;
3   5'bx1_xxx: data_bus=s_data_out_0;
4   5'b00_100: data_bus=m_data_out_2;
5   5'b00_010: data_bus=m_data_out_1;
6   5'b00_001: data_bus=m_data_out_0;
7   default: data_bus=m_data_out_0;
8 endcase
```

d. How to improve the efficiency of the protocol? Can you improve the efficiency by re-designing the handshake protocol?

50. Design for testability is required for the production of all commercial chips. Its goal is to make your design controllable and observable. The methodology of DFT has been well established. To test the digital circuits, all combinations of possible inputs must be evaluated. For example, to test the two-input NAND gate shown in Figure 7.74, all possible inputs are "00", "01", "10", "11", which

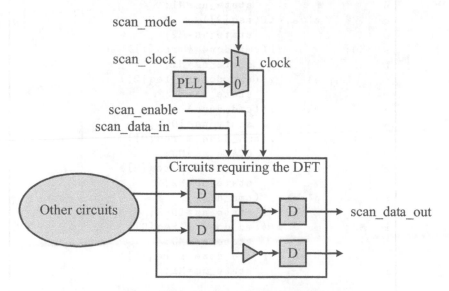

Figure 7.74: Circuit requiring the DFT.

should be controllable. Its corresponding outputs are "1", "1", "1", "0", which should be observable. If all results are correct, no defects will be induced in the NAND gate.

To control the inputs of the NAND and NOT gates, the scan D-FF in Figure 7.75 is required.

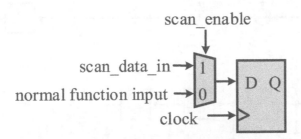

Figure 7.75: Scan D-FF.

Besides, all the FFs in the design must be chained together to control the outputs of all FFs. The scan input data (scan_data_in), i.e., scan output from the previous FF of the scan chain, is shifted in the scan chain by the control signal âĂIJscan_enableâĂİ. That is, the normal function input is bypassed. The reset signal is not shown here. The clock for the normal function is generated by the PLL. To control the clock, the scan_clock is selected when scan_mode is asserted. Other circuits in Figure 7.74 are unknown. Please manually design the DFT for the circuits including NAND and NOT gates in the box in Figure 7.74. You need to replace the D-FF with the scan D-FF and chain all of the FFs. Then, write the test pattern for the circuits under the test.

51. a. Figure 7.76 shows three different structures for implementing a 5-tap decimation filter with decimation factor $M = 2$: (a) original, (b) generalized Noble identity-derived, and (c) folded FIR structures. Write RTL codes and the testbench to verify them. What are the pros and cons of the three different architectures?

  b. Please redesign the above decimation filters using the transposed form.

52. Unknown parameter estimation problem: If received samples, y_1 and y_2, are related to known transmitted data, x_1 and x_2, by

$$
\begin{bmatrix} y_1 \\ y_2 \end{bmatrix} = \begin{bmatrix} x_1 & x_2 \\ x_2 & x_1 \end{bmatrix} \begin{bmatrix} a_1 \\ a_2 \end{bmatrix}
$$

$$
= a_1 \begin{bmatrix} x_1 \\ x_2 \end{bmatrix} + a_2 \begin{bmatrix} x_2 \\ x_1 \end{bmatrix} \tag{7.4}
$$

where a_i, x_i, and y_i, $i = 1, 2$, are all complex numbers. Known transmitted data, x_1 and x_2, are unity, i.e., $|x_1|^2 + |x_2|^2 = 1$. Besides, x_1 and x_2 are orthogonal,

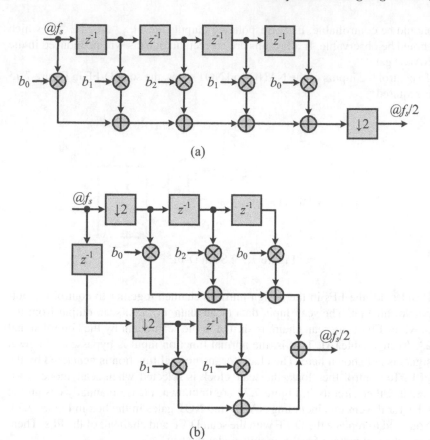

(a)

(b)

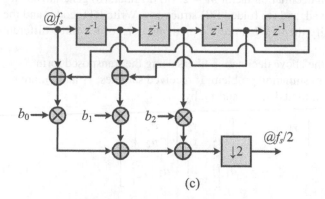

(c)

Figure 7.76: Different structures for a 5-tap decimation filter.

i.e., $x_1^* x_2 + x_1 x_2^* = 0$, where $(\cdot)^*$ denotes the complex conjugate. The solution of unknown parameters, a_1 and a_2, can be obtained by

$$\begin{bmatrix} x_1^* & x_2^* \end{bmatrix} \begin{bmatrix} y_1 \\ y_2 \end{bmatrix} = a_1 \begin{bmatrix} x_1^* & x_2^* \end{bmatrix} \begin{bmatrix} x_1 \\ x_2 \end{bmatrix} + a_2 \begin{bmatrix} x_1^* & x_2^* \end{bmatrix} \begin{bmatrix} x_2 \\ x_1 \end{bmatrix}$$

$$\Rightarrow \quad \begin{bmatrix} x_1^* & x_2^* \end{bmatrix} \begin{bmatrix} y_1 \\ y_2 \end{bmatrix} = a_1 \begin{bmatrix} x_1^* & x_2^* \end{bmatrix} \begin{bmatrix} x_1 \\ x_2 \end{bmatrix} \text{ (By orthogonality)}$$

$$\Rightarrow \quad a_1 = \begin{bmatrix} x_1^* & x_2^* \end{bmatrix} \begin{bmatrix} y_1 \\ y_2 \end{bmatrix} = x_1^* y_1 + x_2^* y_2. \text{ (By unity)} \qquad (7.5)$$

Similarly, it can be shown that

$$a_2 = \begin{bmatrix} x_2^* & x_1^* \end{bmatrix} \begin{bmatrix} y_1 \\ y_2 \end{bmatrix} = x_2^* y_1 + x_1^* y_2. \qquad (7.6)$$

The complex multiplication,

$$x^* y = (x_r + j x_i)^* (y_r + j y_i) = (x_r y_r + x_i y_i) + j(x_r y_i - x_i y_r) \qquad (7.7)$$

where x_r / y_r and x_i / y_i are respectively real and imaginary parts of x/y, is assumed to require 4 real multiplications.

a. You can design a circuit using 16 multipliers and obtain the result in one cycle. Plot your architecture and write down your RTL codes in a module. Please use parameter to define the bit widths of x and y.
b. Identify the critical path in the above architecture.
c. If our goal is to design a circuit with a small area and satisfactory performance, i.e., 4 multipliers, plot your architecture with datapath only. You need not show the control signals.
d. Identify the critical path using the above architecture.
e. Plot your timing diagram and show how you can obtain the same result using the first architecture.
f. If our goal is to design a circuit with the smallest area, i.e., one multiplier, plot your architecture with datapath only. You do not have to show the control signals.
g. Plot the critical path using the above architecture.
h. Plot your timing diagram and show how you can obtain the same result using the first architecture.

53. Complete the designs in the previous exercise.

a. Please completely show your datapath and control signals (by FSM) using the 2nd architecture in problem 52 and verify it using Modelsim (by showing the timing diagram).
b. Please completely show your datapath and control signals (by FSM) using the 3rd architecture in problem 52 and verify it using Modelsim (by showing the timing diagram).

54. Serial-to-parallel cyclic redundant code conversion. The circuit in Figure 7.77 uses serial CRC-4 architecture.

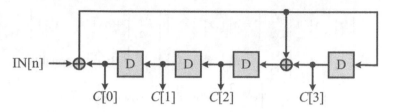

Figure 7.77: Serial CRC-4.

where IN[n] is serial input and $C[3:0]$ is the CRC result, $n = 0,1,2,....$ The circuit can be transformed to one using parallel architecture with 4 inputs, IN[3 : 0], at a time, as shown in Figure 7.78.

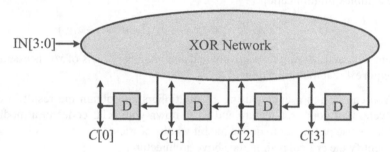

Figure 7.78: Parallel CRC-4.

Based on the serial architecture, we can write

$$C_{n+1}[0] = C_n[1]$$
$$C_{n+1}[1] = C_n[2]$$
$$C_{n+1}[2] = IN[n] \oplus C_n[0] \oplus C_n[3]$$
$$C_{n+1}[3] = IN[n] \oplus C_n[0] \tag{7.8}$$

where $\oplus$ denotes the bitwise XOR operation, and the subscript $n+1$ and n denote the next and current states, respectively. Let $C_0[3:0] = C[3:0]$, we have

$$C_1[0] = C_0[1] = C[1]$$
$$C_1[1] = C_0[2] = C[2]$$
$$C_1[2] = IN[0] \oplus C_0[0] \oplus C_0[3] = IN[0] \oplus C[0] \oplus C[3]$$
$$C_1[3] = IN[0] \oplus C_0[0] = IN[0] \oplus C[0]. \tag{7.9}$$

Similarly, we can express $C_2[3:0]$ using $C[3:0]$. Repeat this until $C_3[3:0]$ can be expressed using $C[3:0]$.

a. What XOR network did you obtain?

b. Verify your result using IN[3 : 0]=4'b1011. Assume that $C[3 : 0] = 4'b1111$, i.e., initial states of D-FFs are set before the CRC calculation starts.

55. Design the square-root approximation (SRA) used to calculate the magnitude of a complex number $z = a + bj$, where a and b are real and imaginary parts, respectively, $j = \sqrt{-1}$, as follows:

$$|z| = \sqrt{a^2 + b^2} \approx \max(0.875x + 0.5y, x) \qquad (7.10)$$

where

$$
\begin{aligned}
x &= \max(|a|, |b|), \\
y &= \min(|a|, |b|), \qquad (7.11)
\end{aligned}
$$

min and max must denote minimum and maximum operations, respectively.

56. A sample tree structure is presented below.

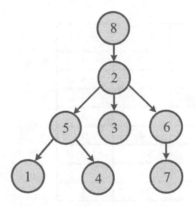

Figure 7.79: A tree data structure.

Design a tree distance analyzer that can output the distance of the longest path of all node pairs in a tree. For example, the tree displayed above has the longest path between nodes 1 and 7, i.e., 4. The specification of interface timing diagram is presented below. The information of all nodes, from nodes 1, 2, 3, ..., are input sequentially. When the signal in_valid is true, the first in_data[6 : 0] is the parent node of the current node, and following in_data[6 : 0] are children nodes. For the leaf node, it has no child nodes. When the information of all nodes are transferred, the signal last is true. After the processing is done, the signal out_valid becomes true and out_data[6 : 0] represents the longest distance. In Figure 7.80, there are 3 nodes. Nodes are transmitted sequentially from node 1, 2, to 3. The first node has 3 child nodes, the second node has 0 child nodes, and the third node has 1 child node. All nodes have only one parent node, and the parent node of the root node is 0. We assume that the maximum number of nodes is 100. Each node has a maximum of 3 child nodes.

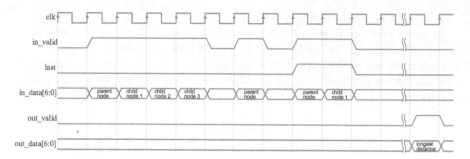

Figure 7.80: Interface timing diagram.

a. Write your RTL codes to build up a table of the tree data structure and its child count. In the table of the sample tree, the parent node of node 8 is 0. Therefore, node 8 is the root node. Sample RTL codes are given below for your reference.

node	parent	child 1	child 2	child 3
1	5	0	0	0
2	8	5	3	6
3	2	0	0	0
4	5	0	0	0
5	2	1	4	0
6	2	7	0	0
7	6	0	0	0
8	0	2	0	0

node	child_cnt
1	0
2	3
3	0
4	0
5	2
6	1
7	0
8	1

Figure 7.81: Table of the sample tree data structure together with its child count.

```
 1 parameter  MAX_NODE = 100;
 2 parameter  MAX_CHNODE = 3;
 3 reg [6:0]  ttab_par [1:MAX_NODE];
 4 reg [6:0]  ttab_ch1 [1:MAX_NODE];
 5 reg [6:0]  ttab_ch2 [1:MAX_NODE];
 6 reg [6:0]  ttab_ch3 [1:MAX_NODE];
 7 reg [1:0]  ttab_chcnt [1:MAX_NODE];
 8 reg [6:0]  ttab_raddr;
 9 reg [1:0]  ttab_caddr;
10 reg [6:0]  root;
11 reg in_valid_r, last_r;
12 integer i1, i2, i3;
```

```
13 always @(posedge clk or posedge reset)
14   if(reset)
15     for(i1=1;i1<=MAX_NODE;i1=i1+1) begin
16       ttab_par[i1]<=0;ttab_ch1[i1]<=0;
17       ttab_ch2[i1]<=0;ttab_ch3[i1]<=0;
18     end
19   else if(in_valid)
20     case(ttab_caddr)
21     2'd0: ttab_par[ttab_raddr]<=in_data;
22     2'd1: ttab_ch1[ttab_raddr]<=in_data;
23     2'd2: ttab_ch2[ttab_raddr]<=in_data;
24     default: ttab_ch3[ttab_raddr]<=in_data;
25     endcase
26 always @(posedge clk or posedge reset)
27   if(reset) ttab_caddr<=0;
28   else if(in_valid) ttab_caddr<=ttab_caddr+1;
29   else ttab_caddr<=0;
30 always @(posedge clk or posedge reset)
31   if(reset) begin
32     ttab_raddr<=1;
33     for(i2=1;i2<=MAX_NODE;i2=i2+1)
34       ttab_chcnt[i2]<=0;
35   end
36   else if(~in_valid & in_valid_r) begin
37     ttab_raddr<=ttab_raddr+1;
38     ttab_chcnt[ttab_raddr]<=ttab_caddr-1;
39   end
40 always @(posedge clk) begin
41   in_valid_r<=in_valid;
42   last_r<=last;
43 end
44 always @(*) begin
45   root=0;
46   for(i3=1;i3<=MAX_NODE;i3=i3+1)
47     if(ttab_par[i3]==0) root=i3;
48 end
49 assign start=~last & last_r;
```

b. For each node, find the top 2 maximum distances between it and its child nodes. For example, in Figure 7.79, node 1 has no child nodes. Therefore, its top 2 maximum distances are both 0. Node 2 has 3 child nodes, 5, 3, and 6, with the maximum distances of 2, 1, and 2, respectively. Therefore, its top 2 maximum distances are both 2. Node 6 has 1 child node. Therefore, its top 1 and top 2 maximum distances are 1 and 0, respectively.

Initiated from the root node, 8, you need to traverse all nodes and find their top 2 maximum distances, max 1 and max 2, in Figure 7.82. The column labeled by "child nodes processed" is a set of counters of all nodes used to record the number of child nodes that have been processed. The counter of a specific node increments when one of its child nodes is done (after finding the top 2 maximum distances of a child node). When all child nodes are processed, i.e., the counter reaches its maximum value indicated by child_cnt, the final top 2 maximum distances of the specified node can be determined. Write your RTL codes to build up the following table. Sample RTL codes are given below for your reference.

node	max 1	max 2		node	child nodes processed
1	0	0		1	0
2	2	2		2	3
3	0	0		3	0
4	0	0		4	0
5	1	1		5	2
6	1	0		6	1
7	0	0		7	0
8	3	0		8	1

Figure 7.82: Table for the top 2 maximum distances between a node and its child nodes.

```verilog
1 reg [1:0] state_ns, state_cs;
2 wire is_IDLE_cs, is_NEXT_cs, is_RETN_cs, is_DONE_cs,
3     is_IDLE_ns, is_NEXT_ns, is_RETN_ns, is_DONE_ns;
4 reg [6:0] dtab_max1[1:MAX_NODE];
5 reg [6:0] dtab_max2[1:MAX_NODE];
6 reg [1:0] dtab_chid[1:MAX_NODE];
7 reg [6:0] cur_node, ch_node;
8 wire [6:0] pa_node, tmp_max;
9 integer i4, i5;
10 parameter ST_IDLE =2'b00; parameter ST_NEXT  =2'b01;
11 parameter ST_RETN =2'b11; parameter ST_DONE  =2'b10;
12 assign is_IDLE_cs=state_cs==ST_IDLE;
13 assign is_NEXT_cs=state_cs==ST_NEXT;
14 assign is_RETN_cs=state_cs==ST_RETN;
15 assign is_DONE_cs=state_cs==ST_DONE;
16 assign is_IDLE_ns=state_ns==ST_IDLE;
17 assign is_NEXT_ns=state_ns==ST_NEXT;
18 assign is_RETN_ns=state_ns==ST_RETN;
19 assign is_DONE_ns=state_ns==ST_DONE;
```

```
20 always @(*) begin
21   state_ns=state_cs;
22   case(state_cs)
23   ST_IDLE: if(start) state_ns=ST_NEXT;
24   ST_NEXT: if(dtab_chid[cur_node]==
25               ttab_chcnt[cur_node] &&
26               cur_node==root)
27             state_ns=ST_DONE;
28           else if(dtab_chid[cur_node]==
29               ttab_chcnt[cur_node])
30             state_ns=ST_RETN;
31   ST_RETN: if(dtab_chid[cur_node]==
32               ttab_chcnt[cur_node] &&
33               cur_node==root)
34             state_ns=ST_DONE;
35           else if(dtab_chid[cur_node]==
36               ttab_chcnt[cur_node]
37             state_ns=ST_RETN;
38           else
39             state_ns=ST_NEXT;
40   ST_DONE: state_ns=ST_IDLE;
41   endcase
42 end
43 always @(posedge clk or posedge reset)
44   if(reset) state_cs <= ST_IDLE;
45   else state_cs <= state_ns;
46 always @(posedge clk or posedge reset)
47   if(reset) cur_node<=0;
48   else if(is_NEXT_ns)
49         cur_node<=is_IDLE_cs?root:ch_node;
50   else if(is_RETN_ns) cur_node<=pa_node;
51 assign pa_node=ttab_par[cur_node];
52 always @(*)
53   case(dtab_chid[cur_node])
54   2'b00: ch_node=ttab_ch1[cur_node];
55   2'b01: ch_node=ttab_ch2[cur_node];
56   2'b10: ch_node=ttab_ch3[cur_node];
57   default: ch_node=0;
58   endcase
59 always @(posedge clk or posedge reset)
60   if(reset)
61     for(i4=1;i4<=MAX_NODE;i4=i4+1) dtab_chid[i4]<=0;
62   else if(is_RETN_ns)
63         dtab_chid[pa_node]<=dtab_chid[pa_node]+1;
64 assign tmp_max=dtab_max1[cur_node]+1;
65 always @(posedge clk or posedge reset)
66   if(reset)
```

```
67     for(i5=1;i5<=MAX_NODE;i5=i5+1) begin
68        dtab_max1[i5]<=0;dtab_max2[i5]<=0;
69     end
70  else if(is_RETN_ns &&dtab_chid[pa_node]==0)
71     dtab_max1[pa_node]<=tmp_max;
72  else if(is_RETN_ns &&dtab_chid[pa_node]==1)
73           if(tmp_max>dtab_max1[pa_node]) begin
74              dtab_max1[pa_node]<=tmp_max;
75              dtab_max2[pa_node]<=dtab_max1[pa_node];
76           end
77           else dtab_max2[pa_node]<=tmp_max;
78  else if(is_RETN_ns) begin
79           if(tmp_max>dtab_max1[pa_node]) begin
80              dtab_max1[pa_node]<=tmp_max;
81              dtab_max2[pa_node]<=dtab_max1[pa_node];
82           end
83           else if(tmp_max>dtab_max2[pa_node])
84              dtab_max2[pa_node]<=tmp_max;
85  end
```

c. According to the top 2 maximum distances of all nodes, the distance of the longest path beneath a node can be decided, which is max 1+max 2 of the node. As presented in Figure 7.83, the longest distance beneath node 2 is 4.

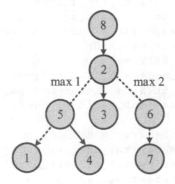

Figure 7.83: Distance of the longest path beneath node 2.

The maximum distance of all node pairs in a tree is the distance of the longest path beneath the root node, which is derived on-the-fly by keeping the maximum distance of all complete nodes, as shown below.

```
1 reg [6:0] ans;
2 wire [6:0] result, out_data;
3 assign result=dtab_max1[cur_node]+
```

```
4                         dtab_max2[cur_node];
5 always @(posedge clk or posedge reset)
6   if(reset) ans<=0;
7   else if((is_RETN_ns|is_DONE_ns) && result>ans)
8     ans<=result;
9 assign out_valid=is_DONE_cs;
10 assign out_data=ans;
```

Complete the whole design with the timing diagram shown below, where dtab_chid denotes the set of counters for the "child nodes processed", and dtab_max1 and dtab_max2 denote the top 1 and top 2 maximum distances of a node (relevant to its child nodes). The timing diagram for establishing the tree tables, ttab_par, ttab_ch1, ttab_ch2, ttab_ch3, and ttab_chcnt, are omitted here.

d. For leaf nodes, the memory space for the "max 1", "max 2", and "child nodes processed" in Figure 7.82 are wasted. Please use a stack to store the "max 1", "max 2", and "child nodes processed" to save the chip area.

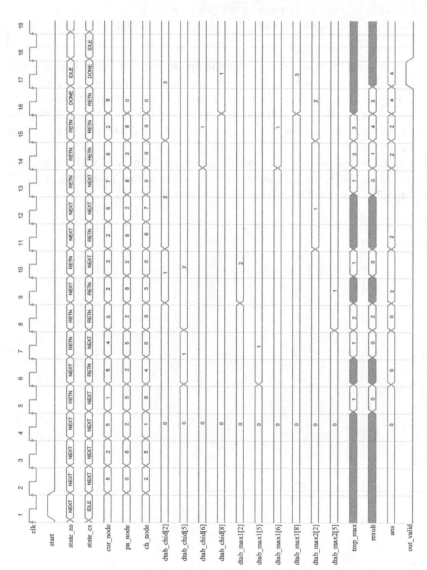

Figure 7.84: Timing diagram of the tree distance analyzer for the sample tree.

8 Advanced System Designs

This chapter discusses several advanced system-level design issues, including DRAM, flash memory, synchronizer design, and a crypto processor. DRAM chips are commonly used for main memory. Flash memory is a solid-state non-volatile computer memory storage medium that can be electrically erased and reprogrammed. Synchronizer design is often encountered in ASIC wherever signals need to transfer from one clock domain to another. We will see that violating setup and hold times may result in the flip-flop entering an illegal unstable state in which its state variable is neither a logic 1 nor a logic 0. The system-level design for the synchronization of signals across different clock domains is comprehensively presented via three sections: single-bit synchronizer, deterministic multi-bit synchronizer, and non-deterministic multi-bit synchronizer (with and without flow control). Embedded co-processor can offload the main processor. We introduce a specialized crypto processor for the Advanced Encryption Standard (AES). Finally, a digital design of component labeling engine is illustrated from its algorithm to RTL design.

8.1 DYNAMIC RANDOM-ACCESS MEMORY

As an off-chip memory, DRAM has the lowest cost per bit. Due to higher capacity and lower cost, DRAMs are most often used as the main memory of computer systems. By contrast, the hard disk has a lower cost per bit than DRAM, its speed is too slow to be used as the main memory. Modern DRAM chips have a capacity of up to 8 Gb, where $G = 10^9$, significantly higher than that can be realized on an SRAM chip. However, such a high capacity also leads to a high access latency.

DRAM and SRAM are volatile memories. SRAMs use a storage cell with 6 transistors (6T) that is similar to the D-type latch. Rather, the storage cell of DRAMs uses a single transistor and capacitor (1T1C), as that shown in Figure 8.1. Consequently, a DRAM cell is much smaller than that of SRAM. However, the access time of DRAMs is longer than that of SRAMs due to high capacity. The complexity for access and control of DRAMs is also higher than SRAMs.

The charge on the DRAM cell determines whether it stores logic 1 or 0. When the transistor is turned off, the capacitor is separated from the bit line to maintain the charge on the capacitor. In order to write to the cell, the DRAM control circuit turns on the transistor through the word line, and then charges and discharges the capacitor through the bit line. To read the data in a cell, the DRAM control circuit precharges the bit line to an intermediate voltage level, and then turns on the transistor. Depending on the charge in the capacitor, the voltage level on the bit line may rise or fall. A sensor detects and amplifies the change in voltage on the bit line to determine the logic level stored in the cell.

Since accessing data will destroy the charge stored in the capacitor, the control circuit needs to restore it before turning off the transistor. This causes the read access

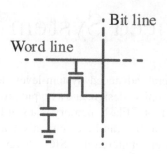

Figure 8.1: A DRAM cell.

time of a DRAM to be much longer than that of an SRAM. Moreover, when the DRAM cell is separated from the bit line by turning off the transistor, the charge stored on the capacitor will still gradually leak. Thus, the control circuit uses a process called refreshing to restore the charge on the capacitor before the charge decays too much. Since DRAM cannot be accessed normally during a refreshing, the refreshing must be interleaved between normal memory accesses. Typically, the refreshing is operated periodically, and the DRAM controller treats it as a high-priority operation than normal memory accesses.

The cells in a DRAM are usually organized into several 2-D arrays, called banks. A bank consists of several rows and columns. There are three steps to read and write a specific address in DRAM, including row activation, column access, and precharge.

- Row activation: a specific row of a bank is activated and read into the sense amplifiers, which destroys the stored charge in capacitors.
- Column access: commands are used to read and write specific columns of the activated row.
- Precharge: the precharge command writes the row back into the bank.

For multiple reads and writes issued to different columns of the same row and bank, activation and precharge are not required. Moreover, rows in different banks should be activated.

As shown in Figure 8.2, an activation command for row 0 of bank 0 is issued in cycle 1. Second activation command for row 6 of bank 3 is issued at cycle 2. After a delay of t_{AC}, a column access command to read column 0 of row 0 of bank 0 is issued in cycle 3. After t_{RA}, data are output in cycle 7, and its burst length is 2. Row 0 of bank 0 must be precharged in cycle 7 before a different row 2 in the same bank (bank 0) can be accessed. The DRAM controller must wait t_{PC} to allow the precharge operation of row 0 of bank 0 to complete before performing another row activation (row 2) on the same bank (bank 0) in cycle 11. If another column in the same row is accessed, no precharge is necessary. For example, the column access command to read column 1 of row 6 of bank 3 in cycle 9 follows that of column 2 of row 6 of bank 3. Accesses of other banks can be interleaved between those of bank 0.

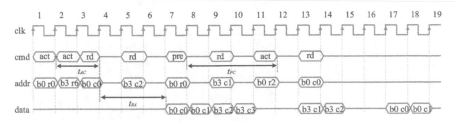

Figure 8.2: Timing diagram of a DRAM chip.

8.2   FLASH MEMORY

Flash memory is a form of electrically erasable programmable ROM that many new applications use. It is organized into storage blocks (commonly of 16, 64, 128, or 256 K bytes) that can be erased at once, and followed by writing a specific memory location in a block. Before aging, flash memory usually only allows a limited number of erasure and programming operations, usually hundreds of thousands of times. There are two kinds of flash memories, NOR and NAND flash, referring to different techniques that make up the memory cells. Flash memories must be erased in whole before being written.

In a NOR flash memory, data can be read (an arbitrary number of times) and written (once per erasure) in a random order. The NOR flash chip has similar signals to an SRAM with a comparable read access time, making it suitable for a program memory of an embedded processor. In a NAND flash memory, on the other hand, locations are written and read one page typically of 2 K bytes at a time. Read access to a given address would take several microseconds by reading the page containing the address, followed by selection of the required data in that address. If all the data in a page are needed, the sequential reading data in this page is comparable in time to reading data in SRAM. Erasing a block and writing a page of data are much slower than writing to SRAM.

Due to the different access behavioral of NAND flash and SRAM, the interface of NAND flash is different from SRAM interface, and the control circuit of NAND flash is also much more complicated. The advantage of NAND flash is that it has a higher density than NOR flash. Thus, NAND flash is better suited to applications that need to cheaply store a large amount of data, such as the solid-state disks (SSDs) and universal serial bus (USB) memory sticks.

8.3   SYNCHRONIZER DESIGN

8.3.1   SYNCHRONIZATION FAILURE

In this section we investigate the abnormal condition that timing constraints are unavoidably violated. For a flip-flop to function properly, its setup time and hold time constraints must be met. These constraints must be carefully guaranteed for synchronous designs. However, for asynchronous interfaces in digital systems, timing

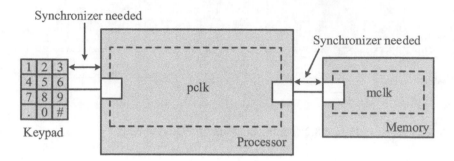

Figure 8.3: Synchronizers are needed between asynchronous and synchronous systems. They are also needed between different clock domains, pclk and mclk.

violations are unavoidable. We will see that violating setup and hold times may result in the flip-flop entering an illegal unstable state in which its state variable is neither a logic 1 nor a logic 0. Even worse, it will stay in the metatable state for an unknown period of time before it finally reaches one of the two stable states (0 or 1). This synchronization failure will cause serious problems in digital systems. If the unstable state of the flip-flop output is sampled, it will cause an indeterminate result.

The synchronization failure happens in two distinct scenarios, as shown in Figure 8.3. First, input signals come from truly asynchronous signal sources. They must be synchronized before being used in a synchronous digital system. For example, a keypad pressed by a human produces an asynchronous signal. However, this signal can transition at any time.

Second, a synchronous signal may move from one clock domain to another. A clock domain is simply a set of signals that are all synchronous with respect to a single clock. For example, in a computer system, the processor may operate in one clock domain, pclk = 3 GHz, whereas the memory system operates in a different one, mclk = 800 MHz. These two clocks have different frequencies. Signals generated by the processor that are synchronous to pclk cannot be directly used in the memory system synchronous to mclk, and vice versa. They must be synchronized with the destined clock domain before being used.

8.3.2   METASTABILITY

After the synchronization failure happens owing to timing constraint violation, most of the illegal states of flip-flops decay to a legal 0 or 1 state. However, it is possible that an illegal metastable state might prolong for an arbitrary amount of time before reaching a legal state.

The CMOS master-slave flip-flop is displayed in Figure 8.4.

After the clock rises, the input transmission gate t1 of the master latch is off and the feedback tristate inverter u3 is enabled. The master latch thus becomes two back-to-back inverters. Additionally, the transmission gate t2 of the slave latch is on and the feedback tristate inverter u5 is disabled. The slave latch thus becomes transparent.

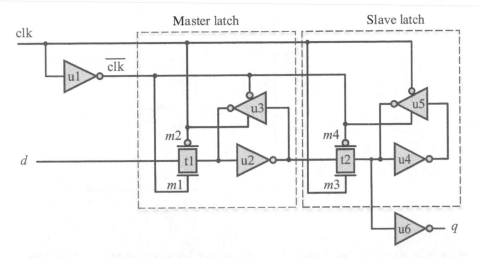

Figure 8.4: A CMOS master-slave flip-flop constructed from two CMOS latches.

So that the equivalent circuit of the flip-flop is that of two back-to-back inverters, as shown in Figure 8.5(a).

Figure 8.5(b) shows the transfer characteristics of the output V_2 of the forward inverter as a function of V_1, i.e., $V_2 = f(V_1)$ (sold line), where $f(\cdot)$ denotes the transfer function of an inverter, and the transfer characteristics of the output V_1 of the feedback tristate inverter as a function of V_2, i.e., $V_1 = f(V_2)$ (dashed line). There are three intersections of the two transfer characteristics on the figure. In the absence of disturbances, these points are stable that the voltages V_1 and V_2 will never change. At any point other than these three stable points, the circuit quickly converges to one of the outer two stable points, i.e., $\Delta V \equiv V_1 - V_2 = +V_{DD}$ or $\Delta V = -V_{DD}$.

For example, if we disturb the state slightly from the middle metastable point, the state will quickly converge to the nearest outer stable point. As presented in Figure 8.6, when V_1 slightly increases, it will decay to $\Delta V = +V_{DD}$, i.e., $V_1 = V_{DD}$ and $V_2 = 0$ through trace 1. Similarly, when V_1 slightly decreases, it will decay to $\Delta V = -V_{DD}$, i.e., $V_1 = 0$ and $V_2 = V_{DD}$ through trace 2. Yet another case, if we disturb the state slightly from either of the two outer stable points, the state returns to that stable point again. A state, like the middle stable state, where a small disturbance causes a system to leave that state, is called metastable.

The behavior of the metastable state can be presented in Figure 8.7. The ball would remain on the top of the hill if it were perfectly balanced. Actually, nothing is perfect, and the ball will eventually roll to one side or the other.

The detailed transistor-level schematic of Figure 8.5(a) is presented in Figure 8.8. We assume that all n-channel and p-channel FETs are perfectly matched such that $k_n = k_p$, where $k_n = \mu_n C_{ox} \left(\frac{W}{L}\right)_n$ denotes the device characteristics of n-channel FET, $k_p = \mu_p C_{ox} \left(\frac{W}{L}\right)_p$ denotes the device characteristics of p-channel FET, μ_n/μ_p are the mobilities of electron/hole, C_{ox} is the gate capacitance per unit

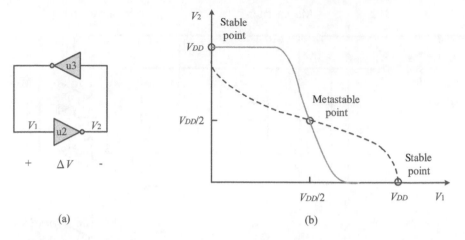

(a)   (b)

Figure 8.5: (a) When the clock is high, the master latch acts as two back-to-back inverters, and the slave latch becomes transparent. (b) Transfer characteristics of the back-to-back inverters.

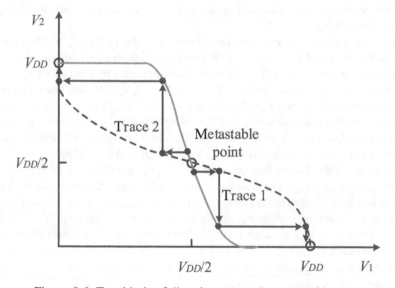

Figure 8.6: Two kinds of disturbances on the metastable state.

area, $\left(\frac{W}{L}\right)_n / \left(\frac{W}{L}\right)_p$ are the aspect ratios of n-channel/p-channel FETs, and the absolute values of the threshold voltage of n-channel FET, V_{tn}, and the threshold voltage of p-channel FET, V_{tp}, are the same, i.e., $V_{tn} = -V_{tp} = V_t$. Also, for simplicity, the parasitic capacitors of two inverters are the same.

Assuming that the inverters u2 and u3 were initially in the metastable state, i.e., $V_1 = V_2 = V_{DD}/2$. Suddenly, at the time $t = 0$, V_1 slightly increases owing to some

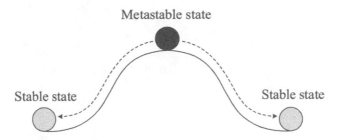

Figure 8.7: A metastable state that is represented by a ball at the top of a hill.

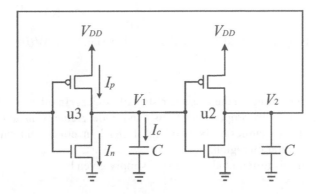

Figure 8.8: Transistor schematic of the master-slave flip-flop when the clock is high.

reason, for example, I_c is produced, so that V_2 slightly decreases accordingly. There-fore, $\Delta V(0) = V_1 - V_2 > 0$ and ΔV will converge toward $+V_{DD}$. Moreover, it can be observed that all transistors are in saturation region. Since $I_p - I_n = I_c$ and $I_c = C\frac{dV_1}{dt}$ for u3, we have

$$\frac{k}{2}(V_2 - V_{DD} + V_t)^2 - \frac{k}{2}(V_2 - V_t)^2 = C\frac{dV_1}{dt}. \tag{8.1}$$

Similarly, for u2, we have

$$\frac{k}{2}(V_1 - V_{DD} + V_t)^2 - \frac{k}{2}(V_1 - V_t)^2 = C\frac{dV_2}{dt}. \tag{8.2}$$

Subtracting Equation 8.2 from Equation 8.1 yields

$$kV_{DD}\Delta V = C\frac{d\Delta V}{dt}. \tag{8.3}$$

Hence, the dynamics of the two back-to-back inverters can be expressed by the following differential equation,

$$\frac{d\Delta V}{dt} = \frac{\Delta V}{\tau} \tag{8.4}$$

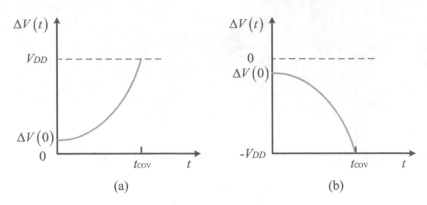

Figure 8.9: Convergence of $\Delta V(t)$ toward a stable state: (a) $\Delta V(0) > 0$ and (b) $\Delta V(0) < 0$.

where $\tau = \frac{C}{kV_{DD}}$ depending on the characteristics of devices. In other words, the rate of change of ΔV is directly proportional to its magnitude. Actually, in addition to the metastable state, the dynamics of the two back-to-back inverters hold whenever the transistors are in saturation region.

The solution of this differential equation is simply given by

$$\Delta V(t) = \Delta V(0)\exp\left(\frac{t}{\tau}\right). \tag{8.5}$$

As displayed in Figure 8.9, when $\Delta V(0) > 0$, $\Delta V(t)$ will converge toward $\Delta V(t) = +V_{DD}$, where t_{cov} denotes the convergence time. By contrast, when $\Delta V(0) < 0$, $\Delta V(t)$ will converge toward $\Delta V(t) = -V_{DD}$.

Therefore, given $\Delta V(0) > 0$, the amount of time that a synchronization failure takes to converge to $\Delta V = +V_{DD}$ is given by

$$t_{\text{cov}} = -\tau\log\left(\frac{\Delta V(0)}{V_{DD}}\right) \tag{8.6}$$

where the natural logarithm, $\log(\cdot)$, denotes the logarithm to the base $e \approx 2.71828$ of a number. Likewise, for $\Delta V(0) \leq 0$, the amount of time that a synchronization failure takes to converge to $\Delta V = -V_{DD}$ can be shown and omitted here. The convergence time t_{cov} plotted against $\Delta V(0)$ is displayed in Figure 8.10. When $\Delta V(0) = 0$, the flip-flop is in the metastable state, and the convergence time $t_{\text{cov}} = \infty$. By contrast, when $\Delta V(0) = \pm V_{DD}$, the flip-flop has already been in the stable state, and the convergence time $t_{\text{cov}} = 0$.

Assuming that a flip-flop initially has a $\Delta V(0)$ uniformly distributed over the interval $(0, +V_{DD})$. Given that the stable state has reached after some time, i.e.,

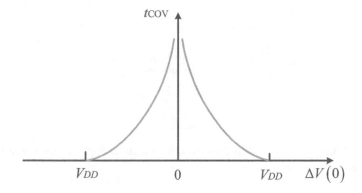

Figure 8.10: Convergence time t_{cov} plotted against $\Delta V(0)$.

$\Delta V(t) = V_{DD}$, the probability of state error, P_{SE}, for the convergence time t_{cov} to the stable state longer than the waiting time, t_w, can be written as

$$
\begin{aligned}
P_{SE} &= P(t_{\text{cov}} > t_w) \\
&= P\left(\frac{\Delta V(0)}{V_{DD}} < \exp\left(-\frac{t_w}{\tau}\right)\right) \\
&= F_U\left(\exp\left(-\frac{t_w}{\tau}\right)\right)
\end{aligned}
\tag{8.7}
$$

where $P(\cdot)$ denotes the probability and $F_U(\cdot)$ is the cumulative distribution function of a uniform random variable, $U = \frac{\Delta V(0)}{V_{DD}}$. Notice that P_{SE} is the same as the probability that $U = \frac{\Delta V(0)}{V_{DD}} < \exp\left(-\frac{t_w}{\tau}\right)$. With U being uniformly distributed between 0 and 1, $F_U(x) = x$. Consequently, P_{SE} is thus simply

$$
P_{SE} = \exp\left(-\frac{t_w}{\tau}\right). \tag{8.8}
$$

The probability of state error P_{SE} decreases exponentially when the waiting time t_w increases. Therefore, a good way to reduce the probability of state error is to increase the waiting time.

8.3.3   PROBABILITY OF ENTERING AN ILLEGAL STATE

An asynchronous input signal is sampled by a flip-flop with clock frequency f_C, setup time t_S, and hold time t_H. The input of a flip-flop should arrive before the setup time and arrive after the hold time. In other words, the input cannot change within the slash area in Figure 8.11, where $t_C = 1/f_C$ denotes the clock period.

During the clock period of the sampling flip-flop, suppose that a transition of the asynchronous input signal is equally likely to occur at any time instance during a

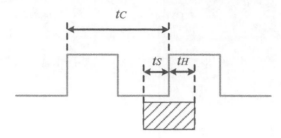

Figure 8.11: Input signal of a flip-flop cannot change during the slash area due to setup time and hold time constraints.

cycle, the probability of timing error, P_{TE}, for the setup time or hold time violation that may cause the sampling flip-flop to enter the unstable state can be written as

$$P_{TE} = \frac{t_S + t_H}{t_C} = f_C(t_S + t_H).$$

(8.9)

If the transition frequency of the asynchronous input signal is f_I, the frequency of timing errors is given by

$$f_{TE} = f_I P_{TE} = f_I f_C(t_S + t_H).$$

(8.10)

Example 8.1. Assuming that a transition of the asynchronous input signal is equally likely to occur at any time instance during a cycle, what is the frequency of timing errors for $t_S = t_H = 0.1$ ns, $t_C = 2$ ns, and $f_I = 10$ MHz?

Solution: By putting the values into Equation 8.9, we find $P_{TE} = \frac{t_S + t_H}{t_C} = \frac{0.2 \text{ ns}}{2 \text{ ns}} = 0.1$. Thus, according to Equation 8.10, the frequency of timing errors $f_{TE} = f_I P_{TE} = 10$ MHz$\times 0.1 = 1$ MHz, which is relatively high.

□

8.3.4   SIMPLE SYNCHRONIZER

We see that, in the previous example, sampling an asynchronous signal might lead to an unacceptably high timing error rate. A practical solution to the problem of frequently entering an illegal state is to allow it to decay to one of the two stable states after a waiting time, t_w.

As shown in Figure 8.12, through a combination of waiting for an unstable state to converge to one of stable states and separating the potentially unstable signals, a simple synchronizer that can reduce the probability of synchronization failure is thus designed. Synchronization of single-bit signals is often achieved using the simple synchronizer. Flip-flop FF1 samples an asynchronous input signal a to produce an output a_r. Signal a_r will be unstable because of the high frequency of timing errors, f_{TE}, with which FF1 will enter the unstable state. To protect remaining parts of a system from the unsafe signal, we wait one (or more) clock periods for any illegal

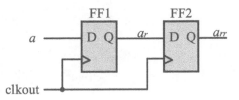

Figure 8.12: A simple synchronizer consisting of two back-to-back flip-flops.

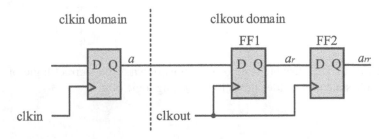

Figure 8.13: Registered output a crossing clkin domain to clkout domain.

states of FF1 to decay before resampling it with FF2 to produce the synchronized output a_{rr}. As a result, the input signal is sampled by the output clock twice, so the simple synchronizer is also called the double synchronizer. The double synchronization scheme isolates the unstable signal a_r from affecting the clkout domain and allows (approximately) a clock period of clkout to wait for the unstable signal, a_r, to converge to one of the stable states.

The RTL codes of the double synchronizer are listed below.

```
1 // Simple or double synchronizer: one-cycle waiting time
2 always @(posedge clkout) begin
3     a_r<=a;
4     a_rr<=a_r;
5 end
```

Figure 8.13 displays the clock domain crossing (CDC) issue. It should be emphasized that the input signal a in clock domain clkin must be a registered output so that there is only one transition in signal a at the clock rising edge, and the instability issue can be reduced to the minimum. Besides, the frequency of clkout is commonly higher than that of clkin so that, if the signal a to be synchronized is a strobe signal with one-cycle high in its clock domain, clkin, the synchronized signal $a_r r$ still can capture the strobe signal.

If the unstable state of a_r settles down to the correct/wrong logic of a, the synchronized signal, a_{rr}, will appear to have the correct logic value sooner/later, as shown in Figures 8.14(a)/(b). When a_r settles down to the wrong logic of a, at the next rising

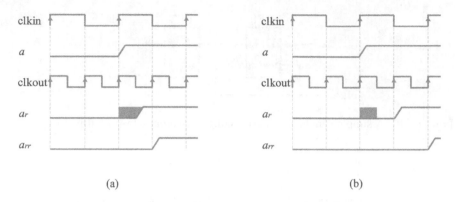

(a)   (b)

Figure 8.14: (a) The unstable state of a_r settles down to the correct logic of a. (b) The unstable state of a_r settles down to the wrong logic of a.

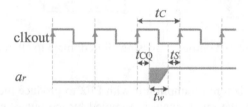

Figure 8.15: Relationship between t_w, t_{CQ}, t_S, and t_C of the double synchronizer.

edge of clkout, it will sample the correct logic of a without any possibility of timing violation.

It is interesting to understand how well the synchronizer works. In other words, the probability of a_{rr} entering an illegal state after a transition on a needs to be derived. This will happen only if (1) FF1 enters an illegal state and (2) this state has not converged to one of stable states before a_r is resampled by FF2. FF1 enter an illegal state with probability P_{TE}, and it will remain in this state after a waiting time t_w with probability P_{SE}. Thus, the synchronization error probability of FF2 entering an illegal state is given by

$$P_E = P_{TE}P_{SE} = \frac{t_S + t_H}{t_C}\exp\left(-\frac{t_w}{\tau}\right). \tag{8.11}$$

The synchronization error frequency of FF2 entering an illegal state is thus

$$f_E = f_I P_E. \tag{8.12}$$

In fact, FF1 has a delay t_{CQ} to reflect its output a_r. Also, the FF2 captures its input a_r at the time instance t_S before the rising edge of clkout. Therefore, the relationship between t_w, t_{CQ}, t_S, and t_C is presented in Figure 8.15.

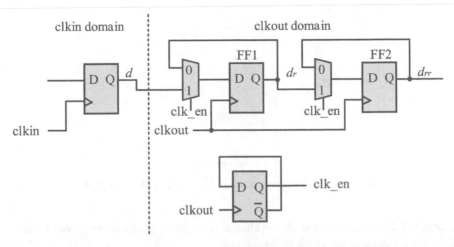

Figure 8.16: Double synchronizer with $N = 2$. Flip-flops in clkout domain are enabled every 2 clock cycles.

Hence, the waiting time t_w is not a complete clock cycle, but rather a clock cycle subtracting the required overhead:

$$t_w = t_C - t_S - t_{CQ} \tag{8.13}$$

where t_{CQ} denotes the clock-to-Q delay.

Example 8.2. If we have $t_S = t_H = t_{CQ} = \tau = 0.1$ ns, $t_C = 2$ ns, and $f_I = 10$ MHz, find the probability of FF2 entering an illegal state and the frequency of synchronization failure.

Solution: We have $t_w = 1.8$ ns and the synchronization error probability of FF2 entering an illegal state is thus given by $P_E = \left(\frac{0.1 \text{ ns} + 0.1 \text{ ns}}{2 \text{ ns}}\right) \exp\left(-\frac{1.8 \text{ ns}}{0.1 \text{ ns}}\right) = 1.523 \times 10^{-9}$. If signal a has a transition frequency of $f_I = 10$ MHz, then the synchronization error frequency is given by $f_E = f_I P_E = (10 \text{ MHz})(1.523 \times 10^{-9}) = 0.0152$ Hz.

□

If the synchronization failure probability is not low enough, we can increase the waiting time to reduce it, because it is inversely proportional to the exponential of waiting time. It is best to add a clock enable signal to the two flip-flops to accomplish this, and the flip-flops are enabled every N clock cycles. Figure 8.16 presents the double synchronizer with $N = 2$. The frequency of clk_en is half that of clk-out. Therefore, flip-flops, FF1 and FF2, in clkout domain are enabled every 2 clock cycles.

This can extend the waiting time to $t_w = Nt_C - t_S - t_{CQ}$, such as that of $N = 2$ in Figure 8.17. Waiting longer with clock enable is more efficient than using multiple flip-flops in series. Moreover, in addition to a reduced number of flip-flops, we only pay the flip-flop overhead $t_S + t_{CQ}$ once in the waiting time t_w, rather than once per flip-flop.

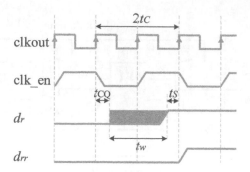

Figure 8.17: Relationship between t_w, t_{CQ}, t_S, and t_C for $N = 2$.

Example 8.3. In our example above, change the simple synchronizer to wait for two clock cycles through the clock enable signal.

Solution: The waiting time becomes $t_w = Nt_C - t_S - t_{CQ} = 2 \times 2 - 0.1 - 0.1 = 3.8$ ns and the synchronization error probability of FF2 entering an illegal state is thus given by $P_E = 0.1\exp(-38) = 3.1391 \times 10^{-18}$. The synchronization error frequency is thus $f_E = f_I P_E = (10 \text{ MHz})(3.1391 \times 10^{-18}) = 3.1391 \times 10^{-11}$ Hz.

□

According to Figure 8.16, the RTL codes of the synchronizer with $N = 2$ and clock enable are presented below. It should be emphasized that the sampling frequency has reduced by half. The sampling frequency must be acceptable for the system specification.

```
1// Simple or double synchronizer: two-cycle waiting time
2// Sampling frequency is reduced by half.
3module sync(d_sync, d, clkout, rst_n);
4output d_sync;
5input d, clkout, rst_n;
6reg d_r, d_rr, clk_en;
7assign d_sync=d_rr;
8always @(posedge clkout or negedge rst_n)
9  if(!rst_n) clk_en<=1'b0;
10  else       clk_en<=~clk_en;
11always @(posedge clkout)
12  if(clk_en) begin
13    d_r<=d;
14    d_rr<=d_r;
15  end
16endmodule
```

In another way, we can increase the waiting by connecting flip-flops in series. For example, the triple synchronization is shown in Figure 8.18.

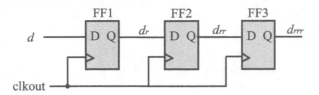

Figure 8.18: Triple synchronization implemented using three flip-flops in series.

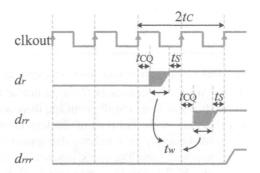

Figure 8.19: Relationship between t_w, t_{cq}, t_S, and t_C for the triple synchronization.

With flip-flops in series, each additional flip-flop adds $t_C - t_S - t_{CQ}$ to our waiting time. In that each flip-flop has a clock-to-Q delay, t_{CQ}, and the input voltage sampled by the flip-flop is the voltage at the setup time, t_S, before the clock rising edge. Therefore, for the synchronization using N flip-flops in series, the waiting time is $N(t_C - t_S - t_{CQ})$. The waiting time of the triple synchronization is displayed in Figure 8.19.

Example 8.4. In our example above, change the simple synchronizer to wait for two clock cycles by using three flip-flops in series.

Solution: We have $t_w = N(t_C - t_S - t_{CQ}) = 2 \times (2 - 0.1 - 0.1) = 3.6$ ns and the synchronization error probability of FF2 entering an illegal state is thus given by $P_E = 0.1\exp(-36) = 2.3195 \times 10^{-17}$. The synchronization error frequency is $f_E = f_I P_E = (10 \text{ MHz})(2.3195 \times 10^{-17}) = 2.3195 \times 10^{-10}$ Hz, which is approximately 10 times that of the previous example.

□

According to Figure 8.18, the RTL codes of the synchronizer with $N = 2$, i.e., three back-to-back flip-flops, are presented below.

```
1 // Simple or double synchronizer: two-cycle waiting time
2 // Three back-to-back flip-flops are used.
3 module sync(d_sync, d, clkout);
4 output d_sync;
```

```
 5 input d, clkout;
 6 reg d_r, d_rr, d_rrr;
 7 assign d_sync=d_rrr;
 8 // Triple synchronization
 9 always @(posedge clkout)
10 begin
11    d_r <= d;
12    d_rr <= d_r;
13    d_rrr <= d_rr;
14 end
15 endmodule
```

The mean time between failures (MTBF) can also be expressed as $1/f_E = \frac{\exp(k_1 t_w)}{k_2 f_1 f_C}$, where k_1 and k_2 are measured constants for a particular flip-flop. For those applications in which reliability is a key requirement and there are many asynchronous inputs, we should study the technical data of implementation fabric we adopt and follow the advice of manufacture on synchronizing inputs. The MTBF is inversely proportional to the input and sampling clock frequencies. Consequently, higher frequencies lead to a shorter MTBF, that is, to more frequent synchronization failure.

The synchronization failure probability and MTBF depends on your system and what it is used for. Generally, we want to make the probability of synchronization failure significantly smaller than some other system failure or error characteristics. For example, in a telecommunication system where the bit-error rate of a line is 10^{-8}, it would suffice to design a synchronizer with a synchronization failure probability P_E of 10^{-9} or lower.

8.3.5 DETERMINISTIC MULTI-BIT SYNCHRONIZER

The simple synchronizer can only synchronize signals with single bit. To synchronize a multi-bit signal with a deterministic sequence, the signal must be ensured that all neighboring current and next states change one bit at a time. As such, the synchronization problem of a deterministic multi-bit signal reduces to that of single-bit signal, so that the double synchronization can be employed; otherwise, a new synchronizer is required. For example, as shown in Figure 8.20, if there is a 3-bit counter that counts from 3 (3'b011) to 4 (3'b100), all of the bits of the counter, cnt, are changing when the clock, clk1, rises. If clk1 and clk2 are asynchronous, 3 bits of cnt_r may all enter unstable states when clk2 rises. During the next rising of clk2, 3 flip-flops of cnt_rr may sample a wrong value if the unstable state of either bits of cnt_r has not settled down or has settled down but converged to wrong stable states.

To solve this problem, the value of the counter can be converted using the popular Gray code sequence that changes one bit at a time for all adjacent states, as shown in Figure 8.21.

Verilog codes for a 3-bit Gray-coded counter, cnt, that generates this sequence are shown below.

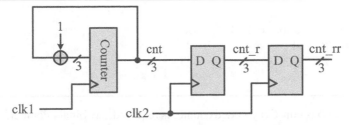

Figure 8.20: Incorrect method of synchronizing a multi-bit signal when multiple bits in the counter are changing concurrently.

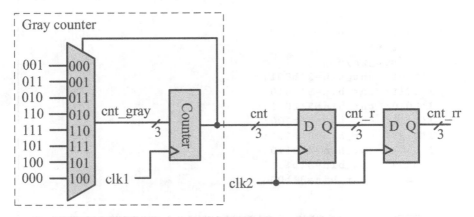

Figure 8.21: Correct method of synchronizing a multi-bit signal when only single bit in the counter can change at a time.

```verilog
// Converting binary to Gray codes before double
// synchronizer
reg [2:0] cnt, cnt_r, cnt_rr, cnt_gray;
always @(posedge clk1 or posedge rst)
  if (rst) cnt <= 3'd0;
  else cnt <= cnt_gray;
always @(*)
  case(cnt)
  3'b000: cnt_gray=3'b001;
  3'b001: cnt_gray=3'b011;
  3'b011: cnt_gray=3'b010;
  3'b010: cnt_gray=3'b110;
  3'b110: cnt_gray=3'b111;
  3'b111: cnt_gray=3'b101;
  3'b101: cnt_gray=3'b100;
  default: cnt_gray=3'b000;
```

```
17   endcase
18 always @(posedge clk2) begin
19   cnt_r <= cnt;
20   cnt_rr <= cnt_r;
21 end
```

If a synchronous non-Gray-coded counter is required, say binary counter, the synchronized Gray-coded counter, cnt_rr, can be converted back into a binary counter, as shown below.

```
1 // Gray to binary conversion
2 reg [2:0] cnt_bin;
3 always @(*)
4   case(cnt_rr)
5   3'b001: cnt_bin=3'b001;
6   3'b011: cnt_bin=3'b010;
7   3'b010: cnt_bin=3'b011;
8   3'b110: cnt_bin=3'b100;
9   3'b111: cnt_bin=3'b101;
10  3'b101: cnt_bin=3'b110;
11  3'b100: cnt_bin=3'b111;
12  default: cnt_bin=3'b000;
13  endcase
```

The n-bit binary-to-Gray-code conversion can be implemented using the Boolean equation

$$\text{gray}[i] = \text{bin}[i+1] \oplus \text{bin}[i],$$

where gray$[i]$ denotes the Gray code, bin$[i]$ denotes the binary data, $i = 0, 1, ..., n-1$, and bin$[n]$=0. The 3-bit binary-to-Gray-code conversion is written in Verilog function, gray, below.

```
1 // Functions used to convert binary to Gray
2 function [2:0] gray;
3   input [2:0] bin;
4   begin
5     gray[2]=bin[2];
6     gray[1]=bin[2]^bin[1];
7     gray[0]=bin[1]^bin[0];
8   end
9 endfunction
```

Similarly, the n-bit Gray-to-binary-code conversion can be expressed using the Boolean equation

$$\mathrm{bin}[i] = \mathrm{bin}[i+1] \oplus \mathrm{gray}[i],$$

where $i = 0, 1, ..., n-1$. The 3-bit Gray-to-binary-code conversion is written in Verilog function, bin, below.

```
1 // Functions used to convert Gray to binary
2 function [2:0] bin;
3   input [2:0] gray;
4   begin
5     bin[2]=gray[2];
6     bin[1]=bin[2]^gray[1];
7     bin[0]=bin[1]^gray[0];
8   end
9 endfunction
```

It can be seen that the critical path of the Gray-to-binary-code conversion increases linearly with the bit width of Gray code, while the critical path of the binary-to-Gray-code conversion is a XOR gate and is constant without regarding to the bit width. The implementation of conversion between binary and Gray codes using the Boolean equation generally has a longer critical path but smaller area than that using the case statement when the bit width becomes wider.

It is simple to generate the Gray code with a sequence of 2^N numbers, where $N \geq 1$ is an integer. However, the desired number of count may not be a power of 2. If we want a Gray code with a sequence of arbitrary even numbers, it can still be derived from the original Gray code with a sequence of 2^N numbers. For example, a Gray code with $N = 3$ is displayed in Figure 8.22. It can be observed that the codes before and after a pair of adjacent codes with the same LSB, either 1 or 0, i.e., circled ones, always differ by exactly one bit.

As a result, the circled codes can be removed so that remaining ones still exhibit the property of a Gray code. For example, if we remove the two circled codes 001 and 011 with the same LSB 1 to have a 6-code sequence, remaining neighboring codes still differ by only one bit. If we further remove 111 and 101 with the same LSB 1, we have a 4-code sequence. Consequently, a Gray code with a sequence of arbitrary even numbers can be eventually obtained. Similar approach can be applied for circled codes with the same LSB 0.

However, it is impossible to derive a Gray code with arbitrary odd number of count in a similar way. For practicality, the Gray code with odd number count can be derived by folding the Gray code with even number count. For example, to determine a 3-code sequence, if a 6-code sequence is 000, 010, 110, 111, 101, and 100, then separated-by-3 codes in the 6-code sequence represent the same binary count. That is, 000 and 111 represent binary 0, 010 and 101 represent binary 1, and 110 and 100 represent binary 2.

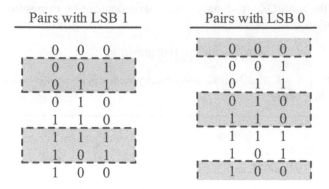

Pairs with LSB 1	Pairs with LSB 0

Figure 8.22: A pair of adjacent Gray codes with the same LSB bit.

8.3.6 NONDETERMINISTIC MULTI-BIT SYNCHRONIZER USING FIFO WITHOUT FLOW CONTROL

When data are random, sampled signals can transit from arbitrary current state to any next state. Therefore, we cannot guarantee that it should be like a counter with a deterministic sequence where only one bit changes using a Gray code. Hence, we cannot use a simple synchronizer on arbitrary random signals with multiple bits. The most common multi-bit synchronizer is the FIFO synchronizer, as shown in Figure 8.23. The key concept behind all of them is moving the synchronization requirement from the multi-bit datapath to synchronization of control path with either a single bit or a Gray-coded sequence.

We assume that the FIFO synchronizer uses a set of registers queue[0] to queue[$N-1$] as the FIFO memory. Data are written into the FIFO memory under control of the input clock, clkin, and read from the FIFO memory under control of the output clock, clkout. A write pointer, wr_ptr, selects which address in the FIFO memory is to be written next, and a read pointer, rd_ptr, selects which address is to be read next. Data are added at the write pointer (or tail) of the FIFO, and removed from the read pointer (or head) of the FIFO. The read pointer is used to select a FIFO output data through select pins of the multiplexer. The write pointer is decoded by the decoder to one-hot to drive the enable signals of registers. Using Gray code for the counters enables them to be synchronized by simple deterministic multi-bit synchronizers in the control path.

A timing diagram showing operation of a FIFO synchronizer with four registers (queue[0] to queue[3]) is shown in Figure 8.24. The input clock, clkin, is commonly slower than the output clock, clkout. On each rising edge of the input clock, clkin, a new data on the input port, fifo_wdata, is written to one of the registers selected by the write pointer, wr_ptr, which repeatedly increments with a Gray-code pattern, 00, 01, 11, 10, 00, in binary. That is, the first data a is written to register queue[0], the second data b is written to queue[1], c is written to queue[3], and so on. The FIFO is implemented using the circular buffer. When the last element queue[2] is written, the next element to be written is the first element, queue[0].

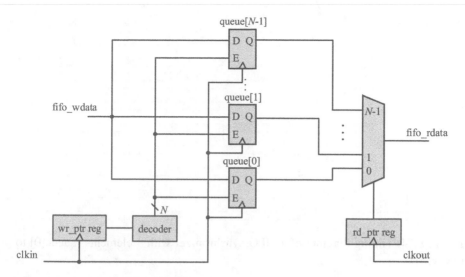

Figure 8.23: Datapath of a FIFO synchronizer.

On the output side, each rising edge of clock clkout advances the Gray-coded read pointer, rd_ptr, to select each register in turn. Initially, rd_ptr is 00, and it selects the contents a of register queue[0] to drive the output port, fifo_rdata. The second rising edge of clkout advances rd_ptr to 01, and selects b from queue[1] to appear on the output. The third edge selects c from queue[3] according to the rd_ptr of 11, and so on. When the last element queue[2] has been read, the next element to be read is the first element, queue[0]. It can be seen that the data stored in queue[0] to queue[3] has been extended to four clock cycles of clkin. By using multiple registers to extend the valid period of the input data, it is possible to make the FIFO synchronizer read data without undergoing any unstable or transition state when selecting them on the output fifo_rdata. Thus, there is no probability of violating setup and hold times in the datapath of clkout if the read pointer selects the required data when it had been stable (after its transition). There are even multiple cycles available for reading a queued data before it is used.

In the FIFO synchronizer, the frequency of clkout is typically higher than that of clkin. As a result, the frequency of read access is typically higher than that of write access. Therefore, in such a condition, the FIFO is guaranteed not to overrun. Consequently, the output and input of FIFO can never be stopped. Otherwise, the flow control mechanism is needed. The need to synchronize is simply moved to the control path. There is a wr_ptr in the clkin domain and a rd_ptr in the clkout domain used for the write access and read access, respectively.

Example 8.5. Please design a FIFO synchronizer without flow control, as shown in Figure 8.25. Since the flow control is not required, the speed of data output is higher than or equal to that of the input data. Please write the RTL codes and determine the worst-case queue depth of the FIFO such that no overrun can occur. The longest

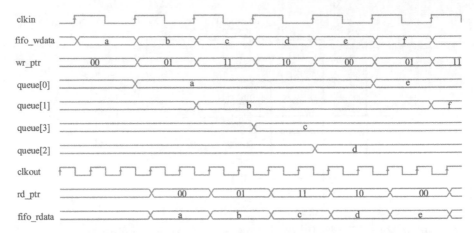

Figure 8.24: Timing diagram of a FIFO synchronizer with 4 elements (queue[0] to queue[3]).

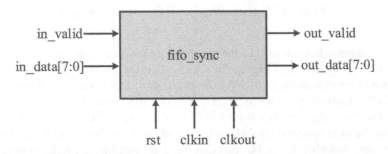

Figure 8.25: Interface of a FIFO synchronizer.

queue depth is desired when the frequencies of clkin and clkout are the same. Also, the frequency of read access is assumed to be the same as that of write access.

The output valid signal, out_valid, is used to indicate the nonempty status of the FIFO queue. The out_valid is true when synchronized wr_ptr (to the clkout domain) is not the same as the rd_ptr. To synchronize wr_ptr, it is encoded using the Gray code. Even a properly designed FIFO synchronizer is ensured not to overrun, the queue depth of the FIFO shall still be large enough because the wr_ptr is double synchronized from clkin to clkout domain, which may incur (worst) 2 cycles delay in clkout domain.

Solution: A FIFO with depth of 10 is demonstrated and implemented using a circular buffer in Figure 8.26. When write pointer, wr_ptr, and read pointer, rd_ptr, are the same, the FIFO may be empty or full. For example, initial write pointer and read pointer are displayed in Figure 8.26, assume that there is no write access so that wr_ptr is fixed. After 4 read accesses, rd_ptr=wr_ptr=2, the FIFO is empty at this time. As another example, assume that there is no read access so that rd_ptr is fixed. After 6 write accesses, rd_ptr=wr_ptr=8, the FIFO is full in this case.

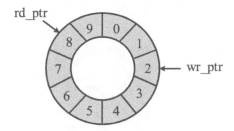

Figure 8.26: The FIFO memory is indexed by write and read pointers.

To easily distinguish the FIFO empty and full status using only read and write pointers (without the queue length counter), a space in FIFO is often purposely left unoccupied. Therefore, when write pointer and read pointer are the same, the FIFO can be decided to be empty. By contrast, when the "next" write pointer and read pointer are the same, the FIFO is full because a space in FIFO is not used. Consequently, the out_valid signal is true when write pointer and read pointer are not the same.

Considering the double synchronization and a burst write, the timing diagram to assert the latest out_valid (owing to double synchronization of wr_ptr) is the worst case for the (longest) queue depth and it is shown in Figure 8.27. The double

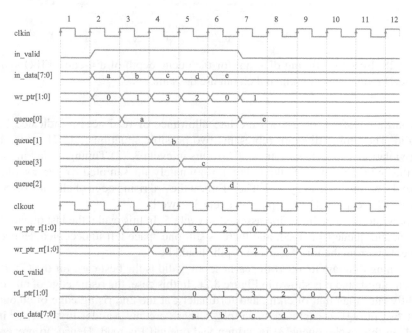

Figure 8.27: Worst-case timing diagram of a 4-entry FIFO synchronizer for determining the queue depth. Frequencies of clkin and clkout are the same.

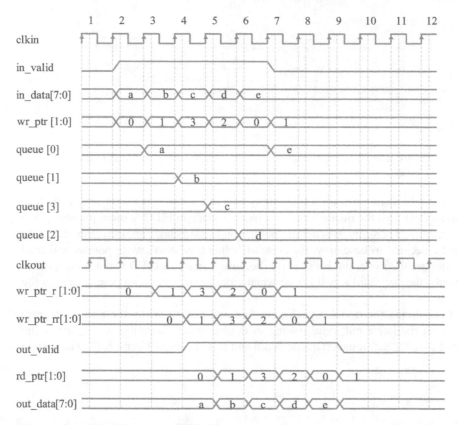

Figure 8.28: Best-case timing diagram for the queue depth of a 4-entry FIFO synchronizer. Frequencies of clkin and clkout are the same.

synchronization of wr_ptr causes the late allowance of read access indicated by out_valid. The timing diagram represents two possible situations: (1) There is no timing violation. Correct "wr_ptr_r= 0" occurs in cycle 3. (2) Timing violation exists at the 2nd rising edge of clkout, but, unfortunately, the sampled wr_ptr_r settles down to the wrong logic in cycle 2. Therefore, at the 3rd rising edge of clkout, correct "wr_ptr= 0" is captured by wr_ptr_r in cycle 3 as well.

As presented, out_valid is first asserted in cycle 5. In this cycle, the last queue[2] is written and queue[0] is read, and there is still one space left unoccupied. Hence, to prevent overrun, the longest queue depth should be 4.

The timing diagram to assert the earliest out_valid is the best case for the (shortest) queue depth and it is shown in Figure 8.28. In this case, the rising edge of clkout is slightly later than that of clkin, and fortunately, at the 2nd rising edge of clkout, correct "wr_ptr= 0" is captured by wr_ptr_r. Therefore, out_valid is first asserted in cycle 4. In this cycle, queue[3] is written and queue[0] is read. Hence, to prevent overrun, the shortest queue depth should be 3.

From above, we will design a FIFO with queue depth of 4 according to the worst-case design criterion. Similar to the fifo_ctrl in Example 7.7, there is a wr_ptr in clkin domain used to indicate the write address, and there is a rd_ptr in clkout domain used to indicate the read address. To reduce the complexity of the synchronizer, only the Gray coded wr_ptr signal is double synchronized to the clkout domain to indicate the nonempty (or out_valid) status of the queue.

When the FIFO is full, write pointer and read pointer are the same. However, when the FIFO is empty, they are also the same. To differentiate the FIFO full status from the FIFO empty status, the FIFO full is commonly asserted when the next write pointer equals the current read pointer. Doing so intends to leave one element unoccupied, and a buffer space is wasted. In the sequel, out_valid is asserted whenever the rd_ptr and the synchronized write pointer, wr_ptr_rr, are not the same. The RTL codes are written below.

```verilog
1 // FIFO synchronizer without flow control
2 module fifo_sync(out_valid, out_data, in_valid, in_data,
3                  clkin, clkout, rst);
4 output out_valid;
5 output [7:0] out_data;
6 input in_valid;
7 input [7:0] in_data;
8 input clkin, clkout, rst;
9 reg [1:0] wr_ptr, wr_ptr_r, wr_ptr_rr, rd_ptr;
10 reg [7:0] queue[0:3];
11 reg [7:0] out_data;
12 //*****************
13 //* clkin domain
14 //*****************
15 always @(posedge clkin or posedge rst)
16   if(rst) wr_ptr <=0;
17   else if(in_valid) begin
18     case(wr_ptr) // Gray coded pointer
19     2'b00: wr_ptr <=2'b01;
20     2'b01: wr_ptr <=2'b11;
21     2'b11: wr_ptr <=2'b10;
22     2'b10: wr_ptr <=2'b00;
23     endcase
24   end
25 always @(posedge clkin)
26   if(in_valid) begin
27   // Case statement can be simply replaced by
28   // queue[wr_ptr] <=in_data;
29   case(wr_ptr) // Gray coded pointer
30     2'b00: queue[0] <=in_data;
31     2'b01: queue[1] <=in_data;
32     2'b11: queue[3] <=in_data;
```

```
33        2'b10:  queue[2] <= in_data;
34      endcase
35    end
36  // *****************
37  //* clkout domain
38  // *****************
39  // Double sync
40  always @(posedge clkout or posedge rst)
41    if(rst) begin
42      wr_ptr_r <=0;
43      wr_ptr_rr <=0;
44    end
45    else begin
46      wr_ptr_r <=wr_ptr;
47      wr_ptr_rr <=wr_ptr_r;
48    end
49  assign out_valid=wr_ptr_rr!=rd_ptr;
50  always @(posedge clkout or posedge rst)
51    if(rst) rd_ptr<=0;
52    else if(out_valid) begin
53      case(rd_ptr) // Gray coded pointer
54        2'b00:  rd_ptr<=2'b01;
55        2'b01:  rd_ptr<=2'b11;
56        2'b11:  rd_ptr<=2'b10;
57        2'b10:  rd_ptr<=2'b00;
58      endcase
59    end
60  always @(*)
61    // Case statement can be simply replaced by
62    // out_data=queue[rd_ptr];
63    case(rd_ptr)
64    2'b00:  out_data=queue[0];
65    2'b01:  out_data=queue[1];
66    2'b11:  out_data=queue[3];
67    2'b10:  out_data=queue[2];
68    endcase
69  endmodule
```

□

Example 8.6. Redesign the above FIFO synchronizer without flow control so that all FIFO spaces can be fully utilized.

Solution: To fully utilize the FIFO space, the queue_length counter must be implemented. To easily generate the out_valid signal, the queue_length counter is located in clkout domain. Since the out_valid signal can be generated using the queue_length counter, double synchronization is not required for wr_ptr. Rather, we synchronize one-bit signal, in_valid, to count the queue_length so that the circuit area can be reduced. The RTL code fragment is written below. Other parts are the same as those RTL codes in the previous example and omitted here.

The synchronized in_valid signal, in_valid_rr, may be too long and span over several clock cycles of clkout because the frequency of clkin is usually slower than that of clkout. Therefore, in_valid_rr should qualify in_valid_rrr, i.e., in_valid_rr&~in_valid_rrr, so that an one-cycle input valid indication can be derived.

```
1 //*****************
2 //* clkout domain
3 //*****************
4 reg in_valid_r, in_valid_rr;
5 reg[2:0] queue_length;
6 // Double sync
7 always @(posedge clkout or posedge rst)
8   if(rst) begin
9     in_valid_r<=0;
10    in_valid_rr<=0;
11    in_valid_rrr<=0;
12  end
13  else begin
14    in_valid_r<=in_valid;
15    in_valid_rr<=in_valid_r;
16    in_valid_rrr<=in_valid_rr;
17  end
18 assign out_valid=queue_length!=0;
19 assign fifo_wr=in_valid_rr&~in_valid_rrr;
20 assign fifo_rd=out_valid;
21 always @(posedge clkout or negedge rst_n)
22   if(!rst_n)
23     queue_length<=0;
24   else if(fifo_wr&&!fifo_rd)
25     queue_length<=queue_length+1'b1;
26   else if(fifo_rd&&!fifo_wr)
27     queue_length<=queue_length-1'b1;
```

□

8.3.7 NONDETERMINISTIC MULTI-BIT SYNCHRONIZER USING FIFO WITH FLOW CONTROL

Generally speaking, the FIFO synchronizer is a popular method that can move and queue multi-bit data from one clock domain to another. When the access speeds of two clock domains are varying, it is sometimes necessary to implement the flow control mechanism to prevent temporarily the FIFO overrun, and FIFO underrun as well. When the write access is faster than the read access, the FIFO will eventually overrun that data will be lost if they are written when the FIFO is full. To avoid data loss, we must apply the flow control mechanism in the input interface. Similarly, the

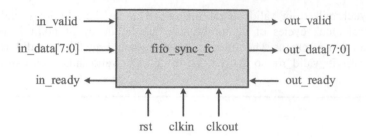

Figure 8.29: Interface of a FIFO synchronizer with flow control.

output interface should also adopt the flow control to prevent underrun that invalid data will be provided if they are read when the FIFO is empty.

The interface of the FIFO synchronizer with valid-ready flow control is shown in Figure 8.29. On both the input and output interfaces, the valid signal is true if the transmitter has valid data on the data bus, and the ready signal is true if the receiver is ready to receive new data. A data transfer takes place only when both valid and ready signals are true.

On the input interface, the in_ready signal indicates the buffer *not* full status in the FIFO queue. It is generated by comparing the write and read pointers. Unfortunately, this comparison is complicated by the fact that write and read pointers are in different clock domains, i.e., clkin and clkout, respectively. By the deterministic multi-bit synchronizer, we generate a synchronized version of read pointer in the clkin domain, rd_ptr_rr. Similarly, on the output interface, the out_valid signal indicates the buffer *not* empty status in the FIFO queue. It is also generated by comparing the write and read pointers. By the deterministic multi-bit synchronizer, we generate a synchronized version of write pointer in the clkout domain, wr_ptr_rr.

Based on the write and read pointers, the in_ready and out_valid signals can be generated. However, if we allow all FIFO entries to be used, the full and empty statuses of the FIFO queue are true when both write and read pointers are the same. Unfortunately, it is hard to discriminate between these two conditions, particularly when the clock frequencies of clkin and clkout are different. Hence, we simply declare the 4-entry FIFO to be full when the next write pointer, next_wr_ptr, and the read pointer are the same, i.e., one entry is intentionally left unoccupied, as shown below. We claim that the FIFO is nonempty when the write and read pointers are not the same.

```
1 // Flow control mechanism
2 wire in_ready , out_valid ;
3 reg [1:0] next_wr_ptr ;
4 assign in_ready =~( next_wr_ptr == rd_ptr_rr );
5 always @(*)
6   case(wr_ptr) // Gray coded pointer
```

```
 7    2'b00: next_wr_ptr =2'b01;
 8    2'b01: next_wr_ptr =2'b11;
 9    2'b11: next_wr_ptr =2'b10;
10    2'b10: next_wr_ptr =2'b00;
11    endcase
12 assign out_valid =~(wr_ptr_rr ==rd_ptr );
```

The synchronization delays the synchronized write and read pointers relative to their original ones, but this delay does not cause queue overrun and underrun. That is, the synchronized rd_ptr_rr and wr_ptr_rr cause the late allowance of write access and read access, respectively. Therefore, the queue full status is relieved later and the queue nonempty status is reported later as well, which will conservatively stop the write access and read access in the input and output interfaces, respectively.

The RTL codes of 4-entry nondeterministic FIFO synchronizer with flow control are written below. Except the flow control mechanism, most parts of the RTL codes in the FIFO synchronizer with flow control are the same as those in the FIFO synchronizer without flow control.

```
 1 // FIFO synchronizer with flow control
 2 module fifo_sync_fc (in_valid , in_data , in_ready ,
 3                      out_valid , out_data , out_ready ,
 4                      clkin , clkout , rst );
 5 // Input interface
 6 input in_valid ;
 7 input [7:0] in_data ;
 8 output in_ready ;
 9 // Output interface
10 output out_valid ;
11 output [7:0] out_data ;
12 input out_ready ;
13 input clkin , clkout , rst ;
14 reg [1:0] wr_ptr , rd_ptr , next_wr_ptr ;
15 reg [7:0] queue [0:3];
16 wire in_wr_en ;
17 reg [1:0] wr_ptr_r , wr_ptr_rr ;
18 wire out_rd_en ;
19 reg [1:0] rd_ptr_r , rd_ptr_rr ;
20 reg [7:0] out_data ;
21 // ****************
22 // * clkin domain
23 // ****************
24 assign in_ready =~(next_wr_ptr ==rd_ptr_rr );
25 always @(*)
26    case (wr_ptr ) // Gray coded pointer
27    2'b00: next_wr_ptr =2'b01;
```

```
28   2'b01: next_wr_ptr=2'b11;
29   2'b11: next_wr_ptr=2'b10;
30   2'b10: next_wr_ptr=2'b00;
31   endcase
32 // Double sync
33 always @(posedge clkin or posedge rst)
34   if(rst) begin
35     rd_ptr_r <=0;
36     rd_ptr_rr <=0;
37   end
38   else begin
39     rd_ptr_r <=rd_ptr;
40     rd_ptr_rr <=rd_ptr_r;
41   end
42 assign in_wr_en=in_valid & in_ready;
43 always @(posedge clkin or posedge rst)
44   if(rst) wr_ptr <=0;
45   else if(in_wr_en) begin
46     case(wr_ptr) // Gray coded pointer
47     2'b00: wr_ptr <=2'b01;
48     2'b01: wr_ptr <=2'b11;
49     2'b11: wr_ptr <=2'b10;
50     2'b10: wr_ptr <=2'b00;
51     endcase
52   end
53 always @(posedge clkin)
54   if(in_wr_en) begin
55     case(wr_ptr) // Gray coded pointer
56     2'b00: queue[0] <=in_data;
57     2'b01: queue[1] <=in_data;
58     2'b11: queue[3] <=in_data;
59     2'b10: queue[2] <=in_data;
60     endcase
61   end
62 // *****************
63 //* clkout domain
64 // *****************
65 assign out_valid=~(wr_ptr_rr==rd_ptr);
66 // Double sync
67 always @(posedge clkout or posedge rst)
68   if(rst) begin
69     wr_ptr_r <=0;
70     wr_ptr_rr <=0;
71   end
72   else begin
73     wr_ptr_r <=wr_ptr;
74     wr_ptr_rr <=wr_ptr_r;
```

```
75   end
76 assign out_rd_en=out_valid & out_ready;
77 always @(posedge clkout or posedge rst)
78   if(rst) rd_ptr<=0;
79   else if(out_rd_en) begin
80     case(rd_ptr) // Gray coded pointer
81     2'b00: rd_ptr<=2'b01;
82     2'b01: rd_ptr<=2'b11;
83     2'b11: rd_ptr<=2'b10;
84     2'b10: rd_ptr<=2'b00;
85     endcase
86   end
87 always @(*)
88   case(rd_ptr)
89   2'b00: out_data=queue[0];
90   2'b01: out_data=queue[1];
91   2'b11: out_data=queue[3];
92   2'b10: out_data=queue[2];
93   endcase
94 endmodule
```

The timing diagram of the nondeterministic FIFO synchronizer with flow control is presented in Figure 8.30. The out_ready signal is assumed to be asserted every 2 cycles.

8.4 COMPUTER ORGANIZATION

8.4.1 EMBEDDED PROCESSOR

Unlike the general-purpose personal computer, a processor in an embedded system has just those resources required to complete its specialized operation, as shown in Figure 8.31. A processor executes according to a program, which is encoded in binary form and stored in the instruction memory. The data upon which the program operates are stored in the data memory. Instruction memory and data memory in an embedded system are typically separated, which is often referred to as the Harvard architecture. We usually store instructions in a ROM or flash memory, and provide a RAM for the data memory because the instructions in an embedded computer are usually fixed during the manufacturing of the system and the memory space of instructions is known in advance. The I/O controller allows the embedded processor to input data to be processed from peripherals and to output the results. The accelerator is a specialized circuit designed to implement specific tasks with higher performance than that can be achieved using the processor.

The interconnect in an embedded computer can employ a simple bus or complex crossbar switch. For a high-performance embedded system, there may be separate buses for connecting the instruction memory, data memory, and the I/O controllers with the CPU, as shown in Figure 8.32.

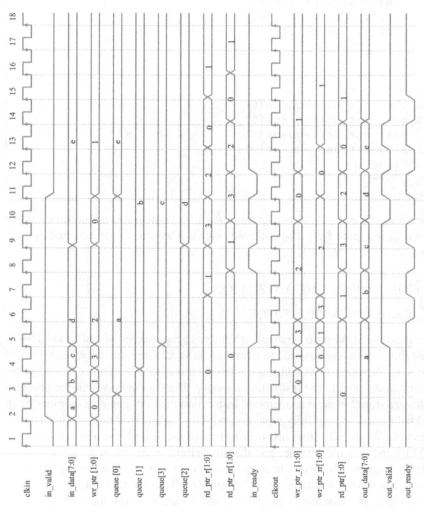

Figure 8.30: Timing diagram of the nondeterministic FIFO synchronizer with flow control.

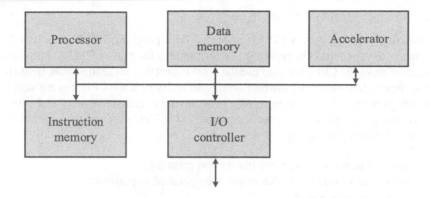

Figure 8.31: Elements of an embedded computer.

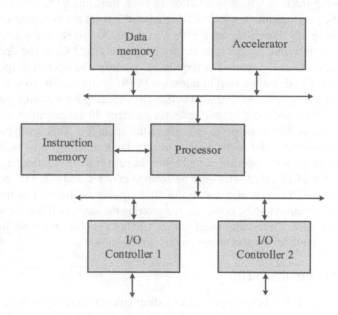

Figure 8.32: A high-performance embedded computer with multiple buses: one for the instruction memory, one for the data memory and an accelerator, and one for I/O controllers.

There are specialized processing elements, named DSPs, optimized for the kinds of operations involved in dealing with digitized signals, such as audio, video or other streams of data from sensors. Even though, applications still often need a general-purpose processor to perform other tasks, such as interacting with the user and overall coordination of system operation. Hence, DSPs are often combined with CPUs in heterogeneous multiprocessor systems.

8.4.2 INSTRUCTIONS AND DATA

The function performed by a CPU is specified by a program, which consists of a sequence of instructions. The repertoire of instructions for a given CPU is called the instruction set of the CPU. We also use the term instruction set architecture (ISA) to refer to the combination of the instruction set and registers of the CPU that are visible to the programmer. The instructions of a program are encoded in binary and stored in successive locations of the instruction memory. The CPU executes the program by repeatedly following these steps:

- *Fetch* the instruction from the instruction memory.
- *Decode* the instruction to determine the operation to perform.
- *Execute* the operation.

In order to keep track of which instruction to fetch next, the CPU has a special register called the program counter, **PC**, in which the address of the next instruction is kept. In the fetching step, the CPU uses the content of the **PC** to do a read access from the instruction memory, and then automatically increments the **PC**. In the decoding step, the CPU determines the resources required to perform the operation specified by the instruction. The decoding step in a low-end CPU is simple. By contrast, in a complex CPU, decoding may involve such actions as checking for resource conflicts and availability of data, and waiting until resources are free. In the execution step, the CPU activates corresponding resources to perform the operation. This involves using control signals generated in the decoding step to select required operands, enable the ALU to perform the required operation, and route the results to destination registers.

In a non-pipelined CPU, these steps are performed in order, and when the instruction is finished, the CPU starts again with the fetching step of the next instruction. Modern high-performance CPUs, however, can overlap the steps as if the steps were performed sequentially. Techniques used within CPUs to execute multiple instructions concurrently include pipelining and superscalar techniques.

8.4.3 CRYPTO PROCESSOR

We will design a simple 8-bit crypto processor to implement the encryption algorithm of the AES. AES has a fixed block size of 128 bits for the plaintext, and a key size of 128, 192, or 256 bits. The 128-bit plaintext can be represented by the following two-dimensional array,

$$
\begin{bmatrix}
a_{0,0} & a_{0,1} & a_{0,2} & a_{0,3} \\
a_{1,0} & a_{1,1} & a_{1,2} & a_{1,3} \\
a_{2,0} & a_{2,1} & a_{2,2} & a_{2,3} \\
a_{3,0} & a_{3,1} & a_{3,2} & a_{3,3}
\end{bmatrix}
\tag{8.14}
$$

where $a_{i,j}$ is an 8-bit binary number, called state in AES, $i, j = 0, 1, 2, 3$.

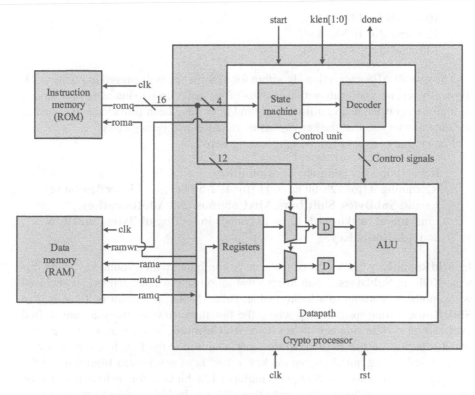

Figure 8.33: Block diagram and interface of crypto processor.

The block diagram and interface of the crypto processor are shown in Figure 8.33. Detailed design of the control unit and datapath will be presented later. The program is stored in the instruction memory, which is implemented using a ROM, while data are stored in the data memory implemented in a RAM. The processor requires a 256×16-bit instruction memory and a 256×8-bit data memory. For the largest key size of 256 bits, we need 15 keys and each key has 128 bits (16 Bytes). Hence, the maximum required space of data memory is $(15 \times 16$ Bytes (for keys) $+ 16$ Bytes (for plaintext)$) = 256$ Bytes. The maximum allowed ROM space for the program is assumed to be 512 Bytes. The one-cycle **start** signal enables the crypto processor. When start is true, the signal, **klen[1:0]**, selects the key size of 128, 192, or 256 bits. The signal, **done**, is asserted after the ciphertext has been stored into the data memory.

8.4.3.1   AES Algorithm

The key size used for an AES cipher indicates the number of rounds that convert the input, i.e., plaintext, into the final output, i.e., ciphertext. The number of rounds is listed below.

- 10 rounds for 128-bit key.
- 12 rounds for 192-bit key.
- 14 rounds for 256-bit key.

The overall AES encryption algorithm for 128-bit key is displayed in Figure 8.34. Typically, an encryption algorithm consists of several rounds to maintain the security of a cipher: confusion and diffusion. Round keys have been provided and stored in the data memory so that the key expansion function will be neglected.

Each round consists of several processing steps:

- Initial round key addition: **AddRoundKey**.
- Remaining 9 (for 128-bit key), 11 (for 192-bit key), or 13 (for 256-bit key) rounds: **SubBytes**, **ShiftRows**, **MixColumns**, and **AddRoundKey**.
- Final round (making 10, 12 or 14 rounds in total): **SubBytes**, **ShiftRows**, and **AddRoundKey**.

In **AddRoundKey**, each byte of the state is combined with a round key using bitwise XOR; in **SubBytes**, a non-linear substitution step where each byte is replaced with another according to a lookup table, called S-box, as shown in Table 8.1; in **ShiftRows**, a transposition step where the last three rows of the state are shifted cyclically a certain number of steps; in **MixColumns**, a linear mixing operation which operates on the columns of the state, combining the four bytes in each column. Based on the initial encryption key, round keys are derived from it using the key expansion function. AES requires multiple 128-bit keys for each rounds and the initial round key addition. We assume that all keys, including initial key and round keys, have been calculated and stored in data memory.

In the **SubBytes** step, each byte $a_{i,j}$ in the state array is substituted with $S(a_{i,j})$ using the 8-bit S-box, as shown in Figure 8.35.

In the **ShiftRows** step, the states in each row are cyclically shifted by a certain offset, as shown in Figure 8.36.

In the **MixColumns** step, each column is transformed using a fixed matrix (matrix left-multiplied by column gives new value of column in the state), and it can be written as

$$
\begin{bmatrix} a'_{0,j} \\ a'_{1,j} \\ a'_{2,j} \\ a'_{3,j} \end{bmatrix} = \begin{bmatrix} 02 & 03 & 01 & 01 \\ 01 & 02 & 03 & 01 \\ 01 & 01 & 02 & 03 \\ 03 & 01 & 01 & 02 \end{bmatrix} \begin{bmatrix} a_{0,j} \\ a_{1,j} \\ a_{2,j} \\ a_{3,j} \end{bmatrix}, \; j = 0, 1, 2, 3 \qquad (8.15)
$$

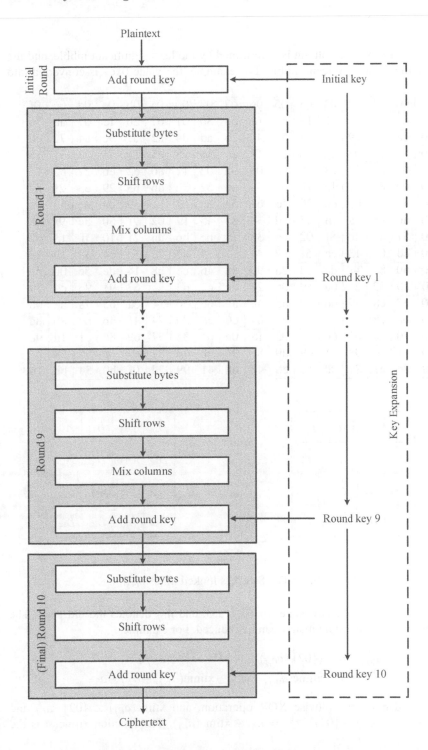

Figure 8.34: Overall AES encryption algorithm of 128-bit key.

Table 8.1: S-box. The column is determined by the least significant nibble, and the row by the most significant nibble. For example, the value 0xc7 is converted into 0xc6.

	00	01	02	03	04	05	06	07	08	09	0a	0b	0c	0d	0e	0f
00	63	7c	77	7b	f2	6b	6f	c5	30	01	67	2b	fe	d7	ab	76
10	ca	82	c9	7d	fa	59	47	f0	ad	d4	a2	af	9c	a4	72	c0
20	b7	fd	93	26	36	3f	f7	cc	34	a5	e5	f1	71	d8	31	15
30	04	c7	23	c3	18	96	05	9a	07	12	80	e2	eb	27	b2	75
40	09	83	2c	1a	1b	6e	5a	a0	52	3b	d6	b3	29	e3	2f	84
50	53	d1	00	ed	20	fc	b1	5b	6a	cb	be	39	4a	4c	58	cf
60	d0	ef	aa	fb	43	4d	33	85	45	f9	02	7f	50	3c	9f	a8
70	51	a3	40	8f	92	9d	38	f5	bc	b6	da	21	10	ff	f3	d2
80	cd	0c	13	ec	5f	97	44	17	c4	a7	7e	3d	64	5d	19	73
90	60	81	4f	dc	22	2a	90	88	46	ee	b8	14	de	5e	0b	db
a0	e0	32	3a	0a	49	06	24	5c	c2	d3	ac	62	91	95	e4	79
b0	e7	c8	37	6d	8d	d5	4e	a9	6c	56	f4	ea	65	7a	ae	08
c0	ba	78	25	2e	1c	a6	b4	c6	e8	dd	74	1f	4b	bd	8b	8a
d0	70	3e	b5	66	48	03	f6	0e	61	35	57	b9	86	c1	1d	9e
e0	e1	f8	98	11	69	d9	8e	94	9b	1e	87	e9	ce	55	28	df
f0	8c	a1	89	0d	bf	e6	42	68	41	99	2d	0f	b0	54	bb	16

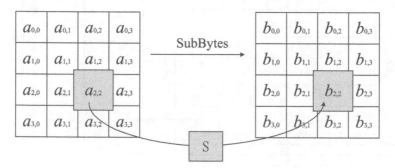

Figure 8.35: The S-box is looked up using $a_{i,j}$.

where $a'_{i,j}$ denotes the new state, $i = 0, 1, 2, 3$, and $a_{i,j}$ denotes the old state. The multiplication by constant matrix can be reduced. For example,

$$
\begin{aligned}
a'_{0,j} &= (\{02\} \cdot a_{0,j}) \oplus (\{03\} \cdot a_{1,j}) \oplus a_{2,j} \oplus a_{3,j} \\
&= \mathrm{xtime}(a_{0,j}) \oplus a_{1,j} \oplus \mathrm{xtime}(a_{1,j}) \oplus a_{2,j} \oplus a_{3,j}
\end{aligned}
\tag{8.16}
$$

where $\oplus$ denotes the bitwise XOR operation, and $\mathrm{xtime}(a_{i,j}) \equiv \{02\} \cdot a_{i,j}$ and $\{03\} \cdot a_{i,j} = (\{01\} \oplus \{02\}) \cdot a_{i,j} = a_{i,j} \oplus \mathrm{xtime}(a_{i,j})$. The function $\mathrm{xtime}(\cdot)$ is the

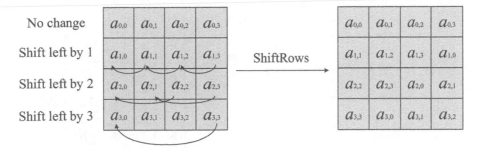

Figure 8.36: States in each row are shifted cyclically to the left. The number of shift differs in each row.

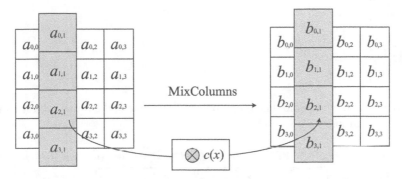

Figure 8.37: Each column of the states can be viewed as being multiplied with a fixed matrix or fixed polynomial, where $c(x)$ denotes the polynomial that linearly combines each columns.

multiplication by 2 in the Galois field and can be derived by

$$
\text{xtime}(a_{i,j}) = \begin{cases} a_{i,j} \ll 1, & \text{if } a_{i,j}[7] \text{ is 1'b0} \\ (a_{i,j} \ll 1) \oplus \{8'h1b\}, & \text{if } a_{i,j}[7] \text{ is 1'b1} \end{cases}, \tag{8.17}
$$

where $\ll$ denotes the left shift operation. The **MixColumns** can also be visualized in Figure 8.37.

In the **AddRoundKey** step, each byte of the state is added by the corresponding byte of the subkey (or round) using bitwise XOR, as shown in Figure 8.38.

8.4.3.2 Processor Design

The processor has been optimized for simplicity instead of performance. The instructions have two kinds of formats, formats A and B, as shown in Figure 8.39. For instructions with format A excluding those jump instructions, they have three fields, opcode, destination register (**Rd**), and source register (**Rs**). For jump instructions (including subroutine call) with format B, they have two fields, opcode and an 8-bit

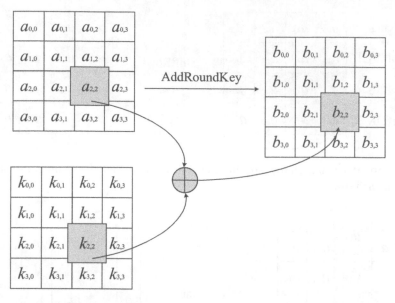

Figure 8.38: Each byte of the state is combined with a byte of the round subkey using the XOR operation.

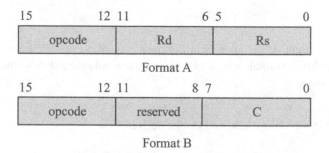

Figure 8.39: Instruction formats of 8-bit crypto processor.

immediate constant, which represents the jump or subroutine call address. For instructions with format A, depending on their opcodes, 6-bit **Rd** and/or 6-bit **Rs** fields may be absent, replaced with a data in the data memory addressed by **Ra** (address register of data memory), or simply replaced with a 6-bit immediate constant.

The primary field of an instruction is the 4-bit opcode, short for operation code that specifies the operation to be performed and, by implication, the layout of the remaining fields within the code word. All registers in the processor have 8 bits. There are general-purpose registers, **R0-R31**, that can store the 128-bit plaintext and 128-bit key, two more general-purpose registers, **R32** and **R33**, the program counter, **PC**, the address register of data memory, **Ra**, the read-only status register, **Ri**, including **E-bit** (equivalence bit) in bit 0, **P-bit** (pause bit) in bit 1, and other bits are reserved, and the read-only round register, **Rr** = 9, 11, or 13 configured by the key size signal, **klen[1:0]**, for 128-bit, 192-bit, and 256-bit key, respectively. The stack memory has only one entry that can support non-nested subroutine call. By keeping the field layout simple and regular, we make the circuit for the instruction decoder simple. In a complex processor with a large number of various instructions, to speedup the instruction decoding, instruction sets are usually encoded by distinct prefix for different categories of instructions.

Based on the AES algorithm, we define the instruction set specialized for it, as shown in Table 8.2, where **Rd** denotes the destination register, **Rs** denotes the source register, **Ra** is the address register of data memory, **(Ra)** denotes the content of **Ra**, **C** represents an 8-bit constant for **jmp**, **jne**, and **jsb** instructions or 6-bit constant for **mvc** and **adc** instructions, **Ri** is the status register, and **PC** is the program counter. Notice that **Rd** and **Rs** can be either **R0-R33**, **Ra**, **PC**, **Ri**, **Rk**, or **Rr**. The register, **Rk**, is the stack register with only one entry used to save and restore **PC** upon executing the instructions, **jsb** and **ret**, respectively. However, it is not allowed to manually update read-only registers, **PC**, **Ri**, **Rk**, and **Rr**. The instructions, **ldm** and **stm**, automatically increment **Ra** without explicitly needing another increment instruction.

To reduce the space of instruction memory, we support the subroutine call using the instruction, **jsb**. However, nested subroutine call is not allowed to reduce the space of stack memory as well. The subroutine call automatically saves the **(PC+1)** (next to the subroutine call) into the stack memory, and restores the stored **PC** when the instruction, **ret**, has been encountered. The **jsb** must be used in tandem with **ret**. The instruction, **wat** sets the **P-bit** in **Ri** and waits for the **start** signal that activates the processor. The instruction, **dne**, asserts the signal, **done**.

Address mapping of the processor is listed in Table 8.3.

When the CPU is reset, it clears the **PC** to 0 to fetch the first instruction from address 0 in the instruction memory, and starts the fetch-decode-execute steps by the **start** signal. The **PC** automatically increments to fetch instructions sequentially unless a jump instruction, **jne** or **jsb**, is encountered.

The control unit in Figure 8.33 has two blocks: state machine and decoder. The state machine has 4 states as shown in Figure 8.40. After the assertion of **start** signal, the processor begins the fetch-decode-execute steps for each instruction until the **wat** instruction is encountered that causes the state machine to transit to the ST_WAIT state. To continue encryption of the next block of plaintext, the **start** signal should be asserted again. The decoder generates control signals to the datapath according to the opcode.

The timing diagrams of instruction set are presented in Figures 8.41–8.43. Notice that the timing diagrams of **mvc**, **mul2**, and **mul3** are similar to that of **mvr**, and the timing diagrams of **jmp** and **jne** are similar to that of **jsb**. Whereas, unlike **jsb**, the instructions, **jmp** and **jne**, do not store the **PC** into the stack register, **Rk**.

Table 8.2: Instruction set.

Instructions	Opcode	Description
ldm Rd, (Ra)	4'b0000	Load data memory addressed by Ra to Rd. Ra is automatically incremented.
stm (Ra), Rs	4'b0001	Store Rs to data memory addressed by Ra. Ra is automatically incremented.
mvr Rd, Rs	4'b0010	Move Rs to Rd.
mvc Rd, C	4'b0011	Move 6-bit constant C to Rd.
cmp Rd, Rs	4'b0100	Compare Rd with Rs. If equal, E-bit in Ri is set.
adc Rd, C	4'b0101	Add Rd with 6-bit constant C and store the result into Rd.
sbt Rd	4'b0110	Substitute Rd using the S-box and store the result into Rd.
ml2 Rd, Rs	4'b0111	Multiply Rs by 2 in GF(2) and store the result into Rd.
ml3 Rd, Rs	4'b1000	Multiply Rs by 3 in GF(2) and store the result into Rd.
xor Rd, Rs	4'b1001	XOR Rs with Rd and store the result into Rd.
jmp C	4'b1010	Unconditionally jump to address specified by 8-bit constant C.
jne C	4'b1011	Jump to address specified by 8-bit constant C when E-bit is false.
jsb C	4'b1100	Jump to subroutine specified by 8-bit constant C. PC+1 is automatically saved.
ret	4'b1101	Return from subroutine call. PC is automatically restored.
dne	4'b1110	Program done. Output the done signal.
wat	4'b1111	Wait for the start signal. Set the P-bit in Ri.

Table 8.3: Address mapping.

Register	Address	Role in AES Algorithm
R0-R31	6'b000000 (6'd0)-6'b011111 (6'd31)	R0-R15: plaintext and ciphertext. R16-R31: key.
R32	6'b100000 (6'd32)	Temporary register used in ShiftRows for cyclically shifting each row.
R33	6'b100001 (6'd33)	Round counter.
Ra	6'b100010 (6'd34)	Address of the data memory. Increment automatically when ldm or stm instruction executes.
PC	6'b100011 (6'd35)	Program counter.
Ri	6'b100100 (6'd36)	Not explicitly used. Whereas E-bit is used to determine the end of the algorithm after comparing R33 and Rr.
Rk	6'b100101 (6'd37)	Stack register used for jsb and ret instructions.
Rr	6'b100110 (6'd38)	Round number configured by the key size signal.

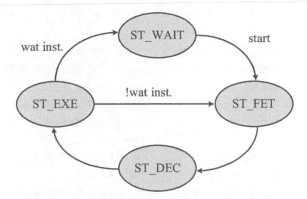

Figure 8.40: State machine of crypto processor.

The detailed datapath in Figure 8.33 is presented in Figure 8.44.

8.4.3.3 RTL Design

In the control unit, the state machine is encoded below.

```
// Control unit: state machine of crypto processor
reg [1:0] state_cs, state_ns;
parameter ST_WAIT=2'b00; parameter ST_FET=2'b01;
parameter ST_DEC=2'b11; parameter ST_EXE=2'b10;
always @(*) begin
  state_ns=state_cs;
  case(state_cs)
  ST_WAIT: state_ns=start?ST_FET:ST_WAIT;
  ST_FET: state_ns=ST_DEC;
  ST_DEC: state_ns=ST_EXE;
  ST_EXE: state_ns=inst_dec15_rr?ST_WAIT:ST_FET;
  default: state_ns=state_cs;
  endcase
end
always @(posedge clk or posedge rst)
  if(rst) state_cs <=ST_WAIT;
  else state_cs <=state_ns;
```

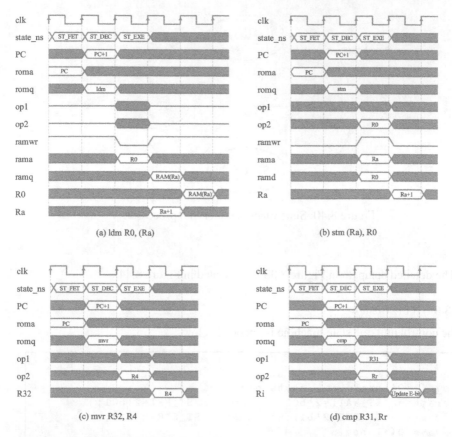

Figure 8.41: Timing diagrams of instructions: (a) **ldm**, (b) **stm**, (c) **mvr**, and (d) **cmp**.

In the control unit, the RTL codes of the decoder are described below. During the state, ST_FET, the **PC** is incremented; during the state, ST_DEC, the opcode is decoded to generate instruction enable signals, inst_dec[15 : 0], write enable signals, wr_en[34 : 0], for **Ra** and **R33**-**R0**, the enable signals to latch operands for the ALU, op1_en and op2_en. The LSB 4 bits of the register **Rr** is encoded according to key size and remaining 4 bits are reserved. The signals, inst_dec[15 : 0] and wr_en[34 : 0], are pipelined.

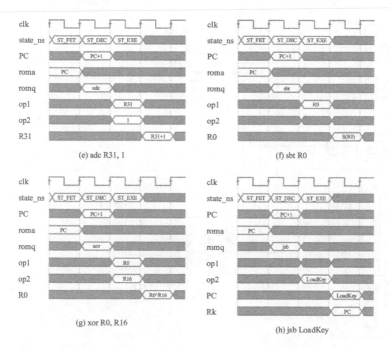

Figure 8.42: Timing diagrams of instructions (continued): (e) **adc**, (f) **sbt**, (g) **xor**, and (h) **jsb**.

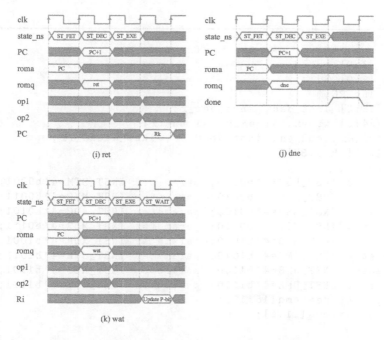

Figure 8.43: Timing diagrams of instructions (continued): (i) **ret**, (j) **dne**, and (k) **wat**.

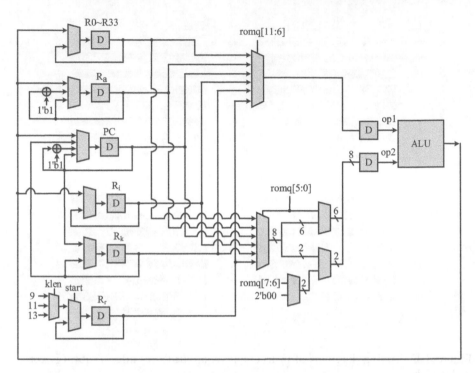

Figure 8.44: Datapath.

```
1// Control unit: decoder of crypto processor
2wire [3:0] opcode;
3wire [5:0] Rd;
4wire inc_PC;
5reg [15:0] inst_dec, inst_dec_r;
6reg [34:0] wr_en, wr_en_r, wr_en_rr;
7reg op1_en, op2_en, inst_dec0_rr, inst_dec15_rr;
8reg [7:0] R[0:37];
9integer i;
10parameter INST_LDM=4'b0000; parameter INST_STM=4'b0001;
11parameter INST_MVR=4'b0010; parameter INST_MVC=4'b0011;
12parameter INST_CMP=4'b0100; parameter INST_ADC=4'b0101;
13parameter INST_SBT=4'b0110; parameter INST_ML2=4'b0111;
14parameter INST_ML3=4'b1000; parameter INST_XOR=4'b1001;
15parameter INST_JMP=4'b1010; parameter INST_JNE=4'b1011;
16parameter INST_JSB=4'b1100; parameter INST_RET=4'b1101;
17parameter INST_DNE=4'b1110; parameter INST_WAT=4'b1111;
18assign opcode=romq[15:12];
19assign Rd=romq[11:6];
```

```
20// Increment PC
21assign inc_PC=(state_ns==ST_FET);
22always @(*) begin
23   inst_dec=16'd0;
24   wr_en=35'd0;
25   op1_en=1'b0;
26   op2_en=1'b0;
27   if(state_ns==ST_DEC) begin
28     case(opcode)
29     INST_LDM: begin
30                 inst_dec[0]=1'b1;
31                 for(i=0;i<=34;i=i+1)
32                     if(Rd==i) wr_en[i]=1'b1; // Update Rd
33               end
34     INST_STM: begin inst_dec[1]=1'b1; op2_en=1'b1; end
35     INST_MVR: begin
36                 inst_dec[2]=1'b1;
37                 for(i=0;i<=34;i=i+1)
38                     if(Rd==i) wr_en[i]=1'b1; // Update Rd
39                 op2_en=1'b1;
40               end
41     INST_MVC: begin
42                 inst_dec[3]=1'b1;
43                 for(i=0;i<=34;i=i+1)
44                     if(Rd==i) wr_en[i]=1'b1; // Update Rd
45                 op2_en=1'b1;
46               end
47     INST_CMP: begin
48                 inst_dec[4]=1'b1;
49                 op1_en=1'b1; op2_en=1'b1;
50               end
51     INST_ADC: begin
52                 inst_dec[5]=1'b1;
53                 for(i=0;i<=34;i=i+1)
54                     if(Rd==i) wr_en[i]=1'b1; // Update Rd
55                 op1_en=1'b1;
56                 op2_en=1'b1;
57               end
58     INST_SBT: begin
59                 inst_dec[6]=1'b1;
60                 for(i=0;i<=34;i=i+1)
61                     if(Rd==i) wr_en[i]=1'b1; // Update Rd
62                 op1_en=1'b1;
63               end
64     INST_ML2: begin
65                 inst_dec[7]=1'b1;
66                 for(i=0;i<=34;i=i+1)
```

```
67                      if(Rd==i) wr_en[i]=1'b1; // Update Rd
68                    op2_en=1'b1;
69                  end
70      INST_ML3: begin
71                    inst_dec[8]=1'b1;
72                    for(i=0;i<=34;i=i+1)
73                      if(Rd==i) wr_en[i]=1'b1; // Update Rd
74                    op2_en=1'b1;
75                  end
76      INST_XOR: begin
77                    inst_dec[9]=1'b1;
78                    for(i=0;i<=34;i=i+1)
79                      if(Rd==i) wr_en[i]=1'b1; // Update Rd
80                    op1_en=1'b1;
81                    op2_en=1'b1;
82                  end
83      INST_JMP: begin inst_dec[10]=1'b1; op2_en=1'b1; end
84      INST_JNE: begin inst_dec[11]=1'b1; op2_en=1'b1; end
85      INST_JSB: begin inst_dec[12]=1'b1; op2_en=1'b1; end
86      INST_RET: inst_dec[13]=1'b1;
87      INST_DNE: inst_dec[14]=1'b1;
88      INST_WAT: inst_dec[15]=1'b1;
89      endcase
90    end
91 end
92 // Pipeline control signals
93 always @(posedge clk or posedge rst)
94    if(rst) begin
95      wr_en_r<=35'd0;
96      wr_en_rr<=35'd0;
97    end
98    else begin
99      wr_en_r<=wr_en;
100     wr_en_rr<=wr_en_r;
101   end
102 always @(posedge clk or posedge rst)
103   if(rst) begin
104     inst_dec_r<=16'd0;
105     inst_dec0_rr<=1'b0;
106     inst_dec15_rr<=1'b0;
107   end
108   else begin
109     inst_dec_r<=inst_dec;
110     // For ldm to latch data mem output
111     inst_dec0_rr<=inst_dec_r[0];
112     inst_dec15_rr<=inst_dec_r[15];
113   end
```

In the datapath, the ROM and RAM interfaces, registers **R0-R33**, **Ra**, **PC**, **Ri**, and **Rk**, and **done** signal are described below.

```verilog
// Datapath: interface signal generation and
// register description
wire [7:0] Ra, PC, Ri, Rk, roma, rama, ramd;
reg ramwr, done;
integer i1;
assign Ra=R[34];assign PC=R[35];assign Ri=R[36];
assign Rk=R[37];
assign roma=PC;assign rama=Ra;assign ramd=op2;
always @(posedge clk or posedge rst)
  if(rst) ramwr<=1'b0;
  else if(inst_dec[1]) ramwr<=1'b1; // stm
  else ramwr<=1'b0;
// R0-R33: R[0]-R[33], Ra: R[34], PC: R[35], Ri: R[36],
// Rk: R[37], Rr: R[38]
always @(posedge clk)
  if(inst_dec0_rr)
    for(i1=0;i1<=33;i1=i1+1)
      if(wr_en_rr[i1])
        R[i1]<=ramq; // Load mem to R[0]~R[33]
  else
    casex(inst_dec_r)
    16'bxxxx_xxxx_xxxx_x1xx , 16'bxxxx_xxxx_xxxx_1xxx :
        for(i1=0;i1<=33;i1=i1+1) // Write to R[0]~R[33]
          if(wr_en_r[i1]) R[i1]<=alu_out;
    16'bxxxx_xxxx_xx1x_xxxx , 16'bxxxx_xxxx_x1xx_xxxx ,
    16'bxxxx_xxxx_1xxx_xxxx , 16'bxxxx_xxx1_xxxx_xxxx ,
    16'bxxxx_xx1x_xxxx_xxxx :
        for(i1=0;i1<=33;i1=i1+1) // Write to R[0]~R[33]
          if(wr_en_r[i1]) R[i1]<=alu_out;
    endcase
always @(posedge clk or posedge rst)
  if(rst) R[34]<=0;;
  else if(inst_dec_r[0]|inst_dec_r[1]) // ldm or stm
    R[34]<=R[34]+1'b1; // Increment Ra
  else if(inst_dec0_rr&wr_en_rr[34]) // ldm
    R[34]<=ramq; // Load to Ra
always @(posedge clk or posedge rst)
  if(rst) R[35]<=1; // Execute from address 1
  else if(inc_PC) R[35]<=R[35]+1'b1; // Increment PC
  else if(inst_dec_r[10]|inst_dec_r[12]) // jmp or jsb
    R[35]<=alu_out; // Load branch addr
  else if(inst_dec_r[11]) // jne
    R[35]<=~R[36][0]?alu_out:R[35]; // Branch or not?
  else if(inst_dec_r[13]) // ret
```

```
45    R[35]<=R[37]; // Return by Rk
46 always @(posedge clk or posedge rst)
47   if(rst) R[36]<=0;;
48   else if(inst_dec_r[4]) R[36][0]<=alu_out[0]; // E-bit
49   else if(start) R[36][1]<=1'b0; // Clear P-bit
50   else if(inst_dec_r[15]) R[36][1]<=1'b1; // Set wat
51 always @(posedge clk or posedge rst)
52   if(rst) R[37]<=0;;
53   else if(inst_dec_r[12]) // jsb
54      R[37]<=R[35];; // Save PC to Rk
55 always @(posedge clk or posedge rst)
56   if(rst) R[38]<=8'd0;
57   else if(start)
58         case(klen)
59         2'b00: R[38]<={4'd0,4'd9};
60         2'b01: R[38]<={4'd0,4'd11};
61         2'b10: R[38]<={4'd0,4'd13};
62         endcase
63 always @(posedge clk or posedge rst)
64   if(rst) done<=1'b0;
65   else if(inst_dec_r[14]) done<=1'b1;
66   else done<=1'b0;
```

In the datapath, the multiplexers used to produce the operands of ALU are described below.

```
1 // Datapath: selection of ALU operands
2 wire [5:0] Rs;
3 wire [7:0] C;
4 reg [7:0] op1_sel, op2_sel_tmp, op2_sel, op1, op2;
5 assign Rs=romq[5:0];
6 assign C=romq[7:0];
7 always @(*) begin
8   op1_sel=0; // Default value
9   op1_sel=R[Rd];
10 end
11 always @(*) begin
12   op2_sel_tmp=0; // Default value
13   op2_sel_tmp=R[Rs];
14 end
15 always @(*)
16   if(inst_dec[3]|inst_dec[5]) begin
17     op2_sel[5:0]=C[5:0];
18     op2_sel[7:6]=2'b00;
19   end
20   else if(inst_dec[10]|inst_dec[11]|inst_dec[12])
```

```
21          op2_sel[7:0]=C[7:0];
22   else     op2_sel[7:0]=op2_sel_tmp;
23 always @(posedge clk)
24   if(op1_en) op1<=op1_sel;
25 always @(posedge clk)
26   if(op2_en) op2<=op2_sel;
```

In the datapath, the ALU is described below, where the S-box is implemented using a lookup table.

```
1 // Datapath: ALU
2 reg [7:0] alu_out;
3 always @(*) begin
4   alu_out=op2;
5   casex(inst_dec_r)
6   16'bxxxx_xxxx_xxx1_xxxx:
7     alu_out={7'd0,(op1==op2)};
8   16'bxxxx_xxxx_xx1x_xxxx:
9     alu_out=op1+op2;
10  16'bxxxx_xxxx_x1xx_xxxx:
11    alu_out=Sbox(op1);
12  16'bxxxx_xxxx_1xxx_xxxx:
13    alu_out=ml2(op2);
14  16'bxxxx_xxx1_xxxx_xxxx:
15    alu_out=ml3(op2);
16  16'bxxxx_xx1x_xxxx_xxxx:
17    alu_out=op1^op2;
18  endcase
19 end
20 // S-Box implemented using table lookup
21 function [7:0] Sbox;
22   input [7:0] inbyte;
23   case(inbyte)
24   8'h00: Sbox=63;8'h01: Sbox=7c;8'h02: Sbox=77;8'h03: Sbox=7b;
25   8'h04: Sbox=f2;8'h05: Sbox=6b;8'h06: Sbox=6f;8'h07: Sbox=c5;
26   8'h08: Sbox=30;8'h09: Sbox=01;8'h0a: Sbox=67;8'h0b: Sbox=2b;
```

27 8'h0c : Sbox=fe ;8'h0d : Sbox=d7 ;8'h0e : Sbox=ab ;8'h0f : Sbox =76;

28 8'h10 : Sbox=ca ;8'h11 : Sbox =82;8'h12 : Sbox=c9 ;8'h13 : Sbox=7d;

29 8'h14 : Sbox=fa ;8'h15 : Sbox =59;8'h16 : Sbox =47;8'h17 : Sbox=f0 ;

30 8'h18 : Sbox=ad ;8'h19 : Sbox=d4 ;8'h1a : Sbox=a2 ;8'h1b : Sbox=af ;

31 8'h1c : Sbox=9c ;8'h1d : Sbox=a4 ;8'h1e : Sbox=72;8'h1f : Sbox=c0 ;

32 8'h20 : Sbox=b7 ;8'h21 : Sbox=fd ;8'h22 : Sbox =93;8'h23 : Sbox=26;

33 8'h24 : Sbox =36;8'h25 : Sbox=3f ;8'h26 : Sbox=f7 ;8'h27 : Sbox=cc ;

34 8'h28 : Sbox =34;8'h29 : Sbox=a5 ;8'h2a : Sbox=e5 ;8'h2b : Sbox=f1 ;

35 8'h2c : Sbox =71;8'h2d : Sbox=d8 ;8'h2e : Sbox =31;8'h2f : Sbox =15;

36 8'h30 : Sbox =04;8'h31 : Sbox=c7 ;8'h32 : Sbox =23;8'h33 : Sbox=c3 ;

37 8'h34 : Sbox =18;8'h35 : Sbox =96;8'h36 : Sbox =05;8'h37 : Sbox=9a ;

38 8'h38 : Sbox =07;8'h39 : Sbox =12;8'h3a : Sbox=80;8'h3b : Sbox=e2 ;

39 8'h3c : Sbox=eb ;8'h3d : Sbox =27;8'h3e : Sbox=b2 ;8'h3f : Sbox=75;

40 8'h40 : Sbox =09;8'h41 : Sbox =83;8'h42 : Sbox=2c ;8'h43 : Sbox=1a ;

41 8'h44 : Sbox=1b ;8'h45 : Sbox=6e ;8'h46 : Sbox=5a ;8'h47 : Sbox=a0 ;

42 8'h48 : Sbox =52;8'h49 : Sbox=3b ;8'h4a : Sbox=d6 ;8'h4b : Sbox=b3 ;

43 8'h4c : Sbox =29;8'h4d : Sbox=e3 ;8'h4e : Sbox=2f ;8'h4f : Sbox =84;

44 8'h50 : Sbox =53;8'h51 : Sbox=d1 ;8'h52 : Sbox =00;8'h53 : Sbox=ed ;

45 8'h54 : Sbox =20;8'h55 : Sbox=fc ;8'h56 : Sbox=b1 ;8'h57 : Sbox=5b ;

46 8'h58 : Sbox=6a ;8'h59 : Sbox=cb ;8'h5a : Sbox=be ;8'h5b : Sbox =39;

47 8'h5c : Sbox=4a ;8'h5d : Sbox=4c ;8'h5e : Sbox =58;8'h5f : Sbox=cf ;

48 8'h60 : Sbox=d0 ;8'h61 : Sbox=ef ;8'h62 : Sbox=aa ;8'h63 : Sbox=fb ;

49 8'h64 : Sbox =43;8'h65 : Sbox=4d ;8'h66 : Sbox =33;8'h67 : Sbox=85;

50 8'h68 : Sbox =45;8'h69 : Sbox=f9 ;8'h6a : Sbox =02;8'h6b : Sbox=7f ;

51 8'h6c : Sbox =50;8'h6d : Sbox=3c ;8'h6e : Sbox=9f ;8'h6f : Sbox=a8 ;

52 8'h70 : Sbox =51;8'h71 : Sbox=a3 ;8'h72 : Sbox=40;8'h73 : Sbox=8f ;

53 8'h74 : Sbox =92;8'h75 : Sbox=9d ;8'h76 : Sbox =38;8'h77 : Sbox=f5 ;

54 8'h78 : Sbox=bc ;8'h79 : Sbox=b6 ;8'h7a : Sbox=da ;8'h7b : Sbox =21;

55 8'h7c : Sbox =10;8'h7d : Sbox=ff ;8'h7e : Sbox=f3 ;8'h7f : Sbox=d2 ;

56 8'h80 : Sbox=cd ;8'h81 : Sbox=0c ;8'h82 : Sbox =13;8'h83 : Sbox=ec ;

57 8'h84 : Sbox=5f ;8'h85 : Sbox =97;8'h86 : Sbox=44;8'h87 : Sbox=17;

58 8'h88 : Sbox=c4 ;8'h89 : Sbox=a7 ;8'h8a : Sbox=7e ;8'h8b : Sbox=3d ;

59 8'h8c : Sbox=64;8'h8d : Sbox=5d ;8'h8e : Sbox =19;8'h8f : Sbox=73;

60 8'h90 : Sbox=60;8'h91 : Sbox=81;8'h92 : Sbox=4f ;8'h93 : Sbox=dc ;

61 8'h94 : Sbox =22;8'h95 : Sbox=2a ;8'h96 : Sbox=90;8'h97 : Sbox =88;

```
62   8'h98 : Sbox =46;8'h99 : Sbox=ee ;8'h9a : Sbox=b8;8'h9b : Sbox =14;
63   8'h9c : Sbox=de ;8'h9d : Sbox=5e ;8'h9e : Sbox=0b;8'h9f : Sbox=db;
64   8'ha0 : Sbox=e0;8'ha1 : Sbox =32;8'ha2 : Sbox=3a ;8'ha3 : Sbox=0a ;
65   8'ha4 : Sbox =49;8'ha5 : Sbox=06;8'ha6 : Sbox=24;8'ha7 : Sbox=5c ;
66   8'ha8 : Sbox=c2 ;8'ha9 : Sbox=d3 ;8'haa : Sbox=ac ;8'hab : Sbox =62;
67   8'hac : Sbox=91;8'had : Sbox=95;8'hae : Sbox=e4;8'haf : Sbox=79;
68   8'hb0 : Sbox=e7 ;8'hb1 : Sbox=c8 ;8'hb2 : Sbox =37;8'hb3 : Sbox=6d ;
69   8'hb4 : Sbox=8d;8'hb5 : Sbox=d5 ;8'hb6 : Sbox=4e ;8'hb7 : Sbox=a9 ;
70   8'hb8 : Sbox=6c ;8'hb9 : Sbox=56;8'hba : Sbox=f4 ;8'hbb : Sbox=ea ;
71   8'hbc : Sbox=65;8'hbd : Sbox=7a ;8'hbe : Sbox=ae ;8'hbf : Sbox =08;
72   8'hc0 : Sbox=ba ;8'hc1 : Sbox =78;8'hc2 : Sbox =25;8'hc3 : Sbox=2e ;
73   8'hc4 : Sbox=1c ;8'hc5 : Sbox=a6 ;8'hc6 : Sbox=b4;8'hc7 : Sbox=c6 ;
74   8'hc8 : Sbox=e8 ;8'hc9 : Sbox=dd ;8'hca : Sbox =74;8'hcb : Sbox=1f ;
75   8'hcc : Sbox=4b;8'hcd : Sbox=bd ;8'hce : Sbox=8b;8'hcf : Sbox=8a ;
76   8'hd0 : Sbox =70;8'hd1 : Sbox =3e ;8'hd2 : Sbox=b5;8'hd3 : Sbox=66;
77   8'hd4 : Sbox =48;8'hd5 : Sbox=03;8'hd6 : Sbox=f6 ;8'hd7 : Sbox=0e ;
78   8'hd8 : Sbox=61;8'hd9 : Sbox=35;8'hda : Sbox=57;8'hdb : Sbox=b9 ;
79   8'hdc : Sbox =86;8'hdd : Sbox=c1 ;8'hde : Sbox=1d ;8'hdf : Sbox=9e ;
80   8'he0 : Sbox=e1 ;8'he1 : Sbox=f8 ;8'he2 : Sbox =98;8'he3 : Sbox =11;
81   8'he4 : Sbox =69;8'he5 : Sbox=d9 ;8'he6 : Sbox=8e ;8'he7 : Sbox=94;
82   8'he8 : Sbox=9b;8'he9 : Sbox=1e ;8'hea : Sbox=87;8'heb : Sbox=e9 ;
83   8'hec : Sbox=ce ;8'hed : Sbox =55;8'hee : Sbox=28;8'hef : Sbox=df ;
84   8'hf0 : Sbox=8c ;8'hf1 : Sbox=a1 ;8'hf2 : Sbox =89;8'hf3 : Sbox=0d ;
85   8'hf4 : Sbox=bf ;8'hf5 : Sbox=e6 ;8'hf6 : Sbox =42;8'hf7 : Sbox=68;
86   8'hf8 : Sbox =41;8'hf9 : Sbox=99;8'hfa : Sbox=2d ;8'hfb : Sbox=0f ;
87   8'hfc : Sbox=b0 ;8'hfd : Sbox=54;8'hfe : Sbox=bb;8'hff : Sbox =16;
88   endcase
89 endfunction
90 // xtime or X2 function
91 function [7:0] ml2;
92   input [7:0] inbyte;
93   reg [7:0] shiftone;
94   begin
95     shiftone=inbyte <<1;
96     ml2=shiftone^{8'h1b&{8{inbyte[7]}}};
```

```
97   end
98 endfunction
99 // X3 function by adding the results of X2 and X1
100 function [7:0] ml3;
101   input [7:0] inbyte;
102   reg [7:0] ml2_result;
103   begin
104     ml2_result=ml2(inbyte);
105     ml3=ml2_result^inbyte;
106   end
107 endfunction
```

8.4.3.4   AES in Assembly

Programs can be written in assembly language and translated into a sequence of binary-coded instructions by an assembler. Based on the ISA, the main program of the AES algorithm in Figure 8.34 is written using assembly language.

The first instruction, **wat**, waits for the start signal. The plaintext is put in the first 16 Bytes of the data memory. The maximum required space of $15 \times 16 = 240$ Bytes allocated for the keys follows the plaintext, as shown in Figure 8.45. The plaintext is loaded into **R0-R15**. Then, the subroutine, **LoadKey**, is called to load the key into **R16-R31**. The 16 states of plaintext are stored in addresses 0, 1,..., 15 of the data memory. Total 13, 15, and 17 keys, including initial key and remaining round keys, for 128-bit, 192-bit, and 256-bit key size, respectively, are stored in following addresses.

Subsequently, the AES algorithm starts and calls the subroutine, **AddRoundKey**, to XOR plaintext and key. Next, the 9, 11, and 13 main rounds (specified by **Rr**) are performed for 128-bit, 192-bit, and 256-bit key size, respectively. During the

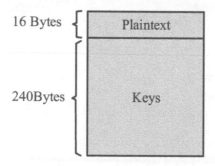

Figure 8.45: Layout of data memory.

MainRound, the subroutine calls, **SubBytes**, **ShiftRows**, **MixColumns**, and **Load-Key** and **AddRoundKey**, are executed. Then, the last round, including subroutine calls, **SubBytes**, **ShiftRows**, and **LoadKey** and **AddRoundKey**, is performed.

Finally, the ciphertext in **R0-R15** is stored into the data memory starting from address 0, the **done** signal is asserted by instruction **dne**, and jumps to the main program to wait for the next plaintext.

In following assembly codes, comments start with the "#" character and extend to the end of the line. Notice that similar and repeated instructions are omitted to save the space and represented by "...". We can place a label followed by a colon before an instruction. The label is the designation for the address of the instruction. We assume that the assembler can work out the address for us. We can then refer to the label in instructions.

```
# wait for start signal
Main:              wat
# load plaintext
                   mvc  Ra, 0
                   ldm  R0, (Ra)
                   ldm  R1, (Ra)
                        ...
                   ldm  R15, (Ra)
# load initial key
                   jsb  LoadKey
# xor plaintext and initial key
                   jsb  AddRoundKey
# repeat 9 rounds for 128-bit key,
# 11 rounds for 192-bit key, and
# 13 rounds for 256-bit key
                   mvc  R33, 0
# subroutine: MainRound
# A loop that executes Rr times
MainRound:         jsb  SubBytes
                   jsb  ShiftRows
                   jsb  MixColumns
                   jsb  LoadKey
                   jsb  AddRoundKey
                   adc  R33, 1
                   cmp  R33, Rr
                   jne  MainRound
LastRound:         jsb  SubBytes
                   jsb  ShiftRows
                   jsb  LoadKey
                   jsb  AddRoundKey
```

```
#  store  ciphertext  into  data  memory
            mvc  Ra,  0
            stm  (Ra),  R0
            stm  (Ra),  R1
            . . .
            stm  (Ra),  R15
            dne
            jmp  Main
```

The subroutine, **LoadKey**, shown below loads the key into **R16-R31**.

```
LoadKey:              ldm  R16,  (Ra)
                      ldm  R17,  (Ra)
                      . . .
                      ldm  R31,  (Ra)
                      ret
```

The subroutine, **AddRoundKey**, shown below XORs the plaintext stored in **R0-R15** and the key stored in **R16-R31**.

```
AddRoundKey:          xor  R0,  R16
                      xor  R1,  R17
                      . . .
                      xor  R15,  R31
                      ret
```

The subroutine, **SubBytes**, shown below substitutes the plaintext stored in **R0-R15** by S-box.

```
SubBytes:             sbt  R0
                      sbt  R1
                      . . .
                      sbt  R15
                      ret
```

The subroutine, **ShiftRows**, shown below left shifts each row of the plaintext stored in **R0-R15** using different steps.

```
# shift 2nd row
ShiftRows:        mvr  R32, R4
                  mvr  R4,  R5
                  mvr  R5,  R6
                  mvr  R6,  R7
                  mvr  R7,  R32
# shift 3rd row
                  mvr  R32, R8
                  mvr  R8,  R10
                  mvr  R10, R32
                  mvr  R32, R9
                  mvr  R9,  R11
                  mvr  R11, R32
# shift 4th row
                  mvr  R32, R15
                  mvr  R15, R14
                  mvr  R14, R13
                  mvr  R13, R12
                  mvr  R12, R32
                  ret
```

The subroutine, **MixColumns**, shown below mixes the elements in each column of the plaintext stored in **R0-R15** using a constant matrix with values 0x01, 0x02, and 0x03. When deriving the new states of the first column (**R0**, **R4**, **R8**, and **R12**), the old states of the first column must remain their values. Therefore, the new states of the first column will be temporarily stored in **R16**, **R20**, **R24**, and **R28**; the new states of the second column will be temporarily stored in **R17**, **R21**, **R25**, and **R29**, and so on. Finally, after all new states in **R16-R31** are available, they will be copied into **R0-R15**.

```
# mix 1st column
MixColumns:       ml2  R16, R0  # 1st element
                  ml3  R20, R4
                  xor  R16, R20
                  xor  R16, R8
                  xor  R16, R12
                  ml2  R20, R4  # 2nd element
                  ml3  R24, R8
                  xor  R20, R0
                  xor  R20, R24
                  xor  R20, R12
                  ml2  R24, R8  # 3rd element
```

```
                    ml3  R28,  R12
                    xor  R24,  R0
                    xor  R24,  R4
                    xor  R24,  R28
                    ml2  R28,  R12 # 4th element
                    ml3  R0,  R0 # R0 no longer needed
                    xor  R28,  R0
                    xor  R28,  R4
                    xor  R28,  R8
# To mix the 2nd (3rd or 4th) column,
# change R0 to R1 (R2 or R3), R4 to R5 (R6 or R7),...
# in above codes.
                    ...
# Move R16~R31 to R0~R15, respectively.
                    mvr  R0,  R16
                    mvr  R1,  R17
                    ...
                    mvr  R15,  R31
                    ret
```

Considering the major tasks performed by the assembly codes, **SubBytes**, **ShiftRows**, **MixColumns**, **LoadKey**, **AddRoundKey**, and load and store plaintext and ciphertext, respectively, the number of instructions to be performed is slightly more than 771 instructions, which corresponds to $771 \times 3 = 2313$ cycles. If the clock frequency is 200 MHz, the throughput of the AES encryption is around 128 bits/(2313 cycles $\times$ 5 ns/cycle) $\approx$ 11 Mbps.

8.5 DIGITAL DESIGN OF COMPONENT LABELING ENGINE

At the end of this chapter, we demonstrate a complete digital design. We want to design a component labeling engine (CLE) that can identify all the foreground objects in a 16×16 binary image, shown in Figure 8.46, which is stored in a 256×8 SSRAM. A single pixel occupies an entry of the SSRAM and has a value of 0 (background) or 1 (foreground), that is, the stored values are 8'd0 and 8'd1, respectively. The pixels of the image, from left to right and top to bottom, are arranged in the SSRAM with a series of addresses ranging from 0 to 255.

Every disjoint objects must be given a unique identification number larger than zero, as shown in Figure 8.47. The identification numbers do not need to be consecutive but must be unique. The identification numbers must finally be stored in the same SSRAM where the original pixel values are stored.

There are 8 cases in which the central pixel (black one) with foreground value is determined to be connected to an adjacent object (with foreground value), as shown in Figure 8.48. Adjacent pixels must be classified as the same object.

X axis

	00	01	02					...						14	15
00	0	0	0	0	0	0	0	0	0	0	0	0	0	0	0	0
01	0	0	0	1	0	0	0	1	0	0	0	0	0	0	0	0
02	0	0	1	1	0	0	0	1	1	0	1	0	0	0	0	0
	0	1	1	0	0	0	1	1	1	1	1	0	0	0	0	0
	0	0	0	0	0	0	0	0	0	0	0	0	1	0	0	0
	0	0	0	1	1	0	0	0	0	0	1	1	1	0	0	0
	0	0	0	0	1	0	1	0	0	1	1	0	1	1	0	0
	0	1	0	1	1	1	1	0	0	1	0	0	0	1	0	0
⋮	0	1	1	1	0	0	0	0	0	0	1	1	1	0	0	0
	0	0	0	0	0	0	0	0	0	0	0	0	0	0	0	0
	0	1	1	0	0	0	0	0	1	0	0	0	0	0	0	0
	0	0	1	0	0	0	1	1	1	0	0	0	0	0	0	0
	0	0	1	0	0	0	1	0	1	0	0	0	0	0	0	0
	0	0	0	1	0	1	0	0	0	1	0	0	0	0	0	0
14	0	0	0	0	1	0	0	1	1	1	0	0	0	0	0	0
15	0	0	0	0	0	0	0	0	0	0	0	0	0	0	0	0

Y axis

Figure 8.46: A 16×16 binary image.

8.5.1   BLOCK DIAGRAM AND INTERFACE

The system block diagram and the interface of the CLE are displayed in Figure 8.49.

8.5.2   ALGORITHM DESIGN

Based on the 8 possible situations in which the central pixel is positioned adjacent to neighboring pixels when scanning all pixels of an image from left to right and top to bottom, we use the pattern shown in Figure 8.50 to detect the connectivity of a pixel (shown as black) to its previous adjacent pixels. Compared to the nine-square division in Figure 8.48, the adopted pattern in Figure 8.50 uses the pixels that were available because future pixels have not been read. The pattern in Figure 8.50 will slide from left to right and top to bottom until all pixels of an image have been scanned. This process continues until all connected neighboring pixels can be

X axis

	00	01	02					...							14	15
00	0	0	0	0	0	0	0	0	0	0	0	0	0	0	0	0
01	0	0	0	1	0	0	0	2	0	0	0	0	0	0	0	0
02	0	0	1	1	0	0	0	2	2	0	2	0	0	0	0	0
	0	1	1	0	0	0	2	2	2	2	2	0	0	0	0	0
	0	0	0	0	0	0	0	0	0	0	0	0	3	0	0	0
	0	0	0	4	4	0	0	0	0	0	3	3	3	0	0	0
	0	0	0	0	4	0	4	0	0	3	3	0	3	3	0	0
	0	4	0	4	4	4	4	0	0	3	0	0	0	3	0	0
⋮	0	4	4	4	0	0	0	0	0	0	3	3	3	0	0	0
	0	0	0	0	0	0	0	0	0	0	0	0	0	0	0	0
	0	8	8	0	0	0	0	0	8	0	0	0	0	0	0	0
	0	0	8	0	0	0	8	8	8	0	0	0	0	0	0	0
	0	0	8	0	0	0	8	0	8	0	0	0	0	0	0	0
	0	0	0	8	0	8	0	0	0	8	0	0	0	0	0	0
14	0	0	0	0	8	0	0	8	8	8	0	0	0	0	0	0
15	0	0	0	0	0	0	0	0	0	0	0	0	0	0	0	0

Y axis

Figure 8.47: Final object identification numbers of the 16×16 binary image.

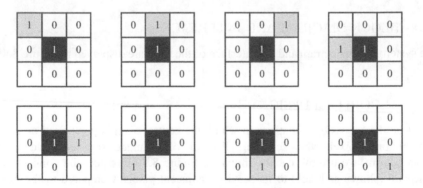

Figure 8.48: Pixels that are adjacent to the central one.

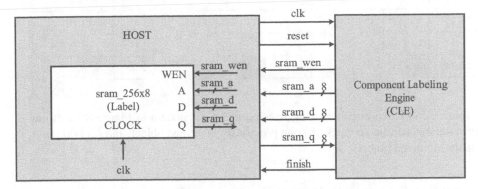

Figure 8.49: Block diagram and interface of the CLE.

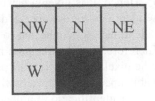

Figure 8.50: Pattern used to detect the connectivity of a pixel (marked as black). Notably, NW, W, N, and NE represent north-west, west, north, and north-east, respectively.

determined because, using this method, it is known with complete confidence that the remaining pixels can be used to identify all previously connected pixels.

The SSRAM will store the given identification numbers of all pixels. To detect the object identification number of the current pixel, the identification numbers of its neighboring 4 pixels must also be available. Therefore, a FIFO buffer implemented by $(16+1) \times 8$ registers is required to fulfill the algorithm. The FIFO can store the object identification numbers of all pixels prior to the current pixel up to that of the north-west one in the previous row. The FIFO advances every clock cycle, so the following 4 identification numbers in the FIFO are needed: the first, the second, the third, and the last, which correspond to the NW, W, N, and NE pixels, respectively. The method only needs to read the original pixels once, reducing the detection time to the bare minimum.

For these examples, we assume the maximum number of temporarily identifiable objects to be 254, i.e., from 8'd1 to 8'd254. Notably, the number of temporarily identifiable objects may be different from the final identified objects because some can be merged owing to "the late detection of connectivity", a concept which will be introduced later. The object identification number, 8'd255, is reserved to represent the background. The object identification number, 8'd0, is not used for debugging purpose.

If the value of the pixel being identified is 0, then its identification number will be given 8'd255, but if it is 1, there are several different possibilities, as shown in

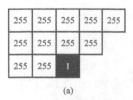

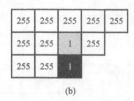

| | |
| (a) | (b) |

(c)

Figure 8.51: Three possible cases detected using the pattern in Figure 8.50: (a) no previously identified objects, (b) one previously identified object, and (c) two previously identified objects.

Figure 8.51. For case (a) (in Figure 8.51(a)), the pixel is identified as "unconnected to any previous pixels" because its surrounding identification numbers are all given by the background one, 8'd255. Hence, it is given a new, temporary, identification number, 8'd1, for the first new identification number, 8'd2 for the second, and so on. For case (b), the pixel is identified as "connected to one previous pixel with identification number 8'd1". Therefore, the identification number of the previously identified object is assigned to the pixel. For case (c), the pixel is identified as "connected to two previous, presumably unconnected, pixels with identification numbers 8'd1 and 8'd2." Hence, the smallest identification number, 8'd1, of the previously identified object is assumed to be assigned to the pixel. Notably, it can be proven that the maximum number of previous pixels that had previously been considered to be unconnected but are now connected due to their relation to the new pixel under detection is two. This is referred to as "the late detection of connectivity." These two previously identified objects with different object numbers need to be merged later.

Using this detection method may result in the late detection of connectivity. Therefore, a label table (label_tab) needs to be used to record the identification numbers, which will need to be merged, owing to newly detected connections. The label table has 254 entries with addresses ranging from 1 to 254. Its contents are initialized based upon their corresponding addresses, as shown in Figure 8.52.

The obj_id_cnt counts the temporarily identified objects and points to (or represents) the new, temporary, identification number. If the pixel value under identification is 0, then it is given identification number 8'd255. Hence, the original pixel value is replaced by 8'd255 and written into the FIFO and the same SSRAM address. As such, the global picture of the connectivity is saved in the SSRAM, whereas the FIFO stores the local connectivity. If the pixel under identification is 1, for case (a) (in Figure 8.51(a)), the pixel under identification is given a new temporary identification number, obj_id_cnt, and written into the FIFO and the same SSRAM address. Hence, the original pixel value is replaced by obj_id_cnt. Then, obj_id_cnt increases by 1. For case (b) (in Figure 8.51(b)), the pixel is identified as "connected to one previous pixel with identification number 8'd1". Therefore, the identification number, 8'd1, of the previously identified object is assigned to the pixel and written into the FIFO and the same SSRAM address. Thus, the obj_id_cnt keeps the same value. For case (c) (in Figure 8.51(c)), the smallest identification number, 8'd1, of the previously iden-

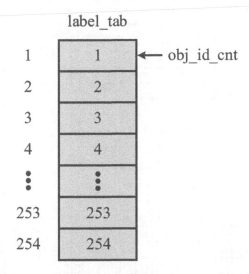

Figure 8.52: Label table and its initial contents.

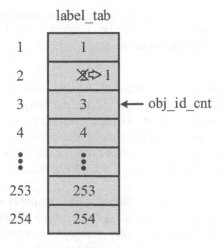

Figure 8.53: Recording the information in label_tab for merging two connected objects with different identification numbers, 8'd1 and 8'd2, later using label_tab.

tified object is assigned to the pixel and written into the FIFO and the same SSRAM address. Thus, the obj_id_cnt still keeps the same value.

To merge the connected objects with different identification numbers for case (c) (in Figure 8.51(c)), the content of label_tab addressed by the larger identification number, 8'd2, is replaced by the smaller one, 8'd1, to indicate that the identification number, 8'd2, will be merged with the identification number of 8'd1, as shown in Figure 8.53.

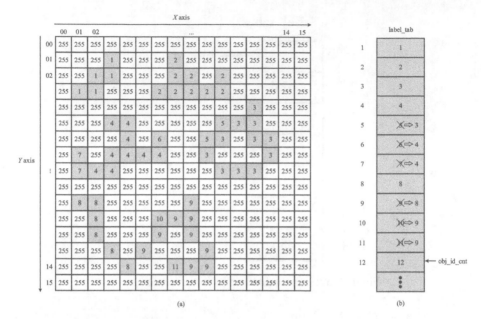

(a)   (b)

Figure 8.54: After determining the object identification number for each pixel: (a) contents of SSRAM and (b) label_tab. Initial contents in label_tab are overwritten by those object numbers that need to be merged.

Till now, the label_tab has only included objects connected pairwise. That is, the pattern which has been used to detect the connectivity of pixels only guarantees the connectivity of adjacent pixels, but this does not guarantee that their object identification numbers are the same. For example, the contents of SSRAM and the label_tab of the binary image in Figure 8.46 become the ones shown in Figure 8.54(a) and 8.54(b), respectively. The obj_id_cnt is 12, which means that there are 11 temporarily identified objects.

To merge all connected objects using the same object number, the label_tab shown in Figure 8.55 must be thoroughly scanned so that a unique identification number can be used for all connecting objects. To accomplish this, each entry in the label_tab is scanned from that pointed to by the (obj_id_cnt−1) until the minimum identification number, i.e., 1, for all connecting objects has reached. When scanning a specific entry, its content is looked up and compared to its address. If they are not the same, its content will be used as the next address. This process continues till the entry that its content and address have the same value. Such an entry represents the unique (and minimum) identification number that the specific entry must use.

For example, the temporarily identified object number, 8'd11, must be finally merged with the object number, 8'd8, shown in Figure 8.55(a). This can be achieved by looking up the content of entry addressed by 8'd11, which indicates that 8'd11 should be merged with object number 8'd9. Then, the content of the entry addressed by 8'd9 indicates that 8'd9 should be merged with object number 8'd8. Furthermore,

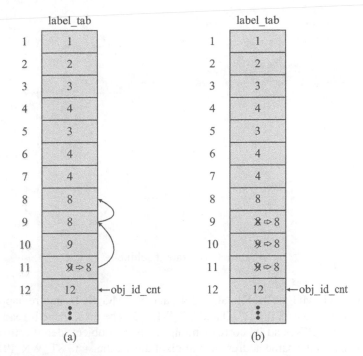

Figure 8.55: Merging of (a) temporarily identified object number, 8'd11 and (b) all temporarily identified objects. The goal is to derive a unified object number for all connected pixels.

the content of the entry with the address 8'd8 indicates that 8'd8 should be merged with object number 8'd8. At this time, the scanning for object number 8'd11 stops when the address and its content become identical. Finally, the entry for the temporarily identified object number, 8'd11, is written into 8'd8, the minimum identification number. This process continues until all temporarily identified object numbers (from obj_id_cnt−1 = 11 to 1) have been merged, as shown in Figure 8.55(b). Eventually, the label_tab specifies that object numbers (from 11 to 1), 11, 10, and 9 should be merged with 8, 8 (the minimum object number itself) should be merged with 8, 7 and 6 should be merged with 4, 5 should be merged with 3, 4 should be merged with 4, and so on.

Finally, the identification numbers stored in SSRAM are remapped to those specified in the label_tab and the background identification number, 8'd255, is remapped to 8'd0.

8.5.3   RTL DESIGN

We use a state machine to control the operation of the CLE, as shown in Figure 8.56. The state machine proceeds through three main stages: scanning all pixels including states ST_RD_PIX and ST_WR_PIX, merging all identified objects including states

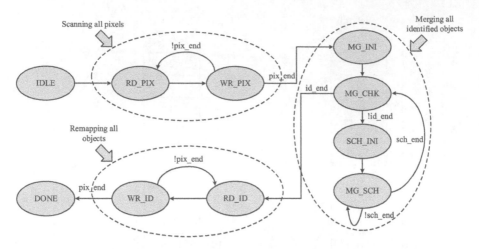

Figure 8.56: State machine.

ST_MG_INI, ST_MG_CHK, ST_SCH_INI, and ST_MG_SCH, and remapping all objects including states ST_RD_ID and ST_WR_ID. The pixel value is read during the state ST_RD_PIX, and its corresponding temporary object identification number is written into the same address as the pixel during the state ST_WR_PIX until all pixel values have been read and their object numbers identified. Therefore, once the original pixel has been read and overwritten, its original pixel value is no longer needed. However, since remaining pixels, particular those in the next row, will use data related to previous pixels, information regarding previous pixels (their temporarily identified object numbers, not pixel values) should also be stored in a FIFO for future use.

The stage of merging all identified objects implements the process of finding the minimum object number for all connected objects (from obj_id_cnt−1 to 1) in Figure 8.55. The process is indeed a two nested loops that, for each temporarily identified objects (from obj_id_cnt−1 to 1), find its minimum object number till an entry in lab_tab that has the same content and address.

The stage of remapping all objects is very simple and just remaps all temporarily identified objects in SSRAM according to the lab_tab.

Using the appropriate algorithm, the architecture of the CLE is displayed in Figures 8.57–8.58. There are two major components in this design: FIFO buffer for storing the local connectivity, and the label_tab for recording all identification numbers. The datapath of the FIFO buffer and SSRAM interface are presented in Figure 8.57. The FIFO has 4 read ports, FIFO[0], FIFO[1], FIFO[2], and FIFO[DEPTH], where DEPTH= 16, for the NW, N, NE, and W object numbers. The SSRAM write data 8'd255 (for background object number), obj_id_cnt (for case (a)), and obj_id_min (for cases (b) and (c)) are used in the state ST_WR_PIX, and write data 8'd0 (for remapped background object number) and lab_tab[sram_d] (for remapped object number) are used in the state ST_WR_ID.

The datapath of the label_tab is presented in Figure 8.58.

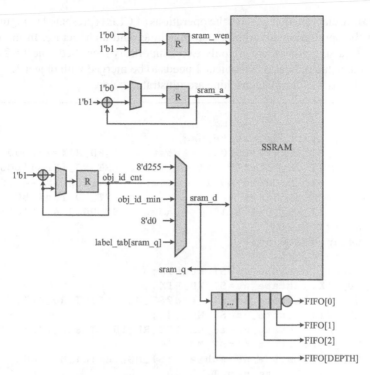

Figure 8.57: Architecture of the datapath: FIFO buffer and SSRAM interface.

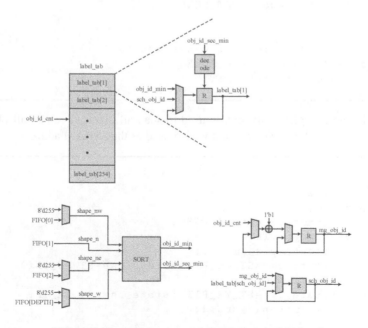

Figure 8.58: Architecture of the datapath: label_tab.

The timing diagram that governs the operations of CLE is presented in Figure 8.59 based on the appropriate algorithm, state machine, and architecture. In the timing diagram, we assume that there are only two temporarily identified objects: 2 and 1. Also, the label_tab indicates that object 2 needs to be merged with object 1.

The RTL codes of the state machine are illustrated below.

```verilog
// State machine encoding
reg [3:0] state_cs, state_ns;
parameter ST_IDLE=4'b0000;parameter ST_RD_PIX=4'b0001;
parameter ST_WR_PIX=4'b0011;parameter ST_MG_INI=4'b0010;
parameter ST_MG_CHK=4'b0110;parameter ST_SCH_INI=4'b0111;
parameter ST_MG_SCH=4'b0101;parameter ST_RD_ID=4'b0100;
parameter ST_WR_ID=4'b1100;parameter ST_DONE=4'b1101;
always @(*) begin
  state_ns=state_cs;
  case(state_cs)
  ST_IDLE:    state_ns=ST_RD_PIX;
  ST_RD_PIX:  state_ns=ST_WR_PIX;
  ST_WR_PIX:  state_ns=pix_end?ST_MG_INI:ST_RD_PIX;
  ST_MG_INI:  state_ns=ST_MG_CHK;
  ST_MG_CHK:  state_ns=id_end?ST_RD_ID:ST_SCH_INI;
  ST_SCH_INI: state_ns=ST_MG_SCH;
  ST_MG_SCH:  state_ns=sch_end?ST_MG_CHK:ST_MG_SCH;
  ST_RD_ID:   state_ns=ST_WR_ID;
  ST_WR_ID:   state_ns=pix_end?ST_DONE:ST_RD_ID;
  ST_DONE:    state_ns=ST_DONE;
  endcase
end
always @(posedge clk or posedge reset)
  if(reset) state_cs<=ST_IDLE;
  else state_cs<=state_ns;
```

A pixel counter register, pix_cnt, is used to scan all pixels or remap all objects according to the label_tab. The pix_cnt is also used as the SSRAM address.

```verilog
// pix_cnt used to generate control signal
reg [7:0] pix_cnt;
wire pix_end;
assign pix_end=pix_cnt==8'd255;
always @(posedge clk or posedge reset)
        if(reset) pix_cnt<=0;
  else if(state_cs==ST_WR_PIX&&state_ns==ST_MG_INI)
          pix_cnt<=0; // Redundant
  else if(state_cs==ST_WR_PIX||state_cs==ST_WR_ID)
          pix_cnt<=pix_cnt+1;
```

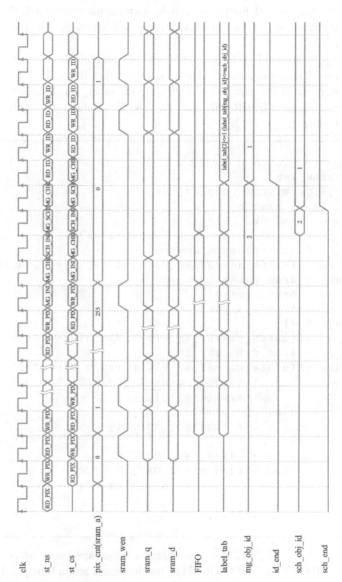

Figure 8.59: Timing diagram of CLE.

The "scanning all pixels" operation reads each original pixel value, determines its object identification number, and writes the object identification number into both the SSRAM and FIFO. The temporary identification number is determined using the shape presented in Figure 8.50. During the state ST_WR_PIX, if the pixel value under identification is 0, then it is given the identification number 8'd255; if the pixel under identification is 1, there can be three possible results, which are presented in Figure 8.51.

During the state ST_WR_ID, the temporary identification number 8'd255, i.e., the reserved background object identification number BG_OBJ_ID, is remapped to 8'd0; otherwise, it is remapped according to the label_tab. Therefore, the SSRAM is written at states ST_WR_PIX and ST_WR_ID. The pix_cnt is also used for the SSRAM address.

```verilog
1 // SRAM interface
2 reg sram_wen;
3 reg [7:0] sram_d, obj_id_cnt;
4 wire [9:0] sram_a;
5 parameter BG_OBJ_ID=8'd255;
6 always @(posedge clk or posedge reset)
7         if(reset) sram_wen <=0;
8   else if(state_ns==ST_WR_PIX || state_ns==ST_WR_ID)
9           sram_wen <=1;
10  else    sram_wen <=0;
11 assign sram_a=pix_cnt;
12 always @(*)
13         if(state_cs==ST_WR_PIX && sram_q[0]==1'b0)
14           sram_d=BG_OBJ_ID;
15  else if(state_cs==ST_WR_PIX && sram_q[0]==1'b1) begin
16               if(obj_id_min==BG_OBJ_ID) // Case (a)
17                   sram_d=obj_id_cnt;
18           else // Cases (b) and (c)
19                   sram_d=obj_id_min;
20       end
21  else if(state_cs==ST_WR_ID)
22           sram_d=sram_q==BG_OBJ_ID?8'd0:
23                       label_tab[sram_q];
24  else // Dont care
25           sram_d=8'd0;
```

In state ST_WR_PIX, the four identification numbers, stored in FIFO[0], FIFO[1], FIFO[2], and FIFO[DEPTH], for the pixels around the pixel under detection are sorted by the function, SORT, which outputs the sorted object′s IDs. The minimum object ID, obj_id_min, is the first one of the sorted results. The second minimum value, obj_id_sec_min, that is different from the obj_id_min, is found by comparing all the sorted results with obj_id_min. It is worth pointing out that for those pixels under detection in the first column, the identification numbers of the

north-western and western pixels are absent and assumed to be BG_OBJ_ID, and
the identification numbers for the northern and north-eastern pixels are respectively
FIFO[1] and FIFO[2], while for those pixels under detection in the last column, the
identification number of the north-eastern pixel is also absent and assumed to be
BG_OBJ_ID.

The register, obj_id_cnt, counts the number of used identifications. If the pixel
value is 1, when obj_id_min is BG_OBJ_ID, i.e., 8'd255, all four identification numbers for the pixels around the target pixel are BG_OBJ_ID. Hence, a new identification number is used and obj_id_cnt increases by 1. In addition to being written
into the SSRAM, the identification number is also written into the FIFO to store
the local connectivity of remaining pixels. The label_tab stores the locally merged
identification numbers. When obj_id_min and obj_id_sec_min are different and do
not equal BG_OBJ_ID, the larger identification number should be merged with the
smaller one by writing obj_id_min into address obj_id_sec_min of label_tab, which
records this information.

```verilog
1 // FIFO buffer and label_tab
2 wire is_first_column , is_last_column ;
3 wire [7:0] shape_nw , shape_n , shape_ne , shape_w;
4 wire [31:0] shape_all_data ;
5 wire [7:0] sort_result [0:3] , obj_id_min , obj_id_sec_min ;
6 reg [7:0] FIFO [0:DEPTH] , label_tab [1:254];
7 integer i1, i2;
8 parameter DEPTH=16;
9 assign is_first_column =pix_cnt [3:0]==4'd0 ;
10 assign is_last_column =pix_cnt [3:0]==4'd15 ;
11 // Watch out for first and last columns
12 assign shape_nw=is_first_column ?BG_OBJ_ID :FIFO [0];
13 assign shape_n=FIFO [1];
14 assign shape_ne=is_last_column ?BG_OBJ_ID :FIFO [2];
15 assign shape_w=is_first_column ?BG_OBJ_ID :FIFO [DEPTH];
16 assign shape_all_data ={shape_nw ,shape_n ,shape_ne ,
17                        shape_w};
18 assign {sort_result [0] ,sort_result [1] ,sort_result [2] ,
19         sort_result [3]}=SORT (shape_all_data );
20 assign obj_id_min =sort_result [0];
21 always @(*) begin
22   obj_id_sec_min =sort_result [0];
23   if (sort_result [1] !=obj_id_min )
24     obj_id_sec_min =sort_result [1];
25   else if (sort_result [2] !=obj_id_min )
26     obj_id_sec_min =sort_result [2];
27   else if (sort_result [3] !=obj_id_min )
28     obj_id_sec_min =sort_result [3];
29 end
30 always @(posedge clk or posedge reset)
```

```
31          if(reset)
32              // Object id 0 is not used, 255 is reserved
33              obj_id_cnt<=1;
34      else if(state_cs==ST_WR_PIX&&sram_q[0]==1'b1&&
35              obj_id_min==BG_OBJ_ID)
36              obj_id_cnt<=obj_id_cnt+1;
37 always @(posedge clk or posedge reset)
38          if(reset)
39              for(i1=0;i1<=DEPTH;i1=i1+1)
40                  FIFO[i1]<=BG_OBJ_ID;
41      else if(state_cs==ST_WR_PIX) begin
42              for(i1=0;i1<=DEPTH-1;i1=i1+1)
43                  FIFO[i1]<=FIFO[i1+1];
44              FIFO[DEPTH]<=sram_d;
45          end
46 always @(posedge clk or posedge reset)
47          if(reset)
48              for(i2=1;i2<=254;i2=i2+1)
49                  label_tab[i2]<=i2;
50      else if(state_cs==ST_WR_PIX&&sram_q[0]==1'b1 &&
51          obj_id_min!=BG_OBJ_ID&&obj_id_sec_min!=BG_OBJ_ID
52          &&obj_id_sec_min!=obj_id_min)
53              label_tab[obj_id_sec_min]<=obj_id_min;
54      else if(state_cs==ST_MG_SCH&&state_ns==ST_MG_CHK)
55              label_tab[mg_obj_id]<=sch_obj_id;
56 // Sort the obj ids
57 function [31:0] SORT; // Function call definition
58   input [31:0] shape_all_data;
59   reg [7:0] temp_data;
60   reg [7:0] data[0:3];
61   integer i, j;
62   begin
63     data[0]=shape_all_data[31:24];
64     data[1]=shape_all_data[23:16];
65     data[2]=shape_all_data[15:8];
66     data[3]=shape_all_data[7:0];
67     for(i=3;i>0;i=i-1)
68       for(j=0;j<i;j=j+1)
69         if(data[3-j]<data[3-j-1]) begin
70           temp_data=data[3-j-1];
71           data[3-j-1]=data[3-j];
72           data[3-j]=temp_data;
73         end
74     SORT={data[0],data[1],data[2],data[3]};
75   end
76 endfunction
```

The register, mg_obj_id, stores the current identification number that is being searched for the minimum identification number that should be used for merging. At state ST_MG_INI, the identification numbers in the label_tab are checked for merging using the mg_obj_id initialized based upon the number of identification numbers, obj_id_cnt−1. The operation progresses in reverse order from the last to the first identification number. During each transition to ST_MG_CHK, mg_obj_id decreases by 1 so that the next smaller identification number is checked.

When mg_obj_id reaches the smallest identification number, the merging stops. For each current identification number being searched to find the minimum identification number that can be used for merging, the register sch_obj_id loads the content of the label_tab which it points to, i.e., label_tab[sch_obj_id]. When sch_obj_id and label_tab[sch_obj_id] are equal, it indicates that the minimum identification number used for merging has been found and the search stops. Therefore, the merging process of label_tab actually implements two nested for loops.

```
1 // Merging of label_tab
2 reg [7:0] mg_obj_id , sch_obj_id ;
3 wire id_end , sch_end ;
4 reg finish ;
5 always @(posedge clk or posedge reset)
6         if (reset) mg_obj_id <=0;
7    else if (state_ns ==ST_MG_INI) mg_obj_id <=obj_id_cnt -1;
8    else if (state_ns ==ST_MG_CHK && state_cs ==ST_MG_SCH)
9         mg_obj_id <=mg_obj_id -1;
10 assign id_end=mg_obj_id ==8'd1 ;
11 always @(posedge clk or posedge reset)
12         if (reset) sch_obj_id <=0;
13    else if (state_ns ==ST_SCH_INI) sch_obj_id <=mg_obj_id ;
14    else if (state_ns ==ST_MG_SCH)
15         sch_obj_id <=label_tab [sch_obj_id ];
16 assign sch_end=sch_obj_id ==label_tab [sch_obj_id ];
17 always @(posedge clk or posedge reset)
18         if (reset) finish <=1'b0 ;
19    else if (state_ns ==ST_DONE) finish <=1'b1 ;
```

Finally, during state ST_WR_ID, the object identification numbers stored in the SSRAM are remapped based upon the rules specified by the label_tab except that the identification number, BG_OBJ_ID, is remapped to 8'd0. Also, the control signal, "finish", asserts when the state machine enters the state ST_DONE.

8.6   FURTHER READING

- Clive (MAX) Maxfield, *How to generate Gray Codes for non-power-of-2 sequences*, EDN Network, United States, 2007. Accessed on: June 17, 2021. [Online]. Available: https://www.edn.com/how-to-generate-gray-codes-for-non-power-of-2-sequences/

- David Money Harris and Sarah L. Harris, *Digital design and computer architecture*, 2nd Ed., Morgan Kaufmann, 2013.
- John F. Wakerly, *Digital design: principles and practices*, 5th Ed., Prentice Hall, 2018.
- Mark Gordon Arnold, *Verilog digital computer design: algorithms into hardware*, Prentice Hall, 1999.
- Michael D. Ciletti, *Advanced digital design with the Verilog HDL*, 2nd Ed., Prentice Hall, 2010.
- Peter J. Ashenden, *Digital design: an embedded systems approach using Verilog*, Morgan Kaufmann Publishers, 2007.
- Ronald W. Mehler, *Digital integrated circuit design using Verilog and Systemverilog*, Elsevier, 2014.
- Stephen Brown and Zvonko Vranesic, *Fundamentals of digital logic with Verilog design*, McGraw-Hill, 2002.
- William J. Dally and R. Curtis Harting, *Digital design: a systems approach*, Cambridge University Press, 2012.

PROBLEMS

1. a. If $\Delta V(0) = e^{-1} V_{DD}$, find the time for the circuit to converge to $\Delta V(t) = V_{DD}$.
   b. What about $\Delta V(0) = e^{-2} V_{DD}$?
   c. What about $\Delta V(0) = 0.25 V_{DD}$?
2. For the stable states, $\Delta V(t) = +3 V_{DD}$ or $\Delta V(t) = -3 V_{DD}$. What is the smallest value of $\Delta V(0)$ that converges in less than 5τ?
3. What is the frequency of timing error, f_{TE}, for $t_S = t_H = 0.1$ ns, $t_C = 5$ ns, and $f_I = 1$ MHz?
4. Please verify the functions, bin_to_gray and gray_to_bin, in Section 8.3.5.
5. Calculate the MTBF for a system with $f_I = 100$ kHz, $f_C = 1$ GHz, $t_S = t_H = 50$ ps, $\tau = 100$ ps, and $t_{CQ} = 80$ ps that uses three back-to-back flip-flops for a synchronizer.
6. We want to synchronize a binary sequence from clkin domain to clkout domain. Please identify the potential problems in the following deterministic multi-bit synchronizer and fix them.

```
1 always @(posedge clkin or posedge rst)
2   if (rst) cnt <= 3'd0;
3   else cnt <= cnt + 1;
4 always @(*)
5   case (cnt)
6   3'b000 : cnt_gray = 3'b000;
7   3'b001 : cnt_gray = 3'b001;
8   3'b010 : cnt_gray = 3'b011;
9   3'b011 : cnt_gray = 3'b010;
10  3'b100 : cnt_gray = 3'b110;
11  3'b101 : cnt_gray = 3'b111;
12  3'b110 : cnt_gray = 3'b101;
13  3'b111 : cnt_gray = 3'b100;
14  endcase
15 always @(posedge clkout) begin
16   cnt_r <= cnt_gray;
17   cnt_rr <= cnt_r;
18 end
```

7. Please redesign the nondeterministic multi-bit synchronizer using 5-entry FIFO with flow control.
8. Assume that the FIFO is guaranteed not to overrun. Please redesign the nondeterministic multi-bit synchronizer using FIFO without flow control.

   a. The frequency of clkout is 2 times that of clkin. What's the queue depth of your design?
   b. The frequency of clkout is 3 times that of clkin. What's the queue depth of your design?

9. Assume that $t_S = 50$ ps, $t_H = 20$ ps, $\tau = 40$ ps, $t_{CQ} = 20$ ps, $f_I = 200$ MHz, and $f_C = 2$ GHz. Calculate the MTBF for the following synchronizers.

   a. Waiting one cycle for synchronization.
   b. Waiting five cycles for synchronization.
   c. Using five back-to-back flip-flops for synchronization.

10. When using a two-bit simple synchronizer to transfer a two-bit Gray-coded signal across clock domains, what is the minimum amount of time that needs to elapse between bit toggles? That is, what is the maximum clock rate at which the Gray codes can advance?

11. Consider a FIFO synchronizer that uses simple synchronizers composed of three back-to-back flip-flops to synchronize the read and write pointers. Assuming the input and output clocks are running at approximately the same frequency ($\pm10\%$), what is the minimum FIFO depth that will support data transport at full rate?

12. Please design a Gray code sequence with 5 elements.

13. Please verify the 8-bit crypto processor by finishing remaining RTL codes and assembly codes, and translating the assembly codes into binary machine codes that can be executed directly by the processor. The binary machine is converted from the assembly code using the instruction format, opcode, and address mapping of registers.

14. The status register, **Ri**, is updated upon the execution of **cmp** instruction. Hence, if the **cmp** instruction executes in a subroutine, the contents of **Ri** produced in the main program become invalid. To restore **Ri** (or other registers) after a subroutine, it (or they) must be automatically saved into the stack memory when **jsb** instruction executes. Please expand the stack register to 2 entries that can store and load **Ri** as well as **PC** to/from the stack memory when encountering **jsb** and **ret** instructions, respectively.

15. Please redesign the 8-bit crypto processor, including the ISA, RTL codes, and assembly codes, such that the AES decryption algorithm can be implemented.

16. Please redesign the 8-bit crypto processor, including the assembly codes, and instruction and data memories if needed, such that the AES operation mode of cipher block chaining (CBC) for 2 blocks of plaintext can be implemented. The 2 blocks of plaintext are put in the first two 16 Bytes of the data memory. Then, the 16-Byte initial vector follows. The maximum required space of $15 \times 16 = 240$ Bytes allocated for the keys follows the initial vector.

17. Please redesign the 8-bit crypto processor such that both the AES encryption and decryption algorithms can be implemented. There are two 256×8 ROMs for encryption and decryption assembly, respectively. There are also two 256×8 RAMs for plaintext (to be encrypted) and ciphertext (to be encrypted), respectively. The opcodes of encryption and decryption are shared such that the 8-bit crypto processor needs not to be extended to 16 bits. To switch between encryption and decryption, an input signal can select the mode, and required ROM and RAM.

18. Please redesign and extend the crypto processor to 32 bits such that an instruction can process 4 states of plaintext at a time. What's the throughput of your design? How much performance has been improved?

19. The instruction stages of the original 8-bit crypto processor are not pipelined. Please redesign a pipelined 8-bit crypto processor such that the fetch-decode-execute steps can be performed concurrently. What's the throughput of your design? How much performance has been improved?

20. Please redesign the 8-bit crypto processor, including the ISA, RTL codes, and assembly codes, such that the data encryption standard (DES) encryption algorithm can be implemented.

21. Please redesign the CLE such that the temporary identification number of background can be given by 8'd0.

22. Please redesign the CLE such that a smaller FIFO with 3×8 registers that store the object IDs of NW, N, and W pixels is needed. To this, the memory must be accessed twice, once for reading the pixel value under detection and once again for the object ID of the NE pixel. Please compare the new design with the original CLE using a FIFO of $(32 + 1) \times 8$ registers.

23. Rewrite the Verilog codes of the CLE using the named block for all **for** loops.

24. Please design an edge decoder that can compute the derivatives of the intensity signal in the x and y directions for detecting abrupt changes in intensity, particularly at the boundaries of objects. Subsequent analysis should be able to determine what the objects are. We assume a monochrome image of 480×640 pixels, each of 8 bits. The pixels of an image, from left to right, top to bottom, are to be stored in a 76800×32 SRAM. Four pixels are in an SRAM address. Pixel values are interpreted as unsigned integers ranging from 0 (black) to 255 (white). We can use the Sobel edge detector, which approximates the derivative in each direction for each pixel by a process called convolution. This involves multiplying 9 adjacent pixels by 9 coefficients, which are often represented by two 3×3 convolutional masks, G_x and G_y (shown in Figure 8.60), and then summing the 9 products to form two partial derivatives for the derivative image, D_x and D_y.

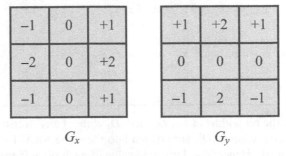

$$G_x \qquad\qquad G_y$$

Figure 8.60: Sobel convolutional masks, G_x and G_y.

The magnitude of the derivative of image pixels can be written as

$$|D| = \sqrt{D_x^2 + D_y^2}. \qquad (8.18)$$

However, since we are just interested in finding the maxima and minima in the magnitude, a sufficient approximation is

$$|D| = |D_x| + |D_y|. \qquad (8.19)$$

Note that the pixels around the edge of the image do not have a complete set of neighboring pixels, so we need to treat them separately. The simplest approach is to set the derivative value, $|D|$, of the edge pixels to 0. A pseudo code is presented below. Let $P[r][c]$ denote pixel value in the original image, and $D[r][c]$ denote pixels in the derivative image, where the row index, r, ranges from 0 to 479, and the column index, c, ranges from 0 to 639. Also, let $G_x[i][j]$ and $G_y[i][j]$ denote the convolutional masks for the x and y axes, respectively, where $i, j = -1, 0, +1$.

```
1 // Set the derivative value of the edge pixels to 0
2 r=0; // First row
3 for(c=0; c<=639; c=c+1) D[r][c]=0;
4 r=479; // Last row
5 for(c=0; c<=639; c=c+1) D[r][c]=0;
6 c=0; // First column
7 for(r=0; r<=479; r=r+1) D[r][c]=0;
8 c=639; // Last column
9 for(r=0; r<=479; r=r+1) D[r][c]=0;
10 // Other pixels
11 for(r=1; r<=478; r=r+1) begin
12   for(c=1; c<=638; c=c+1) begin
13     sum_x=0; sum_y=0;
14     for(i=-1;i<=1;i=i+1) begin
15       for(j=-1;j<=1;j=j+1) begin
16         sum_x=sum_x+P[r+i][c+j]*G_x[i][j];
17         sum_y=sum_y+P[r+i][c+j]*G_y[i][j];
18       end
19     end
20     D[r][c]=abs(sum_x)+abs(sum_y);
21   end
22 end
```

a. Determine the bit widths of D_x, D_y, and $|D|$ without any overflow.
b. The derivative values, $|D|$, are written into the same SRAM with 8 bits for each derivative. Hence, the derivative value of each pixel is truncated into 8 bits. Like the original pixels, four directive values are stored in each SRAM address. Please design an edge detector without any constraints on the number of times memory can be accessed.

c. Please redesign the edge detector with a constraint on the number of times memory can be accessed, such that each memory is only allowed to be read once.

25. Design and verify the video edge detection based on the Sobel accelerator.

26. Design and verify the video edge detection based on the Sobel accelerator using a model in which the pixels can only be read once.

9 I/O Interface

The way of transferring information between internal storage and external I/O devices is called I/O interface. The I/O interface interacts with physical world through I/O devices, such as the human interfaces of display and keypad.

A bus is a communication system that can transfer data within or between computers. Some buses are used for connecting separate chips on a circuit board. Others connect separate boards in a system. Bus specifications and protocols vary, depending on the requirement of their intended use. Off-chip buses use tristate drivers for signals that have multiple data sources. For example, the PCI bus is used to connect add-on cards to a computer. On-chip buses are used to connect sub-modules within an IC. They have separate input and output signals that allow to use multiplexers and demultiplexers to connect components. Examples include the AMBA buses specified by ARM, the CoreConnect buses specified by IBM, and the Wishbone bus specified by the OpenCores organization.

To easily integrate components designed by different teams, a number of common bus protocols have been specified. Components connected using buses should conform to the same bus protocol. Otherwise, some interface glue logics may be required. The specification of a bus protocol includes a signal list for connecting compliant components, and a description of the operation sequences and signal timings to implement various bus operations. The address width of a bus determines the memory space it can address, and the data width of a bus results in different speeds of transferring data.

This chapter introduces the I/O controller for the keypad. Additionally, an I/O processor is used to program or control the I/O controller. The multiplexed, tristate, and open-drain buses, and several serial transmission protocols are presented. The main difference between the programs in embedded systems and general purpose computers is that the embedded software must be able to react promptly when an event occurs. Therefore, we introduce the I/O interfaces of embedded software, such as polling, interrupt, and timer, for embedded systems. Finally, an accelerator of FFT processor is illustrated from its algorithm to RTL design.

9.1 I/O CONTROLLER

The I/O controller of a keypad uses switches to detect the pushed buttons, as shown in Figure 9.1. In order to reduce the number of signals, particularly for a large keypad, the switches are usually arranged in a matrix form. To scan the closed contacts in the matrix, the I/O controller drives one row line low at a time. The way the row signals, $row[3:0]$, are generated is that each row is sequentially selected at a time by the I/O controller. Then, the column signals, $col[2:0]$, are latched by the I/O controller to determine the pushed button. For example, when the second row is selected by asserting a logic 0 on the signal row[1] and leaving the rest of the row lines logic 1,

DOI: 10.1201/9781003187196-9

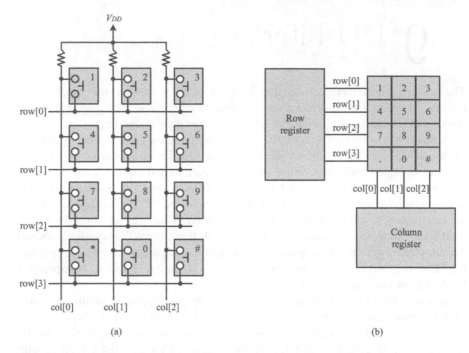

(a)   (b)

Figure 9.1: (a) Keypad switches arranged in a scanned matrix. (b) A keypad matrix with an output register, row register, for driving row lines and an input register, column register, for latching column lines.

i.e., row[3 : 0] = 4'b1101, if either digit 4, 5, or 6 has been pushed, its corresponding column signals will be pulled low and detected. When all of the key switches are open, all column lines are pulled high by the resistors.

The row signal is controlled by a processor through its I/O interface, as shown in Figure 9.2. The data buses, din[7 : 0] and dout[7 : 0], have 8 bits. When cen is true, a write (wen = 1'b1) or read (wen = 1'b0) I/O command has been issued. There are 3 I/O ports provided by the controller, and they are decoded by the address signal, addr[1 : 0]. The port numbers 0, 1, and 2 are used to access the status register, row register, and column register, respectively. Bit 0 of the status register indicates a valid column signal, col[2 : 0], that has been sampled. Bits 7 to 1 of the status register are reserved. Bits 3 to 0 of the row register drive the row signal, row[3 : 0]. Bits 7 to 4 of the row register are reserved. Bits 2 to 0 of the column register stores the valid column signal, col[2 : 0], and bits 7 to 3 are reserved.

However, a user can push the button or switch at a random time. Even worse, as the switch closes, the contact may bounce back and forth several times. This may cause the circuit to open and close several times before finally staying in the stable and closed position. Hence, the column signals should be synchronized to eliminate the timing failure and debounced to generate a stable column signal. The minimum

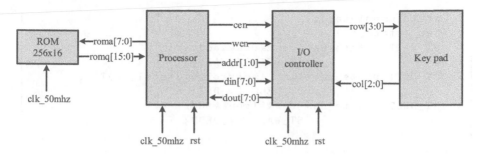

Figure 9.2: I/O interface of the keypad controller.

scanning period for each row is assumed to be 2 ms, and the debouncing interval is 1 ms.

The steps of the processor used to decide the pushed keys are: 1) configure the row register; 2) wait for a valid and debounced column signal by reading the status register. Bit 0 of the status register automatically clears after being read; 3) read the stable column register. Debounced column signal can be obtained by comparing two column signals separated by 1 ms. If they are the same, a debounced column signal has been derived; otherwise, additional 1 ms needs to wait for the contact to settle down.

We develop a Verilog model for the keypad controller that can generate a stable signal to indicate the status of 12 keys, as shown below. The frequency of system clock is 50 MHz.

```verilog
1// Module of I/O controller
2module io_ctrl(row, dout, col, cen, wen, addr, din,
3                clk_50mhz, rst);
4output [3:0] row;
5output [7:0] dout;
6input [2:0] col;
7input [1:0] addr;
8input [7:0] din;
9input cen, wen, clk_50mhz, rst;
10reg [3:0] row_reg;
11reg [15:0] cnt;
12wire time_1ms;
13reg [2:0] col_r, col_rr, col_old, col_reg;
14reg [7:0] dout;
15reg [1:0] state_ns, state_cs;
16reg col_valid;
17parameter ST_WAIT=2'b00; parameter ST_DET=2'b01;
18parameter ST_DEBD=2'b11;
19always @(*) begin
```

```
20   state_ns=state_cs;
21   case(state_cs)
22   ST_WAIT: state_ns=(cen&&wen&&addr==1)?
23                     ST_DET:ST_WAIT;
24   ST_DET: state_ns=(time_1ms&&col_old==col_rr)?
25                     ST_DEBD:ST_DET;
26   ST_DEBD: state_ns=(cen&&!wen&&addr==0)?
27                     ST_WAIT:ST_DEBD;
28   endcase
29 end
30 always @(posedge clk_50mhz or posedge rst)
31   if(rst) state_cs <=ST_WAIT;
32   else state_cs <=state_ns;
33 // Row register
34 assign row=row_reg;
35 always @(posedge clk_50mhz or posedge rst)
36   if(rst) row_reg <=0;
37   else if(state_cs==ST_WAIT&&state_ns==ST_DET)
38     row_reg <=din[3:0];
39 // Read data
40 always @(posedge clk_50mhz or posedge rst)
41   if(rst) dout <=0;
42   else if(cen&&!wen)
43     case(addr)
44     2'd0: dout <={7'd0,col_valid};
45     2'd1: dout <={4'd0,row_reg};
46     2'd2: dout <={5'd0,col_reg};
47     endcase
48 // Counter for 1 ms
49 always @(posedge clk_50mhz or posedge rst)
50   if(rst) cnt <=0;
51   else if(time_1ms) cnt <=0;
52   else if(state_cs==ST_DET&&state_ns==ST_DET)
53     cnt <=cnt+1;
54 assign time_1ms=cnt==49999;
55 // Double synch
56 always @(posedge clk_50mhz)
57 begin
58   col_r <=col;
59   col_rr <=col_r;
60 end
61 // Old col signal
62 always @(posedge clk_50mhz)
63   if(time_1ms) col_old <=col_rr;
64 // Detected col register
65 always @(posedge clk_50mhz or posedge rst)
66   if(rst) col_reg <=3'b111;
```

```
67    else if(state_cs==ST_DET&&state_ns==ST_DEBD)
68        col_reg<=col_rr;
69  // Valid bit for detected col register
70  always @(posedge clk_50mhz or posedge rst)
71    if(rst) col_valid <=1'b0;
72    else if(state_cs==ST_DET&&state_ns==ST_DEBD)
73        col_valid <=1'b1;
74    else if(state_cs==ST_DEBD&&state_ns==ST_WAIT)
75        col_valid <=1'b0;
76  endmodule
```

9.1.1 SIMPLE PROCESSOR

To implement a processor dedicated to the keypad I/O controller, we define the instruction set in Table 9.1. Similar to the instruction set defined in Chapter 8, the instruction set in this section also has two kinds of formats as that shown in Figure 8.39. For instructions with format A excluding those jump instructions, they have three fields, opcode, destination register (**Rd**), and source register (**Rs**). For jump instructions with format B, they have two fields, opcode and an 8-bit immediate constant, which represents the jump address. For instructions with format A, depending on their opcodes, 6-bit **Rd** or 6-bit **Rs** fields may be simply replaced with a 6-bit immediate constant. The port number of I/O instructions, **out** and **inp**, has 6 bits. Consequently, the maximum number of ports is $2^6 = 64$.

Table 9.1: Instruction set.

Instructions	Opcode	Description
mvc Rd, C	4'b0000	Move 6-bit constant C to Rd.
cmpc Rd, C	4'b0001	Compare Rd with 6-bit constant C. If Rd and C are equal, E-bit in Ri is set; if Rd is larger than C, P-bit in Ri is set; otherwise, N-bit in Ri is set.
jmp C	4'b0010	Unconditionally jump to address specified by 8-bit constant C.
jne C	4'b0011	Jump to address specified by 8-bit constant C when E-bit is false.
jp C	4'b0100	Jump to address specified by 8-bit constant C when P-bit is true.
jsb C	4'b0101	Jump to subroutine specified by 8-bit constant C. PC+1 is automatically saved.
ret	4'b0110	Return from subroutine call. PC is automatically restored.
out C, Rs	4'b0111	Output Rs to output port specified by 6-bit constant C.
inp Rd, C	4'b1000	Input port specified by 6-bit constant C to Rd.

The primary field of an instruction is the 4-bit opcode, short for operation code that specifies the operation to be performed and, by implication, the layout of the remaining fields within the code word. All registers in the processor have 8 bits. There are general-purpose registers, **R0-R3**, the program counter, **PC**, and the read-only status register, **Ri**, for the comparison instruction, including **E-bit** (equivalence bit) in bit 0, **P-bit** (positive bit) in bit 1, **N-bit** (negative bit) in bit 2, and other bits are reserved. The stack memory has only one entry, i.e., stack register **Rk**, that can support non-nested subroutine call. Notice that **Rd** and **Rs** can be either **R0-R3**, **PC**, **Ri**, or **Rk**. However, it is not allowed to manually update read-only registers, **PC**, **Ri**, and **Rk**.

Address mapping of the processor is listed in Table 9.2. The register, **Rk**, is the stack register with only one entry used to save and restore **PC** upon executing the instructions, **jsb** and **ret**, respectively.

Table 9.2: Address mapping.

Register	Address	Remark
R0-R3	6'b000000 (6'd0)-6'b000011 (6'd3)	General purpose registers
PC	6'b000100 (6'd4)	Program counter
Ri	6'b000101 (6'd5)	Status register
Rk	6'b000110 (6'd6)	Stack register used for jsb and ret instructions

Upon reset, the processor starts the fetch-decode-execute steps from the **PC**= 0. The **PC** automatically increments to fetch instructions sequentially unless a jump instruction, **jmp**, **jne**, **jp**, or **jsb**, is encountered.

The timing diagrams of instruction set are presented in Figure 9.3. Notice that the timing diagrams of **jmp**, **jne**, and **jp** are similar to that of **jsb**. Whereas **jmp**, **jne**, and **jp** do not store the **PC** into the stack register, **Rk**.

The detailed datapath of the processor is presented in Figure 9.4.

9.1.1.1 RTL Design

In the control unit, the state machine is encoded below. The CPU executes the program by repeatedly performing the steps of fetch, decode, and execute.

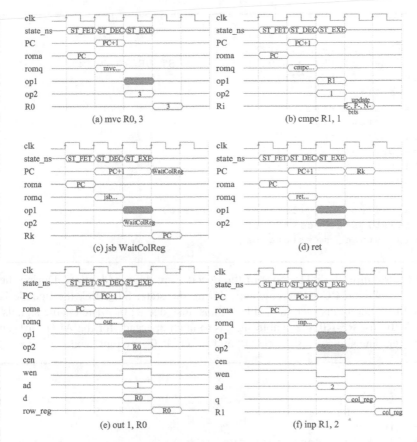

Figure 9.3: Timing diagrams of instructions: (a) **mvc**, (b) **cmpc**, (c) **jsb**, (d) **ret**, (e) **out**, and (f) **inp**.

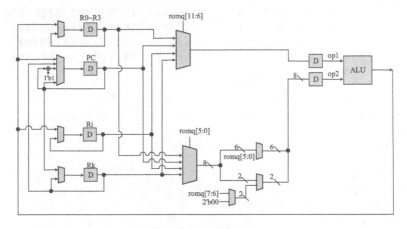

Figure 9.4: Datapath.

```
1 // Control unit: state machine
2 reg [1:0] state_ns , state_cs ;
3 parameter ST_FET=2'b00; parameter ST_DEC=2'b01;
4 parameter ST_EXE=2'b11;
5 always @(*) begin
6   state_ns=state_cs ;
7   case(state_cs)
8   ST_FET: state_ns=ST_DEC ;
9   ST_DEC: state_ns=ST_EXE ;
10  ST_EXE: state_ns=ST_FET ;
11  endcase
12 end
13 always @(posedge clk or posedge rst)
14  if(rst) state_cs <=ST_FET ;
15  else state_cs <=state_ns ;
```

In the control unit, the RTL codes of the decoder are described below. During the state, ST_FET, the **PC** is incremented; during the state, ST_DEC, the opcode is decoded to generate instruction enable signals, inst_dec[8 : 0], write enable signals, wr_en[3 : 0], for **R3-R0**, the enable signals to latch operands for the ALU, op1_en and op2_en. The signals, inst_dec[8 : 0] and wr_en[3 : 0], are pipelined.

```
1 // Control unit: decoder
2 wire [3:0] opcode ;
3 wire [5:0] Rd ;
4 wire inc_PC ;
5 reg [8:0] inst_dec , inst_dec_r ;
6 reg [3:0] wr_en , wr_en_r , wr_en_rr ;
7 reg op1_en , op2_en , inst_dec8_rr ;
8 integer i;
9 parameter INST_MVC=4'b0000; parameter INST_CMPC=4'b0001;
10 parameter INST_JMP=4'b0010; parameter INST_JNE=4'b0011;
11 parameter INST_JP =4'b0100; parameter INST_JSB=4'b0101;
12 parameter INST_RET=4'b0110; parameter INST_OUT=4'b0111;
13 parameter INST_INP=4'b1000;
14 assign opcode=romq[15:12] ;
15 assign Rd=romq[11:6] ;
16 assign inc_PC=(state_ns==ST_FET); // Increment PC
17 always @(*) begin
18   inst_dec=9'd0 ;
19   wr_en=4'd0 ;
20   op1_en=1'b0 ;
21   op2_en=1'b0 ;
22   if(state_ns==ST_DEC) begin
23     case(opcode)
```

```
24     INST_MVC: begin
25                   inst_dec[0]=1'b1;
26                   for(i=0;i<=3;i=i+1)
27                      if(Rd==i) wr_en[i]=1'b1; // Update Rd
28                   op2_en=1'b1;
29                end
30     INST_CMPC: begin
31                   inst_dec[1]=1'b1;
32                   op1_en=1'b1; op2_en=1'b1;
33                end
34     INST_JMP: begin inst_dec[2]=1'b1; op2_en=1'b1; end
35     INST_JNE: begin inst_dec[3]=1'b1; op2_en=1'b1; end
36     INST_JP:  begin inst_dec[4]=1'b1; op2_en=1'b1; end
37     INST_JSB: begin inst_dec[5]=1'b1; op2_en=1'b1; end
38     INST_RET: inst_dec[6]=1'b1;
39     INST_OUT: begin inst_dec[7]=1'b1; op2_en=1'b1; end
40     INST_INP: begin
41                   inst_dec[8]=1'b1;
42                   for(i=0;i<=3;i=i+1)
43                      if(Rd==i) wr_en[i]=1'b1; // Update Rd
44                end
45     endcase
46   end
47 end
48 // Pipeline control signals
49 always @(posedge clk or posedge rst)
50   if(rst) begin
51     wr_en_r<=4'd0;
52     wr_en_rr<=4'd0;
53   end
54   else begin
55     wr_en_r<=wr_en;
56     wr_en_rr<=wr_en_r;
57   end
58 always @(posedge clk or posedge rst)
59   if(rst) begin
60     inst_dec_r<=9'd0;
61     inst_dec8_rr<=1'b0;
62   end
63   else begin
64     inst_dec_r<=inst_dec;
65     // For inp to latch data from output port
66     inst_dec8_rr<=inst_dec_r[8];
67   end
```

In the datapath, the ROM and I/O interfaces, registers **R0-R3**, **PC**, **Ri**, and **Rk** are described below.

```verilog
1  // ROM and I/O interfaces, and register description
2  // R0-R3: R[0]-R[3], PC: R[4], Ri: R[5], Rk: R[6]
3  reg [7:0] R[0:6];
4  reg [5:0] addr;
5  reg wen, cen;
6  wire [7:0] din;
7  integer i1;
8  assign Rs=romq[5:0];
9  assign roma=PC;
10 assign PC=R[4]; assign Ri=R[5]; assign Rk=R[6];
11 always @(posedge clk or posedge rst)
12   if(rst)
13     wen<=1'b0;
14   else if(inst_dec[7]) wen<=1'b1; // out
15   else wen<=1'b0;
16 always @(posedge clk or posedge rst)
17   if(rst)
18     cen<=1'b0;
19   else if(inst_dec[7]|inst_dec[8]) cen<=1'b1; // out&inp
20   else cen<=1'b0;
21 always @(posedge clk)
22   if(inst_dec[7]) addr<=Rd; // out
23   else if(inst_dec[8]) addr<=Rs; // inp
24 assign din=op2;
25 always @(posedge clk or posedge rst)
26   if(rst)
27     for(i1=4;i1<=6;i1=i1+1) R[i1]<=0;
28   else if(inc_PC) R[4]<=R[4]+1'b1;
29   else if(inst_dec8_rr)
30     for(i1=0;i1<=3;i1=i1+1)
31       if(wr_en_rr[i1]) R[i1]<=dout;
32   else
33     casex(inst_dec_r)
34     9'bx_xxxx_xxx1:
35         for(i1=0;i1<=3;i1=i1+1)
36           if(wr_en_r[i1]) R[i1]<=alu_out;
37     9'bx_xxxx_xx1x: R[5][2:0]<=alu_out[2:0];
38     9'bx_xxxx_x1xx: R[4]<=alu_out;
39     9'bx_xxxx_1xxx: R[4]<=~R[5][0]?alu_out:R[4];
40     9'bx_xxx1_xxxx: R[4]<=R[5][1]?alu_out:R[4];
41     9'bx_xx1x_xxxx: begin
42         R[4]<=alu_out; R[6]<=R[4];
43     end
44     9'bx_x1xx_xxxx: R[4]<=R[6];
45     9'bx_1xxx_xxxx: ; // No register to update
46     endcase
```

In the datapath, the multiplexers used to produce the operands of ALU are described below.

```
1 // Operands selection for ALU
2 reg [7:0] op1_sel, op2_sel_tmp, op2_sel, op1, op2;
3 wire [7:0] C;
4 assign C=romq[7:0];
5 always @(*) begin
6   op1_sel=0; // Default value
7   op1_sel=R[Rd[2:0]];
8 end
9 always @(*)begin
10   op2_sel_tmp=0; // Default value
11   op2_sel_tmp=R[Rs[2:0]];
12 end
13 always @(*)
14   if(inst_dec[0]|inst_dec[1]) begin
15     op2_sel[5:0]=C[5:0];
16     op2_sel[7:6]=2'b00;
17   end
18   else if(inst_dec[2]|inst_dec[3]|inst_dec[4]|
19           inst_dec[5])
20         op2_sel[7:0]=C[7:0];
21   else    op2_sel[7:0]=op2_sel_tmp;
22 always @(posedge clk)
23   if(op1_en) op1<=op1_sel;
24 always @(posedge clk)
25   if(op2_en) op2<=op2_sel;
```

In the datapath, the ALU consisting of only a comparator is described below.

```
1 // ALU
2 reg [7:0] alu_out;
3 always @(*) begin
4   alu_out=op2;
5   casex(inst_dec_r)
6   9'bx_xxxx_xx1x: alu_out={5'd0,(op1<op2),(op1>op2),
7                           (op1==op2)};
8   endcase
9 end
```

9.1.1.2 I/O Control Program in Assembly

Programs can be written in assembly language and translated into a sequence of binary-coded instructions by an assembler. Based on the ISA, the main program of keypad controller is written in assembly language below. The directive **equ** is used to define a constant. The registers, **R0**, **R1**, and **R2**, store the row register, status register, and column register of the I/O controller, respectively. Rows are scanned by configuring the row register in the I/O controller. After a valid and debounced column register has acquired, **R2** can be used to decide the pushed key in corresponding row.

In the assembly codes, comments start with the "#" character and extend to the end of the line. Notice that similar and repeated instructions are omitted to save the space and represented by "...". We can place a label followed by a colon before an instruction. The label is the designation for the address of the instruction. We assume that the assembler works out the address for us. We can then refer to the label in instructions.

```
# port address definition
KEY_STATUS       equ   0
ROW_REG          equ   1
COL_REG          equ   2
Main:            mvc   R0, 14 # select 1st row
                 out   ROW_REG, R0
                 jsb   WaitColReg
                 cmpc  R2, 6 # key in the 1st column
                             # has been pressed
                 cmpc  R2, 5 # key in the 2nd column
                             # has been pressed
                 cmpc  R2, 3 # key in the 3rd column
                             # has been pressed
                 mvc   R0, 13 # select 2nd row
                 ...
                 mvc   R0, 11 # select 3rd row
                 ...
                 mvc   R0, 7 # select 4th row
                 ...
                 jmp   Main # repeat scanning all rows
```

After setting a row register, the subroutine, **WaitColReg**, shown below waits until a valid column register has been detected and indicated by bit 0 of the status register in I/O controller.

```
WaitColReg:      inp   R1, KEY_STATUS
                 cmpc  R1, 1
                 jne   WaitColReg
                 inp   R2, COL_REG
                 ret
```

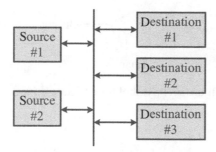

Figure 9.5: A bus interconnect.

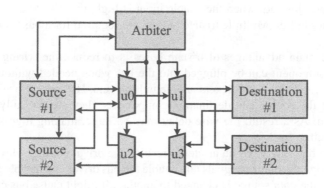

Figure 9.6: Detailed implementation of the bus.

9.2 BUSES

Bus is an interconnect that can move data between components. The most simple bus we have seen thus far is a point-to-point connection where one component acts as the source of data and another one acts as the destination. However, in many systems, it is necessary to use a common interface to connect multiple sources to multiple destinations, shown conceptually in Figure 9.5. The interconnect carries both data and control signals to sequence the operations on the bus. Three solutions that can avoid bus contention are presented below.

9.2.1 MULTIPLEXED BUSES

Detailed implementation of the bus is presented in Figure 9.6. The arbiter is used to resolve the conflict when multiple sources want to drive the bus at the same time. When a source gains the ownership of the bus, its signals to the destination are selected by the multiplexer u0 (whose select pins are controlled by the arbiter), and then, routed to the destination by the demultiplexer u1 (whose select pins are controlled by the arbiter as well).

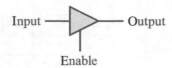

Figure 9.7: Symbol for a tristate driver.

9.2.2   TRISTATE BUSES

A second solution to establish a bus is to use the tristate buffer, as shown in Figure 9.7. Driving the enable signal of the tristate driver low can place it in a high-impedance state. Instead, when the enable input is high, the tristate driver behaves like an ordinary buffer. Multiple tristate buffers are required for a bus with multiple bits.

One of the main advantages of tristate buses is to reduce the wiring complexity. Also, a component can be plugged into the bus when needed without needing any glue logic, such as multiplexers and demultiplexers. However, since bus wires connect all of the source and destination components, they are typically long and heavily loaded. As a result, the wire delay may be large, making high-speed data transfer difficult.

The tristate bus still needs an arbiter to resolve the driver conflict. However, it is difficult to design the control signals that enable the bus driver and disable other non-drivers. When the data source is changed to another, it might cause bus contention. There will be an overlapping interval that some bits of the enabled drivers may be driving opposite logic levels to those of disabled drivers. The overlap will cause a direct current between power supply and ground, which might even damage the circuit.

The control signals must prevent the bus contention by guaranteeing there is only one driver at any time. That is, it must be ensured that the old bus driver is disabled and in a high-impedance state before a new driver can be enabled. Consequently, we need to take into account the timing of the control signals involved in disabling (t_{off}) and enabling (t_{on}) drivers, as shown in Figure 9.8. It is better to provide a handover period ($t_{handover}$) between the enabling of different source drivers. A conservative approach is to defer enabling the new driver until a clock cycle or longer after the old driver is disabled.

Additionally, a floating bus belonging to an unspecified logic level can cause switching problems for some designs. The bus signal might float to a voltage around the switching threshold of the transistors of bus destination inputs. We can avoid the unspecified logic level on a bus signal by attaching a weak keeper to it, as shown in Figure 9.9. The bus keeper will maintain the logic level of the bus source driver after all drivers are disabled and in high-impedance states. The transistors in the bus keeper are small and have relatively high on-state resistance. The logic is easily over-ridden by the tristate bus driver because the bus keeper cannot source or sink much current.

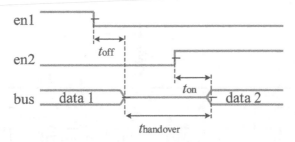

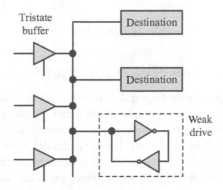

Figure 9.8: Handover period used to prevent the bus contention.

Figure 9.9: A bus keeper used to maintain a valid logic level.

Tristate buffers are synthesizable. However, it is better to use multiplexers instead of tristate buffers in an on-chip bus when developing the RTL because tristate buffers are difficult to test. Moreover, not all implementation fabrics, such as many FPGA devices, provide tristate drivers for internal connections. They only provide tristate drives for the chip I/O to connect externally with other chips. If we want to design a circuit implemented in different fabrics with minimal change, it is best to avoid tristate buses.

9.2.3 OPEN-DRAIN BUSES

A third solution that can avoid bus contention is to use open-drain drivers, as shown in Figure 9.10. The wand net is obtained by using the open-drain drivers. The driver connects its drain terminal of a transistor to the bus signal. When all of the transistors are turned off, the resistor pulls the bus signal high; when any of the transistors turns on, it pulls the bus signal low. If multiple drivers try to drive a low logic level, their transistors simply share the sink current from the power supply. Hence, we obtain the wand logic of inputs, i.e., $y = a_0 a_1 a_2 a_3$.

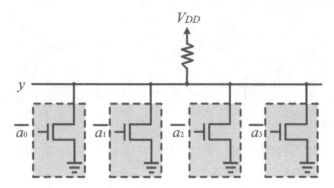

Figure 9.10: Open-drain bus.

9.3 SERIAL TRANSMISSION TECHNIQUES

Parallel transmission gives us the fastest data transfer rate in terms of bits per second. However, it increases the wiring complexity that can significantly increase circuit area and make the circuit layout and routing more complicated. As a consequence, delay has been increased and crosstalk between parallel wires becomes worse as well. For parallel transmission between chips, it requires more I/O pads and pins, and larger PCB traces and area. Even worse, there exists an issue of skew between parallel signals. By contrast, the serial transmission that sends one bit at a time over a single wire can get grid of the above difficulties in parallel transmission under the condition of a possibly lower data transfer rate.

9.3.1 SERIAL TRANSMISSION PROTOCOLS

We can use shift registers to convert a parallel signal to a serial one, and vice versa. On the transmitter side, we load the parallel data into a shift register and shift one bit out at a time. The output bit at one end of the register drives the signal. On the receiver side, the signal is shifted into a shift register. When all the bits have arrived, the parallel data is available. Serial transmission can optimize the signal path so that signal can be transferred at a very high data rate, such as more than 10 gigabits per second. We use the term serializer/deserializer (serdes) for shift registers used in this way.

Example 9.1. A 32-bit data is serially transmitted between two sides of a system. The timing diagram of the transmission scheme is presented in Figure 9.11. Assume that both transmitter and receiver are in the same clock domain. The strobe signal, **load_en**, indicates that a data is ready to transmit. The transmitter outputs the first bit from the least significant bit bit. When a **load_en** strobe occurs, the signal, **tx_valid**, indicates the serial data valid for 32 cycles to shift the serial data in on the receiver. After the transmission is complete, the receiver generates a strobe signal, **rx_valid**.

 Solution: The RTL codes of the transmitter are displayed below, within which we need a 32-bit shift register with parallel load control.

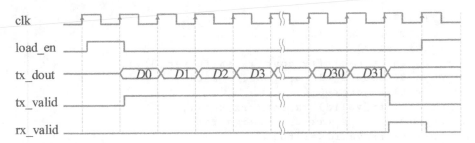

Figure 9.11: Timing diagram of the serial transmission.

```
1 // Module of 32-bit serial transmission
2 module TX(tx_valid, tx_dout, load_en, tx_din, clk, rst);
3 output tx_valid, tx_dout;
4 input load_en, clk, rst;
5 input [31:0] tx_din;
6 reg tx_valid;
7 reg [31:0] tx_shift_reg;
8 reg [4:0] tx_cnt;
9 assign tx_dout=tx_shift_reg[0];
10 always @(posedge clk or posedge rst)
11   if(rst) tx_shift_reg<=0;
12   else if(load_en) tx_shift_reg<=tx_din;
13   else if(tx_cnt!=0) tx_shift_reg<=tx_shift_reg>>1;
14 always @(posedge clk or posedge rst)
15   if(rst) tx_cnt<=0;
16   else if(load_en) tx_cnt<=5'd31;
17   else if(tx_cnt!=0) tx_cnt<=tx_cnt-1;
18 always @(posedge clk or posedge rst)
19   if(rst) tx_valid<=1'b0;
20   else if(load_en) tx_valid<=1'b1;
21   else if(tx_cnt==0) tx_valid<=1'b0;
22 endmodule
```

On the receiver side, we also need a 32-bit shift register, as shown below.

```
1 // Module of 32-bit serial receiver
2 module RX(rx_valid, rx_dout, tx_valid, tx_dout, clk,
3          rst);
4 output rx_valid;
5 output [31:0] rx_dout;
6 input tx_valid, tx_dout, clk, rst;
7 reg rx_valid;
8 reg [31:0] rx_shift_reg;
```

```
9  reg [4:0] rx_cnt;
10 always @(posedge clk)
11   if(tx_valid)
12     rx_shift_reg<={tx_dout,rx_shift_reg[31:1]};
13 always @(posedge clk or posedge rst)
14   if(rst) rx_cnt<=0;
15   else if(tx_valid) rx_cnt<=rx_cnt+1;
16 always @(posedge clk or posedge rst)
17   if(rst) rx_valid<=1'b0;
18   else if(rx_cnt==31) rx_valid<=1'b1;
19   else rx_valid<=1'b0;
20 endmodule
```

□

9.3.2   TIMING SYNCHRONIZATION

With a low wiring complexity, the serial transmission still has the timing synchronization problem between the transmitter and receiver. The timing synchronization acquires the transmission boundary and the sampling time of each incoming bits. There are three basic ways to synchronize the transmitter and receiver. First, the clock can be transmitted on a separate signal wire as shown in the previous section.

The second method is that the transmitter signals the beginning of a serial transmission, and the receiver keeps track of the individual bit intervals agreed upon a predefined standard. The boundary of the transmission is delimited by the start bit and stop bit that indicate the beginning and end of transmission, respectively. Transmitter and receiver typically have independent clocks several times faster than the serial bit rate. The sender uses its clock to transmit data, and the receiver uses its clock to determine the best time instance to sample data after acquiring occurrence of the start bit, as shown in Figure 9.12, where eight bits are transmitted each time. The signal waveform adopts the non-return to zero (NRZ) line code. The signal is held at a high voltage level when there is no data to transmit. The start bit indicates the beginning of transmission by going low for one bit interval. After that, each data bits are transmitted for one bit interval with bits 0 and 1 represented by low and high voltage levels, respectively. Finally, the stop bit indicates the end of transmission by going low for one bit interval.

At the receiver end, the receiver monitors the voltage level of the signal. When the receiver detects a low voltage level of the start bit, it prepares to receive the

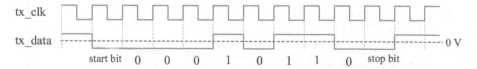

Figure 9.12: Transmission of NRZ serial data, 00010110.

Figure 9.13: Manchester encoding of the serial data, 00010110.

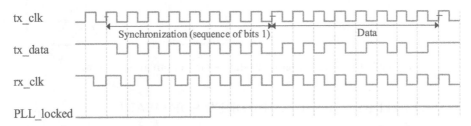

Figure 9.14: Synchronization of the clocks of transmitter and receiver by a PLL.

data. It waits until the middle of each bit interval and samples the signal into the receiving shift register. The receiver uses the stop bit to return to the idle state. The clocks of transmitter and receiver might have slightly different frequencies, i.e., clock drift, and are not related in phase. The clock drift does not matter provided that each transmission does not last too long. Historically, computers have a component called the universal asynchronous receiver/transmitter (UART) for serial communications ports which were popular for the digital modem. The firmware can program the bit rate and other transmission parameters.

The third scheme is transmitting the clock together with data using the Manchester encoding. The Manchester line code represents a bit 0 with a transition from low to high in the middle of the bit interval, and a bit 1 with a transition from high to low, as shown in Figure 9.13. Since there is an indication of the transition in the middle of a bit, and hence, the sampling time of each bit, this avoids the need for complex clock synchronization.

Since the clock information of a transmitter is embedded in the line code, the receiver must be able to recover the transmitted clock and data from the received signal. The receiver employs the famous phase-locked-loop (PLL), which is an oscillator whose frequency and phase can be adjusted to line up with a reference clock signal. For the synchronization purpose, the transmitter sends a continuous sequence of encoded data with bit 1 before sending normal data. The PLL on the receiver side locks onto the sequence of encoded 1 bits (indicated by the PLL_locked signal) to give a reference clock that can be used to determine the bit intervals of transmitted data, as shown in Figure 9.14.

The advantage of Manchester encoding is that it can save a separate clock wire. The disadvantage is that the bandwidth of Manchester encoding is double that of conventional NRZ encoding. Manchester encoding has been adopted in numerous serial transmission standards, including the Ethernet standard.

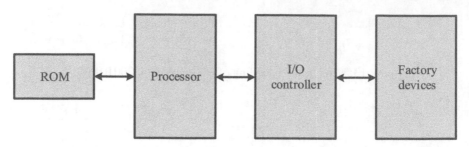

Figure 9.15: Block diagram of the factory automation system.

9.4   I/O INTERFACE OF EMBEDDED SOFTWARE

After introducing the hardware aspects of I/O, we will turn our attention to the corresponding embedded software. The main difference between the programs in embedded systems and general purpose computers is that the embedded software must be able to react immediately when an event occurs. We focus on several mechanisms for synchronizing embedded software with I/O events in this section.

9.4.1   POLLING

Polling of the embedded software is the simplest mechanism for I/O synchronization. The embedded program uses a busy loop to repeatedly monitor the status input from a controller to see if an event has occurred. If multiple events occur, the program will sequentially process the events one at a time.

Example 9.2. In Figure 9.15, a factory automation system monitors two devices in the system based on the processor with the instruction set in Table 9.1. The system has a temperature sensor for the first device and a pressure sensor for the second device. The sensor data are sampled by an I/O controller. The program reads the temperature of the first device, represented as an 8-bit unsigned integer in °C, from an input register at address 8 in the I/O controller. For the second device, the processor monitors its pressure, represented as an 8-bit unsigned number in u(4.4) format, from an input register at address 9 in the I/O controller. If the temperature of the first device is higher than 60 °C or the pressure of the second device is larger than 1.5 atm, the alarm bell is enabled by writing logic 1 to bit 0 of an output register at address 10 in the I/O controller, and writing 0 disables it. Develop an embedded program to monitor the inputs and activate the alarm bell when any abnormal condition arises.

Solution: The polling loop must repeatedly read the input registers even there is no abnormal events. The assembly codes are shown below.

```
# port address definition
TEMP_REG                equ     8
PRES_REG                equ     9
```

```
ALAR_REG            equ   10
Main:               inp   R0,  TEMP_REG  # poll temperature
                    cmpc  R0,  60        # compare with 60
                    jp    SetAlarm       # set alarm if
                                         # larger than 60
                    inp   R1,  PRES_REG  # poll pressure
                    cmpc  R1,  24        # compare with 1.5
                                         # for u(4.4) format
                    jp    SetAlarm       # set alarm if
                                         # larger than 2.0
                    out   ALAR_REG, 0    # clear alarm
                    jmp   Main           # loop
```

The subroutine, **SetAlarm**, shown below sets the alarm and jump to the main loop instead of returning to the instruction next to the subroutine. Doing so sets the alarm without clearing it until the abnormal condition has been removed.

```
SetAlarm:           out   ALAR_REG, 1    # set alarm
                    jmp   Main           # loop
```

Polling is so simple that no extra circuits are required except the input and output registers of the I/O controller. However, the processor must be continuously executing even there is no events to process. Moreover, if the program is busily processing another event, it will not be able to respond immediately,

9.4.2 INTERRUPTS

The use of interrupts is the most common way for the I/O synchronization mechanism. The processor can execute its normal tasks. When an event occurs, the corresponding I/O controller interrupts the processor. The processor stops what it was doing, then starts executing an interrupt handler, and finally resumes its internal status and jumps to the instruction before the occurrence of interrupts. Some processors provide different priorities to different controllers so that a higher-priority event can interrupt service of a lower-priority event, but not vice versa.

To implement the interrupt mechanism, the processor has following features.

- The signal, **int_req**, is generated by wired-AND function of the individual controllers' requests that connect to the signal with an open-drain or open-collector driver.
- The processor must be able to prevent the interrupt while it is executing certain non-interruptable sequences of instructions. Examples are instructions that update information shared between an interrupt handler. If the processor is halfway through updating such information, the interrupt handler will

see incomplete information. So processors generally have instructions that
can disable interrupts (**disi**) and enable interrupts (**eni**).

- The program counter (**PC**) and status register (**Ri**) before the interruption
must be automatically saved before going to the interrupt service routine
(ISR) and restored later upon a return from interrupt (**reti**) instruction. For
simplicity, the nested interrupt is not supported. Hence, the interrupt handler
automatically disables interrupts upon the assertion of **int_req** and enables
interrupts upon **reti**.

- For simplicity, the ISR is placed at address 1 in the instruction memory. So,
the instruction at address 0 in the instruction memory is a jump instruction
to the main program.

- To store registers used in the interrupt handler, they must be saved and restored by **push** and **pop** instructions, respectively.

- To allow multiple interrupt sources, each controller must provide status information in a status register that indicates whether it has requested an interrupt. An interrupt is acknowledged and cleared through writing its interrupt
status register.

9.4.2.1 Simple Processor with Interrupt

In addition to the instruction set designed in Section 9.1.1, we provide several instructions to support the interrupt, as shown in Table 9.3.

Table 9.3: Instruction set.

Instructions	Opcode	Description
reti	4'b1001	Return from interrupt. PC and Ri are automatically restored.
disi	4'b1010	Disable interrupt.
eni	4'b1011	Enable interrupt.
push Rs	4'b1100	Push Rs into stack memory.
pop Rd	4'b1101	Pop Rd from stack memory.

Also, as shown in Figure 9.16, a stack memory, **stk_mem**, with 6 entries are
provided to store the program counter, status register, and other registers used in the
ISR. The stack memory adopts the last-in first-out policy, and has only one pointer,
stk_ptr, that points to the top of the available entry in stack, i.e., the write address
of the stack memory. The pointer automatically increments and decrements upon the
instructions, **push** and **pop**, respectively. Initially, the **stk_ptr** is 0.

The timing diagrams of the instructions in Table 9.3 are shown in Figure 9.17.
A new state ST_INT of the state machine is used to notify that an interrupt event
has happened as indicated by the signal, **int_req_g**. As a result, the **int_dis** signal
is set to prevent the nested interrupt, the **PC** goes to the ISR at address 1 of ROM,
PC and **Ri** are respectively stored in the addresses, **stk_ptr** and **stk_ptr**+1, of the
stk_mem, and the **stk_ptr** points to the next write address, **stk_ptr**+2. The ISR is

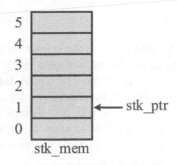

Figure 9.16: Stack memory and stack pointer.

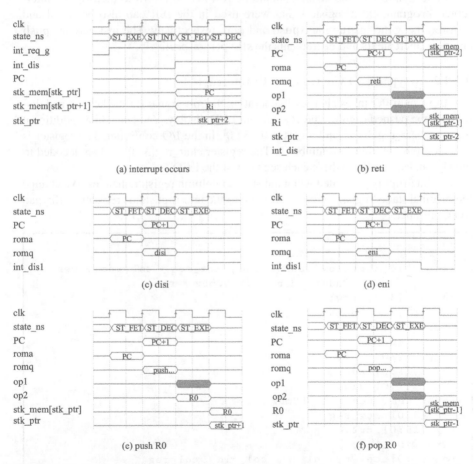

Figure 9.17: Timing diagrams of instructions: (a) interrupt event occurs, (b) **reti**, (c) **disi**, (d) **eni**, (e) **push**, and (f) **pop**.

left by the instruction **reti**, which leads to reverse actions compared to those of an interrupt event.

The signal, **int_req_g**, is a gated signal of the original interrupt request, **int_req**, and two interrupt disable signals, **int_dis** and **int_dis1**, as shown below. Either interrupt disable signals can disable the interrupt. The signal, **int_dis**, is maintained by the processor. When an interrupt occurs, **int_dis** will be set to prevent the nested interrupt; when encountering the instruction **reti**, it is cleared. By contrast, the signal, **int_dis1**, is maintained by the program. It is set upon the instruction **disi** and cleared upon the instruction **eni**. The instructions, **disi** and **eni**, appear in tandem.

```
1 assign int_req_g=int_req&~int_dis&~int_dis1;
```

In addition to **PC** and **Ri** that should be restored to return to the original interrupted program, extra registers that were used in the ISR can also be saved and restored using the instructions, **push** and **pop**, respectively. The instructions, **push** and **pop**, increments and decrements the **stk_ptr**, respectively.

9.4.2.2   Keypad I/O Controller with Interrupt

The I/O Controller takes charge of generating the row signal for the keypad and displaying the pushed digit on the 16-segment LED display. You can add an additional register, char_reg[3 : 0], and a port, led[15 : 0], in the I/O controller. The register is accessed through the port number 3. The register char_reg[3 : 0] is then decoded to the signal, led[15 : 0], to drive each segment of the LED.

The interrupt is generated when the state of column register changes. We change the original status register at port number 0 to the interrupt status register of Keypad I/O Controller.

```
1 // I/O controller with interrupt
2 module io_ctrl(row, dout, led, int_req, col, cen, wen,
3                 addr, din, clk_50mhz, rst);
4 output [3:0] row;
5 output [7:0] dout;
6 output [15:0] led;
7 output int_req;
8 input [2:0] col;
9 input [1:0] addr;
10 input [7:0] din;
11 input cen, wen, clk_50mhz, rst;
12 reg [3:0] row_reg;
13 reg [15:0] cnt;
14 wire time_1ms;
15 reg [2:0] col_r, col_rr, col_old, col_reg,
16          col_reg_old[0:3];
```

```
17 reg [7:0] dout;
18 reg [1:0] state_ns , state_cs;
19 reg int_req;
20 reg [15:0] led;
21 parameter ST_WAIT=2'b00; parameter ST_DET=2'b01;
22 parameter ST_DEBD=2'b11; parameter ST_INT=2'b10;
23 always @(*) begin
24   state_ns=state_cs;
25   case(state_cs)
26   ST_WAIT: state_ns=ST_DET;
27   ST_DET: state_ns=(time_1ms&&col_old==col_rr)?
28                     ST_DEBD:ST_DET;
29   ST_DEBD: state_ns=
30     (row_reg==4'b1110&&col_reg!=col_reg_old[0] |
31      row_reg==4'b1101&&col_reg!=col_reg_old[1] |
32      row_reg==4'b1011&&col_reg!=col_reg_old[2] |
33      row_reg==4'b0111&&col_reg!=col_reg_old[3])?
34                     ST_INT:ST_WAIT;
35   ST_INT: state_ns=(cen&&wen&&addr==0)
36                     ST_WAIT:ST_INT;
37   endcase
38 end
39 always @(posedge clk_50mhz or posedge rst)
40   if(rst) state_cs<=ST_WAIT;
41   else state_cs<=state_ns;
42 assign row=row_reg;
43 always @(posedge clk_50mhz or posedge rst)
44   if(rst) row_reg<=4'b1110;
45   else if(state_cs==ST_WAIT&&state_ns==ST_DET)
46     row_reg<={row_reg[2:0],row_reg[3]};
47 always @(posedge clk_50mhz or posedge rst)
48   if(rst) char_reg<=4'b0000;
49   else if(cen&&wen&&addr==3)
50     char_reg<=din[3;0];
51 // Drive the 16-segment LED display
52 always @(*)
53   case(char_reg)
54   4'd0: led={1'b1,1'b1,1'b1,1'b0,
55              1'b0,1'b0,1'b1,1'b0,
56              1'b1,1'b1,1'b0,1'b0,
57              1'b0,1'b1,1'b1,1'b1};
58   ...
59   endcase
60 always @(posedge clk_50mhz or posedge rst)
61   if(rst) dout<=0;
62   else if(cen&&!wen)
63     case(addr)
```

```
64   2'd0:dout<={7'd0,int_req};
65   2'd1:dout<={4'd0,row_reg};
66   2'd2:dout<={5'd0,col_reg};
67   2'd3:dout<={4'd0,char_reg};
68   endcase
69 always @(posedge clk_50mhz or posedge rst)
70   if(rst) cnt<=0;
71   else if(time_1ms) cnt<=0;
72   else if(state_cs==ST_DET&&state_ns==ST_DET)
73     cnt<=cnt+1;
74 assign time_1ms=cnt==49999;
75 always @(posedge clk_50mhz)
76 begin
77   col_r<=col;
78   col_rr<=col_r;
79 end
80 always @(posedge clk_50mhz)
81   if(time_1ms) col_old<=col_rr;
82 always @(posedge clk_50mhz or posedge rst)
83   if(rst) col_reg<=3'b111;
84   else if(state_cs==ST_DET&&state_ns==ST_DEBD)
85     col_reg<=col_rr;
86 always @(posedge clk_50mhz)
87   if(state_cs==ST_INT&&state_ns==ST_WAIT)
88     case(row_reg)
89     4'b1110:col_reg_old[0]<=col_reg;
90     4'b1101:col_reg_old[1]<=col_reg;
91     4'b1011:col_reg_old[2]<=col_reg;
92     4'b0111:col_reg_old[3]<=col_reg;
93     endcase
94 always @(posedge clk_50mhz or posedge rst)
95   if(rst) int_req<=1'b0;
96   else if(state_cs==ST_DEBD&&state_ns==ST_INT)
97     int_req<=1'b1;
98   else if(state_cs==ST_INT&&state_ns==ST_WAIT)
99     int_req<=1'b0;
100 endmodule
```

9.4.2.3   Program with Interrupt in Assembly for Two I/O Controls

The I/O controller of factory automation system, as shown in Example 9.2, generates the interrupt when alarms have been detected in either device. The port number of the interrupt status register is 11.

As presented in Figure 9.18, based on the processor with interrupt, we want to implement the I/O controllers of the keypad and the above factory automation system.

The assembly codes are written below.

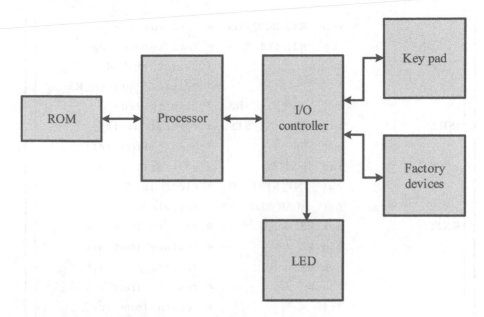

Figure 9.18: Block diagram of the keypad and factory automation system.

```
INT_STS1        equ   0
ROW_REG         equ   1
COL_REG         equ   2
CHA_REG         equ   3
TEMP_REG        equ   8
PRES_REG        equ   9
ALAR_REG        equ   10
INT_STS2        equ   11
                jmp   Main
ISR:            push  R0              # save in stk_mem
                push  R1              # save in stk_mem
                push  R2              # save in stk_mem
                push  R3              # save in stk_mem
ISR1:           inp   R0, INT_STS1    # read keypad int.
                cmpc  R0, 1           # check keypad int.
                jne   ISR2            # set alarm if
                out   INT_STS1, 0     # clear int.
```

```
               inp   R1, ROW_REG    # read row reg.
               inp   R2, COL_REG    # read column reg.
               ...                  # decide pushed
                                    # button & put in R3
               out   CHA_REG, R3    # display led
ISR2:          inp   R0, INT_STS2   # read alarm int.
               cmpc  R0, 1          # check alarm int.
               jne   EXITI          # exit int.
               out   INT_STS1, 0    # clear int.
               out   ALAR_REG, 1    # set alarm
EXITI:         pop R3               # restore from stk
               pop R2               # restore from stk
               pop R1               # restore from stk
               pop R0               # restore from stk
               reti                 # return from int.
Main:          ...                  # normal function
               jmp   Main           # loop
```

9.4.3 TIMER

An embedded system often needs to respond at periodic intervals based on a real-time clock. The programmable timer generates an interrupt to the processor, and then the interrupt handler performs any required periodic procedures.

Example 9.3. Develop the Verilog model of a real-time clock controller. The controller generates a timer with 20 μs period derived from a 50 MHz system clock. The programmable timer is implemented using a down counter loadable with an 8-bit output register, called the counter value register. Writing to the counter value register causes the counter to be loaded. After the down counter reaches 0, it reloads the value from the counter value register and produces an interrupt. The counter has an interrupt status register. Writing to the interrupt status register clears the interrupt. The controller also has an interrupt mask register. When bit 0 of the register is 1, interrupts from the controller are masked, and when it is 0, they are enabled.

Solution: The Verilog model is displayed below. The interrupt status register, interrupt mask register, and counter value register are placed at the port numbers, 16, 17, and 18.

```
1// Real-time clock controller
2module rtc_ctrl(dout, int_req, cen, wen, addr, din,
```

```
3                    clk_50mhz, rst);
4 output [7:0] dout;
5 output int_req;
6 input [4:0] addr;
7 input [7:0] din;
8 input cen, wen, clk_50mhz, rst;
9 reg [9:0] base_cnt;
10 wire time_20us;
11 reg [7:0] timer_cnt, int_val;
12 wire time_out;
13 reg [7:0] dout;
14 reg int_mask;
15 reg int_req_reg;
16 always @(posedge clk_50mhz or posedge rst)
17   if(rst) dout<=0;
18   else if(cen&&!wen)
19     case(addr)
20     5'd16:dout<={7'd0,int_req};
21     5'd17:dout<={7'd0,int_mask};
22     5'd18:dout<={int_val};
23     endcase
24 always @(posedge clk_50mhz or posedge rst)
25   if(rst) base_cnt<=0;
26   else if(time_20us) base_cnt<=0;
27   else base_cnt<=base_cnt+1;
28 assign time_20us=base_cnt==999;
29 always @(posedge clk_50mhz or posedge rst)
30   if(rst) timer_cnt<=8'hff;
31   else if(cen&&wen&&addr==5'd18) timer_cnt<=din;
32   else if(time_out) timer_cnt<=int_val;
33   else timer_cnt<=timer_cnt-1;
34 assign time_out=timer_cnt==0;
35 always @(posedge clk_50mhz or posedge rst)
36   if(rst) int_val<=8'hff;
37   else if(cen&&wen&&addr==5'd18) int_val<=din;
38 always @(posedge clk_50mhz or posedge rst)
39   if(rst) int_mask<=1'b0;
40   else if(cen&&wen&&addr==5'd17) int_mask<=din[0];
41 assign int_req=int_req_reg&~int_mask;
42 always @(posedge clk_50mhz or posedge rst)
43   if(rst) int_req_reg<=1'b0;
44   else if(time_out) int_req_reg<=1'b1;
45   else if(cen&&wen&&addr==5'd16) int_req_reg<=1'b0;
46 endmodule
```

□

9.5   ACCELERATORS

The embedded processor sequentially handles all tasks. However, many time-consuming or critical tasks can be accelerated by a customized hardware. Doing so can also offload the load on a processor. The key to the acceleration performance is parallelism: independent tasks can be performed in parallel.

A processor can benefit from instruction-level parallelism by performing fetching, decoding and executing stages concurrently. That is, based on the pipelining technique, when fetching a new instruction, the preceding instruction can be decoded, and the instruction before the preceding one can be executed at the same time. A high-end processor might fetch, decode, and execute several instructions at once by multiple decoding units and ALUs. Even so, the advantage of lower cost still makes custom hardware accelerators an efficient solution for many critical tasks, particular for those regularly structured data, such as the video data. The performance of accelerators is only limited by the data dependencies and the availability of data.

We can quantify the performance gain of an algorithm achieved by accelerating the kernel, i.e., the critical part that is to be accelerated. Suppose a system takes time t to execute the algorithm, and that a fraction, f, of that time is spent in executing the kernel. Executing codes other than the kernel spends a fraction of $1 - f$. Hence, the original execution time can be written as

$$t = ft + (1 - f)t. \tag{9.1}$$

If our accelerator speeds up execution of the kernel by a factor α, the total execution time t' with accelerator reduces to

$$t' = \frac{ft}{\alpha} + (1 - f)t. \tag{9.2}$$

The overall speedup s is the ratio of the original execution time to the reduced one as

$$s = \frac{t}{t'} = \frac{ft + (1 - f)t}{\frac{ft}{\alpha} + (1 - f)t} = \frac{1}{\frac{f}{\alpha} + (1 - f)}. \tag{9.3}$$

This formula is also called Amdahl's Law.

Example 9.4. Suppose we have two kernels in an algorithm. One takes 50% of the execution time and another takes 10%. Using a hardware accelerator, we could speed up execution of the first kernel by a factor of 2 or the second kernel by a factor of 5. Which accelerator gives the best overall performance improvement?

   Solution: The overall speedup s_1 from the first kernel is

$$s_1 = \frac{1}{\frac{0.5}{2} + (1 - 0.5)} \approx 1.33.$$

Accelerating the second kernel gives an overall speedup s_2 as

$$s_2 = \frac{1}{\frac{0.1}{5} + (1 - 0.1)} \approx 1.09.$$

Since $s_1 > s_2$, accelerating the first kernel is more efficient.

$\square$

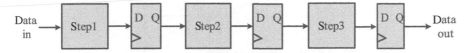

Figure 9.19: Three-stage pipelined structure of an accelerator.

There are two major schemes for implementing parallelism. The first technique is simply duplicating components that perform on different independent data. Compared to that without duplication, the speedup achieved is ideally equal to the number of components that are replicated.

The second technique for implementing parallelism is to break the overall task into a sequence of simpler stages where each stage can perform concurrently like a pipeline, as shown in Figure 9.19 where a three-stage pipelined structure is displayed. The overall execution time by the pipeline for a given data takes approximately the same time as that a non-pipelined one. However, if one data can be supplied at every clock cycle, the pipeline can complete one data every cycle. Thus, the speedup compared to the non-pipelined version is ideally equal to the number of stages. This scheme is suitable for applications that involve complex processing steps that can be broken into simpler ones. Some applications contain independent complex tasks. We can replicate the pipeline to obtain the benefits of both parallel and pipelining schemes.

Moving data between memory and the accelerator by software is an inefficient approach. Instead, the accelerator typically contains a direct memory access (DMA) under software control to transfer data to and from memory automatically by hardware. The software simply configures the DMA through control registers in an accelerator, and then monitors the status register in the accelerator. If the DMA shares the same bus with the processor for accessing the memory, an arbiter is required to resolve the access conflicts, as shown in Figure 9.20.

Example 9.5. We want to design an 8-point FFT accelerator. The N-point FFT is a fast algorithm for the discrete Fourier transform expressed as

$$X(k) = \sum_{n=0}^{N-1} W_N^{nk} x(n), k = 0, 1, ..., N-1,$$

where $x(n)$ and $X(k)$ are time- and frequency-domain data, respectively, $j = \sqrt{-1}$ and $W_N = e^{-j2\pi/N}$. The structure of the 8-point FFT is shown in Figure 9.21. The brute-forced discrete Fourier transform algorithm above requires N^2 complex multiplications, while the FFT algorithm has $\log_2(N)$ stages and each stage needs $N/2$ complex multiplications.

The interface of FFT accelerator is shown in Figure 9.22. The input data$[31:0]$ includes both real (x_r) and imaginary (x_i) parts of x, i.e., data $[31:0]=\{x_r[7:-8], x_i[7:-8]\}$, where x_r and x_i have fixed-point representation of s(8.8). The output fft_di, $i = 0, 1, ..., 7$, also includes both real (X_r) and imaginary

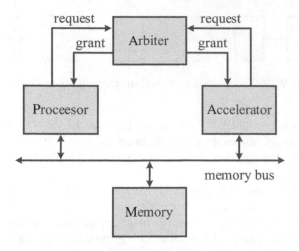

Figure 9.20: A system with an arbiter for the memory bus.

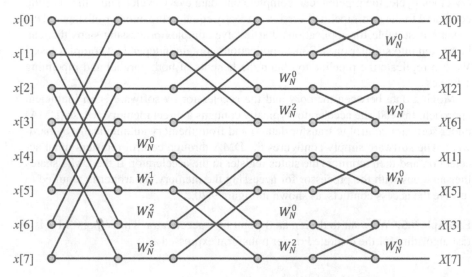

Figure 9.21: Structure of the FFT accelerator.

(X_i) parts of X, i.e., $\{X_r[7:-8], X_i[7:-8]\}$, where X_r and X_i have fixed-point representation of $s(8.8)$.

The interface timing diagram is displayed in Figure 9.23. The input data are sequential input while output data are parallel output.

Solution: The most fundamental unit of FFT is the butterfly operation shown in Figure 9.24, where $(\cdot)^*$ denotes the complex conjugate operation. Each butterfly needs two input data and two output data. The output data simply overwrite the registers that stores corresponding input data. This is called in-place FFT.

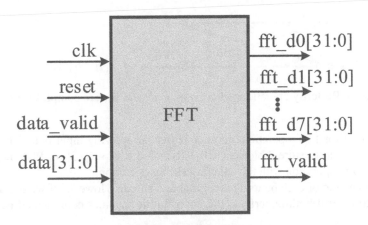

Figure 9.22: Interface of the FFT accelerator.

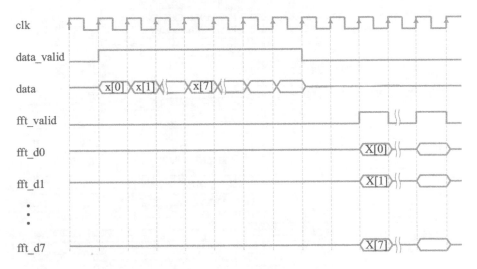

Figure 9.23: Interface timing diagram.

Our design goal is to process input streaming data using a circuit area as small as possible. In each stage of FFT, there are 4 butterfly operations. Consequently, the total number of butterfly operations for a block in 3 stages is $4 \times 3 = 12$. There are 8 cycles to input a block of FFT data, resulting in 8 cycles to complete the processing of a FFT block. Therefore, during each cycle, we must complete $\lceil 12/8 \rceil = 2$ butterfly operations, where $\lceil \cdot \rceil$ denotes the ceiling function.

The timing diagram of the circuit with 2 butterflies is presented in Figure 9.25. As shown, the inputs of two butterflies are scheduled in a regular form such that it is simpler for the hardware design. We must store 2 blocks of FFT data because, when the second block has arrived, the first block is still in progress. Therefore, when one

Figure 9.24: Butterfly operation, where a, b, c, d, and W_N are complex numbers.

buffer is used for FFT operation, another buffer is receiving input data. The ping pong buffers used to store 2 blocks (R[0]~R[7] and R[8]~R[15]) of FFT data can overlap the I/O operation with the data processing operation.

The processing of each butterfly is regular and simple. However, if we use a state machine to control both butterflies, the control unit becomes complicated because

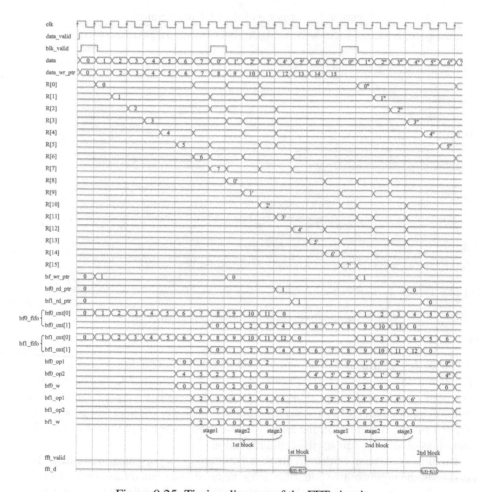

Figure 9.25: Timing diagram of the FFT circuit.

there are too many states for the combination of the operations of two butterflies. By contrast, it can be seen that the processing of a block for each butterfly is simple. For butterfly 0, when a new block comes in, it just waits 5 cycles, then starts processing points (R[0],R[4]) (0 and 4 in Figure 9.25), (R[1],R[5]) (1 and 5 in Figure 9.25), (R[0],R[2]) (0 and 2 in Figure 9.25), (R[1],R[3]) (1 and 3 in Figure 9.25), (R[0],R[1]) (0 and 1 in Figure 9.25), and finally (R[2],R[3]) (2 and 3 in Figure 9.25) sequentially in a fixed pattern. For butterfly 1, when a new block comes in, it just waits 6 cycles, then starts processing points (R[2],R[6]) (2 and 6 in Figure 9.25), (R[3],R[7]) (3 and 7 in Figure 9.25), (R[4],R[6]) (4 and 6 in Figure 9.25), (R[5],R[7]) (5 and 7 in Figure 9.25), (R[4],R[5]) (4 and 5 in Figure 9.25), and finally (R[6],R[7]) (6 and 7 in Figure 9.25) sequentially. Butterflies 0 and 1 parallel execute and the operation of the same block for butterfly 1 is one cycle later than that of butterfly 0.

The datapath of the FFT accelerator is presented in Figure 9.26(a). To make things simpler, the input data are stored in a ping pong data buffer (R[0]~R[7] and R[8]~R[15]) implemented using FIFO with 16 entries, i.e., R[0]~R[15]. In Figure 9.26(b), the FIFO, data_fifo, has a write pointer, data_wr_ptr, but has one read pointer for each butterfly, i.e., two read pointers, bf0_rd_ptr and bf1_rd_ptr, in total. Hence, the processing of two butterflies can be decoupled. The proposed architecture can make two butterflies temporarily process different blocks.

The write pointer, data_wr_ptr, of data FIFO advances when data_valid is true. The read pointer, bf0_rd_ptr/bf1_rd_ptr, of data FIFO for butterfly 0/1 advances when a block has been completed by butterfly 0/1. The accomplishment of a block of butterfly 0 is indicated by bf0_cnt_sel== 11, and, for butterfly 1, it is indicated by bf1_cnt_sel== 12. Therefore, the time instances that two butterflies accomplish the same block are different, as shown in the timing diagram. When butterfly 0 is processing one block, butterfly 1 can process another using the proposed architecture. This makes two butterflies seem to independently perform their operations.

Also, we decouple the processing of two butterflies using two additional butterfly FIFOs, bf0_fifo and bf1_fifo, one for each butterfly. Each FIFO has 2 entries, such as bf0_cnt[0] and bf0_cnt[1] for butterfly 0, and bf1_cnt[0] and bf1_cnt[1] for butterfly 1. One entry is dedicated to one block, so that the states of two block data of a butterfly can be separately recorded and decoupled. Such a design makes the pipelining of two neighboring blocks easier and more regular. The datum in the butterfly FIFO is simply an up counter that is enabled when a new block comes in, indicated by blk_valid, and advances automatically until it counts up to a value that its correspond butterfly has accomplished its operation, i.e., 11/12 for butterfly 0/1, respectively. Each butterfly FIFO has one read pointer and one write pointer. The write pointer, bf_wr_ptr, is the same for both bf0_fifo and bf1_fifo and advances when a new block has arrived, indicated by blk_valid. The read pointers, bf0_rd_ptr and bf1_rd_ptr, of butterfly FIFOs are the same as those used for the data FIFO.

After the architecture design, we need to determine the bit widths of every variables. Both real ($W_{N,r}^n$) and imaginary ($W_{N,i}^n$) parts of the twiddle factor, $W_N^n = W_{N,r}^n + jW_{N,i}^n$, have fixed-point representation of s(2.16). The outputs, $c = c_r + jc_i$ and $d = d_r + jd_i$, can be expressed using inputs, $a = a_r + ja_i$ and $b = b_r + jb_i$, and

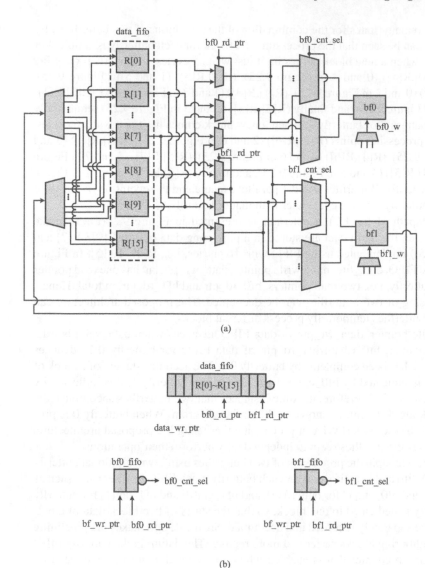

(a)

(b)

Figure 9.26: Architecture of the circuit: (a) datapath and (b) control unit. The bf0_fifo contains two entries: bf0_cnt[0] and bf0_cnt[1]. The bf1_fifo contains two entries: bf1_cnt[0] and bf1_cnt[1].

the twiddle factor, $W_N^n = W_{N,r}^n + jW_{N,i}^n$, as shown below.

$$
\begin{aligned}
c_r &= a_r + b_r, \\
c_i &= a_i + b_i, \\
d_r &= (a_r - b_r)W_{N,r}^n + (b_i - a_i)W_{N,i}^n, \\
d_i &= (a_r - b_r)W_{N,i}^n + (a_i - b_i)W_{N,r}^n.
\end{aligned}
$$

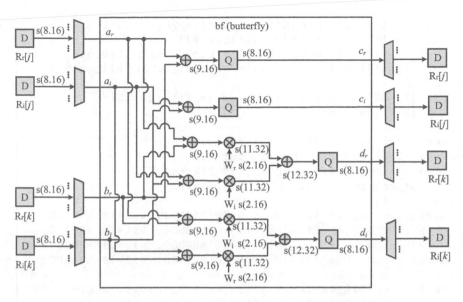

Figure 9.27: Architecture and bit width of the butterfly.

To reduce the quantization error, the fractional part of data registers, $R[0] \sim R[15]$, in the data FIFO should be 16 bits. Hence, the bit width design of the datapath is planned in Figure 9.27, where the block Q quantizes input using the truncation.

Finally, the RTL codes are written below. It can be observed that, according to the timing diagram, only half of the next block data have input when the previous block data are output. Therefore, the optimal number of registers needs only 12 registers, i.e., $R[0] \sim R[11]$. Consequently, to save the space of data buffer, the ping pong buffer can be changed to a 12-entry FIFO. The new architecture is left as a problem at the end of this chapter.

```
1 // Module of FFT processor
2 module fft(fft_valid , fft_d0, fft_d1, fft_d2, fft_d3,
3             fft_d4, fft_d5, fft_d6, fft_d7,
4             data_valid, data, clk, reset);
5 output fft_valid;
6 output [31:0] fft_d0, fft_d1, fft_d2, fft_d3;
7 output [31:0] fft_d4, fft_d5, fft_d6, fft_d7;
8 input data_valid;
9 input [31:0] data;
10 input clk, reset;
11 reg fft_valid;
12 reg [7:-16] Rr[0:15],Ri[0:15];
13 reg [7:-16] bf0_op1r,bf0_op1i,bf0_op2r,bf0_op2i;
```

```verilog
14 reg [7:-16] bf1_op1r,bf1_op1i,bf1_op2r,bf1_op2i;
15 reg [7:-16] bf0_wr,bf0_wi,bf1_wr,bf1_wi;
16 wire [7:-16] bf0_out1r,bf0_out1i,bf0_out2r,bf0_out2i;
17 wire [7:-16] bf1_out1r,bf1_out1i,bf1_out2r,bf1_out2i;
18 // Data queue
19 reg [7:-16] data_fifor[0:15],data_fifoi[0:15];
20 reg [3:0] data_wr_ptr;
21 // Butterfly queue
22 reg [3:0] bf0_cnt[0:1],bf1_cnt[0:1];
23 wire [3:0] bf0_cnt_sel,bf1_cnt_sel;
24 wire blk_valid,bf0_blk_end,bf1_blk_end;
25 reg bf_wr_ptr, bf0_rd_ptr,bf1_rd_ptr;
26 integer i;
27 parameter signed [1:-16] wr0=18'h10000, wi0=18'h00000;
28 parameter signed [1:-16] wr1=18'h0B504, wi1=18'h34AFC;
29 parameter signed [1:-16] wr2=18'h00000, wi2=18'h30000;
30 parameter signed [1:-16] wr3=18'h34AFC, wi3=18'h34AFC;
31 // Two butterflies
32 bf bf0(.cr(bf0_out1r),.ci(bf0_out1i),.dr(bf0_out2r),
33        .di(bf0_out2i),.ar(bf0_op1r),.ai(bf0_op1i),
34        .br(bf0_op2r),.bi(bf0_op2i),
35        .wr(bf0_wr),.wi(bf0_wi));
36 bf bf1(.cr(bf1_out1r),.ci(bf1_out1i),.dr(bf1_out2r),
37        .di(bf1_out2i),.ar(bf1_op1r),.ai(bf1_op1i),
38        .br(bf1_op2r),.bi(bf1_op2i),
39        .wr(bf1_wr),.wi(bf1_wi));
40 always @(posedge clk or posedge reset)
41   if(reset) fft_valid<=0;
42   else if(bf1_blk_end) fft_valid<=1'b1;
43   else fft_valid<=0;
44 // FFT output data selection
45 assign fft_d0=
46 {bf1_rd_ptr?data_fifor[0][7:-8]:data_fifor[8][7:-8],
47 bf1_rd_ptr?data_fifoi[0][7:-8]:data_fifoi[8][7:-8]};
48 assign fft_d1=
49 {bf1_rd_ptr?data_fifor[1][7:-8]:data_fifor[9][7:-8],
50 bf1_rd_ptr?data_fifoi[1][7:-8]:data_fifoi[9][7:-8]};
51 assign fft_d2=
52 {bf1_rd_ptr?data_fifor[2][7:-8]:data_fifor[10][7:-8],
53 bf1_rd_ptr?data_fifoi[2][7:-8]:data_fifoi[10][7:-8]};
54 assign fft_d3=
55 {bf1_rd_ptr?data_fifor[3][7:-8]:data_fifor[11][7:-8],
56 bf1_rd_ptr?data_fifoi[3][7:-8]:data_fifoi[11][7:-8]};
57 assign fft_d4=
58 {bf1_rd_ptr?data_fifor[4][7:-8]:data_fifor[12][7:-8],
59 bf1_rd_ptr?data_fifoi[4][7:-8]:data_fifoi[12][7:-8]};
60 assign fft_d5=
```

```
61 {bf1_rd_ptr?data_fifor[5][7:-8]:data_fifor[13][7:-8],
62 bf1_rd_ptr?data_fifoi[5][7:-8]:data_fifoi[13][7:-8]};
63 assign fft_d6=
64 {bf1_rd_ptr?data_fifor[6][7:-8]:data_fifor[14][7:-8],
65 bf1_rd_ptr?data_fifoi[6][7:-8]:data_fifoi[14][7:-8]};
66 assign fft_d7=
67 {bf1_rd_ptr?data_fifor[7][7:-8]:data_fifor[15][7:-8],
68 bf1_rd_ptr?data_fifoi[7][7:-8]:data_fifoi[15][7:-8]};
69 // Butterfly 0 input data selection
70 always @(*) begin
71   case(bf0_cnt_sel)
72   4'd6: begin
73            bf0_op1r=(bf0_rd_ptr)?Rr[8]:Rr[0];
74            bf0_op1i=(bf0_rd_ptr)?Ri[8]:Ri[0];
75            bf0_op2r=(bf0_rd_ptr)?Rr[12]:Rr[4];
76            bf0_op2i=(bf0_rd_ptr)?Ri[12]:Ri[4];
77            bf0_wr=wr0;bf0_wi=wi0;
78         end
79   4'd7: begin
80            bf0_op1r=(bf0_rd_ptr)?Rr[9]:Rr[1];
81            bf0_op1i=(bf0_rd_ptr)?Ri[9]:Ri[1];
82            bf0_op2r=(bf0_rd_ptr)?Rr[13]:Rr[5];
83            bf0_op2i=(bf0_rd_ptr)?Ri[13]:Ri[5];
84            bf0_wr=wr1;bf0_wi=wi1;
85         end
86   4'd8: begin
87            bf0_op1r=(bf0_rd_ptr)?Rr[8]:Rr[0];
88            bf0_op1i=(bf0_rd_ptr)?Ri[8]:Ri[0];
89            bf0_op2r=(bf0_rd_ptr)?Rr[10]:Rr[2];
90            bf0_op2i=(bf0_rd_ptr)?Ri[10]:Ri[2];
91            bf0_wr=wr0;bf0_wi=wi0;
92         end
93   4'd9: begin
94            bf0_op1r=(bf0_rd_ptr)?Rr[9]:Rr[1];
95            bf0_op1i=(bf0_rd_ptr)?Ri[9]:Ri[1];
96            bf0_op2r=(bf0_rd_ptr)?Rr[11]:Rr[3];
97            bf0_op2i=(bf0_rd_ptr)?Ri[11]:Ri[3];
98            bf0_wr=wr2;bf0_wi=wi2;
99         end
100  4'd10: begin
101           bf0_op1r=(bf0_rd_ptr)?Rr[8]:Rr[0];
102           bf0_op1i=(bf0_rd_ptr)?Ri[8]:Ri[0];
103           bf0_op2r=(bf0_rd_ptr)?Rr[9]:Rr[1];
104           bf0_op2i=(bf0_rd_ptr)?Ri[9]:Ri[1];
105           bf0_wr=wr0;bf0_wi=wi0;
106        end
107  4'd11: begin
```

```verilog
108             bf0_op1r=(bf0_rd_ptr)?Rr[10]:Rr[2];
109             bf0_op1i=(bf0_rd_ptr)?Ri[10]:Ri[2];
110             bf0_op2r=(bf0_rd_ptr)?Rr[11]:Rr[3];
111             bf0_op2i=(bf0_rd_ptr)?Ri[11]:Ri[3];
112             bf0_wr=wr0;bf0_wi=wi0;
113         end
114   default: begin
115             bf0_op1r=(bf0_rd_ptr)?Rr[8]:Rr[0];
116             bf0_op1i=(bf0_rd_ptr)?Ri[8]:Ri[0];
117             bf0_op2r=(bf0_rd_ptr)?Rr[12]:Rr[4];
118             bf0_op2i=(bf0_rd_ptr)?Ri[12]:Ri[4];
119             bf0_wr=wr0;bf0_wi=wi0;
120         end
121   endcase
122 end
123 // Butterfly 1 input data selection
124 always @(*) begin
125   case(bf1_cnt_sel)
126   4'd7: begin
127             bf1_op1r=(bf1_rd_ptr)?Rr[10]:Rr[2];
128             bf1_op1i=(bf1_rd_ptr)?Ri[10]:Ri[2];
129             bf1_op2r=(bf1_rd_ptr)?Rr[14]:Rr[6];
130             bf1_op2i=(bf1_rd_ptr)?Ri[14]:Ri[6];
131             bf1_wr=wr2;bf1_wi=wi2;
132         end
133   4'd8: begin
134             bf1_op1r=(bf1_rd_ptr)?Rr[11]:Rr[3];
135             bf1_op1i=(bf1_rd_ptr)?Ri[11]:Ri[3];
136             bf1_op2r=(bf1_rd_ptr)?Rr[15]:Rr[7];
137             bf1_op2i=(bf1_rd_ptr)?Ri[15]:Ri[7];
138             bf1_wr=wr3;bf1_wi=wi3;
139         end
140   4'd9: begin
141             bf1_op1r=(bf1_rd_ptr)?Rr[12]:Rr[4];
142             bf1_op1i=(bf1_rd_ptr)?Ri[12]:Ri[4];
143             bf1_op2r=(bf1_rd_ptr)?Rr[14]:Rr[6];
144             bf1_op2i=(bf1_rd_ptr)?Ri[14]:Ri[6];
145             bf1_wr=wr0;bf1_wi=wi0;
146         end
147   4'd10: begin
148             bf1_op1r=(bf1_rd_ptr)?Rr[13]:Rr[5];
149             bf1_op1i=(bf1_rd_ptr)?Ri[13]:Ri[5];
150             bf1_op2r=(bf1_rd_ptr)?Rr[15]:Rr[7];
151             bf1_op2i=(bf1_rd_ptr)?Ri[15]:Ri[7];
152             bf1_wr=wr2;bf1_wi=wi2;
153         end
154   4'd11: begin
```

```
155          bf1_op1r=(bf1_rd_ptr)?Rr[12]:Rr[4];
156          bf1_op1i=(bf1_rd_ptr)?Ri[12]:Ri[4];
157          bf1_op2r=(bf1_rd_ptr)?Rr[13]:Rr[5];
158          bf1_op2i=(bf1_rd_ptr)?Ri[13]:Ri[5];
159          bf1_wr=wr0;bf1_wi=wi0;
160        end
161     4'd12: begin
162          bf1_op1r=(bf1_rd_ptr)?Rr[14]:Rr[6];
163          bf1_op1i=(bf1_rd_ptr)?Ri[14]:Ri[6];
164          bf1_op2r=(bf1_rd_ptr)?Rr[15]:Rr[7];
165          bf1_op2i=(bf1_rd_ptr)?Ri[15]:Ri[7];
166          bf1_wr=wr0;bf1_wi=wi0;
167        end
168     default: begin
169            bf1_op1r=(bf1_rd_ptr)?Rr[10]:Rr[2];
170            bf1_op1i=(bf1_rd_ptr)?Ri[10]:Ri[2];
171            bf1_op2r=(bf1_rd_ptr)?Rr[14]:Rr[6];
172            bf1_op2i=(bf1_rd_ptr)?Ri[14]:Ri[6];
173            bf1_wr=wr2;bf1_wi=wi2;
174          end
175     endcase
176 end
177 // Reformatting data_fifo to R, which is used by the
178 // butterfly input data
179 always @(*)
180   for(i=0;i<16;i=i+1) begin
181     Rr[i]=data_fifor[i];
182     Ri[i]=data_fifoi[i];
183   end
184 // Write pointer of data_fifo
185 always @(posedge clk or posedge reset)
186   if(reset) data_wr_ptr<=0;
187   else if(data_valid) data_wr_ptr<=data_wr_ptr+1'b1;
188 //****************************************************
189 // Writing of data_fifo
190 // data_fifo needs to store the fft input data and
191 // output of butterflies
192 //****************************************************
193 always @(posedge clk) begin
194 // data_fifo[0]
195   if(data_valid&data_wr_ptr==0) begin
196     data_fifor[0]<={data[31:16],8'h00};
197     data_fifoi[0]<={data[15:0],8'h00};
198   end
199   else if(bf0_rd_ptr==0&&(bf0_cnt_sel==4'd6||
200     bf0_cnt_sel==4'd8||bf0_cnt_sel==4'd10)) begin
201     data_fifor[0]<=bf0_out1r;
```

```
202        data_fifoi[0]<=bf0_out1i;
203    end
204 // data_fifo[1]
205    if(data_valid&data_wr_ptr==1) begin
206        data_fifor[1]<={data[31:16],8'h00};
207        data_fifoi[1]<={data[15:0],8'h00};
208    end
209    else if(bf0_rd_ptr==0&&(bf0_cnt_sel==4'd7||
210        bf0_cnt_sel==4'd9)) begin
211        data_fifor[1]<=bf0_out1r;
212        data_fifoi[1]<=bf0_out1i;
213    end
214    else if(bf0_rd_ptr==0&&bf0_cnt_sel==4'd10) begin
215        data_fifor[1]<=bf0_out2r;
216        data_fifoi[1]<=bf0_out2i;
217    end
218 // data_fifo[2]
219    if(data_valid&data_wr_ptr==2) begin
220        data_fifor[2]<={data[31:16],8'h00};
221        data_fifoi[2]<={data[15:0],8'h00};
222    end
223    else if(bf0_rd_ptr==0&&bf0_cnt_sel==4'd8) begin
224        data_fifor[2]<=bf0_out2r;
225        data_fifoi[2]<=bf0_out2i;
226    end
227    else if(bf0_rd_ptr==0&&bf0_cnt_sel==4'd11) begin
228        data_fifor[2]<=bf0_out1r;
229        data_fifoi[2]<=bf0_out1i;
230    end
231    else if(bf1_rd_ptr==0&&bf1_cnt_sel==4'd7) begin
232        data_fifor[2]<=bf1_out1r;
233        data_fifoi[2]<=bf1_out1i;
234    end
235 // data_fifo[3]
236    if(data_valid&data_wr_ptr==3) begin
237        data_fifor[3]<={data[31:16],8'h00};
238        data_fifoi[3]<={data[15:0],8'h00};
239    end
240    else if(bf0_rd_ptr==0&&(bf0_cnt_sel==4'd9||
241        bf0_cnt_sel==4'd11)) begin
242        data_fifor[3]<=bf0_out2r;
243        data_fifoi[3]<=bf0_out2i;
244    end
245    else if(bf1_rd_ptr==0&&bf1_cnt_sel==4'd8) begin
246        data_fifor[3]<=bf1_out1r;
247        data_fifoi[3]<=bf1_out1i;
248    end
```

```verilog
249 // data_fifo[4]
250   if(data_valid&data_wr_ptr==4) begin
251     data_fifor[4]<={data[31:16],8'h00};
252     data_fifoi[4]<={data[15:0],8'h00};
253   end
254   else if(bf0_rd_ptr==0&&bf0_cnt_sel==4'd6) begin
255     data_fifor[4]<=bf0_out2r;
256     data_fifoi[4]<=bf0_out2i;
257   end
258   else if(bf1_rd_ptr==0&&(bf1_cnt_sel==4'd9||
259     bf0_cnt_sel==4'd11)) begin
260     data_fifor[4]<=bf1_out1r;
261     data_fifoi[4]<=bf1_out1i;
262   end
263 // data_fifo[5]
264   if(data_valid&data_wr_ptr==5) begin
265     data_fifor[5]<={data[31:16],8'h00};
266     data_fifoi[5]<={data[15:0],8'h00};
267   end
268   else if(bf0_rd_ptr==0&&bf0_cnt_sel==4'd7) begin
269     data_fifor[5]<=bf0_out2r;
270     data_fifoi[5]<=bf0_out2i;
271   end
272   else if(bf1_rd_ptr==0&&bf1_cnt_sel==4'd10) begin
273     data_fifor[5]<=bf1_out1r;
274     data_fifoi[5]<=bf1_out1i;
275   end
276   else if(bf1_rd_ptr==0&&bf1_cnt_sel==4'd11) begin
277     data_fifor[5]<=bf1_out2r;
278     data_fifoi[5]<=bf1_out2i;
279   end
280 // data_fifo[6]
281   if(data_valid&data_wr_ptr==6) begin
282     data_fifor[6]<={data[31:16],8'h00};
283     data_fifoi[6]<={data[15:0],8'h00};
284   end
285   else if(bf1_rd_ptr==0&&(bf1_cnt_sel==4'd7||
286     bf0_cnt_sel==4'd9)) begin
287     data_fifor[6]<=bf1_out2r;
288     data_fifoi[6]<=bf1_out2i;
289   end
290   else if(bf1_rd_ptr==0&&bf1_cnt_sel==4'd12) begin
291     data_fifor[6]<=bf1_out1r;
292     data_fifoi[6]<=bf1_out1i;
293   end
294 // data_fifo[7]
295   if(data_valid&data_wr_ptr==7) begin
```

```
296       data_fifor[7]<={data[31:16],8'h00};
297       data_fifoi[7]<={data[15:0],8'h00};
298    end
299    else if(bf1_rd_ptr==0&&(bf1_cnt_sel==4'd8||
300       bf1_cnt_sel==4'd10||bf1_cnt_sel==4'd12)) begin
301       data_fifor[7]<=bf1_out2r;
302       data_fifoi[7]<=bf1_out2i;
303    end
304 // data_fifo[8]
305    if(data_valid&data_wr_ptr==8) begin
306       data_fifor[8]<={data[31:16],8'h00};
307       data_fifoi[8]<={data[15:0],8'h00};
308    end
309    else if(bf0_rd_ptr==1&&(bf0_cnt_sel==4'd6||
310       bf0_cnt_sel==4'd8||bf0_cnt_sel==4'd10)) begin
311       data_fifor[8]<=bf0_out1r;
312       data_fifoi[8]<=bf0_out1i;
313    end
314 // data_fifo[9]
315    if(data_valid&data_wr_ptr==9) begin
316       data_fifor[9]<={data[31:16],8'h00};
317       data_fifoi[9]<={data[15:0],8'h00};
318    end
319    else if(bf0_rd_ptr==1&&(bf0_cnt_sel==4'd7||
320       bf0_cnt_sel==4'd9)) begin
321       data_fifor[9]<=bf0_out1r;
322       data_fifoi[9]<=bf0_out1i;
323    end
324    else if(bf0_rd_ptr==1&&bf0_cnt_sel==4'd10) begin
325       data_fifor[9]<=bf0_out2r;
326       data_fifoi[9]<=bf0_out2i;
327    end
328 // data_fifo[10]
329    if(data_valid&data_wr_ptr==10) begin
330       data_fifor[10]<={data[31:16],8'h00};
331       data_fifoi[10]<={data[15:0],8'h00};
332    end
333    else if(bf0_rd_ptr==1&&bf0_cnt_sel==4'd8) begin
334       data_fifor[10]<=bf0_out2r;
335       data_fifoi[10]<=bf0_out2i;
336    end
337    else if(bf0_rd_ptr==1&&bf0_cnt_sel==4'd11) begin
338       data_fifor[10]<=bf0_out1r;
339       data_fifoi[10]<=bf0_out1i;
340    end
341    else if(bf1_rd_ptr==1&&bf1_cnt_sel==4'd7) begin
342       data_fifor[10]<=bf1_out1r;
```

```
343    data_fifoi[10]<=bf1_out1i;
344  end
345 // data_fifo[11]
346  if(data_valid&data_wr_ptr==11) begin
347    data_fifor[11]<={data[31:16],8'h00};
348    data_fifoi[11]<={data[15:0],8'h00};
349  end
350  else if(bf0_rd_ptr==1&&(bf0_cnt_sel==4'd9||
351    bf0_cnt_sel==4'd11)) begin
352    data_fifor[11]<=bf0_out2r;
353    data_fifoi[11]<=bf0_out2i;
354  end
355  else if(bf1_rd_ptr==1&&bf1_cnt_sel==4'd8) begin
356    data_fifor[11]<=bf1_out1r;
357    data_fifoi[11]<=bf1_out1i;
358  end
359 // data_fifo[12]
360  if(data_valid&data_wr_ptr==12) begin
361    data_fifor[12]<={data[31:16],8'h00};
362    data_fifoi[12]<={data[15:0],8'h00};
363  end
364  else if(bf0_rd_ptr==1&&bf0_cnt_sel==4'd6) begin
365    data_fifor[12]<=bf0_out2r;
366    data_fifoi[12]<=bf0_out2i;
367  end
368  else if(bf1_rd_ptr==1&&(bf1_cnt_sel==4'd9||
369    bf0_cnt_sel==4'd11)) begin
370    data_fifor[12]<=bf1_out1r;
371    data_fifoi[12]<=bf1_out1i;
372  end
373 // data_fifo[13]
374  if(data_valid&data_wr_ptr==13) begin
375    data_fifor[13]<={data[31:16],8'h00};
376    data_fifoi[13]<={data[15:0],8'h00};
377  end
378  else if(bf0_rd_ptr==1&&bf0_cnt_sel==4'd7) begin
379    data_fifor[13]<=bf0_out2r;
380    data_fifoi[13]<=bf0_out2i;
381  end
382  else if(bf1_rd_ptr==1&&bf1_cnt_sel==4'd10) begin
383    data_fifor[13]<=bf1_out1r;
384    data_fifoi[13]<=bf1_out1i;
385  end
386  else if(bf1_rd_ptr==1&&bf1_cnt_sel==4'd11) begin
387    data_fifor[13]<=bf1_out2r;
388    data_fifoi[13]<=bf1_out2i;
389  end
```

```
390 // data_fifo[14]
391   if(data_valid&data_wr_ptr==14) begin
392     data_fifor[14]<={data[31:16],8'h00};
393     data_fifoi[14]<={data[15:0],8'h00};
394   end
395   else if(bf1_rd_ptr==1&&(bf1_cnt_sel==4'd7||
396     bf0_cnt_sel==4'd9)) begin
397     data_fifor[14]<=bf1_out2r;
398     data_fifoi[14]<=bf1_out2i;
399   end
400   else if(bf1_rd_ptr==1&&bf1_cnt_sel==4'd12) begin
401     data_fifor[14]<=bf1_out1r;
402     data_fifoi[14]<=bf1_out1i;
403   end
404 // data_fifo[15]
405   if(data_valid&data_wr_ptr==15) begin
406     data_fifor[15]<={data[31:16],8'h00};
407     data_fifoi[15]<={data[15:0],8'h00};
408   end
409   else if(bf1_rd_ptr==1&&(bf1_cnt_sel==4'd8||
410     bf1_cnt_sel==4'd10||bf1_cnt_sel==4'd12)) begin
411     data_fifor[15]<=bf1_out2r;
412     data_fifoi[15]<=bf1_out2i;
413   end
414 end
415 // Timing for writing two butterfly queues is the same
416 assign blk_valid=data_valid&data_wr_ptr[2:0]==0;
417 // Write pointer of two butterfly queues
418 always @(posedge clk or posedge reset)
419   if(reset) bf_wr_ptr<=0;
420   else if(blk_valid) bf_wr_ptr<=~bf_wr_ptr;
421 // Processing of a block using butterfly 0 completes
422 assign bf0_blk_end=bf0_cnt_sel==11;
423 // Processing of a block using butterfly 1 completes
424 assign bf1_blk_end=bf1_cnt_sel==12;
425 // Read port of butterfly queue of butterfly 0
426 assign bf0_cnt_sel=~bf0_rd_ptr?bf0_cnt[0]:bf0_cnt[1];
427 // Read port of butterfly queue of butterfly 1
428 assign bf1_cnt_sel=~bf1_rd_ptr?bf1_cnt[0]:bf1_cnt[1];
429 // Read pointer of butterfly queue of butterfly 0
430 always @(posedge clk or posedge reset)
431   if(reset) bf0_rd_ptr<=0;
432   else if(bf0_blk_end) bf0_rd_ptr<=~bf0_rd_ptr;
433 // Read pointer of butterfly queue of butterfly 1
434 always @(posedge clk or posedge reset)
435   if(reset) bf1_rd_ptr<=0;
436   else if(bf1_blk_end) bf1_rd_ptr<=~bf1_rd_ptr;
```

```
437 // Butterfly queue of butterfly 0
438 always @(posedge clk or posedge reset)
439   if(reset) begin
440     bf0_cnt[0]<=0;
441     bf0_cnt[1]<=0;
442   end
443   else begin
444     if((blk_valid&&bf_wr_ptr==0)||bf0_cnt[0]!=0)
445       bf0_cnt[0]<=(bf0_cnt[0]==11)?0:(bf0_cnt[0]+1);
446     if((blk_valid&&bf_wr_ptr==1)||bf0_cnt[1]!=0)
447       bf0_cnt[1]<=(bf0_cnt[1]==11)?0:(bf0_cnt[1]+1);
448   end
449 // Butterfly queue of butterfly 1
450 always @(posedge clk or posedge reset)
451   if(reset) begin
452     bf1_cnt[0]<=0;
453     bf1_cnt[1]<=0;
454   end
455   else begin
456     if((blk_valid&&bf_wr_ptr==0)||bf1_cnt[0]!=0)
457       bf1_cnt[0]<=(bf1_cnt[0]==12)?0:(bf1_cnt[0]+1);
458     if((blk_valid&&bf_wr_ptr==1)||bf1_cnt[1]!=0)
459       bf1_cnt[1]<=(bf1_cnt[1]==12)?0:(bf1_cnt[1]+1);
460   end
461 endmodule
462 // Butterfly module
463 module bf(cr,ci,dr,di,ar,ai,br,bi,wr,wi);
464 output signed [7:-16] cr,ci,dr,di;
465 input signed [7:-16] ar,ai,br,bi,wr,wi;
466 reg signed [8:-16] tmp_cr,tmp_ci;
467 reg signed [11:-32] tmp_dr,tmp_di;
468 assign cr=tmp_cr[7:-16];assign ci=tmp_ci[7:-16];
469 assign dr=tmp_dr[7:-16];assign di=tmp_di[7:-16];
470 always @(*) begin
471   tmp_cr=ar+br;tmp_ci=ai+bi;
472 end
473 always @(*) begin
474   tmp_dr=(ar-br)*wr+(bi-ai)*wi;
475   tmp_di=(ar-br)*wi+(ai-bi)*wr;
476 end
477 endmodule
```

□

9.6   FURTHER READING

- David Money Harris and Sarah L. Harris, *Digital design and computer architecture*, 2nd Ed., Morgan Kaufmann, 2013.
- John F. Wakerly, *Digital design: principles and practices*, 5th Ed., Prentice Hall, 2018.
- Peter J. Ashenden, *Digital design: an embedded systems approach using Verilog*, Morgan Kaufmann Publishers, 2007.

PROBLEMS

1. A 16-segment LED display, shown in Figure 9.28, can display alphabetic and numeric characters. Extend the keypad I/O controller to display the pushed digit on the LED display. You can add an additional register, char_reg[3 : 0], and a port, led[15 : 0], in the I/O controller. The register is accessed through the port number 3. The register char_reg[3 : 0] is then decoded to the signal, led[15 : 0], to drive each segment of the LED.

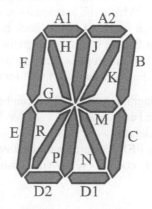

Figure 9.28: A 16-segment LED display.

2. Design the I/O controller for the factory automation system in Section 9.4.1.
3. Design the processor with interrupt using the instruction set in Section 9.4.2.
4. Write down the assembly codes for the keypad controller, alarm controller, and real-time clock controller. The period of the real-time clock is 2 ms. The main program starts by initializing controllers and interrupts. The interrupt handler is located at address 1 of instruction memory. On responding to an interrupt, it checks the interrupt status registers of each I/O controller to determine the interrupt source, starting with the real-time clock controller. The handler then proceeds to check for other interrupt sources before returning to the interrupted program. The ISR of the real-time clock simply sets a flag **rtc_flag** which will then be used by the processor for further real-time processing. After processing, the processor clears the flag **rtc_flag**.
5. The original butterfly of FFT accelerator requires 4 real multipliers. Redesign the butterfly using 3 real multipliers and evaluate the gate count that can be saved.
6. Change the output of 16-point FFT to be serial, which is suitable for SRAM interface. Redesign the FFT accelerator using the minimum number of data registers.
7. Change the data buffer of 8-point FFT from the ping pong buffer with total of 16 memory space to a 12-entry FIFO.
8. Integrate the FFT accelerator in the previous problem with the simple processor with interrupts in Section 9.4.2. The processor and the accelerator share the same 256×8 data memory as that shown in Figure 9.20. The arbiter gives the highest

priority to the processor. The accelerator has two output registers for the FFT processing, including interrupt status register and command register. The interrupt status register has done-field at bit 0, and other bits are reserved. The command register has start-field at bit 0, and block number-field at bits 7-5. Every time-domain FFT block needs 16×32 bits, i.e., 64 Bytes. Hence, the maximum block number in a 256-Byte data memory is 4. After the processor has prepared the time-domain data for the accelerator, the processor programs the accelerator via the command register through the start-field and block number-field. When the start-field is set, DMA in the accelerator reads data and the FFT starts processing according to that specified in the block number-field. When the accelerator is done, the done-field of the interrupt status register is set, which then interrupts the processor. The interrupt is cleared through writing the interrupt status register. After that, the accelerator can wait for the next FFT calculation.

a. Redesign the timing diagram so that a block can be processed earlier and the number of registers can be reduced.
b. Redesign the FFT accelerator.
c. Integrate the processor, FFT accelerator, and the data memory.
d. Write done the assembly codes to verify your design.

10 Logic Synthesis with Design Compiler

A RTL design described with high-level constructs, such as always block and continuous assignment, allows us to design according to its functionality without considering too much about the implementation method. Actually, you only need to describe the circuit function you want without having to worry about how you are going to implement the design in an early stage. The details, i.e., logic gates and their interconnections, in implementing the circuit function will be determined later using logic synthesis.

This does not mean that we can arbitrarily use all the constructs of HDL in our designs. Many Verilog features are only suitable for the high-level behavioral modeling in testbench, and cannot be synthesized into an equivalent gate-level circuit. Consequently, it requires that the RTL models be written using a subset of Verilog constructs, and only codes using a template structure can be inferred to its corresponding hardware. For example, the synthesis tool, Synopsys DC, requires that synchronous registers be expressed using always blocks with either a positive or negative edge-triggered clock signal. This chapter assumes that you have a synthesis tool and cell library at hand.

First, this chapter emphasizes design guidelines for synthesis. Next, the steps for the synthesis methodology of timing, area, and power optimization, including reading design, describing design environment, constraining design, compiling design, reporting and analyzing design, and saving design, are introduced. Particularly, the synthesis commands used for the dynamic and static power optimization are presented. Finally, synthesis skills for solving setup time violations, hold time violations, multiple port nets, large for loops, and naming rules are exemplified.

10.1 DESIGN FOR SYNTHESIS

To begin, we list the guidelines for synthesizable designs as follows.

- Knowing synthesizable Verilog constructs: synthesizable Verilog constructs include parameter declaration, wire, tri, wand, wor, reg, input, output, inout, continuous assignment, module and gate instantiations, always, function and task, for loop, if-else, case, casex, casez, etc. Synthesizable Verilog primitives include and, or, not, namd, nor, xor, xnor, bufif0, bufif1, notif0, and notif1. Synthesizable Verilog operators include binary bit-wise ($\sim$, &, |, $\wedge$, $\sim\wedge$), unary reduction (&, $\sim$&, |, $\sim$|, $\wedge$, $\sim\wedge$), logical (!, &&, ||), arithmetic (+, −, *, /, %), relational (>, <, >=, <=), equality (==, !=), logical shift ($\ll$, $\gg$), arithmetic shift ($\lll$, $\ggg$), concatenation ({}), replication({{}}), conditional (?:) operators, etc.

DOI: 10.1201/9781003187196-10

- Knowing non-synthesizable Verilog constructs: non-synthesizable Verilog constructs include delay, initial, repeat, wait, fork and join, event, force and release, user defined primitive (UDP), time, triand, trior, tri1, tri0, trireg, nmos, pmos, cmos, rnmos, rpmos, rcmos, pullup, pulldown, rtran, tranif0, tranif1, rtranif0, rtranif1, forever, case equality (===) and case inequality (!==) operators, modulus operator, etc.
- Understanding wire (including tri, wand, wor) and reg declaration: a wire declaration is used in continuous assignments, and reg declaration is used in procedural blocks, such as always blocks and functions. If multiple sources drive the same net, it must be declared as either tri, wand, or wor net type.
- Combinational logic inference: the reg data type may not be exactly synthesized to a real hardware register. If you do not use the posedge or negedge keywords in the sensitivity list of an always block, a combinational logic is implied. You must use blocking assignments within an always block to infer a combinational logic. A sensitivity list must be specified completely; otherwise, RTL simulations and gate-level simulations may mismatch. Another way to infer a combinational logic is through a continuous assignment or function.
- Register inference: a register (flip-flop) is implied if you use the @(posedge clk) or @(negedge clk) in the sensitivity list of an always block. You must use non-blocking assignments for those outputs of real hardware registers to infer flip-flops within always blocks.
- Avoiding inferring latches: if a variable assigned within an always block without @(posedge clk) or @(negedge clk) in the sensitivity list is not fully specified, a latch is inferred.
- Avoiding inferring combinational loops: the output of a combinational loop is undetermined and problematic for the static timing analysis.
- For loop statement: in synthesis, for loops with a fixed number of iteration are unrolled and then synthesized. Therefore, loop index must be of the integer type, and its low_range, high_range and step values must be constant.
- Case and if-else statements, and conditional operator: they can be nested and provide complex conditional operations. They are usually used to model multiplexers.
- Combinational circuits with registered output: you can write a single always block with @(posedge clk) or @(negedge clk) in the sensitivity list to describe combinational circuits together with registered output if the next state of the register (or combinational output) is not explicitly used. Alternatively, you can use two always blocks to separately describe the combinational (without @(posedge clk) or @(negedge clk) in the sensitivity list) and sequential (with @(posedge clk) or @(negedge clk) in the sensitivity list) circuits. Finite state machines are commonly written in this style.
- Compiler (or synthesis) directives: if you do not specify all possible branches for if and case statements, to prevent lathes, you can use "synopsys full_case" directive to specify the full case. But you must ensure that

other branches will never occur. Additionally, if DC cannot determine that case branches are parallel, a priority multiplexer will be synthesized. By contrast, you can declare a case statement to enforce a parallel case with the "synopsys parallel_case" directive.

* DesignWare (DW) library: DesignWare contain many technology-independent soft macros, such as adders and multipliers, etc., that can be synthesized into gates using your target library. The DesignWare library enables the user to synthesize large and complex arithmetic operations by Verilog behavioral modeling, such as divider and modulus, etc. Each macro, such as an adder, contains multiple architectures which allow DC to evaluate speed and area tradeoffs and choose the most suitable implementation. We can invoke DesignWare components through inference and instantiation (for a complex function, such as the trigonometric operation).

10.2 DESIGN FLOW CONSIDERING SYNTHESIS

When the physical design cannot meet our requirements, it must be modified and optimized. This is a process of making trade-offs of one property for another. There are three main objective functions, such as timing, area, and power, of a design that we often seek to optimize through the design constraints. These properties are related to each other and often conflict with each other. Decisions made early in the flow, starting with architecture exploration and partitioning, usually have the greatest impact. For example, if we compare the parallel and pipelining architectures, it can be expected that the parallel architecture has higher performance, but it will also cost a greater area. If we want a design with good performance and moderate area, the pipelined design will probably be the best choice.

If it is found that our design goals are not achievable toward backend implementation, we may need to go back to an earlier frontend stage, and the previous design choices need to be revised. When we move to the later stages of the design flow, it will be difficult to make significant changes to the design. If fine-tuning the design cannot solve the problem, we have to revisit earlier stages to make more substantial changes. The actual design flow is often cyclical and non-linear.

An overview of logic synthesis is presented in Figure 10.1. The DesignWare library contains building blocks such as datapath and intellectual property blocks that are tightly integrated into the synthesis environment. DC maps Synopsys design block or generic technology (GTECH) library (without timing information) to gate-level design with a user specified technology library (with timing information). Libraries contain three categories of cells: standard cells, I/O cells, and full-custom hard IP macros. The cell information contained in libraries are denoted as abstraction, timing model, power model, and logic model.

The steps for synthesis are listed below. All steps are introduced in this section, except the setting design constraints and design compiling, which will be introduced in the next section. Notice that the DC commands are written using the tool command language (Tcl).

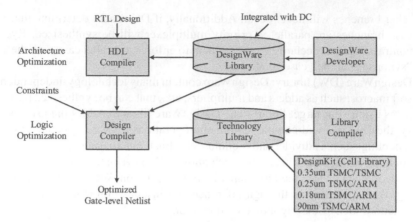

Figure 10.1: Logic synthesis overview.

- Read your design.
- Describe the design environment.
- Constrain the design.
- Compile the design.
- Report and analyze the design.
- Save the design.

10.2.1   DESIGN OBJECTS

Before introducing the synthesis steps, design objects are illustrated first. The module, fir2, is written below. The design objects in it are displayed in Figure 10.2 and listed below.

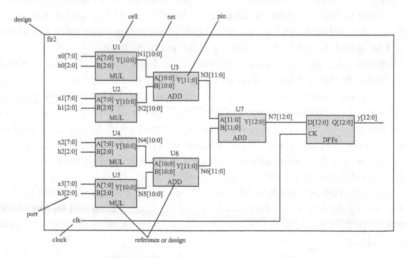

Figure 10.2: Design objects in fir2.

- Design (or reference): a circuit that performs one or more logical functions.
- Cell: an instantiation of a design.
- Port: the input, output, or inout of a design.
- Pin: the input, output, or inout of a cell.
- Net: the wire that connects ports or pins.
- Clock: waveform applied to a port or pin identified as a clock source.

```
1 module fir2(y, x0, x1, x2, x3, h0, h1, h2, h3, clk);
2 output [12:0] y;
3 input  [7:0]  x0, x1, x2, x3;
4 input  [2:0]  h0, h1, h2, h3;
5 input         clk;
6 reg    [12:0] y;
7 always @(posedge clk)
8   y <= (x3*h3+x2*h2)+(x1*h1+x0*h0);
9 endmodule
```

10.2.2 READING DESIGN

You can read netlists or other design files into DC as follows.

```
read_file -format verilog design.v
```

You can read more designs as follows if necessary.

```
read_file -format verilog design1.v design2.v ...
```

DC now supports the AutoRead as follows, where design is your top module name and your_rtl_dir is the directory containing your design files.

```
read_file -autoread -top design -recursive \
                              {your_rtl_dir}
```

Alternatively, instead of directly reading the design, you can analyze the design that checks Verilog for syntax and synthesizability. Subsequently, you can elaborate the design to bring it into DC memory using GTECH components. For example, you can analyze then elaborate your design as follows.

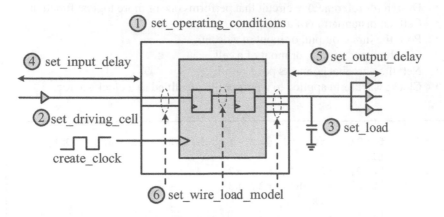

Figure 10.3: Design Environment.

```
analyze  −format  verilog  design.v
elaborate  design  −architecture  verilog
```

If there are multiple instances referencing the same design, you must enable the DC to distinguish among them. Physical designs must each be unique by separating their components, even they have the same function. Using the following command will allow multiple distinctive instances referencing the same design for synthesis.

```
uniquify
```

10.2.3   DESCRIBING DESIGN ENVIRONMENT

The defaults may not be realistic conditions for your design. You must manually specify operating environment that can affect the components selected from the target library and area/timing of your design, as shown in Figure 10.3.

You can specify the operating condition using the following command. In this command, slow.db/fast.db is used for the maximum/minimum (max/min) delay calculation under the worst/best-case operating condition.

```
set_operating_conditions  −max_library  slow  −max  slow  \
                           −min_library  fast  −min  fast
```

If your input is driven by an input pad consisting of PDIDGZ in the TSMC 0.18 μm process, you can set the input driving strength as follows. In this command, pin

C of input pad, PDIDGZ, in the I/O pad library, tpz973gvwc, drives the input port named your_input_port_name.

```
set_driving_cell  −library tpz973gvwc  −lib_cell PDIDGZ \
                  −pin {C} [get_ports your_input_port_name]
```

You can also appoint all primary input ports using [all_inputs] to the same driving cell as follows.

```
set_driving_cell  −library tpz973gvwc  −lib_cell PDIDGZ \
                  −pin {C} [all_inputs]
```

If your output is loaded using an output pad of PDI16DGZ in TSMC 0.18 μm process, you can set the output load as follows. In this command, pin I of output pad, PDI16DGZ, in I/O pad library, tpz973gvwc, loads the all primary outputs.

```
set_load [load_of "tpz973gvwc/PDI16DGZ/I"] \
         [all_outputs]
```

There are three paths: FF1 to FF2, FF2 to FF3, and FF3 to FF4 of the design illustrated in Figure 10.4. Provided that the clock is perfectly synchronous, to guarantee that all signals are stable before the rising edge of the clocks, the path delay from FF1 to FF2 will be $t_{CQ} + M + N = 1 + 4 + 6 = 11$ ns. Considering the setup time, $t_S = 0.5$ ns, the clock period for FF1 to FF2 must be larger than $11 + 0.5 = 11.5$ ns. From FF2 to FF3, the path delay will be $t_{CQ} + X = 1 + 11 = 12$ ns. Considering the setup time, the clock period for FF2 to FF3 must be larger than $12 + 0.5 = 12.5$ ns. From FF3 to FF4, the path delay will be $t_{CQ} + S + T = 1 + 3 + 7 = 11$ ns. Considering the setup time, the clock period for FF3 to FF4 must be larger than $11 + 0.5 = 11.5$ ns. Taking all three paths into consideration, the minimum clock period will be 12.5 ns.

In the above design, to correctly constrain the paths from FF1 to FF2 and FF3 to FF4, you can specify the input and output max delays for the setup time as follows.

```
set_input_delay  −clock clk −max 5 [get_ports in]
set_output_delay −clock clk −max 7.5 [get_ports out]
```

In addition to the setup time, requirements for the hold time must also be satisfied. For the design in Figure 10.5, to correctly constrain the paths from FF1 and FF2 to FF3, you can respectively specify the input max and min delays for the setup time and hold time as follows.

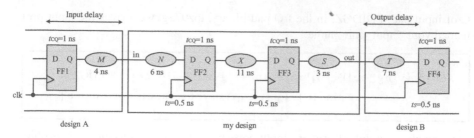

Figure 10.4: Input and output delays of the design.

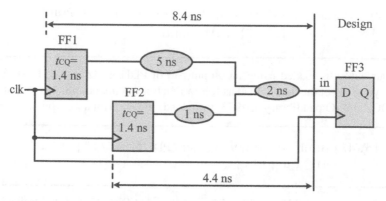

Figure 10.5: Max and min input delays of the design. The max input delay is usually used for the setup time check, and the min input delay is used for the hold time check.

```
set_input_delay  −clock  clk  −max 8.4 [ get_ports  in ]
set_input_delay  −clock  clk  −min 4.4 [ get_ports  in ]
```

The wiring of a design also contributes to the load of the outputs. To configure the wire load, you can specify the wire load model using the following command. In the command, the wire load model, tsmc18_wl10, in the slow.db library is chosen. It should be noted that the wire load is determined using the area of your design in the synthesis stage, which is not so accurate. An accurate wire load is unique for every wires and can only be obtained after the placement and routing of your design has been done.

```
set_wire_load_model  −name tsmc18_wl10  −library  slow
```

There are three wire load modes: top, segmented, and enclosed. These are specified depending upon the area of your design. As shown in Figure 10.6, there is a wire

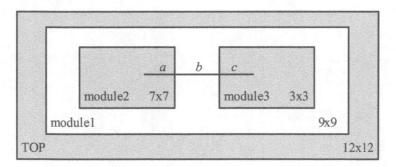

Figure 10.6: Wire load modes.

separated into three parts, a, b, and c. Besides, the wire load modes of each modules according to their circuit areas are also displayed.

The top mode specifies that wires use the wire load model of the top-level design. For example, if the wire load mode is top, the wire load models of a, b, and c will all follow 12x12 model of the top-level design. The segmented mode specifies that wires use the wire load models of the block that encloses each of them. For example, if the wire load mode is segmented, the wire load models of a, b, and c will be 7x7 (of module2), 9x9 (of module1), and 3x3 (of module3) model, respectively. The enclosed mode specifies that wires use the wire load model of the block that encloses all of them. For example, if the wire load mode is enclosed, the wire load models of a, b, and c will all be 9x9 (of module1). Consequently, the wire load mode of top is the most conservative and more stringent, whereas the wire load mode of segment is the most aggressive and less strict.

10.2.4   REPORTING AND ANALYZING DESIGN

Before introducing how to report a design, it must be emphasized that all error and warning messages must be carefully examined. All error messages must be dealt with and fixed. Some warning messages must also be fixed until it is absolutely clear that any remaining warning messages do not indicate serious problems and can safely be waived.

10.2.4.1   Design Report

A design can be reported using the report_design command, through which the operating conditions and wire load model can be carefully checked. You can use report_hierarchy to show the components used in each blocks and their position in the overall hierarchy. The ports of the design can also be reported using the report_port -verbose command. The report_port command will check the load as well as the input and output delay constraints. Clock constraints can be reported using the report_clock command. An example of a clock report is given in Figure 10.7.

```
------------------------------
Reports : clocks
Design  : TOP
Version : C-2009.06-SP2
Date    : Mon May 11 11:03:43 2020
------------------------------

Attributes:
    d - dont_touch_network
    f - fix_hold
    p - propagated_clock
    G - generated_clock

Clock          Period      Waveform        Attrs       Sources
------------------------------------------------------------------
ext_clk        10.00       {0,5}           d f         {ext_clk}
int_clk        20.00       {0,10}          G d f       {int_clk}
------------------------------------------------------------------

Generated      Master                      Generated       Master      Waveform
Clock          Source                      Source          Clock       Modification
------------------------------------------------------------------
int_clk        ext_clk     {CLK_GEN/u1/Q}  ext_clk     divide_by (2)
------------------------------------------------------------------
```

Figure 10.7: There is one external clock, ext_clk, and one generated clock, int_clk in the clock report.

High fanout nets should be identified and reported in the following manner. The capacitance of the high fanout nets designated as ideal networks will be shown to be 0.

```
report_net_fanout  -high_fanout
```

After reading your designs, check_design command reports error and warning messages that are important and should be carefully analysed. For example, if you instantiate a module with more ports than its definition, an error message is reported, while a warning is reported if a port is not connected to any nets. After setting constraints, check_timing should be used to verify that there are no unconstrained paths.

Clock gating (introduced later) should be reported as follows.

```
report_clock_gating  -gating_elements
```

An example of a clock gating report is shown in Figure 10.8.

10.2.4.2   Timing Report

Setup time can be reported using the report_timing command as follows. To report the hold time, you can change the option to "-delay min".

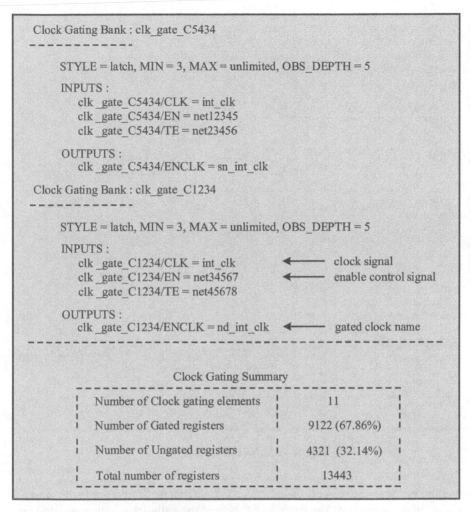

Figure 10.8: Clock gating report.

```
report_timing  -delay max
```

An example of the setup time report is shown in Figure 10.9. By default, only one maximum or minimum delay path (depending on the operating condition) of the design is displayed. The option "-max_paths" is used to show more paths. In this report, the start point is enable signal and the end point is timer/time_1ms_reg[0]/D. To analyze another path, specify the starting point using the option "-from" and the ending point using the option "-to". The column specified by "Incr" represents the incremental delay of the combined net and cell delays of each component. The column

```
Startpoint:  enable (input port clocked by clk)
Endpoint:  timer/time_1ms_reg[0]
             (rising edge-triggered flip-flop clocked by clk)
Path Group: clk
Path Type: max
```

Des/Clust/Port	Wire Load Model	Library
top	G5K	slow

Point	Incr	Path
clock clk (rise edge)	0.0000	0.0000
clock network delay (ideal)	1.0000	1.0000
input external delay (ideal)	1.0000	2.0000 f
enable (in)	0.0129	2.0129 f
...		
timer/time_1ms_reg[0]/D (QDFFX1)	2.6016	4.6145 f
data arrival time		4.6145
clock clk (rise edge)	4.0000	4.0000
clock network delay (ideal)	1.0000	5.0000
clock uncertainty	-0.1000	4.9000
timer/time_1ms_reg[0]/CK (QDFFRBX1)	0.0000	4.9000 r
library setup time	-0.0820	4.8180
data required time		4.8180
data required time		4.8180
data arrival time		-4.6145
slack (MET)		0.2035

Figure 10.9: Setup time report.

specified by "Path" represents the total path delay from the start point to the output of a specific component. The letter, r or f, behind the path delay indicates rising or falling transition for the output signal of a component. The SDF file can be referred to for individual net and cell delays.

In this report, the start point, enable signal, has an input delay of 1 ns. The end point (D input of flip-flop time_1ms_reg[0] or time_1ms_reg[0]/D) arrives at 4.6145 ns after the clock rising edge. The clock network (introduced later) has a period of 4 ns, a latency of 1 ns, and a clock uncertainty of 0.1 ns. According to the setup time requirement of time_1ms_reg[0], the data time_1ms_reg[0]/D is required to arrive at 4.8180 ns. Since the data arrives earlier than required, the timing constraint is satisfied and the slack= 4.8180 − 4.6145 = 0.2035 is positive (or met).

An example of a hold time report is shown in Figure 10.10. The hold time can be checked with the minimum delay in the best-case operating condition using the fast.db library. The report shows a register (time_1ms_reg[1]/CK) to register (time_1ms_reg[2]/D) path. The end point (time_1ms_reg[2]/D) arrives at

```
Startpoint: timer/time_1ms_reg[1]
           (rising edge-triggered flip-flop clocked by clk)
Endpoint: timer/time_1ms_reg[2]
           (rising edge-triggered flip-flop clocked by clk)
Path Group: clk
Path Type: min

Des/Clust/Port    Wire Load Model       Library
-----------------------------------------------------
top               G5K                   fast

Point                                          Incr        Path
-----------------------------------------------------------------------
clock clk (rise edge)                          0.0000      0.0000
clock network delay (ideal)                    1.0000      1.0000
timer/time_1ms_reg[1]/CK (QDFFRBX1)            0.0000      1.0000 r
timer/time_1ms_reg[1]/Q (QDFFRBX1)             0.0975      1.0975 f
           ...
timer/time_1ms_reg[2]/D (QDFFRBX1)             0.0344      1.1319 f
data arrival time                                          1.1319

clock clk (rise edge)                          0.0000      0.0000
clock network delay (ideal)                    1.0000      1.0000
clock uncertainty                              0.1000      1.1000
timer/time_1ms_reg[2]/CK (QDFFRBX1)            0.0000      1.1000 r
library hold time                              0.0016      1.1016
data required time                                         1.1016
-----------------------------------------------------------------------
data required time                                         1.1016
data arrival time                                         -1.1319
-----------------------------------------------------------------------
slack  (MET)                                               0.0303
```

Figure 10.10: Hold time report.

1.1319 ns after the clock rising edge. According to the hold time requirement of time_1ms_reg[2], the data time_1ms_reg[2]/D is required to arrive at 1.1016 ns. Since the data arrives later than required, the timing constraint is satisfied and the slack$= 1.1319 - 1.1016 = 0.0303$ is positive (or met).

The following command will generate a timing report that reports only paths which have setup-time violations. To report only paths with hold-time violations, change the option to "-min".

```
report_constraints  -all_viol  -max  -verbose
```

10.2.4.3 Area Report

A chip area report can be generated as follows.

```
report_area  -hier
```

Library(s) used:

   slow (File: /user/A/design/slow.db)

Number of ports:	35
Number of nets:	46
Number of cell:	5
Number of references:	5
Combinational area:	1456.864521
Noncombinational area:	1674.896431
Net interconnect area:	89642.658422
Total cell area:	3131.760952
Total area:	92774.419374

Figure 10.11: Area report.

In the report shown in Figure 10.11, only the total cell area needs to be considered. The net interconnect area will not be a problem because it depends on the wire load model, which cannot yet be determined.

The chip area depends on the semiconductor process. Therefore, it is usually unfair to compare the chip areas of two designs fabricated using different processes. On the contrary, the gate count is independent of the semiconductor process, and will usually give a good impression on the area size of the circuit. The gate count is roughly determined by the number of 2-input NAND (NAND2X1) gates, and can be calculated by

$$\text{gate count} = \text{chip area}/\text{NAND2X1 area}. \tag{10.1}$$

The NAND2X1 area can be looked up in the document of the cell library.

10.2.4.4 Power Report

The power consumption can be reported as follows.

```
report_power  −hier
```

An example of a power consumption report is given in Figure 10.12. The report is calculated using the load of each nets, which mainly depends on the area of your circuits. Moreover, the switching activity of your design is not known to the synthesis tool. In the sequel, a more accurate dynamic power must depend on the switching activity of your design, which can be derived by simulations.

Cell internal power = 343.9944 uW   (45%)
Net switching power = 420.4376 uW   (55%)

Total dynamic power = 764.4321 uW   (100%)

Cell leakage power   =   6.3256 uW

Figure 10.12: Power consumption report.

10.2.5 SAVING DESIGN

The new design can be saved to a file before quitting DC. To write the synthesized gate-level netlist in Verilog format for gate-level simulations, the "write" command is used. This will output the netlist into the file "design.vg" as follows. The file extension is specified as ".vg" to emphasize that it is a Verilog gate-level netlist instead of a Verilog RTL model.

```
write  −format verilog  −hierarchy  −output  design.vg
```

The synthesis constraints can be verified using the pre-sim. You can write the SDF of your design in "design.sdf" for pre-sim as follows.

```
write_sdf  −version 2.1  −context verilog  design.sdf
```

During the pre-layout phase, by default, the interconnect delays (INTERCONNECT field in the SDF file) are not to be written out separately in the SDF file. Rather, they are included as part of the IOPATH delay of each cell because of the fact that the interconnect delays are calculated according to the wire load model.

By contrast, the interconnect delays after layout are determined based on the routed design. In the sequel, the interconnect delays should be written out separately in the post-layout SDF file.

STA tools may be able to take into account path delays which have negative values, whereas timing simulation tools may have to interpret such negative delays as zero. Thus, although by using the timing data in the same SDF file, different interpretations may exist between STA and simulation tools and result in small differences in analysis results. We must pay attention to the warning messages when writing SDF file or back-annotating SDF file but negative delays are treated as zero. When this condition happens, timing violations may occur but STA analysis has no negative slacks. Including the interconnect delay into the cell delay when writing the SDF file may get rid of such a problem. Otherwise, you may opt to use a simulator that can back annotate negative delays and checks, such as the Synopsys VCS Verilog simulator. To annotate the negative delay and check, -negdelay and +neg_tchk options must be respectively used as displayed below, where test.v, chip.vg, and library.v are testbench, gate-level netlist of design, and cell library model, respectively. The option, -R, enables the VCS to run the executable file immediately after VCS links together the executable file, and the option, +v2k, enables new Verilog features in the IEEE 1364-2001 standard.

```
vcs -R test.v chip.vg -v library.v +typdelays (or +mindelays or +maxdelays)
-negdelay +neg_tchk +v2k
```

The design constraints of the design can also be written into a script file, i.e., Synopsys design constraints (SDC) file for layout tool or STA, as follows.

```
write_sdc design.sdc
```

10.3   SETTING DESIGN CONSTRAINTS

Design constraints are goals that the DC uses to optimize a design for inclusion in the target technology library. There are two kinds of constraints: design rule constraints (DRCs) and optimization constraints. Design rule constraints show the technology-specific restrictions, such as the maximum transition, maximum fanout, and maximum capacitance. The DRCs are characterized by the library vender and specified in the library; therefore, we need not specify them in the synthesis script file unless we want to specify more stringent ones. For example, we can limit the maximum fanout to 4 to reduce the loading of a high-fanout signal.

Optimization constraints specify design goals and requirements, such as the maximum and minimum delay (confined by clock constraints), maximum area, and maximum power. The DC attempts to meet all constraints during the compiling step.

10.3.1   OPTIMIZATION CONSTRAINTS

10.3.1.1   Creating Clock

In synchronous designs, we need to accurately specify the details of the clock scheme in the early design stage in order to achieve timing convergence, including the period, waveform, uncertainty (or skew+jitter), latency, and input and clock transitions. Clock jitter refers to a small deviation from true periodicity of a presumably periodic clock source. All register-to-register paths are simply constrained by clocks. The following command defines a clock, clk, with a period of 10 ns.

```
create_clock  -period 10 [get_ports clk]
```

The following command defines a clock, clk, with a period of 10 ns and duty cycle of 40%.

```
create_clock  −period 10 −waveform {0 4} \
              [ get_ports clk ]
```

During the synthesis stage, the clock network must be ideal without requiring the insertion of any buffers to reduce the load of the high-fanout clock net. High fanout networks, such as clock and reset signals, are solved by inserting buffers during the layout stage. The ideal network is indicated to the synthesizer via the set_ideal_network as follows.

```
set_ideal_network [ get_ports clk ]
```

Additional, you must tell the synthesizer buffers are not to be inserted into the clock network as follows.

```
set_dont_touch_network [ get_ports clk ]
```

It is best to set the driving of the clock network to infinity to get an ideal clock delay as follows.

```
set_drive 0 [ get_ports clk ]
```

10.3.1.2 Clock Latency

Clock latency is the propagation time from the actual clock origin to the clock pins of flip-flops in the design. Clock latency includes the source latency and network latency. The source latency is the delay from the actual clock origin to the clock port, such as the delay introduced by a phase-locked loop or other clock gating logic, and the network latency models the clock tree delay, as displayed in Figure 10.13.

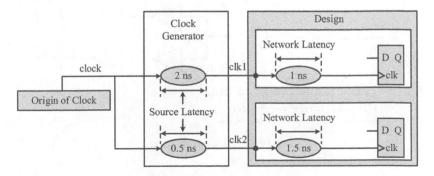

Figure 10.13: Clock latency.

The clock latency in Figure 10.13 can be described below. Notably, the named clock, ori_clk, is a virtual clock that has been defined but not associated with any pin/port. The create_generated_clock specifies that clk1 and clk2 be generated using a virtual clock, ori_clk, but clk1 and clk2 have the same frequency as ori_clk. In this example, clk1 and clk2 have source latencies of 2 and 0.5 ns, respectively, and they have clock tree delays of 1 and 1.5 ns, respectively.

```
create_clock  -name  ori_clk  -period 10
create_generated_clock  -source  ori_clk  -divide_by 1 \
                        [get_ports clk1]
create_generated_clock  -source  ori_clk  -divide_by 1 \
                        [get_ports clk2]
set_clock_latency  -source 2 [get_ports clk1]
set_clock_latency  -source 0.5 [get_ports clk2]
set_clock_latency  1 [get_ports clk1]
set_clock_latency  1.5 [get_ports clk2]
```

10.3.1.3 Clock Transition

Clock transition refers to the rising and/or falling time of a clock. Knowing the actual clock transition time enables a more accurate delay estimate. We assume that the clock transition is displayed in Figure 10.14.

The clock transition can be modeled below.

```
set_input_transition  0.5  [get_ports  clk]
set_clock_transition  0.1  [get_ports  clk]
```

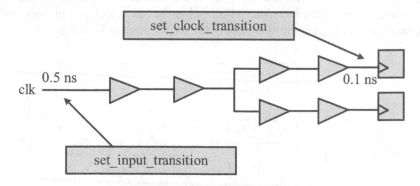

Figure 10.14: Clock transition.

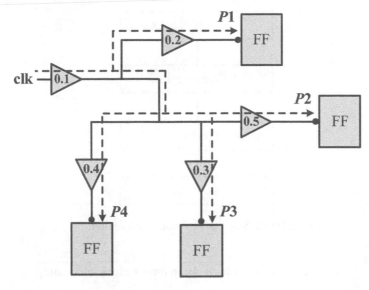

Figure 10.15: Clock skew.

10.3.1.4 Clock Uncertainty

The clock uncertainty (or skew+jitter) is the maximum difference either between the arrival of clock signals at sequential cells in one clock domain or between different clock domains. During synthesis, clock uncertainty is used to predict the possible differences between the clock arriving times of adjacent flip-flops. During RTL simulations, the clocks are assumed to arrive at all flip-flops at the same time. That is, the clock uncertainty is assumed to be 0. However, after the clock tree synthesis (CTS) for the high-fanout clock network, there will be some clock skew due to potential different latencies in all branches of the clock tree. For example, in Figure 10.15, the clock latencies of the clk for each flip-flop are different: $P1 = 0.3$ ns, $P2 = 0.6$ ns, $P3 = 0.4$ ns, and $P4 = 0.5$ ns. Therefore, the clock skew is $0.6 - 0.3 = 0.3$ ns. Clock jitter is the timing variations of a set of clock signal edges from their ideal value, i.e., the clock period. If the frequency of a clock source is 25 MHz (or period is 40 ns) with a jitter of 200 part per million (ppm), it will contribute to the clock uncertainty of 40 ns $\times$ 200 $\times$ 10^{-6}=8 ps.

Taking the clock uncertainty after the CTS into consideration, clock uncertainty incurred from the clock skew and jitter can be added to the clock network as follows.

```
set_clock_uncertainty 0.308 [get_ports clk]
```

Hence, considering the clock uncertainty, clock-to-Q delay, and the setup time constraints of a flip-flop, the clock period requirement should be modified as follows.

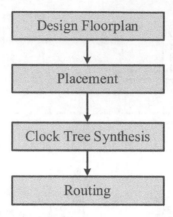

Figure 10.16: Steps in physical implementation.

clock-to-Q delay + critical path delay + setup time + clock uncertainty
< clock period.

Likewise, considering the clock uncertainty and clock-to-Q delay, the hold time constraint must be modified as follows.

clock-to-Q delay + path delay > hold time + clock uncertainty

The role of CTS in physical implementation is presented in Figure 10.16. The routing of CTS has a higher priority than that of normal signals. After placement, CTS is performed to obtain a clock tree with minimum skew by balancing the clock routing from the source to all FF leaves. When designing the floorplan, the physical partitions of sub-blocks can be specified using region/group constraints for those timing-critical paths.

10.3.1.5   Impacts of Clock Tree Modeling

For the circuit in Figure 10.17, assume the clock port, clk, has a source latency of 2 ns, a network latency of 3 ns, and a clock uncertainty of 1 ns. The requirement of setup time for all flip-flops is 0.5 ns.

The clock can be described as follows.

```
create_clock  -period 10  -waveform {0 5} [get_ports clk]
set_clock_latency  -source 2 [get_ports clk]
set_clock_latency 3 [get_ports clk]
set_clock_uncertainty 1 [get_ports clk]
```

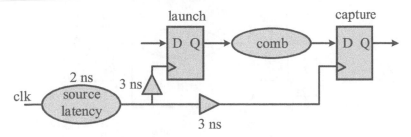

Figure 10.17: A circuit with clock latency.

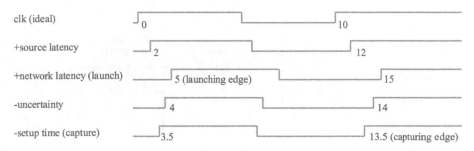

Figure 10.18: Specified clock waveform for the setup time constraint.

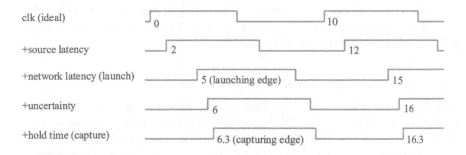

Figure 10.19: Specified clock waveform for the hold time constraint.

The clock waveform is displayed in Figure 10.18. The worst case for the setup time of the capturing clock is that it advances an amount of clock uncertainty, i.e., 1 ns. If the setup time requirement is 0.5 ns, the D input of the capturing FF must arrive before 13.5 ns.

The worst case for the hold time of the capturing clock is that it lags, producing an amount of clock uncertainty, i.e., 1 ns. If the hold time requirement is 0.3 ns, the D input of the capturing FF must arrive after 6.3 ns, as shown in Figure 10.19.

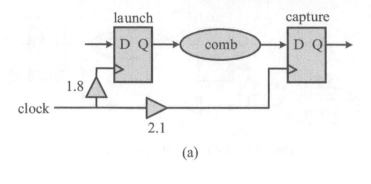

(a)

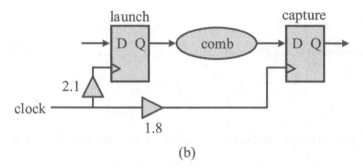

(b)

Figure 10.20: Impact of clock uncertainty. (a) The clock latency of the launching FF is 0.3 ns shorter than that of the capturing FF. (b) The clock latency of the launching FF is 0.3 ns longer than that of the capturing FF.

10.3.1.6   More on Impacts of Clock Tree Modeling

The clock skew may impact the setup time and/or hold time constraints. However, it may still be utilized to solve a few timing critical paths after the CTS, as shown in Figure 10.20. Figure 10.20(a) displays that the clock latency of the launching FF is 0.3 ns shorter than that of the capturing FF. Therefore, the effective clock period of the path is 10.3 ns for a nominal clock period of 10 ns. As a result, the setup time constraint is less stringent than that for a clock without any skew. By contrast, the clock latency of the launching FF is 0.3 ns longer than that of the capturing FF in Figure 10.20(b). Its effective clock period is thus only 9.7 ns. The setup time constraint is more stringent than that without clock skew.

To sum up, if a clock arriving at the capturing FF is earlier than that at the launching FF, the positive clock skew (clock latency of launching FF − clock latency of capturing FF > 0) impacts the clock period constraint. Although not ideal, the negative clock skew (clock latency of launching FF − clock latency of capturing FF < 0) can be seen as somewhat helpful, as it may relieve the clock period constraint. It is unnecessary to employ the clock skew to solve the hold time violations, which can be simply solved by inserting buffers.

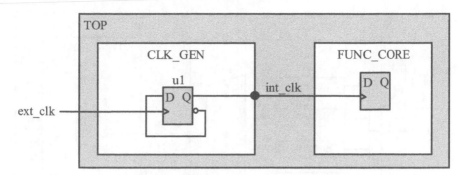

Figure 10.21: A derive clock, int_clk.

Nevertheless, the use of clock skew to solve the setup time problem requires special care. It may impact the paths with start point from the capturing FF. Moreover, the clock skew should be carefully confirmed under all operation modes, such as the scan mode.

10.3.1.7 Derived Clock

It's a common practice for a derived clock, int_clk, to be generated by a primary clock, ext_clk, as shown in Figure 10.21.

The divide-by-2 clock, int_clk, is generated by a 100 MHz primary clock, ext_clk. This can be specified as follows.

```
create_clock −period 10 [get_ports ext_clk]
create_generated_clock −source ext_clk −divide_by 2 \
                       [get_pins CLK_GEN/u1/Q]
set_ideal_network [get_ports ext_clk]
set_ideal_network [get_pins CLK_GEN/u1/Q]
set_dont_touch_network [get_ports ext_clk]
set_dont_touch_network [get_pins CLK_GEN/u1/Q]
set_drive 0 [get_ports ext_clk]
set_drive 0 [get_pins CLK_GEN/u1/Q]
```

There are often multiple clock sources for a logic as well, as shown in Figure 10.22.

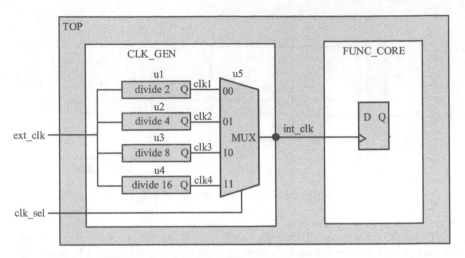

Figure 10.22: Multiple clock sources.

These clocks can be specified as follows.

```
create_clock  −period 10 [get_ports ext_clk]
create_generated_clock  −source ext_clk  −divide_by 2 \
                        [get_pins CLK_GEN/u1/Q]
create_generated_clock  −source ext_clk  −divide_by 4 \
                        [get_pins CLK_GEN/u2/Q]
create_generated_clock  −source ext_clk  −divide_by 8 \
                        [get_pins CLK_GEN/u3/Q]
create_generated_clock  −source ext_clk  −divide_by 16 \
                        [get_pins CLK_GEN/u4/Q]
```

To analyze the timing in this case, the most stringent clock is selected for synthesis as follows.

```
set_case_analysis 3 [get_ports clk_sel]
```

Sometimes, we prefer to manually instantiate the multiplexer for the clock generator. In this case, you can tell the DC not to touch the cells you instantiated as follows.

```
set_dont_touch [get_cells CLK_GEN/u5]
```

If some cells in the library are not preferred, for instance, the JK flip-flops, they can be excluded from the synthesis by using the following command.

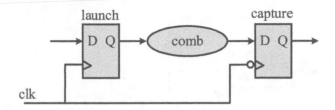

Figure 10.23: Paths between positive and negative edge clocks.

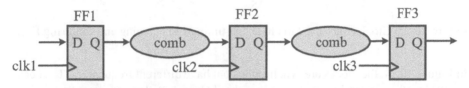

Figure 10.24: A design with 3 clocks.

```
set_dont_use [get_cells slow/JKFF*]
set_dont_use [get_cells fast/JKFF*]
```

The paths between positive and negative edge clocks need not be specially indicated, as shown in Figure 10.23. The DC can perform the STA correctly. Derived negated clocks can be automatically identified by DC as well. You only have to describe the clock port as follows. Even so, it is still discouraged to use both the positive and negative edges of a clock source because to do so the clock period must be reduced by a factor of 2. Moreover, derived negative-edge triggered FFs are difficult for chip testing.

```
create_clock −period 10 [get_ports clk]
```

A derived gated clock (introduced later) can also be automatically identified by DC. You only have to describe the original clock port.

10.3.1.8 Multiple Clock Design

A design with 3 clocks is described below. It is also shown in Figure 10.24.

```
create_clock −period 10 [get_ports clk1]
create_clock −period 20 [get_ports clk2]
create_clock −period 25 [get_ports clk3]
```

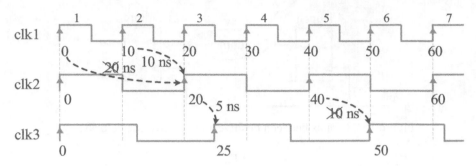

Figure 10.25: Clock edges used to check the timing of launching and capturing FFs.

In Figure 10.24, the clocks are synchronous but have different frequencies. To check the timing, the most stringent clock edges should be selected to guarantee that timing constraints are met under all circumstances. For example, as displayed in Figure 10.25, from FF1 to FF2, the most critical timing is launched from the 2nd clock edge of clk1 to the 2nd clock edge of clk2, i.e., 10 ns, instead of from the 1st clock edge of clk1 to the 2nd clock edge of clk2, i.e., 20 ns. Likewise, the most critical timing from FF2 to FF3 is 5 ns.

When clocks are asynchronous, the simple or FIFO synchronizer introduced in Chapter 8 must be used. However, the most stringent clock edges may be extremely close, making it hard to satisfy the timing constraints. Fortunately, those paths across different clock domains are false paths that will be introduced later.

10.3.1.9   Propagated Clock after CTS

After the CTS, the real delays of clock buffers and real clock skews can be identified, and their estimates no longer need to be used. This enables the properties of physical implementation to be more accurately characterized. For example, suppose that the clocks and input/output delays listed below had been specified before the CTS. The clock uncertainty is 0.3 ns composed of a clock jitter of 0.1 ns and an estimated clock skew of 0.2 ns.

```
create_clock  −name ori_clk  −period 10
create_generated_clock  −source ori_clk  −divide_by 1 \
                        [get_ports clk]
set_clock_latency 1 [get_clocks clk]
set_clock_uncertainty 0.3 [get_clocks clk]
set_input_delay  −clock ori_clk  −max 5  −min 4 \
                        [get_ports in]
set_output_delay  −clock ori_clk  −max 7.5  −min 6 \
                        [get_ports out]
```

After CTS, suppose that the real clock tree latency is found to be around 1.5 ns. The constraints can now be modified by removing the estimated clock latency, skew, and input and output delays. The set_propagated_clock uses the real clock skews of FFs, so only the clock jitter in the clock uncertainty needs to be modeled. A new virtual clock, ori_clk1, can be created to be referenced by the input and output signals. A clock latency of 1.5 ns can be added to ori_clk1, so that the clock (ori_clk1) of the input and output signals will be synchronous with that (clk) of the design. Consequently, in addition to those constraints used before the CTS, additional constraints can be specified as follows.

```
create_clock -name ori_clk1 -period 10
remove_clock_latency [get_clocks clk]
remove_clock_uncertainty [get_clocks clk]
remove_input_delay [get_ports in]
remove_output_delay [get_ports out]
set_clock_latency 1.5 ori_clk1
set_clock_uncertainty 0.1 [get_clocks clk]
set_propagated_clock [get_clocks clk]
set_input_delay -clock ori_clk1 -max 5 -min 4 \
                [get_ports in]
set_output_delay -clock ori_clk1 -max 7.5 -min 6 \
                 [get_ports out]
```

10.3.1.10   Maximum Delay of a Combinational Circuit

A pure combinational circuit has no clocks. Hence, the paths in it can not be constrained by the clock specification. To constrain pure combinational circuits, the first method is to specify the maximum delay for each paths in the combinational circuit as follows.

```
set_max_delay 3 -from [all_inputs] -to [all_outputs]
```

Of course, you can use a virtual clock, and input and output delays to constrain a pure combinational circuit as the second method as follows.

```
create_clock -name clk -period 5
set_input_delay -clock clk -max 1 \
                [all_inputs]
set_output_delay -clock clk -max 1 \
                 [all_outputs]
```

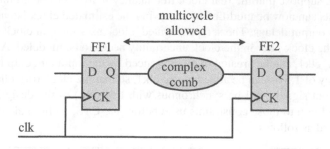

Figure 10.26: Multicycle path.

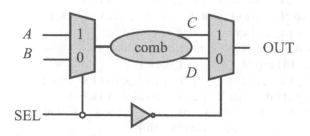

Figure 10.27: False path.

10.3.1.11   Timing Exceptions

In some designs, combinational logic delay between two registers is allowed more than one clock cycle, as shown in Figure 10.26.

If the path delay of the complex combinational logic in Figure 10.26 is larger than one clock cycle, the clock period constraint will be violated. However, if a timing exception is made and it is allowed a multicycle path, the timing violation can be waived. Suppose that the combinational logic delay is allowed 2 clock cycles; in such a case the multicycle paths can be set as follows.

```
set_multicycle_path  2  -from [get_pins FF1/CK] \
                        -to [get_pins FF2/D]
```

A false path is also a timing exception that timing constraints along the path will be ignored. For example, if the timing paths from *A*, through *C*, to OUT are false paths in Figure 10.27, we can set the false paths as follows.

```
set_false_path  -from [A]  -through {C}  -to [OUT]
```

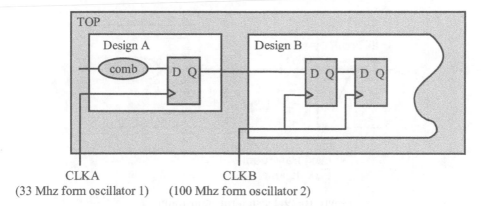

CLKA   CLKB
(33 Mhz form oscillator 1)   (100 Mhz form oscillator 2)

Figure 10.28: False path across different clock domains.

The paths across different clock domains are commonly false paths, as shown in Figure 10.28. The simple or FIFO synchronizer introduced in Chapter 8 guarantees the functionality of signals crossing different clock domains.

We can set the false paths of all signals from clock domain CLKA to clock domain CLKB as follows.

```
set_false_path  -from [get_clocks CLKA] \
                -to [get_clocks CLKB]
```

If there are also signals from clock domain CLKB to clock domain CLKA, we can set the false paths of all signals from clock domain CLKB to clock domain CLKA as follows.

```
set_false_path  -from [get_clocks CLKB] \
                -to [get_clocks CLKA]
```

In asynchronous interfaces, the clock edges of launching and capturing FFs can become so small that timing violations will eventually happen. However, since the unstable problem of signals across different clock domains has been solved by the synchronizer, their timing violations are false alarms. These false alarms are constrained by false paths to the synthesis tool.

To eliminate false alarms during gate-level simulations with timing information back annotated, the first FF (facing the asynchronous clock) in the synchronizer should be replaced with a cell having the same original functionality but without timing checks. The models of FFs without timing checks will need to be manually crafted. Similarly, the cells referring to them in the gate-level netlist will have to be manually replaced.

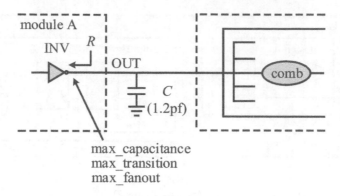

Figure 10.29: Design rule constraints.

10.3.2 DESIGN RULE CONSTRAINTS

Vendors impose design rules that restrict how many cells a cell can be connected to based on capacitance, transition, and fanout, as shown in Figure 10.29.

More conservative design rules may be applied to accommodate the interface environment a given block will encounter. This has the advantage of preventing the cells in a design from operating close to their limits, where performance degrades rapidly. An example is shown below.

```
set_max_capacitance 1.2 [get_ports A/OUT]
set_max_transition 0.2 [get_ports A/OUT]
set_max_fanout 6 [get_ports A/OUT]
```

10.4 COMPILING DESIGN

During optimization, there exists a constraint priority listed in descending order as follows. DC tries to meet all constraints but, by default, gives emphasis to design rule constraints because they are essential requirements for a functional design.

- Design rule constraints.
- Timing constraints.
- Power constraints.
- Area constraints.

The optimization of timing, area, and power to meet their constraints are presented below.

10.4.1 TIMING OPTIMIZATION

The purpose of timing optimization is to ensure that a design achieves the necessary performance constraints or specifications. In other words, the goal is to maximize

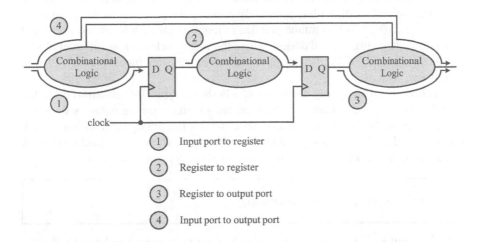

Figure 10.30: Various paths constrained in a synchronous design.

the number of operations per clock period, or, conversely, to minimize the clock pe-riod per operation. Changes made in the architecture exploration stage of the design flow will have the greatest impact on the performance, such as the application of parallelism, which is only limited by the data dependency. Since parallelism requires additional resources which take up area and consume power, increasing parallelism is contrary to reducing area and power consumption. By contrast, the pipelining tech-nique can usually obtain a good performance under the premise of moderate increase of area and power consumption. Clearly, tradeoffs must be made between parallelism and pipelining techniques.

We need to estimate the achievable clock frequency because it is part of the perfor-mance analysis for candidate architectures. In another way that, according to system requirements, the clock frequency can also be specified in advance. Whatever way we adopt, the clock period will be used as a design constraint for subsequent stages of the design flow.

When we move in accordance with the design flow, the emphasis of the design criteria will shift gradually from performance to timing. In a synchronous design, the clock period constrains the propagation delay of the combinational circuit between the registers. This includes paths from input ports through combinational logic to register inputs, paths from register outputs to register inputs, paths from register out-puts through combinational logic to output ports, and paths from input ports directly through combinational logic to output ports, as shown in Figure 10.30.

Especially in cases in which different blocks are designed by different design-ers, it is important to guarantee that the combined path from a register output in one block to a register input in another block meets the clock period constraint. One way to do this is to allocate a timing budget for each block by specifying the maximum output delay of a path from a register output to its output port in one block, and the maximum input delay of a path from an input port to a register input in another block. Since it is sometimes difficult to accurately estimate the propagation delays of combinational circuits, it is a common practice to require that each block has registered outputs. In a large high-speed design, where the wiring delay across different blocks may be significant, it may also be appropriate to require that inputs are registered in each blocks.

Optimizing and analyzing the timing of a design is typically performed using the static timing analysis. In Figure 10.30, there are 4 kinds of timing paths for the static timing analysis. The static timing analysis estimates the timing information of each cells specified in the technology library, together with simple wire load models. A typical compiling command using the medium effort is displayed below.

```
compile  −map_effort medium
```

At the synthesis stage, since the design has not been placed and routed, the delays of cells and wires can only be estimated. However, using the estimates will be sufficient to guide the timing optimization at this stage. To cope with possible mismatches between the estimated and real delays, the clock period constraint can be conservatively configured to 90% of its target. The static timing analysis determines whether the clock period constraint has been met, and surely you can identify the critical paths in your design. If necessary, you can then modify your design to reduce its critical path delay.

In the physical design stage, we can configure the aspect ratio and (area) utilization of the design and choose the locations of hard macros and soft designs via floorplanning. After floorplanning, the interconnect wires between blocks can be globally routed. If there is no routing congestion, detailed placement and routing can be performed. However, this process is very computationally intensive. When the physical design has been established, real delay values of components and wires can be extracted. We can then repeat the static timing analysis using the accurate delays to verify the timing constraints again.

If the synthesized netlist or physical design do not meet the timing constraints, we can still fine tune the timing using different synthesis or placement and routing commands. However, if the constraints still can not be met by the design, there may be no choice but to revisit earlier stages of the design flow and choose different architectures at higher levels of abstraction.

10.4.2   AREA OPTIMIZATION

The cost of a chip is proportional to the wafer fabrication cost, and hence, the chip area. Moreover, a chipâĂŹs yield is inversely proportional to the chip area. A larger chip wastes more area near the wafer edge and dissipates more heat. In addition, a larger chip usually requires more pins which leads to a costly package. It also dissipates more heat and needs even more package cost. If a chip has defects, the cost of its fabrication, testing, and packaging will be completely wasted. Considering all factors, the final chip cost is approximately proportional to the square of the chip area. No doubt, if possible, the smaller the chip area the better.

Similar to the timing of a design, choices made earlier in the design flow affect the chip area most. At the synthesis stage, we can specify constraints on the area in the synthesis tool, as shown below. When the delays of the design have been optimized, cells with smaller area will replace those in non-timing critical paths.

```
set_max_area 0
compile −map_effort medium
```

At the physical design stage, the chip area can be optimized through intervention in the floorplanning, and placement and routing of the circuit. However, only fine tuning of the chip area will be possible. For a design with simple wiring complexity, a high (area) utilization can be achieved, while, for a design with high wiring complexity, a low (area) utilization is usually traded-off for timing.

10.4.3   POWER OPTIMIZATION

As digital systems continue to become smaller and more complex, power consumption becomes an increasingly important issue. The power consumed by a circuit will be converted into heat, which needs to be dissipated by the chip and package. Many of the previously mentioned methods of minimizing the chip area are still useful for reducing the power consumption. Because a larger chip has more transistors, it will therefore consume more power. There are still other approaches to reduce the power consumption, such as identifying the idle period for each block of a system. The clocks of an idle block can be turned off, and the voltage levels of idle blocks can be lowered or even switched off. Alternatively, when the performance requirements are not high, the power management can be achieved by an adjustable clock generator to control the clock frequency.

Although turning off some blocks in the system can save a lot of power consumption, it is a complicated procedure. In particular, if an active block is connected to the powered down blocks, the interface signals must be disabled to avoid spurious activation in the active block. Further, when power is supplied to the block that is turned off, it takes a considerable amount of clock cycles to restore it to normal operation.

10.4.3.1   Power Model

In a digital system, the dynamic power consumption used for turning on and off transistors is the main source of power consumption. The greater the fanout load driven by an output, the higher the power required to transit the load between logic 0 and 1 levels. In a clocked synchronous digital system, a global clock signal needs to drive many flip-flops. Within them, several transistors switch their states at clock edges even the outputs of flip-flops do not change. However, these internal transitions in flip-flops unavoidably consume power.

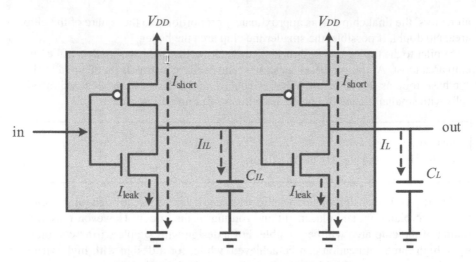

Figure 10.31: Power model of a CMOS buffer.

As Figure 10.31 shows, there are two main kinds of power consumption: dynamic and static. The power model of a CMOS buffer has dynamic power consumption which includes the dynamic switching power used to charge the output load C_L (by I_L) and internal load C_{IL} (by I_{IL}) of a cell, and the short-circuit power consumption (due to I_{short}) in a cell. The dynamic switching power used for charging a load C is characterized by

$$P_D = \frac{1}{2}\alpha f C V_{DD}^2, \qquad (10.2)$$

where α represents the toggle rate, f is the clock frequency, C is the capacitive load, and V_{DD} is the supply voltage. To reduce the dynamic power used to charge the loads, one can reduce the switching activity, clock frequency, capacitive load, or the supply voltage. The technique used to adapt to various operating requirements by adjusting the clock frequency and supply voltage is called dynamic voltage and frequency scaling (DVFS).

When charging the output or internal loads, both NMOS and PMOS may turn on for a short period of time leading to a short current I_{short}. Consequently, the short-circuit power consumption occurs and, during the short circuit period, it is characterized by

$$P_S = \alpha f I_{short} V_{DD}. \qquad (10.3)$$

The static power consumption includes the leakage power (due to I_{leak}) even when there is no signal transition. The leakage power is a complex function (and ignored here) of the supply voltage V_{DD}, the threshold voltage V_t of transistors, and the aspect ratio $\frac{W}{L}$.

Dynamic power optimization is achieved using clock gating for the RTL codes, gate-level optimization using the synthesis tool, and the multi-V_{DD} multi-supply

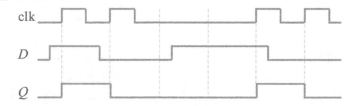

Figure 10.32: Timing diagram for a flip-flop with a gated clock.

(MVMS) library. Static power optimization reduces power leakage by using the multi-Vt library, including cells with different threshold voltages. Through the use of a multi-Vt library, low Vt cells on critical paths can improve their timing, while high Vt cells on non-critical paths can save power. Hence, the low-leakage and high-performance design can be achieved together with a multi-Vt library.

Statistically, clock gating can save from 20% to 40% of dynamic power, depending on your design, while gate-level optimization using the synthesis tool can save 2% to 6% of dynamic power. Reducing the leakage power using the synthesis tool can save 20% to 80% of static power.

10.4.3.2 Clock Gating

Another common way of reducing the power consumption of CMOS logic is through clock gating, which involves turning off the clock to a portion of FFs whose stored values do not need to be updated. We can use a clock-enable signal to control the activity of a single register. When using clock gating, the components see no clock transitions when the clock is turned off. As shown in Figure 10.32, the clock is gated off for two cycles. During that interval, the register consumes no dynamic power because no signals (including those in a register) need to transition, not even clock signals.

Gating a clock is not as simple as inserting an AND gate in the clock signal. Also, given the delay in an AND gate, the resulting clock edges will have an offset from those of the ungated clock and leads to a higher clock skew, making it difficult to meet timing constraints. Moreover, if a gating control signal is generated through combinational logic, this approach can cause glitches in the gated clock signal, as shown in Figure 10.33. The glitch may cause the unwanted triggering of the register. The solution is to not to express the clock gating in the RTL model of the circuit. Rather, we should treat clock gating as a part of power optimization to be implemented by clock gating insertion tools during the synthesis. Several synthesis tools can perform this kind of power optimization.

To optimize power consumption in digital circuits, clock gating can be automatically performed by Power Compiler of Synopsys if your RTL codes obey certain coding styles. For example, you can use if statements, conditional operators, or case statements in always blocks, as shown below, to infer the glitch-free clock gating. One requirement is that the clock to be gated and the clock that generates the enable

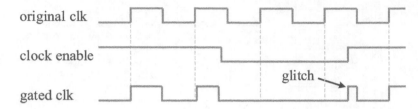

original clk

clock enable

glitch

gated clk

Figure 10.33: Glitch on a gated clock should be avoided.

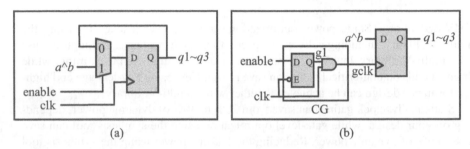

(a)   (b)

Figure 10.34: Schematics (a) without clock gating and (b) with clock gating.

signal should be the same.

```
1 // Three ways to infer the clock gating
2 always @(posedge clk)
3   if(enable) q1<=a^b;
4 always @(posedge clk)
5   q2<=enable? a^b:q2;
6 always @(posedge clk)
7   case(enable)
8   1'b0: q3<=q3; // Redundant
9   1'b1: q3<=a^b;
10  endcase
```

The derived circuits with and without clock gating are displayed in Figure 10.34.

In addition to an AND gate, the clock gating uses a latch as well. In Figure 10.35, the clock gating produces no glitches on the gated clock, gclk.

The script for automatic clock gating is displayed below.

```
insert_clock_gating
compile
```

The script can also be written as follows.

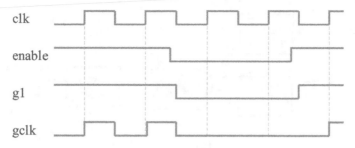

Figure 10.35: No glitch on a gated clock.

```
compile  -gated_clock
```

The clock gating can be manually inserted into the RTL codes, although this is generally discouraged. However, if it is determined that this is the preferable solution, the following command should be used before compiling to synthesize the gated clock.

```
replace_clock_gates  -global
```

10.4.3.3 Dynamic Power Optimization

High switching activity in a design causes an increase in overall dynamic power consumption, making it necessary to implement design features that can reduce the excessive switching activity. To accurately optimize the switching activity, we need to determine the most realistic power model for the switching activity. An addition operation may be considered which can be implemented with 3- or 4-stage full adders, as shown in Figure 10.36. In Figure 10.36(a), the high activity input goes through three full adders, while, in Figure 10.36(b), the high activity input only goes through one full adder so that the power consumption can be reduced.

We can optimize the RTL power consumption using the synthesis tool as shown below.

```
set_dynamic_optimization true
compile  -map_effort medium  -area_effort low \
         -power_effort high
```

For the design in Figure 10.37 as another example, only one of the arithmetic operations is required depending on the sel[1 : 0] signal at every clock cycle.

To stop data from feeding into the DW arithmetic components through operand isolation, the DC can automatically insert activation logic, as the AND gates used

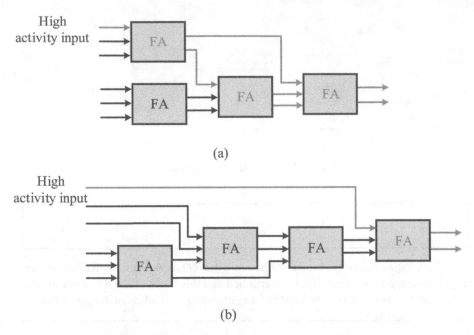

(a)

(b)

Figure 10.36: Addition operation to accommodate the switching activity, where FA denotes the full adder: (a) before optimization and (b) after optimization.

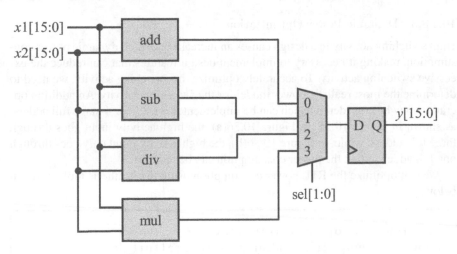

Figure 10.37: A circuit that can adopt the operand isolation.

to isolate the operands of the adder shown in Figure 10.38. However, the operand isolation might impact the logic depth of the combinational circuit.

The script for the operand isolation is displayed below. For weight=1 of the set_operand_isolation_slack command, if the timing slack is 0.5 worse than before,

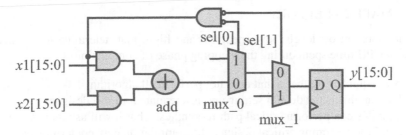

Figure 10.38: Activation logic inserted.

the operand isolation will be terminated. If weight=0, the tool can decide whether the operand isolation will be performed.

```
set do_operand_isolation true
read_file -f verilog design.v
source design_constraints.tcl
set_operand_isolation_style -logic adaptive
# weight: 0~1
set_operand_isolation_slack 0.5 -weight 1
compile
```

At the gate-level, we can incrementally optimize the power consumption, as shown below.

```
set_dynamic_optimization true
compile -inc
```

10.4.3.4 Power Analysis

Finally, a power analysis tool can estimate the circuit's power consumption based on signal transitions. A good way to acquire signal transitions is to monitor the values of signals during simulation of the netlist of the circuit. To accomplish this, you need to dump the VCD file during simulation. Then, you can convert the VCD file to the switching activity interchange format (SAIF) file using the Synopsys vcd2saif utility.

The power analysis tool can then calculate the power consumption from the technology library together with the wire load model for the interconnecting signals as follows. The file "design.saif" is the SAIF file.

```
create_power_model
read_saif -input design.saif -instance your_design
report_rtl_power
```

10.4.4 MAPPING EFFORT

There are three effort levels: low, medium, and high, that determine the relative amount of CPU time spent during the mapping phase of compilation.

- Low: a quicker synthesis that does not perform all algorithms.
- Medium: this is the default setting and is adequate for most designs.
- High: this can perform critical path re-synthesis, but it will use more CPU time. In some timing critical designs, the compilation may not terminate.

To reduce the synthesis time, multi-core synthesis is supported through the use of the following command, where 4 CPU cores are available to be used for synthesis.

```
set_host_options  -max_cores 4
```

We can also direct the tool to optimize logics across block boundaries.

```
compile  -boundary_optimization
```

For the cases in Figure 10.39, boundary logics can be optimized.

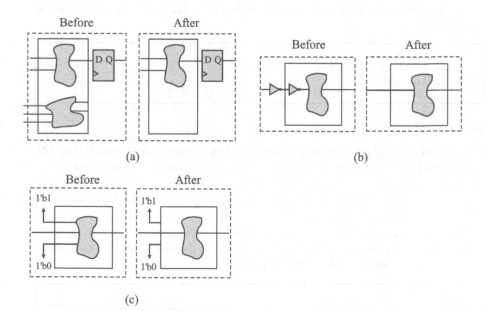

(a)   (b)

(c)

Figure 10.39: (a) Unconnected output ports are removed, (b) redundant inverters are optimized, and (c) constants are propagated to reduce logic.

DC-Ultra enables synthesis for timing critical, ultra high-performance designs, as follows. By default, DC-Ultra will automatically ungroup all modules to obtain an ultra high-performance design. It is suggested that the netlist generated by DC-Ultra be carefully verified using formal equivalence checking with its RTL codes, particular for a very complicated design.

```
compile_ultra
```

The DC-Ultra has several options including

```
-scan                        # for test-ready compile
-no_autoungroup              # for turning off the
                             # ungrouping
-no_boundary_optimization    # for turning off the
                             # boundary optimization
```

10.4.5   SOLVING SETUP TIME VIOLATIONS

You can opt to perform incremental gate-level optimization without logic level optimization as follows.

```
compile -incremental_mapping -map_effort high
```

Alternatively, the design hierarchy of a design can be broken by flattening the design. The logic flattening allows the compiler to obtain a better optimized design.

```
ungroup -all -flatten
compile -incremental_mapping -map_effort high
```

The implementation shown in Figure 10.40 has several critical constraints: a clock period of 10 ns, clock-to-Q delay, t_{CQ}, of 1 ns, input delay of 1 ns, and setup time, t_S, of 1 ns as well. If the worst negative slack of your design is still too large, or there are too many paths with negative slack, it is best to go back and redesign at the architectural exploration stage.

During the synthesis stage, it is often best to apply the optimize_registers for retiming of the registers, as shown in Figure 10.41.

The compile or compile_ultra command only optimizes the combinational logics, and does not change the location of registers. There are three commands for the register retiming which can move registers: optimize_registers, pipeline_registers,

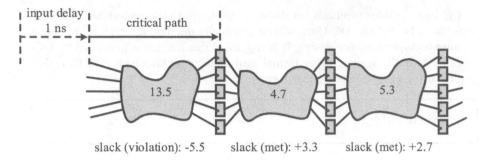

Figure 10.40: Implementation with a large negative slack.

and balance_registers. In addition to changing the location of registers, the opti-mize_registers command will optimize the area and incrementally compile the design as well. Using a different approach, the pipeline_registers command only inserts registers for a purely combinational logic. The balance_registers command only changes the location of registers without optimizing the area or incrementally compiling the design.

If the setup time constraint is not met, the clock speed can be lowered to solve the setup time violation, although the system specification will remain unsatisfied.

10.4.6   SOLVING HOLD TIME VIOLATIONS

A hold time violation is usually considered using the best-case operating condition, because, in this condition, the delay is minimum, which has the worst negative impact on the hold time constraint. To perform only hold time fixing and ignore other design rules, the set_fix_hold command must be specified. After setup time violations have been corrected, you can then incrementally compile again for hold time fixing as follows.

```
set_operating_conditions  best
set_fix_hold
compile  -inc  -only_hold_time
```

Typically, buffers are inserted in those paths with the hold time violation where the path delay of combinational logic is too small. If the hold time constraint is not met, the circuit may fail to operate at any clock speed due to the hold time violation. Hence, hold time violations must be solved in all situations.

10.4.7   SOLVING MULTIPLE PORT NETS

Occasionally designs will occur in which some output ports are driven by the same net, an output port is driven directly by an input port, or an output port is driven by a constant value, as shown in Figure 10.42.

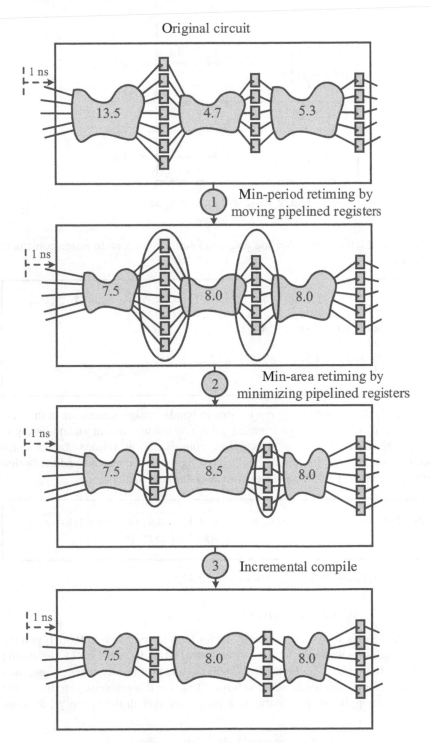

Figure 10.41: Retiming using optimize_registers.

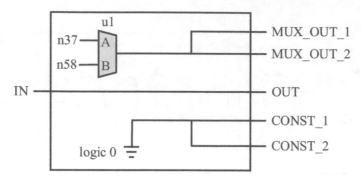

Figure 10.42: Multiple port nets.

In these cases, the written Verilog gate-level netlist may contain assign constructs as follows.

```
1 output MUX_OUT_1 , MUX_OUT_2 , OUT , CONST_1 , CONST_2 ,...
2 MUX U1 (.Y(MUX_OUT_1), .A(n37), .B(n58));
3 assign MUX_OUT_2=MUX_OUT_1 ;
4 assign OUT=IN ;
5 assign CONST_1=1'b0 ;
6 assign CONST_2=1'b0 ;
```

Unfortunately, layout tools may not be able to handle assign statements in the Verilog netlist. To ensure that your netlist does not contain assign statements, you can separate the multiple port nets during compilation as follows. In the command, the option "-all" fixes both feedthrough signals and constants and the option "-buffer_constants" buffers constants instead of duplicating them.

```
set_fix_multiple_port_nets  −all  −buffer_constants  \
                            [get_designs *]
```

The synthesized logic is presented in Figure 10.43.

10.4.8 SOLVING LARGE FOR LOOPS

By default, the maximum iteration limit of a for loop for synthesis is 4096. If you are describing a design with a for loop with iteration of 8192, though the RTL simulation performs well for a large for loop, the DC will fail and prompt an error message, such as "Loop exceeded maximum iteration limit". To solve this problem, you can set the hdlin_while_loop_iterations variable to a higher number in the synopsys_dc.setup file as follows

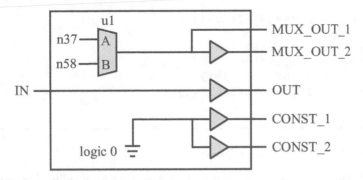

Figure 10.43: Preventing assign statements in gate-level netlist using buffers.

```
set hdlin_while_loop_iterations 8192
```

Unfortunately, though the iteration limit of a for loop can be extended, it still has a hard maximum limit of 10000. If your design contains a for loop with iteration of 16384 shift registers shown below, the synthesis will eventually interrupt with the above error message again.

```
1 always @(posedge clk) begin
2   a[0]<=in;
3   for(i=1;i<16384;i=i+1)
4     a[i]<=a[i-1];
5 end
```

To get around this issue, you can separate one big for loop into several smaller for loops as follows.

```
1 always @(posedge clk) begin
2   a[0]<=in;
3   for(i=1;i<4096;i=i+1)
4     a[i]<=a[i-1];
5 end
6 always @(posedge clk) begin
7   a[4096]<=a[4095];
8   for(i1=1;i1<4096;i1=i1+1)
9     a[4096+i1]<=a[4096+i1-1];
10 end
11 always @(posedge clk) begin
12   a[8192]<=a[8191];
13   for(i2=1;i2<4096;i2=i2+1)
```

```
14      a[8192+i2]<=a[8192+i2-1];
15 end
16 always @(posedge clk) begin
17   a[12288]<=a[12287];
18   for(i3=1;i3<4096;i3=i3+1)
19     a[12288+i3]<=a[12288+i3-1];
20 end
```

10.4.9   SOLVING NAMING RULES

Some tools may not accept the naming style of your gate-level netlist. For example, the bus name, bus[2], may not be accepted. You might need to change it to bus_2_. In this case, you can set new naming rules as follows.

```
set_bus_inference_style {%s_%d_}
set_bus_naming_style {%s_%d_}
```

Then, you can apply new naming rules before writing out your netlist as follows.

```
change_names −hierarchy −rules script_of_your_rules
```

10.5   ADAPTIVE THRESHOLD ENGINE

We want to design an adaptive threshold engine (ATE) to separate the foreground image from a grayscale one, as shown in Figure 10.44. The threshold is the simplest way to segment an image. Binary images can be created from grayscale images using the threshold.

The image is assumed to have 8×8 pixels. The threshold is calculated by the average of the maximum and minimum pixel data, i.e.,

$$\text{threshold} = \frac{\text{max} + \text{min}}{2}$$

where max and min denote the maximum and minimum pixel data, respectively.

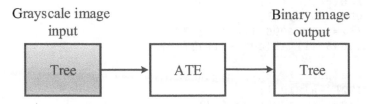

Figure 10.44: Functionality of ATE.

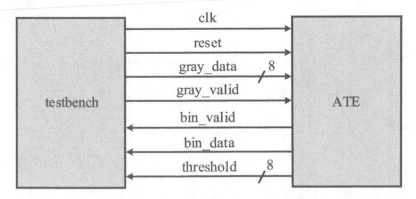

Figure 10.45: System block diagram.

Based on the threshold, the data, bin_data, of binary image is determined by the pixel data, gray_data[7 : 0], of grayscale image as

$$\text{bin\_data} = \begin{cases} 0, & \text{gray\_data} < \text{threshold} \\ 1, & \text{gray\_data} \geq \text{threshold} \end{cases} . \tag{10.4}$$

The system block diagram is shown in Figure 10.45
The I/O interface is presented in Table 10.1.

Table 10.1: I/O interface.

Signal name	I/O	Description
clk	I	System clock.
reset	I	Active-high reset signal.
gray_valid	I	Indicate the validation of gray_data[7 : 0]. The number of valid data is 64.
gray_data[7 : 0]	I	Gray data for ATE. Valid when gray_valid is true.
bin_valid	O	Indicate the validation of bin_data and threshold[7 : 0].
bin_data	O	Binary data of the binary image.
threshold[7 : 0]	O	Threshold data.

The interface timing diagram is displayed in Figure 10.46. There are 64 grayscale pixel data, d[i], $i = 0, 1, ..., 63$, and 64 binary data, b[i], $i = 0, 1, ..., 63$. Along with binary data, the threshold is valid for 64 cycles.

Since the threshold can be determined only after 64 pixel data have been received, 64 pixel data must be stored into a FIFO to decide the binary data. The streamline FIFO does not need flow control. Read access of 64 pixel data from FIFO follows write access of 64 pixel data, and hence, only one pointer, wrrd_ptr, is required and it is shared for both read and write accesses. The FIFO is implemented below, where the macro, CLOG2, is defined in Chapter 3.

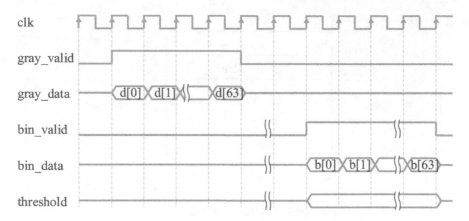

Figure 10.46: Interface timing diagram.

```
1// FIFO with one pointer
2parameter DEPTH=64; parameter BITS=8;
3parameter DEPTH_BITS=`CLOG2(DEPTH);
4reg [DEPTH_BITS-1:0] wrrd_ptr;
5reg [BITS-1:0] fifo_rdata;
6reg [BITS-1:0] fifo_mem[0:DEPTH-1];
7reg gray_valid_r;
8wire rd_stb;
9// FIFO write & read pointer
10always @(posedge clk or negedge rst_n)
11  if(!rst_n)
12    wrrd_ptr <=0;
13  else if(gray_valid|bin_valid)
14    wrrd_ptr <=wrrd_ptr+1'b1;
15assign bin_valid=~gray_valid&(rd_stb|~(wrrd_ptr==0));
16assign rd_stb=~gray_valid&gray_valid_r;
17always @(posedge clk or negedge rst_n)
18  if(!rst_n) gray_valid_r <=0;
19  else gray_valid_r <=gray_valid;
20// FIFO write port and read port
21// FIFO write operation
22always @(posedge clk)
23  if(gray_valid) fifo_mem[wrrd_ptr] <=gray_data;
24// FIFO read operation
25always @(*)
26  fifo_rdata=fifo_mem[wrrd_ptr];
```

The ATE algorithm is implemented below. Notably, the fraction part of threshold is unconditionally truncated. The outputs, bin_valid, bin_data, and threshold are combinational outputs. A pipeline stage can be inserted if registered outputs are needed.

```verilog
1// ATE algorithm
2reg [BITS-1:0] max, min;
3wire [BITS:0] sum;
4wire [BITS-1:0] threshold;
5reg bin_data;
6// Maximum pixel
7always @(posedge clk)
8   if(gray_valid&&wrrd_ptr==0)
9     max<=gray_data;
10   else if(gray_valid&&(gray_data>max))
11     max<=gray_data;
12// Minimum pixel
13always @(posedge clk)
14   if(gray_valid&&wrrd_ptr==0)
15     min<=gray_data;
16   else if(gray_valid&&(gray_data<min))
17     min<=gray_data;
18// Threshold value
19assign sum=max+min;
20assign threshold=sum>>1;
21// Binary data
22always @(*)
23   if(fifo_rdata<threshold) bin_data=1'b0;
24   else bin_data=1'b1;
```

The synthesis script is written below.

```
### Create Clock ###
set cycle 10
create_clock -period $cycle [get_ports clk]
set_ideal_network          [get_ports clk]
set_dont_touch_network     [get_ports clk]
set_drive            0      [get_ports clk]
set_clock_uncertainty 1     [get_ports clk]
set_clock_latency     0     [get_ports clk]
set_fix_hold               [get_ports clk]
### Design Environment ###
set_input_delay -clock [get_clocks ] -max 4 \
   [remove_from_collection [all_inputs] [get_clocks ]]
set_input_delay -clock [get_clocks ] -min 2 \
   [remove_from_collection [all_inputs] [get_clocks ]]
```

```
set_output_delay  −clock [get_clocks  ]  −max 4 \
   [all_outputs]
set_output_delay  −clock [get_clocks  ]  −min 2 \
   [all_outputs]
set_load [load_of "slow/INVX1/A"] [all_outputs]
set_driving_cell  −library slow  −lib_cell INVX1 \
   −pin {Y} \
   [remove_from_collection [all_inputs] [get_clocks  ]]
set_operating_conditions  −min_library fast \
   −min fast  −max_library slow  −max slow
set_wire_load_model  −name tsmc18_wl10  −library slow
### Compile Design ###
compile  −map_effort medium
```

10.6 FURTHER READING

* Donald E. Thomas and Philip R. Moorby, *The Verilog hardware description language*, 5th Ed., Kluwer Academic Publishers, 2002.
* John F. Wakerly, *Digital design: principles and practices*, 5th Ed., Prentice Hall, 2018.
* M. J. S. Smith, *Application-specific integrated circuits*, Addison-Wesley, 1997.
* Michael D. Ciletti, *Advanced digital design with the Verilog HDL*, 2nd Ed., Prentice Hall, 2010.
* National Chip Implementation Center, *Lecture notes: cell-based digital integrated-circuit design and implementation*, 2015.
* Samir Palnitkar, *Verilog HDL: a guide to digital design and synthesis, 2nd Ed.*, Pearson, 2011.
* Stephen Brown and Zvonko Vranesic, *Fundamentals of digital logic with Verilog design*, McGraw-Hill, 2002.
* Vaibbhav Taraate, *Digital logic design using Verilog: coding and RTL synthesis*, Springer, 2016.
* Zainalabedin Navabi, *Verilog digital system design: RT level synthesis, testbench, and verification*, McGraw-Hill, 2005.

PROBLEMS

1. Identify design objects for the circuit in Figure 10.47.

  a. Make a list of all the ports in the design.
  b. Make a list of all the cells that have the letter "U" in their names.
  c. Make a list of all the nets ending with "CLK".
  d. Make a list of all the "Q" pins in the design.
  e. Make a list of all the references.

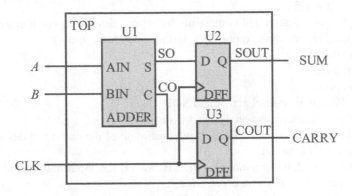

Figure 10.47: A sample circuit.

2. Synthesize the following modules.

  a. Specify your constraint file with the maximum delay from all input to all output of 5 ns. The input delay constraint is 1 ns and the output delay constraint is 1.5 ns.
  b. Report all timing paths to the output port.
  c. Report all timing paths through the module decode_3_8/u0.

```
1 module decode_3_8(E, X, Y);
2 output [7:0] Y;
3 input    E;
4 input [2:0] X;
5 wire E1, G1, G2;
6 not u0(E1, X[2]);
7 and u1(G1, E, X[2]);
8 and u2(G2, E, E1);
9 decoder_2_4 u0(G1, X[1:0], Y[7:4]);
10 decoder_2_4 u1(G2, X[1:0], Y[3:0]);
11 endmodule
12 module decoder_2_4(Y, E , X);
13 output [3:0] Y;
14 input E;
```

```
15 input [1:0] X;
16 assign Y=E?1'b1<<X:4'h0;
17 endmodule
```

3. Synthesize the module, fir2, in Section 7.3.3 using the following steps.

   a. Specify your constraint file with a clock frequency of 100 MHz and clock uncertainty of 0.3 ns. The input delay constraint is 1 ns and the output delay constraint is 1.5 ns.
   b. Analyze your design and constraints by report_design, report_hierarchy, report_port, report_clock, report_net_fanout, and check_timing.
   c. Report timing.
   d. Report area.
   e. Report power.
   f. Write Verilog gate-level netlist and SDF.
   g. Run the dynamic timing analysis (pre-sim).
   h. Use the VCD file to get a better power estimate of the gate-level design than that of the RTL model.

4. Repeat Problem 3 for the module, fir2. However, the input and output delays should reference the negative clock edge.

5. Repeat Problem 3 for the module, fir2. However, set the timing exception of false path to those from the input coefficients of the FIR filter, h_0, h_1, h_2, and h_3, because they are constants and do not change during the operation.

6. Repeat Problem 3 for the module, fir2, but in this case the clock signal, clk, is generated by the following clock generator, clk_gen. Suppose that the clock frequencies of clk0, clk1, clk2, clk3 are 100, 200, 300, and 400 MHz, respectively.

   a. Integrate modules, fir2 and clk_gen, into a module named chip.
   b. Modify your script file to synthesize chip.
   c. Run pre-sim to confirm that your design can operate at all clocks without any timing violations.

```
1 module clk_gen(clk0, clk1, clk2, clk3, sel, clk);
2 output clk;
3 input clk0, clk1, clk2, clk3;
4 input [1:0] sel;
5 always @(*)
6    case(sel)
7    2'b00:clk=clk0;
8    2'b01:clk=clk1;
9    2'b10:clk=clk2;
10   2'b11:clk=clk3;
11   default:clk=clk0;
12   endcase
13 endmodule
```

7. Repeat Problem 3 for the module, fir2. However, the clock signal, clk, is generated by the following clock generator, clk_gen1. The clock, clk1, is a divide-by-2 generated clock from clk. Suppose that the clock frequency of clk0 is 100 MHz.

   a. Integrate modules, fir2 and clk_gen1, into a module named chip.
   b. Modify your script file to synthesize chip.
   c. Run pre-sim to confirm that your design can operate under $sel = 0, 1$ without any timing violations.

```
1 module clk_gen1(clk0, sel, clk, rst_n);
2 output clk;
3 input clk0;
4 input sel;
5 input rst_n;
6 reg clk1;
7 always @(posedge clk0 or negedge rst_n)
8   if(!rst_n) clk1 <=1'b0;
9   else clk1 <=~clk1;
10 always @(*)
11   case(sel)
12   1'b0:clk=clk0;
13   1'b1:clk=clk1;
14   default:clk=clk0;
15   endcase
16 endmodule
```

8. Plot the timing diagrams of the circuits with and without clock gating in Figure 10.34. Verify the glitch-free clock gating in Figure 10.34(b).

9. Suppose a clocked synchronous design uses registers with a setup time of 1.2 ns and a clock-to-Q delay of 0.6 ns. The clock has an uncertainty of 0.3 ns. Three register-to-register paths in the combinational circuits have propagation delays of 2.6 ns, 1.9 ns, and 3.3 ns.

   a. What is the maximum clock frequency at which the datapath can be operated?
   b. If the path with a delay of 3.3 ns is optimized so that its delay is reduced to 2.3 ns, what is the maximum clock frequency for the optimized datapath?

10. Suppose a clocked synchronous design in Figure 10.48, in which registers have a setup time of 200 ps and a clock-to-Q delay of 100 ps, has a timing constraint in which the clock frequency is 800 MHz. The propagation delays through combinational elements in the datapath and control path are displayed in the figure. The control path uses a Mealy FSM.

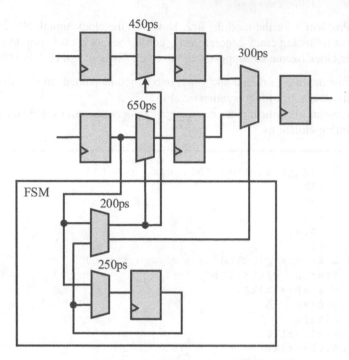

Figure 10.48: A sample circuit.

a. Identify the critical path in the system.
b. Are timing constraints for the clock frequency met?
c. If the FSM were changed to be a Moore FSM, what would the achievable maximum clock frequency be? Could the critical path change? Could the constraints be met?

A Basic Logic Gates and User Defined Primitives

CMOS logic gates lie at the heart of modern digital designs. This appendix presents the transistor-level designs of basic logic gates. In addition to built-in gate-level primitives, we can use UDPs to augment the set of predefined primitives.

A.1 BASIC LOGIC GATES

A well-structured logic circuit must be restoring, so that degraded input levels will result in restored output levels. To achieve this, the voltage on the output must be driven by a supply voltage, i.e., positive supply (V_{DD}) or ground (GND), not by one of the inputs. A static CMOS gate circuit realizes a logic function $f(\cdot)$ while generating a restoring output that is compatible with its input as shown in Figure A.1. When function $f(\cdot)$ is true, a PMOS network connects output terminal Y to the V_{DD}. When function $f(\cdot)$ is false, an NMOS switch network connects output terminal Y to the GND. It is important that the functions realized by the PMOS network and the NMOS network are complements, so that a short circuit from V_{DD} to GND can be avoided. A short circuit results in a large amount of current, which can cause permanent damage to the circuit.

The most famous IC digital logic family is the complementary metal-oxide semiconductor or CMOS. The digital logic family is characterized by fanin, fanout, propagation delay, power dissipation, and noise margin.

Fanin is the number of inputs available in a gate. Fanout specifies the number of standard loads that the output of a gate can drive without impairing or overloading its normal operation. A standard load is usually defined as the amount of current needed by an input of another similar gate. The fanout depends on the amount of electric current that a gate can source or sink when driving other gates.

The maximum fanout of a logic gate measures its load driving capability. The output of one logic gate is connected to the inputs of other logic gates. A logic gate provides a limited amount of output current, whereas the inputs of logic gates it drives require a certain amount of input current for normal operation. The maximum fanout of a logic gate is therefore the maximum number of inputs of other logic gates that can be connected to the output of it. For example, we assume that the manufacture's data sheet specifies a typical input capacitance, C_{in} of 3 pF. Moreover, if the AND gate has a maximum propagation delay of 4.0 ns measured with a load capacitance C_L of 30 pF. Hence, the maximum fanout of the AND gate is $C_L/C_{in} = 30$ pF/3 pF= 10. In practice, other stray capacitance between the output of a gate and inputs of other gates, such as the wire load, would lower the maximum fanout.

Propagation delay is the average transition delay time for a signal to propagate from input of a logic gate to its output. For example, if the input of an inverter

DOI: 10.1201/9781003187196-A

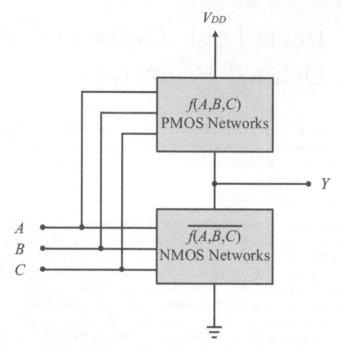

Figure A.1: CMOS gate circuit.

transitions from logic 0 to 1, its output will transition from logic 1 to 0 after the propagation delay due to the load of the inverter.

Power dissipation is the power consumed by the gate that must be available from the power supply. There are two main kinds of power consumption: dynamic and static. The static power contains the leakage power. The dynamic power is consumed due to signal transitions, including the dynamic switching power and transient short-circuit power.

Spurious electrical signals can induce undesirable voltages on the connecting wires due to the inductance between logic gates. These unwanted signals are re-ferred to as noise. Noise margin is the maximum external noise added to an input of a logic gate that does not cause an undesirable change in its output.

We briefly introduce several CMOS logic gates here. To understand their oper-ations, we can know that 1) the NMOS conducts when its gate-to-source voltage is positive (and larger than its threshold voltage), 2) the PMOS conducts when its gate-to-source voltage is negative (and smaller than its threshold voltage), 3) either NMOS or PMOS is turned off if its gate-to-source voltage is zero.

- Inverter
  The basic CMOS logic gate is an inverter or NOT gate, which consists of one PMOS transistor and one NMOS transistor. When the input is low, both gates of PMOS and NMOS are 0 V. The gate-to-source voltages of NMOS,

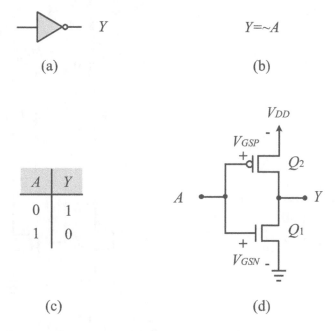

$$A \quad \longrightarrow \hspace{-0.3em} \triangleright\hspace{-0.3em}\circ \hspace{-0.3em}- \quad Y \hspace{5em} Y{=}{\sim}A$$

(a)   (b)

A	Y
0	1
1	0

(c)   (d)

Figure A.2: NOT gate: (a) symbol, (b) description in Verilog, (c) truth table, and (d) CMOS schematics.

V_{GSN}, and PMOS, V_{GSP}, are 0 V and $-V_{DD}$ V, respectively. Hence, NMOS turns off while PMOS turns on. Under this situation, the output voltage becomes V_{DD} V. When the input is high, the reverse condition occurs, and the output voltages is 0 V. The net result is the logical NOT function.

- Buffer gate
  The buffer is constructed using two back-to-back inverters. Its Boolean equation is the inverse of a NOT gate. The net result is the logical buffer function. A buffer can decrease the propagation delay of a logic gate when the gate is driving a large capacitive load.
- NAND gate
  The NAND gate composes of two NMOS transistors connected in series between GND and the drain-output, and ensures that the drain-output is only driven low (logical 0) when both gate inputs, A and B, are high (logical 1). The complementary parallel-connection of the two PMOS transistors between V_{DD} and drain-output ensures that the drain-output is driven high (logical 1) when one or both gate inputs are low (logical 0). The net result is the logical NAND function.
- AND gate
  The AND gate is constructed using a NAND gate and a NOT gate in series. Its Boolean equation is the inverse of a NAND gate.
- NOR gate

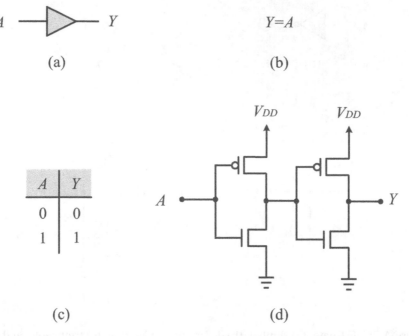

Figure A.3: Buffer gate: (a) symbol, (b) description in Verilog, (c) truth table, and (d) CMOS schematics.

The NOR gate composes of parallel-connection of the two NMOS transistors between GND and the drain-output ensures that the drain-output is only driven low (logical 0) when either gate inputs, A and B, is high (logical 1). The complementary series-connection of the two PMOS transistors between V_{DD} and drain-output means that the drain-output is driven high (logical 1) when both gate inputs are low (logical 0). The net result is the logical NOR function.

- OR gate
  The OR gate is constructed using a NOR gate and a NOT gate in series. Its Boolean equation is the inverse of a NOR gate.
- Multiplexer gate
  The multiplexer (mux) gate is a selector and constructed using an OR gate, two AND gates, and a NOT gate. When S is logical 1, $Y = B$; and when S is logical 0, $Y = A$.
- XOR gate
  The XOR gate composes of parallel-connection of the two NMOS transistors in series between GND and the drain-output, and ensures that the drain-output is only driven low (logical 0) when the gate inputs, A and B, are both high (logical 1) or they are both low (logical 0). The PMOS transistors are connected in a complementary fashion to those of NMOS transistors. The net result is the logical XOR function.

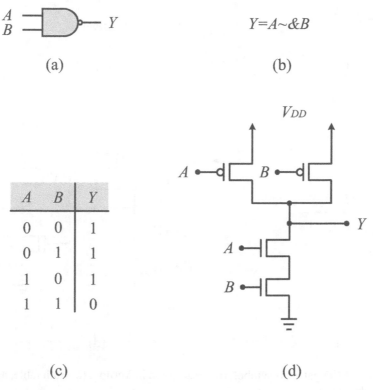

$$Y=A\sim\&B$$

(a)   (b)

A	B	Y
0	0	1
0	1	1
1	0	1
1	1	0

(c)   (d)

Figure A.4: NAND gate: (a) symbol, (b) description in Verilog, (c) truth table, and (d) CMOS schematics.

- XNOR gate
  The XNOR gate composes of parallel-connection of the two NMOS transistors in series between GND and the drain-output, and ensures that the drain-output is only driven low (logical 0) when the gate inputs, A and B, have reverse logical values. The PMOS transistors are connected in a complementary fashion to those of NMOS transistors. The net result is the logical XNOR function.
- Transmission gate
  Transmission gate can enable the bidirectional signal transmission. The CMOS transmission gate works like a voltage-controlled switch. It consists of one NMOS and one PMOS transistors with common source and drain connections. The gates of the two transistors are controlled by E and $\overline{E}$, respectively. The idea is that both transistors are non-conducting when $E = 1$. Hence, the output Y is in the high-impedance state. On the contrary, both transistors are conducting when $E = 0$. In this situation, the output Y is directly connected to input A. The transmission gate is not a static CMOS gate because its output is not a restored logic function of its input.

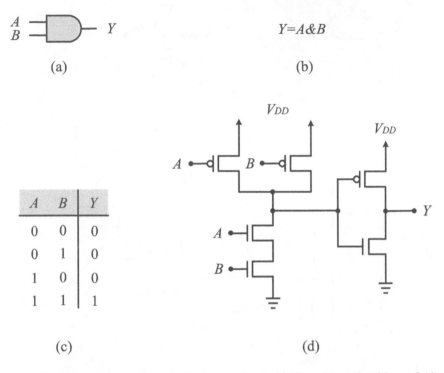

Figure A.5: AND gate: (a) symbol, (b) description in Verilog, (c) truth table, and (d) CMOS schematics.

A question may arise, "why are there two parallel paths through NMOS and PMOS concurrently?" First, it is obvious that parallel paths through NMOS and PMOS can provide a larger current for drawing or sinking the output load of a transmission gate.

Second, as shown in Figure A.12(a), when $E = 0$, $A = 1$, and $Y = 0$, the charge passes through NMOS so Y changes from 0 V to V_{DD} V. It must be emphasized that the MOS, either NMOS or PMOS, used in a transmission gate is symmetric that its source and drain terminals are interchangeable. During this occasion, the source and drain terminals of NMOS are on the right-hand-side and left-hand-side, respectively. The gate-to-source voltage V_{GSN} gradually decreases as well. However, the NMOS must conduct when $V_{GSN} \geq V_{TN}$, where $V_{TN} > 0$ denotes the threshold voltage of NMOS. There-fore, if the transmission gate pulls Y high through the NMOS, Y will be a weak one because $V_{SN} \leq V_{GN} - V_{TN} = V_{DD} - V_{TN}$, which is less than V_{DD}, where V_{SN} and V_{GN} are the source voltage and gate voltage of NMOS.

As shown in Figure A.12(b), if the charge passes through PMOS to pull Y high when $E = 0$, $A = 1$, and $Y = 0$. The source and drain terminals of PMOS are on the left-hand-side and right-hand-side, respectively. The

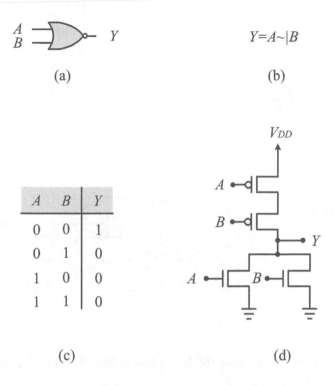

$$Y = A \sim | B$$

(a)   (b)

A	B	Y
0	0	1
0	1	0
1	0	0
1	1	0

(c)   (d)

Figure A.6: NOR gate: (a) symbol, (b) description in Verilog, (c) truth table, and (d) CMOS schematics.

PMOS must conduct when $V_{GSP} \leq V_{TP}$, where $V_{TP} < 0$ denotes the threshold voltage of PMOS. Since $V_{GSP} = 0 - V_{DD} = -V_{DD} \leq V_{TP}$ is a constant, so that PMOS always conducts and the charge will pass through it until Y reaches V_{DD}, which is a strong one.

Similarly, as shown in Figure A.13(a), when $E = 0$, $A = 0$, and $Y = 1$, the charge passes through NMOS so Y changes from V_{DD} V to 0 V. During this occasion, the source and drain terminals of NMOS are on the left-hand-side and right-hand-side, respectively. The gate-to-source voltage $V_{GSN} = V_{DD}$ is a constant. Consequently the NMOS will always conduct and the current flows through it until $V_Y = 0$ V, which yields a strong zero. By contrast, as shown in Figure A.13(b), if the charge passes through PMOS to pull Y low when $E = 0$, $A = 0$, and $Y = 1$. The source and drain terminals of PMOS are on the right-hand-side and left-hand-side, respectively. The PMOS must conduct until its gate-to-source voltage $V_{GSP} \leq V_{TP}$. Therefore, Y will be a weak zero because $V_{SP} \geq V_{GP} - V_{TP} = -V_{TP} > 0$, which is higher than 0 V, where V_{SP} and V_{GP} are the source voltage and gate voltage of PMOS.

In summary, in a transmission gate, the PMOS is good to pass logic 1 and NMOS is good to pass logic 0. To provide both strong logic 1 and logic 0, PMOS and NMOS are connected in parallel.

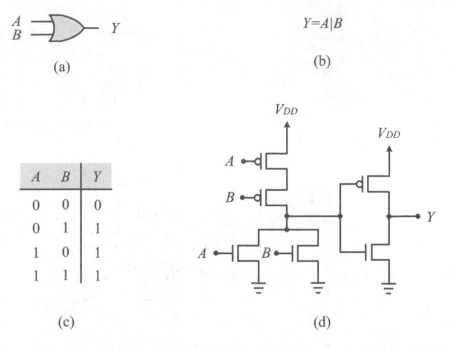

Figure A.7: OR gate: (a) symbol, (b) description in Verilog, (c) truth table, and (d) CMOS schematics.

- Tristate buffer gate
  The tristate buffer is constructed using a buffer and a transmission gate. In computer engineering, a tristate bus is realized using multiple tristate buffers. The tristate buffer is not a static CMOS gate because its output is not a restored logic function of its input. If more than one enable of different sources is asserted simultaneously, the bus conflict happens. For example, when a source wants to drive the bus logic 1 while another wants to drive the bus logic 0, a short circuit may cause static current to flow from the power supply of one gate to the ground of another. The voltage level of the bus will be undetermined and the power dissipation significantly increases. Even worse, the large current may vaporize metal traces and damage the chip. Because of the potential short circuit, tristate buffers should be avoided, particularly for those enable signals with a large clock skew. If there is no choice but to use the tristate buffers, an idle cycle (with all enable signals low) is inserted between the assertion of one enable signal and another.
- D-Type edge-triggered flip-flop

The D-Type edge-triggered flip-flop is constructed using 6 NAND gates, i.e., 3 SR latches.

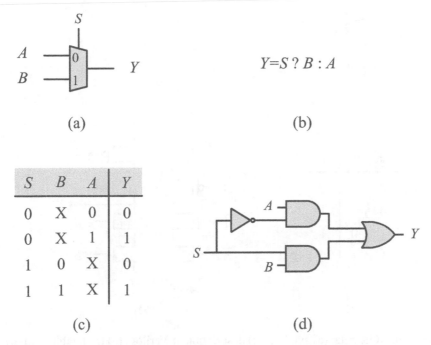

$$Y=S\ ?\ B:A$$

(a)   (b)

S	B	A	Y
0	X	0	0
0	X	1	1
1	0	X	0
1	1	X	1

(c)   (d)

Figure A.8: Multiplexer gate: (a) symbol, (b) description in Verilog, (c) truth table, and (d) schematics.

A.2   USER DEFINED PRIMITIVES

In Verilog structural modeling, you can use built-in gate-level primitives or your own UDPs. UDPs are useful for ASIC library cell design as well as small- and medium-scale chip designs. You can use UDPs to augment the set of predefined primitives. UDPs are self contained and do not instantiate other modules. You can design your own combinational and sequential UDPs. You can instantiate a UDP just like you do for a built-in primitive.

The function of a UDP is described in a truth table. A UDP can have only one output. If the functionality requires more than one output, then additional primitives need to be connected to the output of the UDP, or several UDPs can be used together. UDP can have 1 to 10 inputs. All inputs and outputs must be scalar and unidirectional. The Z logic value is not supported and it will be treated as X. The output port must be listed first in the port list. To model sequential logic, its output can be initialized to a known state at the start of simulation using the initial statement. UDPs are non-synthesizable.

UDP is defined outside of a module. Its output becomes X for any input combination not described in the table. In each row, the inputs are specified first, and then the output follows, as shown below. The inputs and output are separated by colon, ":". In the table, ? represents 0, 1, or X.

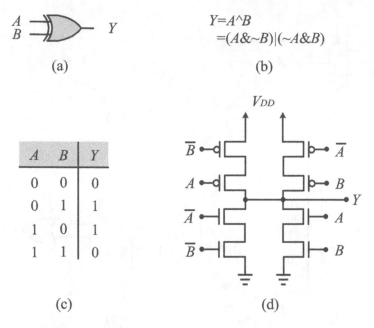

$Y=A^\wedge B$
$=(A\&{\sim}B)|({\sim}A\&B)$

(b)

A	B	Y
0	0	0
0	1	1
1	0	1
1	1	0

(c)   (d)

Figure A.9: XOR gate: (a) symbol, (b) description in Verilog, (c) truth table, and (d) CMOS schematics.

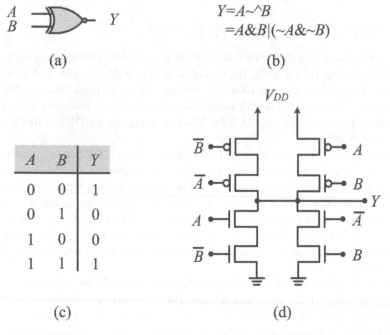

$Y=A{\sim}^\wedge B$
$=A\&B|({\sim}A\&{\sim}B)$

(b)

A	B	Y
0	0	1
0	1	0
1	0	0
1	1	1

(c)   (d)

Figure A.10: XNOR gate: (a) symbol, (b) description in Verilog, (c) truth table, and (d) CMOS schematics.

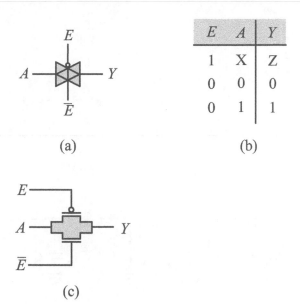

E	A	Y
1	X	Z
0	0	0
0	1	1

(a)   (b)

(c)

Figure A.11: Transmission gate: (a) symbol, (b) truth table, and (c) CMOS schematics.

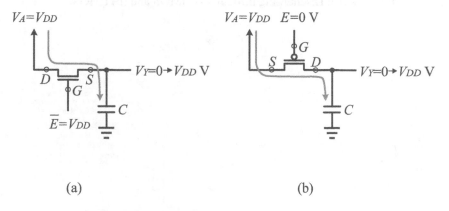

(a)   (b)

Figure A.12: Charging through (a) NMOS and (b) PMOS.

```
1 primitive multiplexer(o, x, y, s);
2 output o;
3 input x, y, s;
4 table
5 // x, y, s : o
6    0  ?  1 : 0;
```

```
 7     1   ?   1  :  1;
 8     ?   0   0  :  0;
 9     ?   1   0  :  1;
10     0   0   x  :  0;
11     1   1   x  :  1;
12 endtable
13 endprimitive
```

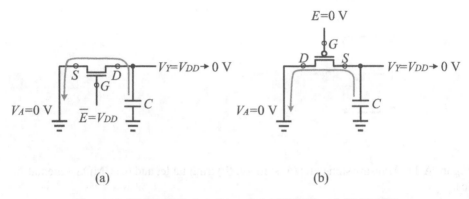

(a)   (b)

Figure A.13: Discharging through (a) NMOS and (b) PMOS.

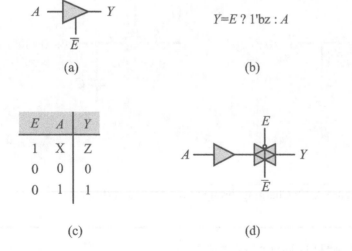

$A \rightarrow Y$ $Y = E ? 1'bz : A$

$\overline{E}$

(a)   (b)

E	A	Y
1	X	Z
0	0	0
0	1	1

(c)   (d)

Figure A.14: Tristate buffer gate: (a) symbol, (b) description in Verilog, (c) truth table, and (d) schematics.

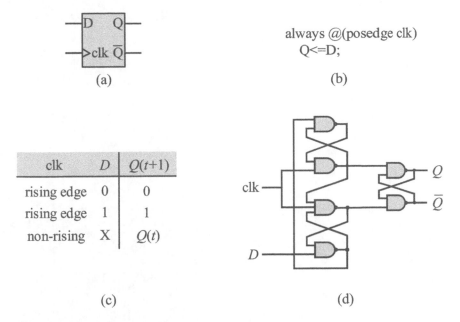

always @(posedge clk)
Q<=D;

(b)

clk	D	Q(t+1)
rising edge	0	0
rising edge	1	1
non-rising	X	Q(t)

(c)   (d)

Figure A.15: D-Type edge-triggered flip-flop gate: (a) symbol, (b) description in Verilog, (c) function table, and (d) schematics.

A.3   FURTHER READING

- Donald E. Thomas and Philip R. Moorby, *The Verilog hardware description language*, 5th Ed., Kluwer Academic Publishers, 2002.
- John F. Wakerly, *Digital design: principles and practices*, 5th Ed., Prentice Hall, 2018.
- John Michael Williams, *Digital VLSI design with Verilog: a textbook from Silicon Valley Polytechnic Institute*, 2nd Ed., Springer, 2014.
- M. Morris Mano and Michael D. Ciletti, *Digital design*, 4th Ed., Prentice Hall, 2006.
- M. J. S. Smith, *Application-specific integrated circuits*, Addison-Wesley, 1997.
- Stephen Brown and Zvonko Vranesic, *Fundamentals of digital logic with Verilog design*, McGraw-Hill, 2002.

B Non-Synthesizable Constructs

In addition to those non-synthesizable codes described in the main text, extra non-synthesizable ones are given in this appendix.

B.1 NON-SYNTHESIZABLE VERILOG STATEMENTS

- delay
- initial
- forever

  A forever loop executes a statement (or block of statements) until the simulation ends. The following code segment describes generation of a clock with period of 20 time units.

```
1 reg clk;
2 initial begin
3   clk=0;
4   forever begin
5     #10 clk=1;
6     #10 clk=0;
7   end
8 end
```

- while

  A while loop executes a statement (or block of statements) as long as its expression is true. Its syntax is shown below.

```
1 while(expression) begin
2   statements
3 end
```

The following code segment describes the generation of a clock with period of 20 time units.

```
1 reg clk;
2 initial begin
3   clk=0;
4   while(1) begin
```

DOI: 10.1201/9781003187196-B

```
5     #10 clk=1;
6     #10 clk=0;
7   end
8 end
```

- repeat

  A repeat loop executes a statement (or block of statements) a fixed number
  of times. Its syntax is shown below. If the iteration_number is a constant,
  it can be synthesized. However, it is recommended to use repeat loop in
  testbench only.

```
1 repeat(iteration_number) begin
2   statements
3 end
```

- wait

  In the following example, after the assertion, and then, deassertion of the
  active-low reset signal, reset_n, normal function follows.

```
1 initial begin
2   wait(!reset_n); // Wait for the assertion of
3                   // active-low reset_n
4   wait(reset_n);  // Wait for the deassertion of
5                   // reset_n
6   // Normal function here
7 end
```

- fork and join

  Originally, descriptions inside an initial block are processed sequentially.
  However, descriptions inside fork-join pair in an initial block are executed
  in parallel. In the following example, a is assigned 1 at the time unit 2, and
  b is assigned 2 at the time unit 4, instead of 6.

```
1 initial
2 fork
3   #2 a=1;
4   #4 b=2;
5 join
```

- event

  You can define your own events and write Verilog codes in an event-driven
  style. A named event is a data type that you can then trigger in a procedural

block to cause an action. It must be declared before you can reference it. The -> operator is the trigger of the named event. The syntax of the named event is displayed below.

```
1 always @(event_name) begin
2   statements
3 end
```

An example is demonstrated below.

```
1 event receive_data;
2 event check_data_format;
3 always @(posedge clk)
4 begin
5   // receive_data and check_data_format events are
6   // generated when last_data_packet is true.
7   // Descriptions inside are executed in parallel.
8   if(last_data_packet)
9   begin
10     ->receive_data;
11     ->check_data_format;
12   end
13 end
14 always @(receive_data)
15 begin
16   // Statements to receive data
17 end
18 always @(check_data_format)
19 begin
20   // Statements to check data format
21 end
```

- force and release
  If some condition rarely happens, you can force signal values by the force statement. The force statement is handy in functional simulations. In the following example, the first line forces bit 0 of data in the hierarchical instance name, A0.B0, to 1'b1. Then, after 200 time units, the forced value of bit 0 is released, so its original data is recovered.

```
1 force A0.B0.data[0]=1'b1;
2 #200 release A0.B0.data[0];
```

- Verilog primitives: nmos, pmos, etc.
- pullup and pulldown

B.2   FURTHER READING

- Michael D. Ciletti, *Advanced digital design with the Verilog HDL*, 2nd Ed., Prentice Hall, 2010.
- Ronald W. Mehler, *Digital integrated circuit design using Verilog and Systemverilog*, Elsevier, 2014.
- Vaibbhav Taraate, *Digital logic design using Verilog: coding and RTL synthesis*, Springer, 2016.

C Advanced Net Data Types

This appendix presents three advanced net data types, including tri, wand, and wor. If multiple sources drive the same net, it must be declared as either tri, wand, or wor net type.

C.1 EXAMPLES

A net can physically have three states: 0, 1, and Z (high impedance). The high-impedance state is symbolized by Z in Verilog. The high-impedance state is used to model open circuit, which means that the net connected to an output of a logic gate with high-impedance state appears to be disconnected, and inputs of other logic gates connected to the high-impedance net are not affected by it.

The tri data type is used when all variables that drive the tri net must have a value of high-impedance, Z, except one, which must be ensured by the designer, as shown below.

```
1 // Only one driver can drive the tri net
2 module test_tri(tri_out, condition)
3   output tri_out;
4   input [1:0] condition;
5   reg a, b, c;
6   tri tri_out;
7   assign tri_out=a;
8   assign tri_out=b;
9   assign tri_out=c;
10  always @(condition)
11  begin
12    a=1'bz; b=1'bz; c=1'bz; // Default assignments
13    case (condition)
14      2'b00:a=1'b1;
15      2'b01:b=1'b1;
16      2'b10:c=1'b1;
17    endcase
18  end
19 endmodule
```

When condition is 2'b00, *a*, *b*, and *c* are 1, Z, and Z, respectively. That is, only *a* drives tri_out, and *b* and *c* are high impedance (Z). When conditions are 2'b01, 2'b10, and 2'b11, only *b*, *c*, and none drive tri_out, respectively. The tristate wire, tri, with states (0, 1, Z) is implemented using a tristate buffer.

When multiple wires drive the same net, an unknown X happens. As shown below, wires *a* and *b* drive the same wire, *w*.

DOI: 10.1201/9781003187196-C

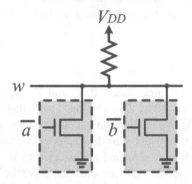

Figure C.1: Use case of wand net.

Figure C.2: Open-drain drivers.

```
1 wire w;
2 assign w=a;
3 assign w=b; // Error exists
```

The conflict can be resolved by the wand or wor declarations depending on the drive strengths of drivers. The wand net is used in the following situation.

```
1 wand w;
2 assign w=a;
3 assign w=b;
```

Wires a and b are wired as an AND logic exists virtually to generate wire-and w depending on the drive strengths of a and b, as shown in Figure C.1.

The wand net is also obtained by using the open-drain drivers, as shown in Figure C.2. The wire w is logic 1 by connecting it to V_{DD} only when both $\overline{a}$ and $\overline{b}$ are logic 0. Otherwise, w is logic 0. That is, the net result is the logic $w = \overline{\overline{a}\,\overline{b}} = ab$.

The wor net is used in the following situation.

```
1 wor w;
2 assign w=a;
3 assign w=b;
```

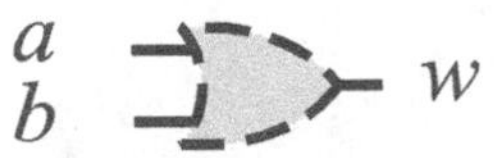

Figure C.3: Use case of wor net.

Inputs a and b are wired as an OR logic exists virtually to generate wire-or w depending on the drive strengths of a and b, as shown in Figure C.3.

C.2   FURTHER READING

- John Michael Williams, *Digital VLSI design with Verilog: a textbook from Silicon Valley Polytechnic Institute*, 2nd Ed., Springer, 2014.
- Samir Palnitkar, *Verilog HDL: a guide to digital design and synthesis*, 2nd Ed., Pearson, 2011.

D Signed Multipliers

This appendix is dedicated to the synthesis of unsigned and signed multipliers. The multiplier is one of the most important arithmetic units in DSP systems. Therefore, the systolic array structures of unsigned and signed multipliers are presented.

D.1 SYNTHESIS OF SIGNED MULTIPLIERS

Multiplication of unsigned numbers by hand is the same as that in hardware. When n-bit number times n-bit number, the result is $2n$ bits. There exists a rule for unsigned number multiplication: when number of bits for addition is not enough, just pad (sign bit) 0, as shown in Figure D.1.

Multiplication of unsigned numbers (4×4 multiplier) in hardware uses the systolic array, as shown in Figure D.2, where $PS_{i,k}$ denotes the k-th bit of the partial sum, PS_i, $i = 0, 1$, and $k = 0, 1, 2, 3$. Notably, $PS_{i,0}$ is P_{i+1}. The systolic array can be simply pipelined. For example, you can insert 2-stage pipeline using registers (at the dashed lines) to the architecture of the unsigned number multiplication. Attentions should be paid to P_0 and P_1 that they also need a 2-stage pipelines, and P_2 needs an 1-stage pipeline. After pipelining, the circuit is much like a systolic array, where clock resembles the heartbeat.

Figure D.3 illustrates two methods for the multiplication of signed numbers (5×5 multiplication) by hand. Method 1 just sign extends to the maximum bit number you need. By contrast, method 2 uses the partial product and only sign extends when required. In this example, multiplicand is negative and multiplier is positive. Comparing these two methods, method 2 needs only 4 5-bit adders, which is smaller than method 1. However, the sign extension of method 2 is irregular and not suitable for hardware implementation.

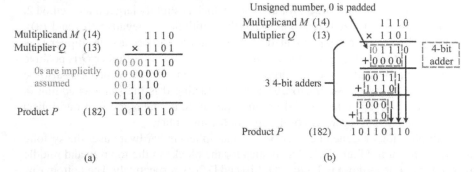

(a)   (b)

Figure D.1: Unsigned number multiplication: (a) by hand (b) in hardware.

DOI: 10.1201/9781003187196-D

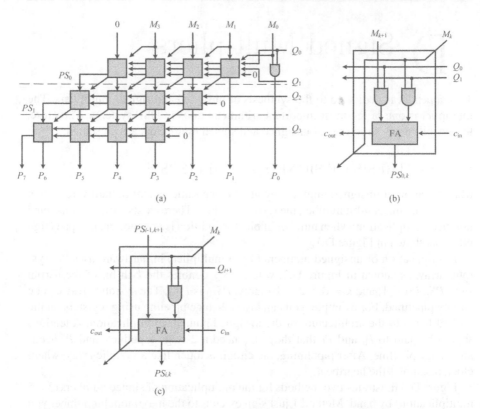

Figure D.2: Circuits of unsigned number multiplication: (a) structure of the circuit, (b) schematics for the blocks in the top row, and (c) schematics for the blocks in remaining rows.

Figure D.4 illustrates method 3 for a regular 5×5 signed number multiplier using the partial product, which is suitable for hardware implementation. As displayed, method 3 requires 4 6-bit adders for all cases, which is slightly larger than method 2.

It must be emphasized here that when the multiplier is negative ((c) and (d)), the last adder should be implemented using the subtractor, because multiplier Q is negative and its sign bit represents a value of -2^{n-1}. When multiplier Q is positive ((a) and (b)), the partial product produced by its sign bit is 0, which can also be implemented using the subtractor, because subtracting 0 is the same as adding 0. Hence, from above, the last partial product (produced by the sign bit of multiplier) should be subtracted regardless of the sign of the multiplier.

Multiplication of signed numbers (5×5 multiplier) in hardware uses the systolic array, as shown in Figure D.5. Schematics for the blocks in the top row and middle row are the same as those in Figures D.2(b) and D.2(c), respectively. The bottom row implements the subtractor for the last partial product by inverting every bits of the last partial product (using the NAND gate) and connecting the carry in of the adder to logic 1.

[Method 1] Sign extend to the bit number you need.

[Method 2] Partial products and partial sums are sign-extended. When number of bits for addition is not enough, just sign extend it.

Multiplicand M (-14)   1 0 0 1 0
Multiplier Q (13)   × 0 1 1 0 1
                                   1 1 1 1 1 1 0 0 1 0
                                   0 0 0 0 0 0 0 0 0
                                   1 1 1 1 0 0 1 0
                                   1 1 1 0 0 1 0
                                 + 0 0 0 0 0 0
Product P (-182)   1 1 0 1 0 0 1 0 1 0

Multiplicand M (-14)   1 0 0 1 0
Multiplier Q (13)   × 0 1 1 0 1

4 5-bit adders

          1 1 0 0 1 0   5-bit
        + 0 0 0 0 0   adder
          1 1 1 0 0 1
        + 1 0 0 1 0
          1 0 1 1 1 0
        + 1 0 0 1 0
          1 0 1 0 0 1
        + 0 0 0 0 0

Product P (-182) 1 1 0 1 0 0 1 0 1 0

Problem: sign extension is irregular and not suitable for hardware implemetation.

Figure D.3: Two methods for the signed number multiplication (5×5 multiplication) by hand: (a) sign extending to the maximum bit number you need and (b) sign extending partial products and partial sums. Multiplicand is negative and multiplier is positive.

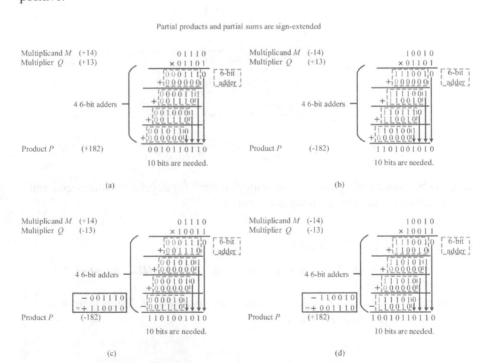

Partial products and partial sums are sign-extended

Multiplicand M (+14)   0 1 1 1 0
Multiplier Q (+13) × 0 1 1 0 1

4 6-bit adders

Product P (+182) 0 0 1 0 1 1 0 1 1 0
10 bits are needed.

(a)

Multiplicand M (-14)   1 0 0 1 0
Multiplier Q (+13) × 0 1 1 0 1

4 6-bit adders

Product P (-182) 1 1 0 1 0 0 1 0 1 0
10 bits are needed.

(b)

Multiplicand M (+14)   0 1 1 1 0
Multiplier Q (-13) × 1 0 0 1 1

4 6-bit adders

          − 0 0 1 1 1 0
          = + 1 1 0 0 1 0
Product P (-182) 1 1 0 1 0 0 1 0 1 0
10 bits are needed.

(c)

Multiplicand M (-14)   1 0 0 1 0
Multiplier Q (-13) × 1 0 0 1 1

4 6-bit adders

          − 1 1 0 0 1 0
          = + 0 0 1 1 1 0
Product P (+182) 1 0 0 1 0 1 1 0 1 1 0
10 bits are needed.

(d)

Figure D.4: Method 3: regular 5×5 signed number multiplier using the partial product for hardware implementation. In this example, there are 4 different cases: (a) positive multiplicand and positive multiplier, (b) negative multiplicand and positive multiplier, (c) positive multiplicand and negative multiplier, and (d) negative multiplicand and negative multiplier.

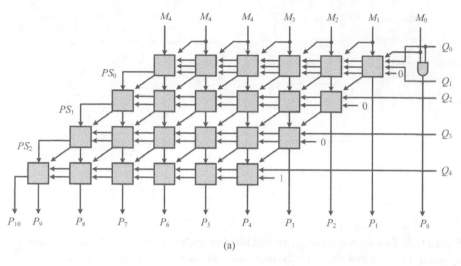

(a)

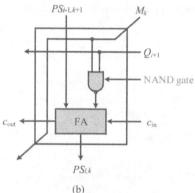

(b)

Figure D.5: Circuits of signed number multiplication: (a) structure of the circuit and (b) schematics for the blocks in the bottom row.

D.2   FURTHER READING

- Joseph Cavanagh, *Computer arithmetic and Verilog HDL fundamentals*, CRC Press, 2010.
- Stephen Brown and Zvonko Vranesic, *Fundamentals of digital logic with Verilog design*, McGraw-Hill, 2002.

E Design Principles and Guidelines

It is essential to conform to the design guidelines using a good coding style to describe the RTL codes for the combinational and sequential logics. These guidelines will improve the performance, reusability, readability, and testability of your design. Therefore, we present design guidelines fulfilled using the good Verilog coding style for synthesizable modules that can ultimately map to physical hardware. The Verilog sample codes throughout this book follow this style, while a different and free style can be used in the testbench.

Legal Verilog codes may contain both good and bad coding styles. Therefore, beyond legal Verilog codes, we present what good Verilog codes are via design principles and guidelines. Based on these principles and guidelines, designers can develop good and maintainable codes. Many design houses adopt their own coding styles to manage the quality of their digital designs. Some EDA vendors also provide style checking tools, called lint tools, that verify whether Verilog codes meet a set of coding rules.

To handle different design versions throughout the design flow, a digital design project is typically managed using some sort of revision management tools, such as the Concurrent Version System (CVS). The revision management tool coordinates the work of team members by maintaining a repository of different code versions. After a change has been confirmed in his/her own copy of the codes, they can independently commit and then integrate the revised codes. Synchronization is achieved by the tool, and old copies are backed up to the repository automatically.

E.1 BASIC PRINCIPLES

We list serval fundamental but essential design principles here.

- **Hardware mindset**: Don't forget you are designing the hardware. A workable digital circuit depends on two essential factors: function and timing. Thinking about the functions of input and output can help bridge the gap between concept and its physical realization. In fact, digital circuits are executed in parallel. On the contrary, computer programs execute sequentially. As Verilog is used to describe the behavioral of hardware, don't treat Verilog as another "software" language, such as C language.
- **Architecture exploration**: There exists tradeoffs between designs that adopt different architectures, such as pipelining or parallelism, which have different performances and require different hardware resources. Consequently, the timing diagram should be designed accordingly. To this, you must understand what your module will be synthesized to, analyze which

DOI: 10.1201/9781003187196-E

resources should be shared or optimized, and determine how to implement a component, for example, using an SRAM or flip-flops as a storage. Experienced designers can even predict the timing paths of various architectures.

- **Architecture design**: Once the system has been specified, it must be divided into manageable subsystems or modules. This can be thought of as a divide-and-conquer process in which a potentially overwhelmingly large and complex overall system is divided into manageable subsystems which can then be designed separately. Before writing your RTL modules, in addition to how to describe them, you must know what kinds of circuits you are defining, such as a combinational or sequential logics. Doing so can let you know which signals are respectively outputs of combinational and sequential logics. Then, using the blocking assignment to describe combinational logics and the non-blocking assignment to describe sequential logics, such as flip-flops. This can be achieved by plotting the architecture of your circuit. Remember that if one cannot clearly determine what circuits are modeled by the Verilog codes, then the CAD tools are unlikely to synthesize a correct circuit that he/she is trying to obtain. Last but not least, remember that designs with regularity and simplicity are beautiful.

- **Timing diagram**: The functionality of designs that can conform to its specification is of paramount importance. However, it is also critical that the required tasks are performed in the right time slot. This can be fulfilled by plotting the timing diagram of the design. After knowing the operation sequence, control signals that govern the operations can be designed using, for example, the finite state machine.

- **Verification plan**: Through the architectural and timing diagrams of your design, the responses of the design will be very predictable. After that, think about how your design will go wrong and try to provide some assertions to check error conditions in your modules. Besides the verification methodology, the verification plan typically consists of a spreadsheet listing all test patterns for each functionality of the system.

- **Synthesis skills**: Synthesis tools are constraint-driven. Therefore, we should know very well how to set correct constraints. Beyond that, we can also learn to gain an effective design by different synthesis commands or synthesis strategies. Modern logic synthesis tools do a great job of optimizing combinational logics, including arithmetic and logic circuitry. However, synthesis tools are still not good at making high-level optimizations, such as pipelining or parallelism. The capability of synthesis tools in terms of resource sharing and logic partition still has some limitations. In the sequel, they should be implicitly described using a good coding style.

- **Circuit analysis**: When we move in accordance with the design flow, the emphasis of the design criteria will shift gradually from performance to timing. The designer should be able to analyze the area, timing, and power of the derived circuit by the synthesis tool. Much can be learned by gaining clearer pictures about the RTL model and its gate-level netlist.

- **Design readability**: During the development of a project, a module may be revised many times. Moreover, a design may be used in different projects and maintained by other engineers. To make it easy, the readability of the module is very helpful. The design functionality should be clear and descriptive. Consistent naming rules must be obeyed for comprehensive designs, including module and signal names, and parameter names. Comments should clarify the purpose of every statements, instead of just duplicating what the code expresses.

E.2 DESIGN GUIDELINES

We separately present design guidelines and coding guidelines below.

First, though a file can consist of more than one module designs (or definitions), it is strongly recommended that a file should contain a module definition and the filename is the same as the module name in it. Doing so makes the management of your designs easier.

The top-level module should contain only instantiation and wiring of sub-blocks. If there exists some glue logics, group them into a module. Therefore, no design or glue logic should be described in the top-level module so that sub-blocks can be synthesized separately and the top-level module only has to link them. A module of clock generator, for example, clk_gen, is dedicated to describe the clock schemes. As such, the complex clock schemes that may generate various derived clock sources through multiplexers or frequency dividers can be easily investigated. Similarly, a module of reset generator, rst_gen, can be used to describe the complex reset schemes as well.

If you are a (fresh) designer, it is strongly recommended that you should plot the architectural diagram of, at least, the datapath unit. Doing so can clearly understand what components are included and where a potential critical path is in a design. In addition to physical timing specification, such as the setup time and hold time constraints of flip-flops, a timing diagram can clearly demonstrate the relation between inputs and outputs, and the sequence of operations of a pipelined RTL design. Therefore, it is also strongly recommended to plot the timing diagram of the design before writing its RTL codes. Doing this can clearly understand the evolution of signals over time so that right things can be performed at the right times. If a performance issue raises, some pipeline stages might need to be adjusted.

There are various ways to describe the behavior model of combinational circuits, including continuous assignment, always block, and function. The function allows designers to write more reusable and maintainable codes. By contrast, there is only one way to write the behavior model of sequential circuits, i.e., always block.

It's a good practice to adopt the port mapping by name, which needs not worry about the actual port positions (that may change in different design versions) in the instantiated modules. Otherwise, functional errors may occur when ports are wrongly connected.

A for loop is "unrolled" and the loop index declared as an integer is dummy and does not represent any hardware components. To make the for loop synthesizable (and unrollable), the loop index must be constant rather than variable. The maximum iteration limit of a for loop for synthesis is 4096. If your design contains a for loop with iteration of 16384, you may separate one big for loop into several smaller for loops.

Combinational loop is not allowed. You may need to declare different signal names for the inputs and inputs of a combinational logic. Otherwise, sequential logics can be adopted to break the timing loop.

It's better to manually optimize the circuits rather than depending too much on the tool. For example, the following two pieces of codes demonstrate the same functionality. However, it's a good practice to explicitly select the operands of a function, sum3, as shown below.

```
1 wire [1:0] sel;
2 wire [3:0] a, b, c;
3 reg a_sel, b_sel, c_sel;
4 wire [1:0] out;
5 always @(sel or a or b or c) begin
6   case(sel[1:0])
7   2'b00: begin
8             a_sel=a[0];
9             b_sel=b[0];
10            c_sel=c[0];
11          end
12  2'b01: begin
13            a_sel=a[1];
14            b_sel=b[1];
15            c_sel=c[1];
16          end
17  2'b10: begin
18            a_sel=a[2];
19            b_sel=b[2];
20            c_sel=c[2];
21          end
22  default: begin
23            a_sel=a[3];
24            b_sel=b[3];
25            c_sel=c[3];
26          end
27  endcase
28 end
29 assign out=sum3(a_sel,b_sel,c_sel);
```

Rather, the following piece of codes is optimized by the synthesis tool to derive a combinational logic, sum3, with its operands selected by the sel signal. Therefore, the two pieces of codes may infer the same logic. Even so, at the first glance, sum3 seems to be called (or instantiated) 4 times.

```verilog
1 // Optimization depends on the tool
2 wire [1:0] sel;
3 wire [3:0] a, b, c;
4 reg [1:0] out;
5 always @(sel or a or b or c) begin
6   case(sel[1:0])
7   2'b00: out=sum3(a[0],b[0],c[0]);
8   2'b01: out=sum3(a[1],b[1],c[1]);
9   2'b10: out=sum3(a[2],b[2],c[2]);
10  default: out=sum3(a[3],b[3],c[3]);
11  endcase
12 end
```

Completely specify the sensitivity list of a combinational logic to avoid mismatches between RTL and gate-level netlists. Also, to prevent latches, the outputs of combinational circuits MUST be fully specified, which is the behavioral of combinational circuits. By contrast, if the outputs are not fully specified, latches are induced because outputs will keep their original values for those unspecified conditions. This is the behavioral of latches, which are sequential circuits and can be used as memory elements. Explicitly specifying full conditions, or implicitly assigning default values is a good coding style for combinational circuits.

Initial blocks are non-synthesizable and they must not appear in the RTL codes. The functionality of a variable described using always block should be completely contained in one always block. For example, the reset and normal functions of a register should not be separately described using two always blocks.

Typically, the POR and hardware reset (asserted by the reset push button) are applied using the asynchronous reset, while normal function uses the synchronous reset to reset (or clear) a block or a portion of the digital circuits. Specifically, for active-low POR and hardware reset, they are AND-ed to generate the asynchronous reset.

A net cannot have more than one driver unless it is declared as tri, wand, or wor net types.

It's a good coding style to separate the next state and current state of a flip-flop, particularly for inexperienced designers. Doing so makes the inference of combinational circuits and sequential circuits clearly, as shown below. The confusions about blocking an non-blocking assignments are avoided.

```verilog
1 assign next_count=clear?0:counter+1;
2 always @(posedge clk or negedge reset_n)
3   if (!reset_n) counter<=0;
4   else counter<=next_count;
```

By contrast, the following description hides the next state and the combinational circuit that produces it.

```
1 always @(posedge clk or negedge reset_n)
2   if(!reset_n) counter <=0;
3   else if(clear) counter <=0;
4   else counter <= counter +1;
```

In additional to binary encoding of state machine, the Gray code encoding and one-hot encoding can be adopted. The Gray code can reduce the dynamic power of a state machine and one-hot encoding can achieve a faster sequential circuit because the decoders used to generate the control signals of a state machine are not needed.

Grouping variables with the same control signals together in an always block can save simulation time and is also a good coding style. For example:

```
1 always @(posedge clk)
2   if(!reset_n) begin
3     counter1 <=0;
4     counter2 <=0;
5   end
6   else if(enable) begin
7     counter1 <= counter1 +1;
8     counter2 <= counter2 +2;
9   end
```

Instead, put dissimilar variables into different always blocks. For the example in Figure E.1:

For the example in Figure E.2, we assume that "state_cs==S0" and "enable" are mutually exclusive. So, variables, a and b, are controlled by different signals and they should better be described using two always blocks.

For the example in Figure E.3, it's good to only describe changed conditions, while unchanged condition is implicitly implied.

The if-else statement and conditional operator imply the multiplexer. Good style takes advantage of if-else priority that can be commonly shared, as shown in Figure E.4.

Sharing common parts of complex expressions using assignments to intermediate variables is a good style. For example, in the following original codes:

```
1 assign addr1=(base1*256)+(base2<<4)+offset1;
2 assign addr2=(base1*256)+(base2<<4)+offset2;
```

It can be observed that the result $(base1 \times 256) + (base2 \ll 4)$ is a common part of the two expressions. We can declare an additional variable, base, for the common part and share it in the two expressions as follows:

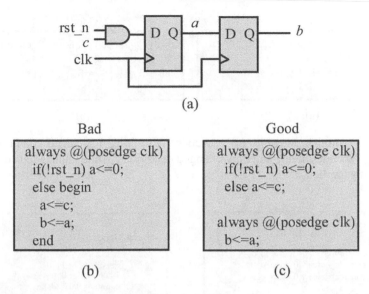

(a)

Bad	Good

```
always @(posedge clk)
  if(!rst_n) a<=0;
  else begin
    a<=c;
    b<=a;
  end
```

```
always @(posedge clk)
  if(!rst_n) a<=0;
  else a<=c;


always @(posedge clk)
  b<=a;
```

(b)   (c)

Figure E.1: Coding dissimilar flip-flops, *a* (with synchronous reset) and *b* (without synchronous reset): (a) circuits, (b) bad codes putting dissimilar variables into the same always block, and (c) good codes putting dissimilar variables into different always blocks.

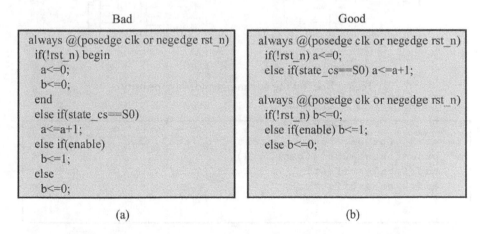

Bad	Good

```
always @(posedge clk or negedge rst_n)
  if(!rst_n) begin
    a<=0;
    b<=0;
  end
  else if(state_cs==S0)
    a<=a+1;
  else if(enable)
    b<=1;
  else
    b<=0;
```

```
always @(posedge clk or negedge rst_n)
  if(!rst_n) a<=0;
  else if(state_cs==S0) a<=a+1;


always @(posedge clk or negedge rst_n)
  if(!rst_n) b<=0;
  else if(enable) b<=1;
  else b<=0;
```

(a)   (b)

Figure E.2: Additional example: (a) bad codes putting dissimilar variables, *a* and *b*, into the same always block and (b) good codes putting dissimilar variables, *a* and *b*, into different always blocks.

Bad	Good

always @(posedge clk or negedge rst_n)
  if(!rst_n) a<=0;
  else if(state_cs!=S0) a<=a;
  else a<=a+1;
	always @(posedge clk or negedge rst_n)
	  if(!rst_n) a<=0;
	  else if(state_cs==S0) a<=a+1;

(a)	(b)

Figure E.3: Another example: (a) bad codes describing unchanged condition first and (b) good codes describing only changed conditions, while unchanged condition is implicitly implied.

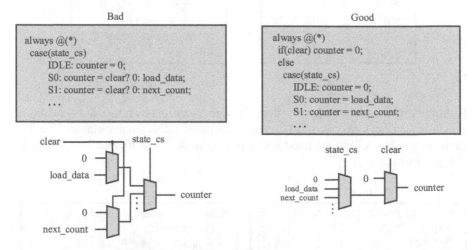

Figure E.4: Taking advantage of if-else priority.

```
1 always @(base1, base2, offset1, offset2) begin
2   base=(base1*256)+(base2<<4);
3   addr1=base+offset1;
4   addr2=base+offset2;
5 end
```

The variable, base, is not an input of the combinational circuit. It is an intermediate variable, since it is assigned a new variable each time the block is activated. Then, base is used in subsequent expressions. For this reason, the variable does not need to be included in the event list. We need to use blocking assignments in the description of combinational circuits, since we use the assigned values sequentially.

Modern logic synthesis tools are very good at optimizing small combinational modules. Instead, they do poorly on large modules. Thus, these modules should be written in the manner that is easiest to synthesize. Keeping modules smaller also lets them more readable. It is known well what they will be synthesized to as well. Large

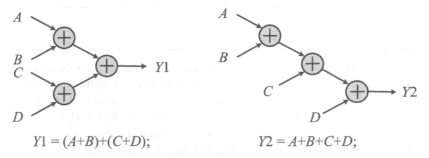

$$Y1 = (A+B)+(C+D);$$ $$Y2 = A+B+C+D;$$

Figure E.5: Balanced adders.

modules should be structural by instantiations of other modules connected by wires. There is no doubt what a structural module synthesizes to.

Datapath typically needs not reset to save the area cost. On the contrary, external and internal control signals MUST be reset. For example, in the following piece of codes, so_valid is the generated output control signal, cur_st and counter are internal control signals. They must be reset to prevent unknown conditions. By contrast, so_data needs not be reset provided that whenever so_valid is true, so_data has a valid value. This must be ensured by designers.

```
1 always @(posedge clk or posedge rst)
2   if(rst) counter <=0;
3   else if(state_cs ==S0) counter <=0;
4   else if(state_cs ==S1) counter <= counter +1;
5 always @(posedge clk or posedge rst)
6   if(rst) so_valid <=0;
7   else if(counter ==7) so_valid <=1;
8 always @(posedge clk)
9   so_data <= buffer [counter];
```

The case statement implies the multiplexer, and a design with balanced path delays is good for timing. For example, a multiplexer inferred by the parallel case statement has a more balanced delay (and hence a shorter longest delay) than that using the if-else-if statement.

Moreover, balanced design using the bracket is good for timing. For example, the expression $Y1 = (A+B)+(C+D)$, which has the critical path with two adders, is better than $Y3 = A+B+C+D$, which has the critical path with three adders, as shown in Figure E.5.

The comparator might be implemented using the XNOR or XOR gates to reduce the circuit delay. The XNOR and XOR gates compare whether two bit are the same or different, respectively. In the following example, the signal $a[7:0]$ is compared to a constant 8'hA5 using XNOR.

```
ı assign is_the_same =&(a~^8'hA5);
```

By inserting FIFO buffers between pipelined stages, variation in throughput can be eliminated. This can achieve a full throughput without stalling the upstream pipeline stage and starving the downstream pipeline stage. Besides, an FIFO is also pretty good at decoupling the interactions between pipelined stages. Hence, the FIFO can simplify a complex design greatly if one can adequately utilize it.

The FIFO controller can be implemented using read and write pointers, and the queue length counter. Such a FIFO design can fully utilize the FIFO space. Another popular FIFO controller is realized using only read and write pointers without the queue length counter. However, when read and write pointers are the same, the FIFO may be either empty or full. To differentiate the FIFO full status from the FIFO empty status, the FIFO full is asserted when the next write pointer equals the current read pointer. Such FIFO design intends to leave one element unoccupied, and a buffer space is wasted.

Try to use a smaller memory to build up the larger memory with increased band-width and capacity through both the bit-slicing and banking techniques. A smaller memory can enhance or reduce the access time of it. Also, disable those memory banks that are not accessed can save the memory access power. However, too many hard macros, such as SRAMs, might increase the difficulties in physical implementation at the layout stage.

About I/O signals of a module, output signals should better be flip-flopped (or registered) outputs to prevent any timing issues. Important control signals, such as control signals of a memory interface, for example, write and read enable signals, should also be flip-flopped (or registered) outputs.

If a low-level RTL (or gate-level) design is desired, instantiate the logic gates using Verilog primitives instead of those in the cell library. Hence, the design can be technology independent and portable and can be optimized by the tools.

We typically use the intra-assignment delay to model the clock-to-Q delays of sequential circuits. To model the output delay of a combinational circuit described using the continuous assignment, the inter-assignment delay is usually adopted.

Constant decimal numbers (e.g., −12) are treated as signed numbers. But constant based numbers (with or without size) (e.g., −'d12) are treated as unsigned numbers. Hence, do not use base when you refer to a negative number. When assigning RHS to LHS, if the bit width of RHS is smaller than LHS and the result of RHS is signed, signed number is sign extended; if the bit width of RHS is smaller than LHS and the result of RHS is unsigned, unsigned number is zero extended; if the bit width of RHS is larger than LHS, RHS is truncated.

Scan chains can be inserted by allocating pins for the scan mode (scan_mode), scan clock (scan_clk), scan enable (scan_en), scan inputs (scan_in), and scan outputs (scan_out). If there exists more than one scan chains (to save the test time), multiple scan inputs and outputs are needed. The numbers of flip-flops in different scan chains should be balanced. To make the design controllable, the clocks of all

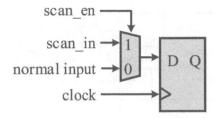

Figure E.6: Scan flip-flops.

flip-flops should be triggered by the external scan clock using the multiplexers as follows.

```
1// The system has two clock domains, clk1 and clk2.
2// For normal function, they are respectively driven by
3// ori_clk1 and ori_clk2.
4// For scan test, they are both driven by the scan_clk.
5assign clk1=scan_mode?scan_clk:ori_clk1;
6assign clk2=scan_mode?scan_clk:ori_clk2;
```

For the modules with flip-flops, three additional ports are dedicated to the scan test as shown below, including scan_en, scan_in, and scan_out, which are used by the scan chains compiled by the synthesis tool.

```
1module scan_test(scan_out, scan_en, scan_in, ...);
2output scan_out;
3input scan_en, scan_in;
4...
5endmodule
```

These three ports will be automatically connected to scan flip-flops in Figure E.6 during the scan chain insertion. When scan_en is true, scan_in is selected. Therefore, during the scan mode (configured by scan_mode=1), at every positive edge of scan_clk, the scan_in is latched by the scan flip-flop. For those flip-flops in a scan chain, their stored data will be shifted in and out at the clock edge. Doing so makes all data stored in flip-flops controllable.

During the scan mode, when scan_en is false, the normal function input driven by the output of a combinational logic is selected and captured subsequently at the clock edge. Since the inputs of a combinational logic are connected to the outputs of controllable scan flip-flops, the normal function input is predictable and can be used to confirm if defects exist in combinational and sequential logics or not.

After the placement and routing, the scan chain may be reordered to reduce the wire lengths according to their physical locations.

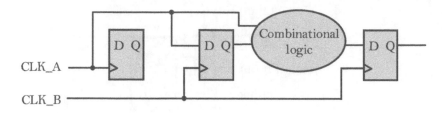

Figure E.7: Clock coding style.

E.3   OTHER CODING AND NAMING STYLES

For a synchronous design, mixing positive-edge triggered and negative-edge triggered flip-flops should be avoided. Otherwise, clock period may be reduced. Besides, it may be problematic for chip testing and should be carefully treated. Clock gating should also be avoided unless power optimization is needed. Some tools may have limitations to handle these special designs.

Clocks fed to data inputs of registers directly or indirectly, as shown in Figure E.7, could lead to timing violations and race conditions. Such a design should be avoided or carefully treated if you have to do that.

If you are using Synopsys Design Compiler (DC) as your synthesis tool, you can prevent lathes by "synopsys full_case" directive to specify all possible branches for if and case statements provided that you know the other branches will never occur. Besides, you can declare a case statement as parallel case with the "synopsys parallel_case" directive.

Parameterized design is a good coding style. Parameterization increases reusability. For example, $w1$ can be set as a $(n+1)$-bit wire if we change $m1$ to n (i.e., if $m1=10$, $w1$ becomes a 11-bit wire; if $m1=4$, $w1$ becomes a 5-bit wire). Parameters can be overwritten when the parameterized module is instantiated. As shown below, the parameter m1 is changed to 10 by instantiation.

```
1// Parameter m1 is changed to 10 by instantiation.
2param_test #(10) param_test (...);
```

It is much more readable to use symbolic constants. Symbolic names can be connected to constant values as either constants (using Verilog 'define) or as parameters (using the parameter statement).

```
1'define RED_LIGHT_TIME 9
2if(counter=='RED_LIGHT_TIME)
3...
```

Often, a long signal is broken into a number of subfields. For example, a 16-bit instruction may be split into an 4-bit opcode, 2 6-bit addresses. Consider the following statement:

```
1 case (instruction [15:12])  ...
```

This is harder to understand, and there is a danger of getting wrong indices, particularly for a new definition of the opcode subfield. Codes become much more readable when symbolic names are defined for these subfields. We can declare a new signal, opcode, as follows.

```
1 wire [3:0] opcode=instruction[15:12];
2 case (opcode)  ...
```

Naming skill is important for a project. For example, you can use lowercase letters for all signal names and port names, while uppercase letters for constant names. For active-low signals, the signal name is suffixed with an underscore followed by a lowercase character, e.g., rst_n. Your code will be much more readable if your signal names describe their functionality. Consider, for example, the statement

```
1 base=(base1*256)+(base2<<4);
```

is much more illustrative than

```
1 b=(b1*256)+(b2<<4);
```

Statements are easier to understand if they fit in one line. While easily readable, long names can make code appear cluttered. With an appropriate naming rules and supporting documents, not-too-short or abbreviated names can still be readable as in the following, where ba denotes the base address.

```
1 ba=(ba1*256)+(ba2<<4);
```

Interaction between initial (in the testbench) and always blocks (in the design) may induce a race condition. To solve the race condition, we can either assign the primary input of a design at a time instance other than clock edges or try to use non-blocking assignments in testbench.

Only use timescale in the top (testbench) module, and it is inherited to all sub-modules.

Well-written code should have lots of high-quality comments. Comments should describe design rationale and goal. Consider the following code fragment:

```
1 assign out1=sel?a+b:c+d;  // sel==1, do a+b;
2                           // sel==0, do c+d
3 assign out2=sel?a-b:c-d;  // sel==1, do a-b;
4                           // sel==0, do c-d
```

These comments do not convey any information. They just describe the codes and should be deleted. Also, at the first glance, there are 4 arithmetic units (2 for both out1 and out2) in the codes. Now, consider the following new codes and comments:

```
1 // First, the operands, op1 and op2, are factored
2 // manually and shared for out1 and out2.
3 // Second, arithmetic units are optimized manually
4 // because some synthesis tools may work badly for
5 // the optimization of continuous assignments.
6 // Consequently, only one adder and one subtractor
7 // are required and explicitly described by codes.
8 assign op1=sel?a:c;  // Share common operands for
9                      // out1 and out2
10 assign op2=sel?b:d;  // Share common operands for
11                      // out1 and out2
12 assign out1=op1+op2;// Only one adder is needed
13 assign out2=op1-op2;// Only one subtractor is needed
```

New codes and comments give the big picture view of the codes. First, the operands, op1 and op2, are factored manually and shared for out1 and out2. Second, arithmetic units are optimized manually so that only one adder and one subtractor are required.

E.4 FURTHER READING

- William J. Dally and R. Curtis Harting, *Digital design: a systems approach*, Cambridge University Press, 2012.

Index